Thomas Borghoff

Evolutionary Theory of the Globalisation of Firms

Herausgeber / Editors:

Prof. Dr. Profs. h. c. Dr. h. c. Klaus Macharzina
Universität Hohenheim, Stuttgart

Prof. Dr. Martin K. Welge
Universität Dortmund

Prof. Dr. Michael Kutschker
Universität Eichstätt, Ingolstadt

Prof. Dr. Johann Engelhard
Universität Bamberg

In der mir-Edition werden wichtige Ergebnisse der wissenschaftlichen Forschung sowie Werke erfahrener Praktiker auf dem Gebiet des internationalen Managements veröffentlicht.

The series mir-Edition includes excellent academic contributions and experiential works of distinguished international managers.

Thomas Borghoff

Evolutionary Theory of the Globalisation of Firms

Bibliografische Information Der Deutschen Bibliothek
Die Deutsche Bibliothek verzeichnet diese Publikation in der Deutschen Nationalbibliografie;
detaillierte bibliografische Daten sind im Internet über <http://dnb.ddb.de> abrufbar.

Bibliographic information published by Die Deutsche Bibliothek
Die Deutsche Bibliothek lists this publication in the Deutsche Nationalbibliografie;
detailed bibliographic data is available in the Internet at <http://dnb.ddb.de>.

Dissertation Universität Dortmund, 2004

Dr. Thomas Borghoff ist Dozent an der Wirtschafts- und Sozialwissenschaftlichen Fakultät der Universität Dortmund sowie an der School of Marketing and International Business (SMIB), Victoria University of Wellington, New Zealand.

Dr. Thomas Borghoff is Senior Lecturer and Scientific Assistant at the Faculty of Economics and Social Sciences, University of Dortmund, and Senior Lecturer at the School of Marketing and International Business (SMIB), Victoria University of Wellington, New Zealand.

Abonnenten von mir – Management International Review erhalten auf die in der mir-Edition veröffentlichten Bücher 10 % Rabatt.

Subscribers to mir – Management International Review are entitled to a 10 % price reduction on books published in mir-Edition.

1. Auflage August 2005

Alle Rechte vorbehalten
© Betriebswirtschaftlicher Verlag Dr. Th. Gabler/GWV Fachverlage GmbH, Wiesbaden 2005

Lektorat: Ulrike Lörcher / Renate Schilling

Der Gabler Verlag ist ein Unternehmen von Springer Science+Business Media.
www.gabler.de

Das Werk einschließlich aller seiner Teile ist urheberrechtlich geschützt. Jede Verwertung außerhalb der engen Grenzen des Urheberrechtsgesetzes ist ohne Zustimmung des Verlags unzulässig und strafbar. Das gilt insbesondere für Vervielfältigungen, Übersetzungen, Mikroverfilmungen und die Einspeicherung und Verarbeitung in elektronischen Systemen.

Die Wiedergabe von Gebrauchsnamen, Handelsnamen, Warenbezeichnungen usw. in diesem Werk berechtigt auch ohne besondere Kennzeichnung nicht zu der Annahme, dass solche Namen im Sinne der Warenzeichen- und Markenschutz-Gesetzgebung als frei zu betrachten wären und daher von jedermann benutzt werden dürften.

Druck und buchbinderische Verarbeitung: Wilhelm & Adam, Heusenstamm
Gedruckt auf säurefreiem und chlorfrei gebleichtem Papier
Printed in Germany

ISBN 3-8349-0013-3

Vorwort der Herausgeber

Die internationale Geschäftstätigkeit ist für Unternehmen, die davon berührten Länder und die Weltwirtschaft zum Schlüsselfaktor des Erfolgs geworden. Die Herausgeber beabsichtigen mit der Schriftenreihe **mir-Edition**, die multidimensionalen Managementanforderungen der internationalen Unternehmenstätigkeit wissenschaftlich zu begleiten. Die **mir-Edition** soll zum einen der empirischen Feststellung und der theoretischen Verarbeitung der in der Praxis des internationalen Managements beobachteten Phänomene dienen. Zum anderen sollen die hierdurch gewonnenen Erkenntnisse in Form von systematisiertem Wissen, Denkanstößen und Handlungsempfehlungen verfügbar gemacht werden.

Diesem angewandten Wissenschaftsverständnis fühlt sich seit nunmehr dreißig Jahren auch die in über 40 Ländern gelesene und jüngst von 1380 US-Professoren als "best rated journal" im internationalen Management platzierte internationale Fachzeitschrift **mir** - Management International Review - verpflichtet. Während dort allerdings nur kurzgefasste Aufsätze publiziert werden, soll hier der breitere Raum der Schriftenreihe den Autoren und Lesern die Möglichkeit zur umfänglichen und vertieften Auseinandersetzung mit dem jeweils behandelten Problem des internationalen Managements eröffnen. Der Herausgeberpolitik von **mir** entsprechend, sollen auch in der Schriftenreihe innovative und dem Erkenntnisfortschritt dienende Beiträge einer kritischen Öffentlichkeit vorgestellt werden. Es ist beabsichtigt, neben Forschungsergebnissen, insbesondere des wissenschaftlichen Nachwuchses, auch einschlägige Werke von Praktikern mit profundem Erfahrungswissen im internationalen Management einzubeziehen.

Das Auswahlverfahren sieht vor, dass die Herausgeber gemeinsam über die Veröffentlichung eines in der Reihe erscheinenden Werkes entscheiden. Sie laden zur Einsendung von Manuskripten in deutscher oder englischer Sprache ein, die bei Auswahl jeweils in der Originalsprache publiziert werden.

Die Herausgeber hoffen, mit dieser Schriftenreihe die fachliche Diskussion und praktische Lösung von Problemen des internationalen Managements zu stimulieren, und wünschen der **mir-Edition** eine positive Aufnahme in den Zielgruppen von Wissenschaft, Praxis und Studium des internationalen Geschäfts.

Klaus Macharzina, Martin K. Welge,
Michael Kutschker, Johann Engelhard

Foreword of the Editors

Recognizing the importance of international business for firms, countries and the global economy at large, the Series aims at covering the managerial requirements, objectives and tools of international business activity from the standpoint of applied research. The goal of **mir-Edition** is to explore and analyze the real world phenomena of international management and to offer on a more general level systematic knowledge and advice in terms of practical recommendations to problem solution.

This basic understanding of research has also guided the editorial policy of **mir** - Management International Review - which has had its readers in more than 40 countries for thirty years. While in the Journal naturally there is only room for relatively short treatment of the respective subject matters the Series opens up the possibility for comprehensive and in-depth study and discussion of international management problems. Similar to the editorial policy of **mir** the volumes of the Series should contribute in an innovative manner to the progress of discovery both in the theoretical and practical dimension. It is therefore intended to include in the Series excellent academic contributions, particularly of the young generation of researchers, but also experiential works of distinguished international managers.

Similar to the high aspiration level which has been achieved in **mir** and which has led to the Journal being ranked number one in International Management by 1380 US professors recently, only contributions of very high quality will be accepted in the Series. The selection decision will be made collectively by the Editors. Manuscripts are invited in English and German; they will be published in the original form.

The Editors sincerely hope to stimulate the discussion and to assist in the solution of problems in the area of international management by way of the Series. They wish that **mir-Edition** will receive a positive welcome among the major target groups which comprise academics, students and managers in international business.

Klaus Macharzina, Martin K. Welge,
Michael Kutschker, Johann Engelhard

Preface

For many years, globalization has been the focus of political and academic discussion. Surprisingly, the theoretical foundation of the process of globalisation is still in its infancy. There is no framework integrating the process of globalization and the globalization of firms, and linking the coevolutionary interaction of both levels. Therefore, the objective of Thomas Borghoff's study was to systematize the heterogeneous landscape and to develop a theoretical frame of reference explaining properties and mechanisms of the process of globalization of firms and their coevolutionary development with the globalizing environment. The study is, therefore, clearly positioned in the area of theory development.

Based on theories such as general and social systems theory, evolutionary theories, dynamic organization theories, and the knowledge based view - all of which have not been developed in the context of globalization - the author develops an evolutionary theory of globalization. In the center of the theory stands the development of specific globalization capabilities. According to the author, these capabilities are as follows: (1) global entrepreneurial capabilities, (2) internationalization capabilities, (3) global network capabilities, and (4) capabilities of global evolutionary dynamics. These capabilities are put in a management perspective, in order to develop requirements for managing the globalization process.

To my knowledge, such an evolutionary theory of globalization has not been developed yet. The author succeeded in developing a coherent dynamic theory of globalization by integrating different streams of theoretical work from other disciplines. Therefore, the study is a significant step in the direction of a sounder theoretical foundation of the field of international management in general and the subject of globalization more specifically. That is why this study deserves a broad attention among international management scholars around the world.

Prof. Dr. Martin K. Welge

Preface of the author

The motivation to write about globalisation was easy to find, as it is a phenomenon that touches everyone's life. Personally, I regard it as the most important process in the history of social evolution and I was keen to know more about the game in which we are all taking part. In the context of International Management, the focus moves to the evolution of individual firms on global scale. Of course, the globalisation of an individual firm is embedded in the underlying globalisation process of social life, which exerts strong influences and provides basic mechanisms for the globalisation of each individual social actor. In a first step, these general evolutionary principles of globalisation are analysed in Chapter 2.

International Management research has been traditionally focused on two main areas: (1) the development of globally dispersed activities (internationalisation) and (2) the co-ordination and integration of globally dispersed activities (management of multinational enterprises or 'MNEs'). Chapter 3 outlines internationalisation strategy research and internationalisation theories while Chapter 4 depicts global network research inter- and intraorganisational level. One main aspect, which has largely been neglected by research on the globalisation of firms is the underlying dynamic of this process. The increase in global complexity, heterogeneity, or the pace of globalisation is generally taken as a given or as a contingency but is rarely explained in its underlying dynamics. Chapter 5 serves to analyse different theories that provide insights in these dynamics. Evolutionary theories, dynamic organisation theories, and the knowledge-based view from a management perspective all provide hints the underlying dynamics of the evolution process, which have to be adapted to an international or global perspective. Chapter 6 provides an evolutionary approach to the globalisation of firms on the basis of framework built on evolutionary and systems theory. Firms are conceptualised as both allopoietic and autopoietic systems whose globalisation process may be explained, respectively.

This publication contains only two thirds of the original contents in order to make it more compact and to adapt it to the format of the MIR Edition. Main 'victims' of this reduction are dynamic organisation theories and general evolutionary perspectives from the knowledge-based view. Nonetheless, these perspectives are very valuable in the explanation of evolutionary processes in globalisation and may be published in another format.

I would like to thank several persons who made this work possible and who helped me a lot. First of all, I would like to thank Prof. Dr. Martin K. Welge for supervising my doctoral thesis and even more for the patience and the faith that he had in my work. I would also like to thank Neriman Cetinkaya, Daniela Greco, and Sylvia Liedmeyer who helped me in my search for literature and in the formatting of my thesis. In addition, my colleagues Dr. Nicola Berg, Steffi Rabbe, Dr. Anja Schulz, and Stefan Achenbach supported me in balancing my professional duties and the development of my thesis. I would particularly like to thank my parents who made my qualification possible and my sister Claudia who opened the first doors to 'real' international business for me. Most of all, I would like to thank my wife Cristina for both designing most tables, figures, and the references and – even more – for the tolerance, inspiration, and strength that she gave me in the time of writing the thesis.

Dr. Thomas Borghoff

Contents

1 Introduction 1
2 What is globalisation? 11
   2.1 Characteristics of globalisation 11
      2.1.1 Definitions of globalisation 12
      2.1.2 Distinction between globalisation and similar concepts 16
         2.1.2.1 Distinction between globalisation and internationalisation 16
         2.1.2.2 Globalisation versus localisation and regionalisation 18
            2.1.2.2.1 Globalisation and regionalisation 20
            2.1.2.2.2 Globalisation and localisation 24
            2.1.2.2.3 Hybrid global and local structures 27
   2.2 Globalisation as an evolutionary historical process 29
      2.2.1 First stage: early international trade 30
      2.2.2 Second stage: formation of global systems 32
         2.2.2.1 Colonialism and entrepreneurial capitalism: 15th until mid-19th century 32
         2.2.2.2 Incipient globalisation: mid-18th century to the mid-19th century 34
         2.2.2.3 Early economic globalisation 35
         2.2.2.4 Full-scale globalisation: mid-20th century – present 37
         2.2.2.5 Development of a global economic context 38
         2.2.2.6 Formation of MNEs and evolution of the world competitive structure 41
   2.3 An evolutionary perspective on globalisation 46
   2.4 Implications for a management of globalisation 53
   2.5 Summary 58
3 Internationalisation 61
   3.1 Internationalisation strategies 65
      3.1.1 International market entry strategies 65
      3.1.2 International business strategies 68
      3.1.3 Multidimensional internationalisation strategy 74
      3.1.4 Contribution to an evolutionary perspective 77
   3.2 Processual internationalisation theories 78
      3.2.1 Internationalisation of 'born globals' 79
         3.2.1.1 Entrepreneurs as drivers of early internationalisation 84
         3.2.1.2 Networks as drivers of early internationalisation 85
      3.2.2 Stage theories of internationalisation 88
         3.2.2.1 International product life cycle (Vernon) 89
         3.2.2.2 Stage models of organisational structures 91

3.2.2.2.1 Stage models of activity modes in foreign markets 91
3.2.2.2.2 Stage models of formal organisation structures 93
3.2.2.2.3 Evolution of organisational cognitive structure 98
3.2.2.3 Learning-based stage models 100
3.2.2.3.1 Behavioural theory of foreign direct investment (Aharoni) 101
3.2.2.3.2 Uppsala School 101
3.2.2.3.3 Helsinki School 111
3.2.2.3.4 Innovation School 115
3.2.2.3.5 Empirical limits of incremental stage models 119
3.2.2.4 Discontinuous stage models of internationalisation 122
3.2.2.4.1 GAINS Paradigm (Macharzina/Engelhard) 122
3.2.2.4.2 Dynamic internationalisation theory (Kutschker) 124
3.2.2.4.3 Internationalisation as a strategy process 126
3.2.3 Contribution to an evolutionary perspective 128
3.3 Resource-based theory of internationalisation 132
3.3.1 Extension of economic theories by resource-based view 132
3.3.2 Extension of incremental stage models by resource-based view 133
3.3.3 Contribution to an evolutionary perspective 139
3.4 Summary 139
4 Global networks 142
4.1 Interorganisational networks 144
4.1.1 Local networks 144
4.1.1.1 Context and forms of local networks 155
4.1.1.2 Innovation in local networks 159
4.1.1.3 Local path-dependence 167
4.1.2 Business networks 173
4.1.3 Strategic networks 179
4.1.3.1 The interorganisational network as a political economy (Benson) 179
4.1.3.2 Networks between markets and hierarchies (Thorelli) 181
4.1.3.3 The 'dynamic network' (Miles/Snow) 182
4.1.3.4 Segmentary, polycentric, integrated networks (SPINs) 183
4.1.3.5 Strategic network (Jarillo) 184
4.1.4 Contribution to an evolutionary perspective 185
4.2 Global intraorganisational networks: MNEs 187
4.2.1 Strategy in MNEs 191
4.2.2 The 'Process School' of international management 198
4.2.2.1 The diversified multinational corporation (DMNC) (Doz/Prahalad) ... 198
4.2.2.2 The transnational corporation (TNC) (Bartlett/Ghoshal et al.) 205

- 4.2.2.3 The MNE as a heterarchy and 'multi-centre structure' (Hedlund et al.) 212
- 4.2.2.4 Other network concepts of MNEs 217
- 4.2.2.5 Critical reflection upon the Process School 219
- 4.2.3 Intraorganisational roles in MNEs 220
  - 4.2.3.1 Headquarters-subsidiary relations 223
  - 4.2.3.2 Subsidiary roles 225
    - 4.2.3.2.1 Subsidiary initiatives 227
    - 4.2.3.2.2 Subsidiary mandates 229
    - 4.2.3.2.3 Subsidiary role typologies 233
    - 4.2.3.2.4 Subsidiary evolution 242
  - 4.2.3.3 Critical reflection upon MNE role research 248
- 4.2.4 Contribution to an evolutionary perspective 248
- 4.3 Summary 251
- 5 Global evolutionary processes 254
  - 5.1 Evolutionary theories 254
    - 5.1.1 Economic evolutionary theories 257
      - 5.1.1.1 Organisational routines 261
      - 5.1.1.2 Technological trajectories 264
      - 5.1.1.3 Evolutionary mechanisms 265
      - 5.1.1.4 Foundation of organisations 268
    - 5.1.2 Social evolutionary theories 271
      - 5.1.2.1 General social evolutionary theory 271
      - 5.1.2.2 Theory of structuration (Giddens) 278
      - 5.1.2.3 Organisational transformation 283
        - 5.1.2.3.1 Organisational life cycle 283
        - 5.1.2.3.2 Theories of organisational change 283
        - 5.1.2.3.3 Concepts of dynamic organisation 287
          - 5.1.2.3.3.1 Relentlessly shifting organisations (Brown/Eisenhardt) 287
          - 5.1.2.3.3.2 Continuous morphing (Rindova/Kotha) 288
      - 5.1.2.4 Evolutionary mechanisms 289
      - 5.1.2.5 Management of evolution 294
    - 5.1.2 Contribution to an evolutionary perspective 296
  - 5.2 The knowledge-based view of management 299
    - 5.2.1 Theoretical roots: resource-based and knowledge-based view 300
      - 5.2.1.1 The roots of the resource-based view 300
      - 5.2.1.2 The roots of the knowledge-based view 303
    - 5.2.2 Knowledge in the global context 304
      - 5.2.2.1 Knowledge in the global economy 304

XV

			5.2.2.1.1 National origins	305

- 5.2.2.1.1 National origins 305
- 5.2.2.1.2 Cultural differences 307
- 5.2.2.2 Globalisation knowledge of firms 311
  - 5.2.2.2.1 Internationalisation knowledge 311
  - 5.2.2.2.2 Network knowledge in MNEs 315
    - 5.2.2.2.2.1 Knowledge creation in MNEs 318
    - 5.2.2.2.2.2 Diffusion of knowledge in the global network 319
  - 5.2.2.2.3 Knowledge-based theory of the MNE 324
- 5.2.3 Contribution to an evolutionary perspective 324
- 5.3 Summary 327

6 Evolutionary theory of firm globalisation 329

- 6.1 Properties of firms as social systems 333
  - 6.1.1 Theoretical basis of a social systems perspective 333
    - 6.1.1.1 Firms as open systems: General systems theory 334
    - 6.1.1.2 Theory of living systems 336
    - 6.1.1.3 Theory of autopoietic systems 338
    - 6.1.1.4 The dual character of social systems 340
  - 6.1.2 Properties of firms as allopoietic systems 342
  - 6.1.3 Properties of firms as autopoietic systems 343
    - 6.1.3.1 Meaning as the basis of social systems 343
    - 6.1.3.2 Evolutionary mechanism of social systems 345
    - 6.1.3.3 Complexity of social systems 347
    - 6.1.3.4 Interpenetration of system and environment 348
    - 6.1.3.5 Recursive interplay of action and meaning structure 351
  - 6.1.4 Change and reproduction of global social systems 352
    - 6.1.4.1 Differentiation and integration 353
    - 6.1.4.2 Evolutionary motors 356
  - 6.1.5 Co-evolution of social systems and their environment 359
- 6.2 Globalisation capabilities of social systems 362
  - 6.2.1 Entrepreneurial capability of firms 362
    - 6.2.1.1 Foundation of organisations 364
    - 6.2.1.2 Foundation of networks 369
  - 6.2.2 Internationalisation 374
    - 6.2.2.1 Internationalisation of firms 374
    - 6.2.2.2 Internationalisation of networks 380
  - 6.2.3 Global network capability 381
    - 6.2.3.1 Intrasystemic networking 381
    - 6.2.3.2 Intersystemic networking 385

- 6.2.4 Capability of global evolutionary dynamics 387
  - 6.2.4.1 The life cycle motor 387
  - 6.2.4.2 The teleological motor 388
  - 6.2.4.3 The dialectical motor 391
  - 6.2.4.4 The Darwinian motor 393
  - 6.2.4.5 The autopoietic motor 396
    - 6.2.4.5.1 System – environment 396
    - 6.2.4.5.2 Element – whole 398
    - 6.2.4.5.3 Element – relation 399
    - 6.2.4.5.4 Identity – difference 399
    - 6.2.4.5.5 Allopoiesis – Autopoiesis 400
- 6.3 A management perspective on the globalisation of firms 402
  - 6.3.1 Management of global foundation 402
  - 6.3.2 Management of global differentiation 403
  - 6.3.3 Management of global network capabilities 404
  - 6.3.4 Management of global evolutionary dynamics 405
  - 6.3.5 Management of differences in globalisation 406
- 6.4 Contribution to an evolutionary perspective 407
- 6.5 Summary 410

7 Conclusions 413

References 431

List of figures

Figure 1-1:	Conceptual framework	10
Figure 2-1:	Shrinking map of the world	14
Figure 2-2:	Historical development of global competition	43
Figure 2-3:	Co-evolution of a firm in its task-environment	47
Figure 2-4:	Network-building of MNEs and SMEs	54
Figure 2-5:	Firm capabilities of globalisation	56
Figure 3-1:	Influences on entry mode decisions	67
Figure 3-2:	The dimensions of international strategy	70
Figure 3-3:	Types of international strategy	71
Figure 3-4:	Two dimensions of international strategy	72
Figure 3-5:	Strategic mapping of some international strategies	72
Figure 3-6:	Four generic international competitive strategies	73
Figure 3-7:	Internationalisation strategies in the four-dimensional framework	75
Figure 3-8:	Dynamic internationalisation strategy	76
Figure 3-9:	Conditions of time-spans until internationalisation	83
Figure 3-10:	Degrees of internationalisation	91
Figure 3-11:	Sequences of structural change of American MNEs	93
Figure 3-12:	Relationships between strategy and structure	94
Figure 3-13:	International organisational evolution of European MNEs	95
Figure 3-14:	Structural evolution of nonconglomerate U.S. multinational firms	96
Figure 3-15:	Evolution of organisational forms	98
Figure 3-16:	The basic mechanism of internationalisation – state and change aspects	103
Figure 3-17:	The multilateral aspect of the internationalisation process	108
Figure 3-18:	Lateral rigidity in decision processes	112
Figure 3-19:	Incremental evolution, episodes, and epochs in company evolution	125
Figure 3-20:	Four types of processes captured by different longitudinal approaches	127
Figure 4-1:	The sustainability of sticky places	149
Figure 4-2:	The integration-responsiveness framework	193
Figure 4-3:	The global/local trade-off	194
Figure 4-4:	Integration-responsiveness: strategic focus and organisational adaptation	200
Figure 4-5:	Decentralised federation model	206
Figure 4-6:	Centralised hub model	207
Figure 4-7:	Integrated network model	207
Figure 4-8:	The process of changing head office subsidiary relationship	217
Figure 4-9:	The strategic control dilemma in MNCs	235
Figure 4-10:	Basic and development mandates	237

Figure 4-11:	International subsidiary roles related to different resource flows	238
Figure 4-12:	International strategy and subsidiary roles based on resource flows	239
Figure 4-13:	Stages of development of multinational subsidiary	245
Figure 4-14:	Example of stages in subsidiary development process	246
Figure 5-1:	The dimensions of the duality of structure	279
Figure 5-2:	Evolutionary motors	293
Figure 5-3:	Variations in subsidiary strategic contexts based on knowledge flows	321
Figure 6-1:	Construction of consensual domains	360
Figure 6-2:	Integration of local and global consensual domains	361
Figure 6-3:	General evolutionary capabilities of firms	366
Figure 6-4:	Two-step globalisation	367
Figure 6-5:	Globalisation process of a firm	376

List of tables

Table 2-1:	Definitions of globalisation	15
Table 2-2:	Processes and characteristics of globalisation	15
Table 2-3:	World merchandise trade by region and selected economy	19
Table 2-4:	Economic concentration ratios 1985 and 2000 (percentages)	21
Table 2-5:	Formation of regional trading blocs	23
Table 2-6:	Chronology of incipient globalisation	37
Table 2-7:	Indicators of accelerated globalisation	38
Table 2-8:	World merchandise exports, production and world GDP, 1950-2000	39
Table 2-9:	Selected indicators of FDI and international production, 1982- 2000	39
Table 3-1:	Industry globalisation drivers	68
Table 3-2:	Evolutionary principles in internationalisation strategy	78
Table 3-3:	Responses in organisation structure in the evolution of a global enterprise	97
Table 3-4:	Headquarters orientations in an international enterprise	99
Table 3-5:	Characteristics of the 'Three Es': an overview	124
Table 3-6:	Evolutionary principles in stage theories of internationalisation	131
Table 4-1:	Evolutionary principles in interorganisational network approaches	186
Table 4-2:	Global strategy: an organising framework	192
Table 4-3:	Evolutionary elements in intraorganisational network approaches	250
Table 5-1:	Evolutionary principles in economic and social evolutionary theories	298
Table 5-2:	Inclusion of evolutionary principles in the knowledge-based view	326
Table 6-1:	Properties of open systems	334
Table 6-2:	Dynamic-constituting characteristics of evolving systems	335
Table 6-3:	Inclusion of evolutionary principles on allopoietic and autopoietic level	409

Abbreviations

AFTA	ASEAN Free Trade Area
ANDEAN	The Andean Group
APEC	Asian-Pacific Economic Co-operation
ASEAN	Association of South East Asian Nations
BIS	Bank for International Settlements
Bn.	Billion
CACM	Central American Market
CARRICOM	Caribbean Common Market
CEAO	Communauté Économique de L´Afrique de L´ouest
CEFTA	Central European Free Trade Area
CoE	Centre of Excellence
DMNC	Diversified Multinational Corporation
DOI	Degree of Internationalisation
EC	European Community
ECOWAS	Economic Community of West African States
EEA	European Economic Area
EEC	European Economic Community
EFTA	European Free Trade Association
EU	European Union
FDI	Foreign Direct Investment
FSA	Firm-specific Advantage
FSR	Firm-specific Resources
FTAA	Free Trade Agreement of the Americas
GATT	General Agreement on Tariffs and Trade
GDP	Gross Domestic Product
IT	Information Technology
ICT	Information and Communication Technology
LAIA	Latin American Integration Association
LME	London Metal Exchange
M&A	Merger & Acquisition
MERCOSUR	Mercado do Sur
Mn.	Million
MNC	Multinational Corporation
MNE	Multinational Enterprise
NAFTA	North American Free Trade Agreement
PLC	Product Life Cycle

PTA	Eastern and Southern African Preferential Trade Area
REI	Regional Economic Integration
ROA	Return on Assets
ROI	Return on Investment
ROS	Return on Sales
SME	Small and Medium-sized Enterprise
SSA	Subsidiary-specific Advantage
TNC	Transnational Corporation
UDEAC	Customs and Economic Union of Central Africa
UNCTAD	United Nation Council on Trade and Development
WIR	World Investment Report
WPM	World Product Mandate
WTO	World Trade Organisation

1 Introduction

Globalisation is a phenomenon that has been unfolding for thousands of years, beginning with early trade between ancient cultures and reaching a historical level of economic integration around the year 2000. After a phase of increasing international scope in trade beginning with the eighteenth century, globalisation was derailed by war (in 1914) and by economic policy during recession (in the early 1930). Intensive globalisation as known today began to accelerate from the 1950s with another quantum leap in the 1980s and 1990s. Only since the 1980s, the world economy has become so structurally interdependent *'that the use of the word global, as distinct from international, has become justifiable'* (Dunning 1997c: 33).

Nonetheless, globalisation is **not a steady process**. After growing by 12% in 2000 and by an average of 7% a year throughout the 1990s, the volume of global trade remained virtually stagnant since 2001. While international trade remained at least relatively stable, the main indicator of globalisation in terms of increasing global interdependencies - the development of foreign direct investment (FDI) – was subject to extreme alterations. While FDI outflows in 1982 amounted to a mere $57 bn., it increased to $202 bn. in 1990 and reached a peak level of $1.200 bn. in 2002. Since then, the amount was nearly cut by half to $647 bn. in 2002 (WIR 2001, 2003). As FDI implies a huge resource commitment and the creation of new and intensive interdependencies, it depends much more on expectations and the economic atmosphere than trade. The same applies to cross-border mergers and acquisitions (M&As), which had a volume of $151 bn. in 1990, amounted to a peak level of $1,144 bn. in 2000 and than experienced a steep decline to $370 bn. in 2002 (Ibid.). In the first years of the new millenium, the phase of intensive economic globalisation of the 1980s and 1990s seems to have come to a temporary halt due to stagnating economies undergoing structural changes in large parts of the world and increased uncertainties caused by environmental threats and fears caused by international terrorism. Even with a focus on economic actors, the natural and the globalising social environment cannot be ignored in an analysis of the globalisation process of firms.

Globalisation thus is not a linear, but an alternating phenomenon. Although subject to serious crises due to economic or political perturbations, in the long term it has been increasing, however, with different momentum in the functional social subsystems. In democratic societies with market-based economies, the **economic subsystem** traditionally has the *role of a pacemaker* due to the vital interests and influence of economic actors, often inducing and facilitating the globalisation of political or legal systems. In times of stagnation, economic development clearly dominates the preferences even of political decision-makers in the distribution of efforts and resources across functional social systems. In terms of a social system, society is dependent on economy as it organises the functional process of resource acquisition and production of everything needed for survival so that in times of crises and doubt, other social subsystems often adopt the role of service providers rather than equal building blocks of society. Economic growth allows for allocation of resources to other subsystems.

The **globalisation of a firm** is embedded in the globalisation of its task environment. This process can be described as a co-evolutionary process of a social system in its environment. A historical view of the globalisation of competition seems to prove that it can be interpreted as an evolutionary process of differentiation and integration of social systems (e.g. societies, organisations) that is reinforced by the decreasing rigidity of boundaries. Globalisation not only means a decreasing role of the rigidity of boundaries but as well an expansion and increasing density of global competition. As a result, a '**liquefaction of competition**' can be observed, in which an increasing number of autonomous economic actors, such as decentralised units of multinational enterprises (MNEs), and small and medium-sized enterprises (SMEs), are competing and co-operating in the global context. A *'network competition'* emerges, which can be traced to an increasing expansion and density of economic and other social interactions (Welge/Borghoff 1999, 2001, Borghoff/Welge 2000, 2003). As Chapter 2 further substantiates, developing **global network capability** thus becomes a central demand for firms in the process of globalisation. The feedback-loop of globalisation is accompanied by an increasing dynamic, so that the **capability of global evolutionary dynamics** becomes the second central demand for management. A management of globalisation thus should be based on the **internationalisation capability** in the sense of changes in the extension of international business activities and complemented by the capabilities of global networking and evolutionary dynamics. A management of global firm evolution should be based on these key dimensions of globalisation. MNEs and SMEs in this respect have very different starting points. While in the context of globalisation MNEs are usually observed as *'global networks'*, SMEs are usually ascribed the role of *'internationalisers'*, extending their activity structure to global scale. Nonetheless, changing global configurations of MNEs and increasing emergence of *'micro-multinationals'* and *'born globals'* show that both SMEs and MNEs are subject to all three kinds of globalisation processes.

In **literature**, the comparatively young discussion of *globalisation processes* is embedded in a long tradition of scientific discourse in the field of international business activities. *'The wealth of nations'* by Adam Smith (1776) may be regarded as a first milestone in a long line of explanatory approaches to international trade and business activities. However, until the 1960s the discourse in the field of international business activities was restricted to explanatory approaches of the existence of such activities. The *'take-off'* in **international business**, which developed in the aftermath of the Second World War, especially since the 1960s, has induced an increasing need for concepts to actively handle and organise international activities from a management point of view. Technological and societal developments led an increasing number of industries towards globalisation. Firms within these globalising task environments became entangled in the feedback-loop of adapting to globalisation demands on the one hand and thus reinforcing the globalisation on the other. Competition in this respect provides the mechanism for the feedback loop in which companies have to strive for competitive advantages by global differentiation and integration of their products and activities while at the same time this produces ever-increasing demands for the capabilities in global business. The *feedback-loop of globalisation* thus seems to inhere self-reinforcing dynamics, which still have not been explicitly identified and defined for the process as a whole.

A noticeable intensification of research especially in international management can be observed since the 1970s. Beyond the **explanation** of the **existence of international business** and of **patterns of internationalisation processes**, the management point of view increasingly has been taken into account. Research on explanations of global economic activities has been complemented by research on **strategy** and **organisation of MNEs**. The focus moved from a basically **static orientation in the 1970s** (strategy content and organisational structure) to **processes of organisational and strategic change since the 1980**. An area still neglected is the study of the underlying evolutionary dynamics driving globalisation itself and their implications for international management.

The **globalisation of the firm** and the globalisation of its **task environment** are linked in a **dynamic interplay**, which is embedded in the wider context of the globalisation of society. The latter can be conceived as a phase in the historical evolution of society as a social system, in which the emergence and reproduction of social systems expand from heretofore dispersed, unconnected local contexts (nations, tribes) to a globally differentiated social context. The perspective of globalisation hence presupposes an understanding of social evolutionary processes, which provide the underlying properties and dynamics of change. Though a myriad of publications have been produced with the word evolution or evolutionary in their title, most have only described development and change processes. Only a few have actually integrated **evolutionary principles** in their concepts. The focus of an evolutionary perspective is on the process, not necessarily on the content of social reproduction. A theory of process consists of statements that explain how and why a process unfolds over time (van de Ven 1992: 174). Most approaches to change describe a sequence of manifestations of *what* changes over time but do not identify mechanisms or drivers of these processes.

Another weakness of research on social evolutionary processes is the **fragmentation of specialised fields in literature**. Resuming the contribution of economic theories, management theories, organisation theories, and evolutionary theories to the understanding of the adaptation process of organisations, Lewin/Volberda (1999: 523) come to the conclusion that while these various single-lens perspectives have made profound contribution to the strategy and organisation field, the resolution of the adaptation-selection debate has not progressed very much. Lewin/Volberda believe that **single-theme explanations** for the adaptation-selection phenomenon have reached their **limit** and that progress in the field requires combining and recombining multiple lenses instead of increasing fragmentation (Ibid.). The authors contend that particularly studies of simultaneous evolution or co-evolution of organisations and their environment are still rare (Ibid. 526). In a similar vein, Hagström/Chandler (1998: 1) contend:

'Partial theories of the underlying long-run competitiveness of firms are abound. However, more complete theories of explaining the functioning of, and change in, firms in an ever more internationalized environment still seem elusive. Perhaps we have reached the limit of approaches firmly anchored in one of the various subdisciplines when it comes to the question of understanding the firm as it evolves over time'.

Hinings/Greenwood (2002: 419) even propose a redirection of organisation theory as one major field in which knowledge about social evolution is produced. Their basic criticism states that the development in organisational research is highly contextualised in time and space. The main argument is that the narrowing of organisation research on the understanding how to understand and thus design efficient and effective organisations leads to a **conceptual blindness** with regard to **organisations' embeddedness in the process of social evolution**, a criticism also applicable to management theories (Ibid. 413). This argument is even more valid in the **context of globalisation**. A major concern is seen in the inclusion of long-term and historical perspectives - particularly of globalisation processes - in organisation theory. One way of opening the analysis of organisations in society would be to reframe studies of fields as studies of institutional processes. These would include, for example, the economic system, the legal system, or the political system (Ibid. 418-419).

On balance, there is a huge amount of research from different perspectives and on different aspects of globalisation, leading to a fragmented and often even incommensurable or conflicting understanding of this phenomenon. It often appears that people talk about different subjects when talking about globalisation. The same applies to different theoretical perspectives, which are still open to a symbiotic development of globalisation knowledge.

☞   *Objectives*

On the basis of the identified weaknesses of existing research or at least of the (global) niche left by it, the **overarching objective** of this study is to provide a **comprehensive framework** for the identification and explanation of properties, characteristics, and mechanisms of globalisation processes both of individuals firms and of their co-evolutionary interplay with their environment. This includes two levels: (1) a basic framework has to be developed that allows for the explanation of the globalisation of the firm and its environment as an evolutionary process; and (2) the framework must provide the possibility to symbiotically integrate existing specialised approaches, which explain certain aspects of globalisation. These are basically theories explaining evolutionary processes in the globalisation of firms, i.e. internationalisation, global network evolution, and global evolutionary dynamics. The theories explaining aspects of these processes are evolutionary theories, dynamic organisation theories, system theories, network theories, and theories of globalisation and internationalisation. Due to the given fragmentation in research the **conceptualisation of globalisation processes** has to be developed on two levels: (1) on a *general level*, i.e. a conceptualisation of the evolution of firms as organisations and social systems, (2) in the *context of globalisation* on the basis of existing knowledge about globalisation processes and of knowledge gained on the general level. The **main objective** of this study thus is **theory building** in order to develop a **holistic, evolutionary approach to the globalisation of firms**, which also offers free space for specific theories contributing to such a perspective.

A **second objective** derived from the holistic approach is the **explanation of the whole evolutionary process of the firm**, beginning with its foundation (birth) to its reproduction on global scale. Such a perspective is completely missing. Internationalisation theories already assume a successful national firm, which internationalises in a second step. Literature on MNEs even begins its explanations in the context of already existing globally differentiated structures. Only since the 1990s, global SMEs have become subject of research. Born globals are described as an emergent phenomenon in global entrepreneurship but not in terms of a nucleus of globally differentiated evolution. The global evolution of born globals, traditional 'internationalisers', and MNEs should be explained by the holistic approach without cutting knowledge from the individual theories to a combined minimum.

A **third objective** is to outline **specific theories** contributing to an understanding of **global evolutionary processes** in detail in order to generate a comprehensive knowledge base on globalisation processes. The description of the individual theories may convey their idiosyncratic perspective and their possible value for the description of globalisation processes. From the level of the different individual theories then may emerge an understanding of globalisation processes from the holistic level.

A **fourth objective** of this study is to identify and describe **motors of global evolutionary change**, which actually cause and fuel this process. An understanding of these underlying mechanisms may be quite valuable not only for a better understanding of globalisation processes but also of implications for the strategic management of firms.

A **fifth objective** is the description and explanation of the **co-evolutionary interplay** of the **globalisation as a social phenomenon** and the **globalisation of individual firm** within this stream of social evolution. Literature in organisation theory and international business usually takes environmental complexity and dynamics as a given contingency but does not combine the evolutionary dynamics of the firm with the evolutionary dynamics of its environment. An understanding of this interplay may facilitate a symbiotic evolution of a firm with less flukes and inconsistent actions with regard to its environment and more efficient allocation of resources and attention.

☞ *Conceptual approach*

In research, the **fundament for a chosen observation** has to be provided by a **distinction**. For an observation of the movement or development of an object, a **background** is needed: the environment of the object. For example, to observe and measure the race of a runner you need a track. Thus a stable and observable background is available by the definition of the start, course, and the end of the racetrack, which is linear. This makes the performance of different athletes comparable. However, the observation of the **globalisation of a firm** is much more complicated as the **background itself**, i.e. the economic environment, is **in motion**. Obviously, a static background is not available in the social context. The natural environment seems to be quasi static compared to the enormous pace of social evolution and may not serve well to observe the **meaning-based mechanisms** of the latter. On the contrary, even the evolutionary mechanism of biological reproduction has become subject to the influence of social evolutionary processes such as innovation, learning, and decision-making. These meaning-based mechanisms allow for an **evolutionary pace in social organisation**, which is much faster than biological reproduction where variation may occur only vertically between generations. Social evolution allows for **immediate feedback-loops** on the basis of communication and social action, cutting change processes to a fragment in terms of temporal intervals. In addition to the temporal aspect, intentional change complements the blind evolutionary process in biology by facilitating much more directed developments.

With no adequate static background available, basic mechanisms or directions may be identified in order to develop an understanding of how the globalisation process of a firm in its globalising environment works and how a firm may enhance its viability in this process. As Chapter 2 will show, three **basic globalisation processes** may be identified, which characterise and drive globalisation and thus call for the development of capabilities, which reflect these processes within the firm:

1. *Processes of internationalisation* are changes in the global extension of social systems. These processes induce the spatial differentiation of social actors on global scale and the formation of social systems with worldwide extension (e.g. born globals).
2. *Processes of global network formation* are characterised by growing interdependencies between social actors (individuals, organisations, and states) and growing integration of social communication, activities, and structures on global scale.
3. *Processes of evolutionary dynamics* lead to a compression of time and space (due to transport and communication technologies) and the differentiation and integration of social systems on global scale. Different evolutionary motors drive evolutionary dynamics. These motors are life cycle, teleological, dialectical, autopoietic, and Darwinian (see Chapter 5).

The main objective is the development of a conceptual framework for the description and explanation of evolutionary processes and respective capabilities in the globalisation of firms. Therefore, the three general characteristics of globalisation also provide '*conceptual drawers*' - and thus chapters - for the description of individual theories, which provide specialised knowledge for distinct aspects.

There are two **alternatives** to provide an **integrative and comprehensive view** on theories explaining different aspects of global evolution of social systems. The **first alternative** would afford to develop a conceptual framework developed on the **basis of a specific theory** (e.g. internationalisation theory, economic or social evolutionary theory), which then is filled in eclectically with central propositions from other specialised theories. This would provide a consistent model on the first glance. On the second, however, it would provoke a quite arbitrary and incommensurable use of individual theoretical propositions due to the large number of theories and underlying assumptions describing aspects of globalisation. Arguments from a variety of theories would appear in the same context without their own theoretical fundament, causing confusion about the level and focus of observation. Arguments may become unclear and even misleading. Even more important is that specialised theories may not integrate other theories on a generalised level due to the specialised assumptions. For example, organisation theories may not capture the globalisation of society as a whole as the relevant environment for the globalisation of firms. The same applies to approaches in international business literature; no single one has the theoretical scope to integrate others.

The **second alternative** would call for a **general theory** providing the **framework** and a shared meaning structure of central properties characterising global organisational evolution - and particularly the co-evolution of firm and environment - that would allow for the **transfer of knowledge across different theoretical perspectives**. The development of an evolutionary approach to the globalisation of firms shall not provide another specific theory describing in detail a specific perspective on globalisation such as internationalisation theories or network approaches. Rather, it serves to provide a basic framework, which identifies the main characteristics and drivers of globalisation processes and allows for a consistent transfer of knowledge across different theoretical frameworks. It redirects the focus from the individual tree to the forest while respecting the idiosyncratic position and perspective of each specialised approach. It may provide a **holistic perspective**, where **individual perspectives** appear **symbiotically in one picture**. Such a holistic perspective may be created by providing a joint meaning base with shared basic concepts, which make transfer of knowledge commensurable.

It is clear that the approach and the argumentation can only lead to a meta-approach or **meta-theory,** which provides the integrative language and concepts for the development of a holistic perspective on globalisation while providing free space for specialised theories. Even by definition, **social systems theory** is such an approach, which by its own design is constituted by the difference of whole and part, integrating both in one system. Social systems theory thus provides the language and concepts to describe the holistic view of globalisation processes and thus the holistic level of the framework while creating free space for the specialised elements (theories) within the framework. For example, meaning in social systems may take the specific form of routines in evolutionary economics, '*comps*' in population ecology, or knowledge and competencies in the knowledge-based view with resulting definitions and perspectives. On the basis of meaning, however, all these specific manifestations are subject to the basic social evolutionary processes, which determine their emergence and reproduction. The **identification of general properties and mechanisms** in the evolution of social systems allows for the **transfer of specific knowledge** on the basis of such generalised principles.

Social systems theory in tandem with **evolutionary theories** provide the generalised knowledge transferable across all specialised theories. These, in turn, may provide more specific knowledge, which may be generalised and transferred across all theories or remain valid only within the assumptions of the given perspective. The language and concepts of the holistic theoretical level hence provide means for the diffusion and integration of knowledge while the specialised theories provide the variety. Such a model may itself become autopoietic when this motor sets in, i.e. when variation from one perspective may be diffused to others, causing further variations in other elements via the holistic level of the model and vice versa.[1]

---

[1] In fact, the whole development of the study has been functioning that way, leveraging knowledge from general to specific level and vice versa, in an autopoietic interplay.

After the description of the holistic level of the approach, the study will begin with a description of the elements, i.e. the individual, specialised approaches, which will be outlined within the given framework constituted by the three basic characteristics of globalisation on holistic and firm level. In **Chapter 2**, **globalisation** is described from a **holistic perspective**. Globalisation is presented as a historical process of social evolution, which leads to the expansion of the evolutionary process of differentiation and integration of social systems from a dispersed local to a differentiated global level. Different historical phases may be identified on the basis of technological and social change.

Chapter 3 illuminates processes of **internationalisation**. Traditionally, internationalisation has been used to describe increasing levels of activity in foreign countries, leading to the formation of MNEs. The basic assumption underlying this perspective is that firms first develop activity structures in their home country before they internationalise incrementally. Increasing global interdependencies and dynamics have led to an increasing skipping of stages in the incremental process and to the emergence of born globals. Both phenomena call for alternative explanations. In addition, internationalisation in terms of a process of increasing international complexity of firms neglects the fact that changes in the global dispersion of firm activities may also be negative (de-internationalisation) and a basic element in the reproduction of globally operating firms. This also includes MNEs, which usually are not taken into account in internationalisation literature. Chapter 3 describes literature on internationalisation strategy and internationalisation theory in order to provide a comprehensive overview in this field.

The **global network perspective** will be outlined in **Chapter 4**. Chapter 4 differentiates two general perspectives of network organisation: interorganisational and intraorganisational. In the context of **interorganisational networks** in which the firm is embedded, three levels may be distinguished: (1) local networks, (2) business networks, and (3) strategic networks. All these network levels may be globally differentiated and constitute building blocks in the firm's task environment. Firms may also be conceived as intraorganisational networks. In international business literature, MNEs are usually conceptualised as **intraorganisational networks**, thus paying tribute to the global complexity and heterogeneity of these firms. MNEs are described as transnational corporations, heterarchies, and multi-centre structures. These approaches focus on the complementary interplay of strategy and structure on the basis of learning and context management. Another important contribution in the intraorganisational network view of MNEs is the study of intraorganisational roles within these globally differentiated structures.

The underlying **evolutionary dynamics of globalisation** are the subject of **Chapter 5**. A basic task to explain evolutionary dynamics in globalisation is the identification of mechanisms of social evolution. Economic and social evolutionary theories and the knowledge-based perspective of management are outlined in Chapter 5 in order to extract relevant knowledge for the observation and explanation of globalisation processes. In order to allow the transfer of already existing theoretical concepts, which may provide some insight into the globalisation process of firms, these will be conceived as organisations in the sense of social systems. Based upon this definition, knowledge from different disciplines can be transferred to derive a dynamic view of the globalisation of firms and its implications for management. Chapter 5 begins with the presentation of social and economic evolutionary theories, which contribute concepts of evolutionary change in cultures, industries, and organisations. They also identify main mechanisms of social evolution. The knowledge-based view of strategic management illuminates more specific aspects of organisational evolution and contributes more focused knowledge to the study by providing evolutionary concepts from the management point of view.

Chapter 6 provides an **integrative evolutionary approach of the globalisation of firms** on the basis of social systems and evolutionary theories and includes knowledge from the more specific perspective in order to facilitate a comprehensive understanding of the chosen phenomenon. Figure 1-1 illustrates the conceptual framework of the study.

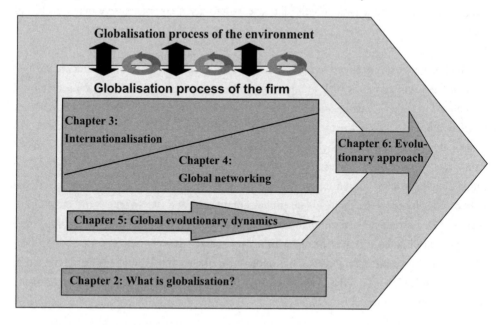

Figure 1-1:   Conceptual framework

2 What is globalisation?

In this chapter, a **historical point of view** serves to develop a basis for an analysis of the driving forces of globalisation and its inherent dynamic forces. The increasing interconnectedness and interdependencies of actors and actions in global competition should not be regarded only in terms of an isolated stage or '*quantum leap*' of economic competition or social transformation taking place over the last two or three decades. It is part of the historical process of continuing social differentiation and integration.

2.1 Characteristics of globalisation

The words '**internationalisation**' and '**globalisation**' are two of the most frequently used terms in contemporary scientific literature. They stand for the need to explain almost every form of social and especially economic change and adaptation. In society, there is a range from '**global culture**' in general, comprising items ranging from common human values to special trends in popular music and fashion. In the economy, '**global integration**' is generally used as the label for the exploitation of economies of scale, scope, and learning on a worldwide basis. As language reflects the actual social evolution, it might be interesting first to know when the words internationalisation and globalisation entered the discourse in the developing '**global community**' and for what reasons.

When new vocabulary gains currency, it is often because it captures an important change that is taking place in the world. New terminology is needed to describe new phenomena. For example, when Jeremy Bentham coined the word '**international**' in 1780, it caught hold because it resonated of a growing trend of those times, namely the **rise of nation-states and cross-border transactions** between them. People have not spoken of 'international relations' before this time since social affairs had not previously been organised so deeply around national communities governed by territorial spaces (Scholte 2000: 43). Adam Smith was the first to reflect on this development in the economic context in his work '*The wealth of nations*' (1776). A rich strand of literature has developed in this tradition, ranging from explanatory theories of international trade and FDI to process models of internationalisation since the 1960s (Chapter 3). All these theories are built on the assumption that enterprises are based in a **home country**. Their activities then included 'inter-national' cross-border arrangements. The cross-border transactions between nations and their enterprises are assumed to be mainly bilateral, due to the fact of serious restrictions in transportation and communication as well as to the idiosyncratic character of national economies (e.g. regulatory systems, entry barriers, consumer preferences). Since the late 1970s the incremental '**rings in the water models**' of internationalisation were complemented by **network models** focusing on global corporate structures and since the 1990s by studies of '**born global**' firms, which operate internationally from their foundation. The global perspective therefore entered international business discourse in the late 1970s and rapidly gained prominence in the 1980s.

Although the word '**global**' is about 400 years old (Bauman 1998: 2) the word '**globalisation**' first appeared in a dictionary in 1961 (Webster 1961: 965). The terms '**globalise**' and '**globalism**' were mentioned first in 1944 (Reiser/Davies 1944: 212, 219). McLuhan (1964) coined the term '**global village**' in order to describe the development of a borderless society. This marked the beginnings of explicit recognition in the contemporary period of the growing significance of the worldwide connectedness of social events and relationships (Kilminster 1997: 257).

The means to this development are provided by the phenomena of world-embracing transportation and communication. These means also allow for an integrative perspective on all activities of internationally operating enterprises. In his article 'The globalisation of markets' in 1983, Leavitt therefore stresses the efforts to exploit economies of scale and scope resulting from global integration and standardisation as the core of a global strategy. Homogenisation of markets and preferences are presented as the fundament of globalisation in this article. In the literature published afterwards, the meaning of '**global strategy**' in terms of '**global integration**' is still dominating in the marketing literature (Kustin 1994: 79-81) whereas in the fields of international business and strategic management the paradox of '**global integration vs. local responsiveness**' has become prominent. The organisational forms and strategic responses in order to cope with this paradox in a dialectical and integrative way are coined as '**transnational**' or '**glocal**'. The term '**globalisation**' thus can be conceived as academically significant since the mid-1980s whereas as a processual term it was still rare in the early 1990s (Waters 2001: 3). The words '**glocal**' and '**glocalisation**' entered '*The Oxford Dictionary of New Words*' in 1991 but became part of business jargon during the 1980s (Robertson 1995: 27).

2.1.1 Definitions of globalisation

A vast number of definitions can be found as '**globalisation**' is representing all kinds of human activity on the one hand and as it is influencing them on the other. Definitions of globalisation therefore differ principally in their scope and their focus. Many of them are confined to particular thematic areas. Burmester (1998: 136) therefore demands a more holistic view on globalisation. In his words, '*the tendency to work within the 'globalisation of...' framework, rather than 'globalisation is ... ', eventually may obscure vital truths of the same variety as a* *failure to see the forest shrinking due to focused interest in the growth of individual trees.'* This perspective appears to be reasonable, as all players in the globalisation process have to come to terms with growing worldwide expansion and density of relations and interdependencies. A focus on particular manifestations of globalisation, i.e. of the economy, thus should be embedded in the wider context of **'globalisation is ... '**.

Intuitively, globalisation is a process fuelled by, and resulting in increasing cross-border flows of goods, services, money, people, information, and culture (Held et al. 1999: 16). Sociologist Giddens (1990: 64, 1991: 21) proposes to regard globalisation as a decoupling or **'distanciation'** between space and time, while geographer Harvey (1989: 260, 284) and political scientist Mittelman (1996: 3) observe that globalisation entails a **'compression of time and space'**, a shrinking of the world. Sociologist Castells (1996: 92) emphasises the informational aspects of the global economy and stresses the resulting informational interconnectedness of economic action and actors. In a similar vein, sociologist Gereffi (1996: 64) writes about **'global commodity chains'**, with production being co-ordinated on a global scale. Management scholar Kobrin (1997: 147-148) describes globalisation as driven not by foreign trade and investment but by increasing technological scale and information flows. Political scientist Gilpin (1987: 389) defines globalisation as the *'increasing interdependence of national economies in trade, finance, and macroeconomic policy'*. Sociologist Albrow (1992: 248) defines globalisation as *'the process whereby the population of the world is bonded into a single society'* that is driven by the *'diffusion of practices, values and technology that have an influence on people's lives world-wide'* (Albrow 1997: 88). Hargittai/Centeno (2001: 1545) are convinced that *'globalisation involves a variety of links expanding and tightening a web of political, economic, and cultural interconnections'*. Harvey (1989: 241) illustrates the process in a diagram, which shows four maps of the world over time, each smaller than the previous one with its size determined by the speed of transportation. The world of the 1960s is about one-fiftieth the size of the world of the sixteenth century precisely because jet aircraft can travel at about 50 times the speed of a sailing ship (Figure 2-1).

Robertson (1992: 8) states that globalisation in the sense of a concept *'refers both to the compression of the world and the intensification of the consciousness of the world as a whole'*. *'In an increasingly globalised world there is a heightening of civilisational, societal, regional, and indeed individual, self-consciousness'* (Robertson 1992: 27). As a consequence, globalisation might be regarded as a self-fuelling process in which the evolution of global structures is providing social and thus economic actors with expectations and perspectives that lead to more planning and implementing of actions with global reach, thus producing further **'global realities'**. According to Waters (2001: 15), *'globalisation involves a phenomenology of contraction'* and *'implies the phenomenological elimination of space and the generalisation of* *time. The phenomenology of globalisation is reflexive. The inhabitants of the planet self-consciously orient themselves to the world as a whole....'* Axtman (1998: 14) adds: *'As we find ourselves in the vortex of time-space compression, the 'globe' has practically become the reference-point for our identity formation.'*

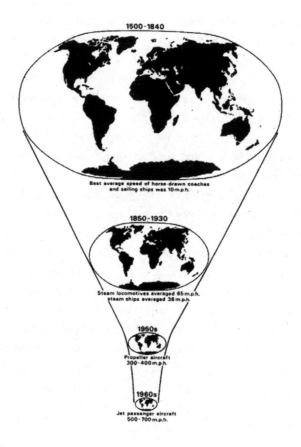

Figure 2-1:   Shrinking map of the world
                (Source: Harvey 1989: 241)

Definitions of '**globalisation**' can be found in a large variety of scientific disciplines as this phenomenon is touching every part of social life and activity. Some of the most prominent definitions are shown in Table 2-1. These examples are only a few out of a vast number of definitions. Mauro Guillén (2001) has counted literally dozens of citations using the term, each often offering a new version of a definition.

Definitions of globalisation

'Globalisation is a social process in which the constraints of geography on economic, political, social and cultural arrangements recede, in which people become increasingly aware that they are receding and in which people act accordingly' (Waters 2001: 5).

'Globalisation may be taken to be the production of an interdependent world system resulting from the process of communication among the people, governments, and institutions of the planet. Globalisation comes about because of the increasingly meaningful communication that takes place between any two points on the globe, particularly regarding political, economic, and scientific activities' (Barnett 2001: 1638).

'Globalisation refers to the multiplicity of linkages and interconnections between the states and societies, which make up the present world system. It describes the process by which events, decisions, and activities in one part of the world come to have significant consequences for individuals and communities in quite distant parts of the globe. Globalisation has two distinct phenomena: scope (or stretching) and intensity (or deepening). (McGrew 1997a: 23).

Table 2-1: Definitions of globalisation

In terms of a historical process beginning at the time of geographically dispersed and isolated societies, globalisation may be condensed to three main processes (Table 2-2):

Globalisation processes:	Characteristics:
Processes of internationalisation (changes in the global differentiation and extension of social systems)	• Spatial differentiation of social actors on global scale • Formation of social systems with world-wide extension (e.g. '*born globals*')
Processes of global network formation	• Growing interdependencies between social actors (individuals, organisations, states) on global scale • Growing integration of social communication, activities, and structures
Processes of evolutionary dynamics	• Compression of time and space (due to transport and communication technologies) • Differentiation and integration of social systems on global scale

Table 2-2: Processes and characteristics of globalisation

2.1.2 Distinction between globalisation and similar concepts

In literature, there is a huge variety of concepts in the field of organisation, which explain different aspects of this phenomenon or describe it from a different angle. Concepts like internationalisation, localisation, regionalisation, or glocalisation sometimes overlap in their explanations and will be outlined and distinguished in the following.

2.1.2.1 Distinction between globalisation and internationalisation

Globalisation is related differently to internationalisation, depending on the perspective taken. Some authors describe globalisation and regionalisation as a special form of internationalisation (Germann et al. 1999: 1). Others conceive globalisation as a new phase of internationalisation, where the integration of globally configured activities is the central characteristic. In the latter view, globalisation has essentially to do with the dynamics of capital accumulation and technological change and is symbolised by the international investment activities of multinational corporations (Chesnai 1995: 78). Globalisation in these views is restricted to the economic area and the activities of multinational corporations.

The concept of internationalisation is rooted in a worldview that is based on nation states that provided the basis of social organisation during the process of modernisation and industrialisation. This concept describes the expansion and development of '**inter-national**' and thus cross-border activities by individuals, organisations, and states. Pettigrew (2000: 611) contends: '*The international world ...has been evolving for 400 years, it is the traditional nation-state that we have known since the Westphalia Treaty*'. He further differentiates between the '**era of internationalisation**' and the current '**era of globalisation**'. The former implied two things: first, expansion of the geographic space where economic, commercial, and an increasing proliferation of other activities were carried out; and second, the existence of national borders. Pettigrew (Ibid.) draws the following distinction:

'*Internationalisation increased the interdependence among societies designed as nation-states, and, in fact, the very word 'internationalisation' seemed to emphasise the impermeability of national, i.e. political spaces. The more recent phenomenon of globalisation is of a qualitatively different order. Globalisation is the result of technological advances, trade liberalisation and deregulation. In this world, corporation can decide to carry out a given industrial function in a given geographic region for economic reasons, notwithstanding any political considerations.*'

Kobrin has proposed a distinction between the globalisation in the late twentieth century – which marks the '**take-off**' of globalisation for many authors – and the previous period of modern expansion of world economy in the nineteenth century commonly assumed to represent the beginning of globalisation. The period in the nineteenth century *'links discrete, mutually exclusive, geographical national markets through cross-border flows of trade and investment'* (Kobrin 1997: 147). By contrast, the global economy of the late twentieth century is driven by the increasing scale of technology, the surge in cross-border collaboration of firms along the value-added chain, and the cross-border integration of information flows. Thus, globalisation has substantive meaning because now *'national markets are fused transnationally rather than linked across borders'* (Ibid. 148, see also Held et al. 1999: 429-31). Similarly, Asheim (1997: 144-45) states that *'internationalisation refers simply to the extension of activities across national boundaries; globalisation involves more than this and is qualitatively different. It implies a degree of purposive functional integration among geographically dispersed activities'.*

Scholte (2000) insists that the difference between globality and internationality needs to be stressed in particular. Whereas international relations are interterritorial relations, global relations are supraterritorial relations. International relations are cross-border exchanges over distance, while global relations are trans-border exchanges without distance. Internationality is embedded in territorial space; globality transcends that geography (Scholte 2000: 49). In this context, Waters (2001: 84) proposes:

'The material flows merely render the global economy internationalised, that is, they elaborate connections between territories that remain bordered, separate and sovereign. Globalisation implies the dedifferentiation of the planet, rendering irrelevant national differences in economic practices so that borders and sovereignty will themselves become irrelevant and will expire.'

In a similar vein, Hirst/Thompson (1996) draw a proper distinction between an inter-national economy and a globalised one. The first type is characterised by elaborated migration, trade, and investment flows between nations in a way that there emerges an international division of labour. By contrast, in an economy that is globalised, these national regulatory processes are subsumed by an autonomous supranational system of transactions and processes. Hirst/Thompson assume the world to be still in the firm grip of the first type. In a similar vein, Kreikebaum (1998: 171) argues that if analysed clearly, globalisation often just takes the form of internationalisation as only a relatively small number of **'global players'** are acting on a real global basis.

Internationalisation processes therefore provide the basis for a global system by the expansion and development of activities of firms and other organisations in different countries on a bilateral or multilateral basis. Globalisation does not only include the international expansion of activities; it also implies an integrative '**one-system perspective**'. For example, such a global system may emerge in the organisational form of a global market, impressively represented by the global capital market.

Another global system may be a global hierarchical organisation like an MNE. Such an MNE may be regarded as one global system (integrative view) as well as a structure of different local and regional subsystems (differentiated view). This dialectical quality is constitutive for contemporary global systems and provides the impetus for their evolutionary dynamic. Their energy is provided by the exploitation of integrative advantages like economies of scale and scope on the one hand and of national differences which provide the basis for market imperfections and possibilities for learning and innovation on the other. '**Pure international**' companies without international/global integration of their activities would mainly be restricted to exploit market imperfections. Consequently this perspective provides the basis for the majority of explanatory internationalisation theories (see Chapter 3). A major weakness of these theories is the underlying perspective of a world dominated by nation-states. In the absence of nation-states no FDI exists. '**Multinational**' or even '**transnational**' enterprises cannot be separated from nation-states (Pitelis 2002: 128). Consequently, an approach to describe the evolution of social systems embedded in a worldwide environment and/or with worldwide extension must be '**global**', comprising all other more focused or bounded perspectives.

2.1.2.2 Globalisation versus localisation and regionalisation

The pace of globalisation on the whole has progressively quickened over time. This does not mean that the development is linear or irreversible. Only since the 1960s globality figures continually, comprehensively, and centrally entered the lives of a large proportion of humanity (Scholte 2000: 87). As noted earlier, over the past two centuries trade as an indicator had alternating phases of territorialisation and globalisation. The same stands for economic globalisation in general. After a phase of increasing international scope in trade beginning with the eighteenth century, globalisation was derailed by war (in 1914) and by economic policy during recession (in the early 1930). Intensive globalisation as known today began to accelerate from the 1950s with another quantum leap in the 1980s and 1990s (see Table 2-3). Only since the 1980s, the world economy has become so structurally interdependent '*that the use of the word global, as distinct from international, has become justifiable*' (Dunning 1997c: 33). In terms of exports and imports, Europe dominates the world market with shares of nearly 40%. Nevertheless it has to be remarked that a major share of European trade is intra-regional trade. North America and Asia changed the positions in exports during the last fifty years in favour of the Asian countries. Latin America's share in international trade was cut by half, while Africa with a drop from 7.3% to 2.3% in world exports de facto became irrelevant in economic terms.

World merchandise trade by region and selected economy 1948, 1953, 1963, 1973, 1983, 1993 and 2000 (billion US Dollars and percentage)

	1948	1953	1963	1973	1983	1993	2000
Exports							
Value							
World	58.0	84.0	157.0	579.0	1835.0	3641.0	6186.0
Share							
World	100.0	100.0	100.0	100.0	100.0	100.0	100.0
North America	27.3	24.2	19.3	16.9	15.4	16.8	17.1
Latin America	12.3	10.5	7.0	4.7	5.8	4.4	5.8
Western Europe	31.5	34.9	41.4	45.4	38.9	43.7	39.5
C./E. Europe/ Baltic States/CIS a)	6.0	8.1	11.0	9.1	9.5	2.9	4.4
Africa	7.3	6.5	5.7	4.8	4.4	2.5	2.3
Middle East	2.0	2.7	3.2	4.1	6.8	3.4	4.2
Asia	13.6	13.1	12.4	14.9	19.1	26.3	26.7
GATT/WTO members c)	60.4	68.7	72.8	81.8	76.0	86.9	90.7
Imports							
Value							
World	66.0	84.0	163.0	589.0	1881.0	3752.0	6490.0
Share							
World	100.0	100.0	100.0	100.0	100.0	100.0	100.0
North America	19.8	19.7	15.5	16.7	17.8	19.8	23.2
Latin America	10.6	9.3	6.8	5.1	4.5	5.2	6.0
Western Europe	40.4	39.4	45.4	47.4	40.0	42.9	39.6
C./E.Europe/ Baltic States CIS a)	5.8	7.6	10.3	8.9	8.4	2.9	3.7
Africa	7.6	7.0	5.5	4.0	4.6	2.6	2.1
Middle East	1.7	2.0	2.3	2.8	6.3	3.2	2.6
Asia	14.2	15.1	14.2	15.1	18.5	23.4	22.8
GATT/WTO members c)	52.9	66.0	74.2	89.1	83.9	91.0	92.0

A) Factors between 1983 and 1993; and (ii) the Baltic States and the CIS mutual trade between 1993 and 2000.
B) Beginning with 1998, figures refer to South Africa only and no longer to the Southern African Customs Union.
C) Membership as of the year stated.
Note: Between 1973 and 1983 and between 1993 and 2000 export and imports shares were significantly influenced by oil price developments.

Table 2-3: World merchandise trade by region and selected economy
(Source: Worldbank Report 2001: 30)

Now, the **phase of intensive economic globalisation** seems to come to a halt, as foreign direct investment flows slumped from more than $1.3 trillion in 2000 to barely half that in 2001. After growing by 12 % in 2000 and by an average of 7% a year throughout the 1990s, the volume of global trade was virtually stagnant in 2001.

Cumulatively, from 1997 to 2001, emerging economies have received a mere $19 billion in bank loans, bonds and cross-border investment in shares. This *'paltry figure'* has to be compared with the $655 billion the same emerging markets received between 1994 and 1997, *'as banks fell over themselves to lend and investors lapped up emerging–market bonds'* (The Economist, February 2nd, 2002: 61). Globalisation thus is not a linear, but an alternating phenomenon. In the long term it is still increasing though with different momentum in the functional social subsystems.

It may be assumed that after the phase of very intensive globalisation in the 1980s and 1990s some saturation in the exploitation of advantages from globalisation has materialised. This may be attributed simply to a temporal downturn in the business cycle or to the possibility that in many segments of the worldwide economy advantages from global integration are being widely exploited yet. In the near future, the globalisation of other societal systems like the political or ethical systems may be more accelerated (and needed) than that of the economy, the traditional pacemaker of globalisation. **Globalisation as a historical process** therefore may take the shape of a classical s-shaped curve of organisational growth.

What about society, if the world happened to be completely globalised one day? There may not be an accelerating process of increasing global system formation any more but the continuous evolutionary social process of differentiation and integration will stabilise again. This had been taken place on a local level for thousands of years before the global quantum leap began. The difference will be that there is an integrating global social system with respective global, regional, local, intermediate or even smaller systems, hence more differentiated *and* integrated on worldwide scale. From this perspective, globalisation simply represents the quantum leap of human social evolution from a local and tribal level to a globally differentiated society. It covers processes of global integration, regionalisation, localisation, and further functional differentiation of social systems.

2.1.2.2.1 Globalisation and regionalisation
Globalisation is still a **selective phenomenon**. Many countries benefit; others do not. A study by the World Bank shows that 24 countries, home to 3 billion people, including China, Argentina, Brazil, India and the Philippines, have substantially increased their trade-to-GDP ratios over the past 20 years. Economies grew by an average of 5% a year during the 1990s

and poverty rates declined. However, another 2 billion people live in countries (e.g. Pakistan, much of Africa) that have become less rather than more globalised. Income per head fell on average by 1% a year during the 1990s and poverty has risen. At the same time, there are **strong indicators for inequality** (UNCTAD 2001a: 19):

- in 1993 the poorest 10% of the world's population had only 1.6% of the income of the richest 10%;
- the richest 1% of the world's population received as much income as the poorest 57%; and
- around 25% of the world's population received 75% of the world's income.

'In short, globalisation is not, and never was, global' (The Economist, February 2nd, 2002: 62). This assertion is underlined by the concentration ratios documented in Table 2-4. In a provocative – or maybe overly realistic – way, Rugman (2001: 1) states that *'globalisation is a myth; it never really occurred anyway.'* He notices that *'the process of globalisation is a triad- and management-driven one. Politics, culture, law, and related issues are indirectly affected by the fallout, but these are secondary effects, and such indirect outcomes should not be confused with the drivers of international economic activities – the MNEs'*.

Concentration ratios of FDI, trade, domestic investment and technology payments, 1985 and 2000 (Percentage)

Item	Inward FDI		Outward FDI		Exports [b]	Domestic investment [c]	Technology payments
	Flows [a]	Stock	Flows [a]	Stock			
top 10 countries							
1985	70.0	70.4	85.0	89.8	58.9	70.7	81.7
2000	73.0	67.7	83.2	81.2	56.2	73.7	80.4
top 30 countries							
1985	94.5	92.6	99.3	98.8	82.2	89.9	99.3
2000	93.0	89.2	98.9	98.1	83.6	91.0	98.8
top 50 countries							
1985	98.8	97.7	100.1[d]	99.8	91.5	96.6	99.99
2000	97.6	96.2	100.0	99.8	91.5	96.7	99.95

a The 1983 – 1985 average for 1985 and the 1998 – 2000 average for 2000.
b Export of goods and non-factor services. 1999 data for 2000.
c Gross fixed capital formation. 1999 data for 2000.
d Due to negative flows for some countries, the share is more than 100 per cent.

Table 2-4: Economic concentration ratios 1985 and 2000 (percentages)
(Source: UNCTAD 2001: 39)

Rugman's economic hard-liner position has strong foundations when only economic facts are considered. Globalisation is reduced to a fraction by considering the fact that the **500 largest MNEs** - based in the United States, the European Union, and Japan - account for more than **80% of the world stock of FDI** and more than **50% of world trade**. This impression is even augmented by the assumption that **most global trade** and **FDI by MNEs** are now **intra-firm** based and conducted in **triad-based** business networks or clusters (Rugman 2001: 2).

Pausenberger (1999: 38) estimates the share of intraorganisational trade to represent about 40% of international trade. Kreikebaum (1997: 173) assumes that one third of global trade is conducted intraorganisationally, within MNEs, and another third between themselves. Consequently, globalisation for Rugman is defined by *'the activities of multinational enterprises engaged in foreign direct investment and the development of business networks to create value across national borders'* (Rugman 2001: 4).

Another main argument of Rugman is that the vast majority of manufacturing and service activity is organised regionally, not globally. MNEs are assumed to be the engines – *'and they think regionally and act locally'* (Rugman 2001: 1). Conti (1997: 17) observes that with the beginning of the 1990s the globalisation process has been marked by a trend towards regional integration and the formation of inter-company networks. The global economy and the trend towards globalisation is not a phenomenon that is totalising and homogenising in nature (Le Heron/Park 1995: 4). On the contrary, it is accompanied by (and even defined by) historically specific patterns of different levels of complexity, which are products of structure stability and coherence (Ibid: 5).

'Accompanied by the de-standardisation of production, the development of national varieties and the greater complexity of products and markets, globalisation makes specific national (regional, company) features the foundation of competition between different entities, where variety is the origin of the production of wealth and competitive advantage' (Conti 1997: 20).

Seen in this way, **regionalisation** has been **proceeding on a par** with the development of a **global economy** (OECD-Observer No. 192, 1995: 20). Castells even considers regionalisation to be a systemic attribute of the global economy (Castells 1996: 102).

Dunning (2000: 14) believes that the contemporary phase of globalisation is a process leading to the structural transformation of firms and nations. As such, it represents a discontinuity in the evolutionary process of globalisation in the sense that it creates new and deeper cross-border relationships and dependencies. Sometimes the transformation takes place at a regional level: much of the integrated production network of MNEs is so focused. Sometimes it occurs at a global level.

An important factor supporting the assumption of regionalisation is the **emergence of large trading blocs** in order to increase the internal market size and to protect against external competition. In the case of the EU this integration goes even far beyond mere economic reasoning by aiming at the development of a pluralistic European society. Buckley et al. (2001: 252, 256) assume that regional economic integration (REI) allows countries to emulate efficiency gains from increasing country size in a number of discrete ways, and to different extents on the levels of markets, such as financial, goods, service and labour markets. REI offers both large and small firms the opportunity to enjoy the advantages of a large 'home' market, whether it is their native home or their adoptive home. REI is therefore a way of increasing the preference of MNEs for local production within the integrating area, and also of increasing relative discrimination against firms outside the area of integration. In their empirical study, Buckley et al. (2001: 270), found evidence that the regional economic integration within North America (NAFTA) had the effect that investment by firms from European countries had been greater than it would have been otherwise.

Year	Organisation	Name
1958	EEC	European Economic Community
		From 1965: European Community (EC)
		From 1992: European Union (EU)
1960	CACM	Central American Market
1960	EFTA	European Free Trade Association
1964	UDEAC	Customs and Economic Union of Central Africa
1967	ASEAN	Association of South East Asian Nations
1969	ANDEAN	The Andean Group
1973	CARRICOM	Caribbean Common Market
1974	ECOWAS	Economic Community of West African States
1974	CEAO	Communauté Économique de L´Afrique de L´ouest
1975	Lomé	Agreement between the EEC and the ACP states
1980	LAIA	Latin American Integration Association
1981	PTA	Eastern and Southern African Preferential Trade Area
1989	APEC	Asian-Pacific Economic Co-operation
1991	MERCOSUR	Mercado do Sur
1993	CEFTA	Central European Free Trade Area
1993	AFTA	ASEAN Free Trade Area
1994	EEA	European Economic Area
1994	NAFTA	North American Free Trade Agreement
2005	FTAA	Free Trade Agreement of the Americas

Table 2-5: Formation of regional trading blocs
(Sources: Ball/McCulloch 1999: 138-150, 390-392; Cateora/Graham 1999: 269-308)

The liberalisation of financial and capital markets, the reduction of trade barriers and the formation of regional and supranational trading blocs were other important factors in the development of an international economic context. A chronological list of the most influential trading blocs is illustrated in Table 2-5.

At an organisational level, regionalisation is very much based upon **regional networks** and **industrial districts**, offering the possibility of co-specialisation and co-operation between firms and other institutions within a limited territory. A distinct institutional environment with idiosyncratic competencies and resources offers a good platform for flexible specialisation within a culturally more homogeneous and trustful atmosphere (see Chapter 4.1).

2.1.2.2.2 Globalisation and localisation

'These are global times' - or more accurately, *'these are global-local times'* (Amin/Robins 1991: 105). What we are seeing is the development of increasingly direct and immediate relations between global and local spheres (local in the sense of being a relational concept, possibly a locality, but also a region, a nation state, or even a panregional area such as Europe). In this process, localities, regions, and nations are being dramatically reshaped. We are not seeing the emergence, or re-emergence, of autonomous and proactive localities or regions. If the '**local**' is being redefined, it is in terms and under the conditions of the forces of globalisation. It is the global dynamic now shaping the structure and dynamic of localities, regions, and nations (Ibid.).

Much of the debate about globalisation has tended to assume that it is a process, which is overriding locality. Robertson (1995: 26-27, 35) does not agree with this perspective and argues that *'global is not counterposed to the local; rather, it is essentially included within the global. ... In this respect globalisation, defined in its most general sense as the compression of the world as a whole, involves the linking of localities'*. The state of the world remains indeed far from anything even approaching spatial liquefaction although the economic interconnections across the globe are expanding at a rapid pace. **Localised processes** of growth and development have been actually **accentuated by globalisation**. This is nowhere more apparent than in the case of those dense concentrations of capital and human labour now multiplying throughout in the guise of large metropolitan areas (Scott 1998: 47). The formation of a global social system is inherently based upon the interplay between the constituting geographic (e.g. regional, local) and functional (e.g. economic, political) subsystems.

As **globalisation** can be defined as a **dialectical process** (Mazlish 1993: 6), the meaning-constitutive difference in international management is '**global integration versus local adaptation**':

- *global integration* in order to gain competitive advantages from economies of scale and scope as well as from global learning (Ghoshal 1987: 428), and
- *local adaptation* based on different environmental conditions and consumer behaviour in different countries.

The distinction can be applied to all products and functional areas (Ghoshal 1987: 429). The dynamic balancing of this paradox is expressed by the term '**glocal**' and represents a main challenge to actors in international business.

The territorial distribution of economic activity structures is the domain of **economic geography**. In economic geography there are two important concerns about location and firm performance. First, economic, entrepreneurial and technological activities tend to agglomerate at certain places, leading to patterns of national and regional specialisation. Second, the performance and development of a firm to a considerable extent seems to be determined by the conditions prevailing in its environment. Furthermore, the conditions in the immediate locality – in the local cluster or local milieu – seem to be important in particular (Malmberg/Sölvell 1997: 119).

The economic geographers Taylor/Conti argue that economic change is now creating new geographies of economic activity. They identify six such **geographies** associated with **economic globalisation** (Taylor/Conti 1997: 2).

1. In *production*, the global reach of TNCs by FDI and co-operation has created an integrated and co-ordinated production.
2. In *finance*, financial and business service organisations have created a global financial system hubbed on a few, key global cities tied into an electronic web.
3. The geography of *control* is marked by the emerging patterns of global control. Shifting patterns and processes of control in TNCs are accompanied by the emergence of new trading blocs and the creation of the '*competition state*'.
4. The geographies of *time-space compression and substitutability* (material for material, source for source, labour for labour) are driven by the enabling technologies of IT, telecommunication, and transportation.
5. New global geographies are also emerging in *capital-labour relations*: international division of labour, global patterns of labour migration and the re-establishment of the '*local*' in understanding the mechanisms of labour markets.
6. Global geographies of *consumption* are stimulated by the development of transnational culture traits.

'These six sets of patterns are emerging geographies of point and counterpoint between the global and the local. All are indicative of global-local tensions – and, indeed, a global-local dialectic – and all are targets of enquiry in an economic geography of globalisation' (Taylor/Conti 1997: 2-3).

The '**global**', therefore, is to be understood in a relational sense. Its extent is not definable a priori but only in terms of the relationships that interconnect its constituent subsystems. The global, in other words, is constituted by characteristics of the systems it connects, modelled upon their specific configurations. The '**local**' too is not a simple physical entity. It is not simply a part of a complex system, but a whole in itself, endowed with its own identity distinguishing it from the environment and other systems (Taylor/Conti 1997: 6). Malmberg/Sölvell (1997: 127) are convinced that the very nature of the innovation process tends to make technological activity locally confined, and suggests that recent globalisation forces have not altered – and presumably cannot alter in the near future – this process in any fundamental way. In a similar vein, Porter/Stern (2001: 28) argue that innovation has become the defining challenge for global competitiveness. From their perspective, companies therefore must evaluate the attractiveness of local environments in creating and commercialising new ideas.

From the resource-based view, Fahy (1998: 125) argues that globally sustainable competitive advantages depend on the possession of certain key resources that have the characteristic of value and barriers to duplication. Intangible resources are more difficult to duplicate than tangible. Especially global networks and reputation as examples of accumulated resources are hard to duplicate. Country-specific resources are diverse and complex as well and may be an important source of advantage. Added to firm-specific resources, the globally scaled firm has access to a complex and diverse resource pool. Two types of **country-specific resources** can be differentiated (Fahy 1998: 128):

1. *country-specific assets* include a country's location and climate, its natural resources, its costs of labour and capital, and government incentives; and
2. *country-specific capabilities* refer to a country's stock of knowledge of technological and management practices. These capabilities tend to be culture-bound, developed slowly over time and diffuse across boundaries of the firm easier than across national borders.

Dunning (1997: 115) is convinced that location '... *in today's innovation-led economy ... is being increasingly influenced by the availability and quality of location-specific 'created' assets; and, most noticeably, the kind of infrastructure which fosters entrepreneurship and knowledge accumulation, and that helps to lower distance-related transaction costs.*'

Globally acting companies can learn from local contexts via their subsidiaries and can transfer the gained knowledge in order to develop competitive advantages. This way they can gain advantages compared to mere locally or regionally acting companies. This resource-based view on globalisation has its antecedents in internationalisation theories in industrial organisation tradition (Hymer 1960, Dunning 1977, 1997).

2.1.2.2.3 Hybrid global and local structures

The **global-local nexus** is unequivocally complex. At its heart is the concept of the **network**, which has gained considerable prominence in economic geographic literature (see Dicken/Thrift (1992), Grabher (1993), Dicken (1994)). Dicken (1994: 217) argues that a critical determinant of local economic development is the relationship between transnational corporations and nation-states. Each can be conceptualised as highly embedded interacting networks as well as competitive institutions that are subject to fundamental global-local tensions. According to Dicken (1986: 184), *'the interrelationships between firms of different sizes and types increasingly span national boundaries to create a set of geographically nested relationships from local to global scales'*. MNEs and SMEs in each of the major organisational segments operate over widely varying geographical ranges and perform rather different roles in a global economy. But the most important point to be made is that the segments are interconnected in complex ways. It is such interconnections, for example, that a very small firm in one country may be directly linked into a global production network whereas most small firms serve only a very restricted geographical area (Dicken 1986: 185).

From a **dynamic perspective**, Mathews (2002: 6-7) contends that the **world economy** and in particular its globally interlinked character may be called a **worldwide web of interfirm connections**. The global economy can be conceived as a network of networks.

In what he calls '**new zoology of the international economy**', Mathews (2002) describes the emerging global network economy with its '**new inhabitants**'. In this view, the incumbents of the global economic arena – the classical, resource-rich MNEs – are increasingly joined by new forms of species. These are *'born globals'*, *'micro-MNEs'*, *'hidden champions'*, *'contractor MNEs'*, *'global niche players'*, and *'late- or newcomer MNEs'* from the global economic *'periphery'* like the Acer Group (Taiwan), Ispat (India), Cemex (Mexico), Li &Fung (Hong Kong), or the Hong Leong Group (Singapore) (Ibid. 21-26). All the latter companies exhibited three key features in their remarkable **'latecomer' internationalisation process** (Mathews 2002: 37-39):

- *accelerated internationalisation* through innovative acquisitions and partnerships;
- *strategic innovation* in business models and practices; and

- *organisational innovation* by devising non-hierarchical, *'lattice like'* structures that optimise the possibilities of achieving rapid global spread, e.g. by global *'cellular'* structures, *'client-server'* organisational architecture or an *'internet protocol'* architecture (Acer).

These **key features** observed by Mathews reflect the **basic globalisation capabilities** of (here: accelerated) internationalisation, network management, and evolutionary dynamics defined above. The common features of the successful latecomers revolve around their capacity to overcome initial disadvantages by exploiting potential advantages such as lack of organisational inertia. The outstanding competitive advantage in this regard is the possibility of expanding globally with an exclusively geocentric approach (Ibid. 40). The **global network competition** therefore gains a very **different profile**. The standard economic view, where firms are treated as atomistic entities engaged in international production operations, is misleading at the best of times (Ibid. 45). For firms engaged in international production, **exchange relationships** become **all-important** (Ibid. 27).

The **network** may be basically conceived as a representation of social interaction between actors. A system seen in this light evolves and expresses itself through a **relational dynamic**, involving agents acting both collectively and individually. Thus local actors or agents interact globally not only as individuals but also as an expression of the territorialised socio-economic relationships in which they are embedded. At the same time, the same local systems interact with each other and with local individual agents who belong simultaneously to both local and global networks. This results in a perspective on global-local interconnection as a mass of complexity and contingency fuelled by recursive relationships (Taylor/Conti 1997: 7). The network structure expresses the relation and the valorisation of **different local identities** that - precisely because of their diversity - can integrate each other and evolve in a **global scenario**. In this light, the territorial dimension represents a priority instrument for the explanation of the present industrial dynamic. If the local is not separated from the global but part of it, it must be concluded that the phenomenon of globalisation generates a new dialectic between local and global (Conti 1997: 20). Taylor et al. (1997: 72) argue that global-local interdependencies are not just an issue of the global, national, and local as separate spatial spheres of social organisation and action, but are an issue of the interconnectedness, linkage and hybridisation between agents and places. *'It is precisely because globalization enhances mutual awareness in the world that diversity in organizational form is expected as countries and firms seek to differentiate themselves in the global economy'* (Guillén 2001a: 6).

Nederveen Pieterse (1995) is conceiving of **globalisation as hybridisation** of different organisational forms with different territorial scope: *'What globalisation means in structured terms,* *then, is the increase in the available modes of organisation: transnational, international, macro-regional, national, micro-regional, municipal, local*' (Ibid. 50).

'*The overall tendency towards increasing global density and interdependence, or globalisation, translates, then, into the pluralisation of organisational forms. Structured hybridisation and the mélange of diverse modes of organisation give rise to a pluralisation of forms of co-operation and competition as well as to novel mixed forms of co-operation*' (Ibid. 52).

From this perspective, globalisation also induces and represents a '**creolisation of global culture**' (Friedman 1995). As an early example, Friedman (1995: 74) describes Marco Polo's gift of pasta from China and the subsequent introduction of pasta into the cuisine of the Italian peninsular. Another example is presented by Rowe/Schelling (1991: 161): '*How do we come to terms with phenomena such as Thai boxing Moroccan girls in Amsterdam, Asian rap in London, Irish bagels, Chinese tacos and Mardi Gras Indians in the United States, or Mexican schoolgirls dressed in Greek togas dancing in the style of Isidora Duncan?*'

Summarised, it might be argued from this perspective that '*material exchanges localize, political exchanges internationalize; and symbolic exchanges globalize*' (Waters 1995: 9).

2.2 Globalisation as an evolutionary historical process

Globalisation is a processual term that can be applied to any social system and activity. It can be conceived as the result of human and social evolution, as it represents the development of a global society linked by communication, activities, and transportation on a worldwide basis. At the same time, globalisation has an immense impact on this evolutionary process. Something new has emerged out of a history of separated and dispersed tribes, kingdoms, and nations. There are still local, national and regional '**niches**' but a new one has emerged providing the resources for an increasing amount of social systems that occupy global space. A historical perspective on globalisation will provide a look on the quality and the extent of the formation of social systems on global scale.

The globalisation of society and especially of the economy is not a new phenomenon, which has just been evolving during the last two or three decades and which is sometimes attributed with a somehow metaphysical character. On the contrary, it should be regarded as a natural process of social evolution. Therefore, '*...we should reject the idea of the 'Globalization Process' as a law-governed change but recognize globalization in sum as an overall historical transformation*' (Albrow 1996: 93).

The **roots of globalisation** are defined differently in literature, depending on the taken perspective. The earliest form of globalisation might be regarded as the diffusion of '*Homo sapiens*' from prehistoric Africa around the globe some 200 million years ago. What followed was the global existence of scattered families, groups, and tribes belonging to the '*mankind*' but these had merely an immediate locational perspective. The perspective ended at the fringes of the habitat. One could also argue, that globalisation begins with the dawn of history (Guillén 2001: 237). From this perspective, the beginning of globalisation in the sense of spatial expansion and integration of social systems therefore is identical with the development of civilisations. The historical process of globalisation can be described in the form of phases or stage models. They differ in terms of the time-span that is covered and the criteria chosen in order to differentiate the phases.

2.2.1 First stage: early international trade

From an economic perspective, as early as 4.000 years ago, there was an evolution of corporate structures in and around ancient **Assyria**, which nowadays may be termed '**multinational**' (Moore/Lewis 1998). Early **Mesopotamia**, in the third millennium BC, was importing raw materials; Babylonian and Indian societies were engaging in trade as far back as 800 BC. The ancient Egyptians, Greeks, and Phoenicians all traded with foreigners and encountered many of the same obstacles of contemporary managers – such as differences in language, culture, customs, and expectations; varying forms of government; and difficult transportation.

The early **Olympic Games** also provide evidence of the extent of international business in earlier times. Held between 776 BC and 394 AD, descriptions suggest a meeting that was part sport, part religion, and largely commerce. People travelled from all the Greek city-states as well as from other countries. '*Not unlike an international trade show today, this meeting provided merchants, entrepreneurs, and salespeople from all over the region an opportunity to show off their wares while making valuable contacts with people with whom they might do business in the future*' (Mendenhall et al. 1995: 7).

By 300 BC Greek traders were in contact with northern India via Arabia and trade between India and China was developing. When the Chinese Han dynasty (206 BC - AD 220) took control of the crucial land corridor between the Himalayas and the Steppes, an East-West corridor over the Eurasian landmass was effectively opened. The '**Silk Route**', as it became known, was a complex patchwork of land and sea routes that linked the Roman Empire in the West with the Chinese Han empire in the East, by way of Anatolia, Mesopotamia, Persia, routes north and south of the Talkiman Desert and into China herself. Branching off from this trade other routes connected up with northern India, South East Asia, Russia, and Arabia. At either end of the route more local networks connected up the peripheral regions of Europe, Japan, and Korea to the Silk Route (Held et al.1999: 152-153).

Some 2,000 years ago Herod built the port of Caesarea Maritima. This served as a major east-west route with Byzantinum and Rome, 60 days away by sea. The harbour handled local products like wine, flax, and grain as well as exotic products like silk and spices brought from Asia by caravan. Closely tied to the trade in silk and spices in Asia there was the movement of jade. Kunlun, the original '*Jade Mountains*', were Asia's sole source of jade from prehistoric times until the 1700s. The camel caravans travelling west on the Silk Route carrying Cathay's fabrics to the Middle East passed through Kunlun. As truckers do today, they sought other cargo for the trip west and packed heavy jade boulders more than 2,000 miles to the emperors' workshops in Beijing (Mendenhall et al. 1995: 6). Marco Polo observed in 1272 that '*chalcedony and jasper, which are carried for sale to Cathay, ...form a considerable ...commerce*' (Newman 1987). The Silk Route therefore only represents a very prominent example within a system of trade routes between Europe and East Asia. Other examples are the '**Amber Route**' from the Baltic to the Mediterranean, and the '**Spice Route**' by sea between Egypt, the Yemen and India. Trade on the Silk Route prospered until the fall of the Western Roman Empire and the Han Empire. Trade was rekindled in the four centuries leading up to AD 1000 and blossomed between AD 1000 and 1350. As Deng (1997) concludes, '*China's long-distance staple trade reveals a system of international exchange ... in fact ... the existence of a China-centred trading system in pre-modern Asia*'.

Over the same period, **seaborne networks of trade** flourished between the Islamic lands of the Fertile Crescent and Arabia, the coastal city-states of India, African kingdoms and Arab entrepots on the East Coast of Africa. In the fourteenth and early fifteenth centuries these trade networks connected directly with China itself so that in the premodern era trading networks had developed linking Europe, Asia and Africa (Held et al. 1999: 153)

Foreman-Peck (1998: xiv) comments that a **characteristic** of the world in these times was its **'intransitivity' of discovery and knowledge**. The volume of long distance trade, travel and communication for most of history was inevitably irregular, small, and restricted to items (or people) of high value in relation to weight and bulk, simply because transport was so expensive. Moreover, pirates and robbers usually added to the inherent dangers of long distance travel, and transit taxes often further impeded traffic. **Geographical obstacles** and **lack of knowledge of what lay beyond**, together with the limits of land and maritime **transport technologies** always limited the extent of the ancient trading connections. Not surprisingly, Australia and the Americas remained outside Eurasian and African trading networks. Within the Americas the absence of any large domesticated animal and the failure to develop wheeled vehicles meant intercivilisational trade on the continent was limited. Andean, Mesoamerican, and South American societies of the pre-Colombian era remained, for the most part, quite discrete worlds (Held et al. 1999: 152). Thus globalisation could not take place until more effective means of transport and communication were invented, the costs of transport and communication had fallen dramatically and some immunity from human or animal predators could be guaranteed (Foreman-Peck 1998: xiv-xv).

The first millennium AD was characterised by an **expansion of the 'world religions'**. Buddhism spread along the trade routes to China, Korea and Japan, Sri Lanka and became prominent throughout East Asia. Islamic expansion in the west began in the seventh century, reaching Spain in the eighth century. Political and cultural centres shifted particular towards the Abbasid rulers at Baghdad, who profited from the Silk Route to China, which remained open. Invading Mongols began accepting Islam in 1295. Islam spread from India to Sumatra in 1523 along well-established trade routes (Ibid. xiv-xv). Trade systems of the Indian Ocean and Southeast Asia produced immense institutional and cultural globalisation in what is usually referred to as the Hinduisation of Southeast Asia and Indonesia (Friedman 1995: 76). From the thirteenth century, **European 'discoveries'** provided the basis for the geographic integration of previously regional hemispheres. After the discoveries of the explorers, traders, and entrepreneurs went to exploit the new possibilities and built the missing fundaments to develop and integrate worldwide activities. A world map was drawn which could be used to develop worldwide activities.

2.2.2 Second stage: formation of global systems

The second stage of globalisation is characterised by the **development of global interdependencies** and the **emergence of systems with global extension**.

2.2.2.1 Colonialism and entrepreneurial capitalism: 15th until mid-19th century

A prominent perspective on globalisation is based on the assumption that the sixteenth century marks the starting point for globalisation. International corporate linkages had been forged, for example, by **Hanseatic merchants** and **Italian banking dynasties** in the fourteenth century (Dunning 1993: 321). According to Friedman (1995: 76), the **mercantile companies** of the fifteenth to the eighteenth centuries were globally institutionalised structures. Nonetheless, according to Malcolm Waters (2001), globalisation, in a strict sense of worldwide activities, is proceeding since the **sixteenth century** and involves processes of economic systematisation, **international relations** between states and an **emerging global culture** and consciousness. '*This process has accelerated through time and is currently in the most rapid phase of its development*' (Waters 2001: 15). Khor (2001: 2) makes a similar point:

'*Economic globalisation is not a new process, for over the past five centuries firms in the economically advanced countries have increasingly extended their outreach through trade and production activities (intensified in the colonial past) to territories all over the world. However, in the past two or three decades, economic globalisation has accelerated as a result of various factors such as technological developments, but especially the policies of liberalisation that have swept across the world.'*

Historians have noted the importance of the **first circumnavigation of the Earth** in 1519-1521 (Mazlish 1993). The discovery of the New World in the late 1400s and 1500s was fuelled by Europe's desire to facilitate trade with the Far East. The Dutch and the English as well as other Europeans began building **worldwide business empires** during this period and these were established by the 1700s and 1800s (Mendenhall et al. 1995: 7). World-system theorists maintain that the expansion of European capitalism in the sixteenth century marks the start of globalisation (Wallerstein 1974). In general it might be stated that the sixteenth century marks the time in history when a **'one-world view'** began to develop and was stimulated by worldwide transport and communication. In the aftermath, globalisation gained momentum and evolved through different phases.

At least **three phases** can be identified within the globalisation process from the sixteenth century onwards (Scholte 2000, Waters 1995: 43-46). J.A. Scholte (2000) terms the first phase **emergence of global imagination**, in which a *'global consciousness began to tease the secular imagination half a millennium ago'* and was reflected for example in the literature of William Shakespeare (Ibid. 62). Ideas of globality also inspired several voyagers of the fifteenth and sixteenth centuries to attempt a circumnavigation of the earth, a feat first accomplished in 1522. The development of a global consciousness was also apparent in **Enlightenment** thought of the eighteenth century. Philosophers such as Turgot and Herder were concerned with the history of humanity as a whole and moreover discerned a trend toward a social unification of the world (Kilminster 1997: 262-4). Turgot (1750: 41) forecast that *'finally commercial and political ties unite all parts of the globe'*. **'World society'** – or **'international society'** in its totality largely crystallised in the period 1815-30 when the **Congress of Vienna** provided an international order that endured for a century (Johnson 1991: xviii-xix). 1880-1918 was another crucial period in the formation of a global consciousness, as consequential shifts with respect to our sense of space and time took place, driven by international negotiations, technological innovations, and the standardisation of time-space relations. *'The world became locked into a particular form of a strong shift to unicity'* (Robertson 1995: 36). In **finance**, Bankers in Italy made long-distance loans between the thirteenth and fifteenth century to England, Flanders, and the Balkans. Eighteenth century commercial houses in Amsterdam and Geneva lent money to governments across Europe as well as to the newly founded American federation. International capital transfer as well as the first international stock exchange operations by the two banks Hope & Co. and Barings were rare and only bilateral. Still, it took a number of days for financial panic to travel several hundred kilometres between London and Amsterdam 1745, 1763, 1772, and 1793 and between London and Paris 1825 (Neal 1985: 222-223).

In the eighteenth century, the invention and diffusion of the **mechanical clock** had the effect of universalising time. Equally, space, as expressed in global maps, became a universal social dimension whose reality is independent of any individual social location (Harvey1989: 228-229).

'The liberation of time and space is an entirely modernising development because it allows the stable organisation of human activity across vast temporal and spatial distances - it is a prerequisite for globalisation' (Waters 2001: 62).

The time from 1500 to the early eighteenth century has been described as the **'commercial era'** (Robinson 1964) or as the **'era of mercantile capitalism and colonialism'** (Waters 1995: 77). International business during this era was essentially restricted to trade and was very much a function of individual entrepreneurs seeking personal fortunes in distant lands. The intermediate time from 1800 to 1875 therefore was also described as the **'era of entrepreneurial and financial capitalism'** (Waters 1995: 77) and laid the fundaments for the development of the multinational enterprises that began to develop. Dunning (1997c: 32-35) terms the time from 1770 and 1875 as the phase of **'entrepreneurial capitalism'**. The commercial era was characterised by a close relationship of European monarchs and entrepreneurs. This resulted in the formation of the great, chartered companies such as the Dutch East India or the British Royal American Company. These companies were granted exclusive trading rights as well as the right to perform consular functions (make alliances, appoint governors, and deploy troops) (Mendenhall et al. 1995: 8-9). Despite the international developments during the commercial era, Kuznets (1967) estimates that at the start of the nineteenth century world export amounted to only 1-2 per cent of world GDP.

2.2.2.2 Incipient globalisation: mid-18th century to the mid-19th century

The second phase in global system formation, which Scholte (2000) terms *'incipient globalisation'*, took place between 1850 and 1950 (Scholte 2000: 65, see also Wilkins 1974: 414). During this period, supraterritoriality made its initial more substantial appearance from the middle of the nineteenth century and spread at mostly gradual rate for the next hundred years. This development was driven by the **technology of globalisation**, the railway, the telegraph and the steam ship (Foreman-Peck 1998: xx). For example, the Suez Canal gave steam ships a major advantage on the Indian routes and contributed to the decline in freight rates.

Robertson (1992: 179) argues that globalisation took off between 1875 and 1925 with the **time zoning of the world** and the establishment of the international dateline, the **near-global adoption of the Gregorian calendar** and the adjustable seven-day week, and the establishment of international telegraphic and signalling codes. The telegraph was introduced in the 1850s. The radio followed in the 1890s. Intercontinental air transport began in 1919 with the first non-stop transatlantic flight. The first transatlantic telegraph cable was laid in 1866, five years later from Europe to China, Japan and Australia. The first transpacific cable followed in 1901. The first international telephone connection between London and Paris was established in 1891, the first transatlantic line in 1926. The first planetary radio event was broadcast in January 1930. The speech of King George V, opening the London Naval Conference was broadcast to 242 radio stations across six continents. Despite all these innovations that served as enablers for increased international communications and transaction, it has to be stated that costs were very high. For example, the price of a telephone call from London to New York was a thousand times higher in the 1920s than in 1996 (Financial Times, 23.12.1996: 17).

2.2.2.3 Early economic globalisation

Waters (1995: 78) defines the time from the mid-19th to the mid-20th century as the era of '**international capitalism**'. It was marked by a rapid expansion of resource-based and market-seeking investments. The period from 1870 to 1914 has even been called the '**high water mark**' of an open, integrated international economy and the '**golden age**' of **international economic integration** (UNCTAD 1993).

'Pre-1914 levels of international trade and investment – both relatively and absolutely – were striking; world trade grew by almost 50 per cent per decade from the mid-nineteenth to early twentieth century and international capital investments by 64 per cent per decade during the forty years before the first World War' (Kobrin 1997: 146).

The **development of global markets** was constitutive for economic internationalisation. A global market for copper consolidated from the 1850s onwards, interlinking shipments from Australia, Chile, Cuba, England and the USA. The London Metal Exchange (LME) was established in 1876 (Scholte 2000: 67). Global pricing dynamics developed at this time in respect of cotton, wheat, and other cereals, especially between the commodities exchanges at Buenos Aires, Cairo, Calcutta, Chicago, Liverpool, New York, Rio de Janeiro, and Winnipeg (Baer/Saxon 1949: 12-13). Global markets in brandname packaged goods started to emerge in the late nineteenth century. Campbell Soup and Heinz foods became household articles across several countries from the mid-1880s. Coca-Cola was marketed in Britain, Canada, Cuba, Mexico, and the USA within twenty years of the drink's introduction in 1886. Office Equipment from Remington Typewriter, agricultural machines from International Harvester and appliances from Western Electric began to be marketed between and across continents from the late nineteenth century (Scholte 2000: 67). By 1880, Singer covered three-quarters of the world market in sewing machines (Porter 1986: 415-16). In 1899, J. Walter Thompson opened the first advertising agency outside the country of origin, presaging the development of transborder commercial promotion campaigns.

A study by Houston/Dunning (1976) showed that of the 13,500 enterprises quoted on the London Stock Exchange in 1914, 3,373 **international firms** operated exclusively or mainly abroad. Mira Wilkins has termed these enterprises '**free-standing companies**'. Unlike conventional multinationals they were set up as operations with no parallel organisation in their home country although managerial control of the operation ultimately resided in the country, which had provided the investment funds. Such a joint stock company was floated as a means of allowing capital holders to take advantage of an investment opportunity abroad (John et al. 1997: 11-12, 23). Some economic historians point to the turn of the twentieth century as the heyday of international trade and investment before the convulsions of World War I and the Great Depression threw the world economy into spiralling protectionism (Williamson 1995: 1, 3, 26; Chandler 1986).

Another important factor in the development of increasing **international trade** was the **harmonisation of prices and interest rates** by the establishment of currency links with precious metals. The certainty of this financial stability undoubtedly facilitated the globalisation process. Exchange rates became tightly fixed to the **gold standard** so that there was a very narrow band of about one per cent wherein the exchange rate would normally fluctuate. Financial links strengthened during the nineteenth century. International capital markets allowed most governments to borrow more cheaply and in larger volumes than if they were restricted to selling bonds to their own citizens. Although default on payments to foreign creditors was more serious, due to intergovernmental pressure for instance, it still was common. Nevertheless, most defaulters, like the newly independent states of Latin America in the 1820s, wanted to return to the market, and were obliged to pay off the arrears on defaulted loans. Overall rates of return on lending to most independent states were reasonable and the private system of disciplining governments by the '**Corporation of Foreign Bondholders**' was effective (Lindert/Morton 1989). American railway company shares were traded in each of the major European stock markets as well as in New York by the end of the nineteenth century. The telegraph ensured that market participants quickly knew about stock price movement in other markets (Neal 1985: 221). A summary of important events is illustrated in Table 2-6.

Chronology of incipient globalisation (1850-1950)	
1851	First world's fair
1852	Establishment of the first manufacturing subsidiary
1863	Start of the first transborder relief organisation
1864	Creation of the first transborder labour organisation
1865	Formation of the first global governance agency
1866	First permanent transoceanic telegraph cable
1870	Emergence of the first transworld monetary regime
1871	First round-the-world tourist excursion
1891	First transborder telephone connection
1896	First global sports event
1899	First transborder radio transmission
1918	Inauguration of air mail
1919	First non-stop transatlantic flight
1920	Inauguration of the League of Nations
1926	First transatlantic telephone call
1929	Creation of the first offshore banking arrangements
1930	Formation of the Bank of International Settlements
1944	Creation of the International Monetary Fund and the World Bank
1945	Formation of the United Nations system
1947	Signing of the General Agreement on Tariffs and Trade
1949	First package holiday
1954	Advent of the Marlboro cowboy
1956	First transoceanic telephone cable

Table 2-6: Chronology of incipient globalisation
(Source: Scholte 2000: 73)

2.2.2.4 Full-scale globalisation: mid-20th century – present

If conceived as the **growth of supraterritorial spaces**, then globalisation has unfolded mainly since the 1960s. One of the most striking contemporary acceleration of globalisation has occurred in respect of electronic communications. The infrastructure has vastly grown. Transoceanic cables became available for telephone from 1956. In 1956 the first cable from Scotland to Newfoundland could carry a maximum of 60 calls simultaneously, the Fibreoptic Link Around the Globe (FLAG) laid in 1996-7 can transmit up to 600,000 conversations concurrently. By 1990 transworld direct-dial calls were available in over 200 countries. The introduction of satellites and fibre-optic cables has hugely increased the carrying capacities of the global communications infrastructure. Internet emerged in the 1980s and expanded hugely in the 1990s, connecting up to 180 million people in 1999. Transoceanic television transmissions via satellite were first achieved in 1962. The first satellite television broadcast occurred in respect of a concert by the Beatles in 1967 (Scholte 2000: 74-75). Table 2-7 contains an overview over central indicators of globalisation in recent history.

Indicators of accelerated globalisation in contemporary history	
Fixed telephone lines	from 150 million in 1965 to 851 million in 1998
Mobile telephones	from 0 in 1978 to 305 million in 1998
Internet users	from 0 in 1985 to 180 million in 1998
Radio sets	from 57 million in mid-1930s to 2,008 million in 1994
Television receivers	from 75 million in 1956 to 1,096 million in 1994
International air travellers	from 25 million in 1950 to 400 million in 1996
Receipts from international travel	from $19 billion in 1970 to $389 billion in 1996
Foreign exchange reserves	from $100 billion in 1970 to $ 1,579 billion in 1997
Daily foreign exchange turnover	from $100 billion in 1979 to $1,500 billion in 1998
Bank deposits by non-residents	from $20 billion in 1964 to $7,900 billion in 1995
Balances on transborder bank loans	from $200 billion in early 1970s to $10,383 billion in 1997
Issuance of global bonds	from 0 in 1962 to $371 billion in 1995
Financial derivatives contracts	from 0 in 1971 to $70 trillion in 1998
World stock of FDI	from $99 billion in 1960 to $5,976 billion in 2000
Transborder companies	from 7,000 in late 1960s to 50,508 in 2001
Transborder civic associations	from 1,117 in 1956 to 16,586 in 1998
Annual species extinction	from 6 in 1950 to 10,000 in 1990

Table 2-7: Indicators of accelerated globalisation
(Source: Scholte 2000: 86, UNCTAD 2001a)

2.2.2.5 Development of a global economic context

Transborder production processes and associated intra-firm trade did not exist in earlier phases of globalisation. They first gained substantial proportions in the 1960s, when supraterritorial co-ordination developed especially in the production of semiconductors and consumer electronics. Subsequently the trend spread to the assembly phase in the manufacturing of clothing, motor vehicles, and appliances. Table 2-8 illustrates the increase of **international trade** (exports) of agricultural products, mining products and manufactures compared to the development of the world overall production and gross domestic product (GDP). While the volume of world GDP and production both increased fivefold, exports were 22 times higher in 2000 than in 1950 (with 1990 as the index basis). International trade grew four times faster than world production and GDP. This is a strong indicator of the **increasing global interconnectedness** of worldwide markets. Particularly co-operations and FDI cause global interdependencies.

World merchandise exports, production and gross domestic product (GDP), 1950-00

(Index, 1990=100)

	Value				Volume								World GDP
	Exports				Exports				Production				
	Total	Agriculture	Mining	Manufactures	Total	Agriculture	Mining	Manufactures	Total	Agriculture	Mining	Manufactures	
1950	2	7	2	1	9	26	18	5	18	37	29	13	19
1955	3	8	3	2	13	30	27	7	24	42	37	19	25
1960	4	10	4	3	18	41	39	11	30	49	45	24	30
1965	6	12	6	4	26	50	49	17	41	55	60	35	39
1970	9	15	10	8	41	61	77	29	54	64	76	49	60
1971	10	16	12	9	44	62	78	32	57	65	79	51	53
1985	56	63	88	49	75	90	79	72	86	90	86	84	84
1990	100	100	100	100	100	100	100	100	100	100	100	100	100
2000	181	135	169	194	196	154	149	210	127	122	116	130	125

Table 2-8: World merchandise exports, production and world GDP, 1950-2000 (Source: UNCTAD 2001: 29)

FDI and international production

Selected indicators of FDI and international production, 1982- 2000 (billions of dollars and percentage)

Item	Value at current prices (Billions of dollars)			Annual growth rate (Per cent)					
	1982	1990	2000	1986-1990	1991-1995	1996-1999	1998	1999	2000
FDI inflows	57	202	1,271	23.0	20.8	40.8	44.9	55.2	18.2
FDI outflows	37	235	1,150	26.8	16.3	37.0	52.8	41.3	14.3
FDI inward stock	719	1,889	6,314	16.2	9.3	18.4	19.8	22.3	21.5
FDI outward stock	568	1,717	5,976	20.5	10.8	16.4	20.9	19.5	19.4
Cross-border M&As①	n.a.	151	1,144	26.4②	23.3	50.0	74.4	44.1	49.0
Sales of foreign affiliates	2,465	5,467	15,680③	15.6	10.5	10.4	18.2	17.2③	18.0③
Total assets of foreign affiliates	1,888	5,744	21,102④	18.2	13.9	15.9	23.4	14.8④	19.8④

① Data are only available from 1987 onward
② 1987-1990 only
③ Based on the following regression result of sales against FDI inward stock for the period 1982-1998:
Sales = 967+2,462*FDI inward stock
④ Based on the following regression result of assets against FDI inward stock for the period 1982-1998:
Assets = -376+3,594*FDI inward stock

Table 2-9: Selected indicators of FDI and international production, 1982- 2000 (Source: UNCTAD 2001: 10)

The development of FDI is illustrated in Table 2-9. Between 1982 and 2000 the amount of

- FDI outflows grew by a factor of 31;
- FDI outward stock grew by a factor of ten;
- sales of foreign affiliates grew by a factor of six; and

- total assets of foreign affiliates grew by a factor of eleven.

It may be argued that the development of not only interlinked but also **globally interdependent markets** has taken a **quantum leap since the 1980s**.

The **global financial system** emerged as the creation of a dollar-centred gold standard was generally accepted in the Bretton Woods Agreements of 1944 and its regime of fixed exchange rates became fully operational in 1959. The US dollar became a global currency. With increasing international trade, by the early 1970s, the value of dollars circulating outside the USA exceeded the value of gold stocks held by the American central bank so that the dollar-gold convertibility was halted. In contrast to the earlier collapses of a gold standard in 1914 and the early 1930s, the globalisation of money continued in the context of floating exchange rates. Other national currencies as the German Mark or the Japanese Yen joined the dollar as global means of exchange and stores of value. The integration of twelve European currencies into the Euro and its introduction in 2002 marks a further step in the deterritorialisation of money. Other forms of supraterritorial money, like traveller's cheques, bankcards or credit cards are also innovations of the last 50 years.

Whereas arbitrage effects could only be exploited by the physical transport of gold during the early gold standards, and money had to be transported physically during the early international trade era, nowadays the volume of transactions on the **global foreign exchange markets** exceeds $1.5 trillion per day. Only two per cent of this transaction volume is based on export activities. Today more is traded in six hours on the world currency markets than the World Bank has lent in its entire history (Clark 1999: 1, McGrew 1997a: 6). The need for accurate information and quick communication has also emphasised the role of so-called **'world cities'** in the financial and corporate system. These centres are equipped with teleports, airports, fixed communication links, as well as a wide array of financial, legal, business, and infrastructural services (Harvey 1989: 294-5).

Global deposits were introduced in the second half of the twentieth century. The world total of bank deposits owned by non-residents rose from $20 billion in 1964 to $7.9 trillion in 1995 (IMF 1993:60-70; BIS 1996: 7). Today several trillion dollars lie in offshore finance centres, which have proliferated from a negligible number before 1950 to 500 offshore banks on the Cayman Islands (aside six branches for local business), over 200 in Luxembourg and over 70 in Guernsey (Roberts 1995). Before 1950, extraterritorial share listings on stock exchanges were very rare. At the end of the twentieth century, externally based companies accounted for nearly half the quotations on the stock exchanges of Amsterdam and Frankfurt, a third of those in Zurich and Paris, and over a fifth of those on the London Stock Exchange (O'Brian 1992: 45).

Today insurance companies, investment and pension funds as well as private investors operate **global portfolios**. The two biggest European clearinghouses, Euroclear and Cedel had accumulated an annual turnover of nearly $60 trillion in 1999 (Euroclear 2000). Globalisation also affected the trade with financial derivatives. **Global markets** in futures, options, and other derivatives now exist in respect of commodities, interest levels, foreign exchange rates, stock market indices, and the likes. The total world annual turnover on organised derivatives alone (not counting the larger number of over-the-counter deals) stood at more than $350 trillion in 1997 (BIS 1998b: 155-6). Transactions between derivative exchanges in different time zones are now operated on a round-the-world, round-the-clock basis.

The same applies to **processes in international production**. In a speech in 1999 Jens Neumann - Member of the Board of Management of Volkswagen AG - described the design process of new cars as follows:

'Teams in three continents work on a specific car design project 24 hours a day non-stop by transferring the data daily into the next time zone from Europe to Mexico and Brazil and back – as well as from China to Europe and back. The data flow around the globe, around the clock, accomplishing the work in less than half of the former development time' (Neumann 1999: 1).

The same applies to the production process, the planning, and optimisation of the flow including the integration of hundreds of suppliers with ordering, disposition and logistics for just-in-time delivery. These are created by computer simulation techniques and managed via Intranet and Extranet (Ibid.). According to Manuel Castells (1996: 92) it may be resumed:

'A global economy is something different: it is an economy with the capacity to work as a unit in real time on a planetary scale.'

2.2.2.6 Formation of MNEs and evolution of the world competitive structure

Particularly technological innovations during the last decades led to a significant dynamisation of the process of the international expansion of business activities and their interdependencies. A short overview over the three most important stages in the evolution of the competitive structure in the world economy since the first formation of MNEs will be presented below (according to Martinez/Jarillo 1989: 504; Porter 1993: 71-73, Macharzina 1993: 30-32).

This overview will convey an impression of the '**global competitive playground**' where corporate evolution takes place.

A **stage model** differentiating three different phases best illustrates the development of **global competitive structures**. Martinez/Jarillo (1989) developed the basic framework for this model. The stages in the model are derived from literature on economic history (Chandler 1977, 1986, 1990; Porter 1986; Wilkins 1974). Strategies and organisational forms characterising company behaviour in the respective phases are denominated according to the underlying pattern of international, multinational, global, and transnational management orientations that were coined by authors of the **Process School of International Management** (Bartlett, Ghoshal, Doz, Prahalad, et al.).

Martinez/Jarillo (1989) identify three **stages of international competition** since 1920 that are based on this pattern. The stage model presented here begins in 1880, as the first **strong phase of internationalisation** took place during this time. The era between 1920 and 1945 was more characterised by **de-internationalisation**. The stage model shall convey a more detailed picture of the evolution of competition in the age of **quantum-leap globalisation**. Figure 2-2 illuminates that the globalisation of competition is not only marked by a fading rigidity of boundaries, but that it has to be observed in the context of the evolutionary processes of social differentiation and integration, now expanding to the maximum level of regional extension.

Before 1880, international business activities were very limited and appeared only in the form of **overseas trade**. There were only comparatively few subsidiaries (with the exception of trading houses). Protectionism and high transaction-costs, primarily due to simple communication and transport technologies, permitted only a low profitability of international business.

An exception was colonial trade in which high profits were generated. It was also used to get access to resources. Around 1880, **most industries** were **local** or **regional** in scope. There were only few economies of scale in production until fuel-powered machines and assembly-line techniques emerged. There were heterogeneous product needs. International media were few and communication was difficult. Transportation was slow and complicated. All these structural conditions created little impetus for the widespread globalisation of industries. Industries with international activities reflected classic comparative advantage considerations and chose export as market entry mode (Porter 1986: 29).

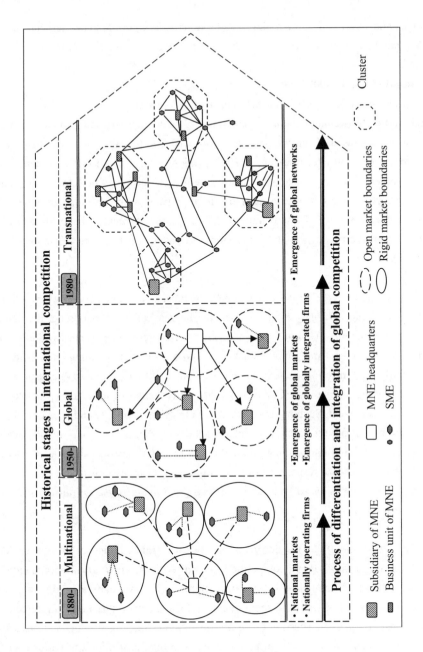

Figure 2-2: Historical development of global competition

The need for '**international management**' was very restricted because of low FDI. The necessary control of the existing subsidiaries was often based on kinship and not on professional management. The importance of international management developed after 1880, when new technologies allowed a rising international trade volume. The period since then can roughly be divided into three stages to demonstrate the importance of the evolutionary mechanism.

Stage 1: multinational, 1880-1950

In a first wave of modern global competition, organisations grew internationally in the late nineteenth and early twentieth century. Economies of scale increased and product needs became more homogenised. Transport facilities improved due to innovation and diffusion of railway, steamships, and later trucking. Communication became easier due to telegraph and telephone. The effective exploitation of those technologies demanded new forms of production and distribution and also a new management and business organisation. Production became more capital-intensive. These conditions led to the development of larger organisations with capital-intensive production and professional management structures (Chandler/Hikino 1997: 35, 56).

According to Chandler (1977: 485-86, 1990: 51), the most significant step in the evolution of the modern multiunit, industrial enterprise was the internalisation of marketing, distribution and purchasing functions of wholesalers and other commercial intermediaries. Such enterprises then invested in research, moved backward into owning and operating units producing raw and semifinished materials and expanded geographically by investing in operational units abroad only after the internalisation of such activities. Economies of scale and scope played a critical role in this context. Such big companies as Ford, Singer, Gillette and Western Electric were among the first to build foreign subsidiaries (Porter 1986: 29). Organisational capabilities then were the driving force in international development of business activities, first functional capabilities, and then responsibilities for coordination, strategic planning, and resource allocation. *'These were the most valuable of all those that made up the organisational capabilities of the new modern industrial enterprise'* (Chandler 1990: 36).

Between the 1920s and 1950s the degeneration towards a **multidomestic pattern** could be observed that moved international competition towards **federations of autonomous subsidiaries** (Porter 1986: 29). The reason for this development was a wave of nationalism and high tariff barriers as a result of wars and economic crises. Cartels and other interfirm agreements inhibited global competition.The first stage of competition therefore was characterised by a strong national focus. The reasons can be attributed to a high protectionism, national differences, and particularly to high transport and communication costs. Foreign subsidiaries of international companies were widely autonomous and with very limited specialisation and exchange activities. Generally, the relations between headquarter and subsidiaries only comprised the transfer of profits.

Stage 2: global, 1950-1980

Between the 1950s and the late 1970s a strong reversal of interwar trends took hold with strong underlying forces of globalisation. Growing similarities in business practices, marketing systems and dramatically increasing economies of scale fuelled the process of increasing **global integration**. The minimum efficient scales of an auto assembly plant more than tripled between 1960 and 1975. The average costs of developing a new drug more than quadrupled. Transport costs plunged thanks to the invention of large bulk carriers, container ships and commercial aircraft (Porter 1986: 30). Especially the invention of the standardised container that integrated all transport systems (trucks, rail, ships, aircraft) led to an enormous decrease in transport time and costs. New technologies reduced the communicative distance completely and costs of communication to a fraction compared to the previous phase. The forces underlying globalisation have been self-reinforcing (Porter 986: 31).

Based upon technological progress and a liberalisation of markets, the advantages of the global integration of business activities grew significantly. Particularly new technologies led to increasing economies of scale, which could also be transferred to the market because of sinking transport and communication costs. As well, GATT agreements also led to a reduction of tariffs from 40% to 8% between 1950 and 1980. In contrast to the multinational stage with international transactions on a more or less pure market basis, the global stage offered profits by integrating value-added activities (particularly upstream) and by a centralisation of the international organisation structure. The global stage was marked by growing interdependencies of markets as well as of the subsidiaries of MNEs. Another characteristic of this stage was the development of global market segments and the formation of **globally integrated MNEs**, which exploited global interdependencies by integrating their own activities on a global basis.

Stage 3: transnational, since 1980

In important global industries large increases in economies of scale have slowed down because of technological limits. The development of flexible production technologies led to a rising efficiency of the production of even smaller quantities. Strategies of global standardisation in many industries are no longer the main option for efficient business activities. An increasing market fragmentation leads to a growing attractiveness of a more flexible and differentiated handling of important dualities in international management (e.g. global versus local or system versus environment). The latter is of increasing importance because the development of '**network competition**' in the transnational phase is accompanied by a relativisation of boundaries. Not only cultural and market boundaries lose their rigidity; particularly organisational boundaries become increasingly blurred. Globalisation leads to a continuing integration of global markets and competition.

Because of increasing intra- and interorganisational interdependencies in global competition, isolated hierarchical and market instruments do not suffice to confront its differentiated demands to organisational evolution. Meffert (1993: 29) observes a trend from formal and structural mechanisms in the 1950s and 1960s to increasing non-structural and informal mechanisms since the 1970 and 1980s. He terms this a change from '*bureaucratic control*' to '*cultural control*'. Firms with global operations develop **global network structures** by internal differentiation and by co-operation. This leads to a greater density of interdependencies in global competition. Companies put into perspective the rigidity of their boundaries and develop new organisational arrangements not in the classical reactive tradition ('*structure follows strategy*') but in a more flexible way by grouping organisational arrangements around their core competencies.

During the multinational stage, the global structure of largely isolated national markets demanded only relatively simple co-ordination modes of economic activities like simple hierarchical structures and local markets with only few global interdependencies. Globally integrated, complex hierarchies were developed to exploit the competitive advantages of this stage, due to the emergence of global markets and the changed conditions in the global stage. The continuing expansion and rising density of global competition in the transnational stage induces the deployment of complex bundles of hierarchical, heterarchical, and market-based mechanisms in international management. The density that has developed in various industries led to the outstanding importance of the competence of constructing and participating in global networks as *the* critical success factor in global business.

2.3 An evolutionary perspective on globalisation

From this perspective, globalisation is conceived as a social evolutionary process on global scale. Regarding the time horizon of globalisation, one can undoubtedly trace far back into human history developments involving the expansion of chains of interconnectedness across wide expanses of the earth. In that sense '**world formation**' has been proceeding for many hundreds, indeed thousands, of years (Robertson 1995: 35). The focus is on the '*world society*' in general or on the '**world economy**' as a social subsystem. Globalisation leads to the formation of global social systems. These are constituted by their subsystems. The global society is constituted by many national and local societies. National subsidiaries and other organisational units constitute multinational companies. Non-governmental organisations are constituted by their national affiliates.

In terms of systems theory, globalisation in general is interpreted as an increasing level of complexity, caused by the multitude of interactions and the resulting variety of possible system states. This leads to a paradox of increasing transparency, caused by the multitude of available information and increasing intransparency, as the consequences of actions are not clear (Steger 1996: 7). Globalisation means an **increase in environmental complexity** for the individual organisation. The consequence is a necessary increase in its own complexity to provide for the requisite variety (Ashby 1956) in the **global context**. Organisations have to continuously adapt their internal representations of reality in the process of co-evolution with the globalising environment. The internal structure and the structural coupling with the environment have to be transformed according to the evolution of these reality constructs.

Analysed on the basis of the **theory of social systems** (Luhmann 1995), globalisation can be viewed as a phase embedded in the social and hence economic evolution. In this concept, social evolution is conceptualised as a **process of continuous functional differentiation and integration of social systems**. The distinguishing feature of this phase in social evolution is that the evolutionary principle of social differentiation and integration is principally not any more restricted by national or cultural boundaries but **extended to global scale** within functional social systems like science, religion, economy, or politics. Especially the economic system - e.g. as compared to the political system - has become extremely independent of national or regional boundaries because of the technological and social developments in recent decades. The result is a process of increasing differentiation and integration on a now principally global basis. Some industries become globally integrated (like the motor industry), some increasingly differentiated (like many leisure or service industries). The same process can be observed on the individual industry-level. In the motor industry, for example, there is integration of production and at the same time a greater variety of products. An individual actor cannot control the described process of differentiation and integration.

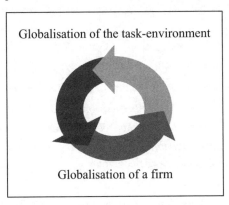

Figure 2-3:   Co-evolution of a firm in its task-environment

There is a '**structural coupling**' between a system and its environment and therefore an interplay between the differentiation and integration processes of both. Figure 2-3 shows the dynamic interplay between the globalisation of a company and its task environment. The result of the **self-reinforcing feedback-loop of globalisation** is the most prominent management problem of last decades: increasing global complexity and dynamics reinforced by the diminishing importance of national, cultural and cognitive boundaries. The possibilities for differentiation and integration rise exponentially. The **success factor 'time'** therefore becomes more and more important. The faster a company can identify and open access to new chances in its respective task environment, the sooner it can build up competitive advantages. Driven by changing modes of competition, globalisation compresses the time and space aspects of social relations (Mittelman 1996: 3). The transformation of the technical and organisational infrastructure of international integration is obvious and needs to be considered in any analysis of globalisation (Hargittai/Centeno 2001: 1549).

'Where previously we might have spoken of a world, on which a variety of lines were drawn, we now need to think of the globe as enmeshed in a web. The new global geography has made relative position within the web simultaneously more difficult to define and much more important' (Hargittai/Centeno 2001: 1550).

In a similar vein, Lübbe (1996: 46) regards globalisation as a process of worldwide network-creation. According to Lübbe, the civilisational evolution can be described as a process of increasing geographical and social expansion of economical, political and cultural interactions (Ibid. 47). The intensity of interactions is expected to be increasing simultaneously to their expansion in the global range. Network extension and the increase of global network density go hand in hand. Based upon these thoughts, Lübbe derives the following heuristic:

'With the increasing density of networks, the disadvantages of not being connected to them rise erratically' (Ibid. 51).

According to Castells (1996: 3), *'global networks of instrumental exchanges selectively switch on and off individuals, groups, regions, and even countries, according to their relevance in fulfilling the goals processed in the network, in a relentless flow of strategic decisions. What follows is a fundamental split between abstract, universal instrumentalism, and historically rooted, particularistic identities. Our societies are increasingly structured around a bipolar opposition between the Net and the Self.'*

Firms therefore have to learn how to transform and balance continuously their self-definition (e.g. products, structures, and competencies) and their embeddedness in the respective network environment (e.g. markets, transactions, and interdependencies). McGrew (1997a: 7-8) underlines the importance of growing global interconnectedness. **Globalisation** from his perspective is characterised by a number of distinctive **attributes**:

1. Social, political and economic activities are becoming '**stretched**' across national frontiers such that events, decisions, and activities in one part of the world come to have immediate significance for individuals and communities in distant parts of the globe.
2. Globalisation involves intensification, or increasing density, in the flows and patterns of interaction or interconnectedness, which transcend the states and communities that constitute the modern world system.
3. The growing extensity and intensity of global interactions is associated with a deepening enmeshment of the local and global so that the distinction between what is internal and what is external is increasingly blurred. Alongside the stretching goes a '**deepening**' such that even though '*...everyone has a local life, phenomenal worlds for the most part are truly global*' (Giddens 1991: 187).
4. Growing interconnectedness generates a host of transnational problems, from proliferation of weapons to global trafficking of narcotics, which can only be resolved by multilateral co-operation. Thus globalisation stimulates the growth of international organisations and multilateral mechanisms for regulating areas of transnational activity.
5. The density and intensity of patterns of global and transnational interconnectedness weave ever tighter and more complex webs of relations between the states, international institutions, communities, non-governmental organisations, and multinational corporations which make up the global system, generating systemic constraints upon all their activities and their autonomy.

Held et al. (1999: 15) add to this list of attributes an acceleration of global interactions and processes as the development of worldwide systems of transport and communication increases the potential velocity of the global diffusion of ideas, goods, information, capital, and people. As a consequence of the growing extensity, intensity and velocity of global interactions and the deepening enmeshment of the local and global, the impact of distant events is supposed to be magnified while even the most local developments may come to have enormous global consequences.

The **rise in global consciousness**, along with higher levels of **material interdependence**, increases the probability that the world will be reproduced as a single system. The particular outcome that separates globalisation in the contemporary period from its earlier manifestations is its **reflexivity**. The phenomenology of globalisation is reflexive. The inhabitants of the planet self-consciously orientate themselves to the world as a whole, for example firms that explore global markets (Waters 2001: 184-85). What is perhaps most distinctive about globalisation is that it intensifies our consciousness of the world as a whole, making us more aware of each other, and perhaps more prone to be influenced by one another without necessarily making us more like each other (Guillén 2001a: 6). Communication networks facilitate linkages to geographically distant areas for labour, production, and marketing purposes. In addition, widespread links yield knowledge of the global arena that can be directed to actions affecting the course of world events (Kick/Davis 2001: 1566).

'If globalization is seen as a process tending toward enhanced mutual awareness in the world, then the reflexive character of action becomes a central concept for understanding how countries and organizations find a place for themselves in the global economy' (Guillén 2001a: 18).

In contrast to the evolution of biological systems based on casual genetic variation and external environmental selection, social systems are constituted by **structures of meaning** that can only be processed by psychic systems (individuals) and social systems. They are therefore open to intended variation and selection of structures of meaning and according actions by their constituents. They are also open to interchange of meaning with other social systems and to the development of '**consensual domains**' (structures of shared ('*objectified*') meaning and expectations (see Chapter 6.1.5). **Institutionalisation** leads to the manifestation and diffusion of generalised meaning in and between social systems on global scale. Hargittai/Centeno (2001: 1548) observe that *'globalisation has been accompanied and supported by an intense process of international isomorphism on practically every level and in almost all aspects of life.'* The process is therefore leading to global structures of consciousness and institutions.

'Globalisation refers in this context to the formation of global institutional structures, that is, structures that organise the already existing global field, and global cultural forms, that is, forms that are either produced by or transformed into globally accessible objects and representations' (Friedman 1995: 75).

According to Hargittai/Centeno (Ibid. 1552), discussion of cultural convergence and organisational isomorphism has never specified how cultural and organisational standards are actually transported across firm and national boundaries. As will be argued in Chapter 6, the evolution of social systems is based upon shared meaning and its communication. Meaningful action by social actors like individuals or organisations then is based upon consensual domains. Globalisation from this perspective leads to the development of '**global consensual domains**' and in general what might be termed a '**global consciousness**'. Institutionalisation processes then lead to a manifestation of globally shared meaning in according institutional structures, like international agreements, organisations, and markets. In this process, globalisation is becoming increasingly institutionalised in social systems and structures and therefore a social reality, which can be now measured quantitatively (e.g. number of MNEs, supranational organisations, subsidiaries, FDI, trade flows) and qualitatively (e.g. diffusion of social practices, cultural traits). The socialisation of the global arena in terms of regularly reproduced praxis is the core of the institutional process of globalisation (Friedman 1995: 76).

There is an increasing acceleration in both concrete global interdependence and consciousness of the '**global whole**' in the twentieth century (Robertson 1992: 8). One aspect is the global diffusion of information. According to a report of the Club of Rome (King/Schneider 1992: 177), in the year 1986 alone there have been as many scientific and technical publications as in the whole history before World War II. As science is a self-referential process, these publications provide the basis for even more publications with references to them. A growing portion of them is reproduced in the field of globalisation.

'In an increasingly globalised world there is a heightening of civilisational, societal, ethic, regional and, indeed, individual self-consciousness. Globalisation in this context is about processes of attribution of meaning that are of a global nature' (Friedman 1995: 73).

There are constraints on social entities to locate themselves within world history and global future. Yet globalisation in and for itself also involves the diffusion of the expectation of such identity declarations (Robertson 1992: 27). As diffusion is crucial to globalisation processes, globalisation proceeds most rapidly in contexts where social relationships are mediated through symbols. Economic globalisation is therefore most advanced in the financial markets mediated by monetary tokens (Waters 2001: 160). On the other hand, firms at the beginning of their internationalisation have to develop international reputation as well as awareness and adaptation of their products in global markets. If local patterns of social organisation are resources for action (like local industrial networks), then successful economic development involves matching logics of social organisations with the opportunities offered by the global economy (e.g. by connecting to global customers) (Guillén 2001a: 14).

From a social systems perspective, the **globalisation of consciousness** evolves in a **recursive interplay with** the **globalisation of social action**. Thought is necessary for purposive action to change and transform a social system.

'Thought in the time dimension is dialectical. It begins with an understanding of the contradiction and proceeds to identify the potential for transformation based on concerted action by self-conscious social forces' (Cox 1996: 27).

Kellner (2000: 82) proposes that *'to properly theorise globalisation we need to conceptualise several sets of contradiction ... '*. Kellner also terms globalisation a '**contradictory amalgam**' of both homogenising forces of sameness and uniformity, and heterogeneity, difference, and hybridity (Ibid: 83). From a systems perspective, globalisation can be described in terms of distinctions that constitute evolutionary dynamics in an ongoing interplay (Khondker 1996, Wiesmann 1993), or as Mlinar (2000: 138) puts it *'in the sense of the unity of opposites'*. For example, excessive local adaptation provokes integrative measures on company-wide level after a while due to missing exploitation of economies of scale and scope and of global learning. On the other hand, excessive global integration of activities impedes local adaptation and therefore provokes processes of localisation in order to become more effective and adaptive. Evans/Doz (1992) call this dynamic balancing of opposites the '**management of dualities**'. Particularly the dialectical links between the local and the global constitute an essential mode for the strategic approach to enterprises (Quérit 1991: 59).

Thinking of globalisation in terms of paradoxes is quite common, as dynamics can be best described in terms of a dialectical process. Political scientist Barber published a book in 1995 with the intriguing title *'Jihad vs. McWorld'*. This seems to be cynic after the assault on the World Trade Centre by Islamistic terrorists but describes our planet as simultaneously *'falling apart and coming together'*. Barber starkly contrasts the economic and technological forces, which are integrating nations into one *'gigantic and homogeneous theme park'*, and the sometimes frightening, but no less widespread, movement towards inter- and intrastate fragmentation along ethnic, tribal, and religious lines. Dunning (1997a: 358-370) predicts that we enter an '**age of paradoxes**' that is especially clear in the globalisation of economic activity. He considers especially four paradoxes, which he believes to be determinating the shape of the political and economic future:

1. Co-operation vs. competition: The paradox of relationships;
2. Globalisation vs. localisation: The paradox of space;
3. The role of governments: The paradox of *'less, yet more'*, and *'centralisation vs. decentralisation'*; and
4. The human consequences of globalisation: The paradox of benefits and disbenefits.

Dunning describes **MNEs** in this context as '**masters of paradoxes**', at least explicitly in the paradox of relationships (Ibid: 360). In the following section, implications for a management will be illuminated. It will also be discussed, in how far the distinction of MNEs as global masters of paradoxes vs. SMEs as local or regional specialists will prove to be true in the process of globalisation.

2.4 Implications for a management of globalisation

The globalisation-process leads to a kind of **'liquefaction of global competition'**, which results in a higher density of interdependencies and interactions between a rising number of globally acting players. Competition in international markets was traditionally the realm of large MNEs, with smaller businesses remaining local or regional. Now, drivers of globalisation are removing the barriers that segmented the competitive environments of small and large firms. *'Firms of all sizes are beginning to share the same competitive space'* (Etemad et al. 2001: 481).

In international management, the traditional view of MNEs as big global monoliths and SMEs as relatively isolated niche-specialists has to be changed in a context where smaller MNE-subunits with greater autonomy and globalising SMEs are on the way to build up interdependencies on a worldwide basis. Dicken/Thrift (1992: 282) observed that larger firms now increasingly populate even those industrial sectors, which, until a few years ago, were still predominantly the domain of SMEs – e.g., like many of the service industries.

On the other hand, the globalised firm has **indistinct and shifting boundaries**. It may be expected to be organised as a network rather than being hierarchical, and it may penetrate and exploit space by proxy or in co-operation with other firms rather than in 'isolation' (Wells/Cooke 1991: 17). Particularly the new information-based industries have demonstrated that the classic concepts of internationalisation and organisation have to be supplemented by more flexible, network-oriented and evolutionary concepts. Dicken/Thrift (1992: 279) argue that *'both intra- and inter-firm structures are best seen as complex networks of enormous diversity. Business organizations organize production systems but are themselves produced through an historical process of embedding.'* They also propose to recognise both the extreme diversity of organisational forms and their dynamic and evolutionary nature.

'Business organizations organize production systems but are themselves produced through a complex historical process of embedding, which involves an interaction between the specific cognitive, cultural, social, political and economic characteristics of a firms 'home territory', those of its geographically dispersed operations and the competitive and technological pressures which impinge on it' (Ibid: 287).

☞ **Dualities in the global network competition**

Companies increasingly have to cope with dualities and paradoxes (Evans/Doz 1992, Cameron 1986, Wiesmann 1993). The popular duality local responsiveness versus global integration has widely been discussed in international management. Another duality in the new '**network-competition**' is stability versus flexibility. Many MNEs have to develop more flexibility by forming smaller and more decentralised units, whereas small and medium-sized enterprises (SMEs) have to get access to international networks mainly by co-operation. Both have to build up new capabilities to adapt to the new form of competition on a global basis, which demands more and more the organisational complexity (intra- and interorganisational) to deliver and to use the profits of both ends of a duality. **Networks of small and large firms** can enhance the competitiveness of both types of organisations. SMEs can specialise more and capture scale economies and international market access that would not be possible without large-firm linkups. MNEs gain flexibility, local adaptation, and economies of scope by accessing a number of highly specialised small firms (Etemad et al. 2001: 487). The following Figure 2-4 shows the respective qualities of MNEs and SMEs to cope with developments in the increasing '**network-competition**'.

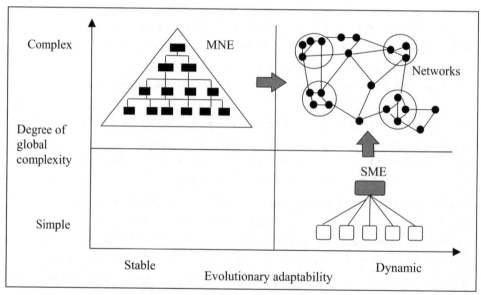

Figure 2-4:   Network-building of MNEs and SMEs

The international extension and integration of relationships in cross-national industry networks does have a strong impact on the internationalisation processes of individual firms in the industry (Madsen/Servais 1997: 580). MNEs and SMEs have a nearly opposite starting point with regards to the development of '**global network fitness**'. MNEs yet have institutionalised international management experience in organisational routines and structures. They have access to internationally dispersed information and resources. They have learned the lessons of internationalisation in the sense of developing international business activities (market selection, market entry, and development processes). The global network competition now demands a balancing of these traditional advantages of MNEs with the advantages of flexible autonomous subunits to strengthen their **global network capability**.

In contrast, most SMEs yet have to develop the **internationalisation capability** because of limited international engagement. On the other hand, they can develop the global network capability right at the beginning of their globalisation process. Etemad et al. (2001: 497) predict that entrepreneurs of the future will be able to draw upon the pooled capabilities and knowledge stock of their entire network, instead of developing the required knowledge themselves. Building upon such enabling networks – mirroring the physical networks of the firms – is a new strategic competence that is bound to challenge SME managers. *'Managers will have to devise new strategies to help develop and maintain network capabilities, in addition to their own internal competencies'* (Ibid: 497).

Particularly new industries in the service and software sector show the great possibilities of **intra- and interorganisational networking**. This enables even start-ups to globalise rapidly without the development of vast organisational hierarchies. These young industries also show the increasing importance of time and therefore of evolutionary dynamics in competition. It does not seem to be happening by chance, that the key dimensions of globalisation are of particular significance in the youngest sectors of the history of global competition.

'Globalization raises the likelihood of actors being aware of each other, potentially offering endless opportunities for them to relate to one another. It compels us to abandon modernist dogmas as to what is the best policy for development, the optimal way to organize markets and industries, the right organizational form, the best managerial practice. It asks us instead to look for the differences across and within countries, regions, communities, industries, and organizations; to look for what makes each of them unique and valuable. Globalization is neither to be opposed as a menace nor to be celebrated as a panacea; it is to be engaged: comprised, located, given form. To be sure, a global world is more unpredictable and ambiguous than the modern world of the recent past. But it allows individuals and organizations to grow out of the straightjackets of location and the modern nation-state, to express themselves in a more boundless way, to pursue their identities without having to conform to a dominant model or paradigm' (Guillén 2001a: 232).

As it has been argued, growing expansion density has marked the evolution of global competition. The underlying evolutionary dynamics seem to gain velocity during this **'quantum leap' of global competition**. Firms can strengthen their ability to identify and define their position in this process by adopting a '**global orientation**' on their operations (Boettcher 1996: 42-50). Globalisation should not only be viewed on the basis of the international expansion of activities. Instead, the observation of globalisation processes a firm follows, should contain three capabilities, which reflect the **firm's capabilities** to cope with the three **basic processes of globalisation** (see also Figure 2-5):

1. development of global business activities (*internationalisation capability*),
2. development of global networks (*global network capability*), and
3. global evolution (*capability of global evolutionary dynamics*).

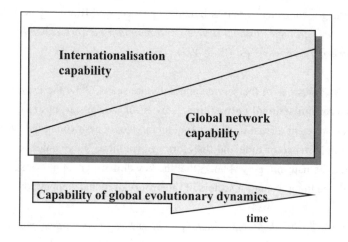

Figure 2-5:   Firm capabilities of globalisation

These three dimensions vary in their importance depending on the state of development a firm faces. Following the '**stage model of internationalisation**' (Johanson/Vahlne 1977, Luostarinen 1979, Cavusgil 1982), it may be argued, that the development of the internationalisation capability is of particular importance for firms at the beginning of their globalisation-process but decreasing during the process of organisational learning and institutionalisation of internationalisation knowledge. On the contrary, the acquisition of the global network capability is of increasing importance during the process because of a growing international complexity in organisation and operations. On a more general level, **internationalisation** may be conceived as a **process of differentiation** while **network formation** implies **processes of integration** of differentiated activities. From a **evolutionary perspective**, both processes are linked in a recursive interplay. In a **sequential perspective**, differentiation always precedes integration as it provides the raw material for integration.

The development of international business activities focuses on individual activities that serve to build up and expand the activity structure in international markets. As a result, a '**configuration**' (Porter 1986) of internationally dispersed activities appears. This component has traditionally been researched on the basis of explanatory approaches in form of internationalisation theories. The '**internationalisation capability**' therefore includes knowledge in market choice, market entry, and selection modes, and the development of a local network position. This capability is of particular importance during the first stages of globalisation. During the course of internationalisation, institutionalisation of this knowledge in routines and organisational structures leads to decreasing marginal returns on this capability at least compared to the increasing returns on the '**global network capability**'. This capability gains importance with the increasing international differentiation and extension of activities that the internationalisation process produces. As described above this capability may also be regarded as the critical success factor in the emerging network competition of today's global markets. Globalisation elevates the role of the ability to network over sheer size. Networks of organisations can certainly undertake large-scale activities without creating large, integrated organisations (Perrow 1992, Powell 1990, Guillén 2001a: 95). In this new form of competition, the global network capability can also be used in the internationalisation process. SMEs, for example, do not have to internationalise by developing complex international organisation structures as the only option like MNEs had to do in earlier stages of global competition. SMEs and autonomous business units can internationalise by building up international network relations.

Network structures gain their advantages from selective specialisation and their flexibility of forming complementary activity structures over time periods. This is a clear advantage over individual firms plagued by sunk costs and organisational inertia. The characteristics of networks might also lead to a very negative influence of time in form of destabilisation. Each organisational form therefore has to cope with the evolutionary dynamics inherent in globalisation. These **dynamic forces** are the **processes of differentiation and integration** in social systems that are currently on a quantum leap to global extension. A management of the evolutionary dynamics in global corporate transformation therefore has to be focused on the dynamic balance of this evolutionary driving principle and on the development of the underlying **capability of evolutionary dynamics**.

During the globalisation process of a firm, organisational units, and activities are differentiated in global as well as in local and cultural contexts. Each differentiation therefore leads to very idiosyncratic relations of the differentiated organisational subsystem and its respective environment(s). The **dynamic management of boundaries** as well as of the relations between internal and external subsystems becomes a core capability in international management. This makes a clear boundary- and self-definition important. Luostarinen (1994: 28) assumes the mastering of dynamics to be the most difficult and challenging task for the management. Dynamics in businesses drive competition, demand, technology development, internationalisation processes, network structures and processes, etc. There should be a match between the competitive advantages of the firm's internal and external action premises. However, because of the existence of dynamics, these premises are continuously changing and thus the competitive edge, which was proper in yesterday's situation, might not necessarily be valid in today's or tomorrow's situation. A continuous evaluation, adaptation, and innovation in order to reproduce the firm's guiding differences therefore are fundamental to its evolutionary capability.

The globalisation of a firm can only be observed within the globalisation process of the social systems. First, it has to be founded by entrepreneurs that can provide resources and network relations to the start-up. In a dynamic interplay first with its founding environment, later with its '*enacted*' environment, the start-up unfolds in the global environment directly as a '*born global*' or indirectly by following a path from national to international competitive positioning. This process of internationalisation is described in Chapter 3. In the course of increasing international commitment, the need for co-ordination rises with the extent, interdependence and diversity of international activities. The global network capability that develops with increasing international activities is described in Chapter 4. Globalising firms develop and reproduce their capability of global evolutionary dynamics, as they are affected by globalisation sooner (born globals) or later (traditional internationalisers). The underlying evolutionary dynamics are illuminated in Chapter 5. Chapter 6 serves to integrate these different levels of observation in an evolutionary approach to the globalisation of firms.

2.5 Summary

The chapter showed that globalisation is a social evolutionary process in which social system formation extends to global scale. It is a historical process that has been unfolding for thousands of years. While international trade already took place in ancient cultures, the formation of social systems with global interdependencies began with technological and organisational innovations in the 15th century. From this perspective, globalisation is an underlying social process including subprocesses such as internationalisation or transnationalisation. The latter concepts presuppose activities between nation states (internationalisation) or across nation states (transnationalisation), which were first founded in the 16th century. Historically, both phenomena are much more specific and temporally bounded than the underlying globalisation process. Globalisation is the historical process in which the evolutionary principle of social differentiation and integration is principally not any more restricted to national or cultural boundaries but **extended to global scale**. It extends from locally dispersed to globally nested social systems from local to global level. Especially the economic system has become independent of national or regional boundaries because of the technological and social developments in recent decades. The result is a process of increasing differentiation and integration on a now principally global basis. Within the global business context this dialectical process is particularly apparent in the duality of global integration vs. local responsiveness. Globalisation is constituted by three subprocesses:

1. **Processes of internationalisation** induce changes in the global extension of social systems by a spatial differentiation of social actors on global scale and by the formation of social systems with worldwide extension (e.g. '*born globals*').
2. **Processes of global network formation** create growing interdependencies between social actors on global scale and a growing integration of their communication, activities, and structures.
3. **Processes of evolutionary dynamics** cause a compression of social time and space and drive the differentiation and integration of social systems on global scale.

The three subprocesses of globalisation apply to all kinds of social systems, from society to organisation level and constitute the globalisation of social systems. On the level of the individual social system, they are reflected in the respective internationalisation capability, global network capability, and capability of global evolutionary dynamics. From a system's perspective, it is thus possible to derive evolutionary principles, which should be explained by an evolutionary theory of the globalisation of firms. Such a theory should capture the whole evolutionary process including the firm's '*birth*' (foundation), its co-evolutionary interplay with its environment, and its reproduction. Accordingly, the evolutionary principles to be explained are

1. **Foundation**: An evolutionary perspective should explain the '*birth*' of an entity. In the case of firms, it is their foundation.
2. **Co-evolution of firm and environment**: Evolution of an entity is only possible in an environmental niche, which provides the necessary resources. A description of the co-evolution of the firm and its respective environment is necessary in order to observe adaptation and to understand change processes.
3. **Global differentiation and integration of firms**: the social evolutionary process is driven by a process of differentiation and integration of social systems. An evolution-

ary perspective on the globalisation of firms has to describe this basic principle of change. On the global level, a basic instantiation of this principle are processes of internationalisation (differentiation) and global network building (integration).

4. **Global evolutionary dynamics of environment and firm**: Evolutionary dynamics follow the principle of differentiation and integration. This principle may be driven by five distinct evolutionary motors, which are explained in Chapter 5.1.2.4:
    - life cycle,
    - teleological (e.g. decision-making),
    - dialectical,
    - variation and selective retention (dominant in biological evolution), and
    - social autopoietic (meaning-based, self-referential reproduction).

The principles of global differentiation, integration, and evolutionary dynamics (3. and 4.) cover the three characteristics of globalisation and their manifestation in firm's properties and capabilities. These basic evolutionary principles serve as a framework to evaluate the contribution of all theoretical perspectives outlined in this publication to an evolutionary perspective of globalisation.

3 Internationalisation

Internationalisation is usually conceived as the expansion of international business activities with a dominant perspective on outward activities in form of export, international cooperative agreements, and FDI. More generally, Beamish (1999: 46) defines internationalisation as the *'... process by which firms both increase their awareness of the direct and indirect influence of international transactions on their future, and establish and conduct transactions with firms in other countries.'* Numerous **indicators of internationalisation** have been developed. Prominent quantitative indicators are (1) foreign sales/value-added, (2) number of employees abroad, (3) participation of foreigners in management, (4) number of foreign subsidiaries, (5) amount of FDI, (6) export share (Krystek 2002: 5).

Such quantification of internationalisation gives an important idea of the amount and intensity of international activities in an enterprise. But internationalisation is not only a phenomenon that is confined to its quantitative share in business activity but also has a strong influence on the enterprise as a whole (Perlitz 1995: 9). The degree of internationalisation of an enterprise is also expressed by its culture, the objectives, strategies, and cognitive orientations. Internationalisation is further exemplified by the worldview and as such comprises a mental orientation towards other countries and cultures in the sense of a **'mental internationalisation'**. Internationalisation therefore induces new management concerns that arise from the contact with foreign countries, cultures, and economic as well as with other social systems (Krystek 2002: 5-11, Simon 1996: 32).

The **degree of internationalisation** (DOI) can also be measured by the use of multi-item scales like that of Sullivan (1994):

$$DOI = FSTS + FATA + OSTS + TMIE + PDIO$$

FSTS: Ratio of foreign sales to total sales
FATA: Ratio of foreign assets to total assets
OSTS: Proportion of overseas subsidiaries to total subsidiaries
TMIE: Top managers' international experience
PDIO: Psychic dispersion of international operations

Sullivan has been criticised by Ramaswamy et al. (1995: 176) because the identification of internationalisation as a unidimensional construct seems methodologically suspect. Especially the measurement of the attitudinal component appears to be questionable.

Another attempt to measure the DOI on a multivariable basis is presented by Kutschker (1994a), who developed the concept of the '**internationalisation mountain**'. Kutschker developed a three-dimensional model of internationalisation based on the number and geographic-cultural distance of countries (markets), the degree of value-added in these markets, and the degree of integration within the firm (Kutschker/Bäurle 1997: 104-110). The **degree of integration** is constituted by four factors (Ibid. 107):

1. Integration increases with the intensity of flows of resources within the firm because the flows of information, which go along with and support the exchange of resources, increase the joint set of knowledge.
2. The integrating effects grow with the number of people involved in the exchange of resources and information between the knots of the international network. It further increases with the frequency and intensity of the exchanges.
3. The joint set of knowledge can develop towards a set of '*contextuating orientations*' (Etzioni 1968: 157-160), which provides a synthesis to the bits of knowledge like values, beliefs, attitudes, and facts. The larger the part of the members of an international firm who share such contextuating orientations, the higher the degree of integration.
4. The higher the integration, the greater is the extent of built-in-flexibility (Kogut 1985a) of the firm's infrastructure.

Graphically the three dimensions generate the '**topography**' of the '**internationalisation mountain**' of a company. The topography visualises the degree of internationalisation along the three dimensions. Kutschker/Bäurle (1997: 108) add '*time*' as a fourth dimension to the model so that the evolution can be visualised as a process of continuous erosion and expansion of the topography over time. The degree of internationalisation changes parallel to changes in the topography. In this model an internationalisation process (like a market entry or a new international co-operation) is represented by a change of the mountain's topography. It may reflect an erosion of any of the three dimensions (Kutschker 1994a: 140). A decrease in the internationalisation profile is an aspect that has been largely neglected by the traditional incremental (expansion) models.

Internationalisation is not always a forward process, but it may also be a backward process followed perhaps by advancing steps, i.e., **de-internationalisation** and **re-internationalisation** may follow internationalisation (Luostarinen 1994: 21). *De-internationalisation* refers to any voluntary or forced actions that reduce a firm's engagement in or exposure to current cross-border activities. Generally, it occurs in a partial way, and may arise in *various forms*, for example (Benito/Welch 1997: 9):

- reduction of operations in a given market or complete withdrawal from it,
- switching to operation modes that entail a lower level of commitment,
- sell-off or closure of foreign sales, service or manufacturing subsidiaries,
- reduction of ownership stake in a foreign venture, and
- seizure by local authorities of assets owned by a foreign firm.

As internationalisation can be conceived as a growth strategy, de-internationalisation is only the rational counterpart in times of falling prices, reduced demand, increased competition or deterioration of relative cost conditions in local markets (Luostarinen 1980: 27, Benito/Welch 1997: 8-10). De-internationalisation is especially important in mature industries (Bell/Young 1998: 15). On the other hand, several factors may constitute an important **impediment to exit** (Caves/Porter 1976, Siegfried/Evans 1994):

- existence of specific assets,
- durable tangible specific assets, such as high sunk costs in machinery,
- intensity of advertising and research and development,
- firm-specific human capital,
- emotional attachment by the management, and
- intangible assets, such as goodwill.

Internationalisation therefore should not be conceived as a linear, teleological process of increasing international growth and complexity. It is rather the **extension of the market boundaries from a local to a global scale** leading to increasing complexity. Still, all activities are subject to resource allocation decisions and therefore always subject to investment *and* disinvestment.

The importance of **de-internationalisation processes** varies between firms with a high or low total amount and percentage of foreign sales and production. Firms with a limited history in internationalisation generally focus on the development of new international activities and not on the disinvestment of the few they have. De-internationalisation for these firms therefore is seldom intended and normally symbolises a kind of failure based on the typical disadvantages of SMEs. Studies by Schulte (2002) and Hirsch-Kreinsen/Schulte (2002) show that for SMEs with a relatively small amount of foreign activities de-internationalisation often marks an outstanding event with different implications. For some SMEs, such an event appears to be traumatic, as it is associated with failure. In the **early steps of internationalisation** this may cause an **impediment to further international engagement** and re-internationalisation. Others take such a situation as a lesson to be learnt and as an occasion of learning-by-doing in order to build up objective and experiential internationalisation knowledge. For most firms, however, unintended de-internationalisation is a mixture of both a failure from which conclusions have to be drawn and a **source of experience** for further internationalisation. SMEs should not be discouraged by initial setbacks in the internationalisation process. Rather, managers in SMEs should focus on **learning** from early experiences and finding effective ways to overcome the disadvantages encountered when initially operating in foreign countries (Lu/Beamish 2001: 582).

Compared to SMEs with a quite limited internationalisation history, '**mini-multinationals**' (Luostarinen 1980: 6, 1984: 27) and large MNEs do not take de-internationalisation as outstanding or even as a failure. These firms are not any more in a position of exploring important markets for the first time. The most important level of strategic decisions in MNEs is the continuous balancing of investment and disinvestment and therefore the reallocation of resources between local and regional markets and globally dispersed organisational units. It can be argued that de-internationalisation should be seen as part of the broader perspective of international strategy, which, with advanced internationalisation, is likely to become an integral part of overall firm strategy. From this perspective, decisions causing changes in the internationalisation profile of a firm can be compared to strategic portfolio planning, with internationally dispersed activities as the relevant bundles of activities (Benito/Welch 1997: 12, 19).

As the pace of global competition accelerates, organisations tend to trace complicated trajectories or migration paths as they search for favourable environmental domains. Analyses based on more stable epochs generally convey the impression that globalisation occurs as a unidirectional process, with expansion being the norm and contraction being the exception. The actual histories of global firms reveal that the **process of globalisation** includes **expansion**, **contraction**, and **frequent changes in direction** as firms enter, exit, and re-enter new markets, businesses, and technologies over time. Global firms operate in multiple domains, often experimenting with different markets before deciding on major expansions in selected areas. Exploration is an accurate way to describe their activities (Hurry 1994: 237).

In general, **literature on internationalisation** has traditionally been **focused on SMEs**, as the impact of internationalisation activities on the individual enterprise is stronger and more outstanding in the phase when international activities are built up for the first time in the evolution of a firm. In MNEs, internationalisation and de-internationalisation activities are conducted on an ongoing basis and are kind of '*business normality*' for them. The idiosyncratic characteristics of MNEs and their context are global complexity and heterogeneity (Doz/Prahalad 1986) so that literature on MNEs traditionally has been more focused on the dispersion and co-ordination of MNE activities. The research on MNEs has widely culminated in the network perspective as a framework to integrate the study of strategy and structure and to illuminate intra- and interorganisational interdependencies in globally dispersed activity structures. Research on change processes in form, extent and intensity of international activities, i.e. (de-) internationalisation processes, is usually confined to SMEs.

3.1 Internationalisation strategies

Internationalisation strategies in the field of international management can be basically differentiated into two categories. The first one, '**international market entry strategies**' are growth strategies that serve to build up and increase international activities. Generally, this type of strategy is discussed in the context of SMEs. The second category, '**international business strategies**', was initially developed to explain strategic behaviour of large diversified MNEs and to provide normative models for their strategic positioning. Basic models, like that of Porter (1986), have also been adapted to the internationalisation perspective. Both categories will be discussed below.

3.1.1 International market entry strategies

The pursuit of **internationalisation processes** can be based on different motivations. General **objectives** might be (Robock/Simmonds 1989: 55, Ghauri 2001: 30):

- market-seeking objectives,
- resource-seeking objectives,
- efficiency-seeking objectives,
- strategic asset-seeking objectives,
- risk avoidance, and
- defence or '*exchange of threat*'.

Dunning (1997a: 218-219) supposes that market and resource seeking investments represent the two main motives for an initial foreign entry by a firm. Efficiency-seeking and strategic asset-seeking investments embrace the two main modes of expansion by established foreign investors. Risk avoidance and defence objectives are especially influential in strategic portfolio planning of MNEs. In the 1960s and 1970s, most FDI was of the first or second types, although regional integration in Europe and Latin America was beginning to lead to some efficiency-seeking FDI. In the 1980s and 1990s, FDI had been increasingly of the third and fourth type. Exceptions include first-time investments by MNEs from developing countries and a new generation of multinational SMEs from industrialised countries (Ibid.).

In the first studies about international strategy, published in the 1970s, the focus was on **international market entry strategies**. International **market selection** and choice of **entry mode** represent the key strategic decisions in connection to a firm's internationalisation (Andersen 1997: 29). Internationalising firms develop their activities in a *logical sequence* of market entry strategies and entry modes depending on foreign market attractiveness, risk, control needs, and international experience. First, firms will choose low risk and low involvement modes of market entry like export or import. After initial success with international trade, firms begin to enter new markets with co-operative entry modes and at last with FDI. For example, an empirical study of internationalisation strategies of Italian clothing companies (Berra et al. 1995: 67) showed that the international growth of SMEs takes place mainly through contractual agreements (68%), more so than with non-co-operative operation (32%), whereas in large firms the non-co-operative strategies slightly prevail (54%). Consequently, the external growth strategy is very important for the SMEs (72%) and somewhat less important for the large firms (54%). A basic conclusion of many studies of strategies for entry into foreign markets has been that lack of knowledge and experience is critical to the development of international operations. Such knowledge is acquired mainly through actual operations abroad and extends the international decision-making capacity (Hedlund/Kverneland 1985: 41). Root (1987: 5-21) describes a '**logical flow model of the entry decision process**':

1. Firms become committed to international markets when they no longer believe that they can attain their strategic objectives by restriction of their activities to the home market. Increasingly, market-seeking objectives are also strong motivators for internationalisation.
2. An international market entry strategy is a comprehensive plan which sets forth the objectives, goals, resources, and policies that will guide a firm's international business operations over a future period long enough to achieve sustainable growth in world markets. For most firms, entry strategy's time horizon is from three to five years (Root 1987).
3. Product/market entry strategies require decisions on
    - the choice of the target product/market,
    - the objectives and goals in the target market,
    - the choice of an entry mode to penetrate the target market,
    - the marketing plan to penetrate the target market, and
    - the control system to monitor performance in the target market.
4. International market entry modes may be classified as export, contractual, and investment modes.

5. Once started in international business, a firm will gradually change its entry mode decisions. First a firm is seeking to minimise risk, later to maximise control over international operations. This also leads to higher resource commitments and risk exposure (stage model of internationalisation). *'In other words, exporting can become an international learning experience, a development process that takes the firm toward more and more international sophistication and commitment'* (Ibid. 53).
6. The foreign market entry plan is an action programme that specifies market-oriented objectives and goals; policies and resource allocations; and a time schedule.

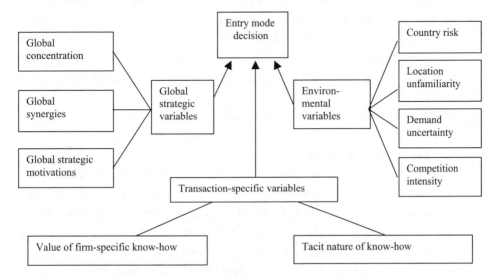

Figure 3-1: Influences on entry mode decisions
(Source: Kim/Hwang 1992: 33)

Kim/Hwang (1992) developed an **eclectic framework of the entry mode choice** stressing the importance of global strategic considerations in choosing a multinational's entry mode (Figure 3-1). Their contention is that **beyond the environmental and transaction-specific factors** assumed to affect the entry mode decision - which is well established in the literature - the **strategic relationship** a multinational envisages between its **operations across borders** in reaching this decision is of increasing importance. Kim/Hwang believe that a multinational's global strategic posture has a major impact on its entry mode choice. This is caused by **increasing internal and external interdependencies in the internationalisation process** and by the fact that strategic actions taken by a multinational in one market can have repercussions in other markets. Kim and Hwang therefore integrate the classical environmental and transaction-specific variables dominating in international business literature with the global strategic variables into their eclectic framework.

In an empirical study, Gaba et al. (2002) found that the **timing of entry** is influenced by a firm's capabilities and/or firm-specific factors (resource-based), by perceptions of the market/environmental opportunities (information processing), and by host country variables (locational factors). One important factor is the **degree of internationalisation**. Firms that have a significant overseas engagement can benefit from the **learning** and **experience** associated with their operations in foreign markets, as well as their extensive market networks. They are assumed to be much more flexible in the exploration and exploitation of international market opportunities that arise from environmental changes. For example, firms with a **higher degree of international experience** were found to be more likely to enter a newly opened international market (here: China) earlier because they can leverage their accumulated knowledge more readily. They can also cross-support and cross-subsidise their entry with their existing operations in other foreign locations (Ibid.). Similar advantages arise from size and scope economies (Ibid. 43-44). The results of the study of Gaba et al. are consistent with resource-based arguments that early entries are different from late entries in terms of their resources and capabilities (Robinson et al. 1992, Liebermann/Montgomery 1998).

3.1.2 International business strategies

With the development of the global network competition in the 1980s, the concentration on a stand-alone perspective of international market entries did not seem to be sufficient any more. The fundamental change in thinking about global competition in the 1980s had been the shift in interest over the decision to invest overseas to the strategic value of operating assets in multiple countries. The **globalisation drivers** presented in Table 3-1 provided the basis for strategies of global integration. The dominant framework for the analysis of global strategies was that of global integration and national adaptation (Kogut 1989: 385)

Market	**Cost**	**Government**	**Competitive**
Homogeneous needs	Economies of scale and scope	Favourable trade policies	Interdependence of countries
Global customers	Learning and experience	Compatible technical standards	Competitors globalised or might globalise
Global channels	Sourcing efficiencies	Common marketing regulations	
Transferable marketing	Favourable logistics		
	Differences in country costs and skills		
	Product development costs		

Table 3-1: Industry globalisation drivers
(Source: Yip 1989: 35-39)

The globalisation drivers offer huge benefits for those firms, which are capable to exploit the potential gains from integrating worldwide activities. Firms following a strategy of global integration can achieve one or more of the following **benefits of global integration** (Porter 1986: 21, Yip1989: 33. Leontiades 1986: 98-99):

- economies of scale in the activity,
- a proprietary learning curve in the activity,
- comparative advantage in where the activity is performed,
- co-ordination advantages of co-locating linked activities such as R&D and production,
- improved quality of products and programs,
- enhanced customer preference,
- increased competitive leverage,
- international sourcing,
- global experience transfer,
- international corporate image,
- global resource focus, and
- international portfolio.

Kogut (1985: 32-36) identifies especially arbitrage and leverage opportunities as drivers for global strategies. **Arbitrage opportunities** can occur in form of production shifting due to changing factor costs or exchange rates, tax minimisation across different countries, differences in local financial markets, and imperfections in the market for information. **Leverage opportunities** are based on global co-ordination of dispersed activities, and the bargaining power by operating dispersed operations. Possible **drawbacks of global strategies** are:

- significant management costs through increased co-ordination,
- reduction in local effectiveness due to lower motivation and morale of local staff,
- standardised products do not satisfy locally differentiated demand,
- concentration distances customers and results in lower responsiveness and flexibility,
- uniform marketing can reduce adaptation to local customer behaviour, and
- integrated moves can mean sacrificing revenues, profits, or competitive position in individual countries (Yip 1989: 34).

Strategic approaches adopted increasingly a holistic view on the internationalisation process and were generally based on the differentiation of two main dimensions of international business activities: the dispersion of international activities and their co-ordination. Porter (1986) developed the basic '**configuration/co-ordination framework**' (Figure 3-2).

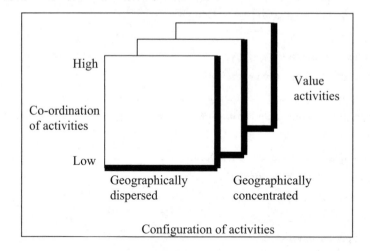

Figure 3-2:   The dimensions of international strategy
(Source: Porter 1986: 60)

The '**configuration**' of a firm's activities worldwide symbolises, where in the world each activity in the value chain is performed, including in how many places. The second dimension, '**co-ordination**', refers to how similar activities are performed in different countries and co-ordinated (Ibid. 17). Figure 3-3 illustrates that all individual value activities are subject to both dimensions.

A firm faces an array of options in both configuration and co-ordination for each activity. **Configuration options** range from concentrated (performing an activity in one location and serving the world from it) to dispersed (performing every activity in each country). In the latter case, each country would have a complete value chain. **Co-ordination options** range from none to very high. At the one extreme, each subsidiary might operate with full autonomy. At the other, the worldwide activities would be tightly co-ordinated and decision-making centralised. Porter developed four normative portfolio strategies on the basis of the dimensions configuration and co-ordination (Figure 3-3). If a firm employs a very dispersed configuration while co-ordinating little or not at all, the firm is competing with a **country-centred strategy.** The domestic firm that only operates in one country is the extreme case of a firm with a country-centred strategy. In general, many SMEs are following this strategic option, though often not consciously by rational decision-making. Many SMEs do not explicitly include the co-ordination dimension during their first steps in internationalisation.

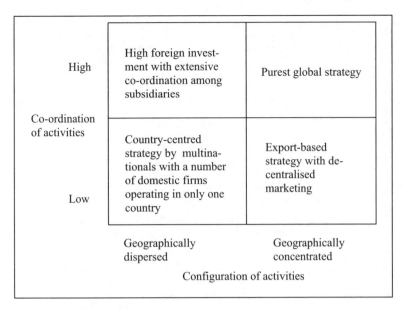

Figure 3-3:   Types of international strategy
(Source: Porter 1986: 60)

Moving from the lower left-hand corner of the diagram up or to the right, strategies are increasingly global. The **purest global strategy**, then, is to concentrate as many activities as possible in one country, serve the world from this home base, and tightly co-ordinate those activities that must be performed near the buyer. According to Porter (1986: 21), a global strategy can be defined more precisely as one in which a firm seeks to gain competitive advantage from its international presence through either concentrating configuration, co-ordination among dispersed activities, or both.

By **dispersion of activities**, a firm can exploit local market potentials and locational advantages in different functional areas. Innovation can be fostered by participation in different **local 'innovative milieus'** or networks (Chapter 4). Dispersion is also encouraged by the risks of performing an activity in only one place: exchange rate risks, political risks, etc.. Co-ordination potentially allows the sharing of know-how among dispersed activities. Different countries, with their inevitably differing conditions, provide a fertile basis for comparison as well as opportunities for arbitraging knowledge obtained in different paces about different aspects of business. Co-ordination may also allow a firm to respond to shifting comparative advantages. On the other hand, co-ordination involves long distances, language problems, and cultural barriers to communication (Porter 1986: 2). Jarillo/Martinez (1991) adapted Porter's international strategy typology to describe typical internationalisation paths of Spanish firms (Figure 3-4).

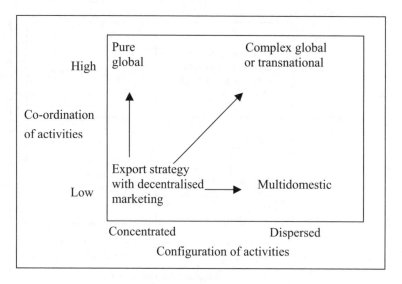

Figure 3-4: Two dimensions of international strategy
(Source: Jarillo/Martinez 1991: 293)

A firm would start the **process of international expansion** at the lower left corner, following an export strategy with decentralised marketing. The firm concentrates all its value-chain activities in its country of origin and exports its products through middlemen like trading companies, agents, and distributors – allowing for a low level of international co-ordination.

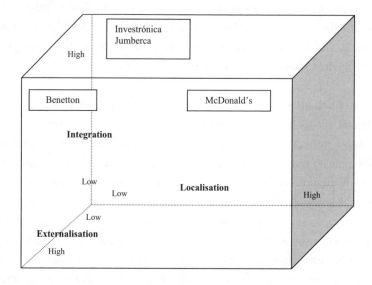

Figure 3-5: Strategic mapping of some international strategies
(Source: Jarillo/Martinez 1991: 297)

Then the three arrows in the box of Figure 3-5 would represent the process of becoming a multinational corporation. Each arrow symbolises a generic strategy the firm can follow to pass from a simple export company to a multinational firm. The internationalisation paths then would follow the logical sequence described in Figure 2-2 ('Historical evolution of global competition'). The results of their empirical study, however, indicated that more than half of the Spanish firms studied did not fit that pattern. A large part never internationalised and others never internalised foreign operations. Jarillo/Marinez therefore added a third dimension '**degree of externalisation of activities**' into the configuration/co-ordination framework in order to describe and explain the observed behaviour (Figure 3-5).

Leontiades (1986) developed a **global-local strategy portfolio** based on the dimensions '*market share objective*' and '*scope*' (Figure 3-6). '**Global high share strategies**' are associated with large MNE and similar to Porter's pure global strategy. Their essence is the worldwide co-ordination of firm resources behind global objectives. The wider scope of worldwide operations opens up several areas of potential advantage.

'**Global niche strategies**' are based on specialisation on certain product niches, technologies, or market segments. They are very attractive for firms with a limited resource base and typical for multinational SMEs.

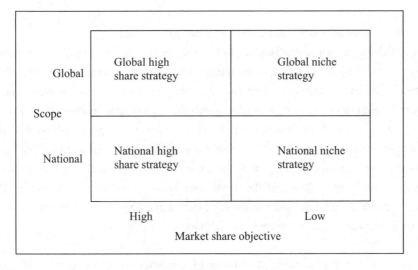

Figure 3-6: Four generic international competitive strategies
(Source: Leontiades 1986: 98)

Welge (1990, 1992) and Boettcher/Welge (1996) provide a comprehensive overview over strategies between global integration and local adaptation. In-depth knowledge of strategic management from a process prospective is further provided by Welge/Al-Laham (2003). In general, **globally operating firms** must have **greater adaptive capabilities**. It must be able to process and sort out a larger number of environmental complexities. It must also have the **capability to detect shifts in environmental factors** that have strategic implications and be capable of responding to the altered environmental state. For this reason the appropriate strategic decision processes are critical for an international firm (Jones et al. 1992: 223). A critical element of formulating an international strategy is to create the **organisational flexibility** and incentives that respond to changes in economic parameters between countries. To this extent, the international firm can be viewed as representing investments in flexibility that permit the exploitation of profit opportunities generated by environmental turbulence (Kogut 1985a: 27).

Strategic market entry decisions normally have intensive **organisational implications** as the international activity profile of the firm is changing. Frese (1994: 4) therefore identifies three important elements of internationalisation decisions: the **regional scope** as measured by the number of foreign markets or production sites, the **configuration** of the value-added activities, and the **co-ordination** of the internationally dispersed activities. In this context, the informational infrastructure is one of the most critical challenges during the transformation into a global competitor (Hasenkamp 1994: 148).

3.1.3 Multidimensional internationalisation strategy

As illustrated above, Kutschker/Bäurle (1997) integrated different strands in international strategy research into a four-dimensional framework, which they term '**internationalisation mountain**'. In this framework, they include the dimensions '*configuration*' and '*co-ordination*' from Porter's strategy portfolio, which the authors term '**value-added**' and '**integration**', respectively. These are combined with the dimension '**geographic-cultural distance of countries**' reflecting the incremental logic of internationalisation strategies and the stage theories of internationalisation with the basic dimension termed '*business distance*' or '*psychic distance*'. By inclusion of the fourth dimension, '*time/velocity*', Kutschker/Bäurle integrate a developmental perspective, which offers a typology of four internationalisation profiles with respective generic strategies to follow (Figure 3-7).

The dimension '**geographic-cultural distance of countries**' is subject to what the authors call '**presence strategies**'. These include '*strategies of target market selection*' and '*entry strategies*', and reflect the internationalisation strategies discussed above.

The dimension '**value-added**' expresses where different value-added activities are located and to which scope. The focus here is on the allocation of resources and activities. '**Alloca-**

tion strategies' consequently reconfigure the relation between the first and second dimension by enlarging, diminishing, and relocating value-added activities within or between countries. The first form of allocation strategies, '**strategies of localisation and globalisation**', reflects the resource allocation in order to exploit advantages from differentiation or standardisation. '**Configurational strategies**', on the other hand, define the relation of concentration or dispersion of activities. The focus here is on decision-making and the relation of centralisation vs. decentralisation. Different roles can be ascribed to headquarters and the subsidiaries according to their individual resource base and contextual factors of their location. Both types of strategies are not independent from another. Globalisation strategies go along with a concentration of activities whereas strategies of localisation call for dispersed, decentralised operations.

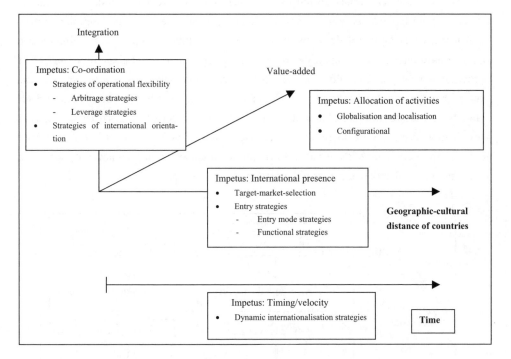

Figure 3-7: Internationalisation strategies in the four-dimensional framework
(Source: Kutschker/Bäurle 1997: 120)

The dimension '**integration**' is influenced by '**co-ordination strategies**'. They determine the way in which dispersed activities are integrated within the international firm. Kutschker/Bäurle draw a distinction between '**surface structure**' and '**deep structure**'. The surface structure constitutes the part of an organisation, which an observer can reconstruct easily. Elements are organisational charts, formalised procedures, and lines of command.

The deep structure of an organisation refers to those soft factors only insiders can perceive, such as values, beliefs, attitudes, and contextuating orientations. The first form of co-ordination strategies, are the '**strategies of operational flexibility**' by Kogut. The second form, '**strategies of international orientation**', gives the internationalisation process a preferred direction by influencing the deep structure of the firm. The deep structure of firms with activities dispersed in different countries and cultural environments tends to be more heterogeneous than the deep structure of national firms. Manipulation of the deep structure provides a strong strategic orientation due to its strong orientational and co-ordinating effect. It is questionable, though, whether the deliberate homogenisation of the heterogeneous subcultures in the international organisation would lead exclusively to positive effects.

Crucial importance is ascribed to the fourth dimension '**time/velocity**'. Strategies from this perspective are termed '**dynamic strategies**' and are normatively derived from the strategic roles that firms occupy in their competitive context. While the strategies influencing the second and third dimension are mainly derived from international business literature on MNEs, the dynamic strategies basically apply to SMEs in their internationalisation process. Internal factors (e.g. resources, potential to internationalise) and external factors (competition) determine the chronological order of activities and the velocity. Therefore, it is necessary to compare the own degree and velocity of internationalisation to the competitors in order to determine the appropriate time, duration, and velocity of strategic action. The necessity for moves in the internationalisation process can be determined on this basis.

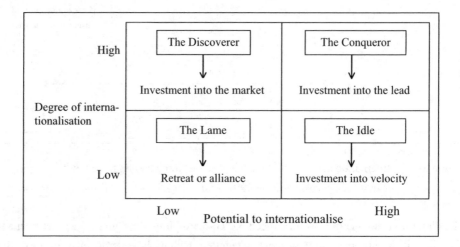

Figure 3-8: Dynamic internationalisation strategy
(Source: Kutschker 1994: 239, Kutschker/Bäurle 1997: 119)

Kutschker (1994:239) and Kutschker/Bäurle (1997:119) developed a **typology of competitive types in the internationalisation process**, which is based on the **dimensions** '*potential to internationalise*' and '*relative degree of internationalisation*' (Figure 3-8). In a second step, generic strategies are ascribed to each of the resulting four types.

'**Discoverers**' face a situation, which is characterised by a relatively high degree of internationalisation and a low potential to internationalise. The international competitive position is strong. Such firms can stabilise and exploit their position while selectively keeping the competitive edge. As resources are scarce, effective strategies are investment into existing subsidiaries and selective establishment of new ones.

'**Conquerors**' have both a relatively high degree of internationalisation and a high potential to internationalise. These firms are in a situation in which investment into their leading position by selectively acquiring competitors or establishment of new subsidiaries are the most reasonable strategic actions available. The other two types - the '**lame**' and the '**idle**' - are characterised by a relatively low degree of internationalisation and therefore lag behind their international competitors.

3.1.4 Contribution to an evolutionary perspective

Literature on internationalisation strategy contributes an **instrumental perspective** to **intended global differentiation**. It provides means to develop systematic modes and sequences for the global extension of activities. Internationalisation strategies basically focus on the **extension of activities** and are **growth strategies**. Only in exceptional cases, negative changes in global differentiation are integrated. None of the three international strategy perspectives refers to evolutionary mechanisms, which drive internationalisation processes or includes emergent elements of globalisation in its perspective. All approaches, however, explicitly allow for the design of system/environment and element/whole relations.

International market entry strategies focus on **differentiation** and provide different modes of market entry by internal or external differentiation. Internal differentiation also includes the foundation of new subsystems in the form of subsidiaries. **International business strategies** add the **integration perspective** and therefore describe strategies on global level instead of focusing only on international extension in the case of market entry strategies. On the other hand, global business strategies convey a more general and conceptual perspective compared to the more practical and instrumental perspective of market entry modes. Similar to the international business strategy literature, the **multidimensional strategy perspective** provides a conceptual view on global differentiation and integration and further integrates the dimensions of time and space. The multidimensional strategy perspective provides a more dynamic view but is more oriented at the observation and classification of an internationalisation profile rather than on strategy making. On balance, internationalisation strategies provide means and instruments for the development of international activities and thus for intended global differentiation and integration. Table 3-2 gives an overview over the inclusion of evolutionary principles in internationalisation strategy perspectives.

	International market entry strategies	International business strategies	Multidimensional internationalisation strategy
Foundation	Subsidiaries	Subsidiaries	Subsidiaries
Co-evolution of firm and environment	Unidirectional, instrumental adaptation and exploitation	Unidirectional, instrumental adaptation and exploitation	Unidirectional, instrumental adaptation and exploitation
Global differentiation of firm	Provide means for development of international activities	Provide concepts and normative strategies for global differentiation	Provides concepts and strategies for global differentiation
Global integration of firm	No	Provide conceptual view and normative strategies for global integration	Provide conceptual view and normative strategies for global integration
Global evolutionary dynamics of environment	No	No	No
Global evolutionary dynamics of firm	Teleological, learning	Teleological, learning	Teleological, learning, time/space dynamics

Table 3-2:   Evolutionary principles in internationalisation strategy

3.2 Processual internationalisation theories

Literature on internationalisation is evolving, and more important, it is increasingly integrative in nature. That is, researchers seem to recognise that internationalisation is too dynamic and broad a concept to be exclusively defined by any one school of research, perspective, or mode of explanation (Coviello/McAuley 1999: 251). While economic internationalisation theories explain the existence of international trade and multinational enterprises (MNEs), they are basically in nature and will not be included in the evolutionary perspective.

Internationalisation as a process of organisational transformation is path-dependent. Path-dependence is the incremental process where the behavioural pattern of firms is contingent upon and a function of its past international experience (Eriksson et al. 2000: 308). In internationalisation, there seem to exist two conceptually distinct forms of path-dependence: **emergent** and **incremental internationalisation**. The classic form of incremental internationalisation, which is marked by a **cumulative process** described in the stage models, is based on the assumption that firms develop their activity structure first in their home country. All their relationships and knowledge are embedded in a culturally homogeneous national or regional context. By a process of **'imprinting'** (Stinchcombe 1965), organisational structure, knowledge, and external relationships reflect national context, e.g. culture, institutional form, and strategic orientation. Then, after the establishment of activities and structure in the home country, the firm begins to explore foreign markets and to integrate knowledge about and from the international context into its knowledge base. Firms internationalise like **'rings in the water'**, i.e. in a slow and gradual manner with respect to geographical markets, market entry mode, and product policy (Madsen/Servais 1997: 561). This perspective is well founded and documented in the **stage models in internationalisation theory**.

Since the 1980s, however, international competitive forces and advantages especially in knowledge-intensive sectors have been so strong that increasingly new ventures market their products internationally from their inception (Karagozoglu/Lindell 1998: 45, Oviatt/McDougall 1994). Although most firms still appear to internationalise in an incremental way, the speed and complexity of firm internationalisation is increasing around the world and a small but increasing number of firms is international at founding (UNCTAD 1993a, OECD 1997). Such firms receive increasing attention and are termed **'international new ventures'** (INV) (Oviatt/McDougall 1994, 1997, McDougall et al. 1994) or **'born globals'**. In contrast to **traditional internationalisers**, these firms are imprinted with globalisation capabilities from inception and thus reflect **emergent internationalisation**.

3.2.1 Internationalisation of 'born globals'

Knight/Cavusgil (1996: 11) give the following definition of **'born globals'**: 'Born globals are small, technology-oriented companies that operate in international markets from the earliest day of their establishment.' An **'international new venture'** (INV) is defined similar to a born global firm as a *'business organisation that, from inception, seeks to derive significant competitive advantage from the use of resources and the sale of outputs in multiple countries'* (Oviatt/McDougall 1994: 47). The two expressions *'born global'* and *'international new venture'* will be used here as synonyms.

Rennie (1993) describes **born globals** as competing on quality and value created through **innovative technology** and **product design**. Such firms are usually **founded in knowledge-intensive industries** and tend to be **highly specialised**. The specialisation of SMEs is necessarily associated with a reduction in the size of the available market. The **core competence** of born globals must therefore be expected to be **narrow and focused** (Madsen/Servais 1997: 577). Thus, they may find it necessary to expand overseas to take advantage of the skills already developed in their home market, as well as to finance their significant R&D outlays.

It is not surprising that technology appears as a critical component of the internationalisation of newly created high-technology SMEs. For these firms, given the rapid rate of obsolescence of innovations, the drive towards foreign markets to exploit their know-how as quickly as possible emerges as a must (Fujita 1998: 58). Madsen/Servais (1997: 580) suppose that the phenomenon of born globals is not limited to high-technology industries, as it has generally been indicated in literature. Also specialised assortments of low-technology products adapted to **homogeneous niche segments** in many countries, and even trading companies may be cases for born globals. On the other hand, the mere participation in a new high-technology industry does not mean that start-ups are international from inception. Especially firms in service industries (like Internet firms or software consultants) encounter high barriers to internationalisation because of the importance of reputation, '*front-room activities*', and embeddedness in their personal and business networks that are typically still local (Kotha et al. 2001, Borghoff/Welge 2003).

Smaller firms lack the resources to compete on equal terms with large MNEs. They must rely on their knowledge of specialised, relatively narrow product niches in order to succeed. Additionally, these firms must internalise the right combination of facilitating technologies, international business know-how, and access to appropriate contacts abroad. Much of the learning associated with this process results from being linked to **information networks** both at home and abroad (Knight/Cavusgil 1996: 23). Many entrepreneurial firms, including family businesses, can overcome the **disadvantage of small size** through their **use of technology**, such as the Internet, to reach consumers beyond their borders. Along with entrepreneurial and managerial characteristics, the application of technology was found to be a key to explaining internationalisation of new ventures (Davis/Harveston 2000: 110, Gallo/Pont 1996).

Based on a study by McKinsey and Company, Knight/Cavusgil (1996: 18) ascribe the following **characteristics** to born globals:

- Management views the world as its marketplace from the outset of the firm's founding; unlike traditional firms, they do not see foreign markets as simple adjuncts to the domestic market.
- Born globals begin exporting one or several products within two years of their establishment and tend to export at least a quarter of total production.

- They tend to be small manufacturers, with average annual sales usually not exceeding $100 million.
- The majority of born globals is formed by active entrepreneurs and tends to emerge as a result of a significant breakthrough in some process or technology.
- They may apply cutting edge technology to developing a unique idea or to a new way of doing business.
- The products that born globals sell typically involve substantial value adding; the majority of such products may be intended for industrial uses.

Born globals have existed for **most time of economic globalisation**. Examples are the famous East India Company that was chartered in London 1600 or the Ford Motor Company that also can be assumed to have been an international new venture at its founding in 1903 (Wilkins 1970, Wilkins/Hills 1964). Since the late 1980s, however, their number has been continuously increasing (Knight 2000: 2, Oviatt et al. 1994: 45-46). Case studies have begun to appear from scholars of entrepreneurship. Some have shown that such ventures form because internationally experienced and alert entrepreneurs are able to link resources from multiple countries to meet the demand of markets that are inherently international (Coviello/Munro 1992, McDougall/Oviatt 1991). This development can basically be traced to the **increase in innovations of information and communication technologies** and the resulting **decrease in global information and communication costs**. Together with decreasing **transport costs** this leads to a **shrinking of global economic space**. For information-based products it leads even to an economic space with zero-time distance. The **increasing homogenisation of many markets** in distant countries has made the conduct of international business easier to understand for everyone (Hedlund/Kverneland 1985). The upshot is that increasing numbers of business executives and entrepreneurs have been exposed to international business. International financing opportunities are increasingly available and human capital is more internationally mobile (Oviatt et al. 1994: 48).

Madsen/Servais (1995: 38) propose that studying born globals, the **time perspective** should be extended **beyond its birth**. Probably, many of its '**genes**' have roots back to firms and networks in which the founder(s) and top managers gained industry experience. '*Basically, in many instances it may be doubtful whether a born global can be considered a new company. In a legal sense the company may be new, but were its skills and capabilities not often born and matured prior to its legal birth*' (Ibid.).

Compared to traditional new ventures, born globals already are instilled with organisational routines, decision rules, and capabilities that are not depending very much on any local or national borders but were gained in the global context. Routines, decision rules, and capabilities can be considered as the '**genes**' of the organisation (McKelvey 1978). Instead of being tied to geographical markets, these genes may be tied to a certain specialised, value-adding process, which the firm solves in the particular, internationalised industry. **Born globals** dispose of **access to global networks**, **knowledge**, and **markets right from the start** while traditional firms need a development process to explore such global resources. As a main driving force of born globals, Knight (1997: 24) identifies their '**international venturesomeness**'. It is defined as *'the propensity of firms to engage in proactive and visionary behaviors in order to achieve strategic objectives in international markets'* (Ibid.). Firms possessing substantial international venturesomeness are supposed to be more market oriented and more aggressive in the exploitation of their firm-specific advantages. In an empirical study, Oviatt/McDougall (1995: 34-38) identified seven **characteristics of successful global start-ups**:

- A global vision exists from inception.
- Managers are internationally experienced.
- Global entrepreneurs have strong international business networks.
- Pre-emptive technology or marketing is exploited.
- A unique intangible asset is present.
- Product or service extensions are closely linked.
- The organisation is closely co-ordinated worldwide.

Classically, a higher propensity and speed towards internationalisation is ascribed to firms with small home markets (Luostarinen 1980, Ayal/Raban 1987) and firms in industries with oligopolistic reaction (Knickerbocker 1973). Also, the possession of proprietary intangible assets, such as technological expertise or entrepreneurial skills, may confer to their owners the oft-cited advantage that foreign firms have over local enterprises and is supposed to be a driver of internationalisation (Calvet 1981: 54). Oesterle (1997) analyses the influence of a new firm's **innovation set** as a further central variable on the **time-span until starting internationalisation**. In his view, the combination of the aspect of innovation as determinant of a firm's evolution with the fact that internationalisation can be another path to growth leads logically to the relation between innovation and the time-span until the start of international activities (Ibid. 131). Oesterle differentiates continuous, modified, and radical or discontinuous innovation, each with different effects on the time-span. **Radical innovations** require the formation of new behavioural patterns caused by the introduction of totally new products or processes. They are likely to create whole new industries or whole new standards of management, manufacturing, and servicing. They diffuse throughout the socio-economic base and represent fundamental changes. **Continuous innovations**, on the other hand, induce only incremental changes while modified innovations are more disruptive without having the power to alter significantly behavioural patterns.

According to Oesterle (Ibid. 133), the **international context** too, should be interpreted as a **force** influencing the **time-span until internationalisation**. The innovation-related influences of the business context can speed up or slow down the internationalisation of innovations and thereby of the firm as the owner of the innovation. Especially the adoption of radical innovations that have to create their market first is very dependent on the business context. Dependent on these innovation-related innovations the internationalisation process of a firm will start very early, later, or never. The example of the initial evolution of Daimler as an innovative pioneer in the automobile industry illustrates that different local contexts were receptive to different degrees to his radical innovations. In the beginning, the innovations of Daimler were not accepted in Germany, but in France. One major influence on innovation and therefore internationalisation is not only the ability to produce innovation but also the **acceptance of the respective cultural and business context** and later the **absorbing capability** of the market (Ibid. 140-141). Two situations can therefore appear in case of radical innovation:

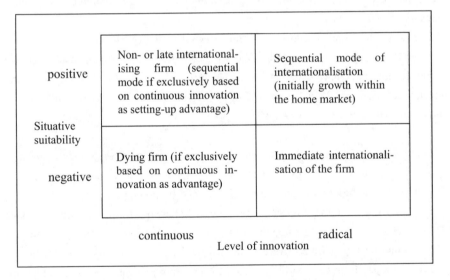

Figure 3-9: Conditions of time-spans until internationalisation
(Source: Oesterle 1997: 144)

1. A **friendly climate** in the country of origin is marked by a high potential of buying power, positive cultural acceptance and no defence actions of competitors. It nurtures the commercial use of innovation first within the home market. A sequential process of internationalisation is more likely to develop.

2. A **hostile climate** in the country of origin is marked by a low potential of buying power (small home market), massive defence actions of competitors (oligopolistic reaction), and negative cultural acceptance. It leads to a commercial use of innovation first within foreign markets. This means the development of born globals due to greater receptiveness of the international market as compared to the home market.

Oesterle integrates the two dimensions '**situative suitability of an innovator's home market**' and '**level of innovation**' in order to derive four typical modes of internationalisation with regard to the time-span to entry (Figure 3-9).

3.2.1.1 Entrepreneurs as drivers of early internationalisation

Oviatt/McDougall (1995) discovered that probably the most important characteristic associated with success is that the **founders** of a global start-up develop and communicate a global vision as to be global one must first **think globally**. Every global start-up they investigated had internationally experienced founders or top managers, and every person interviewed believed that was a necessity. '*Some understanding of the nuts and bolts of cross-border business conduct, such as letters of credit, the risks of exchange rates, and, most important, potential communication and cultural conflicts seem necessary*' (Ibid: 35). The initial inspiration for many of the ventures studied came from the **international experience** of its founder. Calof/Beamish (1994) suggest that an individual's **geocentricity** is associated with international experience. Internationally experienced management teams therefore are viewed as a **key resource** that influences SMEs to engage in behaviours leading to a greater degree of internationalisation (Reuber/Fischer 1997: 820).

McDougall et al. (1994: 479) argue that **entrepreneurs** are people who '*are alert*' about potentially profitable resource combinations when others are not. Research has further shown that this alertness to new business opportunity is influenced by previous experience (Casson 1982, Ronstadt 1988) because that experience provides a framework for processing information. McDougall et al. (1994: 479) assume that **founders of INVs** are more alert to the possibilities of combining resources from different national markets because of the competencies that they have developed from their earlier activities. These entrepreneurs possess an unusual constellation of competencies based on **international experience** and **network resources**. It is therefore further argued that only the entrepreneur possessing these competencies is able to combine a particular set of resources across national borders and form a given INV (Ibid.).

For domestic firms, inertia becomes a problem because it inhibits change to routines appropriate to international environments. **International entrepreneurs**, however, seem to recognise this, and therefore they try to **avoid domestic path-dependence** by establishing ventures, which, at their inception, have routines for managing multicultural workforces, for coordinating resources located in different nations, and for targeting customers in multiple geographic locations simultaneously. In its simplest terms, the founders of INVs believe that ventures will not **develop international competencies** except by **practising international business**. Successful INVs have been shown to make measurable trade-offs among the risks inherent in the countries entered, the entry modes chosen, and the degree of foreign market dependence (McDougall et al. 1994: 481). Contrary to the stage models of internationalisation such behaviour may mean that to a significant degree **international entrepreneurs enact the foreign environment** their ventures face rather than passively accept the risks as exogenous (Oviatt/McDougall 1997: 90).

3.2.1.2 Networks as drivers of early internationalisation

Johannisson (1995: 38) points to the importance of **personal networking** in start-up and internationalisation processes. Personal networks include both social and business relationships, closely intertwined. In his research project looking into the networks that young and prospective entrepreneurs build, Johannisson found that the **most important ties in the personal network** are **considerably older than the venture itself**. This, in turn, supports the thesis that born globals dispose of **international experience and networks from inception**. Birley's study (1985) on the role of networks in the entrepreneurial process concludes that entrepreneurs tend to come from smaller for-profit organisations and they tend to start similar businesses in the same location with previous colleagues as partners. The number of born globals therefore can be expected to rise as more and **more professionals** are **embedded in global business networks**. The choice of networks is a key in understanding the nature of the subsequent firm, because it is during the start-up process that the elements of the firm are set (Ibid. 115). An empirical study by Eriksson et al. (2000) proves that the kinds of **experiential knowledge** developed at the **outset of internationalisation** led to those same kinds of knowledge being further developed in any subsequent internationalisation. According to this study, experiential knowledge types not developed in the early stages of internationalisation are not developed later (Ibid. 323).

Founders make extensive use of **international networks** in order to develop their **global activity structure**, which is in turn closely co-ordinated. Several studies show that **networks** are **central to entrepreneurship** (Carsrud et al. 1987, Aldrich/Zimmer 1986, Aldrich et al. 1987). Vatne (1995: 66-70) provides a model that summarises the relationship between networks and SME internationalisation. This model illustrates **internationalisation as an entrepreneurial process** that is embedded in an institutional and social web that supports the firm in terms of access to information, human capital, finance, and other resources.

Entrepreneurs use their **personal contact networks** to gain knowledge, and seek out and mobilise new partnerships that help the firm grow and expand into foreign markets. A corollary of the importance of social exchange in accessing and co-ordinating resources is that since face-to-face interaction, and social, cultural, and geographic proximity foster the trust needed to facilitate social exchange relationships, the **local resource endowment** is also important. This view of firm growth argues that entrepreneurs learn to leverage their competencies by establishing **dynamic linkages to other firms** in their local production. In the course of internationalisation, these **network linkages** then are extended to **foreign markets** (McNaughton/Bell 1999: 66). According to Obrecht (1994: 27) it is the interactive combination of the '**entrepreneurial resource**' with the '**network resource**' that defines basically the strategic capacity of SMEs. Especially on the international level, the competitive position of SMEs is dependent on its network resources (Ibid. 24).

While knowledge is localised for both start-ups and other firms, start-ups are more closely tied into **local networks** since they depend on networks for critical knowledge inputs. When knowledge flows are localised, firms located in distant regions are excluded from local knowledge networks. It is this local character of networks that is their potential link with globalisation. Therefore, small technology-based firms are attractive acquisition targets for MNEs interested in entering new technological networks (Acs/Preston 1997: 4)

A major feature that distinguishes new ventures from established organisations is the minimal use of internalisation and the greater use of alternative transaction governance structures (Oviatt/McDougall 1994: 53). Entrepreneurs have several disadvantages in the development of international network relations. Beamish (1999: 48-53) points to four major **'liabilities' of entrepreneurs** entering for the first time the **international arena**:

1. **Liability of newness**: Stinchcombe (1965: 148-149) coined this term and described the circumstances from which the liability of newness arises: '*New organisations, especially new types of organisations, generally involve new roles, which have to be learned... The process of inventing new roles, the determination of their mutual relations and of structuring the field of rewards and sanctions so as to get the maximum performance, have high costs in time, worry, conflict and temporary inefficiency... New organisations must rely heavily on social relations among strangers. This means that relations of trust are much more precarious in new than old organisations...One of the main resources of old organisations is a set of stable ties to those who use organisational services*'. New organisations have to develop legitimacy, trust, new knowledge, and access to local resources and networks that are necessary to establish activities in other countries.

2. **Liability of size**: Small organisations have several competitive disadvantages compared to large organisations. Large firms have a larger pool of financial and tangible resources, knowledge and capabilities as well as access to premium labour markets. In contrast, small firms sometimes cannot take full advantage of their existing capabilities, due to the fact that exploitation of these capabilities demands investment in complementary capabilities, which they cannot afford. The lack of slack resources, both managerial and financial, suggests that they are prone to extreme duress in the case of a misstep or sudden changes in the market conditions. Smaller firms also find that they have minimal voice in shaping the competitive environment (Beamish 1999: 50-51).

3. **Liability of foreignness**: The fact that still a majority of entrepreneurs does not enter foreign markets early may be attributed to their lack of business competence or confidence. Foreign market knowledge is usually not one of the biggest assets of domestic entrepreneurs, at least compared to their technological competence. Hymer (1976: 34-35) states that compared to local firms, foreign firms have informational disadvantages due to differences in local contexts. Of a more permanent nature is the barrier arising from discrimination by local government, consumers, and suppliers. Foreign firms have to gain legitimacy and acceptance in a process of learning and institutionalisation. Liabilities of foreignness include high levels of uncertainty that impede effective decision-making, difficulties in dealing with local governments and local partners, and the myriad challenges of adapting products and processes to different cultural and national requirements. Diverse local tastes and preferences, languages and cultures, and business systems and practices increase the odds that foreign firms will make costly errors, encounter substantial delays, or otherwise struggle with their attempts to establish operations abroad (Lord/Ranft 2000: 573).

4. **Liability of relational orientation**: By setting up relationships with one or more firms in the foreign market, the entrepreneur has the potential to simultaneously overcome all these constraints. Network-relations can provide access to new resources, new ways of managing businesses, market information, as well as access to new customers and suppliers. But entrepreneurs entering foreign markets have no proof of qualification and trustworthiness in business relations. They have no experience how to create network relations in the specific foreign market. The development of network relations depends to a great extent on the trust and merits gained from past co-operations. A newcomer has no record of successful co-operations in the new market. Entrepreneurs who enter a new market with co-operative agreements from the start might gain more experience and trust compared to those who enter with a do-it-alone orientation (Beamish1999: 52).

Principally, internationalisation can be conceived as an entrepreneurial process as international activities in foreign markets have to be developed from the start. According to Anderssson (2000: 68), **internationalisation** is an example of strategic change that can be defined as an **entrepreneurial action**. Internationalisation can be conceived as an act of entrepreneurship because it is a strategy in search of opportunities for firm growth and wealth by expanding into new markets. Further, it is a strategy that requires a fundamental departure from existing practices and an act that entails high levels of risk (Lu/Beamish 2001: 567). From this perspective, internationalisation is not an activity that is divided from other activities, but a part or a consequence of a firm's strategy.

Anderson (2000: 80-81) defines three different **types of entrepreneurs** with idiosyncratic strategic orientations. Entrepreneurs in this typology are conceived as the key decision-makers in a firm so that the typology applies not only to start-ups but also to larger firms.

1. The main interest of the **'technical entrepreneur'** is technology. Internationalisation is not the main interest of the entrepreneur, but new products can become known abroad through the international network of which the firm's customer is part. The technical entrepreneur is following an international pull strategy with a preference for low-risk form of foreign entry like export or licensing.
2. The **'marketing entrepreneur'** has found a need in the market and has an idea of how to fill this demand. The internationalisation process and the creation of new channels to reach the customer are followed proactively. The marketing entrepreneur is willing to develop new international ventures and to choose establishment modes such as the greenfield establishment of subsidiaries that require lots of resources. These entry modes make it possible to penetrate markets quickly. Personal preferences and networks may be more important than rational calculation. The marketing entrepreneur prefers an international push strategy.
3. The **'structure entrepreneur'** acts in mature industries and is trying to restructure firms and industries, or the *'rules of the game'*. New business ideas can be developed and implemented by the reorganisation or combination of organisations. From this perspective, internationalisation is not a separate strategic goal but a consequence of the overall strategy. The structure entrepreneur prefers a strategy of international industry restructuring.

3.2.2 Stage theories of internationalisation

Stage theories describe the internationalisation beginning with the first internationally oriented activities of already established firms. These theories do not explain the formation of international new ventures but the internationalisation of firms founded in the national context. In contrast to economic theories, they provide a dynamic perspective on internationalisation and therefore valuable knowledge about the global evolution of firms.

3.2.2.1 International product life cycle (Vernon)

With the concept of the international product lifecycle, Vernon (1966) developed a **first approach** explicitly integrating the time dimension into internationalisation theory. Vernon for the first time developed a **processual view of international business activities**, with the description of a typical international diffusion process of products.

According to the product cycle hypothesis, firms that set up foreign production facilities characteristically do so in reliance on some real or imagined **monopolistic advantage**. The model is based upon the assumption that products are subject to different **developmental stages** with regard to their conditions of production and sales. Vernon assumes that consumer preferences are similar internationally and economies of scale therefore can be exploited. The underlying process comprises four stages:

Stage of innovation: The product cycle hypothesis begins with the assumption that the stimulus to innovation is typically provided by some threat or promise in the market. But according to the hypothesis, firms are acutely myopic; their managers tend to be stimulated by the needs and opportunities of the market closest at hand, the home market. The home market in fact plays a dual role. Not only is it the stimulus for the innovating firm; it is also the preferred location for the actual development of the innovation. A basic assumption in the model is that '*the entrepreneur's consciousness of and responsiveness to opportunity are a function of ease of communication; and further, that ease of communication is a function of geographical proximity*' (Vernon 1966: 192). Firms make use of the national technological network in which they are embedded in order to generate innovations. Production is based in the home country, as the necessary resources, especially know-how, are located in geographical proximity. '*The upshot is that innovations of firms headquartered in some given market tend to reflect the characteristics of that market*' (Vernon 1979: 256).

Stage of exports: Once the innovator has set up his first production unit in the home market, any demand that may develop in a foreign market would ordinarily be served from the existing production unit. As foreign demand for the new product is rising, it is served by exports because missing technological know-how in the host countries impairs offshore production. The firm makes a comparison between the delivered cost of exports and the cost of overseas production in the process of foreign market expansion. Other entry modes like licensing are also considered but often dismissed due to missing know-how in the host countries.

Stage of FDI: Once foreign demand increases first in other advanced countries (Ibid. 197) to an extent that makes local production profitable, entrepreneurs will begin to ask themselves whether the time has come to take the risk of setting up a local production facility. Mass production of the yet *'maturing product'* with low requirements for qualified labour and thus also offshore production is possible now. The diffusion of production sites is following the same logic as the export process. It begins in other industrial nations and later reaches developing countries (Vernon 1979: 258).

Stage of re-imports: Foreign production units first begin to serve third country markets as their production costs make export costs lower than those of exports from the home market due to lower factor costs. Demand in the home market falls below the level of foreign demand (beginning stagnation) so that even economies of scale are better achieved in foreign production units. The increasing competition leads to a relocation of production to developing countries that offer comparative cost advantages.

Vernon constructed a **pragmatic and comprehensive model**, which integrates explanatory, processual, and environmental variables. The theory was based on a model of the global economy with three levels of economic development, which from a contemporary perspective does not seem to be appropriate for most internationally operating firms. In a later article, Vernon (1979) realises the environmental changes that caused a convergence of different market conditions, which formerly provided the basic argument for the hypothesis. Vernon therefore notices that some of the starting assumptions of the product cycle hypothesis are clearly in question (Ibid. 262). The evidence is fairly pervasive that the product cycle hypothesis had **strong predictive power in the first two or three decades after World War II**, especially in explaining patterns of FDI by US firms. Afterwards, different types of MNEs have developed global networks of subsidiaries. Only MNEs serving global markets and with centralised innovatory capacity are assumed to perform consistently with the product cycle pattern. Another remaining trace of the sequence is likely to be provided by the innovating capacities of smaller firms, *'firms that have not yet acquired a capacity for global scanning through a network of foreign manufacturing subsidiaries already in place'* (Ibid. 263). On the contrary, the majority of **contemporary MNEs** are able to introduce **new products** simultaneously on a **geographically differentiated basis**. **Globally dispersed centres of competence** with global strategic responsibility (also for innovation) now contradict the idea of a centralised source of innovation at the home-based headquarters. The evolutionary dynamic of global organisations and its implications for the international management are not explicitly dealt with in the product cycle hypothesis.

3.2.2.2 Stage models of organisational structures

As social systems, firms are constituted by the recursive interplay of meaning and action structures (Chapter 6.1). Consequently, internationalisation processes may be observed on both levels. Stage models have been developed that describe such processes (1) on the level of the **modes of international activity** (2) on the level of the **formal organisation structure**, which reflects the intended activity structure and determines organisational actors, and (3) on the level of **cognitive structures**.

3.2.2.2.1 Stage models of activity modes in foreign markets

Firms that are engaged in international business can make use of a variety of activity or entry modes in foreign markets. These activity modes can be distinguished by their intensity in terms of invested capital, risk, and management capacity (Figure 3–10).

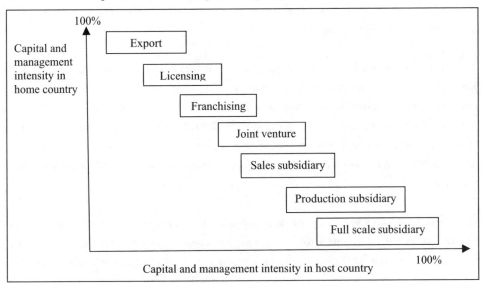

Figure 3-10:   Degrees of internationalisation
                (Source: Meissner/Gerber 1980: 224)

Following this logic, firms begin with **export** as the entry mode with the lowest levels of intensity. An increasing market volume then leads towards more intensive **co-operative arrangements** like licensing, franchising, joint ventures and the foundation of a foreign sales subsidiary. In a next step, increasing competition, governmental action or simply locational advantages require the **development of a subsidiary** with all functions of the value chain. After further increases in the sales volume, an extension of the production capacity makes sense. After some time of stabilisation in the foreign market, the subsidiary begins to develop export activities to third countries and might become a regional centre.

In their empirical study of 78 firms from the U.K. and Continental Europe, Newbould et al. (1978) identified seven different types of **internationalisation paths**, each depending on the respective **sequence in international market entry modes**. They found that firms do not always follow an incremental path from low to high-risk entry modes underlying the learning-based stage models. Instead, a large part of the firms preferred some kind of '*leapfrogging*' in their internationalisation process. In a similar vein, Root (1987: 15) concludes that *'once started in international business, a company will gradually change its entry mode decisions in a fairly predictable fashion. Increasingly, it will choose entry modes that provide greater control over foreign marketing operations'*. Root adds that exporting is an international learning experience, a development process that takes the firm toward more and more international sophistication and commitment. First a firm is seeking to minimise risk, later to maximise control over international activities (Ibid. 53).

Clearly, a **progression from less to more intensive forms of market entry** has an **appealing logic**. The discussion about development paths of SMEs and their limited resource base at the beginning of their internationalisation provide further arguments. Therefore, in literature on the internationalisation of SME, the discussion of different entry modes has been dominating. Research on internationalisation has traditionally focused on the development of dispersion of activities, not on their co-ordination and appropriate mixes or portfolios of international business modes.

Nonetheless, **all entry modes** are **distinct organisational modes** of doing international business and as such they are alternatives or complements and do not necessarily fit into a sequential progressive order. Differences exist between industries, the '*administrative heritage*', and the strategic and cognitive orientations of decision-makers. In an empirical study, Kogut/Singh (1988) found strong support that **cultural distance** and **national attitudes** towards uncertainty avoidance **influence the choice of entry mode**. A survey of FDI in the USA by foreign companies for the years 1981 to 1885 showed significant differences in the preference of the modes joint ventures, acquisition, and greenfield investments. U.K. firms preferred acquisitions (78.7 per cent) to joint ventures and greenfield investments (each 10.6 percent) while French firms clearly prefer joint ventures (70 per cent) and Japanese firms have a nearly equilibrated preference structure towards forms of FDI. These differences are attributed to different scores in **cultural dimensions** like uncertainty avoidance (Kogut/Singh 1988: 417-419, 426).

3.2.2.2.2 Stage models of formal organisation structures

The internationalisation of enterprises always has organisational implications due to the scope and the diversity of business activities in different environments. Several researchers studied the evolution of organisational structures in this process to derive **organisational paths in the internationalisation process**. In their study of 187 US-based multinational enterprises, Stopford/Wells (1972) found that a **close tie between strategy and structure** exists regardless of what industry the firm is in. In contrast to Alfred Chandler's structure-follows-strategy paradigm, they discovered a recursive relationship between structure and strategy. The results showed that '*managers in enterprises following similar strategies in quite different industries have developed similar organizational structures and ownership policies.... Once set up, organizational structure almost certainly influences the choice of strategy of the multinational firm*' (Ibid. 5-6). Stopford/Wells organise the **development of business organisation** in three stages. In *stage 1*, an enterprise is usually small enough to be administered by a single person, typically the owner and founder.

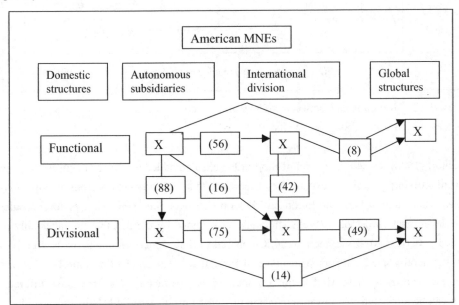

Figure 3-11:   Sequences of structural change of American MNEs
(Source: Stopford/Wells 1972: 28)

In *stage 2*, the enterprise adopts a functional structure. After further growth in size and diversity, the firm develops a divisional structure in *stage 3*. As shown in Figure 3-11, the firms in the study develop their international activities in stage 2 (functional structure) or stage 3 (divisional structure). In the same study, Stopford/Wells also examine the **relationship between strategy and structure** in MNEs. They identify alternative paths from the initial international division, assumed to be the first structure integrating international activities, towards the most complex form of organisation, the global matrix structure (Figure 3-12). The two intermediate organisational forms are based on the formation of worldwide product or area divisions.

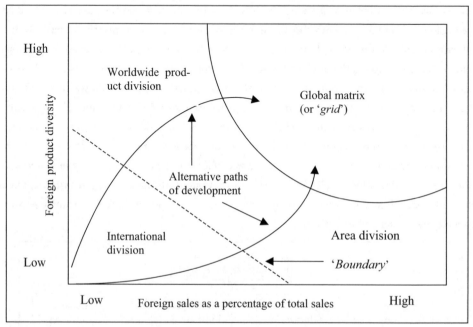

Figure 3-12: Relationships between strategy and structure
(Source: Stopford/Wells 1972: 63)

Egelhoff (1988) revised the model of Stopford/Wells and added a further dimension '**foreign manufacturing**' in order to explain the observation that both product divisions and area divisions in his study of U.S. and European MNEs possessed a high percentage of foreign sales. The deviation from Stopford/Wells' findings is explained by the fact that the latter only included American MNEs in their study. Compared to their American counterparts, European firms generally need a higher percentage of foreign sales in order to become large MNEs. This also applies to those MNEs with a product division structure. The remaining difference then can be attributed to a lower percentage of foreign production by MNEs with worldwide product divisions compared to those with area divisions (Ibid. 10-12).

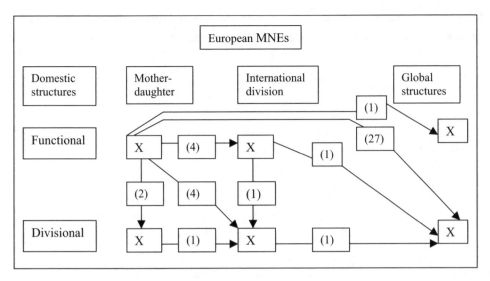

Figure 3-13: International organisational evolution of European MNEs
(Source: Franko 1976: 203, 1976a: 133)

Franko (1976, 1976a) first discovered differences in the internationalisation of organisation structure between U.S. and European firms. He found that the first stage of internationalisation for many European firms was not the **international division** but what he called the **'mother-daughter' structure** in which the heads of foreign subsidiaries reported directly to the head of the parent company (Figure 3-13). The effective design of such mother-daughter relationships was studied by Welge (1981). Other characteristics of this structure are relatively autonomous subsidiaries, informal, personalised relationships, organic rather than mechanistic controls, and the rotation of home-country personnel internationally. Compared to their US competitors, European MNEs largely bypassed the international division and went directly from the decentralised mother-daughter structure to **global structures**. The reason is that American firms adapted their structures to meet the needs of their product diversification strategies before they became involved in foreign operations. In Continental Europe, structure did not follow (diversification) strategy until there was a change in the competitive environment. It was easier for them to decentralise due to a lower degree of complexity of foreign operations (Franko 1976a: 134).

Davidson/Hapeslagh (1982) found that firms that moved from an international division to a global product organisation actually experienced a drop in sales abroad. Such research implicitly argued against a unilinear model of MNE evolution. Other researchers proposed alternative models of structural evolution. Daniels et al. (1984) collected data from ninety-three US

MNEs, and derived an alternative model that positioned the various structural forms differently on the '*product diversity/dependence on foreign sales grid*' (Figure 3-14).

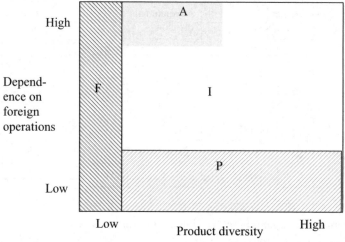

F = Functional; P = Product; I = International division; A = Area

Figure 3-14: Structural evolution of nonconglomerate U.S. multinational firms
(Source: Daniels et al. 1984: 304)

Similar to Stopford/Wells, Brooke/Remmers (1978: 23-36) identify four **types of MNEs** in their study of 51 firms:

- *Type A* has no separate geographical or product-group organisation, and many firms in this category are small or single product. The foreign subsidiary reports to head-office executives with company-wide responsibilities.
- *Type B* comprises companies where the geographical organisation is the main link with foreign operations. International activities are organised by an international division or by area divisions. Some form of B type organisation is preferred when:
    - product divisions are small,
    - geographical spread is large, and
    - the company is mainly in consumer products, or the products are closely related.
- *Type C*, on the other hand, is organised by worldwide product groups. Efficiency gains can be best realised in this structure. One characteristic difficulty of the Type C organisation is a block in communication between head office and the foreign company.

- *Type D* is a complicated mixture of the different projections and resembles the '*grid structure*' described by Stopford/Wells. Like these authors, Brooke/Remmers also identify a development path from Type A (small company) to Type D (very large company), which they conceive as the final stage of development (Ibid. 35). The path is not determined but the direction is clear. '*The transition from one type to another can be sudden ... But usually the change is slower than this, and hence companies are in transition and not readily classifiable* (Ibid. 24).'

Stage	International strategy	Organisation response
1	None	None, or built-in export department
2	Enter foreign markets with direct exports.	Full-function export department or division.
3	Enter some foreign markets with investment in local production; enter other markets with non-investment modes.	International division
4	Serve markets throughout the world from multiple country sources, as guided by a global strategy.	Modified international division, global organisation, or mixed organisation structure.

Table 3-3: Responses in organisation structure in the evolution of a global enterprise (Source: Root 1987: 209)

Root connects the different **stages of organisational structure** to the **respective international strategy** (Table 3-3).:

The strong recursive relation between strategy and structure like in the Stopford/Wells model is even more apparent in the stage model of the Process School in IB (see Chapter 4.2.2). The historical perspective, which identifies a multinational, a global, and a transnational phase, has been presented yet in the preceding chapter. On the basis of the global integration on national differentiation grid, which reflects the dominant guiding distinction in international business since the 1980s, Bartlett (1986) developed a **unilinear evolutionary model** similar in structure, though not content, to the convergence model of Stopford and Wells.

MNEs trying to balance high **demands for both integration and responsiveness** therefore need adequate decision processes, embedded in organisational structures that allow for '**context management**'. The normative structure that allows for a flexible balancing of both the demands for global integration and local responsiveness at the same time is called '**transnational**'. This structure is conceived to be optimal for MNEs that face high demands from both dimensions. Since the 1980, MNEs increasingly move towards the transnational structure, due to the changing environment, in which both dimensions became central to decision-making. MNEs did not adopt this structure from the beginning of their internationalisation, as firms develop structures at their foundation that fit best their environment. In a form of organisational '**imprinting**' (Stinchcombe 1965), this organisational form becomes a '**historical heritage**' (Bartlett/Ghoshal 1987: 14) and is preserved by organisational inertia. Firms that began their internationalisation in the multinational phase therefore developed multinational structures with high autonomy of the subsidiaries and high local responsiveness. Firms that began their internationalisation later in the global phase developed global structures with a high degree of global integration. Both types of MNEs have to move towards the transnational model in order to adapt to the demands of the transnational phase (Figure 3-15)

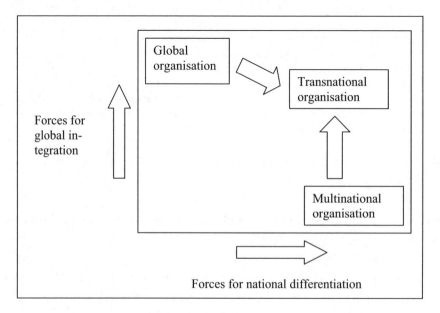

Figure 3-15:   Evolution of organisational forms
              (Source: Bartlett 1986: 377)

3.2.2.2.3 Evolution of organisational cognitive structure

One basic typology in international business is that of the **EPRG-profile** developed by Perlmutter (1969). **International executives** are supposed to develop different **attitudes toward building a multinational enterprise**. These attitudes can be inferred from the assumptions upon which key product, functional, and geographic decisions are made. These states of mind or attitudes may be described as **ethnocentric** (home-country oriented), *polycentric* (host-country oriented), and **geocentric** (world-oriented). According to Perlmutter (1969: 11), they never appear in pure form but are clearly distinguishable. Table 3-4 gives an overview over the characteristics of the three types of headquarters management orientation toward subsidiaries.

Organisation design	Ethnocentric	Polycentric	Geocentric
Complexity of organisation	Complex in home country, simple in subsidiary	Varied and independent	Increasingly complex and interdependent
Authority; decision-making	High in headquarters	Relatively low in headquarters	Aim for a collaborative approach between headquarters and subsidiaries
Evaluation and control	Home standards applied for persons and performance	Determined locally	Find standards, which are universal and local
Rewards and punishments; incentives	High in headquarters, low in subsidiaries	Wide variation; can be high or low rewards for subsidiary performance	International and local executives rewarded for reaching local and worldwide objectives
Communication; information flow	High volume of orders, commands, advice to subsidiaries	Little to and from headquarters; little between subsidiaries	Both ways and between subsidiaries; heads of subsidiaries part of management team
Identification	Nationality of owner	Nationality of host country	Truly international company; identifying with national interests
Perpetuation (recruiting, staffing, development)	Recruit and develop people of home country for key positions everywhere in the world	Develop people of local nationality for key positions in their own country	Develop best people everywhere in the world for key positions everywhere in the world

Table 3-4: Headquarters orientations in an international enterprise
(Source: Perlmutter 1969: 12)

The **ethnocentric** attitude can be found in companies of any nationality with extensive overseas holdings. Managers of the headquarters have an attitude of superiority and think that home nationals are more capable, trustworthy, and reliable than any foreigner in headquarters or subsidiaries. Often, the national identity of the company is particularly stressed like '*this is ... a Swiss company, a German company, an American company, etc.*', and the communication process is dominated by '*advice*', '*counsel*' and directives from headquarters to subsidiary personnel. Foreigners often feel like '*second-class*' citizens (Ibid. 12).

Polycentric firms begin with the assumption that host-country cultures are different and that adaptation is necessary. Local people know what is best for them, and the national subsidiary should be as '**local in identity**' as possible. Polycentric firms, literally, are loosely connected groups with quasi-independent subsidiaries as centres – more akin to a federation (Ibid.)

Geocentric firms do not discriminate for or against personnel, ideas, or capabilities according to national differences. They seek the best people and solutions, regardless of nationality, to solve the company's problems anywhere in the world. The ultimate goal of geocentricism is a worldwide approach in both headquarters and subsidiaries. The firm's subsidiaries are thus parts of a whole whose focus is on worldwide objectives as well as local objectives, each part making its unique contribution with its unique competence (Ibid. 13).

The three types of management orientation vary with regard to function, product, and geography. Differentiated attitudes therefore can be found in a firm according to these dimensions. Inherent in Perlmutter's argumentation is a normative bias towards the geocentric type. He states that there appears to be evidence of a need for evolutionary movement from ethnocentrism to polycentrism to geocentrism (Ibid. 17).

3.2.2.3 Learning-based stage models

Using the number and type of a company's foreign subsidiaries as criteria for differentiation, the **internationalisation process** can be divided into different stages, for example, as follows (Luostarinen 1980: 4-5, Root 1987: 19):

Stage 1: *starting stage* of internationalisation (other than subsidiary operations abroad);
Stage 2: *development stage* of internationalisation (other than manufacturing units abroad);
Stage 3: *growth stage* of internationalisation (manufacturing units in less than six foreign countries); and
Stage 4: *multinational company stage* (manufacturing units in six or more foreign countries).

Firms in the fourth stage fulfil the '**Harvard criteria**' of the multinational corporation (MNC) (Vaupel/Curhan 1969: 3). Compared to MNEs, SMEs develop in different situational contexts, utilising different international business methods, especially export operations, and thus are at different stages of the internationalisation process leading towards the (mini-) multinational enterprise stage (Luostarinen 1980: 6). Three schools of internationalisation research developed on the basis of such incremental stage models and roots in the behavioural theory of the firm (Cyert/March 1963, Aharoni 1966): the **Uppsala School**, the **Helsinki School**, and the **Innovation School**. The first two schools represent combined the 'Scandinavian approach' to internationalisation covering the whole process from first exports to international FDI and production while the latter differentiates different stages that end with extensive export activities. All three approaches are based on the assumption that firms develop an activity structure in their home countries first before they begin to internationalise in a **'centrifugal'** way, beginning with countries close to the home base before incrementally increasing intensity and geographical reach of their activities. The theoretical basis for the incremental, learning-oriented stage model was laid by Aharoni's **'behavioural theory of the firm'** described below.

3.2.2.3.1 Behavioural theory of foreign direct investment (Aharoni)

Aharoni (1966) developed the **first incremental stage theory**, the behavioural theory of FDI. Similar to the scholars in the tradition of industrial organisation, Aharoni tried to explain the existence of FDI. Contrary to the school of industrial organisation, the theory is not based on the assumption that FDI is induced by market imperfections. Like in the behavioural theory of the firm (Cyert/March 1963), Aharoni conceives a company as a political coalition of different interest groups. Consequently, Aharoni focuses on **decision processes of FDI** under conditions of bounded rationality, uncertainty, and diverging interests. Satisfying instead of maximising solutions is thus assumed to be reached in the decision-making processes. These processes are sequentially passing four **stages**: An *initial phase*, an *assessment phase*, a *decision phase*, and a *re-negotiation phase*. The **initial phase** is assumed to be of particular importance and is triggered by four different **initial forces**:

- *external triggers* (e.g. foreign clients, representatives),
- *threats to foreign markets* that were formerly served by exports,
- *bandwagon-effects*, and
- *cross-investments* (in order to counteract FDI by competitors).

In a different study, Steinmann et al. (1977) resume the stage model of Aharoni and expand the decision phase by a **phase of construction** and a **phase of operations**. Based on two empirical studies, Steinmann et al. (1977, 1981) derived categories of indicators for the behaviour and the process in the respective phases. Decisions on centralisation vs. decentralisation, leadership aspects and strategies of market entry and ownership are dominating the management category.

3.2.2.3.2 Uppsala School

The Uppsala School in Sweden is one of three different schools of research that developed in the 1970s with a focus on **incremental internationalisation processes**. Internationalisation is supposed to be the product of a series of incremental decisions (Johanson Vahlne 1977: 23, 1990: 11). Internationalisation is not supposed to be the result of a strategy for optimal allocation of resources to different countries where alternative ways of exploiting foreign markets are compared and evaluated. Rather, it is assumed to be the consequence of a process of incremental adjustments to changing conditions of the firm and its environment. The model is based on two basic assumptions. First, the sequence of stages indicates an **increasing commitment of resources to international markets**. The second assumption is that firms enter new markets with **successively greater psychic distance** (Johanson/Vahlne 1990: 13). Firms face cultural barriers when expanding internationally and learn from their previous experience when gradually expanding into cultural space. Such a centrifugal expansion pattern is assumed to be more successful than a random strategy (Barkema et al. 1996: 162-163. The reasoning is based upon the **behavioural theory of the firm** (Cyert/March 1963, Aharoni 1966) and on the **theory of the growth of the firm** (Penrose 1959).

The Uppsala School conceives internationalisation as a process of incrementally expanding engagement in international business. The model of the internationalisation process focuses on the development of the individual firm, and particularly on its gradual acquisition, integration, and use of **knowledge about foreign markets and operations** as well as on its successively increasing commitment to foreign markets. The basic assumptions of the model are that lack of such knowledge is an important obstacle to the development of international operations and that the necessary knowledge can be acquired mainly through operations abroad. The model is based on the empirical observation of Swedish firms. These firms often developed their international operations in small steps, typically starting with export and gradually increasing the intensity of foreign operations towards more risky and resource-intensive entry modes like joint ventures and FDI (Johanson/Vahlne 1977: 23-24).

Figure 3-16 illustrates how Johanson/Vahlne (1977: 26) conceptualise the internationalisation process as a **dynamic interplay** between **static aspects of internationalisation** (market commitment, market knowledge) and **aspects of change** (current business activities, commitment decisions). Market knowledge and market commitment are assumed to affect both commitment decisions and the way current activities are performed. These in turn change knowledge and commitment. The firm inches forward on its internationalisation path through a cycle of increased commitments yielding greater experiential knowledge, resulting in lower perceived uncertainty, leading to higher resource commitments, and so forth (Erramilli et al. 1999: 29).

The *first state aspect*, **market commitment** increases with the amount of resources committed, with the degree of integration with other activities, and with the degree of specialisation of the resources committed.

The *second state aspect*, **market knowledge**, is of basic interest because commitment decisions are based on several kinds of knowledge (Johanson/Vahlne 1977: 27). Like Penrose (1959: 53), Johanson/Vahlne (1977: 28) distinguish '**objective knowledge**' that can be transferred between individuals and organisational units from '**experiential knowledge**' that can only be gained by personal experience. Experiential knowledge about foreign markets is assumed to be the driving force of the internationalisation process and the critical kind of knowledge in this context (Johanson/Vahlne 1990: 12). An important aspect of experiential knowledge is that it provides the framework for perceiving and formulating opportunities.

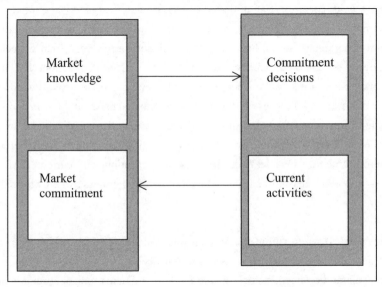

Figure 3-16: The basic mechanism of internationalisation – state and change aspects
(Source: Johanson/Vahlne 1977: 26)

Johanson/Vahlne (1977: 28) also distinguish **general knowledge** and **market-specific knowledge**. Establishment and performance of a certain kind of operation or activity in a country require both. Information gathering proves to be a constant determining factor in the process of export expansion, but exporters' most valuable information is obtained in the field, in the course of business transactions rather than through officially established information services, whether public or private (Denis/Depelteau 1985: 86).

Market-specific knowledge can be gained mainly through **experience** in the market, whereas **knowledge of the operation** can often be transferred from one country to another country. It is the diffusion of this **general knowledge** which facilitates lateral growth; that is, the establishment of technically *similar activities* in dissimilar business environment. In terms of internalisation theory they may constitute organisational firm-specific advantages in international business. There is a direct relation between market knowledge and market commitment. Knowledge can be considered a resource, and consequently the better the knowledge about the market, the more valuable are the resources and the stronger the commitment to the market (Ibid.).

As the *first change aspects*, current business activities are the prime source of experience although there is a lag between most current activities and their consequences, which impedes immediate learning (Johanson/Vahlne 1977: 28-29). It may be argued that experience can be gained alternatively through the hiring of personnel with experience, or through advice from persons with experience. The problem then is the distinction between **firm experience** and **market experience**. The latter can be internalised by hiring or contraction. The main challenge, i.e. integration of market knowledge and firm-specific knowledge, still would require a certain period of learning. Persons working on the boundaries between the firm and its market must be able to interpret information from inside the firm and from the market and to integrate them. Market knowledge and general knowledge of internationalisation therefore have to be acquired through a long **learning process** in connection with current activities. This factor is an important reason why the internationalisation process often proceeds slowly (Ibid.).

The *second change aspects*, **commitment decisions**, depend on what decision alternatives are raised and how they are chosen. It is assumed that decisions are made in response to perceived problems and/or opportunities on the market. Problems and opportunities – that is awareness of need and of possibilities for business actions – are assumed to be dependent on experience. *Firm experience* and *market experience* are relevant. Additional commitments are supposed to be made in small steps unless the firm has very large resources and/or market conditions are stable and homogeneous, or the firm has much experience from other markets with similar conditions. If not, market experience will lead to a step-wise increase in the scale of the operations and of the integration with the market environment where steps will be taken to correct imbalance with respect to the risk situation on the market. Market growth will speed up this process (Johanson/Vahlne 1977: 30-31).

International business activities are assumed to be developed first in countries with a short **'psychic distance'** and to expand incrementally into countries with a larger one. Psychic distance is defined as *'factors preventing or disturbing the flows of information between firms and market'* (Johanson/Wiedersheim-Paul 1975: 18). Examples of such factors are differences in language, culture, political systems level of education, or industrial development. The concept of knowledge is of particular significance in the Uppsala-model. Along the internationalisation process experience and knowledge in international operations are organisationally learned and institutionalised in decision routines and organisational structure. Barkema et al. (1996: 163) showed that the impact of cultural distance varies by mode (start-ups or acquisitions) and ownership structure (wholly owned subsidiaries or joint ventures) of the expansion. Barriers were found to be more pronounced when the venture required '**double-layered acculturation**', and the firm had to accommodate both strange corporate and national cultures. Johanson/Wiedersheim-Paul (1975: 17) assume that the most important obstacles to internationalisation are lack of knowledge and resources. These obstacles are reduced through incremental decision-making and learning about the foreign markets and operations. The process of internationalisation of a firm therefore is expected to begin with export to neighbouring countries or countries that are comparatively well known and similar with regard to business practices etc.. In the stepwise internationalisation process, Johanson/Wiedersheim-Paul (1975: 17-18) distinguish four different stages, which constitute the '**establishment chain**':

1. stage: no regular export activities,
2. stage: export via independent representatives,
3. stage: sales subsidiary,
4. stage: production subsidiary.

In the *first stage*, the firm has made no commitment of resources to the market and it lacks any regular information channel to and from the market. In the *second stage*, the firm has a channel to the market through which it gets regular information about sales influencing factors. It also means a certain commitment to the market. The *third stage* means a controlled information channel to the market by the investment in a sales subsidiary, giving the firm the ability to direct the type and amount of information flowing from the market to the firm. During this stage the firm also gets direct experience of resource influencing factors. The *fourth stage* means a still larger resource commitment and the investment in production facilities (Ibid.).

☞   **Extension by network perspective**

A further cause of path-dependence is the **embeddedness** of firms in relationships and networks. Interaction between firms is contingent upon the interaction that takes place with parties outside the relationship. The internationalisation of firms is path-dependent because it is determined by the reciprocal interaction of the firm and its infrastructure (Eriksson et al.

2000: 309). Network approaches generally postulate that **interconnected exchange relationships** evolve in a dynamic, less structured manner and that increased mutual knowledge and trust lead to greater commitment between international market actors. The internationalisation process not solely depends on the behaviour of the individual firm (Bell/Young 1998: 17). Internationalisation from the network perspective therefore depends on an **organisation's set of network relationships** rather than a firm-specific advantage. Therefore, externalisation occurs. The network perspective offers a complementary view to the economic theories given that the latter do not account for the role and influence of relationship structures in business transactions. Also, internationalisation decisions and activities in the network perspective emerge as patterns of behaviour influenced by various network members, while economic models assume rational decision-making (Coviello/McAuley 1999: 227). Although networks are described in the following Chapter 4, two strands of network research will be sketched briefly because of their adaptation to the internationalisation perspective.

☞ **Strategic linkage theory**

Strategic linkage theory views FDI as an attempt to link to some **strategic resources**, which the firm is lacking, but which are available in a foreign country. The network approach thus views **FDI** as the construction of a **link between domestic and foreign networks** (Nohria/Garcia-Pont 1991). FDI is considered to be a strategic choice that enhances, maintains, or restores the investor's competitiveness in a globalised market, rather than a profit-seeking motive aimed at extracting profits from a foreign market by exploiting its own strategic assets. Strategic linkage theory contends that firms can gain access to desired strategic capabilities by linking to firms with **complementary capabilities**, or by **pooling internal resources with firms** possessing similar capabilities (Porter/Fuller 1986, Nohria/Garcia-Pont 1991). The linkages create a synergy effect that enhances or reshapes the competitiveness of firms bounded by such alliances. Markets can be partitioned into numerous networks, which are mutually nonexclusive and constantly evolve over time (Chen/Chen 1998: 447). Two forms of organisational flexibility in the international experience can be characterised by interfirm linkages. These are the **multidirectional network model** enacted by small and medium businesses and the **licensing-subcontracting model** of production under an umbrella corporation (Benetton) (Castells 1996: 160).

A study of Gomes-Casseres (1997) provides evidence that relatively small firms, as compared to their rivals, tend to use network linkages to gain economies of scale and scope. Comparably larger firms tend to avoid the formation of alliances and prefer to go it alone abroad. A study of Chen/Chen (1998) showed that small Taiwanese firms are keen on forming external network linkages, but are indifferent or incapable of forming internal linkages through FDI. Chen/Chen (Ibid. 463) attribute this behaviour to an assumed trait of Taiwanese firms as being weak in organisational capabilities but strong in external networks. On the other hand, the explication of Gomes-Casseres also seems to apply to small firms in Taiwan. More intercultural studies in this field might be useful to detect differences and similarities in **international networking behaviour**.

☞ Industrial network model

An important extension of the initial work on internationalisation by the Uppsala School has been the study of networks and their evolution. This research developed in the industrial marketing field and is based upon the industrial network model of Håkannson/Johanson (1982, 1993). In fact, much of what passes for marketing or entry decisions can be classified as the process of establishing and maintaining **external networks**. At the heart of inter-company relationships are the contacts between individuals, which typically extend far beyond the confines of any formal company links. The personal relationships, which are established, can play an important role in cementing the company-level connection (Welch 1996: 183). Business relationships are established and developed through interaction. The interaction means that the parties invest time and resources to the relationship. In the domestic context the contacts between the parties are more frequent and informal. The firms also make more adaptations to each other in the domestic market (Johanson 1989: 68). The Uppsala model explains such differences by the **business distance**. This distance has to be bridged in the **international network-building process**.

Johanson/Mattson (1988) relate the internationalisation process of firms to the model of industrial networks. The firm's activities in industrial markets are cumulative processes in which relationships are continually established, maintained, developed, and broken down in order to give satisfactory, short-term economic return, and to create positions in the network, securing the long-term survival and development of the firm (Johanson/Mattson 1988: 292). Instead of regarding the internationalisation as a process between a firm and a somewhat anonymous market, the authors stress the relationships between independent firms forming the network. Due to an **informal division of labour** among involved firms, each firm will become dependent on external resources to the extent to which it builds relationships to other firms in the network. Such relationships often take time and effort to establish and develop; especially in long-term relationships mutual trust and knowledge implies a high degree of commitment and interconnectedness by different types of bonds.

In relation to the internationalisation process of firms, the **Uppsala Model** has to take into account the **network approach** and that concepts like commitment, knowledge, or current activities have to be studied inside the firm itself but also in connection with its co-operation with other firms (Figure 3-17). An extension of the process model to take into account the network aspect should consequently design these concepts multilateral rather than unilateral as in the original model. This means that its state and change aspects must also be understood in an interorganisational setting. Furthermore, networks might not only be confined to a country, but may extend beyond borders. The relationships and the networks can only be understood through experience from interaction inside, and especially so if there is a cultural distance between the actors (Johanson/Vahlne 1990: 18). Differences are supposed to exist between countries and products regarding the international extension, co-ordination and integration of networks. Accordingly, the **degree of internationalisation of the network** has strong implications for the **internationalisation process** of the particular firm. Such a process becomes much more individual, depending on the networks established in the industry as well as the position of the firm in the industry network (Madsen/Servais 1997: 571).

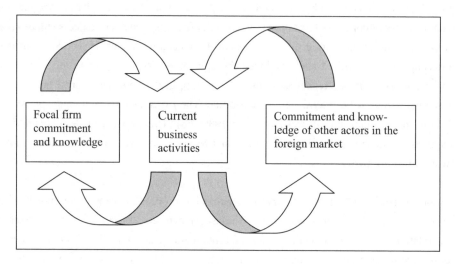

Figure 3-17: The multilateral aspect of the internationalisation process
(Source: Johanson/Vahlne 1990: 19)

When two actors perceive their activities as being interdependent, they are inclined to start exchange with each other. Subsequently, they learn about each other's capabilities and needs. As they learn, they utilise and strengthen the interdependencies of their activities. Thus, there is a **circular causality** between activity interdependencies and exchange relations. These are embedded in other relations within the wider web of industrial activities performed in the network. Through learning, the activities of one actor are eventually modified and adopted to activities of other actors, so that their joint productivity is increased and their interdependence is strengthened (Håkannson/Johanson 1993: 40).

A study by Blankenburg Holm et al. (1996: 262) indicates that the development of cooperative relationships with customers, suppliers, or other business partners may be critical to internationalisation. Moreover, the results show that this may be a matter of managing relationship development processes rather than choosing an appropriate entry mode or organisational form. According to this process view, entry mode selection is primarily an element in a **process of relationship development**. For example, FDI classically is conceived as a means of entering foreign markets in order to exploit firm-specific assets. With the network approach this is only one of several aspects. The investments reflect in large measure the firm's need to reach the demands imposed by the **local industrial environment**, and to handle the relations in the **foreign network** by monitoring, influencing, or even incorporating other actors. Since the company's strength is dependent on links with other companies, the asset cannot be transferred and exploited in another industrial environment without further adaptation and complementation (Forsgren 1989: 36). A newcomer must try to establish a position of some sort, which is difficult in the short run by reason of the long-term, stable relationships in the existing networks (Forsgren/Johanson 1992: 14).

In the course of their internationalisation process firms are becoming engaged in wider networks of business relationships with important consequences for the management as different units with different positions in the networks in different countries become interrelated. In the last phase of internationalisation, former **centre-periphery structures** of international firms change to more complex, reciprocal **multi-centre structures** (Forsgren/Johanson 1992a: 19-20). Within the network approach, the location and type of industrial structure to which the firm belongs is crucial for investment behaviour and cannot be reduced to a question of knowledge about foreign markets (Forsgren 1989: 43).

According to Cantwell (1989:7), multinational expansion can be linked to a **process of cumulative technological change** within the firm, in which innovation and the growth of international production are mutually supportive. By expansion of its own network, each firm extends the use of its own unique line of technological development, and by extending it into new environments it increases the complexity of this development. The expansion of international production thereby brings gains to the firm as a whole, as the experience gained from adapting its technology under new conditions feeds back new ideas for the development to the rest of the system and the network. From this perspective, the evolutionary process of internationalisation can thus be portrayed as a form of 'technological accumulation' (Pavitt 1987) in international networks.

Both the network approach and the internationalisation model stress the cumulative nature of the firm's activities. The latter, however, is a model focusing on the internal development of the firm's knowledge and other resources, while the network approach also offers a model of the market and the relations to that market. The network approach implies that the strategic discretion is constrained by the character of the network in which the firm is operating or into which it intends to enter. This indicates that during the internationalisation of a network, the **timing** of the operations of a firm is important. The timing of activities, their internal co-ordination, and the external co-operation are crucial elements in internationalisation strategy development and implementation. It can also be expected that, because of the **cumulative nature of network processes**, the sequential order of activities in international markets is important. Johanson/Mattson (1988: 309-311) therefore propose that implications of the cumulative nature of network processes should be more investigated.

According to Johanson/Mattson (1986: 249), the internationalisation of the firm means from a network perspective that the firm establishes and develops **positions** in relation to actors in **foreign networks**. This can be accomplished

- by the development of relationships and establishment of positions in country networks that are new to the firm, i.e. *international extension*;
- by the development of relationships in those foreign networks where the firm already has positions; i.e. *penetration*; and
- by connecting and integrating networks in different countries by using the existing relationships of the firm as *bridges* to other networks (Ibid.).

The firm's degree of internationalisation informs about the extent to which the firm occupies certain positions in different national networks, and how important and integrated those positions are. Since a position changes, internationalisation will direct attention to the investments in internal and external assets used for exchange activities. Furthermore, the firm's positions before the internationalisation process starts are important since they show what external assets the firm has access to via relationships which might influence the internationalisation (Ibid.). The **embeddedness** in such **local networks** (*'industrial districts'*, *'local clusters'*, *'local milieus'*, and *'innovation networks'*) and its influence on the internationalisation of firms will be discussed in the following chapter.

According to Johanson/Mattson (1988), the firm's development is to a large extent dependent on its **position in a network** and it can use its market assets (position) in its further development. The firm acquires knowledge about business opportunities through its networks and bases its operations and development on the network of relationships. Internationalisation can be expected to be a result of the characteristics of the network in which the firm operates (Sharma/Johanson 1987: 22). But an actor, who is not engaged in a certain network environment in a foreign country or with a different technology, can comprehend the network with its invisible relationships, connections, and dependencies only very superficially. From this perspective, network entry is very much a **cognitive modelling process** (Håkansson/Johanson 1993: 43). It can be assumed that network structures to some extent are conditioned by technical and cultural factors, but they are also enacted, that is they are formed and modified through the interaction between the actors. The network structure is a result of history. Positions in networks therefore are assets for future action and provide a power basis in exchange relations (Forsgren/Johanson 1992: 8-9). Sharma/Johanson (1987: 28) suggest the following steps as basic for **continuous internationalisation progress**:

1. Map the present network of relationships.
2. Analyse how the present relationships have been developed.
3. Analyse the possibilities the present network of relationships offers as a bridge into new markets.

In general, research indicates that a company's networks are important components of its ability to develop international operations. Because much of their development occurs intangibly, through personal contacts, their extent and value are often not recognised by the senior management of companies. In consequence, decisions can be made, which interfere with the effective operation of the networks (Welch 1996: 185). Research also draws attention to the danger of becoming locked into networks which are by-passed, made irrelevant, or destroyed by institutional, personnel or other changes (Roos et al. 1992).

3.2.2.3.3 Helsinki School

Similar to the Uppsala-model, the Helsinki-School conceives internationalisation as an **incremental process with four central stages**, beginning with a stage of rudimentary organised international operations without foreign investment and culminating in the fourth stage of extensive foreign direct investment (Luostarinen 1980: 5). A further parallel can be found in the assumption that a **learning process** accompanies the internationalisation process. Activity changes are the result of an increase in the company's stock of knowledge (Luostarinen 1980: 9). It is primarily the managerial limit, the level of existent managerial and entrepreneurial knowledge and skill capacity within the enterprise system, which forms a barrier to internationalisation (Luostarinen 1980: 28).

A basic assumption in the Helsinki-model is that the strategic decision-making behaviour of the company is especially characterised by **'lateral rigidity'**, which represents the general aversion of organisational decision-makers to new ideas and their adoption in organisations. The concept has its roots in the behavioural model of decision-making (Cyert/March 1963):

Limited perception ➔ restricted reaction ➔ selective search ➔ limited selection.

Lateral rigidity affects each stage of decision making, so that the prospects for innovative concepts are diminishing from stage to stage (Luostarinen 1980: 33-35). Particularly, strategic decision-making is supposed to be affected by lateral rigidity (Figure 3-18). Laterally rigid decision-making processes are essentially based on the knowledge factor. Imperfection of knowledge causes rigidity and thus plays a central role in every stage of the process. **Organisational learning** along the **internationalisation process** leads to a decreasing rigidity in its course, similar to the diminishing risk- and cost-perception in the Uppsala-model.

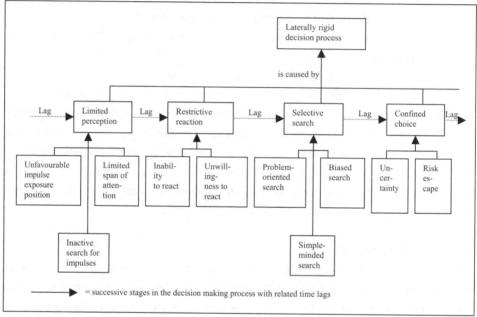

Figure 3-18: Lateral rigidity in decision processes
(Source: Luostarinen 1980: 45)

In general, decision-makers in exporting place far greater value on the information obtained through informal means than they do on formal modes of information collection and transfer. The reliance on **informal modes** is especially evident in situations involving high uncertainty and cultural difference. Research into exporting has also shown that the process of information search, transfer, evaluation, and use is highly influenced not only by the decision-making context, but also by the decision makers themselves – their background, attitudes, values, etc. (Welch 1996: 180-182).Decision-makers with no or little personal networks and individual experience in the international context therefore encounter immense **cognitive barriers to entry**. Positive experience and information decrease the degree of lateral rigidity related to the new action alternative in question whereas negative knowledge reinforces rigidity. Internationalisation therefore is characterised by the special importance of the cognitive aspects for the initiation of decision-making because of the crucial role of knowledge, risks, and organisational learning in international business (Luostarinen 1980: 44-48).

In the **initial stage**, a firm may be able to react to the international business impulse, but may be unwilling to do so because of the mental commitment to domestic business and the prevailing satisfaction with the current domestic situation. The **amount of uncertainty** felt towards international business depends on the knowledge, obtained either through experience or explicit information. The level of resource commitment needed for the implementation of the same operation in foreign markets is perceived to be higher than in domestic markets. The probability of loss is perceived as being greater. Uncertainty and risks are perceived highest in the case of FDI (Luostarinen 1980: 54-57, 119). An increase in managerial and entrepreneurial capacity through an increase in the knowledge of existing personnel and through recruiting experts with extensive strategic internationalisation knowledge and skills, outstanding foreign market experience, and cosmopolitan characteristics from outside the company is thus of primary importance (Luostarinen 1980: 206).

With increasing commitment to international activities the **lateral rigidity decreases** along all stages of the decision-making process (Luostarinen 1980: 59-62). *First*, the perception of international business impulses becomes less limited than before as the firm's exposure position towards international business impulses may be improving. *Second*, reaction to international business impulses may be less restrictive than before due to an increasing ability and willingness to react. Once management gets positive feedback about its abilities in the international context, it gains confidence and is obviously more prepared to increase the international commitment. *Third*, the firm's search for foreign action alternatives becomes more active as knowledge about international markets becomes broader and more structured. *Fourth*, the increasing cognisance of possibilities abroad together with successful market entries reduces the uncertainty and risk related to international business. In general, it is assumed that the degree of lateral rigidity towards internationalisation is usually high at the beginning of the firm's internationalisation but it may decrease through the time as a result of organisational learning.

The concept of '**psychic distance**' in the model of the Uppsala School finds its analogy in the '**business distance**' of the Helsinki School. The business distance is composed of the physical (geographical), cultural, and economic distance.

With regard to the '**physical distance**', the closer a company is located in relation to a foreign country, the greater are its possibilities of being exposed to and searching for international business impulses from that country than from a country with a more distant location. The negative impact of geographical distance is greatest on material and human flows, and also to a minor extent on impulses and knowledge flows (Luostarinen 1980: 128-130). Part of the '**cultural distance**' is the '**institutional distance**', which alone is supposed to have a greater importance than the geographical distance (Luostarinen 1980: 52, 58). The cultural distance is to be seen as a barrier to impulse flows in both directions between two countries.

The '**economic distance**' is created due to differences in the economic environment between the home and target country. Indicators are gross national product (GNP) and the size of the population. Luostarinen (1980: 136) assumes that the greater the economic distance in favour of the target country, the greater the market pull force for the company to enter the market of this country.

The role of '**cultural distance**' is supposed to be very essential for the existence of lateral rigidity and spatial preference in the determination of the geographical structure of the firm's internationalisation pattern.

The '**business distance**' has the same implications for the internationalisation process as the psychic distance in the Uppsala model. Firms begin with activities in markets with a small distance and expand their activities incrementally to more and more distant markets.

The **smallness of home country markets** may form an obstacle to expansion already in the early stages of growth and limit the number of available domestic growth alternatives considerably. This is why internationalisation is assumed to play a more important role as a growth alternative in the firms with small home markets than in the firms with big ones (Luostarinen 1980: 27).

Luostarinen also develops a **model of internationalisation profiles** that is constituted by three **dimensions**:

1. *product* (goods, services, systems, know-how),
2. *operations* (marketing, production),
3. *market investments*.

Empirical research (Luostarinen 1980, Luostarinen/Hellman1994) revealed a process of incremental development not only in terms of the depth of operational mode, but also in terms of the diversity of modes used, as well as in product offerings and the range of markets penetrated. For example, product offerings were divided into four categories: goods, services, systems, and know-how. The offering to foreign markets consistently began in the simplest form – i.e. goods (99 % of the companies) – while sales of services, systems and know-how came later, and approximately in that order (Luostarinen 1980: 95-105).

Luostarinen/Hellman (1994: 19) discovered a relatively consistent **gradual mainstream pattern**, which includes the following **steps**:

1. *Products* are introduced in the order of goods, services, systems and/or know-how.
2. *Operation modes* are utilised in the order of non-direct investment marketing operations (NIMOS), direct investment marketing operations (DIMOS), non-direct investment production operations (NIPOS) and/or direct investment production operations (DIPOS).

Empirical studies generally supported the assumption that the intensity of international activities increases in the course of internationalisation (Luostarinen 1980: 152-154, Luostarinen/Hellman 1994: 5). Based upon the empirical studies, Luostarinen (1980: 183-195) and Luostarinen/Hellman (1984: 12-14) developed a stage model of the **outward internationalisation process**:

1. *starting stage*: physical goods through NIMOS;
2. *development stage*: services and/or DIMOS;
3. *growth state*: systems and/or NIPOS; and
4. *mature stage*: know-how and/or DIPOS.

Welch and Luostarinen (1988) expand the model by integrating the dimensions 'organisational capacity', 'human resources', 'organisation structure', and 'finance'. The new dimensions in the model are not operationalised and instead a reference to approaches of the Process School in international management is offered (Welch/Luostarinen 1988: 159).

3.2.2.3.4 Innovation School
In contrast to the '**Scandinavian School**', the approach of the '**Innovation School**' does not cover the development of the whole range of international business operations up to foreign direct investment in production facilities. Instead, a concentration on the development of export activities is preferred in a more **differentiated stage model of export activities**. Initial involvement in international marketing is conceived as a gradual and sequential process. Such a pattern is thought to be the consequence of greater uncertainty, higher costs of information,

and the lack of experiential knowledge in foreign marketing activities. Export marketing is considered to be the first step in the process of internationalisation. Internationalisation is conceived as a gradual process, taking place in **incremental stages**, and over a relatively long period of time (Cavusgil 1980: 273). The emphasis in the innovation model is on classifying the development into stages, rather than on explaining how firms move from one stage to another (Barkema et al. 1996: 152). The basic model goes back to Rogers (1962: 81-86) and comprises six different stages:

Stage 1: no interest in export activities, neither active nor reactive;
Stage 2: fulfilment of casual export orders, but no active interest in export;
Stage 3: active search for export options (preparations);
Stage 4: experimental exports to some markets;
Stage 5: experienced exporter in these markets;
Stage 6: search for extensive export activities.

Cavusgil (1984: 7-9) proposes that four **categories of influences** at the organisational level are likely to correlate with export behaviour. The *first* are differential firm advantages, like assumed in the theories of FDI. The *second* are managerial aspiration for business goals. The keenness in pursuing basic business goals such as profits, growth, and diversification can be crucial to export market performance. A *third* influence depends on the favourability of management's expectations. Managers tend to form expectation about the profitability, risk, and costs of exporting based upon their own and/or other firm's experiences as well as their perception of potential impact of the constantly changing environment of international markets. The *fourth* influence is based on the extent of resource allocation to exporting. The commitment of managers in terms of the extent of resource allocation for exporting is expected to be influential on export behaviour.

Bilkey/Tesar (1977: 95) assume that a **process of continuous learning** accompanies the development of export activities. According to the authors, a change in values and perceptions of management can also be observed along the intensification of export activities. Bilkey (1978: 44) therefore proposes the integration of the models of the Scandinavian School and the Innovation School because of the conceptual similarity.

Cavusgil (1980) later condenses the incremental export model into five **stages**:

1. *domestic marketing*,
2. *pre-export stage*,
3. *experimental involvement*,

4. *active involvement*, and
5. *committed involvement*.

In his study in 1980, Cavusgil estimated that 88% of the US manufacturing firms still were **non-exporters**. This estimation indicates, that for many firms internationalisation is not of immediate interest although the percentage of exporters since then has risen and is also traditionally higher in other countries.

In the **pre-export stage**, various internal and eternal stimuli are responsible for arousing initial interest in exporting among decision-makers. First, a firm's differential advantages may so serve. Management has to be confident that those advantages are transferable to other markets. Second, the presence of aggressive, venturesome decision-makers in the firm can be a positive stimulus for export initiation. The important internal change-agent tends to be a member of the top management who is interested in and enthusiastic about exporting. Third, the adoption of an international outlook at the top-management level appears to be a critical determinant of initial interest. The firm's international orientation is determined by the firm's background and traditions, and by the foreign attitudes of its top management (Bilkey 1978: 33-34, Bilkey/Tesar1977: 94-95, Cavusgil 1980: 276).

The **experimental involvement** is usually marginal and intermittent. The proportion of foreign sales will not typically exceed 10 per cent. Export is usually restricted to one or two psychologically close foreign countries (Ibid.). Small firms are supposed to be more influenced by *psychological distance* than are large firms (Bilkey 1978: 36).

In the **active involvement stage**, export is extended to new foreign countries, the volume is rising and more resources are committed to the exploration and servicing of foreign markets. This progression will depend on

1. the favourability of experience-based expectations of management concerning exporting;
2. the availability of key firm resources for undertaking the necessary activities unique to this stage; and
3. the willingness of management to allocate such resources.

The **committed involvement stage** may be characterised as the firm's transition into a committed participant in international marketing (Cavusgil 1980: 278). Export has become a normal and integrated part of the firm's posture in business. Management now has to co-ordinate a continuous process of resource allocation to national and international activities. The challenges imposed to management in this stage differ significantly from the previous stages (Swoboda 1997: 7).

Based upon empirical research, Cavusgil et al. (1979) and Cavusgil (1984) developed exporter profiles. A clear distinction could be drawn between the '*most active exporters*' and the '*least active exporters*'. The characteristics of the **most active exporters** include (Cavusgil et al. 1979: 92-95, Cavusgil 1984: 16):

- high level of aspirations for profits and market development,
- very favourable expectations regarding the contribution of exports,
- technology-intensive products,
- relatively big size, and
- systematic market and export planning.

In contrast, **least active exporters** share the following characteristics (Ibid.):

- high level of aspirations for security,
- unfavourable expectations as to the effects of exporting on firm's growth,
- lower share in technology-intensive industries,
- most without systematic export policy or structure.

According to Cavusgil (1984: 17-18), the most important conclusion of these studies is that variation in export activity can be explained, to a significant extent, by organisational and management characteristics. While size appears to be a deterrent in terms of initiating/expanding export activity for very small firms, the relationship between size and export activity remains vague for large companies. Exporting is essentially a developmental process. This may be conceptualised as a **learning sequence** involving either feedback loops or export stages (Bilkey 1978: 42). Cavusgil (1984: 18) identifies the values and expectations of decision-makers as the strongest influence on the internationalisation behaviour.

Under inclusion of other variables (differentiation advantages, preparation intensity), Cavusgil (1984) verifies this thesis by empirically testing ideal profiles of active and passive exporters. This result was confirmed in a study of Bamberger/Evers (1996: 274) who developed ideal profiles according to the stage model of Cavusgil. The study was based on the results of an empirical research project by the STRATOS-Group (1991) on the internationalisation behaviour of companies in eight European countries.

More recently, evidence has been emerging for a departure from the gradualist path as some firms seek to by-pass the steps of deeper commitment, resulting in a speeding up of the whole process (Welch/Luostarinen 1988: 50).

3.2.2.3.5 Empirical limits of incremental stage models

Both Scandinavian schools (Uppsala, Helsinki) are together termed the '**Scandinavian School**' (S-model) by Buckley/Ghauri (1993) because of their similarities and their conceptual closeness. Both the S-models and the **innovation-related internationalisation models** (I-models) conceptualise the basic internationalisation process as an **incremental process**. This type of conceptualisation has been widely used as the basis for much empirical research around the world. Many researchers have accused the stage models for being too **deterministic** and of limited value (Reid 1983, Turnbull 1987, Madsen/Servais 1997). The argument is that the firm has the option of making a strategic choice as to modes of entry and expansion. Reid argues that such a choice is contingent on market conditions and a transaction cost approach is superior to the process model in explaining diversity and variations in internationalisation behaviour. This view is supported by Turnbull's (1987) studies of export organisation in British industries. Madsen/Servais (1997: 562) further argue that the world has changed dramatically since the manifestations of the stage models were formulated in the 1970s. Therefore the manifest stages approach seems to be much less valid today.

Empirical studies testing the incremental stage models provide quite mixed results. In a survey of Hong Kong garment MNEs, Lau (1992) found evidence for a process of incremental commitment among the firms. Barkema et al. (1996) analysed 225 market entries of 14 Dutch firms from 1966 onwards and found evidence consistent with various key assumption of the Scandinavian process model. Firms in their study found cultural barriers when expanding internationally. They learned from their previous experience when gradually expanding into cultural space. The study shows that centrifugal expansion patterns are more successful than a random strategy. When starting a new venture, firms benefit more from previous experience with expansions in other countries in the same cultural block, and least from earlier expansions in blocks that are more proximate to the home country. Against expectations from learning-based models, Erramilli et al. (1999) found prove that South Korean MNEs are more likely to seek majority than minority ownership as the physical distance between South Korea and the host country increases. A study by Gankema et al. (2000) based on Cavusgil's stage model reveals a growing degree of international involvement by the observed SMEs over time. However, the **variation** of this increase is enormous. Some SMEs rocketed from one of the first stages into one of the last stages. Other SMEs stopped the process of internationalisation before they had reached the committed involvement stage.

Empirical evidence provides arguments for the criticism that the Scandivian process model is applicable only to the **early stages of internationalisation** when lack of market knowledge and market resources are still constraining factors (Forsgren 1989). For example, in a study of the internationalisation process of 50 UK firms in the EC, Millington/Bayliss (1990) found no support of a narrowly incremental view, with a step-wise internationalisation process being the exception rather than the rule. With increasing degree of international experience, the initially incremental process that is relying on market experience and incremental adjustment is superseded by formal planning and systematic search. In the final stages of development of international experience may be transferred across markets and between products, thereby enabling firms to leapfrog the incremental process within markets (Ibid. 159).

Furthermore, results of several empirical studies underscore the need to make a **distinction** between **initial** and **later entries**. Eriksson et al. (2001) provided evidence that the learning based stage models are most valuable in early stages of internationalisation. Their study showed that with regard to knowledge accumulation, duration of firms in the internationalisation process has a much stronger effect on those firms with a short duration compared to those with a longer international history. This shows that learning is particular intense in the early stages of internationalisation. *'In fact, the total effect of duration on the knowledge model is insignificant in the long duration firms'* (Ibid. 35). A similar distinction may be drawn with respect to processes of *internationalisation vs. de-internationalisation*. With few exceptions, the latter phenomenon never appeared in mainstream internationalisation theories. They offer explanations of investment and not of disinvestment (Robock/Simmonds 1989: 49). Such a perspective only basically applies to initial steps in internationalisation. Firms that are more advanced in this process have to decide on internationalisation and de-internationalisation on a balanced, ongoing basis. Welge (1989) describes international disinvestment and provides instruments how to cope with them.

Hedlund/Kverneland (1985: 46) expect firms to **'skip' stages** in the establishment chain (agent, sales subsidiary, manufacturing subsidiary) by directly undertaking more ambitious forms of investment in a given country market. They also expect to find a tendency to shorten the time between different stages in the hypothesised chain. These tendencies should be particularly pronounced in large and rapidly growing markets and in companies with extensive international experience and in those subject to competition in global oligopolies. Their study of entry and growth strategies of Swedish firms in Japan showed that these are changing toward more direct and rapid entry modes. About half of the firms investigated went directly from a sales agent to manufacturing in Japan (Ibid. 56). Indeed, there is a possibility that firms skip stages because **global niches** have become narrower and transportation and communication costs have rapidly decreased. The best proof is the rising number of born globals.

Anand/Delios (1997) and Padmanabhan/Cho (1996) found that high levels of **cultural distance** were associated with high control entry modes. In contrast, Kogut/Singh (1988) and Erramilli/Rao (1993) found cultural distance to be related to the use of co-operative modes of entry. In a study of firms from The Netherlands, Germany, Britain, and the U.S., Brouthers/Brouthers (2001) found empirical support for the **cultural distance paradox**. Firms entering markets that are culturally distant and low in investment risk tended to prefer co-operative modes of entry. Conversely, firms entering culturally distant markets high in investment risk preferred wholly owned modes. Investment risk appeared to moderate the relationship between cultural distance and entry mode selection. Furthermore, psychic distance, which is implicit or explicit in most stage models, is much less relevant as global communication and transportation infrastructures improve and many markets become more homogeneous.

The **explanatory scope of S-models** is principally restricted to **smaller and unidimensional firms** (Bell/Young 1998: 6). With the focus on **market seeking activities** only one of the classical four drivers of internationalisation is integrated into the model. Resource seeking, efficiency seeking, and strategic asset seeking international activities are not part of the theoretical underpinnings. The latter are generally supposed to be weak as only some roots are claimed to lie in the behavioural theory of the firm. Furthermore, linkages and **core assumptions** are generally **not made at all clear** (Bell/Young 1998: 10).

Andersen (1993: 217-218) differentiates incremental internationalisation models by their inherent **boundary assumptions**. These are defined as the spatial and temporal reach of the theories' explanations. For instance, Andersen proposes that Innovation models (I-models) apply from the time (or immediate preceding) the idea of exporting is initiated until that international activities are regarded as an ordinary and accepted part of the firm's activities. The spatial delimitation is assumed to be less clear and differentiated in SMEs where export behaviour is influenced by the individual decision-makers and large firms where entry behaviour is supposed to be structurally determined. On the other hand, Anderson regards the theoretical reach of the Scandinavian models (S-models) to be less bounded in time and space (Ibid.) although many authors criticise that also the S-models are only valuable during the first stages, as leapfrogging of stages has proved to be common.

Stage models may be of **limited value** for the explanation of internationalisation processes in **service industries**. In a study of technical consultancy firms, Sharma/Johanson (1987:22) concluded that the internationalisation process model does not say very much about the internationalisation of this kind of firms. Engwall/Wallenstal (1988: 153) draw a similar conclusion on the thesis of psychic distance from their empirical study of major Swedish banks.

They proposed to distinguish manufacturing firms that tend to start out in countries that are culturally close to their own and gradually move further away from banks, which do not show this tendency in their internationalisation process. On the other hand, the gradual process of international commitment was confirmed (Ibid. 154). Andersen (1993), Leonidou/Katsikeas (1996), and Coviello/McAuley (1999) developed excellent overviews over theoretical and empirical research in the area of internationalisation.

3.2.2.4 Discontinuous stage models of internationalisation

In contrast to the incremental models of internationalisation, the discontinuous models are not based on the assumption that there is a smooth incremental process of increasing internationalisation. Internationalisation in these models is conceptualised as a **discontinuous process**, which is marked by **phases of incremental evolution**, alternating with **periods of radical change**. The basic thoughts of this approach to organisational transformation can be traced to (Greiner 1972) and the '**quantum view of structural change**' (Miller/Friesen 1984). In this view, organisations are characterised by an inherent trend towards stability (organisational inertia). The increasing need for adaptation to environmental changes, which is neglected in times of stability, leads to the necessity of '**quantum leaps**' of structural change. During these periods of radical change not only changes the '**surface structure**', which represents a visible and objective level of organisation (e.g. standard operating procedures, formal organisational roles), but also the '**deep structure**' of organisational beliefs, values, and orientations. In two different approaches, Macharzina/Engelhard (1991) and Kutschker (1994, 1996) adapt the discontinuous view of structural change to the process of internationalisation.

3.2.2.4.1 GAINS Paradigm (Macharzina/Engelhard)

Macharzina/Engelhard (1991: 30) assume that internationalising firms adjust to their environment through their decision-makers. Therefore, different aspects of strategic decision-making processes, especially the decision-makers' personal and social idiosyncrasies have to be taken into account. The role of such **international managers** could then be interpreted as '**nerve centres**', which relates to external and internal information. A basic prerequisite for organisational success is the harmonisation of structure, strategy, and the environment. This is the basic task of management.

Macharzina/Engelhard (1991: 30) assume that the **time dimension** is critical for an understanding of the evolutionary dynamics in the reciprocal relationship between decision and the respective results of the following action. The dynamics can only be described by a conceptualisation of the firm's history in terms of a chronology of the interplay between internal (company-specific) and external (environmental) variables.

As it has been argued above, this dimension is of particular importance for the observation of internationalisation processes. The approach of Macharzina/Engelhard (1991) is termed '*gestalt approach of international business strategies*' (GAINS Paradigm). Internationalisation of a firm is assumed to be a process dominated by **phases of incremental development** that are iterating with **phases of fundamental change** ('*transition*'). The incremental or stable phases are characterised by an increasing differentiation of the structures and processes ('**momentum**'). These phases gain stability by the inherent **organisational inertia** and the dominating cultural orientation. The latter is generally marked by self-perpetuating reality constructs that legitimise past action patterns and their adequacy for problem solving. Power relations are basically stabilised and reproduced. In such phases of stability, an increasing pressure for adaptation develops as inertia impedes a continuous adaptation to environmental changes. '**Critical incidents**' then initiate a necessary phase of **quantum leap change** (Macharzina/Engelhard 1991: 32-33).

From the quantum view perspective, organisations normally tend to demonstrate great sluggishness and resistance to change. According to the gestalt rationale, revolutionary or quantum change must occur. Piecemeal-incremental change will be too fragmented and slow, particularly when the adaptive lag has already been great. Conflicts will be the result. The longer the adaptive lag, the more disruptive and comprehensive will be the changes.

Based upon the empirical research of 81 companies, Miller/Friesen formed the '**gestalt**' of six organisational archetypes, using the **dimensions** '*environment*' '*organisation*', and '*strategic decision-making*' as the fundament for their construction (Miller/Friesen 1978: 929). Macharzina/Engelhard add a fourth dimension to this framework for archetype-building to develop their concept of internationalisation. This dimension is called '*management*' and contains the values and beliefs of decision-makers.

The authors identify gestalt configurations of the distinctive profiles by application of the four dimensions to firms in the internationalisation process. Explicitly they agree with the assumptions of the learning-based process models but stress the **iterating incremental and quantum changes** in the internationalisation process. Similar to the innovation school, they derive three **exporter-profiles**: non-exporters, re-active exporters, and active exporters, depending on the configurations of the four dimensions. These types were chosen as preliminary examples for gestalt configurations in the international context, that Macharzina/Engelhard intended to derive from a longitudinal empirical research program, which has not been developed yet (Ibid. 36-38).

3.2.2.4.2 Dynamic internationalisation theory (Kutschker)

Like Macharzina/Engelhard, Kutschker (1996) developed a *'dynamic internationalisation theory'* without strictly following the tradition of incremental stage models. Following the construct of the **'internationalisation topography'** (Kutschker/Bäurle 1997), an increase in the internationalisation profile of a firm can be related to three dimensions, which together form its **'international fingerprint'**. These are the number and geographic-cultural distance of the foreign markets, the extent of value-added in these markets and the degree of integration of activities. The increase of international involvement along these three dimensions is revealed by the inclusion of the fourth dimension *'time'*. Kutschker et al. (1997: 104) developed a typology, which aims at systematising the different kinds of internationalisation processes inherent in this fourth dimension.

	International evolution	International episodes	International epochs
Scope	Small parts of the corporation	Whole units like departments; sometimes even the whole corporation	Whole corporation
Speed	Slow change	Rapid change	Can comprise periods of slow and of rapid change.
Duration	Evolution occurs almost permanently; therefore it is never-ending; the single evolutionary steps, however, are of short duration.	Several months up to several years	Several years
Relevance for future internationalisation	Any single step has only little relevance; the sum of all evolutionary steps can nevertheless be important.	High relevance	Essential

Table 3-5: Characteristics of the 'Three Es': an overview
(Source: Kutschker et al. 1997: 105)

Three **categories of internationalisation processes** are introduced: *international evolution*, *international episodes*, and *international epochs*. The three kinds of processes affect two different **layers in the internationalisation firm**, which are referred to as *'surface structure'* and *'deep structure'*, in a recursive process. The processes differ in the scope of change, in the speed and duration of change and in the relevance they have for the internationalising firm

(Ibid.). '*Scope*' indicates which and how many parts of the firm are altered. With regard to '*speed*', internationalisation processes can change the international fingerprint of the firm abruptly or slowly. The '*duration*' of the three processes can vary from hours to years. The relevance for the future development of the firm can range from minimal to crucial. An overview is presented in Table 3-5.

The '**incremental evolution**' takes place in smaller subunits of the firm and causes *slow changes*. They can result from accidental developments, self-organising mechanisms, and ad-hoc decisions. These variations change the internationalisation profile in an evolutionary and incremental way (Kutschker et al. 1997: 106-107).

Dense clusters of activities, which aim at a rapid change of the international fingerprint, are termed '**international episodes**'. Incremental evolution is interrupted by such episodes from time to time. Episodes are *periods of intensive changes* in the surface structure of a company. Examples are market entries, co-operations, and reconfigurations. International episodes affect *greater parts of a firm* and last from *several months to several years*. They are characterised by a *high speed* and their *importance* for the future internationalisation. The management of such an episode has to take into account the internationalisation process in general and the continuity of the surface structure itself (Kutschker 1996: 18f).

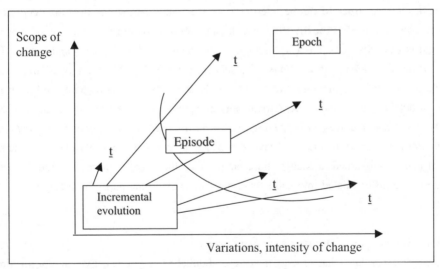

Figure 3-19:   Incremental evolution, episodes, and epochs in company evolution
(Source: Kutschker 1996: 27)

'**International epochs**' represent a third facet of company evolution in form of *longer periods of fundamental transition* that cause a change in the technological core competencies and the strategic orientation. Therefore, not only a change in the surface structure, but particularly of the deep structure of a company is induced. Epochs can comprise both; international evolution and international episodes (Kutschker 1996: 22f, Kutschker et al. 1997: 106). International epochs generally affect the *whole corporation*, they comprise periods of slow and rapid change and they are characterised by a *long duration* (up to 15 years). The differentiation of epochs, episodes, and incremental evolution on the basis of their respective scope and intensity of change is illustrated in Figure 3-19.

The organisational identity of the corporation fundamentally changes from one epoch to the next. A typical example is the development of many SMEs from national to European players in the course of European integration. Another example might be a MNE undergoing a transformation from a global to a transnational structure.

The three processes have different influences on two different organisational layers. The **surface structure** comprises the strategic manoeuvres of a firm, its organisational structure, the traditional formal and technocratic co-ordination mechanisms, the management information systems and business process structures. The different symbolic representations also belong to the surface structure.

While the surface structure can be interpreted as the visible part of the firm the **deep structure** can be conceived as the invisible part. It can only be explored from an internal perspective and is basically constituted by intangible knowledge, cognitive maps, and values. This '*kind of organisational subconscious*' (Kutschker et al. 1997: 108) strongly influences the visible organisational behaviour and is not readily accessible for participants and even less from an outside perspective. Deep structure is defined as '*the specific constellation of data and values (bits of knowledge) prevailing in a corporation and held together by contextuating orientations*' (Ibid.). Both structural layers evolve in a continuous interplay whereas the surface structure is assumed to change more rapidly than the deep structure. In large firms, the latter may be differentiated into sub-deep-structures, which may partly be incommensurable (Ibid.).

3.2.2.4.3 Internationalisation as a strategy process

Mintzberg (1987) states that strategy making is about changing perspectives and/or positions. Internationalisation comprises both changed perspectives and changed positions. Melin (1992) therefore consequently conceives internationalisation as a strategy process. The strategy process determines the ongoing development and change of scope, business idea, action orientation, organising principles, dominating values and converging norms. Internationalisation is a major dimension of the ongoing strategy process of many business firms, but research in strategic management traditionally pays little attention to this important area (Lyles 1990).

Summing up internationalisation research in strategic management, Melin notices a considerable need for research that is responsive to the longitudinal character of internationalisation. From his point of view, **longitudinal research** in this area incorporates at least **four different approaches** (Figure 3-20).

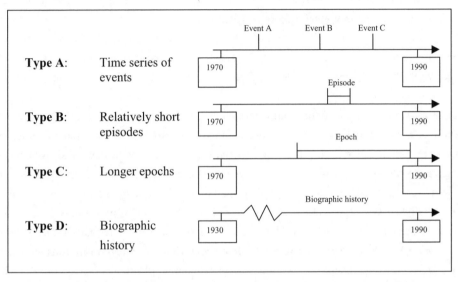

Figure 3-20: Four types of processes captured by different longitudinal approaches (Source: Melin 1992: 102)

- *Type A* represents *a time-series of detached critical events, or states*. Typical are studies of the correspondence between strategy, structure, and performance (Gomez-Meija 1992, Habib/Victor 1991). The process dimension is weakly developed in this type.
- *Type B* represents processes of relatively *short episodes*. Studies typically describe single episodes like an acquisition or several episodes in sequence or in parallel. The time period may vary from weeks to a few years.
- *Type C* comprises processes in the form of *lengthy epochs*. This may be the strategic development of a company under an influential CEO, like Deutsche Telekom under Ron Sommer. An epoch lasts between two and twenty years. A series of epochs may be long periods of evolutionary change disrupted by shorter episodes of revolutionary change.

- *Type D* contains processes seen as *biographic history*. Biographies of firms may capture the whole development from the founding to the present and varies with the firm's age. Research of this type is especially prominent in the area of business history where the evolution of an industry and its most important players is illustrated over its life cycle (e.g. Kipping/Sauviat 1996, Kipping 2002). Malnight (1995) illustrates the incremental evolution of Eli Lilly and Company from an ethnocentric to a geocentric company. With increasing compression of time and space, research of dense or compact histories of start-ups and born globals becomes increasingly valuable in the field of internationalisation (Borghoff/Welge 2003).

Generally, longitudinal studies of internationalisation processes representing types C and D are very infrequent (Melin 1992: 102). Exceptions are studies in the field of business history.

3.2.3 Contribution to an evolutionary perspective

Vernon's cyclic model and the **incremental stage models** describe the internationalisation process by defining certain stages of international engagement. The formation of **fixed stages** brings about that the dynamics themselves, which are driving the evolutionary process, get lost between the fixed stages. Although time is integrated in these models, there is no grip on the evolutionary flow of structural change but only a comparison of momentary stage conditions. Of the three dimensions, the build up of international activities is the core subject. Therefore a largely **unidimensional** and **teleological view of internationalisation** is conveyed. Aspects of interconnective activities occur implicitly in Vernon's PLC in form of market and production interdependencies. The Scandinavian approaches furthermore pay attention to environmental influences by integrating the concepts of psychic distance and business distance - although in a static manner. A **dynamic component** is integrated in the incremental approaches by depicting the core of **internationalisation as a learning process**. Network-building activities have been conceptualised by Scandinavian scholars, whereas the co-evolution of company and environment as the driving force of globalisation does not find explicit attention in these approaches.

The **explanatory value** of the **incremental models** decreases with an increasing degree of internationalisation so that the theory is especially applicable to the **first phases of internationalisation**. Studies on the **institutionalisation process of international management** are still missing with the notable exception of the research done by Rosenzweig/Singh (1992) on the isomorphism of organisation structures of MNE subsidiaries. The **evolution of international organisation structures** has traditionally been described in terms of *stage models* in the development of different types of organisation structures (e.g. international division, global integrated structures). Examples are the studies of Stopford/Wells (1972), Franko

(1976), and scholars of the Process School. Such very rare revolutionary transformations of the organisational structure do not reveal much about the evolutionary dynamics underlying the internationalisation process of firms. Studies on the organisational imprinting in the start-up phase and the continuous interplay of environmental change, organisational innovation, and (de-) institutionalisation are missing in general, in the context of internationalisation even more.

In reviews of internationalisation research, Andersen (1993) and Leonidou/Katsikeas (1996) find that little attention has been paid to **time**. In a similar vein, Oviatt/McDougall (1999) criticise that a dynamic theory of the process of internationalisation relevant to the economic conditions from the 1990s onwards is lacking. For Oviatt/McDougall, *'the accelerated process of internationalisation appears to be a historically significant change in the way business is conducted'* (Ibid. 24). The incremental stage models do not provide a sufficient basis in a context where conditions for international business have changed profoundly. According to Oviatt/McDougall (Ibid. 25), these models rely on assumptions that applied a generation ago.

A basic criticism of all **'dynamic theories'** is that **no initial conditions** are presented, i.e., the models do not explain why or how the process starts, and the sequence of states or conditions is not discussed. The core explanation of the models is that increased market knowledge will lead to increased market commitment, and vice versa. From Anderson's point of view, the explanation is **tautological** because of the definition of market commitment (the amount of resources committed) and the fact that market knowledge could be regarded as an intangible resource. Furthermore, the authors do not discuss factors that may influence the process, as they expect that the internationalisation process, once started, will tend to proceed regardless of whether strategic decisions in that direction are made or not (Andersen 1993: 216-217).

Luostarinen (1994: 20) states that internationalisation should not and cannot always proceed along the lines of the mainstream pattern. In order to adapt to react quickly to the **changing environment**, firms have to be more elastic in their strategic decision-making than in the 1970s. This causes **leapfrogging** in the traditional pattern of internationalisation. The actual progression through the stages has been underexposed, and little has been paid to the **time dimension of the process**.

The **explanatory value** of the **internationalisation model** is assumed to be high in the **early stages** of the internationalisation process, while the explanatory value of the **eclectic paradigm** is high for **MNEs** that have experience from many activities and regions of the world. The internationalisation model rests on behavioural theories while the eclectic paradigm assumes that rational decision-makers have access to perfect information. The latter therefore predicts that the firm will optimise rationally while the internationalisation model places uncertainty avoidance at the centre and assumes that no optimisation will occur.

The **concepts of psychic, business, and cultural distance** are subject to various criticisms. For example, Kogut/Singh (1988: 415) contend that implications for country patterns in entry mode behaviour from psychic distances between countries are not explored. They continue that researchers did not stipulate clearly how the experience of the firm mitigates perceived uncertainty arising from differences in cultures. The authors think that cultural characteristics are likely to influence the entry choice. Kogut/Singh (1988: 429) further consider theories of internalisation and the firm to be culturally robust. Their empirical application in a comparative setting appears to warrant the consideration of cultural differences on the costs and risks, which managers attach to different modes of transacting. In their view, it would be interesting to distinguish between transaction costs that are independent of a firm's country of origin and those that are determined by cultural factors.

In a similar vein, Nordstöm (1991) argues that the world has become much more homogeneous and that psychic distance therefore decreased. Entrepreneurs are more willing and able to enter directly into international markets as the examples of born globals show. The emergence of highly internationalised markets induced as well the development of '**global tribes**' in some segments. According to Nordstöm (1991: 32), the world imploded in terms of psychic distance and what matters from the point of view of understanding and interpreting the actions of business firms is how the actors *perceive* the world. Furthermore it has been argued that the stage models do not take into account interdependencies between different national markets although interdependencies can be expected to have a strong impact on the internationalisation of the firm (Johanson/Vahlne 1990: 15).

Nilsson et al. (1996) assume that not only **different driving forces** are important in the internationalisation process in different firms. From their point of view, the **importance of different forces** also varies over **time** in a single firm.

'The forces behind the pattern of internationalisation change over time. Hence, internationalisation should not be looked upon as one single process, but as a chain of separate but linked processes. The end of a chain represents the point of departure for the next. Internationalisation can be described as a 'sedimentary process' where each company internationalisation becomes a process with many unique elements. To understand the internationalisation process at the corporate level, the firm's specific history and changes in the competitive and regulatory environment must be understood. The importance of firm-specific factors contributes to unexpected outcomes of internationalisation...' (Nilsson et al. 1996: 164).

All described theories fail in the explicit observation of the dynamic co-evolution of a company and its respective environment. The potential for an adequate observation of globalisation processes thus encounters a strong limitation. **No mechanism of innovation, adaptation, and self-reproduction** is explicitly described. Learning-based stage models assume a teleological learning process but do not specify the underlying evolutionary motor. For example, any kind of negative selection that would explain de-internationalisation processes is missing.

	International product life cycle	Stage models of organisational structures	Learning-based stage models
Foundation	Product innovation	No	No
Co-evolution of firm and environment	No	Only internal perspective	Adaptational learning of the firm, network perspective allows for co-evolutionary processes.
Global differentiation of firm	Focus is on product or business, which follows fixed stages of international dispersion.	Entry modes are the means for global differentiation; formal and cognitive structures provide alternative forms of internal differentiation.	Increasing global differentiation from markets with a small to those with a large psychic distance; concentric differentiation
Global integration of firm	No	Entry modes provide means for integration; organisation structures almost reflect integration and provide different forms of integration.	Integration is implicitly reflected by the learning cycle as it presupposes the retention of new elements in a path-dependent process; also external integration in networks.
Global evolutionary dynamics of environment	No	No	No
Global evolutionary dynamics of firm	Life cycle mechanism, deterministic sequence of stages	Implicit teleological and life cycle processes from small to high complexity; dialectical processes are reflected by the underlying dimensions of the typologies	Evolutionary process of learning; co-evolutionary process of action and meaning structure; teleological and life cycle process from low to high distance markets and increasing complexity.

Table 3-6: Evolutionary principles in stage theories of internationalisation

Stage models of internationalisation show that internationalisation may be a **sequential process**, even if the speed and pattern may vary between firms. However, the theories only allow for incrementally increasing international commitment and provide a normative picture. Nilsson et al. (1996: 160) therefore ask to '*increase our knowledge and understanding of how business firms actually internationalise*'. The particular history and culture of the firm is considered to be extremely important by the authors. This perspective is exemplified by Cantwell (1989: 215) who considers the international growth of a firm as a part of an evolutionary process. The following chapters serve to provide a more comprehensive picture of this process from a variety of perspectives. Table 3-6 resumes the main contributions of the stage theories to the understanding of basic evolutionary characteristics of globalisation processes.

3.3 Resource-based theory of internationalisation

In more recent literature, mainstream internationalisation theories are adapted and connected to new theoretical lines of reasoning. The resource-based view and its different theoretical strands have only recently been adapted to the field of internationalisation by a few authors.

3.3.1 Extension of economic theories by resource-based view

The tradition of firm-specific advantages connects with the literature on core competencies arising from the resource-based view and its descendant, the knowledge-based view. This development represents a quite logic extension of the internalisation approach as one main emphasis is on the knowledge factor (Robock/Simmonds 1989: 45). From this perspective, firms can be conceived as internalised bundles of resources, which can be allocated between product groups, and between national markets (Buckley/Casson 1998: 541).

The **organisational capability perspective**, which represents one strand in the knowledge-based view, perceives the firm as a bundle of relatively static and transferable resources. These resources are then transformed into capabilities through dynamic and interactive firm-specific processes (Amit/Shoemaker 1993) where individual skills, organisation and technology are inextricably woven together (Nelson/Winter 1982). The resource-based theory has important implications for questions regarding **boundaries of the firm** and how to differentiate between resources that might support a competitive advantage from other less valuable resources. While the key considerations of the transaction cost theory in selecting entry mode is cost minimisation, the organisational capabilities perspective focuses on the **value of the firm's capabilities** (Andersen 1997: 36-37).

Madhok (1997) introduced the organisational capability perspective to explain *entry mode choices*. Firms with know-how that has a high proportion of intangible resources such as skills and competencies, which are embedded rather than generic, are supposed to have a greater preference for internalisation. This is in accordance with the effects of firm-specific advantages in internalisation theory and of ownership advantages postulated in the eclectic framework. When, on the other hand, the proportion of **embedded market knowledge** compared to **generic market knowledge** is high, firms are expected to show a greater preference for collaborative agreements. According to Madhok (1997: 49), **locational effects** reflect the difficulties of exploiting the firm's existing know-how due to differences between the home and host contexts. He therefore proposes that in the exploitation of an existing advantage, where the potential for erosion in the value of a firm's know-how due to the ownership effect is greater than that due to the locational effect, there will be a greater preference for **internalisation**. On the contrary, there will be a greater preference for **collaboration** when the potential for erosion in the value of a firm's know-how caused by the locational effect is greater than that because of the ownership effect (Ibid.).

In general, a firm must find a balance between exploitation and development of its capabilities. The exploration and development tends to be larger and more critical in dynamic environments. The transaction cost and the organisational capability perspectives differ in their recommendations regarding the preferred degree of internalisation in stable and dynamic environments. In a **dynamic environment** the ownership advantage of the firm may not be sufficiently strong for the creation and realisation of future value, and may need to be complemented by that of other firms (Andersen 1997: 37). Madhok (1997: 51) therefore suggests that where the development/exploitation ratio is high, operations where the underlying motivation is capability development for the generation and realisation of future value will result in a greater preference for collaborations than operations by economising on transaction costs.

3.3.2 Extension of incremental stage models by resource-based view

Similar to the internalisation theory, the stage models are based on the implicit assumptions that (1) resources needed to proceed with internationalisation are available within the firm; and (2) resources available can be readily transferred across countries (Sharma 2001: 76).

From a resource-based view, the dynamics of the internationalisation process are based on the **unique resource collection of firms** (Ibid.). Resources are stocks of available factors owned or controlled by the firm. They consist of assets, organisational processes, and attributes of the firm. In the course of internationalisation, a firm commits a package of tangible and intangible resources abroad. With respect to **tangible resources**, two aspects are important: (1) *speed* with which tangible resources can be transferred; and (2) *scope* of the market served.

According to Sharma (2001: 79), **intangible resources** in the internationalisation process may consist of (1) internationally trained manpower and other management resources; (2) internationally active buyers, suppliers, and other actors among whom the firm enjoys a good reputation, goodwill, and trust; and (3) established brand name. Intangible resources (e.g. implicit knowledge) are imperfectly mobile and limited. Several intangible resources (e.g. administrative routines, human resources) are also subject to learning effects. An increased use of intangible resources results in a **history- or path-dependent** accumulation of reputation, goodwill, and credibility. It demands sustained effort and investment on the part of the firm (Barney 1986). Non-use of these resources leads to decay and erosion in their value (Reed/de Fillippi 1990). It is only when a firm has been operating in a market for years and has consistently kept its promises that it develops such resources as trust and credibility. The mobility of intangible resources may be restricted by organisational culture and routines, sunk costs, reputation, path-dependence, tacit/implicit knowledge and skills, high transaction costs, causal ambiguity, and socially complex production (Lippman/Rumelt 1982, Amit/Schoemaker 1993).

A study by Eriksson et al. (1997) shows that internationalisation is not only a matter of learning about foreign markets and institutions. Knowledge must also be gained about the **internal resources** of the firm, and what the firm is capable of when exposed to new and unfamiliar conditions. The results of the study suggest that a firm must develop structures and routines that are compatible with its internal resources and competencies, and that can guide the search for experiential knowledge about foreign markets and institutions. On a different level, this can be regarded as the need to develop a cognitive framework showing what further knowledge about foreign markets is relevant (Eriksson et al. 1997: 353). A study by Sullivan/Bauerschmidt (1990: 26) reveals internationalisation as shaped by **managers' knowledge** of international conditions, the information gaps of international transactions and characteristics of foreign markets. Consequently, the shape of managers' objective and experiential knowledge drives internationalisation.

Factors such as the duration of foreign operations (Erramilli 1991), the firms' size and age, the number of foreign countries in which they operate (Barkema/Vermeulen 1998) seem to influence the **accumulation of knowledge**. In a series of articles, Eriksson et al. (1997, 2000, 2001) expanded the concept of experiential knowledge and integrated research from organisational learning and the knowledge-based view of the firm.

For example, an empirical study of 362 service firms by Eriksson et al. (1997) delivered proof for the assumption that the level of **risk perception of international activities** is continuously decreasing along the internationalisation process. The analysis shows that a firm's experience of the internationalisation process influences the **perceived cost** in this process. This implies that some experiential knowledge is located in the firm, in its decision-making routines and structures (Ibid. 352). Such routines and structures are first developed by a firm to manage operations in the home market, but are not sensitive to stimuli origination from overseas (Eriksson et al. 2000: 29). The findings indicate that **accumulated internationalisation experience** that affects both business knowledge and institutional knowledge is not related to specific country markets. It is a **firm-specific experience** relevant to all markets. It seems to be reasonable to regard it as a kind of procedural knowledge concerning, for instance, what kind of knowledge a firm needs in different situations.

The study indicates that the perceived costs of internationalisation by decision-makers tend to decrease continuously with increasing experience of the firm in international business. The authors conclude that **international experiential knowledge** is learned organisationally and that it is **institutionalised** in decision-routines and the organisation structure. The international learning process is not confined to the individual experiences of decision-makers but is accompanied by an institutionalisation process of international management (Eriksson et al. 1997: 352). The study further indicates that knowledge has to be gained not only on foreign markets but also on the internal resources of a firm and what the firm is capable of when exposed to new and unfamiliar conditions. A firm therefore must develop structures and routines that are compatible with its internal resources and competence, and that can guide the search for experiential knowledge about foreign markets and institutions. *'On a different level, this can be viewed as the need to develop a cognitive framework showing what further knowledge about foreign markets is relevant'* (Ibid. 353).

Eriksson et al. (2000) examine the effect of variations in the geographical scope of international business operations on experiential knowledge development in the internationalisation of the firm. **Experiential knowledge** is assumed to have three interrelated **components**: internationalisation knowledge, business knowledge, and institutional knowledge (Ibid. 26). The study demonstrates that internationalisation knowledge is a key variable that mediates the effect of variation on the other knowledge variables.

Internationalisation knowledge reveals a firm's capability and resources to engage in international operations (Eriksson et al. 2000: 26, 2001: 23). It operates as a repository in which knowledge may be retained for a period of time and supplies decisional stimuli and responses that are preserved in the firms and have behavioural consequences when revealed. Internationalisation knowledge captures the firm's **'absorptive capacity'** (Cohen/Levinthal 1990) in internationalisation. It highlights the fact that when firms first go abroad, they are likely to be ethnocentric (Perlmutter 1969) because their absorptive capacity is domestic-market based. In the context of experiential knowledge development in the internationalisation process, internationalisation knowledge can be seen as the firm's theory-in-use with regard to international business strategy. Lack of internationalisation knowledge is perceived when the theory-in-use is vague, ill defined or irrelevant (Eriksson et al. 2001: 24). The study of Eriksson et al. (2001) gives rise to the assumption that some basic restructuring of internationalisation knowledge occurs over time. There seems to be a discontinuity of internationalisation knowledge.

Business knowledge concerns competitive situations in specific markets and clients in these markets. In international markets, a lack of knowledge about a particular client's way of making decisions and his idiosyncratic requirement regarding products and services is problematic. Operations in a market allow the internationalising firm to accumulate the kind of institutional and business knowledge it requires and to interpret the information in a firm-specific context. Most firms are aware that business conditions are complex, fluid, and equivocal. They know that the acquisition of foreign knowledge will require interaction with actors abroad. The perceived lack of foreign business knowledge is reduced over time through ongoing foreign operations (Eriksson et al. 2001: 37).

Institutional knowledge is information about the governance structures in specific countries and their rules, regulations, norms, and values. The accumulation of knowledge drives internationalisation (Eriksson et al. 2000: 29-30). Lack of institutional knowledge has a significant effect on the cost of international business. With respect to institutional knowledge, firms are strictly ethnocentric when first going abroad. This ethnocentricity decreases over time as the firms learn about the equivocality of the institutional setting of foreign business (Eriksson et al. 2001: 37). While internationalisation knowledge concerns the firm's strategy with regard to internationalisation, business knowledge and institutional knowledge concern specific foreign markets (Ibid. 26).

In an empirical study of Swedish service firms, Eriksson et al. (2001) showed that firms with a long and a short duration in foreign markets differ substantially with regard to knowledge accumulation. **Duration** was proved to have a much stronger effect in the short than in the long duration group. This shows that learning is particular intense in the early stages of internationalisation. The **development of internationalisation knowledge** appears to be a *discontinuous, stepwise process*. A basic restructuring of internationalisation knowledge seems to occur over time. With regard to **business knowledge**, most firms are already aware that business conditions are complex, fluid, and equivocal (Ibid. 35-37). The kinds of experimental knowledge developed at the outset of internationalisation led to the same kinds of knowledge being further developed in any subsequent internationalisation. Experiential knowledge types not developed in the early stages of internationalisation are not developed later (Eriksson et al. 2000: 323).

Institutional knowledge was proved to have a significant effect on the cost of international business. Firms are strictly ethnocentric when first going abroad. The ethnocentricity decreases over time as the firms learn about the equivocally of the institutional setting of foreign business. The early years of foreign operations appear to be characterised primarily by a feeling of growing knowledge, which, as outcomes of operations are realised, is replaced after some years by a growing awareness of a lack of institutional knowledge and that institutions are more complex than initially expected (Eriksson et al. 2000: 37-38). The **psychic distance paradox** exemplified by study of O'Grady/Lane (1996) about the entry of Canadian retailers in the US market seems to be attributable to unexpected complexity relating to institutional conditions in a country that was initially expected to be quite similar. The perception of a country as having a small psychic distance from one's own can lead decision-makers to a number of faulty assumptions - creating an inability to learn about the country (Ibid. 310).

The behaviour of the international firm is path- or history-dependent because its internationalisation process is based on the stock of the firm-specific tacit or experimental knowledge in the firm. The existing stock of knowledge and the operating environment limit and direct the evolution of the firm (Eriksson et al. 2000: 307-8). **Path-dependence** is the incremental process where the pattern of behaviour by firms is contingent upon and a function of its past international experience. Benito/Gripsrud (1992: 475) found that there is a strong interrelation between the locations of subsequent FDI by firms, although rather in form of an iterating pattern than a '**centrifugal unfolding**' of international activities. Barkema et al. (1996: 163) showed that acquisitions and joint ventures are the types of ventures where firms reduce cultural barriers through learning, with the success of later ventures increasing with the amount of previous FDI of the firm. Learning from previous FDI largely concerns learning about foreign organisational cultures. Andersson et al. (1997: 81) further argue that there are two contextual dimensions impacting on acquisition behaviour and its consequences: extent of previous relationships between the acquiring and the acquired companies and psychic distance.

'Exposure to variation enables internationalising firms to accumulate knowledge from a richer variety of business and institutional actors, so that a double-loop learning process more easily evolves in such firms. Exposure to a richer set of business actors and institutional environments may set in motion a process whereby the internationalising firm's current assumptions regarding business and institutional actors are confronted with a new 'reality'. The feedback process from this questioning may force the firm to reconsider and amend its existing theory-in-use as well as its organisational practices and strategies, compelling it to

develop new technological solutions, products, and ideas. ... A richer knowledge set has a positive effect on the future internationalisation of the firm, because there is a higher probability that the new knowledge required for a new situation may bear some similarity to the current stock of knowledge at the firm' (Ibid. 30-31).

Bilkey (1978) and Naidu/Rao (1993) argue that the **experiential knowledge** that firms gain in the **early years of internationalisation** is extremely important for their subsequent resource commitments in the international market. Sullivan/Bauerschmidt (1990) found that managers' **perceptions of barriers** hinge on their past experience. Internationalisation is shaped by managers' knowledge of international conditions, the information gaps of international transactions and characteristics of foreign markets. *'The gestalt of managers' objective and experiential knowledge drives internationalisation'* (Ibid. 26). Path-dependence therefore can be expected to have a strong effect on resource commitment in foreign markets (Eriksson et al.: 308).

Sharma (2001) developed a '**resource-based model of internationalisation**', which is based on the logic of incremental stage models. From this perspective, the internationalisation process of firms is a continuing process of resource creation, resource accumulation, and its subsequent exploitation by the firm. A disruption in the resource creation – accumulation – exploitation process in a firm will terminate its internationalisation process.

The **first phase** in the evolution of a firm is characterised by a **process of home market accumulation**. This stage, which describes firm operations prior to foreign market entry, was never elaborated in the incremental stage models.

For **initial internationalisation steps**, many options are not available due to the limited resource endowment of firms. The internationalisation process therefore is slow and gradual. This is also caused by resource-based rigidities of intangible resources like organisational culture and routines. The resources accumulated by a firm in the domestic market project the trajectory for the future development of the firm (Ibid. 81). During the first time of discovery of foreign market opportunities the initial steps are reactive and often initiated by external bridge-builders.

From a resource-based perspective, the **choice of a country market** and the respective entry mode depends on the **compatibility with the resource stock of the firm**. Sharma assumes *similarity* and *distance* to be important for the *selection decision*. The capacity to learn about the resources available in foreign markets is contingent upon the structure and configuration of the intangible resources. The **dynamics** in the internationalisation process basically depends on the *interplay between resource commitments to local markets* and the *accumulation of location-specific resources*. A basic similarity to the model of Johanson/Vahlne (1977) is clearly visible.

The firm's **expansion** radiates from the home market in a **systematic fashion**: the operations of the firm are extended *first* to those markets that *best fit* the cognitive and resource character of the company, and *ultimately* those of the *poorest fit*. In effect, the **cumulative experiential knowledge of foreign markets** prepares the firm to manage the incentives and barriers in markets of progressively greater cognitive and physical distance (Sullivan/Bauerschmidt 1990: 20).

3.3.3 Contribution to an evolutionary perspective

Resource-based or knowledge-based perspectives on internationalisation are still in their infancy and deserve much more attention. Knowledge-based contributions in the realm of internationalisation are overwhelmingly extensions of already existing internationalisation theories. They represent a **complementary perspective** to the approaches in the tradition of **industrial organisation** and seem to be an ideal *theoretical basis* for approaches in the tradition of **learning-based reasoning**. They may serve to **combine both lines of reasoning**. Due to the very limited scope of resource-based theory in the international context, there is no motivation for any negative criticism. On the contrary, it has to be criticised that in internationalisation research the inclusion of other theoretical perspectives has been widely ignored. The development of a resource-based approach in internationalisation research therefore seems to be very promising. As indicated in the first chapter, one intended major contribution of this publication is the identification of knowledge form different theoretical fields that can be mobilised for the research of globalisation. Especially from an evolutionary perspective the resource-based view seems to be very promising. An evaluation of the inclusion of evolutionary elements and its possible contribution to an evolutionary globalisation perspective will be discussed in Chapter 5.

3.4 Summary

Processes of internationalisation induce changes in the global extension of social systems by a spatial differentiation of social actors on global scale and by the formation of social systems with worldwide extension (e.g. '*born globals*'). There are basically two streams of literature within the realm of the internationalisation of firms: internationalisation strategy and internationalisation theory. **Internationalisation strategies** may be differentiated in market entry strategies with a focus on international differentiation and a focus on the individual market entry and international business strategies, which generally balance both differentiation and integration of business activities in the global context.

Internationalisation has been subject to theoretical research since the 1950s. In contrast to early economic theories, **processual internationalisation theories** provide a dynamic perspective but generally do so without conceptualisation of an evolutionary motor or mechanism, leading to a basically teleological and predefined course of internationalisation with fixed stages. The **international life cycle** described by Vernon (1966) is constituted by stages documenting the life of a business from its birth to its death along fixed stages. Stage models of organisational structures describe the development and change of organisational structures in the course of internationalisation, usually from a simple to a complex from.

The most comprehensive view on internationalisation processes is conveyed by the **learning-based stage theories** developed by Uppsala School, Helsinki School (together Scandinavian School), and the Innovation School. While the Scandinavian model comprises the whole internationalisation process from first steps to the genesis of a multinational enterprise along fixed stages, the innovation model is restricted to an export perspective. All models conceive internationalisation as an incremental, learning-based process along fixed stages in a centrifugal way with an increasing psychic and business distance to the explored markets. While the innovation models ends with fully developed export activities, the Scandinavian model begins with exports from the home base and ends with the formation of a MNE with subsidiaries in different national markets. Though based on a learning perspective, the models do not provide an explanation for global evolutionary dynamics and suffer from several restrictions. The underlying logic of the models is intriguing and captured very well the context of the 1970s but encounters limitations with increasing dynamics, skipping of stages, decreasing importance of distances, and the emergence of born globals as firms being global from inception rather than expanding in a rings-in-the-water mode.

Literature on born globals is still in its infancy and has to develop a complementary position vis-à-vis traditional internationalisation theory. Born globals are observed with a dominant focus on entrepreneurship and personal networks. The emergence of born global firms is already well researched. Still missing is an observation of globalisation processes after the global emergence. This perspective would be quite interesting as born globals are imprinted with globalisation capabilities from inception and are not marked by a distinction between home-culture and '*foreign*' markets but still are start-ups that have to develop their global activity and meaning structure, particularly with regard to firm-specific capabilities. Therefore, they have to develop globalisation capabilities just like traditional internationalisers, too, with the marked difference that the latter have to overcome the faltline between home-based and globally differentiated activities and structures.

The **discontinuous stage theories** provide an interesting and complementary perspective to the incremental stage models. The **GAINS paradigm** ('*Gestalt approach*') derives different internationalisation profiles but was not developed any further. The **dynamic internationalisation theory** provides a more differentiated view due to the integration of different organisational change concepts from deep structure to surface structure and from incremental to episodical and epochal change. The underlying **strategic process** perspective offers a quite sophisticated spectrum of change concepts. On a stand-alone basis, the discontinuous stage theories represent innovative concepts in the area of internationalisation by import of concepts from organisational change literature but have not matured to consistent theories explaining internationalisation processes. This may also be attributed to a missing adoption of the approaches by other researchers in the international business community.

The **knowledge-based theory of internationalisation** is only emerging and still represents more an extension of economic and learning-based internationalisation theories. It may thus serve as an approach integrating these two distinct research streams. The eclectic character of the knowledge-based view may sustain the development of a more integrative approach to internationalisation. Such an integrative approach to internationalisation may serve as a theoretical '*region*' filling the internationalisation perspective in the evolutionary framework of globalisation developed in the course of this study. Particularly the conceptual closeness between a knowledge-based approach and the meaning-based layout of the evolutionary framework allow for a close and complementary integration.

On balance, the described approaches cover important aspects of internationalisation processes. Learning-based stage theories and literature on SMEs, born globals, and international business strategy also include aspects of network formation as a facilitator of internationalisation. Learning-based stage theories are implicitly based on learning as an evolutionary driver but none of the internationalisation approaches explicitly defines or conceptualises network capabilities or evolutionary mechansisms explicitly.

4   Global networks

In 1998 there were **53,000 MNEs** worldwide with **450,000 foreign subsidiaries**, which had **global sales of $9.5 trillion**. Contrary to earlier times of internationalisation, transnational production outweighs exports as the dominant mode of servicing foreign markets (UNCTAD 1997: 1). These indicators show impressively the degree of economic globalisation and the importance of MNEs. According to Hood/Young (2000: 4), there is little doubt that in various roles the MNE has been a driver, enabler, and promoter of the globalisation processes. In an economy that has achieved a remarkable degree of global integration, **MNEs** have also emerged as critical **brokers** between the **national and local networks** (Kogut et al. 1993: 90).

Though still dominating the global economic landscape, large MNEs have been forced to downsize and flexibilise activities because the competition changed in a way that attributes associated with small size – flexibility, product development, quality and speed – have become increasingly essential. Mathews (2002: 223) even predicts that globalisation in the twenty-first century is likely to be characterised by the increasing integration of a variety of small and medium-sized players in international networks of production, movements of goods, and flows of information and knowledge (Ibid.). From this perspective, what matters most is action orientation and networking among autonomous firms and units (Perrow 1992: 452). As a result, decentralising MNEs take increasingly the shape of **intraorganisational networks**. MNE-units and SMEs also develop increasingly co-operative agreements leading to the formation of **interorganisational networks**.

Giddens (1991: 21-22) contends that *'globalisation has to be understood as a dialectical phenomenon, in which events at one pole of a distanciated relation often produce divergent or even contrary occurrences at another. Globalisation further makes the modes of connection between different social contexts or regions become networked across earth's surface as a whole* (Giddens 1990: 63-64). Robertson (1995: 34-35) sees the global as the **'linking of localities'**. In a similar vein, Held et al. (1999: 21-27) refer to contemporary globalisation as **'thick globalisation'**, especially with regard to the extensity, intensity, and velocity of political, economic, and cultural flows and connections. On balance, the **dialectical character** of economic globalisation with driving **paradoxes** such as MNEs versus SMEs, global versus local, stability versus flexibility, and others, constitutes the main mechanism for economic evolution and leads to a **'liquefaction'** of the emerging global network competition (Borghoff/Welge 2003).

As outlined in Chapter 2, the **globalisation of network competition** can be outlined as a **historical process** of **differentiation and integration of social systems** participating and influencing in the global economy. As early as 1939, Chamberlin identified the acknowledgeable variety among firms and their continuous efforts to differentiate themselves from their competitors as the force, which shapes the behaviour of markets. The main sources of competitive advantage, however, changed in the course of **economic evolution**. Dunning (2000: 22) contends that the main source of wealth creation moved from land in the 17th century, through machines and finance in the 19th and most of the 20th century, to knowledge as embodied in human beings, in physical hardware and in intangible assets. Consequently, in a historical review of the development of modern industrial capitalism, Chandler (1990) identifies the **organisational capabilities** of the enterprise as a unified whole at the **core of the dynamics**. These organisational capabilities were the collective physical facilities and human skills as they were organised within the enterprise. Such organisational capabilities had to be created, and once established, they had to be maintained. One of the most critical tasks of top management has always been to maintain the capabilities and to integrate the facilities and skills into a unified organisation – so that the whole becomes more than the sum of its parts (Porter 1990: 594).

The development and maintenance of **organisational capabilities** did not only help to assure the continuing **growth of the enterprise** but also affected the **growth of the industries** and of the nations in which the new modern industrial enterprise appeared. Such organisational capabilities provided a **dynamic for growth of the industrialised nations** (Porter 1990: 595-596). The organisational capabilities that provided the core dynamics for the continuing evolution of the modern industrial enterprise and of the industries, which it dominated were created primarily in those capital-intensive industries where the interrelated investment in manufacturing, marketing, and management provided powerful competitive advantages (Ibid. 605). A crucial theme of the history of the modern industrial enterprise is that creating and maintaining capabilities is a continuing, long-term process – a process that requires sound long-term perspectives from the decision-makers responsible for the health and growth of their enterprise (Ibid. 627). On balance, one main consequence deriving from economic globalisation is the **central role of knowledge and organisational capabilities in global markets**. The two organisational forms most capable of providing these advantages are traditonally MNEs (intraorganisational networks) and more recently interorganisational networks constituted by formally independent firms. Both network perspectives will be outlined in the following chapter.

4.1 Interorganisational networks

An **interfirm network** may be conceived as an institutional arrangement among distinct but related for-profit organisations, which is characterised by (1) a special kind of network relationship, (2) a certain degree of reflexivity, and (3) a logic of exchange that operates differently from that of markets and hierarchies (Sydow/Windeler 2000: 266). The relationships are the medium and outcome of intensive interorganisational interaction, provide rich information channels, and demand more loyalty and trust. They are typically complex, reciprocal, and relatively stable (Ibid.).

Organising from a network perspective can be understood as social interaction in which agents, managers in particular, try intentionally and reflexively to shape network processes, position and relationships in order to co-ordinate the activities in the network.

The **growth of an interorganisational relationship** is viewed as a **dynamic cyclical process**. A need for resources stimulates communications with organisations that have complementary domains. These communications have the purpose of establishing a formal agreement for financial transactions or informal consensus to refer clients for services. What may start as an interim solution may become a long-term interorganisational commitment of resource transactions and a web of interdependencies, if the process is perceived by the parties to be equitable. Domain similarity, communications and resource dependence proved to contribute to building consensus by parties to the terms of their relationship in a study by van de Ven/Walker (1984: 604).

4.1.1 Local networks
Amin/Roberts (1991: 107) describe the current phase of globalisation as *'a period of epochal change'*. Fundamental to this process is the return to locality, the renaissance of local and regional economies, and the development of increasingly direct and immediate **relations between global and local spheres** (Ibid.).

Just as regionalisation and globalisation of production can be judged to exhibit mutually reinforcing tendencies (Held et al. 1999: 270), also the **localisation of industries** can progress hand in hand with **globalisation**. Localisation progresses with the interfirm linkages within a local area to save transaction costs, to utilise local industrial environment and cultures and to improve innovation potential. Globalisation progresses as interfirm linkages are formed in the global economy beyond national boundaries to increase demand, to reduce production costs, and to limit the uncertainties in innovation and technological development. **Localised net-**

work systems without **global networks** are sometimes vulnerable to external shocks and severe international competitive environments. A localised network should be complemented by a non-local or a global network for its technology, information, and innovation (Park 1996: 477-478). Such a network structure expresses the relation and the valorisation of different local identities, which, precisely because of their diversity, can integrate together and evolve in a global scenario. If the local is not separated from the global but is part of it, then it follows that the phenomena of globalisation generate a **new dialectic between local and global** (Conti 1997: 20).

From a **systems perspective**, openness and closure are inseparable components of an interpretative whole. The organisation of a system and the **structural transformation** it encounters depends on **circular relationships**, which express themselves through **networks of interconnection** and give identity to it. **System dynamics** become interpretable as complex relationships between the global and the local, i.e. they present a socio-economic world that can be understood in terms of relationships and can be represented as networks (Taylor/Conti 1997: 5).

From this perspective, the **local system** is an organised system endowed with a **specific identity** – as the expression of a set of values, knowledge, and institutions. Its evolution on the one hand responds to external stimuli and, on the other, is the basis of the dialectic between the local system and global forces. It follows that, as the local system can be defined by the overlapping of the internal dynamic and the channels of access to globality, the global corporation itself can be understood only by giving theoretical weight to the specific nature of the places in which it is situated and not reduced merely to the network of connections in which codified knowledge flows (Becattini/Rullani 1994: 37). The **'global'**, therefore, is to be understood in a relational sense. Its extent is definable in terms of the relationships that interconnect its constituent subsystems. It is constituted by the systems it connects, modelled upon their specific configurations. At the heart of the **global-local nexus** are the different layers of social systems and networks from the local to the global level (Taylor/Conti 1997: 6-7).

What is fundamental in this **web-like industrial structure** is that it is **territorially spread** throughout the world, and its geometry keeps changing, as a whole and for each individual unit. In such a structure, the most important element for a successful managerial strategy is to position a firm in the web in such a way as to gain competitive advantage for its relative position (Castells 1996: 96). For firms participating in the network competition at various geographic levels, it is central to cope with the fact that *'the new global geography has made relative position within the web simultaneously more difficult to define and much more important'* (Hargittai/Centeno 2001: 1550). Thus, the structure tends to reproduce itself and to keep expanding as competition goes on, so deepening the global character of the economy. For the firm to operate in such a variable geometry of production and distribution, a very flexible form of management is required (Castells 1996: 96). Another important factor is that **production space** in the advanced economies has become increasingly '**slippery**', as the ease to profit from moving plants grows and as new competing lines are set up in lower-cost regions elsewhere (Markusen 1996: 293). **Network positioning** should hence be regarded as a **dynamic process in economic space**.

Unlike internationalisation and multinationalisation, **globalisation** is not just a matter of spatial distribution of activities. Rather, it reflects the impact of several different factors on a large number of regions, creating **spatial differentiation** between the abilities to innovate and to generate innovation processes (Maillat 1996: 70). Organisational and technological knowledge is not uniformly distributed and accessible across countries. **Differential competencies** in organisational co-ordination and technological innovation determine differential possibilities of growth not only of individual firms but also of the entire countries where firms originated (Dosi 1997: 466).

Social-organisational logics enable different types of actors to engage in different activities. They are sense-making frames that provide understandings of what is legitimate, reasonable, and effective in a given context. Firms only adopt practices or organisational forms that make sense to pre-existing actors. If local patterns of social organisation are resources for action, then successful economic development involves matching logics of social organisation with the opportunities offered by the global economy. Rather, countries and their firms are socially and institutionally equipped to do different things in the global economy. Firms from different countries are justly famous for their competitive edge, albeit in different industries and market segments (Guillén 2001a: 14).

Dicken/Thrift (1992: 279) contend that both **intra- and inter-firm structures** are best seen as complex networks of enormous diversity. Geographical industrialisation needs to be seen not only in terms of changing industry trajectories but also in terms of **dynamic webs of power relationships**. Production is organised primarily by business enterprises operating within extremely complex, dynamic networks of internalised and externalised transactional relationships of power and influence. According to Dicken (1994: 221), the variety of developmental trajectories and the spectrum of different forms of governance are best captured by the notion of '*networked interrelationships structured by different degrees and forms of power and influence*'. The interrelationships between firms of different sizes and types increasingly span national boundaries to create a set of **geographically nested relationships from local to global scales**. Segments are interconnected in complex ways. It is through such interconnections, for example, that a small firm in one country may be directly linked to a global production network whereas most small firms serve only a very restricted geographical area (Dicken 1986: 184-185).

The firm's **competitive advantage** in this context is determined not only by interactions with the structures of **global markets** and industry-specific trajectories but also by the **interaction with localised capabilities**. These are primarily based on

- the area's infrastructure and built environment,
- the *natural resources* accessible in the area,
- the area's specific *institutional endowment*, including all the rules, practices, routines, traditions, as well as the entrepreneurial spirits, the culture, and other values to the area, and
- the *knowledge and skills* available in the area (Mariotti/Piscittello 2001: 67).

Local network approaches basically concentrate on two **central processes of 'locational efficiency'**:

- reduction of transaction costs through geographical and social proximity,
- presence of external economies in form of a reduction in average costs and disadvantages of small firms compared to larger ones (Camagni 1991: 2).

In the emerging literature on innovation systems, a dominant approach is that of **national systems of innovation**. Countries differ in terms of their historical experience, language, and culture as well as in terms of organisational forms, interfirm relationships, role of the public sector, institutional set-up of the financial sector, R&D intensity and organisation. More recently, it has been argued that innovation systems could be analysed on the regional level as well. The concept of a **'learning region'**, stresses the importance of interactive learning in spatially delineated industrial systems as the basis for innovation and change in modern developed economies (Malmberg 1997: 575). Camagni (1991a: 122) is convinced that the local spatial context, or the **'local milieu'**, will emerge as a necessary and crucial element in the process of technology creation.

Kelley/Helper (1997), making a distinction between **organisation-specific capabilities** and **place-specific external economies**, find that a firm's propensity to adopt a new technology is a function of organisational capabilities related to size and previous experience with related technologies. They also present empirical evidence in support of the thesis that regional agglomeration economies affect the **adoption of new technologies**. Firms learn better and hence have a higher probability of adopting a new technology when **local management is embedded in a diverse network** of ties to relevant external sources of information and when the region in which the establishment is located is rich in agglomeration economies from localisation and urbanisation.

Particular patterns of conflict, *'truces'*, and mechanisms of incentive governance present an intrinsic **collective nature** grounded in the **institutions of each country**. Together with the **cumulative nature of learning processes**, they contribute to explain the **persistence of national specificity** in organisational set-ups and corporate routines (Coriat/Dosi 1998: 105).

Kogut (1991: 33) proposes that **countries** differ in their underlying **'organising principles'** of work, and that these principles develop within the confines of a **trajectory**. These principles diffuse within an inter-industry network of firms, which, through differing in their products and markets, share common heuristics as applied to how their economic activities are organised. The **diffusion of organising principles** hence embodies the know-how defining a **country's capabilities**. Firms exploit internationally what they have developed domestically, but their capabilities partly reflect their enjoyment of the diffused skills and institutional strengths of their countries of origin (Ibid. 44).

Genosko (1997: 283) conceives **innovative milieus** as the means by which global and regional competition become integrated by the means of networks in which global and regional actors share risks and reduce transaction costs. For example, **MNEs** increasingly concentrate the innovation and development activities for certain business areas in local milieus outside their home countries. The MNEs are thus creating a kind of **'multi home-base' structure** based on centres of competence or centres of excellence in order to foster their innovative capacity. In some cases, MNEs have built up **insider positions** through long-term investment, but more often they become insiders by acquiring local firms with full-fledged operations and established local networks (Malmberg/Sölvell 1997: 132). Differences in institutional frameworks and social capital appear to persist over time, sustaining the difference between the local and international innovation process. As the **subsidiary** accumulates in-depth and unique **knowledge of the local network context**, it gains access to resources and capabilities, which makes it independent and more difficult to control from headquarters (Sölvell/Zander 1998: 410-411).

Biggart/Guillén (1999:725) contend that **organising logics** vary substantially in different *social milieus* and that social organisation unique to a country is not an obstacle to economic action but a resource for action. Rugman/Verbeke (2001: 165) contend that the creation of '**sticky places**' fundamentally depends upon the synergies between strong mobile or non-location bound **firm-specific advantages** (FSAs) and immobile **country-specific advantages** (CSAs). Not all synergies are internalised by the firms involved. The **spatial proximity** between firms in a specific industry and the non-business infrastructure leads to technological and organisational **spillover effects** benefiting the entire, localised industrial district. Rugman/Verbeke (Ibid. 165) distinguish four **types of 'sticky places'** from a sustainability perspective, illustrated in Figure 4-1.

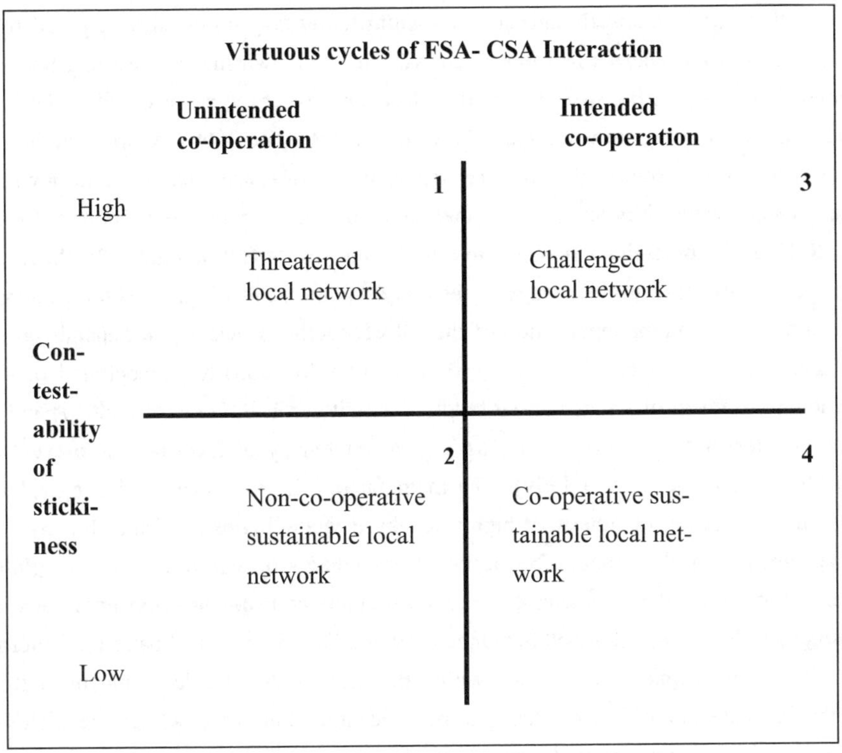

	Virtuous cycles of FSA- CSA Interaction	
	Unintended co-operation	Intended co-operation
High	1 Threatened local network	3 Challenged local network
Contestability of stickiness	2 Non-co-operative sustainable local network	4 Co-operative sustainable local network
Low		

Figure 4-1: The sustainability of sticky places
(Source: Rugman/Verbeke 2001: 165)

The horizontal axis measures the degree of co-operation among the actors in terms of intended efforts to create **virtuous cycles of FSA-CSA interaction**. The vertical axis represents the international contestability of the local network. Local networks with intended co-operation have a much greater robustness with regard to challenges from international competition (Rugman/Verbeke 2001: 165).

MNEs may well act as **intermediaries** in the **international cross-fertilisation of localised knowledge clusters**. MNEs could thus increase the **foreign knowledge absorption capacity of localised innovation clusters** and contribute to the **global diffusion of knowledge**. Such a diffusion process is constrained by the MNE's limited capabilities to absorb and transfer knowledge within their own internal network, especially when dispersed units have distinct approaches to knowledge development and transfer (Ibid. 172).

Firms increase the returns on their own R&D through suitably adapting their underlying tacit capability so that they can absorb and apply the **complementary knowledge** acquired from other locations or from other firms more intensively in their own internal learning process. **Technological diversification** and **internationalisation** have become positively related in MNEs since around 1980 (Cantwell 2002: 237, Cantwell/Piscitello 2000). Apart from the rise in technological interrelatedness, the potential opportunities for **cross-border learning** within MNEs have been enhanced by an increased take-up of information and communication technologies (ICT). **ICT specialisation** seems to amplify the firm's **technological flexibility** by enabling it to fuse together a wider range of formerly separate technologies. Although MNEs have shown a greater internationalisation of their R&D facilities recently, it depends on the type of technological activity involved if the creation is locationally concentrated or dispersed. The development of science-based fields of activity (e.g. ICT, biotechnology) and an industry's **core technology** appear to require a greater intensity of **face-to-face interaction** (Cantwell 2002: 237, Santangelo 1999). The main factors driving occasional geographical dispersion of the creation of otherwise highly localised technologies are either **locally embedded specialisation** that cannot be accessed elsewhere, or **company-specific global strategies** that utilise the development of an organisationally **complex international network for technological learning** (Cantwell/Santangelo 1999). The more typical pattern of international specialisation in innovative activity within the MNE is for the development of technologies that are core to the firm's industry to be concentrated at home, while other fields of technological activity may be located abroad, complementing the home base (Ibid.).

A **cornerstone** in the **management of a geographically complex international network** lies in a **firm's specialisation in ICT**. The opportunities created for the fusion of formerly unrelated types of technology through ICT has made feasible new combinations of activities, at best centres of expertise for which may be geographically distant from one another. The enhanced expertise in ICT seems to provide a company with greater flexibility in the management of its geographically dispersed network, and an enhanced ability to combine distant learning processes in formerly separate activities. Affiliate networks are increasingly used to source new technology. Global learning has become an important mechanism for corporate technological renewal within MNEs (Cantwell 2002: 238). MNEs have recently shifted to a closely integrated network of affiliates designed to facilitate complementary paths of innovation and new competence creation (Ibid. 244, Cantwell/Piscitello 2000).

The most internationally competitive firms in many industries tend to be concentrated in a single or a few countries (Nachum 1999: 1). **Economic space** became a '**relational space**', the field of social interactions, interpersonal synergies, and social collective actions that determine the innovative capability and the economic success of specific local areas (Camagni 1991: 1). A discipline describing the geographic distribution, agglomeration, and embeddedness of economic activities is **economic geography**.

Economic geography is supposed to be initiated by Robert McNee (1960) in terms of a '**geography of enterprise**' (Dicken/Thrift 1992: 280). Spatial perspectives on the firm have received far less attention than either technology-oriented or strategy- and organisation-oriented views of the firms. Economic geography is being rediscovered by other disciplines, thereby ending its relative isolation and opening new possibilities for interdisciplinary dialogue. **Agglomeration advantages** and **external linkages**, or clustering effects, have come to receive greater attention, particularly as regards their relative stability or instability over time. The '**multidimensionality of locational advantages**' and '**spatial trajectories**' are assumed to influence firm behaviour (Hagström/Chandler 1998: 8).

Both the extreme diversity of organisational forms and their dynamic and evolutionary nature have to be recognised. **Business organisations** are themselves produced through a complex **historical process of embedding** which involves an interaction between the specific cognitive, cultural, social, political, and economic characteristics of a **firm's home territory**, those of its geographically dispersed operations and the competitive and technological pressures which impinge upon it (Dicken/Thrift 1992: 287). According to Leamer/Storper (2001: 643), the history of economic geography is a story of **co-ordination over space** and has been shaped by two **opposing forces** (Ibid.):

1. the *constant transformation* of complex and unfamiliar co-ordination tasks *into routine activities* that can be successfully accomplished at remote but cheaper locations, and thus an ongoing tendency toward deagglomeration or dispersion of production,
2. *bursts of innovations* that create new activities requiring high levels of complex and unfamiliar co-ordination, which, in turn, generate bursts of agglomeration.

Competencies and patterns of organisational evolution are distributed **differently across countries** (Coriat/Dosi 1998: 104). In order to interpret these international and interregional differences one must take into account first the properties of the networks in which firms are embedded: these linkages with other firms shape and constrain the opportunities facing each firm to improve its problem-solving capabilities. Second, **national systems of production and innovation** also entail a broader notion of embeddedness of microeconomic behaviours into a set of social relationships, rules, and institutional constraints. In turn, these embeddedness properties contribute to determine the evolution of organisational structures and, together, competencies, and strategies (Coriat/Dosi 1998: 104).

In economic geography there are two important concerns about location and firm performance. The first is that economic, entrepreneurial, and technological activities tend to agglomerate at certain places, leading to patterns of national and regional specialisation. The second is that the performance and development of a firm to a considerable extent seems to be determined by the conditions that prevail in its environment, and that the conditions in the immediate locality – in the local cluster or local milieu – seem to be particularly important (Malmberg/Sölvell 1997: 119).

Agglomeration theory provides a starting point for considerations regarding the existence of *spatial clusters* of related industries. The basic sets for the observation of world production is subject to **regional concentration** (core regions), **spatial clustering** (particular industries tend to co-locate and form spatial clusters), and **path-dependence** (agglomerative process tends to be persistent over time) (Ibid. 121).

Two **types of agglomeration economies** may be distinguished. The *first* relates to general economies of regional and urban concentration and leads to the development of industrial core regions. The *second* type is constituted by specific economies that relate to firms engaged in similar or inter-linked activities, leading to the emergence of spatial clusters of related firms ('new industrial districts', 'innovative milieus'). This local network is typically a territorially agglomerated, local production system established by SMEs (Asheim 1997: 144).

A main argument in industrial geography is that **learning and knowledge creation** are also essential in what are normally regarded as low- or medium-tech industries. The competitive edge of many firms has shifted from static price competition towards dynamic improvement, favouring those, which can create knowledge more quickly than their competitors. An important aspect of economic globalisation is that it tends to convert formerly localised inputs into ubiquities (Malmberg 1997: 574). One of the few remaining genuinely localised phenomena in this increasingly **'slippery' global space economy** is precisely the **stickiness of some forms of knowledge and learning process** (Markusen 1996). The knowledge assets and learning abilities of particular local, regional, or national milieus therefore become a central element in the duality of '**global vs. local**'.

A basic condition for sustained competitiveness has more to do with capabilities leading to **dynamic improvement** than with achieving static efficiency. **Industrial systems** are dynamic arrangements based on knowledge creation rather than fixed flows of goods and services. Benefits of agglomeration are subtle and of a social rather than purely economic nature. The key is supposed to lie in the superior ability of such spatial configurations to enhance learning, creativity, and innovation (Malmberg/Sölvell 1997: 125). According to Andersson (1985), **creative reproduction in a region** depends on five **preconditions**:

1. high levels of competence,
2. many fields of academic and cultural activity,
3. good possibilities for internal and external communications,
4. widely shared perceptions of unsatisfied needs, and
5. a general situation of structural instability, promoting synergies.

In the local milieu, the **fluidity of knowledge** will be improved by the development of a **common code of communication and interaction**, particularly when knowledge is complex or costly to codify. The formal and informal networks between people in a common location, which have often developed through a long-term interaction, and the resulting evolution of **local institutions**, form part of the **social capital** surrounding innovation processes. The importance of **agglomeration economies** in promoting innovations concerns largely **incremental innovation**. Based on informal learning-by-doing and learning-by-using, primarily based on **tacit knowledge** (Asheim 1997: 148). Knowledge embedded in social capital involves a large number of actors within a local milieu and is historically bound to local circumstances, involving unique bonds and accumulated routines. Learning is predominately an interactive and socially embedded process, which cannot be understood without taking into account its institutional and cultural context (Lundvall 1992: 1). Generally, the *diffusion of knowledge within a local milieu is rapid*, while it is typically *slow between a local milieu and another* (Malmberg/Sölvell 1997: 127-128).

In the internationalisation process, with the gradual geographical dispersion of created assets, and as firms become more multinational by deepening or widening their cross-border value-chains, the **structure and content of the location portfolio** of firms becomes more critical to their **global competitive positions**. This applies both from the viewpoint of harnessing new competitive advantages and more efficiently deploying their home-based assets (Dunning 1998: 60).

For **MNEs**, as **brokers of knowledge**, the creation of knowledge may have an impact on **locational advantages** and **internalisation advantages**. If in a specific location the knowledge intensity is high and increasing, this may be an interesting locational endowment for certain types of economic activity. By locating there, the high knowledge intensity may become an important source for (external) **knowledge creation**. New knowledge may also influence the internalisation question, if it creates new circumstances for the strategy decisions on host country production and on the extent of control on foreign activities (Morsink 1998: 16-17). In an MNE network, a set of interlinked economic activities is not located at one specific point in geographical space. Search for the optimal combination of ownership and locational advantages provide the basis for the choice of locations for each activity. The existence for each activity of internalisation advantages determines whether its combination becomes a FDI (Morsink 1998: 22).

The incentive to organise **affiliate specialisation** is to tap into the locally specific and differentiated **stream of innovation in each location**, by specialising in accordance with these local strengths the latter are reinforced. The creation of **tacit capability** is localised and embedded in organisations. This organisational distinctiveness has a location-specific and a firm-specific dimension (Cantwell 1998: 283).

Insofar as knowledge-intensive and knowledge-supporting production has its unique spatial needs, it therefore appears reasonable to assume that both features will impinge on the geographical distribution of FDI and related activities. **Complementary foreign assets** and capabilities sought by MNEs wishing to add value to their core competitive advantages are increasingly of a **knowledge-facilitating kind**, and this is particularly the case as their affiliates become more firmly rooted in host economies (Dunning 1998: 53). A situation of regional divergence emerges in which a dichotomy evolves, distinguishing between **core and periphery regions** (Morsink 1998: 20).

The occurrence of **regional synergies** influences internationalisation processes. Transaction costs can be lowered when companies locate in regions where the bulk of their customers and their production factors are situated. This already creates locational advantages. According to the '**concept of localisation**' (Krugman 1991: 14-23), synergies are created in core regions in the field of labours skills, input provision, and information (including technological spillovers). These synergies create additional locational advantages for the core regions. Globalisation may then lead to a **dispersion of knowledge-intensive production** between and within countries and to a **convergence in cross-border economic structures**. It may equally lead to a concentration of such production in particular countries, and in microregions within those countries, in which case economic structures of the countries and microregions will tend to diverge from, rather than converge with, each other (Dunning 2000: 16).

4.1.1.1 Context and forms of local networks

The **agglomeration** and **path-dependence** of technological and economic development is expressed by the concept of the '**local milieu**'. Maillat (1996: 72) defines '**milieu**' as a **geographical entity** open to the outside world. It has its own know-how, rules and pool of connections. It is attached to a group of actors and contains specific human and material resources. It is subject to continual adjustment, transformation, and development processes triggered by interaction and learning. Interaction is fuelled by the stakeholders' ability to co-operate and to maintain interdependent relations. Learning reflects the ability to adjust behaviour, to implement new solutions, and to create new resources.

A '**local milieu**' is '*the set, or the complex network of mainly informal social relationships on a limited geographical area, often determining a specific external 'image' and a specific internal 'representation' and a sense of belonging which enhances the local innovative capability through synergetic and collective learning processes*' (Camagni 1991: 3). Local milieu therefore is related to but **not synonymous** with '**clusters**' or '**industrial districts**', which are special, largely extra-metropolitan areas in which certain types of firms cluster to gain advantages through co-operation and economies of scale and scope (Ibid.).

Creativity and continuous innovation in such a local or '**innovative milieu**' are the result of a collective learning process. This process is fed by such social phenomena as intergenerational transfer of know-how, imitation of successful managerial practices and technological innovations, interpersonal face-to-face contacts, formal, and informal co-operations between firms, tacit circulation of commercial, financial, or technological innovations. External linkages serve to provide '**negative entropy**' from outside the local network, in terms of new technological opportunities, new organisational models, or new marketing ideas to avoid the '**entropic death**' of a closed system (Camagni 1991: 1-3). Firm networks seem to be the most important instruments (Camagni 1991a: 140).

The **local milieu** performs the following **functions** for firms that are embedded in it (Camagni 1991a: 130):

- a *collective information-gathering and screening function* through informal interchange of information between participants, signalling of 'best practices', co-operative monitoring of markets, and technical change, etc.;
- a *function of signalling* for firms, e.g. in terms of its product image, or reputation;

- a *collective learning process*, mainly through skilled labour mobility within the local labour market, customer-supplier interchange, imitation processes, complementary information, and specialised services provision (transcoding function);
- a collective process of *definition of managerial styles and decision-routines*;
- an informal process of *decision co-ordination*;
- a function of *conversion of external synergies to the need of local firms* (transformer function).

Local milieus are viewed as **generators of innovative behaviour**. Two elements theoretically define their role:

1. *collective learning processes* enhance the local creativity and synergy;
2. processes of *reduction of the elements of dynamic uncertainty* in local contexts (Camagni 1991: 2).

The **innovative milieu** can be seen as the **brain of the local production system** in the sense that this is where the cognitive faculties of the actors are concentrated (Regnier 1996: 73). Innovative milieus have a dual organisation logic combining externalisation with respect to the international environment with organic integration at the local level (Gordon 1991: 183).

While local milieu and innovative milieu characterise the **context of local networks**, '*clusters*' and '*industrial districts*' reflect two distinct **forms of local networks**. Although the terms '*cluster*' and '*industrial districts*' are often used interchangeably, they cover two distinct concepts. **Clusters** can be defined as '*a group of producers making the same or similar things in close vicinity to each other*' (Schmitz 1992: 65). **Industrial districts** are geographical concentrations of firms and supporting agencies producing the same or similar things but which are underpinned by **strong networks** that confer benefits to the participants in the district. Thus all industrial districts are clusters, but not all clusters are industrial districts (McDonald/Burton 2002: 138). However, the differentiation of clusters and industrial districts in most of the literature is not clear and thus will not be used in the following.

Local networks are characterised by distinct competitive advantages. '**Cluster economies**' or '**external agglomeration economies**' result from externalities associated with the presence of a larger number of firms from one industry in a location, as opposed to internal agglomeration economies which represent savings from economies of scale. At its essence, cluster economies rest critically on the idea that there are **localised knowledge spillovers** within industry clusters (Zaheer/Manrakhan 2001: 675). **Tacit knowledge spillovers** are likely to remain localised while codified knowledge will not. Zaheer/Manrakhan (2001: 676) suggest that spatial and temporal proximity will determine where knowledge spreads first, even in the case of codified knowledge. Firms that seek to profit from information or which operate in industries that are critically dependent on augmenting intellectual capital therefore will need to continue to locate in clusters where information or knowledge emerges first. Effective scanning often requires an internalised global portfolio of locations in lead markets, as firm-owned **subsidiaries** can best act as '**antennae**' for local knowledge and information (Ibid. 678). Campbell/Verbeke (2001: 194) stress the major role that **multiple external networks** fulfil for firms, which compete globally, especially firms from small open economies for which the domestic external network may be quite small.

In the local network, the **fluidity of knowledge** will be improved by the development of **common codes of communication and interaction**, particularly when knowledge is difficult or costly to codify, and the build-up of trust between interacting parties is central to the business relation. The local network thus offers an environment for the evolution of a common language, social bonds, norms, values, and institutions, or a social capital, which adds to the process of innovation and new practice creation. Within the local cluster, these institutional arrangements become increasingly specialised and unique, adding **non-imitable competitive advantage** to incumbent firms (Sölvell/Birkinshaw 2000: 87).

The local network can favour the **sharing of means** allocated between different firms in the local network. By exploiting together economies of scale in distribution through cost sharing, the strategies of SMEs can begin to resemble those of larger firms. An initial effect of this strategy would therefore be a tendency toward local co-operation leading to export-oriented co-ordination rather than to international industrial co-operation. The opposite effect can result from the **collective learning process** by these firms. The existence of a local convention of long-term co-operation can facilitate the recourse to partnership modalities with international partners as well (Charbit 1996: 255). Especially three things help account for the **success of SME networks**: *economies of scale through networks*; *trust and co-operation coexisting with competition*; and *welfare effects* that increase the efficiency of the region and industry (Perrow 1992: 460). In each network there is a specific structure of information regarding the locus of capabilities, whether it be financial, productive, or scientific. In this sense, national and regional networks are themselves an expression of social knowledge (Grabher 1993: 25).

Geographical and relational proximity in a local milieu allow for **reduction in uncertainty** and **co-ordination costs** and provide a durable substrate for collective learning (Camagni/Capello 2002: 20). Collective learning and the **transfer of cumulated knowledge** in an innovative milieu are enhanced by an element of continuity and an element that may be interpreted as dynamic synergies. As in the case of learning processes, preconditions exist at the spatial level, which guarantee the development of **dynamic and creative synergies**. These preconditions are embedded in the capability of local firms to co-operate, not only on technical elements, but also on managerial and organisational ones, thanks to their **organisational and cultural proximity** (Camagni/Capello 2002: 21-22).

An empirical study by Camagni/Capello (2002: 36) suggests that **different learning channels** exist in milieus. The collective learning channels are exploited by the smallest and most innovative firms, which take advantage of spatial and territorial assets and use them to overcome the limits of their size. Entrepreneurs learn to leverage their competencies by establishing **dynamic linkages** to other firms in their local production environment (McNaughton/Bell 1999: 66). For large firms, mainly dealing with process innovation, a profile of learning internal to the firm was found to be typical. The study also proved a positive correlation between collective learning and radical innovation activities of small firms as well as between collective learning and factor productivity (Ibid. 37).

Mariotti/Piscittello (2001: 67) contend that the presence of **qualified capabilities** rather than generalised ones provide the local firms with **positive externalities** exploitable in international networks. A strong local dimension characterised by qualified capabilities complements and strengthens the local firm's distinctive competencies and specific advantages. Positive externalities from the local context stem from the presence of qualified localised capabilities such as specialised advanced services, a '**Marshallian atmosphere**', and scientific infrastructures (Ibid.).

The formal and informal networks between people in a common location, which have often been developed through long-term interaction, and the resulting evolution of institutions and business practices, form part of the social capital that surrounds local innovation systems. Whereas knowledge embedded in physical and human capital to an increasing extent travels on the global level through trade, FDI, and migration, knowledge embedded in social capital does not. **Locally embedded knowledge** therefore will remain *scarce, non-imitable, and non-substitutable on global scale* (Sölvell/Zander 1998: 406-407).

An '**invisible infrastructure**' of mediating institutions, or equivalently, a large endowment of social capital is therefore a feature of the locations that MNEs committed to flexibility are likely to seek out. Flexibility is not just an element of corporate strategy but a component of location advantage too. Such location advantages depend crucially on the nature of local institutions and local culture (Buckley/Casson 1998a: 36, Buckley 2000: 19).

4.1.1.2 Innovation in local networks

Rothwell (1994: 43) contends that there is considerable evidence to show that innovation today has become significantly more of a **networking process**. Innovation therefore has to be seen as an interactive process that involves a diverse range of actors with different backgrounds, cutting across organisational boundaries, combining skills, artefacts, knowledge, and experiences in new ways. This interaction is achieved through creating and maintaining networking relationships. Viewed at the aggregate level of a local economy, the *networks* that entrepreneurs develop can be described as the **social capital** of a business community (Routledge/von Amsberg 1996: 1). Generally, knowledge production is more likely in networks involving close linkages among multiple members who do not compete in the same market while networks with weak ties across social communities have been identified as important for knowledge diffusion. The important role of social networks and social communities in technology development has been stressed due to the high share of implicit knowledge in innovations (Newell/Swan 2000: 1290).

When the knowledge base of an industry is both complex and expanding and the sources of expertise are widely dispersed, the **locus of innovation** will be found in **networks of learning**, rather than in individual firms. For example, in a field of rapid technological development, such as biotechnology, the locus of innovation is found within networks of interorganisational relationships that sustain a fluid and evolving community (Powell et al. 1996: 116, 142).

Learning is a **social construction process**. In this view, what is learned is profoundly linked to the conditions under which it is learned. **Knowledge creation** occurs in the context of a community, one that is fluid and evolving rather than bound or static. Sources of innovation do not reside exclusively inside organisations. Consequently, the degree to which firms learn about new opportunities is to a high degree a function of the extent of their participation in activities with other organisations (Powell et al. 1996: 118). Internal capability is indispensable in evaluating research done outside, while external collaboration provides access to news and resources that cannot be generated internally. Firms must learn how to **transfer knowledge** across alliances and locate themselves in those **network positions** that enable them to keep pace with the most promising scientific or technological developments (Powell et al. 1996: 116-117).

When **collaboration** stems from membership in a **common technological community**, partnering is routinised and occurs more readily, with less effort. Collaboration becomes emergent, informal, and non-premediated on the basis of ongoing relationships. Once a firm begins collaborating, it develops experience at co-operation and a reputation as a partner. Subsequently firms develop capabilities for interacting with other firms (Powell et al. 1996: 121).

In the evolution of an industry, both firm-level and industry-level learning practices are evolving as a result of **reciprocal learning**, with boundaries ever more permeable. Increasingly, there appears to be a '**liability of unconnectedness**' at work in dynamic industries and other fields with rapid knowledge expansion (Powell et al. 1996: 143).

Camagni (1991: 8) emphasises that **technological innovation** is increasingly a **product of social innovation**, a process happening both at the intra-regional level in the form of collective learning processes, and through inter-regional linkages facilitating the firm's access to different, though localised, innovation capabilities. In the course of globalisation and technological change, SMEs in the local milieus have to foster their capability to break path-dependence and to change technological trajectory through radical innovation (Asheim 1997: 150). Cooke (1996: 55) contends that **innovative SMEs** differ from non-innovative SMEs by having **dense external networks** involving other innovative SMEs in a variety of relationships involving infrastructural institutions such as universities and private sector research institutes. An **important option for SMEs** is to consequently develop such **relationships** with organisations on the **global level** in order to develop a competitive innovative capacity on the global level and to reduce the dependence of the local context. Inter-organisational networking is of strategic importance to SMEs and supports a strategy of '**learning-by-interacting**' (Asheim 1997: 162). In addition, an **entrepreneurial culture** in both the firm and the local milieus represents a competitive advantage, providing a sustained capability for innovation (Casson 1990: 86-87).

Uncertainty and trial-and-error problem solving, the need to exchange knowledge through face-to-face contact, and repeated interaction with other firms provide an interrelated set of factors, which favours **locally confined innovation processes**. The costs and time associated with local knowledge exchange are further reduced by the evolution of a common code of communication, institutions, norms, and values, i.e. a social capital that adds to the process of accumulated learning (Sölvell/Zander 1998: 409).

Burkhardt/Brass (1990: 111) assume that the **diffusion of a technological change** will occur through **structural patterns of interaction**. Thus, whether or not actors adopt a new innovation is a function of the social context in which they act and communicate. Burkhardt/Brass (Ibid. 120) found prove that **early adopters** to a new technology increase their **network centrality** and their **power** following a change in technology. Powerful, central figures prior to the change were not totally displaced by early adopters, especially depending on the role in the transformation process. Globally operating firms therefore have to develop the distinct capability of dynamic positioning in their network environment.

The **structural evolution of innovation logics** has created a **complex global regional mosaic** as each new round of adjustment and restructuring freezes some regional formations in place, induces adaptation in others, and brings entirely new regions into the ambit of global industrial organisation. The spatial organisation of the industry is differentiated by a conjunction of autonomous regional capabilities, the temporal/structural evolution of global industrial organisation and the application of social learning processes. Successive changes in the logic of innovation have produced a **variegated hierarchy of technological spaces** (Gordon 1991: 182).

As **location matters** especially for **innovation**, companies must broaden their approaches to the management of innovation accordingly by developing and commercialising innovation in the most attractive location. Firms have to take active steps by accessing locational strengths, and proactively enhancing the environment for innovation and commercialisation in locations where they operate. Complementary to **locational differences**, powerful **spillovers** and **externalities across industries** are vital to the rate of innovation (Porter/Stern 2001: 29-30).

While utilising components of the existing spatial hierarchy, the emerging **global structure of network interdependencies** valorises the **specificity of locational attributes in new spaces**. Neither the spatial dispersal of discrete high-technology regional economies nor the spatial decentralisation of specialised production functions can meet the complex innovation requirements of global production chains. As a consequence, networks must increasingly mobilise the unique innovative capabilities of different regional production systems while simultaneously connecting these largely informal mechanisms are insufficient either to initiate or to sustain creative activity as technical-economic complementarities force firms to incorporate extra-regional sources of innovation. The resources available in global inter-firm networks must complement local innovation linkages. Localised agglomeration thus becomes the principle basis for participation in a global network of regional economies (Gordon 1991: 190). Increasingly, **international networks of relationships** are interlocked with **local networks** having a regional dimension (Cappellin 1991: 240).

The expansion of international production brings gains to the firm as a whole, as the experience gained from adapting its technology under new conditions feeds back new ideas for development to the rest of the system. Once they have achieved a sufficient level of technological strength in their own right, firms are particularly keen to produce in the areas from which their major international rivals have emanated, which offer them access to alternative sources of complementary innovation (Cantwell 1989: 11).

The fact that the physical externalities and the know-how of the localised actors are institutionalised within the same territory involves a potential reinforcement process. Moreover, since the externalities are collective goods, they can be appreciated not only by the actors who have contributed to their promotion but also by larger groups so that other local agents may be incited to join the networks. Thus the collective learning process is enlarged and the contribution of new competencies opens the way to more important achievements (Perrin 1991).

☞ **Bridging innovation in local networks and MNEs**
The **technological accumulation approach** addresses the question of why it is that technology is developed in international networks, rather than in a series of separately owned plants. From the perspective of the internalisation theory, the initiating firm is to appropriate a full return on its technological advantage if it is to co-ordinate the successful introduction of its new technology elsewhere, then it must exercise direct control over the network as a whole. In the evolutionary view, technological competence is not an immediate usable intermediate product in its own right, but is rather an input into the collective corporate learning process by which tacit capability and hence technology as a whole is generated. Firms search for profits through innovation and by generating new value-creating technological capabilities (Cantwell 2001: 438-439). A potentially important **source of competitive advantage for MNE** is the **capacity of their foreign subsidiaries to generate innovations** based on stimuli and resources resident in the **heterogeneous host country environments** in which they operate (Frost 2001: 101).

Due to **technological accumulation processes**, technological knowledge bought externally must be adapted to the specific context of the firm's own tacit capability. It has to be incorporated into an existing **stream of innovation**, and this adaptation becomes part and parcel of the on-going process within an established firm of generating its own technology (Cantwell 2001: 440). By extending its network, each firm extends the use of its own line of technological development, and by extending it into new environments it increases the complexity of this development. The expansion of international production thereby brings gains to the firms as a whole, as the experience gained from adapting its technology under new conditions feeds back new ideas for development to the rest of the system. Firms therefore are particularly keen to invest in locations with a high innovative capacity. The notion that the **geographical dispersion of technological development** enhances **innovation** in the network of the **MNE as a whole** is founded on the belief that innovation is both location-specific and firm-specific.

The **increased role of locationally dispersed sourcing of technology** from the major centres of excellence through the networks of more globally integrated MNEs creates a more complex technological system. MNEs therefore accelerate the technological progress due to the integration of locally developed technologies and their **rapid global diffusion**. Though MNEs are often capable to diffuse their technologies with minor adaptations, **networking between local contexts** is a mutual adaptation process. If foreign networks are structurally similar to domestic ones, creating linkages is relatively easy because there is little need for adaptation on either side. Similarity reduces transaction costs and cuts short the learning process envisaged by the cumulative approach to FDI (Chen/Chen 1998: 448). For example, a study by Ghoshal/Bartlett (1988: 365) revealed positive impacts of normative integration through organisational socialisation and dense intra- and inter-unit communication on an MNE's ability to contribute to the innovation tasks of creation, adoption, and diffusion of innovations.

Even where **MNEs** establish networks in which technological activity is locationally specialised across the major centres, this does not destroy the **distinctiveness of their national origins**. Firms follow differentiated paths to learning even when their fields of research are similar. Hence the nature of their tacit capability is path-dependent, and reflects their starting point in nationally differentiated types of expertise (Cantwell 2001: 445). R&D moves overseas much more slowly than production, sourcing, and other business activities. In general, **most MNEs** centralise **core research and product development** in the **home market**, while research oriented toward **customisation** and foreign production support is gradually conducted **locally** (Doremus 1999: 89). The data from the study of Doremus (1999: 107) also imply that technology typically is developed in the home market operations of MNEs and gradually extends abroad in the wake of FDI.

Such **Schumpeterian models of innovation** usually emphasise discontinuity and '**creative destruction**'. For example, the international product life cycle represents an application of the Schumpeterian approach to economic development in the sphere of international trade, based on radical innovation with subsequent diffusion and imitation by other firms. MNEs exploit centrally developed ownership advantages in favourable locations. The model is ignoring **incremental, competing, and co-operative innovations** (Cantwell 1989: 52). Furthermore, firms increasingly gain **advantages from multinationality per se** and the development of a stronger division of labour across a **globally integrated network of activities**, rather than the exploitation of any particular set of technological or similar advantages (Cantwell 1989: 69).

By reorganising themselves around the development of core skills, firms have become much more dependent upon economies of scope, and less dependent on economies of scale. This is especially true for large MNEs and this has undermined the major motive for geographical concentration. This has widened their capacity to innovate, and to diffuse new technological advances more rapidly to all parts of the network, enhancing further technology creation and production. It has also increased their ability to enter into co-operations with other innovative firms to their mutual benefit, as the pattern of their technological accumulation overlaps and becomes more complementary (Ibid. 95).

Production agglomerates in certain sites through a process of cumulative causation. The most dynamic locations continually attract new production facilities and upgrade their existing activity, while at the least successful locations plants close and lack new investment. The strongest firms of an industry are all drawn to the **main international centres of innovation**, and in the process they help to further strengthen the local technological capacity of such centres. The trend will be for the strongest MNEs in each sector to locate both research and production facilities in all major sites of innovative activity in their industry (Ibid. 139-141).

MNEs produce in **centres of innovation** in order to gain access to new sources of technology creation, as well as to more effectively implement their own variety of technology in a different environment (Ibid. 158). Some studies suggested that in an internationally integrated or globalised MNE, the **geographical dispersion of innovation** might come to facilitate the technological development of the firm, since the MNE can tap into **alternative streams of innovation in different centres**, and establish favourable **cross-border interactions** between them. In this event the internationalisation of technological activity will go more substantially beyond the role of facilitating the local exploitation of the MNE's core capabilities, and will instead become a more central part of the process by which its capabilities are developed and extended. The emergence of corporate international networks for technological development has led to the diversification or evolution of firm-specific competencies into new fields of activity, through a restructuring of innovation across geographical sites to better access the local capabilities of each host country (Cantwell/Piscitello 1999: 124).

In the **most successful locations for any industry** technology accumulates rapidly and **domestic firms** gain the **capacity** to become **MNEs** as they begin to expand into international markets. The technology used must be adapted to local conditions. The process of adaptation involves drawing on local types of technology and integrating them with those of the MNE, taking technological development in a direction, which both expands the horizon of the investing firm and widens local capability. By the same token, if firms that are innovating successfully in one location and wish to also draw on the complementary innovations that may be more easily developed in an alternative location, then they must enter into foreign production (Cantwell 1989: 140).

Technology export and import patterns indicate that **cross-border technology flows** certainly have increased over time, yet those flows consistently have stayed within **multinational corporate networks**. Despite the still high degree of centralisation in technology development, **technology** is increasingly **globalised through co-operative forms** of inter-firm transaction in order to share costs and risks as well as to gain access to a wider range of technologies. Most of these alliances are concentrated in a few high-technology industries, particularly information technology, biotechnology, and new materials (Doremus 1999: 107, 112). Given their extensive international production and sourcing networks, MNEs are particularly likely to transfer technology abroad in the form of people, organisational assets, and intermediate goods (Ibid. 133).

The increasing scope from technological interchanges between MNEs has provided greater incentives for companies not to restrict themselves to creating their own intra-firm networks but also to join with other MNEs in **inter-firm networks** in selected areas of parallel lines of activity. This development is even augmented by the trend towards **technology fusion** (Cantwell 2001: 445, Kodama 1992). According to Cantwell (2001: 447), the increasing significance of technological interrelatedness and fusion is one aspect of a new techno-economic paradigm. The **old paradigm** was based on energy and oil-related technologies, and on mass production with its **economies of scale** and specialised corporate R&D. This paradigm has gradually been displaced by a **new paradigm grounded on economies of scope** derived from the interaction between flexible but linked production facilities, and a greater diversity of search in R&D. Individual plant flexibility and network linkages both depend upon the new information and communication technologies.

Firms increase the returns on their **own R&D** through suitably adapting their underlying tacit capability so that they can absorb and apply the **complementary knowledge acquired from other locations or firms** more intensively in their own internal learning process. This is especially pertinent for MNEs developing technology in dispersed locations, as potential opportunities for cross-border learning have been enhanced by an increased use of ICT technologies. **ICT specialisation** seems to amplify the firm's technological flexibility by enabling it to fuse together a **wide range of formerly separated technologies**. The ICT-based paradigm promotes cross-firm and cross-border knowledge flows although knowledge-intensive fields of activities and an industry's core technologies appear to require a greater intensity of face-to-face interaction (Ibid. 447). Cantwell (Ibid. 448) therefore expects the more typical pattern of international specialisation in innovative activities in MNEs to be for the development of technologies that are core to the firm's industry to be concentrated at home, while complementary research tends to be international.

Frost (2001: 103) notes that notwithstanding the intuitive appeal of the argument, **evidence that multinationals actually utilise the technological and institutional diversity to generate innovations is fragmented** and **contradictory**. An empirical study by Frost (2001: 120) supports both the strategic and the embeddedness perspective on external innovation networks. Frost (2001: 115) found evidence that if a subsidiary's innovation is adaptive in nature (exploitation of existing advantages), it will be more likely to draw upon technical ideas originating in the home country than the host country. A further result was that the greater leadership position of the subsidiary was in a particular technical field, the greater was the likelihood that a subsidiary innovation in that field will draw upon technical ideas originating in the host country. Similarly, the greater was the innovation scale of the subsidiary, the greater was the likelihood that its innovations will draw upon technical ideas originating in the host country.

In sum, there are **consistent cross-national variations** in the level and composition of FDI, the degree to which MNEs maintain trade within their own corporate networks, and the extent to which foreign affiliates are integrated with local markets. The study of Doremus (1999: 132) strongly suggests that there are inherent and enduring structural factors that profoundly influence the location decisions and operating styles of MNEs from different countries in the Triad. For example, U.S. and U.K. firms tend to be more integrated with the foreign economies in which they operate, while German and especially Japanese MNEs tend to retain large shares of their innovation and trading operations within their company networks.

A study by Cantwell/Piscitello (1999: 126) proved that by at least the 1980s, the **nature of the competence creation process** seems to have entered a **new phase**, based upon the ability to create an **internal intra-firm but cross-border network** for the development of both geographically and sectorally **dispersed competencies**. MNEs have begun to utilise the internationalisation of technological development as a means of accessing locationally specialised branches of innovation across national boundaries. The result is a more complex integrated and interactive network for the generation of new competence. This new system for corporate development relies on the interrelatedness between specialised activities conducted in particular locations, each of which takes advantage of spatially specific resources or capabilities. In this event internationalisation, diversification, and competence creation - historically with little direct connection between each other - become necessarily interconnected and thus mutually positively related parts of a common process (Cantwell/Piscitello 1999: 127). The study provides evidence that the largest and technologically leading firms have witnessed the emergence of corporate **international networks** for the accumulation of both **geographically and sectorally dispersed technological competencies** (Ibid. 144).

4.1.1.3 Local path-dependence

Local milieus offer a **high innovative capacity** in the industry and the field of capabilities that historically agglomerated in the respective locality. Teece et al. (1994: 16) argue that the local nature of enterprise learning significantly restricts what firms can do. Their future activities therefore are highly dependent on what they have done in the past. Following the notion of **path-dependence**, a firm's **previous investments** and its **repertoire of routines** (its '*history*') constrains its **future behaviour**. This implicates that opportunities for successful new developments will be '*close in*' to previous activities and will thus be transaction and product specific. Learning is a process of trial, feedback, and evaluation. If too many parameters are changed at the same time, the ability of firms to conduct meaningful behaviour is constrained. The same applies to the strategic level where cognitive limits of managers and the costliness of information systems restrict the range of businesses and products that most managers can understand (Ibid. 17). **Ownership advantages** such as core competencies may be expected to have a **strong contextual embeddedness**. Especially the important implicit and tacit components of such organisational knowledge may be locationally '**sticky**'. Stickiness of a given unit of information in a given instance is the incremental expenditure required to transfer that unit of information to a specified locus in a form usable by a given information seeker (von Hippel 1998: 61). Information therefore is sticky when it is costly to acquire, transfer, and use.

Nachum (1999: 21-23) proposes that the **understanding of the nature of ownership advantages** of firms requires a **time-series analysis**. Such a need is supposed to be even more evident in the case of **intangible assets**. Unlike tangible assets, accumulation of intangible assets (e.g. reputation) requires ongoing, conscious efforts over a long period of time. The **initial stages** of the development of ownership advantages of firms take place in the **home country**. Still, the home country is the single most important site for innovation and the most critical source of competitive advantages. The **production of technology** therefore '*remains far from globalised*' (Ibid. 64). As firms expand their international activity, the impact of the home country on their competitiveness diminishes and the impact of other locations increases (Ibid. 160). The more advantages are embodied in culturally specific assets, the stronger the impact of the home countries (Ibid. 206). In a similar vein, Dicken (1994: 117-118) contends that MNEs are not placeless but essentially embedded within their domestic environment. MNEs are thus produced through a **complex historical process of embedding**, in which cognitive, cultural, social, political, and economic characteristics of the **national home base** play a dominant part.

The **specific path of innovation** in each firm and at each location is constrained by a system of technological interrelatedness between companies and types of activity. **Interrelatedness**

between firms is an especially important influence on the **locational specificity of innovation**, as it may be costly to change the prevailing methods in an individual firm or sector without complementary changes elsewhere (Cantwell 1991: 41). To gain full access to a **complementary stream of innovations** the firm requires a **direct local presence**, through a combination of research and related skills and routines in production (Ibid. 53). Evidence was found in the sectoral pattern of intra-industry production between the USA and Germany. American firms have been especially attracted to locate production in Germany in sectors in which German technological activity is comparatively advantaged, while German firms have been similarly disposed to set up U.S. production in those fields in which American technological capability is strongest (Cantwell 1991: 54).

According to Cantwell (1989), who studied the post-war growth of international trade and production of the manufacturing firms of the industrialised countries, MNE expansion can be linked to a process of cumulative technological change within the firm, in which innovation and the growth of international production are mutually supportive (Cantwell 1989: 7). The term of '**technological accumulation**', originally coined by Pavitt (1987), encapsulates the idea that the development of technology within a firm is a cumulative process. Technology encompasses both scientific and organisational factors.

Innovation and technological accumulation is basically an **incremental process**. Even radically new technologies, once they move the purely scientific and experimental stage, often rely on or are integrated with earlier technologies in the course of their development. For this reason, innovation tends to gather certain logic of its own through the continual refinement, extension, and combination of existing technologies. Until there is a new stream of **path-breaking innovation**, firms at the existing frontier of progress tend to establish dynamic advantages. For example, this helps explain why German firms in the chemical industry have maintained a strong tradition for a period of at least a hundred years (Cantwell 1989: 18-19). New products and processes are not independent of one another, and they tend to fall into technological paths or trajectories followed by groups of competing firms and their suppliers and customers (Ibid. 53).

'**Economies of variety over time**' means the **ability of a technology district** to turn out a changing array of outputs in the general product field in which it is specialised so as to outrun the catch-up effect from ever more rapid imitation and convergent productivity. '**Product-based technology learning**' may constitute a dynamic technological advantage of technology districts. It means the ability continuously to reinvent, differentiate, improve, and reconfigure products through a dynamic redeployment of key, specialised production skill and equipment (Storper 1992: 65-66).

Firms located in local networks may exploit '**localised capabilities**' that emerge in the respective region. According to Maskell et al. (1998), the concept of localised capabilities includes the institutional environment, the built structures, the natural resources, and the knowledge and skills of an area. The firm absorbs competencies and resources embodied in its local environment (Mariotti/Piscittello 2001: 676). According to Dierickx/Cool (1989), firm resources are difficult to imitate if they depend on unique historical conditions, the link between resources and competitive advantage is causally ambiguous or the resources are socially complex. These characteristics may give local firms a **comparative advantage** also on the **global level**.

For certain kinds of goods, particular places develop superior innovation or know-how capacities, and are able to keep learning and updating their knowledge faster than competitors, enabling them to take important shares of world markets in those goods. Such local networks may have a few big leaders or they may be comprised of firms of equal size. Usually, they have very complex labour market processes, which also serve to transfer knowledge between firms and enhance the knowledge development capacities of the whole cluster. Such **clustered, knowledge-based industries** are **highly localised as production systems**, but **globalised on the output side**; that is why they show up as **export specialisation**. Their degree of import-openness on the input side is usually lower than their degree of export penetration on the output side. They are cases of local economies, which are motors of world trade (e.g. mechanical engineering industries of Germany or the aircraft industries of Italy) (Storper 2000: 46-47).

It is helpful in outlining the idea of local not on the basis of a rigid dichotomy between local (district) enterprises and non-local enterprises (MNEs), but between different **forms and intensities of embeddedness** (Varaldo 1995: 28):

1. For the *district enterprise, embeddedness* will be *natural* (connected to its entire life cycle), totalising (involving the entire network of its articulations, knowledge, and culture) and thus dependent on local external economies.
2. For the *MNE*, it will assume a *planned character* (strategic choice), selective, and interdependent (on global network level).

Both large and small enterprises are in a process of '**double convergence**' (Conti 1997: 24). Growing environmental complexity induces both SMEs and MNEs to search different styles of behaviour (in time and space), aimed at constructing more effective interactive relations, both with other firms and with the relevant socio-cultural context. In global competition, diversity becomes the basis of competitive advantage and the instrument for the production of economic value (Conti 1995: 3-4). The most effective management of local resources occurs through culturally decentralised organisation, capable of interacting and co-evolving with the local environment. **Key capabilities** in the network environment are what Asanuma (1989) calls '**relation-specific skills**'. They constitute a key economic basis of external accumulation of know-how in these networks.

Research on industrial districts, which are characterised by **network structures of SMEs**, has shown, that the latter can develop **substantial competitive advantages** by **flexible specialisation** and **network learning** (Staber 1998). Recent research indicates that these advantages seem to diminish on the classical regional level, e.g. the regions of Emilia Romagna and Baden Wuerttemberg (Ibid. 721). This might be attributed to the generally decreasing importance of boundaries. On the other hand, co-operation activities of SMEs on and between international industry levels seem to increase.

Even large MNEs partake of wider institutional contexts and systems of externalities, which enable them to generate new commercialisable knowledge (systems of innovation), and these are highly specific to particular countries and regions (Cooke 1996: 47). One of the unique competitive advantages of the large MNE in a knowledge-based, globalising economy is its ability to identify, access, harness, and effectively co-ordinate and deploy resources and capabilities from throughout the world (Ibid. 28). On the other hand there is the question, what '**localised capabilities**' (Maskell et al. 1998) make for strong firm performance in terms of innovations and learning. Malmberg (1997: 576) differentiates three **categories of explanatory dimensions**:

1. *industrial configuration/degree of 'districtness'* as reflected in agglomeration economies and industrial districts literature,
2. *technological infrastructure* of places and regions, and
3. *culture and institutions*.

In industries where the relevant know-how is broadly dispersed, innovation depends on cooperative interaction among different types of organization. The locus becomes a network rather than an individual firm. **Networks** are particularly well suited for **rapid learning** and the **flexible deployment of resources** (Powell/Brantley 1992: 388-389). Where similar businesses are collected together in an **industrial district**, the district serves as an **invisible college**, in which ideas are exchanged and developed: conjecture, refutation, and also criticism are encouraged. In addition to this pattern of competition and collaboration with similar businesses in the generation of new knowledge, firms are linked to suppliers and customers in a network of information and ideas, which provide an **agenda for innovation** (Loasby 1991: 40).

While the importance of international, intra-company information networks has been demonstrated in a number of studies, the link between internal and external networks and processes has yet to be adequately explored, as Macdonald (1992: 54) in a broader information network context has noted: *'There has been much investigation of internal and external information networks ... though precisely how the two may be connected still remains an area ripe for research'.*

The **international domain** adds an extra dimension of complexity to **intra-company information networks**, because of the need to overcome **country-related cultural** and **other communication barriers**, even though there might be a strong, overall company culture promoting cohesion, as well as ready-made cross-country organisational linkages (Welch 1996: 187). The internal dynamics of the firm, complemented by internal/external dynamics of open-system networking models of industrial organisation, propagate a **virtuous circle of regional economic growth dynamics** particular relevant to the **'knowledge-driven' economy**. Growth involves some combination of new firms and growth of existing firms. New and rapidly growing firms emerge from and develop within an industrial infrastructure constituted by a larger population of specialist and affiliated enterprises. A firm's capabilities are shaped in a mutually interdependent process. These **inter-firm processes** involve simultaneously **resource co-ordination** and **capability creation** (Best 2002: 185-186).

Best (Ibid.) characterises the extension of the internal growth dynamics of the firm to the region and inter-firm networking processes. The entrepreneurial firm is driven by a technology/market dynamic. The term dynamic connotes an ongoing historical process in which both technology and market are mutually redefined. Firms pursue unique capabilities but the process of developing such capabilities creates new productive opportunities in terms of a refined match between product or services performance and customer demand, existing and inchoate. In the process of redefining the product, the market, too, is re-characterised. The new market opportunities feed back to motivate changes in productive capabilities setting in motion a new dynamic. In this process the firm has to resolve the dilemma that unique capabilities are both the source of competitive advantage and a constraint on future development (Ibid. 186-187).

The idea of an **internal/external dynamic** captures the interactive process between **firm** and **region**, which propagate growth. The capability-creating process of the entrepreneurial firm is the source of the internal dynamics, but the firm exists within a large system of inter-firm relations and dynamics, which condition its opportunities. Thus a firm's opportunities to specialise and develop its unique capabilities are shaped externally by the constellation of enterprises and capabilities with which it can partner. The new firm creation process is itself an aspect of mutual adjustment (Ibid. 190).

The new productive and market opportunities not exploited by the entrepreneurial firm become opportunities for new firms in a process of technological diversification. New firms and spin-offs can trigger a process of **industrial 'speciation'** or the emergence of new industry subsectors (Best 2002: 187). A study of 19 industrial districts in Italy by Corò/Grandinetti (1999: 117) provided also evidence of a **key transformation** in all observed districts. The traditionally rather **closed local networks are all opening-up** and relating increasingly with external holders of knowledge and resources.

Patterns of corporate technological specialisation are differentiated and firm specific, groups from common countries of origin have certain **country-specific features** in the form of their expertise, and the profiles of specialisation persist over time, reflecting a **path-dependent technological accumulation** or corporate technological trajectories (Cantwell 2002: 235).

The **growth dynamic of the entrepreneurial firm** is increasingly propagated to the larger industrial system. In the course of this process, **inter-firm networking** develops as it offers greater efficiency and flexibility for *co-specialisation, new product development*, and *innovation*. A range of **intra- and inter-firm dynamic processes** underlies **capability development** at both the enterprise and regional levels. **Regional specialisation** results from path-dependence, the unique combinations, and patterns of intra- and inter-firm dynamics, which underlie enterprise and regional specialisation (Best 2002: 188-190).

In a study of the **German 'Ruhrgebiet'**, the *'industrial heartland of Germany'* based on coal, iron and steel, Grabher (1993a) shows that the **initial strengths** of industrial districts of the past – their industrial atmosphere, highly developed and specialised infrastructure, the close inter-firm linkages and strong political support by regional institutions – turned into stubborn **obstacles to innovation**. Regional development became **'locked in'** by the very socio-economic conditions that once made these regions stand out against the rest. These districts fell into the trap of **'rigid specialisation'**. This *'rigid specialisation trap'* was caused by a threefold lock-in of regional development (Ibid. 256-264):

1. The *'functional lock-in'* was produced by a co-specialisation of functions and investments and led to a neglect of the adaptation to the dynamics of the economic environment.

2. The '*cognitive lock-in*' developed on the basis of a common orientation that was reinforced by social processes such as '*groupthink*'. The handicap was caused by the '*weakness of strong ties*', which prevent a dynamic co-evolution with the external environment. Personal cohesiveness and well-established relations within the coal, iron, and steel complex provided the basis for mutual orientations involving a common language and shared mental maps.

3. The '*political lock-in*' evolved along the historical trajectory of the economic development of the Ruhr area and was effectively supported by co-operative relations between industry, the federal government, regional and local planning authorities, unions, and professional associations, all meeting in a culture of consensus on the given technological trajectory.

The study by Grabher illustrates that adaptation to a specific economic environment may undermine a region's adaptability. Adaptation endangers adaptability through what Grabher (1993a: 265) terms a '**process of involution**'. While the system optimises the fit into its environment, it loses its adaptability. The internal coherence of the system results in a '**pathological homeostasis**'. Adaptation leads to an increasing specialisation of resources and a pronounced preference for innovations that reproduce existing structures, a process similar to the development of a dominant design with a technological lock-in on industry level. The difference exists in the intensive social embeddedness and '**social contracts**' between different social actors on the district level.

From a **regional policy view**, *agglomerated learning capability* becomes a condition for both dominating the relevant global economic networks and securing the cumulative industrial development of the '*home base*', by attracting and supporting the best quality domestic and overseas firms (Amin/Thrift 1995: 275). Industrial districts can thus be sustained as '**learning regions**'. Traditional **contextual knowledge** and the **codified knowledge of the global economy** could thus be integrated in a framework of territorially **embedded regional systems of innovation**. Such learning regions are supposed to be in a much better position than traditional industrial districts to avoid a lock-in of development caused by localised path-dependence (Asheim 1997: 165-166). Porter/Stern (2001: 29) stress the importance of the common innovation infrastructure and especially of the cluster-specific environment for innovation in core industries of an economic region.

4.1.2 Business networks

In the '**markets-as-networks**' research tradition, initially developed by researchers in industrial and international marketing research, individual firms are connected to other firms in networks of exchange relationships between firms. Johanson/Mattson (1988) conceptualise

industrial markets as **networks of relationships**. Networks of multidimensional exchange relationships between actors who control heterogeneous, interdependent resources constitute the generic structure of production systems and carry out interlinked activities for value creation and consumption (Mattson 1998: 243). The underlying concept of exchange relationship can be viewed as a set of more or less **implicit rules**, which are related to the exchange in the same way as language is related to communication. A basic assumption of the network model is that those rules imply a **mutual orientation**, including mutual knowledge, trust, and interest awareness of actors to each other (Johanson 1989: 73).

In any field of industrial activity can be identified a network of connected interaction relations between firms engaged in industrial activities, which is called '**industrial network**' (Håkansson 1990: 371). The industrial network consists of the actors and the relations among them, but it also consists of certain activities/resources and the dependencies between them. Each actor controls certain activities and resources directly, but because the dependencies to some extent mean control, the actor has an indirect control over the counterparts' activities and resources. An industrial network comprises, then, both an activity/resource dimension and an actor dimension. Both dimensions are tightly related to each other. An industrial network is a web of relatively interdependent activities performed on the basis of a certain constellation of resources (Håkansson/Johansson 1993: 38).

The **boundaries of the network** may be drawn on the basis of technology, country, a focal organisation, and the like. All such boundaries are arbitrary. Different actors therefore will identify different boundaries as a result of perspectives, intentions, and interpretations. The industrial network is a **product of history**. The actors have memories of their interaction, developed knowledge about other actors, and have made investments in the relations with their partners. In this historical development, there is an inherent tendency to structuring, making the links stronger and more stable, as well as strengthening the power of established actors. On the other hand, other actors, both internal and external, may change and even break up the network (Håkansson 1990: 371).

Industrial networks are not designed according to a master plan or strategic decision. They **emerge** and develop as a consequence of interaction between semiautonomous, interdependent industrial actors. In industrial networks, each actor controls some resources directly and some resources indirectly via dependence relations with other actors, thus constituting a power structure. An interest structure is formed by conflicting and common interests (Ibid.).

In the process of **network evolution** the parties form **bonds of various kinds**. *Technical bonds* are related to the parties' knowledge about their business, *social bonds* in the form of personal confidence, *administrative bonds* related to the administrative routines and procedures of the firms, and *legal bonds* in the form of contracts between the firms (Johanson/Mattsson 1987: 35, Håkansson 1990: 373). Knowledge and experience is shared among actors in an industrial network, constituting the basis for **industry recipes** and **consensual domains** (Borghoff/Welge 2003).

Each actor has a **position** in a specified network that can be described by its relationships to other actors and by the actor's functional and quantitative roles in the production system. Strategic objectives can be defined in terms of network positions. The actor's strategic actions are aimed at influencing exchange relationships and positions in networks (Mattson 1998: 244). *Two levels* can be distinguished with regard to **network positions** (Johanson/Mattson 1986: 245, 1988: 307):

1. The *micro-positions* of a firm are characterised by
   - the role the firm has for the other firm,
   - its importance for the other firm, and
   - the strength of the relationship with the other firm.
2. The *macro position* is also affected by interdependencies:
   - the identity of the other firms in the network,
   - the role of the firm in the network,
   - the importance of the firm in the network, and
   - the strength of the relationships with other firms in the network.

The **positions** characterise the **roles** that the firms play in the network and are consequences of earlier activities in the network. It takes time, effort, and resources to establish, maintain, and change positions (Johanson/Mattson 1985: 187). They are the base for the present and future activities and are *defined by*

- the functions performed by the firm for other firms,
- the importance of the firm in a network,
- the strength of the relationships with the other firms, and
- the identity of the firms with which a particular firm has direct of indirect relations (Johanson/Mattson 1985: 188, Mattson 1989: 122-123).

The **structuredness of a network** refers to how interdependent the positions of different firms are. In **tightly structured networks**, there is a clear division of labour between firms, technologies are well defined, and bonds are strong. Entry and exit of firms are not frequent.

Loosely structured networks have low interdependence, unclear roles, weak bonds, and frequent changes in membership (Johanson/Mattson 1986: 247, Mattson 1989: 123). The social structure of a network is also an expression of knowledge. The **competitive strengths** of a company lie partly in the nature of its **relations** with other firms and institutions. Firms build up over time **unique assets** in terms of knowing where to find certain technologies or buyers, how to co-operate for the development of new products or whom to fund in external, university-based research centres (Kogut et al. 1993: 77).

The firm has a **strategic identity** with regard to the views about the **firm's role and position** in relation to other firms in the industrial network. The strategic identity is formed and developed through the interaction with other firms (Håkansson 1990: 373). A firm's activities are **cumulative processes** in the sense that relationships are constantly being established, maintained, developed and broken in order to give satisfactory, short-term economic returns and to create positions in the network that will ensure the long-term survival and development of the firm (Johanson/Mattson 1993: 257). Different actors interpret the web itself - as well as the connections between activities and resources - in different ways because of differences in either knowledge or intentions. The network is continuously changing in that relations are broken or created, and network actors change because of changes in resources or in the intentions of the actors (Forsgren 1989: 35, Håkansson/Johanson 1993: 38). From a dynamic point of view, it is more important how individual co-operations are related to each other than how each of them is designed (Håkansson 1990: 376).

In developing the business relationship the partners adapt their resources, routines, and processes to each other in a **process of mutual specialisation**. The changes are usually gradual, implying that over time, the firms adapt their business activities to each other's way of doing business thereby modifying their capabilities. The mutual adaptation in ongoing business relationships therefore is also a mutual development of the partner's capabilities. Such a relationship is an important asset. It is a **platform for future transactions** and **knowledge development**. It creates knowledge and develops competence that may be of wider significance for the firm's capability (Andersson et al. 1997: 72). Although each business relationship provides unique, tacit knowledge, the **combined knowledge** from a *set of business relationships* gives the business firm its **specific capability** (Ibid. 75).

Relating the activities of two parties to one another entails adaptations and the *establishment of routines on both sides*. **Reciprocal knowledge** and **capabilities** are revealed and developed jointly and in *mutual dependence*. Through their relationship either party can to some degree gain access to the other's resources. Actors can therefore mobilise and use resources controlled by other actors in the network. The distinctive capabilities of an organisation are developed through its interactions in the relationships that it maintains with other parties. The **identity of the organisation** is thus also created **through relations** with others. Firm's activities are a cumulative process by which relationships are established, maintained, developed, or disrupted (Mattson1989: 122).

Strategic action is generally defined as efforts by actors to influence their relations to the environment. In the network perspective, this means that strategic actions are efforts to **influence actor's network positions**. Network oriented strategic action aims at influencing actors, relationships, and network structures (Johanson/Mattson 1991: 265, 273). **Entrepreneurial action** in terms of the act of **connecting earlier unconnected relationships** and networks is needed for the positioning of the firm and its units (Ibid. 273, Snehota 1990).

Innovations in logistics as well as through information and communication technology, particularly the Internet, now offer global outreach to even the smallest of companies (Lovelock/Yip 1996: 73). The use of Internet tends to expand the geographic market because it reduces the importance of location, at least for the initial sale, bringing many more companies into competition with one another (Porter 2001: 66). Strategic positioning becomes all the more important (Ibid. 71). Mattson (1998) stresses that **strategic change** is equal to **major change in the firm's network positions**.

The **development of exchange relationships** and **network positions** can be viewed as an **investment process**. The position of the actor gives some power over resources controlled by other actors (Ibid. 270-271). An organisation's performance is conditioned by the totality of the network as a context since the other parties also operate under similar conditions in the same context of interdependence (Håkansson/Snehota 1989: 191). Organisational effectiveness is thus managed by framing the context rather than by designing (planning) a future pattern of activities. The framing of a context is a social process and is carried out by individuals but it is coded and stored collectively. Continuous interaction with other parties constituting the context with which the organisation interacts endows the organisation with meaning and a role (Ibid. 198).

Interorganisational networks are the **evolutionary products of embedded organisational action** in which new alliances are increasingly embedded in the same network that has shaped the organisational decisions to form those alliances (Gulati/Gargiulo 1999: 1441). The social network of alliances is dynamic and evolves as new alliances are formed. Over time, **embedded relationships** accumulate into a **network** that becomes a growing repository of information on the availability, competencies and reliability of prospective partners (Ibid. 1440). A firm's position in the network is thus the result of both its own past alliances and those of other firms in the network. Since new ties alter the very social network that moderates their formation, there is an **active interplay between action and structure** over time (Gulati 1995: 620). In a feedback loop, new alliances alter the social structure that influenced their creation (Ibid. 624). Gulati/Gargiulo (1999: 1439) show that the probability of a new alliance between specific organisations increases with their interdependence and also with their prior mutual alliances, common third parties, and joint centrality in the alliance network.

☞ Strategic clusters and flagship firms

Many industries are characterised by the development of **strategic clusters of firms** that form around a **multinational flagship firm**. Similar to the clusters discussed in the context of local networks, a strategic cluster is defined as a group of firms within a small geographic region, all of which participate in the same industry or a closely related group of industries. Each cluster includes a flagship firm (or a small number of firms), which plays a **dominant role** in exports from the cluster, as well as a number of other firms that participate in business dealing with the flagship firms. The **flagship firms** compete **globally**, so their strategies and internal organisations need to reach the benchmark of international standards. In this context, a business network is the web of strategic relationships that tie the members of a cluster together. Network linkages are achieved through the harmonisation of the strategies of the firms within a cluster (Rugman/d'Cruz 2000: 17-18).

Business networks can be structured hierarchically, with an MNE as the network broker or flagship firm at the centre of the net made up by key suppliers, key customers, competitors (co-operations), and the non-business infrastructure. The **flagship firm and five partners business network model** proposed by Rugman/d'Cruz (2000) is based on *Porter's 5-forces model*. The *difference* is the focus on a *co-operative* and *collective action perspective* in the flagship network as opposed to the Porter model in which the basic competitive approach is positioning of the firm to maximise its own relative bargaining power. Examples of flagship networks are MNEs like Benetton, IKEA, and, in general, East Asian business networks (Ibid. 12). The partners are linked together by a common global strategy and purpose. The MNE flagship has the resources and position to lead the network and strategically manage its activities. It makes the network competitive by benchmarking network activities and processes to global standards, restructuring the production and service operations to different network partners, and adopting a paradigm of relationship-based co-operation. **Advantages** offered by flagship networks are shorter product-development cycles, rapid technology diffusion, quicker product obsolescence, and the proliferation of quality producers worldwide. Collaboration within the business network allows partners to **accelerate organisational learning** through access to the resources and expertise of other organisations (Ibid. 1-2).

From the perspective of the flagship firm, a range of activities can be transferred to network partners. The scope of activities within the network firms shrinks as a consequence of the success of the cluster in sharing strategies. What remains in a **process of flexible specialisation** will represent the core competencies of the flagship firm: strategic management, nurturing of the major technologies from which distinctive competencies are based, capital- and knowledge-intensive operations, and maintenance of the network itself (Ibid. 28).

4.1.3 Strategic networks

Contrary to local networks that are bound by geographical boundaries and business networks that encompass all firms working in an industrial field, **strategic networks** are **purposely developed** by firms in order to sustain their activity structure.

Nohria/Garcia-Pont (1991: 105) describe the **network of global strategic linkages** in industry structures. Strategic linkages are conceived as a way for firms to respond to the simultaneous need for global-scale efficiencies, worldwide learning, and local responsiveness. Firms gain **access to desired strategic capabilities by creating linkages** with firms that have **complementary capabilities** or by **pooling their resources** with firms with similar capabilities. Strategic linkages enable firms to manage competitive uncertainty by establishing negotiated environments. 'Strategic groups' are based on similarities in the strategic capabilities of firms and are akin to the ecologist's notion of a niche. '**Strategic blocks**' are based on similarities in their strategic linkages. A strategic block is a set of firms that are connected more densely to each other than to other firms in the industry. **Complementary blocks** are composed of firms from different strategic groups, while **pooling blocks** are composed of firms from the same strategic group (Ibid.).

Complementary to the exploration and exploitation of **global strategic linkages**, an area where the use of networks is of utmost importance is in **entrepreneurship**. Networking is, in most cases, the method entrepreneurs use to get access to external resources, necessary in the pursuit of their opportunities. Thus the realisation of the importance of **networking** and the understanding of the **skills involved in making it** succeed are two of the **most important entrepreneurial skills** (Jarillo 1988: 39). Several forms of strategic networks have been described in literature and will be outlined in the following.

4.1.3.1 The interorganisational network as a political economy (Benson)

Benson (1975) provided a first corner stone in the study of interorganisational networks. Benson conceives an interorganisational network as a **political economy** concerned with the **distribution** of two **scarce resources**, money, and authority. **Authority** refers to the legitimisation of activities, the right and responsibility to carry out programs of a certain kind, dealing with a broad problem area or focus. **Power** permits one organisation to reach across agency boundaries and determine policies or practices in weaker organisations.

The basic unit of analysis is the network of organisations. Such a unit consists of a number of distinguishable organisations having a significant amount of interaction with each other. **Organisations**, the actors of the political economy, pursue an adequate supply with resources. Their interactions and sentiments are dependent upon their respective **market positions** and **power** to affect the flow of resources. The interorganisational network itself is **embedded in a larger environment** consisting of authorities, legislative bodies, associations, and the public. The flow of resources into the network depends on changes in the external environment. Interorganisational relations are viewed as existing in an equilibrium framework (Ibid. 229-230). An interorganisational network is equilibrated to the extent that participant organisations are engaged in highly co-ordinated, co-operative interactions based on normative consensus and mutual respect. Benson (Ibid. 235-236) identifies four **dimensions of interorganisational equilibrium**:

- *domain consensus*: agreement among participants in organisations regarding the appropriate role and scope of an agency;
- *ideological consensus*: agreement among participants in organisations regarding the nature of the tasks confronted by the organisations and the appropriate approaches to those tasks;
- *positive evaluation*: the judgement by workers in one organisation of the value of the work of another organisation; and
- *work co-ordination*: patterns of collaboration and co-operation between organisations. Work is co-ordinated to the extent that programmes and activities in effectiveness and efficiency.

The components tend to vary with a balancing tendency that may move a network toward or away from equilibrium, or stabilise it at a given equilibrium level. The components are dependent on the alignment of political-economic forces, which place restrictive limits upon the range of possible variation in the components (Benson 1975: 238).

The **environment** in Benson's network model is important insofar as it affects the supply of the resources money and authority to a network and the distribution of power within a network. The model therefore is basically rooted in **strategic contingency theory**. The **structure of the environment** contains the following dimensions of variation (Benson 1975: 239-240):

1. *Resource concentration/dispersion* is the extent to which control over resource disbursements to the network resides in one or a few participants.
2. *Power concentration/dispersion* is the extent to which some participants in the environment dominate others.
3. *Network autonomy/dependence* is the extent to which the network is controlled by environmental forces.
4. *Environmental dominance patterns* can be equated with the types of participants exercising power in the environment.
5. *Resource abundance/scarcity* is the amount of resources at the disposal of the environment.
6. *Control mechanisms*, incentive versus authoritative, are the means of control by the environment over networks.

4.1.3.2 Networks between markets and hierarchies (Thorelli)

The organisation of economic production and transaction is traditionally divided in the **market-based organisation** (market) and the **hierarchical organisation** (hierarchy or firm). A hierarchy produces *internal agency* and *co-ordination costs*, while the market produces *transaction costs*. **Networks** represent a *third, co-operative mode of organisation* and are either conceived as a distinct organisational form or as a hybrid mode of organisation. Independent of the question if network organisation is a distinct form, networks nearly always represent a hybrid of market, hierarchical, co-operative, and informal modes of organisation.

Thorelli (1986) conceives the network as a special type of system, one whose internal interdependencies generally change over time. It is viewed as consisting of '*nodes*' or **positions** occupied by social actors and links manifested by **interaction between the positions**. **Positioning of the firm** in the network is supposed to be as significant as the positioning of the **products**. Networks may be tight or loose, depending on the quantity (number), quality (intensity), and type (closeness to the core activity of the parties involved) of interactions between the positions or members. According to Thorelli (1986: 38), **power** is the central concept in network analysis. It is conceived as the ability to influence the decisions or actions of others. The more typical phenomenon is interdependence. Power, information, money, and utilities flow along the links of the network.

Networks are characterised by a **division of labour**, which implies that each firm has a mission. Mission is defined as domain plus specific objectives to be attained within the domain. It may be defined in terms of product, clientele, functions performed, territory, and time. For a network to exist there must be at least a partial **overlap in domain**. A position is a decision centre and a location of power to create and/or influence networks. It depends on the domain, the positions of the company in other networks, and the power of the firm relative to other firms in the same network. Thus position, like power, is a relational and relativistic concept. Both position and power are based on the economic base, technology expertise, trust, and legitimacy and are manifested by differential advantages in these areas. Links between positions, or nodes, involve economic performance, knowledge transfer, forging or exploitation of trust, and the flow of legitimacy. They are based on relationships over time and differ from individual transactions. **Network memberships** are characterised by four **distinct dynamic processes**: entry, positioning, repositioning, exit (Thorelli 1986: 40-42).

4.1.3.3 The 'dynamic network' (Miles/Snow)

Miles/Snow (1986: 62) describe a '**dynamic network**' as '*a new organisational form - a unique combination of strategy, structure, and management processes*'. Characteristics of such a dynamic network are vertical disaggregation, internal and external brokering, full-disclosure information systems, and market substitutes for administrative mechanisms. According to Miles/Snow, firms in a given industry develop different **strategic roles**. While organisation theorists traditionally distinguish generalist and specialist organisations, the authors define three **generic strategies**:

- *Defenders* offer a limited, stable product line and compete primarily on the basis of value and/or cost. They rely heavily on the functional structure and its accompanying managerial characteristics of centralised decision-making and control, vertical communications and integration, and high degrees of specialisation.
- *Prospectors* are '*first-to-the-market*' with a new product or service and differentiate themselves from their competitors by using their ability to develop innovative products and technologies. Prospectors use more flexible structures such as autonomous work-groups or product divisions with highly decentralised planning and control.
- *Analysers* pursue a second-in strategy imitating and improving upon the products of their competitors. They employ a mixed structure such as the matrix wherein project, program, or brand managers act as integrators between resource groups and program units.

Each firm has a **synergistic role** to play that might be described as implicit interdependence among competitors. This means that each **industry** requires an **ideal mix of competitive strategies**. The mix of competitive strategies is supposed to shift from a high proportion of prospectors to a high proportion of defenders with the maturing of an industry (Miles/Snow 1986: 66). The authors recommend explorative mechanisms like intrapreneurship, external co-venturing, idea markets, and innovator roles such as idea champions, sponsors, and orchestrators because competition as a whole is subject to increasing speed and complexity (Ibid. 72).

Snow et al. (1992: 11-14) identify three **distinct types of networks**:

- The *internal network* typically arises to capture entrepreneurial and market benefits internally and without much outsourcing. Instead, competence centres and internal markets provide the necessary efficiency and innovative capacity.
- The *stable network* employs partial outsourcing and is established to inject flexibility into the value chain. Often, a set of vendors is nestled around a large core firm, either providing inputs to the firm or distributing its outputs.
- The *dynamic network* is characterised by a lead firm that identifies and assembles assets owned largely by other companies. Lead firms typically rely on a functional core skill, or in some cases the skill of pure brokering. Dynamic networks can provide both specialisation and flexibility. Each network node practices its particular expertise.

Managers in network structures typically operate across rather than within hierarchies. They can therefore be thought of as brokers with **different broker roles**. As an '*architect*', a manager has an entrepreneurial role and facilitates the emergence of specific operating networks. Managers who act primarily as '*lead operators*' take advantage of the groundwork laid by the architects (although the two roles may overlap considerably). The lead operator formally connects specific firms together into an operating network, whereas '*caretakers*' focus on the continual enhancement of networks to ensure their smooth and effective operation (Snow et al. 1992: 14-17). In the **global competition**, both *network architect* and *lead operator* will require *extensive international knowledge* and *experience*. Architects must keep abreast of available skills and resources around the world, and operators must understand how cross-cultural relationships are forged and maintained. *Caretakers* have to nurture a *sense of community* among the members of the network, based on shared culture, objectives and rewards (Snow et al.1992: 18).

4.1.3.4 Segmentary, polycentric, integrated networks (SPINs)

Gerlach/Palmer (1981) introduce the concept of the '*segmentary, polycentric, integrated network*' (SPIN). **Semiautonomous segments** that differentiate themselves by splitting and appending new segments constitute such networks. Segments overlap and intertwine complexly so that many people are members of several segments at the same time. A person can be leader in one segment and a follower in another. SPINs are polycentric with **leadership of 'temporary first among equals'** rather than a permanent, paramount leader. Individual segments are woven into *loose* and *informal networks* by personal interactions among leaders, overlapping membership, shared ideologies, common causes and effective channels for communication and logistical support. SPINs have five **characteristics** (Gerlach/Palmer 1981: 364-365):

- SPINs foster effective coping with new environments by stimulating innovation and entrepreneurship.
- SPINs are reliable by redundancy and duplication of functions and resources.
- SPINs can penetrate and recruit from a broad range of people.
- SPINs are protected from suppression or co-optation of the total organisation by its redundancy, multiplicity of leaders, self-sufficiency of individuals and segments.
- SPINs escalate efforts and generate forward motion through rivalries and competition.

On balance, the concept of Gerlach/Palmer comes very close to the normative '**esoteric network model**' underlying many network concepts from the mid-1980s to the mid-1990s, where the organisation is conceived to be fluid, amorphous or boundaryless without a clear underlying conception.

4.1.3.5 Strategic network (Jarillo)

Jarillo (1988: 32) conceptualises networks as a mode of organisation that can be used by managers or entrepreneurs to position their firms in a stronger competitive stance. **Strategic networks** are *'long-term, purposeful arrangements among distinct but related for-profit organisations that allow those firms in them to gain or sustain competitive advantage vis-à-vis their competitors outside the network'* (Jarillo 1988: 32). They are long-term relationships based on implicit contracts without specific legal ties (Jarillo 1987: 83). Such a network is the result of a boundary-spanning process of differentiation and integration of economic activities by the constituting **network firms**. This process is also termed '**systemic rationalisation**' and enhances the strategic flexibility and innovative capacity of strategic networks (Sydow 1991: 239-240, Altmann/Sauer 1989).

Essential to this concept of strategic network is that of the '**hub firm**', which is the firm that sets up the network, and takes a pro-active attitude in the care of it. The hub firm has special **relationships with the other members** of the network. Those relations have most of the **characteristics of a hierarchical relationship**: relatively unstructured tasks, long-term perspective, relatively unspecified contracts. The relations have all the characteristics of investments since there is always asset specificity to the know-how dealing with a given partner instead of a new one. The contracting parties remain independent organisations with only partial overlapping of activities (Jarillo 1988: 34). Exchange relations are largely market-based. A strategic network allows a firm to specialise in those activities of the value chain that are essential to its competitive advantage, reaping all the benefits of specialisation, focus, and size. The other activities are then farmed out to specialised members in the network that carry them out more efficiently. All the firms in the network enjoy the added flexibility of not having fixed commitments to non-core activities. Network arrangements are efficient and lower costs as trust and common standards lower transaction costs while the market test is still applicable to the exchange relations. On the other hand, networks allow for **co-specialisation** and **shared learning processes** (Jarillo 1988: 36). Strategic networks therefore generally not only develop an **interorganisational structure** but also a kind of **interorganisational culture** (Sydow 1991: 240).

4.1.4 Contribution to an evolutionary perspective

The **liquefaction of competition** driven by globalisation is characterised by the development of a **global network competition**. The **emergence** and **reproduction of interorganisational networks** is a main element in this process. The interrelationships between firms of different sizes and types increasingly span national boundaries to create a set of **geographically nested relationships** from local to global scales (Dicken 1986: 184). The interorganisational perspectives of local, business, and strategic networks reflect this differentiated interorganisational landscape from local to global scale. Table 4-1 resumes the integration of evolutionary principles within the three network perspectives. However, such principles may be included explicitly, implicitly or left out totally. In the latter case, it may be worth reflecting the applicability of evolutionary principles.

	Local networks	Business networks	Strategic networks
Foundation	Entrepreneurship and innovation in local innovative milieu.	No	No
Co-evolution of firm and environment	Strong embeddedness of local firms in their milieu, co-evolution of the organisations within the local context.	Firms are part of a business network. Positioning of the firm, creation, and reproduction of relations with other network firms is critical.	Loosely coupled co-evolutionary interplay of the firm and its network partners to generate competitive advantages and to reduce risk vis-à-vis the wider competitive environment.
Global differentiation of firm	MNEs may choose local networks as niches for their subsidiaries. Firms in local networks may participate in globally differentiated networks.	Business networks develop co-specialisation in an industry. Differentiation of a firm occurs on the basis of globally differentiated specialisation, positioning, power bases, and relations on industry level.	Co-specialisation of firms within and across industries, generation of competitive advantages by individual and mutual differentiation in products, activities, markets, or competencies.
Global integration of firm	No	Implicit integration in the co-specialisation of the business network.	Integration is implicitly reflected by the learning cycle as it presupposes the retention of new elements; also external integration in of the firm in networks.
Global evolutionary dynamics of environment	No mechanism defined. Implicit assumption: VSR mechanism, historical process of co-specialisation (differentiation) and integration as firms are part of a local meaning and activity system. Possible: Local system may even expose autopoietic traits.	No mechanisms defined. Implicit assumption: technological path-dependencies Possible: dynamics may be explained by all evolutionary mechanisms, even autopoietic (e.g. industry recipes).	No mechanisms defined. Implicit assumption: teleological mechanism as strategic networks are instruments for the attainment of defined goals. Possible: as loosely coupled social systems, strategic networks have an identity and may expose all evolutionary mechanisms.
Global evolutionary dynamics of firm	No mechanism defined. Implicit assumption: Firm is structurally coupled with the local milieu and subject to unspecified evolutionary mechanisms. Possible: all evolutionary mechanisms.	No mechanisms defined. Implicit assumption: Evolutionary dynamics due to structural coupling with technologically path-dependent industrial network.	No mechanism defined. Implicit assumption: teleological co-evolution of network firms Possible: all evolutionary mechanisms.

Table 4-1: Evolutionary principles in interorganisational network approaches

4.2 Global intraorganisational networks: MNEs

The **early focus** on the explanation of international production and the **existence of MNEs** was based on the efforts of **economists**. With the possible exception of **contingency theory**, no paradigm from the major theories about organisations and environments has had a major impact on the study of MNEs, and no research on MNEs has drawn significant attention from organisation theorists (Ghoshal/Westney 1993: 1). Environmental forces for **global integration** and for **local responsiveness** mark **contingencies** for the behaviour and organisation of MNEs from the perspective of the **Harvard-based 'Process School'** with roots in Lawrence/Lorsch's (1966) **'differentiation/integration framework'** and Bower's (1970) emphasis on **organisational processes**. In tandem with Porter's configuration/co-ordination framework, the duality of global integration vs. local responsiveness (adaptation) began to dominate the research on MNEs.

Hamel/Prahalad (1983: 342-343) and Prahalad/Doz (1987: 18-24) identify factors that typically influence the need for integration of global activities and for national responsiveness. **Factors** favouring **global integration** include extra-national scale economies, asset and technology intensity, multinational customers, universal customer needs, global competitors, and low trade barriers. Factors that typically determine the need for **responsiveness** include the need for product adaptation, lack of scale economies, fragmentation of the business, nationally distinctive distribution channels, availability of product substitutes, host government demands, and relatively low technology dependence of affiliates on central R&D.

Due to their internal differentiation and the **global dispersion** of organisational units and cooperations, **MNEs** were soon conceptualised as **multinational networks**. The need for balancing the dominating duality global integration vs. local responsiveness in MNE-networks provided a fertile ground for several concepts of **strategy** and **organisation** in MNEs. The emerging **ideal type** of the *'transnational'* (Bartlett 1986, Bartlett/Ghoshal 1989), *'multifocus'* (Prahalad/Doz 1987) or *'heterarchic'* (Hedlund 1986) firm balances the duality by simultaneously exploiting advantages from both dimensions that are assumed to be orthogonal. The old Chandler paradigm of **'structure-follows-strategy'** is substituted by a **recursive interplay of strategy and structure**.

Despite disagreements in terminology, research from this perspective seem to have developed an agreement on the following **characteristics** of the described **'ideal type' of MNE** (Ghoshal/Westney 1993):

- *Dispersion*: The MNE has globally dispersed subunits (subsidiaries) in each major market, national technology system. The capacity to innovate and to exploit innovations is dispersed in the multinational network.
- *Interdependence*: Subunits are linked to each other and to the headquarters by flows of people, technology, and products, such that key activities are performed in the location with the locational and organisational advantage. The interdependence between the dispersed units creates the '*integrated network*' configuration (Bartlett 1989).
- *Tight coupling of subunits*: Each part of the MNE is expected to respond quickly to stimuli encountered in another part. This requires intensive communication and closely co-ordinated reward systems.
- *Cross-unit learning*: One main advantage of the integrated network is the capacity to develop and diffuse innovations swiftly and to adapt and improve them in this process. An important role of subsidiaries is to exploit their local environment to foster innovations that can be leveraged in the network.
- *Structural flexibility*: The emphasis is on organisational processes rather than on a particular formal structure. Flexibility in decision-making, shared values and perspectives of upper-level managers at headquarters and the subsidiaries, and shared perspectives based on socialisation and cross-unit experience are more important than formal means of organisation.

The size and complexity of MNEs mean that **linkages** and **interdependencies** can be *neither planned nor centrally managed*. Which linkages are going to be useful at a particular point in time for a specific task between two or more subunits is unpredictable, and probably needs to be **self-adjusting**. Management in MNEs thus calls for providing **decentralised, delegated decision contexts** within which opportunities for **linkages** between subunits will *arise* at various points and levels in organisation and time (Doz/Prahalad 1993: 26-27).

Studying the **process of balance** across apparently **conflicting demands** is seen as more important than studying the management demands created by one element of the business (e.g., technology intensity) at a time (Doz/Prahalad 1993: 45-46).

Zaheer (2000: 340-341) proposes a further competitive advantage, termed '**economies of diachronic scope**'. These include benefits that arise from **locating activities across time zones** and which provide **speed of response** when there is need for managerial co-ordination across a global value-adding network. **Information advantages** can accrue to firms that locate and co-ordinate across time zones. Further the true realisation of economies of scale or scope across a global value chain relies on rapid, real-time managerial co-ordination. The **synchro-**

nisation of the individual circadian rhythms, social rhythms, and work rhythms may lead to competitive advantages as do **overlapping work times** across different time zones. The businesses that would benefit clearly are those in which activities are costlessly transmittable across borders, those that rely on information, those operating with codified rather than tacit knowledge, and those in which the throughput requirements are not tied to a particular physical asset (Ibid. 344). For example, in a study of information seeking among banks in the global currency area, Zaheer/Zaheer (1997) found that synchronisation of firm activity across time zones with market activity was positively correlated to measures of a firm's alertness to information.

MNEs may exploit '**time zone economies**' by developing '**global relay strategies**' across time zones. Such economies are particularly *realisable* in industries where the *activity is costlessly fungible across borders* by the effect of increasing throughput within the firm to achieve economies of scale and scope. There are also economies to be gained from increasing the speed of response to a global network of suppliers and customers, both through its effect on throughput through the value-adding system and through its effect on relationship quality and social capital, which can further facilitate co-ordination. A further benefit from location across time zones could arise from the creation of an information advantage through the acquisition of private information or foreknowledge that is facilitated from such location (Zaheer 2000: 349). Europe enjoys a privileged position in the global day, with the centrality of its time zone, and may serve as the location of meta-co-ordination roles (Ibid. 350).

MNEs are of interest as distinctive organisational entities in so far as they authoritatively integrate economic resources and activities in quite different locations that involve managing contrasting kinds of employees and competing and co-operating with varied sorts of firms in differently organised markets. It is the **co-ordination of major activities across significantly different institutional contexts** through organisational routines that potentially makes **MNEs distinctive kinds of organisations**. In general, MNEs are more likely to become distinctive kinds of organisation when they locate major proportions of key assets and activities in quite different kinds of business system, allow foreign subsidiaries to adapt to local conventions, and learn from these novel developments by adapting and integrating them through organisation-wide routines and procedures (Whitley 2001: 32).

MNEs are physically **dispersed** in environmental settings that represent very *different economic, social, and cultural milieus*; they are **internally differentiated** in complex ways to respond to both environmental and organisational differences in different businesses, functions, and geographic locations. As a result of such dispersal and differentiation, they possess **internal linkages** and **co-ordination mechanisms** that represent and respond to many different kinds and extents of dependence and interdependence in **interunit exchange relationships** (Ghoshal/Bartlett 1993: 79).

The globalised firm has **indistinct and shifting boundaries**. It is expected to be networked or distributed in organisational structure rather than being hierarchical, and it may penetrate and exploit space by proxy or in co-operation with other firms rather than in 'isolation' (Wells/Cooke 1991: 17). A major advantage of the multiplant firm in general and the MNE in particular is that it can make substantial adjustments *in situ* without necessarily engaging in locational shift. The most common **locational shifts** within an MNE network are

- *investment* at a new location,
- *disinvestment* of an existing plant, and
- *acquisition* of plants belonging to another firm (Dicken 1986: 212).

MNEs can also be considered not as rational goal-directed actors but as specific forms of **transnational communities**. Underlying this terminology is the sense that forms of social action and identity are increasingly co-ordinated across national boundaries and it is therefore important to understand the modes of social organisation, mobility, and communication that enable these processes to proceed. MNEs constitute a form of **social space**. Inside this space, a **huge diversity of activities** takes place. As the transnational space by definition incorporates **distinct institutional settings**, it sets up potential interactions across national boundaries. Over time, these **boundaries** are **subject to renegotiations** and **change** as new sites are brought into the MNE and resources are reallocated across existing sites. **Creating order** with such a transnational social space, either synchronously or diachronically, is a precarious practice. It depends on the social and geographical space encompassed and how far practices, routines, norms, and values from within these spaces are different, transferable, adaptable, or resistant to change. An important question in this context is how the **boundaries of transnational communities** are structured, managed, redefined, and negotiated and how social relationships within these spaces differ. This depends on how social institutions penetrate organisational relationships, how institutions structure different actors and their interests in organisational contexts and how stretching firms over national boundaries leads to new structures, actors, and possibilities of action (Morgan 2001: 10-11). Reorganisation, rationalisation, and the resulting **spatial change** are an inevitable aspect of the **evolution of MNEs** (Dicken 1986: 214).

Malnight (1995:43) describes the **transition from decentralised to network-based MNE structures**. Malnight argues that the focus of the process shifts over time, initially focusing on building organisational linkages and adjusting the quantity and nature of resources within dispersed units, and later shifting toward reallocating resources and roles across units. The reallocation is dependent on the development of specialised resources and organisational mechanisms enabling their effective interaction. The observed direction of change is being driven by gradual adjustments in multiple aspects of a firm's operations. Poor financial performance ('crises') and changing management are drivers of entering each phase of the transition process, thus also supporting a **punctuated equilibrium view** (Ibid. 60).

4.2.1 Strategy in MNEs

Compared to firms at the beginning of their internationalisation process, **MNEs** have much **more variety** in their **strategic options**. They dispose of globally dispersed assets, activities, and communication structures. The **global internalisation of transactions** and the presence in **multiple global and local networks** provide access to an **immense variety of resources**. From this perspective, a global strategy can be defined as one in which a firm seeks to gain **competitive advantage** from international presence through either *concentrating configuration*, *co-ordination* among dispersed activities, or *both* (Porter 1993: 76). According to Kogut (1990: 49), **multinationality** itself can be a **source of advantage**. Kogut (1990) identifies four '**international sequential advantages**', which can be exploited by internationally operating firms: economies of scale, economies of scope, learning, and multinational dispersion.

- The significance of *economies of scale* in serving world markets is closely linked to a focus on standardised products and global rationalisation. International market expansion and segmentation provides potential for growth and thus larger sales volumes (Kogut 1990: 50).
- *Economies of scope* can be seen not only in terms of static joint economies, but also as affecting the costs of sequential product entries. By lowering the costs of future entries, dynamic scope economies permit the introduction of global products whose volume alone may not justify the costs of entry (Kogut 1990: 53).
- *Learning effects* classically increase the efficiency of operations. In global markets the focus changed increasingly from the efficiency perspective to the innovative capacity of MNEs. MNEs as global brokers of information and knowledge have a unique capacity to develop, adopt, combine, and diffuse new knowledge across national borders. In a process of global knowledge accumulation and diffusion, MNEs are main drivers of innovation and globalisation.
- *Multinational dispersion* of activities provides MNEs with the capacity to exploit comparative advantages between locations and operational flexibility by reallocation of resources and activities. Multinationality thus provides a unique benefit in the form of the possibility to gain from uncertainty (Kogut 1990: 55).

Sölvell/Birkinshaw (2000: 92) assume that as we move into a knowledge economy the benefits **MNEs** gain from multinationality will be far more a function of their ability to **manage practices across borders** rather than activities. The authors thus stress the importance of knowledge in the globalisation process.

Ghoshal (1987: 428) provides an **organising framework for the development of global strategies** (Table 4-2). Three basic goals of MNEs (efficiency, risk optimisation, and learning) can be pursued by the exploration and exploitation of three distinct sources of competitive advantages (national differences, scale economies, scope economies). The key to success is assumed to be the management of the interactions between these different goals and means.

Strategic objectives	Sources of competitive advantage		
	National differences	Scale economies	Scope economies
Achieving efficiency in current operations	Benefiting from differences in factor costs, wages, and cost of capital	Expanding and exploiting potential scale economies in each activity	Sharing of investments and costs across products, markets, and businesses
Managing risks	Managing different kinds of risks arising from market or policy-induced changes in comparative advantages of different countries	Balancing scale with strategic and operational flexibility	Portfolio diversification of risks and creation of options and side-bets
Innovation, learning, and adaptation	Learning from societal differences in organisational and managerial processes and systems	Benefiting from experience-cost reduction and innovation	Shared learning across organisational components in different pro-, ducts, markets, or businesses

Table 4-2: Global strategy: an organising framework
(Source: Ghoshal 1987: 428)

One **key asset of MNEs** is the **diversity of environments** in which it operates. This diversity exposes the firm to multiple stimuli, allows it to develop diverse capabilities, and provides it with a broader learning opportunity than is available to a purely domestic firm (Ghoshal 1987: 431). **Diversity of internal capabilities**, following the logic of population ecology, will enhance the probability of survival by enhancing the chances that it will be in possession of the capabilities required to cope with an uncertain future state. Similarly, **diversity of resources and competencies** may also enhance the firm's ability to create joint innovations, and to exploit them in multiple locations (Ghoshal 1987: 431). igure 4-2 exemplifies that the benefits from global integration and local responsiveness may be explored and exploited on different levels, from the industry level to the individual task at hand.

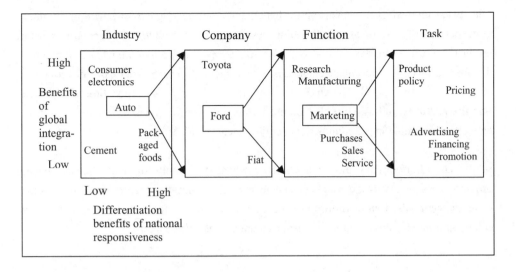

Figure 4-2: The integration-responsiveness framework
(Source: Ghoshal 1987: 429)

According to Kogut (1985: 15), the **design of international strategies** is based on the **interplay** between the **comparative advantages of countries** (*location-specific advantages*) and the **competitive advantages of firms** (*firm-specific advantages*). The geographical dispersion and the allocation of resources to value-added and functional activities are greatly dependent on these potential advantages, which are not necessarily independent of each other. The outstanding feature of global competition is assumed to be the uncertainty over these advantages (Kogut 1985: 27). Consequently, the key operating dimensions in a global strategy proposed by Kogut are to recognise the potential profit opportunities and to create the organisational flexibility that responds to changes in the environment.

The unique content of a global versus a purely domestic strategy lies less in the methods to design long-term strategic plans than in the construction of flexibility, which permits the firm to exploit the uncertainty over future changes in global strategic variables, like exchange rates, competitive moves, or government policy (Kogut 1985a: 27). Kogut (Ibid. 28, 33-35) identifies two **kinds of flexibility** that are critical to a **global strategy**:

- *arbitrage of market imperfections* by production shifting, tax minimisation, financial arbitrage, information arbitrage;
- *exploitation of leverage opportunities* by which a firm's position in one national market is enhanced by its position in a second through global co-ordination and political bargaining.

The **operating flexibility** stems from the benefits of co-ordinating the flows within a multinational network. The value of such flexibility rests not only on *exploiting differentials* in factor, product, and capital markets, but also on the *transfer of learning and innovations* throughout the firm, as well as the enhanced *leverage* to respond to competitors' and governments' threats (Kogut 1989: 384). The **challenge** from this perspective is the **creation of organisational structures and systems** that permit the exploitation of opportunities inherent in the network of operating in different national environments (Ibid. 387).

MNEs face a **fundamental dilemma**. On the one hand, their multinationality creates valuable **opportunities to arbitrage markets** and to exercise **competitive leverage**. On the other hand, the **centralised co-ordination** of these activities entails **significant costs** in communicating information between globally dispersed units (Kogut 1985a: 36).

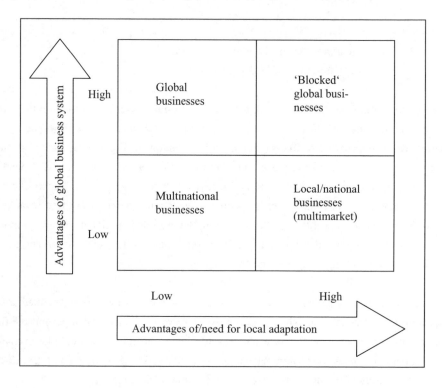

Figure 4-3: The global/local trade-off
(Source: Henzler/Rall 1986: 55)

Henzler/Rall (1986: 55) developed a **portfolio of generic businesses** on the basis of the distinction global integration versus local adaptation (Figure 4-3). Businesses where strong local adaptation is inappropriate and globalising forces can be exploited to a great advantage are termed '*global businesses*'. Businesses that require some degree of local adaptation and where globalisation of all functions offers no decisive competitive advantage are termed '*multinational businesses*'. Businesses in which both dimensions are strong are termed '*blocked global businesses*'. These businesses would be global from a purely economic point of view if they were not constrained by law or government purchasing policies. Businesses with a need for high local adaptation and no major arguments in favour of global integration are true '*local businesses*' (Henzler/Rall 1986: 55-56).

To each of these **archetypal businesses** can be attributed a **generic strategy** (Meffert 1986: 194-195, Macharzina 1996: 203-204). The '**international strategy**' is pursued by firms with a generally ethnocentric focus on their activities. Foreign activities are regarded as an add-on to the domestic market. Products and practices are not adapted to international differences.

The '**multinational strategy**' is based on a structure of autonomous national subsidiaries and a low degree of global integration. Subsidiaries develop their own local strategies with little integration into a global strategic framework and co-ordination across the globally dispersed units. The '**global strategy**' basically ignores national boundaries and optimises global efficiency of operations. It is accompanied with a high degree of standardisation and centralisation. The '**blocked global strategy**' is an alternative for firms in technology-intensive industries with the potential for global standardisation but with barriers to important national markets, typically in industries like telecommunications or defence.

A study by Roth (1992: 546) provided evidence that different patterns of configuration and co-ordination exist, with firms selectively co-ordinating some activities globally, some activities regionally, and allowing other activities to be managed locally. This approach is termed '**selective globalisation**' – global strategy implementation centred on a subset of the value chain. According to Roth, a firm must initially understand its distinctive competencies and then build its global strategy around the location-specific and firm-specific advantages developed through the functional activities associated with these distinctive competencies (Ibid.). Structural cross-relationships between national subsidiaries are essential (Henzler/Rall 1986: 67). For most companies, going global requires a change in strategic orientation due to different strategic and organisational heritage (Leontiades 1986: 100).

Prahalad/Bettis (1996) contend that firms with a high strategic variety might even develop different '**dominant logics**' that are defined as '*the way in which managers conceptualize the business and make critical resource allocation decisions*' (Ibid. 405). The dominant logic is stored via schemata and hence can be thought of as a structure. However, some of what is stored is process knowledge. Hence, the dominant logic can be considered as both a **knowl-**

edge structure and a **set of elicited management processes**. Typically, the dominant top management logic in a diversified firm tends to be influenced by the largest business or the '*core business*' which was the historical basis for the firm's growth and internationalisation. Along the process of growth and internationalisation, a firm may develop various, distinct dominant logics in business units and subsidiaries. A primary challenge to a **global strategy** is the integration and harmonisation of different strategic visions and initiatives across the globally dispersed units (Ibid.).

In general, an organisation that operates **internationally** must have **greater adaptive capabilities**. It must be able to process and sort out a larger number of environmental complexities. It must also have the capability of detecting shifts in environmental factors that have strategic implications and be capable of responding strategically to the altered environmental state. For this reason the appropriate **strategic decision processes** are critical for an international firm (Jones et al. 1992: 223).

Strategic decision-making can be conceived as an '**advocacy process**' between two competing perspectives, i.e. clear **cohesive global strategy** versus **adaptational flexibility**. By confronting conflicting views constructively organisations learn. Doz et al. (1989: 19) therefore consider **multi-dimensionality** and **flexibility** as the **key requirements of the strategic decision process**. The **balancing of dualities** like stability versus change in decision-making processes is a prerequisite for a firm's self-organised influence on evolution (Beyer 1981: 190-191).

Gustavsson et al. (1994: 257) conclude that firms are neither absolutely global nor totally local but rather display elements of both extremes in different activities of its international behaviour. What Gustavsson et al. (Ibid. 256) term '**glocalisation**' tends to be seen as applying to the spectrum of control in the international firm, ranging from the complete central authority of the global firm to the virtual autonomy of dispersed subsidiaries. The glocalisation process, implying an ongoing search for a better balance between global and local, is assumed to be the predominant learning process in international firms. In a dynamic world, the secret may lie in the ability to exploit a variety of international business structures simultaneously and to change their global or local emphasis (Ibid. 284-285). The key element of the organisational capability lies in its ability to shift the locus and logic of decision from a national concern to a global view and vice versa, from decision to decision (Doz 1986: 214).

Given the variety and conflicts of perspectives and interests in MNEs, Kim/Mauborgne (1991, 1993) developed the concept of '**procedural justice**' to explore the impact of process fairness on multinational's ability to conceive and execute effective worldwide strategies. Procedural justice is defined as the extent to which the dynamics of the multinational's strategy-making process for its subsidiary units are judged to be fair by subsidiary top management. The *fair process* effect can be defined as the tendency for perceptions of procedural justice to enhance perceptions of outcome fairness and favourability and hence to contribute both directly and indirectly to the outcome satisfaction of organisational members (Kim/Mauborgne (1993: 244). Procedural justice has five **distinct characteristics**:

- two-way communication exists in the multinational's strategy-making process;
- subsidiary units can legitimately challenge the strategic views of the head office;
- the head office is knowledgeable of the local situation of subsidiary units;
- subsidiary units are provided an account of the MNE's final strategic decisions; and
- the head office is fairly consistent in making decisions across subsidiary units Kim/Mauborgne (1993: 422).

The very nature of the strategic requirements increasingly characterising global strategies – consummate co-operations among global units – makes higher-order attitudes of commitment, trust, and social harmony increasingly central to the effective working of global strategies. The distinctive power of hierarchy has dissipated in MNEs. According to Kim/Mauborgne (1993: 238), procedural justice therefore has great potential importance for the effective execution of global strategies. Especially three **fundamental requirements** can be consistently discerned (Kim/Mauborgne (1993: 242):

- effective and efficient exchange relations among the nodes of the multinational's global network,
- swift actions in a globally co-ordinated manner, and
- the increasing sacrifice of subsystem for system priorities and considerations.

The *empirical study* by Kim/Mauborgne (1993: 251) substantiated the *significant positive influence* of procedural justice in decision-making of MNEs on organisational commitment; trust in head office management, social harmony, outcome satisfaction, and on strategic decision outcome, itself increasing trust and outcome satisfaction. Kim/Mauborgne (1991: 138, 1993: 443) provided significant evidence that the exercise of procedural justice significantly augments the integration of local perspectives in strategy development and subsidiary compliance with MNE's strategic decisions.

4.2.2 The 'Process School' of international management

The '**Process School**' of MNEs emerged on the basis of a process perspective in policy research (Bower 1970) developed at Harvard Business School. Researchers like Bartlett, Doz, Ghoshal, and Prahalad developed a distinct '**paradigm**' focused on the **management of MNEs** from a **top management perspective**. In contrast to former approaches, the Process School gained its name by a **focus on organisational** and **administrative processes** rather than formal organisation structures. Strategy, they claim, cannot be separated from its context, which includes not only external environmental demands but also internal organisational processes and the factors, like quality of management, culture, and history that shape those processes (Bartlett/Ghoshal 1991: 9). Scholars associated with the Process School advocate the underlying duality of the **global integration/local responsiveness framework**, which is assumed to dominate all important elements of management in MNEs.

In order link their diverse organisational perspectives and resources in a way that would allow them to leverage their capabilities for achieving global co-ordination and national flexibility, companies have to develop **transnational organisational capability** – an ability to manage across boundaries (Bartlett/Ghoshal 1988: 56). This capability is supposed to be the 'key to long-term success'. The most important requirement of the transnational organisation is a need for the organisational configuration to be based on a *principle of reciprocal dependence* among units (Ibid. 66). **Dynamic interdependence** is considered as the basis of a transnational company – one that can *think globally* and *act locally* (Ibid. 69).

4.2.2.1 The diversified multinational corporation (DMNC) (Doz/Prahalad)

Considering the multidimensionality and the heterogeneity of the DMNC has led Doz/Prahalad (1991: 147) to specify **particular demands on the DMNC organisation** and on its management. From their perspective an organisational theory of the DMNC has to take into account:

- *structural indeterminacy*: no single unidimensional structure, or simple concepts of structure are likely to be useful;
- *internal differentiation*: management processes need to differentiate between various countries, products, and functions;
- *information intensity*: the importance of information flows, both formal and informal, as a source of competitive advantage and as an implicit structure;
- *latent linkages*: decentralised self-structuring processes facilitate the emergence of appropriate linkages as the need for them arises;

- *networked organisation* and *'fuzzy boundaries'*: external relationships are explicitly incorporated in the management tasks;
- *learning and continuity* (Ibid.).

Initially, Prahalad (1976) focused on the **management of processes** that influence strategic choices in a **global matrix**, which was considered to be the most advanced structural form to cope with the complexity of DMNCs. The starting point was the observation that strategic decision-making processes in matrix structures became an obstacle due to different power bases of the constituting organisational dimensions. A second focus was on power shifts between these dimensions due to environmental changes or internal changes in preferences and politics. Prahalad identified **two sources of complexity** matrix managers have to cope with: *one* arises from changes in worldwide markets and competition, and the *second* arises from the need to co-ordinate the activities of all subsidiaries worldwide. These conflicting considerations were called '**managerial diversity**' and '**managerial interdependence**'. Prahalad (1976: 74-76) developed a typology of organisational forms based on the effect of managerial diversity and interdependence on relative power of organisational dimensions.

The **early stages** of developing a **multinational strategy**, in which the degree of international activity is still small, are characterised by a low diversity and little benefits from interdependence. As the scope of foreign operations expands the desire for diversity may increase simultaneously. If accompanied by a low desire for worldwide co-ordination, then the locus of relative power will reside in the area group. Limited managerial resources and international experience, or culture-bound products may be reasons for this preference. After a **period of rapid expansion** typically follows a **period of worldwide consolidation** and development of a more standardised approach. In businesses with relative advantages from global integration this may lead to a business or product emphasis. Finally, the '**transition stage**' is marked by attempts of MNEs to **combine high interdependence** with **high managerial diversity**. Prahalad assumes this combination as desirable but emphasises the inevitable problems of focus in assigning responsibility for decisions and performance. After a phase of strategic uncertainty the responsibility for decisions has to be assigned to one of the components (Prahalad 1976: 74-76).

Doz (1980: 27) identifies a **conflict** between requirements for economic survival and success (**economic perspective**) and the adjustments made necessary by the demands of host governments (**political imperative**). Doz (1980: 27-30, 1986: 12-17) develops three **types of multinational strategies** depending on the strength of these two dimensions:

- A *'worldwide integration strategy'* is chosen to respond primarily to the economic imperative and to improve the international competitiveness by achieving economies of scale and greater political influence. Multinational integration is defined as the specialisation of plants across borders into an integrated multinational production/distribution network. Integration may involve product or process specialisation.
- A *'national responsiveness strategy'* gives much more leeway to the subsidiaries to respond to the political imperative by having them behave almost as if they were national companies. There are few pressures on the subsidiaries to maximise economic efficiency for the MNE as a whole. Optimisation takes place locally. Still, advantages from integration like the pooling of financial risks, co-ordination of export marketing, spreading of research, and development costs or the transfer of specific skills between subsidiaries can be exploited.
- A *'multifocal strategy'* or *'administrative co-ordination strategy'* trades off internal efficiency for external flexibility. By selecting a multifocal strategy, firms avoid becoming locked into a particular choice and seek both the benefits of integration and the flexibility of responsiveness in an ad hoc way. Administrative adjustments are aimed at providing some of both benefits. Limited adjustments, individual strategic decisions, and a strategy 'to have no set strategy' provide the MNE with a *'Janus-face'* and increase the MNE's flexibility in finding balances between the economic and the political imperative (Ibid. 37).

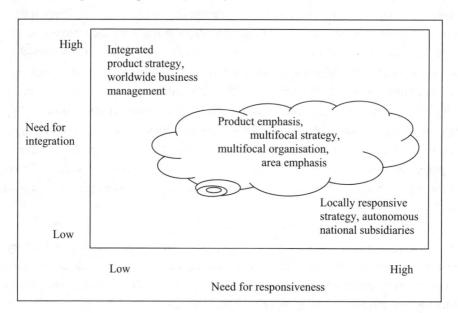

Figure 4-4: Integration-responsiveness: strategic focus and organisational adaptation (Source: Prahalad/Doz 1987: 25)

Prahalad/Doz (1987: 5) add the '**organisational imperative**' as a third imperative to international management. While the interplay of economic and political imperatives allows managers to identify a feasible set of strategic options for a business, the ability to implement that strategy depends on the quality of the organisation. The ability of the organisation to redeploy resources, to redirect the energies of its people, and to adapt to new competitive conditions limits the feasibility of **strategic change**. Figure 4-4 illustrates strategic focus and organisational adaptation within the integration-responsiveness grid of Prahalad/Doz (Ibid. 25). Different **factors** may **change the location** of a business in the *IR grid*:

- changes in the underlying industry economics,
- impact of governments,
- shifts in the competitive focus of customers,
- resegmentation of a business,
- learning, and
- change of the '*rules of the game*' (Prahalad/Doz 1987: 25).

A **basic focus** of the Process School is on the **relationship between headquarters and the subsidiaries**. Prahalad/Doz (1981: 5) assume that as subsidiaries mature and become autonomous with respect to strategic resources, the head office's ability to control the strategies of subsidiaries is significantly reduced. The head office, faced with the inability to exert control over the subsidiaries on the basis of the subsidiaries' dependence on strategic resources, must find substitute mechanisms. The creation of a **sophisticated organisational context** is assumed to be central to compensate for the **erosion of head office's capacity to control subsidiaries**. Such an organisational context can be created by blending organisational structure, information systems, measurement and reward systems, and career planning and a fostering of common organisational culture (Ibid.).

Doz/Prahalad (1986: 120-125) identify three dimensions that determine strategic variety and hence the form of strategic control: countries, businesses, and modes of market participation. Within the first dimension, different **types of subsidiaries** represent the country markets: '*export platforms*', '*large integrated subsidiaries*', '*large self-contained subsidiaries*', and '*small importing subsidiaries*'. The second dimension, which creates variety between strategic control requirements, represents interbusiness differences. The **types of businesses** representing this dimension are '*purely local*', '*local with global competition*', '*multifocal*', and '*global*'. Different types of ownership, ranging from collaborative agreement to fully owned subsidiaries constitute the third dimension (Ibid. 122-125).

Doz/Prahalad (1986: 125) assume **resource dependence** to be the most crude and widespread **tool for strategic control**. Yet, as the subsidiary matures and becomes bigger, the need for financial and technical resources to be provided from head office decreases. Another tool for control, **systems and procedures** such as planning, budgeting, measurement, and evaluation equally becomes less useful as variety and complexity of the strategic control tasks increase. A third approach is the **reliance on key individuals**, in particular where resource dependence and procedures fail. Doz/Prahalad conclude that with increasing required variety of strategic control configuration, human resource management has a key role to play in the continuation of the success of MNEs as institutions (Ibid.).

Hamel/Prahalad (1983) contend that the **imperatives of integration and responsiveness** exist full strength within each activity and each single functional task, eventually leading to **strategic ambiguity**. Strategic ambiguity results, when the MNE, or individual businesses, face competing imperatives. **Organisational ambiguity** is the consequence. Alternatively, when a common strategic imperative exists across businesses and functional tasks, the MNE and its businesses may be characterised as possessing **strategic clarity**. Strategic clarity facilitates **organisational clarity**. Strategic and organisational ambiguity also occurs when the strategic logic of a business or functional area is changing (e.g. from foreign national to global). Head office is then assumed to recognise the emerging global logic of a previously foreign national business.

Managers in DMNCs have to be sensitive not only to the **relationships between headquarters and subsidiaries** at any one point in time but to **changes** in that relationship caused by changes in the underlying structure of a business and its competitive demands (Prahalad/Doz 1987: 158). **Flexibility** in this context requires the ability to **shift between orientations**, almost on a decision-by-decision basis (Prahalad/Doz 1987: 169).

For Prahalad/Doz (1987: 268-269), the **ideal organisation** is hence based on a **comprehensive decision-making culture** that is not bound by constraints imposed by the formal structure of systems. **Principles** that govern the **process of management** and **conflict resolution** are:

- a *multiple advocacy process* or pluralism that allows multiple perspectives and sources of tension surrounding an issue to be explicitly examined;
- a *fluid power structure* that allows an opportunity for anyone to challenge the existing logic and current wisdom in the organisation;
- a *certain legitimacy to dissent*;

- a *certain discipline in the organisation*, which cannot work unless each employee feels bound to implement the decision taken.

Prahalad/Doz (1981: 9) assume that an **organisation is an aggregation of four orientations**, while Prahalad/Doz (1987) and Doz/Prahalad (1987) later concentrated only on the first three of these orientations:

- *cognitive* (nature of information that managers collect and use, or their 'world view'),
- *strategic* (the way managers decide to compete, e.g. on a local-for-local or global basis),
- *power* (people who have the power to commit strategic resources), and
- *administrative* (administrative procedures such as career progression).

Prahalad/Doz (1981: 10) assume **strategic change** to be initiated by an alteration of any one of the four orientations. In order for the change process to be completed, the power orientation must be changed. **Head office managers** can use a variety of three distinct **types of administrative mechanisms**:

- '*Data management mechanisms*' include mechanisms that generate and regulate the flow of information. They structure and provide data that are pertinent to the global performance of the company. Examples are accounting systems, planning and budgeting systems, or management information systems.
- '*Manager management mechanisms*' shift the expectations of managers towards the intended strategic direction. They include the power to assign managers to key positions, executive compensation plans, management development plans, career progression, performance evaluation, and socialisation patterns.
- '*Conflict resolution mechanisms*' serve to resolve conflicts inherent in complex organisational structures. They are used for the development of decision-making structures that serve to balance the priorities from global integration and national responsiveness. Examples are task forces, planning committees, integrators, co-ordinating groups, and decision responsibility assignments (Ibid., Doz/Prahalad 1981: 15-16).

In a transformation process, **perceptions change first**. A precondition for strategic redirection seems to be a change of perspective on the environment, a shift in the cognitive maps in use within the organisation. A study of transformational processes in European MNEs by Doz/Prahalad (1987: 75) confirmed views of **strategic change as a learning process**. According to these authors, change processes follow a **sequence of four stages**: *incubation* (introduction of a new vision), *variety generation* (strategic options), *power shifts* (management), and *refocusing* (legitimisation and implementation of new strategy) (Ibid. 69-74).

At the core, DMNCs must have a complex and **multidimensional view** of the **resource allocation process** – both in terms of the *units of analysis* for resource allocation and in terms of *time frames* that senior managers use. Distribution and technology investments often have a longer time frame than manufacturing and product market investments (Prahalad/Doz 1987: 65). The work of a DMNC's top management can be best described as coping with complexity and balancing the often conflicting demands for providing focus to specific businesses by differentiating the organisational and administrative context, and at the same time maintaining some semblance of uniformity and order. The **dimensions** along which **multinational complexities** arise are

- the *strategic variety* imposed by the number of distinct businesses with different IR profiles;
- the *rate of change* in the competitive dynamics in the businesses in the DMNC's portfolio;
- the *differences in the DMNC's geographical markets* in the various businesses in its portfolio (Prahalad/Doz 1987: 145).

MNE's **global scanning capabilities** give them advanced notice and detailed information in the most profitable manufacturing locations, while their multinational nature will let them relocate easily without showing particular commitment to any country. **Integration** also offers an MNE the opportunity to bias **financial results** of subsidiaries to decrease the total MNE tax exposure, e.g. by transfer pricing and subsidiary remittances (Prahalad/Doz 1987: 73-74). Reflecting on the demands from globalising competition, Hamel/Prahalad (1989: 69, 74) contend that for smart competitors, the goal is not competitive imitation but competitive innovation and the development of distinct **core competencies**, which can be *exploited globally*.

Doz et al. (1981: 65) contend that the conflict between host country demands and competitive forces turns **strategic decision-making** in the MNE into an **advocacy process** between two *competing perspectives*. Multi-dimensionality and flexibility are the key requirements of the desired strategic decision process. By confronting conflicting views constructively the organisation is expected to learn (Ibid. 65-66). *'A multifocal approach to world markets and to global competition is necessarily dialectical'* (Prahalad/Doz 1987: 97). Managers must explicitly examine the tradeoffs between local needs and global integration demands on an ongoing basis (Prahalad/Doz 1987: 173).

Due to the central role of decision-making, Doz et al. (1981: 67-73) distinguish **types of decision-making**, depending on the degree of complexity of the business and the frequency of decisions requiring balancing between national demands and competitive pressure:

- *Substantive decision-making*: Top management ensures that the management groups representing each of the critical decision perspectives are strong enough to develop and advocate a particular viewpoint.
- *Substantive decision arbitration*: Delegating the important balancing responsibility to trusted arbitrators solves some of the problems of substantive decision management.
- *Temporary coalition management*: Due to complex or competitive environments top management has to retreat from direct involvement in the decision-making process and builds in asymmetry influencing the composition of the groups that make decisions.
- *Decision context management*: This type describes an environment in which top management is concerned with the process of decision-making as much as with the substance. This approach attempts to create an overall organisational environment that motivates managers of various perspectives to initiate interaction on major problems on which differences in perspective are critical. Successful decision context management hinges upon two complementary top management tasks. First, the nurturing of a corporate value system, which creates a legitimate organisational structure provides a sense of common identity. Second, the legitimisation of the duality of perspectives by embedding them into the structure with numerous, overlapping administrative systems, which collectively create a co-operative environment.

4.2.2.2 The transnational corporation (TNC) (Bartlett/Ghoshal et al.)

In a study on **multinational structural change** in MNEs, Bartlett (1981) found a more **evolutionary pattern of organisational transformation** than the heretofore-described processes of '*reorganisation*' from one organisational archetype to another. Bartlett identified three distinct but closely interrelated **changes**: new management skills and perspectives, modifications of organisation structures and systems, and a change of the organisation 'climate'. The case studies provide evidence that the purpose of these changes in the formal and informal structures and systems was to allow the organisation's **decision-making process** to evolve from a unidimensional to a multidimensional focus akin to those described by Doz/Prahalad. The **dominant management mode** changed from substantive decision management by senior management in the initial phase towards a temporary coalition management mode, which in turn gave way to **decision context management** in the final. A main challenge was to build an appropriate decision-making environment in order to create an organisational climate in which flexible, constructive, and co-operative interaction between managers with different perspectives was institutionalised (Ibid. 139).

Bartlett (1986: 372) contends that a company's organisation is shaped not only by its external task environment, but also by its **'administrative heritage'**, which he defines as the path by which the company's international operations (its organisational history) and the ingrained values, norms, and practices of its management (its management culture) were developed.

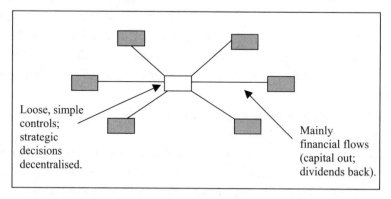

Figure 4-5: Decentralised federation model
(Source: Bartlett 1986: 374)

Bartlett exemplifies the importance of the administrative heritage by presenting three **archetypal organisation models**. The first model, **'decentralised federation'**, represents an organisation and management pattern of a federation of independent national subsidiaries, each focused primarily on its local market (Figure 4-5). The federative model is assumed to be typical for European MNEs whose major international expansion occurred in the first half of the 20th century. Central management had a limited ability to intervene in the subsidiary management and relied on an internal culture that emphasised personal relationships rather than formal structures (Bartlett 1986: 373).

On the other extreme, Bartlett sketches the **'centralised hub model'** (Figure 4-6), building on advantages from global integration and centralisation. The key parts of the company's value-added chain, typically upstream activities like product design or manufacturing, are retained at the centre, or are tightly centrally controlled. The centralised hub model represents typically Japanese companies that developed international activities in the 1960s and 1970s when the global competitive environment provided advantages from global integration (Ibid. 374). Both the decentralised federation and the centralised hub firm are characterised by pooled interdependencies and a '*hub-and-spoke structure*' without significant exchange and co-ordination between the subsidiaries.

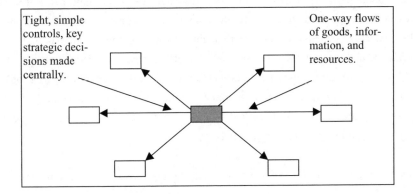

Figure 4-6:   Centralised hub model
(Source: Bartlett 1986: 375)

Since the 1980, Bartlett states the development of a competitive environment in which the forces for global integration remained important, but that has also experienced a re-emergence of several influences that require companies to be more nationally responsive as well. The resulting need to balance global integration and national responsiveness is best met by the '**integrated network model**' (Figure 4-7).

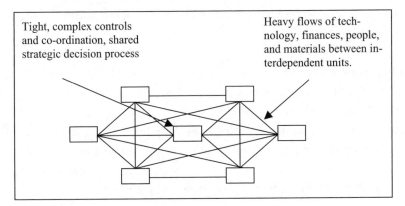

Figure 4-7:   Integrated network model
(Source: Bartlett 1986: 381)

The federative, centralised hub, and integrated network model resemble the multinational, global, and transnational firm as described in Chapter 2. The transnational organisation is capable to develop the organisational capabilities to respond to diverse national interests and demands while simultaneously co-ordinating and controlling these activities to allow the companies to act as efficient and effective global competitors. In contrast to its multinational and global counterparts, the **transnational organisation** builds and legitimises **multiple diverse internal perspectives** able to sense the complex environmental demands and opportunities. Its physical assets and management capabilities are distributed internationally but are interdependent, and it requires a robust and flexible internal integrative process (Bartlett 1986: 377-378). A study by Harzing (2000: 116) proved that Bartlett/Ghoshal's **typology of multinational companies**, based on in-depth case studies of nine MNEs, could be confirmed in a large-scale empirical setting. The **ideal type of a transnational company** has the following characteristics (Ghoshal/Westney 1993: 11):

- *global dispersion of activities* with capacity to innovate and exploit innovations globally;
- *interdependence between linked subunits* with cross-flows of people, technology, and products; key activities are performed by subsidiaries in locations with locational and organisational advantages linked by co-ordination strategies and reward systems;
- *tight coupling of subunits* based on close communication linkages often accompanied by a looser array of strategic partnerships aimed at cross-unit learning;
- *cross-unit learning* and the capacity to transfer innovations originating in one part of the system to other subunits, and to adapt and improve them in that process is a potential advantage of the integrated network;
- *structural flexibility* based on a priority of organisational processes over organisational structures.

The **most important task** of a transnational organisation is to develop a **management process** that can resolve the diversity of interests and perspectives and integrate the dispersed responsibilities. Management must be able to differentiate its operating relationships and change its decision-making roles by function, across businesses, among geographic units, and over time. The management process must be able to change from product to product, from country to country, and even from decision to decision. The required **decision making process** must be based on three **interdependent management processes**:

1. The *self-regulatory capability* in which top management's role is to establish an *appropriate organisational context* for delegated decisions by
   - the establishment of clear objectives and priorities,
   - the development in key management positions of individuals with broad perspectives, and

- the promotion of explicit norms and rules relating to the required organisational process;
2. A *managed organisational process* in which the key management task is to structure roles and relationships in specific key decisions;
3. A *supportive but constrained escalation process* that allows top management to intervene directly in the content of certain decisions (Bartlett 1986: 385-392).

Bartlett (1986: 393-396, 1981: 124, and 1992: 109) describes the different **tools and processes** used to build and manage the **transnational** using a physiological model based on three **components**:

- *Structuring the organisational anatomy* comprises the development of a formal organisational macrostructure (line organisation) and complementary micro-structural tools such as task forces, or committees that may become supplementary decision-making forums.
- *Developing an organisational physiology* includes the design of communication channels through which much of the organisation's decision-making process operates. The adaptation of administrative systems, hierarchical channels, and informal relationships can facilitate an extensive and direct control over the volume, content, and direction of information flows.
- *Organisational psychology* greatly affects the way a firm operates. For internationally operating firms this is a particularly important attribute. Employees with a variety of different cultural backgrounds have to develop a common basis of knowledge, norms, values, and expectations. In a dispersed and dynamic organisational environment, normative integration and shared expectation may prove more effective for co-ordination than prescribed structures. '*The transnational is not so much a type of structural configuration as a management mentality*' (Ibid. 399).

In a review of the evolution of the studies on **mechanisms of co-ordination in MNEs**, Martinez/Jarillo (1989: 500) found evidence that there has been **different emphasis across the years** on different mechanisms of co-ordination. The authors observed an 'evolution' in the focus of the research from the simpler to the more complex devices, a trend from unidimensional to multidimensional perspectives, and from structural/formal to a mixture of structural/formal with informal/subtle mechanisms.

☞ **Complementary perspective: The MNE as an interorganisational network**

Ghoshal/Bartlett (1993: 79) believe that a complex entity like an MNE can be more appropriately conceptualised as an interorganisational grouping rather than as a unitary organisation and by exploring them by concepts of **organisation-sets** and **interorganisational networks**. Ghoshal/Bartlett therefore conceptualise the **MNE as a network of exchange relationships** among different organisational units, including the headquarters and the different national subsidiaries that are collectively embedded in a structured context. This context represents an **external network** consisting of all the organisations such as customers, suppliers, regulators, and competitors with which the different units of the MNE have to interact.

From a **contingency perspective**, Ghoshal/Bartlett (1993: 80-81) hypothesise that the **configuration of organisational resources** and the **nature of interunit exchange relations** can be explained by **attributes of the external network**. Based on insights from the **institutionalisation theory**, relational networks in the institutional environment are assumed to play an important role in influencing the structure and behaviour of organisations. The uniqueness of the MNE as an organisational form arises from the fact that its **different constituent units** are embedded in **different national environments** in which the structures of these relational networks can be very different. In the course of globalisation, these local relational networks are **increasingly interconnected** in complex ways. The differences between local systems and the interconnections among them provide the central tension in organisational relations of the MNE. The **distribution of power within the network** due to centrality, resource endowment, and ability to reduce uncertainty for the MNE has a decisive influence on the organisation of exchange relations in the net.

The MNE has **national operating units**, which are embedded in a unique context and, for any specific type of exchange relationship, has its **unique organisation set (OS)**. The **density of a given OS** is defined as the *extensiveness of exchange ties* within its elements. Density measures the extent to which actors within a set are connected to one another. The **different organisation sets** of the different units may themselves be interconnected through **exchange ties.** Due to such linkages among different local organisation sets, all members of all the organisation sets collectively constitute the '**external network**' within which the MNE network is embedded. It can be differentiated between the '**within density**' of individual local organisation sets and the '**across density**' across all the different sets that collectively constitute the external network.

When **interaction densities within** the different national organisation sets are **low**, the social contexts exerts only limited influence and economic optimisation leads to a **concentration of resources** in the most efficient locations. The overall resource configuration will show relatively low dispersal and high specialisation. When the **densities are high**, the **activities** will be **fragmented** and more resources allocated to national markets so as to provide the variety that is necessary to match the structures of the organisation sets.

When the **linkages across the different national organisation sets** are **sparse**, the MNE's **resource configuration** will be **dispersed** as in the case of high within density. The case of low within density and high across density leads to high specialisation and a low dispersal. The MNE will locate its resources according to the resource niches in different countries. Many of these national resource niches will be eliminated. In the case of high within and high across density, it is not necessary to establish a comprehensive range of resources in each market since exchange linkages can now be established across borders. In general, with high across densities, the logic of resource allocation becomes inappropriate. Instead, the resource configuration is greatly influenced by the nodal characteristics of the complex external network (Ghoshal/Bartlett 1993: 91-92).

Within and across densities in the different national organisation-sets of an MNE predicate the **relative power** of the **headquarters** and the **operational units**, and the **nature of resource flows** generated by the resulting distribution of power leads to the **pattern of isomorphic fit** described above. Ghoshal/Bartlett (1993: 94) expect that **dense relationships** with the members of their **local organisation-sets** can be expected to **enhance the powers of the national units** of the MNE. The efficacy of the hierarchical power of the headquarters to counteract the linkage-based power of the subsidiary is contingent on the density of interactions among members of the subsidiary's organisation-set. Powerful subsidiaries based on strong interdependencies with local firms will use their power to reduce their dependence on the other MNE units and bargain for a full range of resources to become more autonomous. When all or most of the units of the MNE are located in environment of high within density, the consequence is expected to be a high level of dispersal of resources on a local-for-local basis (Ibid. 95).

Power in the MNE network arises from the power to control critical resources in exchange relations and from structural power based on the centrality and position in the network. **Subsidiaries** with different degrees of power in the network will be assigned **different roles**, ranging from an '*implementor*' to a '*global leader*' with world product mandates (Ghoshal/Bartlett 1993: 98).

Kobrin (1991: 19) developed an indicator for the **measurement of transnational integration**. He posits that the greater the **relative volume of cross-border intrafirm resource flows**, the greater the degree of transnational integration. Furthermore, intra-industry trade is assumed to be an indicator of the presence of global competition (Ibid. 20). According to Kobrin, transnational integration implies more than interdependence in the sense that events in one unit significantly influence those in another; it implies dependence of subsidiaries on the multinational system for information, technology, management, funds, and products (Ibid. 19).

4.2.2.3 The MNE as a heterarchy and 'multi-centre structure' (Hedlund et al.)

Within the context of the **MNE** as a '*global learning vehicle*', Sölvell/Zander (1995: 18) identify two distinct schools of thought. One view is that the well-established MNE continues to make a clear distinction between core and peripheral activities for upgrading of competitive advantage on a global scale ('**home-based MNE**'). The other perspective reflects that of the Process School, arguing that MNEs build increasingly complex and fluid organisational structures and management processes in order to cope with a more complex international environment and to combine global integration and local differentiation. For example, when subsidiaries have started carrying out core activities such as R&D and advanced manufacturing, the distinction between core and peripheral activities has become blurred (Sölvell/Zander 1995: 24). The decision-making and co-ordinating dimensions of the **heterarchical MNE** are perhaps the most critical because they highlight its unique properties and provide the basis for the '*competitive advantage of multinationality*' (Sölvell/Zander 1995: 31). The heterarchical organisation seems to be a particularly good arena to make the transfer of tacit knowledge effective through its **holographic characteristics** and organisational culture (Sölvell/Zander 1995: 32).

Hedlund (1993: 214) observes that MNEs are increasingly marked by **'messy' organisational structures**, blending of dimensions, toleration of inconsistencies, overlaps, and non-institutionalised ambiguities. Interdependencies between subsidiaries are multidimensional and reciprocal. From this perspective, the **MNE** appears as a **mechanism for the selection of governance modes** and is hence a selection mechanism rather than a selected mechanism (Ibid. 225). Organisational memory, the capacity for information transfer, mechanisms to encourage shared goals and organisational culture become increasingly valuable for the MNE's capability of self-renewal. The organisational form that represents best the **principle of continuous self-renewal in complex systems** is the holographic organisation, also termed 'heterarchy' (Ibid. 214).

Hedlund's idea of the MNE as a heterarchy builds on the concept of '**holons**' (Koestler 1978), which are parts that are self-regulating, relatively autonomous, and exhibiting properties not deducible from lower units. At the same time, they are parts of larger wholes. The members of a hierarchy, like the Roman god Janus, all have two faces looking in opposite directions: the face turned towards the subordinate levels is that of self-contained whole; the face turned upward toward the apex, that of a dependent part. This '**Janus effect**' is characteristic of sub-wholes in all types of hierarchies. Koestler (1967: 48) proposes the term 'holon' to refer to such Janus-faced entities. Patterns of rule-governed behaviour lend the group stability and cohesion, and define it as a **social holon**, with an individuality of its own. Constituent holons are defined by fixed rules and flexible strategies (Ibid. 55). The **dichotomy of 'wholeness and partness'** (autonomy – dependence) constitutes the **'Janus-principle'**. Its dynamic expression is the polarity of the self-assertive and integrative tendencies (Koestler 1967: 58). Hedlund views this *'holon property'* of Koestler as fully consistent with the heterarchy model that he developed (Hedlund 1986: 10, 12). **MNEs as heterarchies** show the following **properties** (Hedlund 1986: 21-27, 1993: 229-232):

1. The heterarchical MNE has *many centres*. Foundations of competitive advantage no longer in any one country, but in many. New ideas and products may come up in many different countries and later be exploited on a global scale. A geographically diffused pattern of expertise is built up, corresponding to unique abilities in each node of the network, leading to a multi-centre structure.
2. *Subsidiaries* are given *strategic roles*, not only locally, but also for the MNE as a whole. Corporate level strategy has to be implemented and formulated in a geographically scattered network.
3. Heterarchy implies *different kinds of centres* and consists of a *mix of organising principles*. There is no overriding dimension superordinate to the rest but temporary subordination and simultaneous sub- and superordination.
4. Heterarchy is characterised by *different degrees of coupling* between organisational units with flexibility in the selection of governance modes. A heterarchical MNC is a meta-institution, which continuously creates new institutional arrangements. This speeds up the process of institutional evolution in terms of a Lamarckian development, where experience is accumulated, experiments fully exploited, and memory over generations kept intact.
5. Organisation is in a *continuous flux* along time and environmental changes.
6. *Integration* is achieved primarily through *normative control*, and only secondarily through calculative and coercive/bureaucratic regulations.
7. Heterachy exposes *holographic properties*. Information about the whole is contained in each part. Organisation is often circular rather than transitive.
8. The heterarchical firm is best described by the metaphor *'firm as a brain'* rather than *'brain of the firm'*. Thinking is not only restricted to one exclusive centre, but goes on in the whole enterprise. Thinking goes together with and directly informs action.
9. *Coalitions* with other companies and other types of actors are frequent.
10. *Strategy-formulation* is guided by *radical problem-orientation*.

The **watchmaker parable** (Simon 1962: 90-91) shows the hierarchical principle that hierarchical breakdown of a process into stable intermediate forms tends to conserve the original system and make it resistant to change. In human systems, forethought can dramatically increase the speed of evolution and decrease the need for hierarchy (Hedlund 1993: 220). The **MNE** can be understood as a **mechanism for constantly selecting governance modes** for an array of innumerable and changing transactions. This type of meta-institution is what is required when tasks, information, technological interfaces, etc., cannot be pre-specified and must change at non-trivial speed. Many organisational units are both a co-ordinating and direction centre and a subordinated part, and the **composition of roles changes** often enough and *overlaps* to such an extent that segregation into different hierarchical chains becomes impractical (Hedlund 1993: 225-226).

Heterarchy is characterised by the following aspects (Hedlund 1993: 229-232):

1. *Multidimensional*: Components are related along three primary dimension: knowledge, action, and position of authority.
2. *Asymmetrical order*: Units in a heterarchy may or may not be ordered in the same way along the three dimensions.
3. *Temporary subordination and simultaneous sub- and super-ordination*: The order will vary over time and circumstance.
4. *Non-transitivity, circularity*: The order will not necessarily be transitive. The organisation will often be circular.
5. *Horizontality*: The relations between units may be multidimensional and of several kinds.
6. *Normative, goal-directed integration*: A heterarchy is given cohesion and is protected from mere anarchy by normative integration. Shared objectives and a common organisational culture are important mechanisms.

Hedlund/Ridderstråle (1997: 343) hypothesise that the MNE increasingly will have to build its adaptive capability on the principle of '**redundancy of functions**' rather than on '*redundancy of parts*'. Organisational units should contain units capable of **both creation and exploitation**, rather than units specialised in either direction. The challenge is to combine these two functions across related businesses and within as well as across countries or regions (Ibid. 344). Innovation and creation cannot be provided by optimal configuration of a corporate hierarchy. Instead, Hedlund/Ridderstråle (Ibid. 351) assume the heterarchy to be a better model for self-renewal as heterarchy provides a way of thinking about the integration of exploitation and creation.

Similarly, Sölvell/Zander (1995: 25-26) assume that each unit having different responsibilities according to the dimensions of exploitation and experimentation, and also by each unit assuming **different roles** in the creation of new technologies explains the absence of any uniformly superordinate structure. Within the context of experimentation, the roles of different units and their function can change over time.

The **best mode of co-ordination** within units is relatively '**organic**', built on physical co-location and informal networks. The principle of internalising reciprocities is, however, difficult to implement in an MNE because geographical distance weakens all the mechanisms integral to the mutual co-ordination mode: co-location is by definition impossible; personal networks are harder to form; common language and the transfer of tacit knowledge becomes problematic, etc. An archetypal mechanism for co-ordination becomes the temporary, multi-functional, and international project, with resources drawn from the operational structures of the firm (Hedlund/Ridderstråle 1997: 343). In the MNC, this principle necessitates intense dedication to facilitating transfers of personnel (not only managers) across organisational and geographic boundaries (Ibid. 349).

Hedlund (1992) distinguishes three **fundamental structures** in an organisation. The social structure, or **structure of authority**, is mostly organised in a pyramid-like fashion. The **action structure** increasingly is not congruent with the social one. The **knowledge structure** is assumed to be the most important one as hierarchical decision-making is increasingly insufficient in complex MNEs. Disentangling the concept of hierarchy is more necessary the greater the change and geographical and organisational diffusion of knowledge and capacity for strategic actions (Hedlund/Ridderstråle 1997: 352).

The heterarchic organisational models move away from centralised structures toward maximum authority and responsibility in the operating parts, consistent with the need to secure cohesion and coherence across the whole. Organisations utilising such concepts have been described as exhibiting qualities of holograms, hypertext, and object-oriented engineering. These innovations result in the creation of small, highly focused, self-acting units (holons) that co-operate together. Similar to Hedlund, Mathews (2002: 140) terms these units cells due to the similarity of their behaviour with that of cells in a biological organism. The **cellular organisation** is characterised by its **defining features** as follows (Mathews 2002: 141):

1. The operating entities are discrete cells, which are quasi-autonomous and self-sufficient.
2. The relations between cells are direct business relations of contract and subcontract, forming a network.

3. The whole maintains its integrity through shared governance; a co-ordination centre, which acts as the brain or nerve centre of the organisation, provides strategic co-ordination. It has limited powers of intervention and initiative in order to maintain the organisation's integrity and identity.

This description can by definition apply to any level of the organisation. Mathews therefore implicitly builds his **organisational model** on the **principle of 'self-similarity'** in complex systems. Other systemic characteristics as cellular self-sufficiency, self-governance through network communication, and integration shall offer advantages in terms of responsiveness and adaptability because it is the cells themselves that are supposed to respond or adapt to new situations without hierarchical delays. These features bias the organisation toward entrepreneurship, distributed ownership, learning, and mutual trust (Mathews 2002: 143).

☞ **Multi-centre structures**

Early in their development, the **foreign subsidiaries** more or less constitute the parent company's long arm and are very dependent on the parent company for products and knowledge. Later, as the subsidiaries develop and adjust their operations to the local national markets they will gradually disengage from the operation of the mother company and become more independent relative to the parent company than before. Some subsidiaries grow in a way that gives them a dominant position above the local level. The former periphery develops into new centres of power. The **earlier centre-periphery structure** changes to a structure with centres in several different countries. The **multi-centre structure** can be especially prominent in highly internationalised firms where there are several geographically separated subsidiaries, more or less interdependent through their respective business networks in which they are embedded (Forsgren/Holm 1990: 341). The development of international firms into multi-centre structures is also labelled '**internationalisation of the second degree**' (Forsgren et al. 1991).

A **federation** can be best analysed as an **organisation-set** in which the **different units**, e.g. divisions or subsidiaries within divisions, are **embedded in local networks**. Depending on the unit's position within the network and how this network is related to the whole organisation the unit can exercise influence over its own and other unit's strategy and structure, sometimes in opposition to the formal hierarchy (Forsgren/Holm 1990: 340).

From a **political perspective**, there are two consequences of a foreign unit becoming a dominant part of the network. First, it will exert greater influence over the network's operations, Second, the central management will experience a greater need to gain access to the unit's local, critical resources, e.g. information, to be able to influence its activities (Forsgren/Holm 1990: 340).

In line with the multi-centre structure, Ghauri (1990) developed a network approach assuming that a **foreign subsidiary** has a **three-dimensional relationship**: (1) with the *head office*, (2) with *local authorities*, and (3) with the *local network* (Ibid. 261). In a **sequential process**, subsidiaries, through adaptation to local markets, first acquire a **prominent position** in the local network (Figure 4-8).

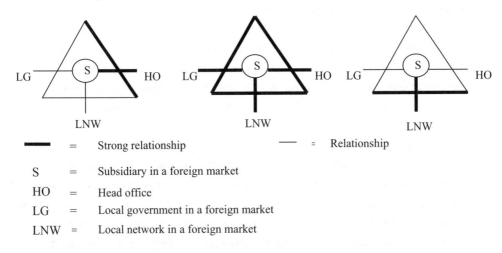

Figure 4-8: The process of changing head office subsidiary relationship
(Source: Ghauri 1990: 271)

In the **first stage**, the start of the internationalisation, the *most important relationship* for the subsidiary is the one with the *head office*. As the subsidiary gains more experience in the local market, it may acquire a stronger position in the local network and become less dependent on the head office. In the resulting **second stage**, the subsidiary most likely gives *equal importance* to the head office, the local network, and the local government. In the **third stage**, the subsidiary gains more experience, knowledge, and a better stance in the *local network* and thus, that relationship becomes the *most pivotal* one. In some cases, the relationship with the head office is replaced by its relationship with a regional centre (Ibid. 271).

4.2.2.4 Other network concepts of MNEs

Hedberg et al. (1997: 13) developed the concept of the '**imaginary organisation**'. The perspective of the imaginary organisation refers to a system in which assets, processes, and actors critical to the focal enterprise exist and function both inside and outside the limits of the enterprise's conventional landscape formed by its legal structure, its accounting, its organisational charts, and the language otherwise used to describe the enterprise. The 'leader' or 'architect' (used interchangeably) of an imaginary organisation creates a strategic map showing how a new business arrangement will be put together. The leader also has a conception of the core competence of the own unit. This competence is later supplemented by the contributions of the partners and partner enterprises co-operating in the arrangement. The next step is to define a customer base, one or more delivery systems, and the methods of communication with customers (Hedberg et al. 1997: 15). Basically, the model of the imaginary organisation resembles that of the '**virtual organisation**'.

The '**stratocracy**' is characterised by (1) multiple roles and temporary assignments, (2) project teams and task forces, (3) co-ordination mechanisms based on informal interaction, (4) limited role of line staff. The fluid and hybrid structure is marked by small entrepreneurial units and is dominated by the '*rule of the doers*' (Bahrami/Evans 1987: 56-57, 65).

Lateral decision processes are the global glue bringing the appropriate people together in a collaborative effort (Poynter/White 1990: 76). In the '**horizontal organisation**', decisions are impacted by three key attributes: (1) lateral (global/local) decision processes, (2) horizontal network, and (3) shared decision premises (White/Poynter 1989: 55). In order to create shared values as a basis for decision-processes, an institutional approach for socialising new members is often most feasible for multinational companies operating in geographically dispersed locations with language and cultural differences. An organisational context that promotes lateral decision-making oriented towards that achievement of competitive advantage worldwide is crucial (Poynter/White 1990: 74). Performance should not be evaluated by locally reported results, but rather by the accumulation of actions consistent with the pursuit of worldwide advantage (Ibid. 76).

Boettcher (1996) provides the most sophisticated instrument for the analysis of global intraorganisational networks with his **global network framework** (GNF). It is built on the basis of a conceptualisation of headquarters and subsidiaries as nodes or actors and three different network levels. The vertical network is organised along the value-added chain. The horizontal network provides the context for co-ordination of value-added activities and the underlying communication and decision network represents the nerve system of the MNE. The GNF is conceptionally more open than the other described network concepts and does not expose the normative character of other intraorganisational network models. Paul (1998) adapts this model to a functional perspective and focuses on the network management of value-added functions. Boettcher et al. (1993) and Welge et al. (1996, 1998) further stress the importance of a global orientation as the overarching co-ordination mode on the global level.

4.2.2.5 Critical reflection upon the Process School

The view of the MNE as an intraorganisational network and the development of strategies and organisational archetypes on the basis of the duality **global integration vs. local adaptability** have been dominating research on MNEs for the last 25 years. Its appeal is twofold.

First, the conceptualisation of the MNE as a network allows for a much better observation and description of its huge global complexity without being fixed by the hierarchical limits of organisation. It is possible to conceptualise organisational units and their interdependencies in a much more differentiated way. The network perspective allows for the definition of networks on different levels, allowing for overlapping roles of units, e.g. the dual roles of subsidiaries as parts of both the MNE and the local network. It is further possible to differentiate MNEs on the basis of organisational actors, products, or competencies without being limited by hierarchical structures. Most approaches, however, cling to the dialectic of headquarters vs. subsidiaries, thus reproducing the inertial perspective of earlier approaches to strategic decision-making in MNEs. Much conceptual freedom gained by introducing the network model has been left unexplored due to the restriction to the popular teleological focus.

Second, the construction of the conceptual frameworks on the basis of the central duality **global integration vs. local differentiation** has provided the means to reduce all global complexity to just one guiding difference, which serves to build anything from strategy to organisation or human resource management. With the notable exception of Hedlund's heterarchy, most approaches did not distinguish this guiding difference from the traditional guiding difference in strategic management of centralisation/decentralisation and mixed up basically independent dimensions. The resulting products are normative strategies and organisational archetypes based on only one guiding difference. Due to this dominance, all other guiding differences were basically left out, producing a vacuum around this approach in international business theory, particularly as other theoretical approaches have only half-heartedly being linked with the MNE perspective. Since the early 1990s, however, authors increasingly link organisation theory and evolutionary theories to the MNE perspective. These approaches will be described in Chapter 5.

In a **reflection upon the Process School**, Forsgren (1992: 479-480) and Melin (1992: 110-111) particularly criticise that

- the need and possibilities of integration is strongly overemphasised compared to differentiation;

- despite a tendency towards multi-centre structures, the headquarters' possibility to design the structure and systems is accentuated in such a way that a beneficial integration is created;
- mainly clinical or phenomenological research methods have been used;
- organisation and strategic management theory have been avoided;
- striving for managerial relevance has led to a normative bias;
- normative bent seems to be increasing with an increased degree of speculation in conceptual frameworks without empirical support;
- despite an emphasis on the dynamic dimension of strategy and structure the process orientation is in fact rather restricted. The only exception is the change process study by Doz/Prahalad (1987).

What is most intriguing is the fact that although coined 'Process School' by the constituting authors themselves, the process perspective is absent in analyses and theory generation. The focus is on administrative processes but the knowledge about the transition of organisational structures is certainly insufficient. Particularly the interplay between internal and external forces or between strategic and structural changes is completely missing (Melin 1992: 113).

Despite these weaknesses and failure, the process school has developed a processual view on strategy and organisation in MNEs as multinational networks, which heretofore had not existed. Particularly the multi-centre view further explores the conceptual freedom offered by the network perspective by integrating global MNE network and local subsidiary levels of observation. It may thus not be counted as an element of the Process School although it has been developed in its tradition. Process research before had been restricted to internationalisation theories and decision-making in headquarters-subsidiary relations. The Process School has introduced the network perspective in MNE research and conceptualised differentiated headquarters and subsidiary relations, thus paving the way for subsequent research on intraorganisational roles, which are described in the following section.

4.2.3 Intraorganisational roles in MNEs

A main influence on the evolutionary capabilities comes from the **interplay of the MNE's subsystems**, particularly among the geographically dispersed subsidiaries. **Research on MNE subsidiary management** can be differentiated into three **major streams** (Birkinshaw/Hood 1998: 4-9):

1. *Headquarter-subsidiary relationship research* focuses on aspects of dyadic relationships between headquarters and the individual subsidiaries. From this hierarchical and

basically static perspective, the control of subsidiaries by headquarters is central to the research.
2. *Subsidiary role research* concentrates on internal, corporate, and environmental factors explaining different subsidiary roles and relationships within network structures.
3. *Subsidiary development research* observes changes in roles and activities of subsidiaries in network structures over time.

With the development of the **network perspective** on MNEs, the focus of research on MNE subsidiaries changed from a situation of the firm as a bundle of headquarter-subsidiary relationships into more complicated system with **reciprocal dependencies** between units in different countries (Forsgren/Pedersen 1998: 141).

Research on subsidiary roles was **first** predominantly focused on '**product mandates**'. Although there is no common definition of what characterises a subsidiary with a product mandate, most of the literature seems to emphasise aspects of autonomy rather than interdependence vis-à-vis the rest of the MNE network. The definition is not primarily a question of specialisation between subsidiaries within an MNE, but rather a question of completeness of functions within one and the same subsidiary (Forsgren/Pedersen 1998: 142).

Within the **network perspective**, **subsidiary roles** became to be **differentiated**. Compared to the product mandate literature, the basic difference seems to be that interdependence rather than autonomy characterises the pattern of relationships within MNEs. Subsidiaries are part of an overall strategy in a learning organisation. Networks of information, communication, and knowledge within the MNE become crucial. The initial question in product mandate literature about how a subsidiary can contribute to the local economy and to overall MNE profits through autonomy is replaced by the question of how the local subsidiary can contribute to the global competitiveness of the MNE through interdependence (Forsgren/Pedersen 1998: 145). Subsidiaries are simultaneously actors in the internal MNE network, the business network, and the local network. Subsidiaries have multiple roles, are linking pins with a bridging function.

In an **integrated MNE network** each affiliate specialises in accordance with the specific characteristics of local production conditions, technological capabilities, and user requirements. The network benefits from **economies of scale** through the local concentration of particular lines of activity, **economies of locational agglomeration** through an interchange with others operating in the same vicinity in technologically allied fields, and **economies of scope** through the international intra-firm co-ordination of related but geographically separated activities. The **experience** acquired in a specialised activity in one location creates technological spillovers that can be passed on to other parts of the MNE network elsewhere (Cantwell 1998: 279, Cantwell/Piscitello 1999: 126). It has been shown that since the 1970s, in industries in which such net advantages to multinational integration were available, multinationality has been a source of competitive success and faster growth (Cantwell/Sanna-Randaccio 1993).

The extent to which affiliates of MNEs specialise within their industry across national boundaries in accordance with the comparative advantage of local expertise tends to be greater for the leading MNEs that originate from the major locational centres of excellence for their industry. The particular role of the largest and best-known MNEs in the formation is attributable partly to their capability to devote the resources needed to organise a complex organisational network. Another factor is their wide range of **global absorptive capacity** and established diversity of competencies to be able to effectively utilise and bring together a variety of new streams of innovation, each to some extent specific to their own particular local institutional setting or environment (Cantwell/Piscitello 1999: 126).

Nohria/Ghoshal (1994: 492-493) assume that **differences between subsidiaries** basically depend on the **complexity of subsidiaries' local environments** and on the **levels of resources possessed by subsidiaries**. An increase in the complexity of a subsidiary's local environment induces an increase in the importance of local knowledge and causes a greater influence of the subsidiary. An increase in its resource level leads to greater local institutional pressure and less dependence on the head office. MNEs are hence assumed to differentiate the structure of headquarters-subsidiary relations to fit the context of subsidiaries in order to enhance the performance of each subsidiary and of the MNE as a whole.

Resource-based theories regard differentiated networks of subsidiaries as a major method of developing **competitive advantages**. Multinational corporations that develop differentiated networks transform some of their subsidiaries into **centres of competence**. These subsidiaries develop core activities that play an important role in the operations in all, or significant parts, of the MNE. Therefore, subsidiaries located in areas capable of development into centres of competence become central to the overall objectives of MNEs. Subsidiaries selected to be centres of competence have desirable resources based on local networks that are founded on trust and access to inputs that are useful in achieving the goals of MNEs. Pools of skilled labour, access to high-quality products, and membership of local networks that include organisations and agencies that help to achieve the strategic objectives of the parent company provide attractive locations for MNEs. When desirable resources cannot readily be transferred to other parts of the firm it is beneficial to develop subsidiaries into centres of competence and to use output from these centres to satisfy demands of the operations in the firm network. MNEs take advantage of the different cultures and business environments in which their subsidiaries operate to develop intra-firm networks that make the best use of the resources available to them (McDonald/Burton 2002: 135-136).

4.2.3.1 Headquarters-subsidiary relations

One main stream in the study of structural and strategic relations between organisational units of MNEs has been focused on the headquarter-subsidiary relationships. **Centralisation** in decision-making versus subsidiary autonomy, formalisation of decision-making according to explicit routines and lines of authority, and integration of activities across the multinational network have been **main research targets** (Birkinshaw 1994b: 119-123).

Headquarters and **subsidiary managers** may perceive both the same country and the corporate network quite differently: they each define their own relevant task environment (Kobrin 1988: 112). Accurate assessment of pressure for fragmentation is difficult. Considerable geographical and cultural distances as well as differences in individual cognitive orientation and organisational position make a *common perception*, or even agreement as to causal relations and effects, *improbable*. Environmental assessment is a subjective and largely qualitative process. **Subsidiary management** is in a unique position at the **interface** of the **local environment** and the **organisation** as local managers are the only individuals who function in both systems (Kobrin 1988: 117). The collection of **local initiatives** and their integration into a **corporate strategy** does not necessarily lead to a real global strategy. The same applies to the administrative systems. For example, a study by Schwarzer (1993: 12) suggests that many MNEs gave their subsidiaries a great leeway in the development of information and communication systems that have led to problems in their integration. The difficulty in international management is to balance the perspective of **global business strategies** that are pursued across all local markets and the perspective of **country-based strategies**, which in their sum constitute a global strategy (Lorange/Probst 1990: 149). In parallel, this balance has to be continuously achieved in the organisational context.

With regard to **cultural differences**, Kriger (1988: 358) found in a study on the **role of subsidiary boards** also consistently significant differences to exist between the overall approach of North American MNEs and Japanese MNEs, with European MNEs generally falling somewhere between the two. Essentially, Japanese MNEs have a strong desire to dig deep roots into the host countries in which they operate whereas North American MNEs, on the whole, were found to be less likely to view a particular host country as requiring such deep roots.

From the traditional **global vs. local perspective**, headquarters focused on control over subsidiary initiatives and actions in order to achieve the integration of MNE actions, resulting in a **high degree of centralisation** in *'global companies'* or *'***laissez-faire***'* in *'multinational* *companies*' (Martinez/Jarillo 1989). The **dominant dimension in headquarters-subsidiary relations** therefore was the **degree of centralisation** and, in turn, **subsidiary autonomy**. For example, Garnier (1982: 906) found evidence that a given subsidiary will have little autonomy if (1) it belongs to a large and dispersed MNE, (2) it manufactures fairly standardised products, (3) the activities of members are largely integrated, (4) it has been created to serve a market larger than the local host market, (5) the parent holds a large portion of the equity.

On the other hand, a study by Gates/Egelhoff (1986: 87) suggests that if MNEs introduce more product lines in foreign markets or modify products to fit differing local environments, such strategic changes are likely to require more decentralisation of decision-making. Similarly, MNEs that allow substantial outside ownership in foreign subsidiaries or attempt to grow through acquisition of foreign firms are also likely to decentralise decision-making. Summarising, Hedlund (1981: 45, 58) found a **positive relationship between the autonomy of subsidiaries** and

- the simplicity of the technology used by the MNE,
- the lack of international experience of the parent company,
- the degree of market fragmentation,
- the lack of links of interdependence or common environmental condition,
- the smallness of the MNE,
- the tendency to internationalise through acquisitions rather than by building up own companies,
- lack of integration with the MNE in terms of product flows,
- low market share of the subsidiary,
- establishment of the subsidiary through acquisition,
- lack of involvement in the core technology of the parent firm,
- lack of technology transfer between the subsidiary and the parent firm,
- size and relative size of the subsidiary,
- low intensity of competition in the local market,
- low concentration of suppliers in the local market,
- high performance of the subsidiary.

From a traditional perspective, the foreign subsidiary will naturally have a much simpler organisation than the home base, but it is likely to mirror head office to some extent. The **mirror effect** may not be produced by instructions from head office, but by an almost unconscious development along the line of communication (Brooke/Remmers 1978: 36). After some time, subsidiaries that are able to contribute knowledge to the group as a whole may develop a certain power base because of this. R&D capacity is a critical strategic resource, which gives headquarters a basic control over the activities of a subsidiary and thus augments the dependence of the subsidiary (Hedlund 1981: 52). The **accumulation of resources**, technological expertise, and relations in clusters and business networks provide subsidiaries increasingly with **positional power**. This development depends recursively on the external context of the subsidiary and its role within the MNE network.

The **mediating role of headquarters** as a broker and co-ordination centre for the management of the multinational network hence is primarily based on the **resource allocation** and **differentiation of subsidiary roles** (Kogut 1990: 61).

Lorange/Probst (1990: 152) promote a **shift** from a relatively strong emphasis on organisational structure to relatively more emphasis on management interaction processes, from '**organisational entities of subsidiaries**' to '**global networks of executives**' as a metaphor for understanding and learning. The benefits to a firm from developing an ability to transfer relevant information and experience from one situation to the next are high. A large firm may wish to avoid the penalties of inconsistent responses that may ensue, particularly when the intensity and the reach of an issue or event are unforeseeable. A determination or standardisation of responses in such cases is impossible (Mahini 1988: 13, 73). Roth/Nigh (1992: 295) found clear support for arguments associating more **effective headquarter-subsidiary relationships** with (1) greater levels of co-ordination between headquarters and the subsidiary, (2) greater use of personal integrating mechanisms, and (3) lower levels of conflict between headquarters and subsidiary.

4.2.3.2 Subsidiary roles

Moore/Heeler (1998: 1) propose that the three classical levels of potential **advantages for MNEs** (firm-specific, country-specific, and internalisation advantages) should be complemented by a fourth level, which is constituted by **subsidiary-specific advantages (SSAs)**. In the view of Moore (2001: 288), the SSAs constitute an additional level in the eclectic paradigm (Dunning 1977). SSAs reside at the subsidiary level, are unique, and are not shared across the MNE as are firm-specific advantages, nor found across a national industry, as are location advantages (Ibid., Moore 2001: 281). He (1998: 31) contends that a **unique social context** can be an important foundation for organisations' **mutual learning**. Subsidiaries are hence assumed to develop idiosyncratic knowledge, capabilities, and competencies that are embedded in their local context.

The term '**subsidiary role**' has two distinct meanings. From a parent company's point of view, the **role is assigned to the subsidiary** on the basis of its proven capability and market potential. From the subsidiary's perspective, its role appears as an **emergent form** that the subsidiary develops over time as a function of its own efforts as well as those of the corporate parent. Similar to different meanings of role, also the **role formation process** may be distinguished from a **parent perspective** *(intended processes)* and a **subsidiary perspective** *(emergent process)*. The emergent process begins with the build-up of special expertise over time in a business unit or subsidiary. The intended process occurs entirely through the efforts of top management (Birkinshaw 1994a: 5).

Birkinshaw (2000: 75) argues that MNEs can be modelled as a federation or a network of interdependent subsidiary units, whose geographical location matters because it is the link to the local context, and the development of location-specific capabilities, that provides the basis for the subsidiaries' competitiveness. The **subsidiary units** are participating simultaneously in three different **internal markets**. The most common market is the '**market for intermediate products and services**' where subsidiaries develop supplier-customer relationships.

The '**market for charters**' is most visible in cases of new investments, e.g. a new production plant or an R&D centre. In such cases, multiple subsidiary units and inward investment bodies are bidding for the investment (Ibid. 71). Charters are defined as the business, or elements of a business that the subsidiary undertakes on behalf of the MNE and for which it has responsibility. Examples are licences, franchises, or mandates (Ibid. 65). While new investments are commonly competed for, increasingly existing charters are deemed to be mobile and open for competition. Subsidiaries need to be understood as a set of resources and capabilities embedded in a local context, with a potentially contestable charter (Birkinshaw 2000a: 115). Single-function subsidiaries may evolve into higher-value multiple function units through functional upgrading. A major influence derives from spillovers in the respective local clusters.

The '**market for capabilities and practices**' is most visible in cases of best-practice transfer between subsidiaries. The challenge is to provide the appropriate incentives to encourage best-practice transfers between units. These include structural approaches such as the creation of centres of excellence or the enactment of internal brokers. Incentives can also be created by evaluating the propensity of organisational actors to co-operate with others (Birkinshaw 2000: 72-72).

According to Birkinshaw (2000a: 21), the **subsidiary** sits at the **interface of three markets**:

1. the *local market*, consisting of competitors, suppliers, customers, and regulatory bodies in the host country,

2. the *internal market*, which is composed of head office operations and all corporate-controlled affiliates worldwide, and
3. the *global market*, consisting of competitors, customers and suppliers that fall outside the local and internal markets.

4.2.3.2.1 Subsidiary initiatives

Birkinshaw (1997: 207) stresses the potential of **entrepreneurship at the subsidiary level** to enhance local responsiveness, worldwide learning and global integration, a much broader role than previously envisioned. The author further contends that the use of contextual mechanisms to create differential subsidiary roles has its limitations because each initiative type is facilitated in different ways. Birkinshaw defines an *initiative* in this context as '*a discrete, proactive undertaking that advances a new way for the corporation to use or expand its resources*' and (1) has significant international value-added potential and (2) was instigated without instruction from the parent company (Birkinshaw 1994a: 8).

Building on a terminology by Thompson (1967), Delany (2000: 233-237) developed a **classification for subsidiary initiatives**:

1. *Domain developing* includes (1) the pursuit of new business opportunities in the local markets, (2) bid for corporate investment, (3) extension of the mandate, and (4) reconfiguration of operations.
2. *Domain consolidating* comprises (1) performance improvement, and (2) input into corporate decisions.
3. *Domain defending* comprises (1) retention of operations, (2) retention of reporting, and (3) finding a new patron or corporate customer for its capabilities.

Many subsidiary managers interviewed by Delany (2000: 237) had experienced the decline and termination of mandates either within their own subsidiary or in previous organisations. They felt that, unless they continued to increase the dependence of the parent on the subsidiary, by increasing the value of its contribution, and increase its mandate, such a threat would emerge.

Birkinshaw (2000: 22-30) developed four **distinct categories of initiatives** by differentiation along the dimensions of '*locus of opportunity*', meaning the market in which the initiative opportunity emerged, and the '*locus of pursuit*', meaning the market where the process was realised.

Local market initiatives are developed in order to serve local customers and are pursued in the local market place. Important facilitators are a moderate level of subsidiary autonomy and a well-established set of capabilities. Outcomes are new products or services for local customers. Local market initiatives are an important means for the local adaptation of MNEs (Ibid. 22-23).

Global market initiates are driven by unmet product or market needs among non-local suppliers and customers. A high level of subsidiary autonomy and of proven capabilities in the relevant areas are facilitators for successful global market initiatives by subsidiaries, e.g. in the case of global product mandates. As an immediate effect of global market initiatives, a specific business area, and the capabilities associated with it, are developed further. This can also enhance worldwide learning processes (Ibid. 23-25).

Internal market initiatives arise through market opportunities identified in the corporate system. These can be caused by changes in the external environment, inducing an internal reconfiguration of activities and responsibilities. The most critical facilitator is the credibility of the subsidiary from the headquarters' perspective and a global orientation among the senior management of the parent firm. Internal market initiatives are fundamentally geared towards reconfiguring and rationalising the activity structure in the MNE (Ibid. 25-28).

Global-internal hybrid initiatives are focused on market opportunities outside the subsidiary's home market, like in the case of global initiatives. Like internal initiatives, the locus of pursuit is internal in that it involves convincing head office managers, not external customers. The facilitating conditions are similar to those of internal market initiatives. Outcomes are reconfigurations on the level of large-scale projects, with subsidiaries claiming a stronger role within a broader-scope corporate initiative (Ibid. 28-30).

In an empirical study, Birkinshaw (1997: 216) provided evidence that **internal** and **hybrid initiatives** exhibited a higher level of integration than previous studies suggested, and relied on geocentrically minded parent company managers to be successful. **Local market initiatives** appeared to be facilitated by a careful balance between autonomy and integration, while **global market initiatives** were exhibited only where the subsidiary was very autonomous. The latter finding is surprising, indicating that subsidiaries cannot easily build world mandate businesses while at the same time remaining integrated with the rest of the corporation (Ibid. 220). If a subsidiary is highly integrated with its parent, it can easily pursue internal market and hybrid initiatives, but less easily undertake local or global market initiatives, which are externally focused (Ibid. 221, 225).

The **resistance** from other organisational actors against **subsidiary initiatives** can be modelled as a **corporate immune system**, which is defined as the set of organisational forces that suppress the advancement of creation-oriented activities such as initiatives. Two levels of resistance constitute the corporate immune system. The first level is constituted by interpreted dispositions underlying behavioural traits of corporate managers, like ethnocentrism, suspicion of the unknown, and resistance to change. The second level represents manifestations, i.e. actions or inaction taken by corporate managers that provide resistance to the initiative, like rejection, delay or request for greater justification, lobbying and rival initiatives, and lack of recognition (Birkinshaw 2000: 39-42).

A survey by Birkinshaw/Fry (1998: 54) showed that subsidiary initiatives are generally championed by individuals in the early stages, testing the idea in a small way, using subsidiary resources and commitment - without the knowledge of headquarters. Then, as the project takes shape, they seek allies – typically local customers – and sometimes personal contacts or mentors in the home office. Finally, once they have demonstrated their project's viability, they present it formally to HQ managers and ask for investment funds and support (Ibid.).

4.2.3.2.2 Subsidiary mandates

Birkinshaw (1996: 467) defines a **subsidiary mandate** as *'a business, or element of a business, in which the subsidiary participates and for which it has responsibilities beyond its national market'*. The term could also be redefined as *'a licence to apply the subsidiary's distinctive capabilities to a specific market opportunity'* (Birkinshaw 1996: 489). Delany (2000: 225-226) distinguishes three **basic types of subsidiary mandates**:

1. **advanced**:
   - *strategic independent*: a subsidiary, which has the freedom and resources to develop lines of a business for either local, multi-country, or global market.
   - *product specialist*: a subsidiary that develops, produces, and markets a limited product line for global or multi-country markets.
2. **intermediate**:
   - *enhanced mandate*: a subsidiary that does not have control of the entire value chain for a multi-country or global business but has activities in a number of parts of the value chain.
3. **basic**:
   - *miniature replica*: a subsidiary that produces and markets some of the parent's product lines in and for a local market.

- *marketing satellite*: a subsidiary, which sells into the local market products that are manufactured centrally.
- *rationalised operator*: a subsidiary, which carries out a designated set of operational activities for a multi-country or global market. Its principal market is the internal market.

Birkinshaw (1996: 490) found support for his hypothesis that the **life cycle concept** may also be applied to **subsidiary mandates**. The implication is not assumed to be that every mandate will eventually lost given that (1) many resources are physically inert, making their transfer impossible, (2) some resources are more adaptable than others, and (3) strong political forces are at work in the MNE and in host countries that constrain the relocation of activities to other countries.

World product mandates

Poynter/Rugman (1982: 54) define that the world product mandate (WPM) strategy requires the local subsidiary of a foreign-owned firm to be the worldwide centre for the research and development, manufacturing, and sales of a product series of products. This strategy is viewed from the perspective of the multinational corporate parent but calls for considerable decentralised decision-making. Poynter/Rugman (1982: 57) stress the costs of mandating and especially of re-allocating mandates do to transition costs and costs arising from the decentralisation of functions. Poynter/Rugman (1982: 60) differentiate three **kinds of mandates**:

1. *full WPM* where the subsidiary carries out R&D, strategic management, production, and international marketing functions for the product either worldwide or possibly for a geographic area.
2. *partial WPM* where the subsidiary carries out, for example, R&D and production but where international marketing and strategic management is run by the MNE parent.
3. *production mandate* where the subsidiary carries out the worldwide or area production for a particular product with little pure product research carried out but sometimes concentrating on product and process development work.

Centres of excellence (CoE)

Fratocchi/Holm (1998: 190) assume that the existence of foreign centres implies a change in the driving forces of the firm's development, away from the home-based headquarters and in favour of foreign subsidiaries. If foreign centres are common, they represent an important dynamic aspect in the internationalisation of the firm.

Fratocchi/Holm (Ibid. 193) define a '**centre of excellence**' (CoE) as a *'foreign subsidiary in the international firm that masters a high operational competence which other units of the firm depend for their activities'*. CoE includes generating knowledge and carrying out activities, which other firm units depend upon. If the competence relates to a single functional area the subsidiary is called a **'single-functional'** CoE. If the competence relates to several functions it is called a **'multi-functional'** CoE.

Frost et al. (2002: 997) define a **centre of excellence** as *'an organisational unit that embodies a set of capabilities that has been explicitly recognised by the firm as an important source of value creation, with the intention that these capabilities be leveraged by and/or disseminated to other parts of the firm.'* The formation of CoEs is shaped by conditions in the subsidiary's local environment as well as by various aspects of the subsidiary's relationship with other parts of the multinational firm.

Moore (2001: 275) proposes the **CoE** as a potentially important mechanism for a subsidiary to develop **subsidiary-specific advantages** (SSAs*)*. Following Moore/Birkinshaw (1998: 84), a **centre of excellence** is *'an entity that is recognised for its distinctive knowledge, and is mandated to leverage and/or make available its knowledge throughout the firm'*. One of the critical issues in capturing global or international mandates is that sister subsidiaries, especially larger ones, feel a sense of fairness about the process, in line with the conduct of '**procedural justice**' (Kim/Mauborgne 1991, 1993). Research by Moore/Heeler (1998) and Birkinshaw/Fry (1998) suggests that for sister subsidiaries to accept that one subsidiary enjoy a global or international mandate the mandated subsidiary must have displayed superior competencies (Moore 2001: 283). A study of CoEs within the UK by Moore (2001: 288) supported the contention that competencies are central to a subsidiary earning or capturing a more strategic role within the MNE and that CoEs are one important mechanism to develop, utilise, and signal competencies.

Andersson/Forsgren (2000: 329) argue that the **role of a subsidiary as a centre of excellence** can be based on the **characteristics** of a subsidiary's internal resources, its relationships with the rest of the MNE, and the business context in which the subsidiary is embedded. The subsidiary's ability to create unique value by linking resources and activities located at different places in the external and internal environment is assumed to be a basic capability of a subsidiary needed to gain such a role (Ibid. 332). A study by Birkinshaw (1996: 490) suggests that the **real engine of subsidiary growth** is its **distinctive capabilities**, and that for a mandate to be effective it must be built around those capabilities.

Relationships with external counterparts in the business environment can be used by the subsidiary to enhance its role as a centre of excellence. The role the subsidiary plays in the MNE can be explained to a great extent by the resources and capabilities that the subsidiary is able to inoculate in the MNE network because of its external network, an effect also termed as '**network intrusion**' (Forsgren et al. 1997). External embeddedness of the subsidiary emerged as an important pillar for the subsidiary's possibilities to be considered important to the MNE as well as a prerequisite to influence the behaviour of the MNE (Andersson/Forsgren 2000: 341-342).

The study also suggests that **headquarters' knowledge about subsidiaries' business context** becomes extremely important for developing a strategy of the whole division. Interestingly, in 40 percent of the cases, unfamiliarity of one or more of the subsidiary's most important business partners is stated by the responding headquarters. In 39 percent of 397 relationships in thirteen Swedish MNEs, the difference between the answers on the business partner's importance as indicated on a five-point scale by both subsidiary and headquarters was two. This indicates that headquarters' knowledge about the subsidiary's most crucial relationships is far from complete and even more so when embeddedness is high (Ibid. 343, 345).

Following Birkinshaw (1994a: 6), '**emergent centres of excellence**' arise through the organic growth of a capability followed by its formal recognition. This kind of centre is very effective at delivering within their traditional sphere of operation but likely to be less effective at delivering the required capability in other spheres. On the other hand, corporate management imposes '**intended centres of excellence**' either through targeted investment or through acquisition. While less effective and efficient in delivering the desired corporate capability, the adoption by other entities of the desired capability will be more readily achieved through intended centres of excellence due to their early formal legitimisation (Ibid. 8).

Moore/Birkinshaw (1998: 84-87) distinguish three types of **CoE in global service firms**. **Charismatic centres of excellence** are simply individuals who are internationally recognised for their knowledge or expertise in a certain area and whose knowledge is leveraged on a global basis. Charismatic CoEs are characterised by both a low specificity and codifiability of knowledge. **Focused centres of excellence**, the most common type, are typically based around a single area of knowledge, also called a capability or best practice. The objective is to identify and build on emerging knowledge and make it available globally. Focused CoEs are characterised by a high specificity and a low codifiability of knowledge. In **virtual centres of excellence**, the core individuals live and work in different locations, and while they know each other and meet intermittently, their principal means of interaction is through electronic media. Virtual CoEs are characterised by both a high specificity and codifiability of knowledge. Knowledge of the missing combination (low specificity/high codifiability) is provided by publicly held databases.

According to Frost et al. (2002: 998), a **major shortcoming in CoE research** is the adoption of the **subsidiary as a whole** as the main **unit of analysis**, as MNEs are moving to ever more complex and sophisticated value chain configurations. *First*, multiple centres may coexist within a particular subsidiary. *Second*, a CoE may be only one aspect of the overall capability profile and mandate of a particular subsidiary. The authors found evidence that the formation of CoEs in MNEs can be understood as a cumulative, evolutionary process. The development and recognition of subsidiary capabilities can be viewed as a cumulative, path-dependent process (Ibid. 1003, 1016).

4.2.3.2.3 Subsidiary role typologies

Bartlett/Ghoshal (1986: 92) propose that corporate management faces three big **challenges** in guiding the dispersion of responsibilities and **differentiating subsidiaries' tasks**. The *first* is in setting the strategic direction for the company by identifying its mission and business objectives. The *second* is in building the differentiated organisation by designing diverse roles, distributing the assignments, and by giving the managers responsible for filling them the legitimacy and power to do so. The *third* challenge is in directing the process to ensure that the several roles are co-ordinated and that the distributed responsibilities are controlled.

Birkinshaw (1997: 210) distinguishes two different perspectives in the research on subsidiaries in MNEs. **Subsidiary role research** views the subsidiary as having a role in the MNE. This perspective is described as (1) having an implicit parent company perspective, (2) being based on the belief that the subsidiary's role is determined by the parent company and essentially assigned to the subsidiary in question, (3) assuming that the subsidiary's role is enacted through the definition of an appropriate set of co-ordination and control mechanisms. **Subsidiary strategy research**, on the other hand, focuses directly on the subsidiary level of analysis. The subsidiary has much more leeway for strategic choice. It has ongoing managerial responsibilities but at the same time it has the responsibility to respond to entrepreneurial opportunities as they arise. Birkinshaw resumes that the fact that subsidiary role research favours control and subsidiary strategy research favours autonomy is essentially a function of the opposing perspectives of parent and subsidiary managers (Ibid.).

According to Taggart (1997: 51-52), a **subsidiary model** has two **basic purposes**. *Firstly*, it allows the MNE head office to allocate appropriate roles to its subsidiaries worldwide in a way that maximises its overall competitive advantage. *Secondly*, it gives each subsidiary management team a variety of scenarios that can be pursued in maximising its own competitive advantage and increasing its bargaining power vis-à-vis head office within, and occasionally beyond, agreed corporate guidelines.

The head office assigns a subsidiary's role while subsidiary strategy suggests some level of choice or self-determination on the part of the subsidiary (Birkinshaw 2001: 389). Several trends limit the subsidiary's degrees of freedom in shaping its market positioning. Examples are the emergence of global customers and the mirroring global integration of the supply chain, e-commerce, and global competitors (Ibid. 391).

In line with the reasoning of the process school, Jarillo/Martinez (1990: 503) propose that to analyse the **strategy at subsidiary level**, two **basic dimensions** have to be observed. The *first* is the geographical localisation of activities; and the *second* is the degree of integration of those activities performed in the country with the same activities in other subsidiaries of the firm. Relating these two dimensions, Jarillo/Martinez develop three **types of subsidiary strategy**:

1. *Autonomous strategy*: Subsidiary carries out most of the functions of the value chain in a manner that is relatively independent of its parent organisation or other subsidiaries. It is typical for multinational firms.
2. *Receptive strategy*: Few of these functions are performed in the country and they are highly integrated with the rest of the firm. It is typical for global firms.
3. *Active strategy*: Many activities are located in the country and they are carried out in close co-ordination with the rest of the firm, thus constituting an active node in a tightly knit network. It is typical for transnational firms.

Birkinshaw (2001: 381) observes that the **concept of strategy** has **changed**. Most MNEs have moved towards some variant of the global business unit structure in their international operations, and a corresponding dilution in the power and responsibilities of the country manager. The result is that the national subsidiary as such no longer exists in most important markets. Instead, there is a series of **discrete value-adding activities** each of which reports through its own business unit or functional line. While the issues around managing MNE subsidiaries are as important as ever, Birkinshaw assumes that the **problem of defining the subsidiary** is becoming more acute. He defines the subsidiary as a discrete value-adding activity outside the home country, in other words at the level below the national subsidiary (Ibid.).

From the traditional headquarters-subsidiary control perspective, Prahalad/Doz (1981: 11) classify MNEs and their various businesses on the basis of the '**strategic control dilemma**', which is caused by the **integration/responsiveness paradox** (Figure 4-9). Strategic control is defined as the extent of influence that a head office has over a subsidiary concerning decisions that affect subsidiary strategy (Ibid. 5).

Type 1: *Fragmented* are those MNEs where the possibilities of substantive control are low and the sophistication of head office managers in using organisational context is also low.

Type 2: *Dependent subsidiary relations* develop where the sophistication of the organisational context is low, but the subsidiaries continue to be dependent on the head office for strategic resources, typically in technology intensive businesses or where subsidiaries are small.

Type 3: *Autonomous subsidiary relations* develop where the subsidiaries are self-sufficient in strategic resources and their dependence on head office is low. While the subsidiaries are autonomous, head office managers can still exercise significant influence over subsidiary strategy.

Type 4: *Integrated subsidiary relations* develop where the MNE has built a high degree of substantive and organisational context control capability.

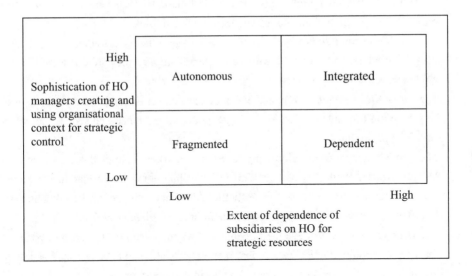

Figure 4-9: The strategic control dilemma in MNCs
(Source: Prahalad/Doz 1981: 11)

From the *same traditional control perspective*, **Doz/Prahalad** (1986: 120-125) contend that different **types of subsidiaries** partly determine the **strategic variety** and the **form of strategic control** in MNEs:

235

- *Export platforms* are an integral part of a global manufacturing network and require extensive strategic control.
- *Large integrated subsidiaries* contain significant R&D, manufacturing, and other functions and constitute a large market. They may require substantial strategic control but may also be the locus of strategic initiatives. The challenge is to ensure active and effective participation of these subsidiaries into the formulation of global strategies, and the transfer of information and knowledge.
- *Large self-contained subsidiaries* are prevented by protectionism from being fully part of a global network. Strategic control therefore may not be critical.

Small importing subsidiaries act as internal agents for the MNE. While their small size may make strategic control look unimportant, they have to be controlled as parts of the overall global pattern of activities and as parts of a global defence perimeter against competitors (Ibid. 120-121). **White/Poynter** (1984) developed a typology with five **types of subsidiaries**:

1. The *miniature replica* is a business that produces and markets some of the parent's product lines or related product lines in the local market. The business is a small-scale replica of the parent but may not be engaged in all activities.
2. The *marketing satellite* is a business that markets into the local trading area products manufactured centrally. Only downstream operational activities are conducted in this type of subsidiary.
3. The *rationalised manufacturer* produces a designated set of component parts or products for a multi-country or global market. Product scope, functional scope, and value-added scope are limited.
4. The *product specialist* develops, produces, and markets a limited product line for global markets. Products, markets, and basic technologies are similar to the parent company, although exchanges between the subsidiary and the parent company are rare. The subsidiary is generally self-sufficient in terms of value added.
5. The *strategic independent* has the freedom and resources to develop lines of business for a local, a multi-country, or a global market. It is allowed unconstrained access to global markets and freedom to pursue new business opportunities.

Delany (1998) observes the evolution of multinational subsidiaries in Ireland, building his **typology** on the basis of the White/Poynter typology but changing some elements:

1. The *rationalised manufacturer* is extended to a *rationalised operator*, encompassing both manufacturing and other functional activities.
2. The *product specialist* will not require the autonomy suggested in the original model.

3. A further category – *enhanced mandate* – is introduced and is defined as a subsidiary that does not have control of the entire value chain but only in parts of it (Ibid. 246).

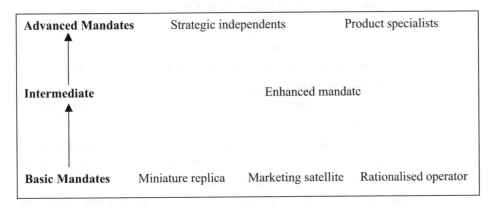

Figure 4-10: Basic and development mandates
(Source: Delany 1998: 248)

Of 28 subsidiaries observed in the study, 27 used a start-up strategy as rationalised operators, miniature replicas, or marketing satellites. These are termed the *basic mandates* for start-up operations (Delany 1998: 247). In its **growth process**, a subsidiary may follow **different basic trajectories** (Figure 4-10).

D'Cruz (1986: 77-78) distinguishes four **types of subsidiaries**, based on the **form of planning systems** in use:

1. *Truncated businesses* do not have a formal system for developing business plans.
2. *Miniature replicas* have systems for annual planning, but have neither formal nor informal strategic planning systems.
3. *Mature, non-strategic subsidiaries* have mature, sophisticated systems of annual business planning, and perform strategic planning on an informal or ad hoc basis.
4. *Strategically managed subsidiaries* have formal systems for strategic planning.

D'Cruz further develops a **subsidiary mission grid**, based on the dimensions '**extent of market involvement**' (local, regional, global), and '**decision-making autonomy**' (low, high). The six resulting types of **subsidiary missions** are

- local: *import, local service,*
- regional: *satellite, branch plant,*
- global: *globally rationalised, world product mandate* (Ibid.).

Bartlett/Ghoshal (1986: 90-92) developed a **typology** focusing on the **differential strategic importance of country markets** in terms of the MNE's overall objectives and linked this with the **level of competence of the local affiliate** in each case:

1. *Strategic leader* can be a highly competent national subsidiary located in a strategically important market. In this role, the subsidiary serves as a partner of head office in developing and implementing strategy.
2. *Contributor* is a subsidiary operating in a small or strategically unimportant market but having a distinctive capability.
3. *Implementor* is a subsidiary in a less strategically important market with just enough competence to maintain its local operation. The implementor's efficiency is as important as the creativity of the strategic leaders or contributors.
4. The *black hole* represents important markets, in which a strong local presence is essential for maintaining the firm's global position, but in which the firm has no significant position. It is therefore not an acceptable strategic position.

Taggart (1997: 55) criticises that this model is perhaps more helpful to an MNE at corporate level in terms of marshalling its network to support global objectives, but yields fewer insights to local managers seeking to increase bargaining power within the MNE.

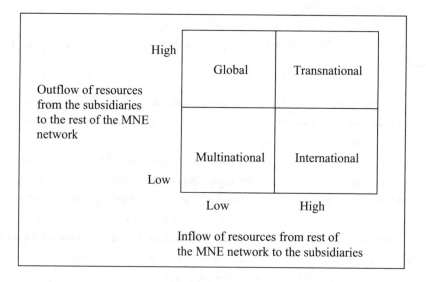

Figure 4-11: International subsidiary roles related to different resource flows
(Source: Randøy/Li 1998: 78)

Randøy/Li (1998: 78-82) developed a **portfolio of subsidiary roles** based on **resource flows** between a **focal subsidiary** and the **MNE network** (Figure 4-11). The portfolio extents the Bartlett/Ghoshal organisational typology as it relates to the intensity and direction of the overall resource flows within the MNE. Resource transfer is measured by product flows, knowledge flows, and capital flows. **Randøy/Li** (Ibid. 82) then develop a **second portfolio** based on the **degree of dispersion** and the **degree of co-ordination of activities** in order to derive basic strategies on corporate and subsidiary level (Figure 4-12).

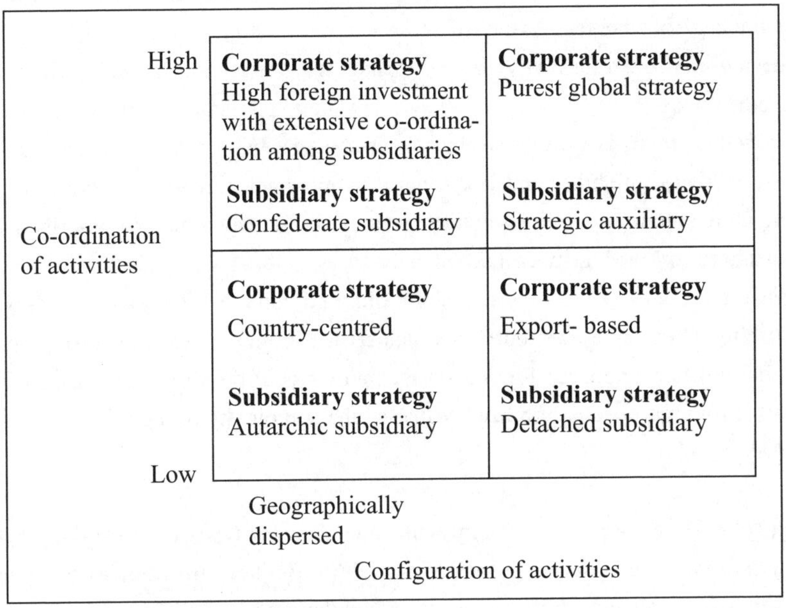

Co-ordination of activities — High	**Corporate strategy** High foreign investment with extensive co-ordination among subsidiaries	**Corporate strategy** Purest global strategy
	Subsidiary strategy Confederate subsidiary	**Subsidiary strategy** Strategic auxiliary
	Corporate strategy Country-centred	**Corporate strategy** Export-based
Low	**Subsidiary strategy** Autarchic subsidiary	**Subsidiary strategy** Detached subsidiary
	Geographically dispersed — Configuration of activities	

Figure 4-12: International strategy and subsidiary roles based on resource flows (Source: Randøy/Li 1998: 82)

Decisions on organisation structure tend to alter two basic capabilities of the organisation's relationship with its environment. **Observability** is the capability of the firm to see and foresee changes in its environment. **Controllability** is the firm's capability to respond to its environment (Fannin/Rodrigues 1986: 84). Birkinshaw (2002) focuses on the observability and mobility of knowledge assets, the impact these factors have on the way individual R&D centres are structured, and how they relate to one another in the international network. Birkinshaw focuses the meaning of *observability* on the extent to which the knowledge of the R&D centre can be understood through observation, while *mobility* is the extent to which the knowledge base of the R&D centre can be separated for its physical settings. For example, an R&D unit whose knowledge base is very low in mobility should potentially be given a high level of autonomy, while one that is high in observability may benefit from being closely integrated with other R&D units.

Birkinshaw (2002: 251) differentiates three **types of R&D centres**:

1. *Self-contained centres* have deep roots in the local economy, and even if there is a change of ownership their activities tend not to change significantly. This kind of centre tends to be rather capital intensive, and involved in industrial, rather than high technology businesses. Assets of these centres lack *fungibility* of assets. These are specialised around narrowly defined technological areas and are difficult to redeploy in other areas.
2. *Modular centres* are the opposite of self-contained centres, in that their knowledge base is high in mobility and low in observability. Such centres are typically younger and more commonly seen in high technology areas. Assets may be described as fungible and redeployed fairly easily.
3. *Home base centres* are typically large, old, and complex. They are typically located close to the corporate head office, which reflects both their historical roots and the interdependencies between R&D and other activities of the firm. There is a low level of both observability and mobility because of the complexity of the interrelationships between the parts.

Surlemont (1998) developed a typology with four different types of **subsidiary roles**. The different types are differentiated on the basis of the **influence subsidiaries exert on other units in the MNE network**. Influence itself is constituted by **participation power** in decision-making processes, the **domain of influence** in terms of the number of units controlled, and the **scope of influence** representing the number of activities or types of behaviour controlled. The empirical study shows that the **evolutionary path of centres** will be completely different according to the growth strategy adopted in the early stage.

Strategic centres of excellence are characterised by a small scope of specialised activities that they manage for other subsidiaries. Such low-scope centres are likely to demonstrate expertise and knowledge of the latest techniques in some specific areas and have a large domain. They cultivate critical resources that are first class according to their MNE's standards and leverage these resources within the MNE network for the benefit of the whole.

The purpose of **administrative centres** is to respond to the organisational needs of decentralisation, integration, and differentiation. Such centres like regional headquarters are established in MNEs for operational purposes. With increasing scope, a centre tends to become more generalist and may influence the management of a broad range of activities through co-ordination and control, but their influence is confined to a limited, and often fixed, number of subsidiaries. The domain of such a centre tends to be low and constrained by structuring considerations of the MNE (Ibid. 166).

Dormant centres exert no influence within the MNE network. These centres have a low scope and a small domain. Such subsidiaries may be *implementors* in the typology of Bartlett/Ghoshal (1986) or master an expertise in specific areas without exerting any influence in the MNE network. Surlemont (1998: 167) terms the latter type also *centre of lost opportunity* because its competencies are not globally leveraged and its potential rents are not properly appropriated.

Global headquarters are centres that concentrate in their hand most decisions, for most activities, and for most subsidiaries. Global headquarters are characterised by a large domain and scope (Surlemont 1998: 167).

Taggart (1997) developed a **typology** focusing on the **subsidiary autonomy** and relates it to the **procedural justice dimension** developed by Kim/Mauborgne (1991):

- *partner subsidiary*: it represents the ideal combination of high procedural justice and high autonomy. Head office and the highly proactive affiliate have excellent relationships.
- *collaborator subsidiary*: compared to the partner subsidiary, the collaborator will be more pliable and co-operative at lower levels of autonomy.
- *vassal subsidiary*: few local managers would wish to find themselves in the low procedural justice and low autonomy quadrant of the model. The head office-subsidiary interface is characterised by dissent, mistrust, and a master-servant relationship.
- *militant subsidiary*: With higher levels of autonomy, disagreements at the interface are likely to be strident, though often resolved in the subsidiary's favour.

A measure of the importance or *status of a subsidiary* may well lie in the *volume of outflows and inflows of network knowledge* (Taggart 1997: 52). An empirical study by Taggart (1998) with subsidiaries of foreign-owned firm located in the UK showed that the *detached subsidiary* was seen as a temporary phase, while the *strategic auxiliary* was either the preferred end point or eventual target of a large proportion of the sample (Ibid. 45).

Birkinshaw/Hood (2000: 141) found evidence that **subsidiaries in leading-edge clusters** are **more strongly embedded** in their local cluster, are **more autonomous**, and are **more internationally oriented** than subsidiaries in other industry sectors. Both levels of R&D and cluster membership were found to be strong predictors of international orientation, though the level of R&D was proved to be stronger. Birkinshaw/Hood (2000: 150) found further evidence that there is a **strong negative correlation** between **cluster dynamism** and **foreign ownership level** and a **positive relationship** between **cluster dynamism** and a **high level of subsidiary autonomy**. Clusters with high levels of foreign ownership have subsidiaries that are in general less autonomous and have weaker capabilities.

4.2.3.2.4 Subsidiary evolution

An empirical study by Birkinshaw/Hood (2000: 141) indicated that typologies of subsidiary roles should give increased consideration to environmental factors. Birkinshaw (1997: 225) suggests a more **dynamic approach to role and context management**, given that the subsidiary's opportunity set and internal capabilities are continually evolving. Luostarinen/Marschan-Piekkari (1999: 2) further remark that there has been **little consideration** of the **dynamic relationship** between the **host country** (target region or global markets) and **subsidiary evolution**. Birkinshaw et al. (1998) and Luostarinen/Marschan-Piekkari (1999: 2) distinguish three **perspectives on the driving forces of subsidiary evolution**: (1) *parent-driven processes*, (2) *subsidiary-driven processes*, and (3) *host country-driven processes*. The three mechanisms interact to determine the subsidiary's role at a given point in time. The **interplay** between the levels is assumed to create a *cyclical process* through which the subsidiary's role changes over time.

The question of interdependence between the parent company and the dispersed units can be connected with the **internationalisation process** of the firm. The **relation** between the **centre** and the **periphery** varies with the degree of internationalisation and international experience (Forsgren 1989: 57-58). **Headquarters-subsidiary relations** are significantly influenced by the **firm's degree of the internationalisation** and the **context and history of its subsidiaries**. According to Kobrin (1988: 108), during the early stages of international expansion, subsidiaries in most MNEs have a great autonomy and independence. On the other hand, subsidiaries may begin as export platforms (Doz/Prahalad 1986), miniature replicas, or marketing satellites with only basic mandates (Delany 1998) so that the autonomy described by Kobrin may basically apply to the multinational type of MNEs but not to international, global, or transnational ones.

Generally, overseas subsidiaries are dependent on the parent company's provision of semi-manufactured goods and technical competence in the preliminary stage. The **internationali-**

sation is based on gradual exploitation of a **company-specific asset**, located at, and controlled by the **parent company**. The company-specific asset is crucial for the internationalisation, since the company has a cognitive and relational disadvantage compared to local competitors. The **subsidiaries' role** in this process is operative and the **dependence** between the centre and the subsidiaries is basically sequential, as inputs and knowledge are sent from the centre to the subsidiaries (Forsgren/Johanson 1992a: 21).

With **increasing internationalisation**, the subsidiaries become stronger, less dependent on headquarters, more institutionalised, more interdependent, and develop their own business and local networks. Interdependencies are pooled, sequential, and reciprocal and become more varied. Increasingly, the internationalising firm takes the form of a **multinational network**. As a company becomes more multinational, there is strong a priori support for the notion that its activities become more interdependent. There is increasingly a shift from pooled to sequential interdependencies and beyond. A **global perspective** necessitates that the system must ultimately achieve reciprocal interdependence, at least in some key respects. As the company increases the number of subsidiaries, the pressures to formalise by standardising systems – and then to simplify the control process – are ever stronger (Hulbert/Brandt 1980: 123-125). This predominant control perspective of the 1970s and 1980s has been increasingly complemented by elements of self-organisation.

When **subsidiaries grow**, the local business environments also become important for the subsidiary's development of competence. To the extent that other units become dependent on the subsidiary, it will be the predominant link for the use of this competence within the firm. The more important the competence of the subsidiary, generated in its local network of business relationships, the more important the subsidiary will be for the whole international firm (Fratocchi/Holm 1998: 192). The subsidiary gains more autonomy and also positional, or structural, power within the MNE network as it controls strategic resources, relationships, and contingencies. Subsidiaries are assigned strategic roles and become central to the development and exploitation of knowledge and markets (Forsgren 1989: 59). In the **last phase of internationalisation**, Forsgren/Johanson (1992a: 20) assume that **centre-periphery structures** of international firms change to more complex, reciprocal **multi-centre structures**.

An empirical study by Cray (1984: 97) provided evidence that **large subsidiaries** tend to be controlled less than their smaller counterparts. Assuming that less corporate control allows room for local negotiation, this should make them more responsive to local control. At both the parent and subsidiary levels technological complexity was found to be associated with dense networks of integration. Cray concludes that the choice, thus, seems to be between large, technologically complex subsidiaries that have more direct control over their own functions but are closely tied to other subsidiaries, or small, technologically simple firms that are subject to a greater degree of direct control.

As an organisation increases its overseas presence, the process of co-ordination and communication with its overseas subsidiaries becomes strained. With increasing **variety of markets**, the MNE correspondingly alters both its **knowledge flows** and its required level of **host country responsiveness** (Hamilton/Kashlak 1999: 173). **Strategy** is often **locally determined**, subsidiary managers may have the authority to make substantial capital commitments if funds are raised nationally, and independent product development may take place. **Strategic unification** requires some degree of **centralised control**. While the degree of centralisation may vary substantially, implementation of a global or unified strategy entails a shift in the locus of control from the periphery to the centre (Kobrin 1988: 108). In addition, Andersson et al. (2002: 992) propose that head office must take part and develop its own relationships with important customers and suppliers in the subsidiary's network because competence developed in these relationships is to a large amount of tacit nature. Fratocchi/Holm (1998: 206) contend that the **subsidiary business relationships** play an important role for the **long-term strategy**. **Headquarters** thus only exerts limited degree of control and to maintain it, the most important issue for it is to continuously update their **knowledge** about the content and development of the **business relationships** of the most important **subsidiaries** of the firm.

Kristensen/Zeitlin (2001: 190) argue that there is '*strong evidence that the existence of diverse subsidiary logics is a quite general phenomenon in the maturing phase of global expansion of MNEs*'. According to their study, headquarters' global strategies produce a variety of unintended local consequences as well as local strategies cause unintended consequences on the global level. MNEs are therefore much more accurately seen as a **network of variation** with casual causes and effects but with an integrating outlook on a **joint horizon** provided by the formulation of intended goals, strategies, and organisational procedures. Thus, even within highly centralised MNEs an increasing **diversity of evolutionary logics** will emerge from the unintended consequences of their global expansion. **Cultural distance** affects managerial decisions, work values, patterns of negotiations, conflict within and failure of international joint ventures, overseas entry mode, and degree of partner reciprocity. The degree of cultural distance is assumed to be an antecedent condition affecting the MNE selection of a control and governance system (Hamilton/Kashlak 1999: 175). This diversity of cultures and evolutionary logics produces **different subsidiary positions**, leading to different intended and emerging subsidiary roles with respect to their external context and the MNE network. Delany (1998, 2000) developed an **eight-stage model of MNE subsidiaries**. In a first step, **three basic phases of development** are identified by the study of Delany (1998: 256):

Phase 1: building credibility of the subsidiary,
Phase 2: gradual build-up of competence of the subsidiary,
Phase 3: strategic development.

These three basic phases are then refined in an **eight-stage model**:

- *Stages 1-3* comprise the *basic mandate*. These stages involve the subsidiary being established and subsequently carrying out its basic mandate at increasing levels of performance. The subsidiary is established as either a rationalised operator, a marketing satellite, or a miniature replica, each representing entry strategic positions.
- *Stages 4-5* begin when the subsidiary has demonstrated superior performance and gained credibility in its original mandate. The subsidiary moves beyond the basic mandate to gain an *enhanced mandate*, moving into different activities.
- *Stages 6-8* differ in the degree of strategic importance of the subsidiary. The subsidiary increases its strategic role by becoming either a product specialist or a strategic independent. In these stages, the subsidiary reaches an *advanced mandate status*.

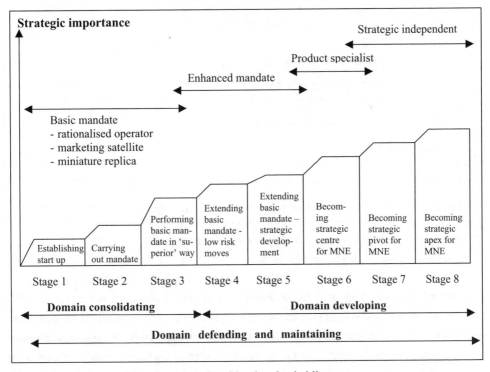

Figure 4-13: Stages of development of multinational subsidiary
(Source: Delany 1998: 258)

The detailed model is illustrated in Figure 4-13. It is important to note that regardless of where a subsidiary has arrived at in terms of its stage of development, it can slip back through lack of performance, environmental change, or organisational restructuring. The model offers a **growth model**, which is not linear or unidirectional.

Sargeant (1990: 47) describes the development process of subsidiary culture as passing through the three **stages** (1) *child* (product and sales mentality), (2) *adolescence* (branch mentality), and (3) *adulthood* (self-contained business mentality).

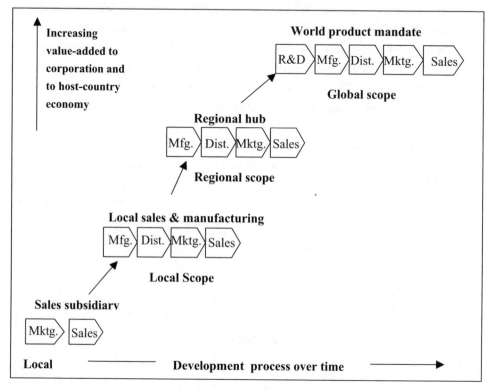

Figure 4-14: Example of stages in subsidiary development process
(Source: Birkinshaw 1998: 272)

The **subsidiary co-evolves with its environment** and gradually plays a more and more important role in the local economy. The subsidiary typically goes through a development process where it gains **enhanced value-added scope** and **greater decision-making autonomy**, and this process is both driven by and a source of benefit to the local economy. This process of subsidiary development varies significantly from country to country (Birkinshaw 1998: 270, 293). Birkinshaw (1998: 272-274) describes this process on the basis of **increasing value-added**, which may be defined by **two dimensions**: the extent of value chain that is undertaken by the subsidiary, and the geographical scope for which the subsidiary has responsibility. A subsidiary development may follow a typical trajectory as illustrated in Figure 4-14. Subsidiary development may occur as a bottom-up, entrepreneurial process that Birkinshaw (1998: 273-274) terms **subsidiary driven development**. On the contrary, a **parent-driven development** is a top-down process involving the allocation of resources and responsibilities to the subsidiary on the basis of strategic decisions taken at head office.

In their study on the business evolution process of Sony in the USA, Chang/Rosenzweig (1998: 327) found evidence that subsidiary evolution along the dimensions of functional migration and line of business entry is a dynamic and adaptive process, with actions, feedback, evaluation, and further actions. The continual adaptation was found evident, to both external and internal factors. A further key result is *'the essential role played by individual champions whose visions and persistent managerial action helped guide the process, overcoming the inertia, scepticism and lack of trust which characterised the organisation'* (Ibid.).

As outgrowth of an existing organisation, **subsidiaries** are born and imprinted with particular predilections and orientations. At the same time, they encounter specific conditions and chronologies in the host country not previously experienced by the parent, which may impose new constraints and apply unanticipated pressures. The imprinting of the subsidiary, both genetically and environmentally, signals the start of the **learning process**. The genetic code of the subsidiary is located in the philosophies, policies, and practices of its various operating systems (Beechler et al. 1998: 338).

Subsidiary evolution is driven by the interaction of head office assignments, subsidiary choice, and local environment determinism. Subsidiary evolution can be defined as the result of an **accumulation or depletion of capabilities over time** (Birkinshaw 2000: 83). These capabilities are to some extent distinct from those of the other units in the MNE network and partly identical or overlapping. A subsidiary is locked in its **local technological trajectory** but also embedded in the **trajectory of the overall MNE network**. The **interface** between the resources and capabilities of the subsidiary and its local context is very **sticky**. Meanwhile, the interface between the subsidiary's charter and its resources and capabilities is semi-fluid in that charters can and do change (Birkinshaw 2000: 115).

Birkinshaw (2000: 88-93) identifies five **generic subsidiary evolution processes**. These are differentiated as a function of the two dimensions '**change in capabilities**' and '**charter change**'. These processes are:

1. *parent-driven investment* in the enhancement of charter and capabilities,

2. *subsidiary-driven charter extension* following an extension of capability development,
3. *subsidiary-driven charter strengthening* by reconfiguration,
4. *parent-driven disinvestment*, and
5. *atrophy (of capabilities) through subsidiary neglect* due to subsidiary's management lack of attention.

4.2.3.3 Critical reflection upon MNE role research

MNE role research has provided a complementary view to the headquarters-centred research dominating the field of international management by adding a subsidiary perspective. At the centre is the evolution of individual subsidiaries, which may develop initiatives, gain mandates, and adopt different roles in the MNE network. MNE role research thus provides a very important new perspective but has been criticised on different levels. For example, Schmid et al. (1998: 95-100) criticise several **weaknesses of subsidiary role typologies**:

- *Underlying dimensions of typologies* generally appear to be *arbitrary*. This is particularly caused by missing theoretical reasoning with regard to the dimensions that differentiate types of subsidiaries.
- Many *role concepts simplify too much* by reducing the reality to a few normative roles.
- Generally, role typologies have their roots in contingency theory with an inherent *linear causal thinking*.
- The majority of role concepts reflect a *top-down perspective*.
- Empirical studies suffer from weaknesses in the *choice of constructs*, the *operationalisation*, and the *definition of the samples*.
- Most typologies are *developed inductively*.

Except for the described weaknesses, subsidiary role typologies open a new perspective by directing the attention towards subsidiaries. A further advantage is the possibility to apply role differentiation to management structures and processes particular in order to develop differentiated co-ordination mechanisms (Ibid. 94-95). MNE role research includes teleological, Darwinian, and life cycle mechanisms and thus provides insights into evolutionary dynamics in MNE networks. These are even explicitly integrated in models of subsidiary evolution. MNE role research therefore represents a very valuable extension of intraorganisational network research from an evolutionary perspective and also introduces the difference between whole and part by explicitly adopting both a headquarters and a subsidiary perspective.

4.2.4 Contribution to an evolutionary perspective

MNE research from an intraorganisational perspective has traditionally stressed global and local differentiation, integration, change processes, and decision-making. **Global strategy**

research focuses on balancing the dual pressures for local adaptation and global integration. Strategy and organisation structure are interdependent so that local, global, or transnational strategies call for a different configuration and co-ordination of globally dispersed activities. Global strategy hence integrates demands from both differentiation (internationalisation) and integration (network formation) in an already existing MNE network. Foundation and initial internationalisation steps are not included in this teleological perspective, which only allows for intended change.

The same applies to the approach of the **Process School**, which is also based on the strategic and organisational balance of the dominant global integration vs. local responsiveness duality. Along these two dimensions, the Process School developed normative strategies and organisational archetypes with a focus on a context management that allows for both an integrative administrative context provided by headquarters and self-organisation across the locally embedded subsidiaries. Foundation and internationalisation aspects are not included in this perspective. Evolutionary dynamics only enter the models as contingencies but are not explained or integrated in the framework. However, the network perspective is explicitly adapted to MNEs and offers a more differentiated view on MNEs as than the traditional headquarters-subsdiary perspective. Particularly co-ordination in MNE networks and thus the integration aspect of globalisation gains a central role in this approach. The co-evolutionary interplay with the environment focuses on the dual role of subsidiaries as parts of both MNE and local network as an impression of the underlying integration vs. responsiveness framework but misses a dynamic component.

Subsidiary role research provides a complementary perspective to the headquarters dominated approach of the Process School by basically differentiating a headquarters and a subsidiary perspective. From the first perspective, mandates and roles are assigned to subsidiaries, from the latter they emerge in the historical trajectory of the subsidiary. Subsidiary role research thus integrates teleological and evolutionary dynamics. This also becomes apparent in the models of subsidiary evolution, which further include a life cycle perspective in their design. Foundation and internationalisation are not subject to subsidiary role research.

The evolutionary interplay with the subsidiary environment is designed with respect to both the internal MNE environment and the external local environment but still lacks an explicit focus on co-evolutionary dynamics. Table 4-3 provides an overview over the integration of evolutionary principles into the respective intraorganisational approaches.

	Strategy in MNEs	Process school	Intraorganisational role models
Foundation	No	Subsidiary level	Subsidiary level
Co-evolution of firm and environment	Strategic change based on the dialectic of global integration vs. local adaptation.	Interdependencies with globally differentiated environment cause isomorphic pressures, strategic contingencies as well as power and control relations.	MNEs react to environment by differentiating organisational roles and assigning them different tasks with different geographic scope.
Global differentiation of firm	Differentiation on global or local level is one of the two main dimensions in strategy on the basis of the dominating guiding difference.	Global differentiation is already a defining property of MNEs. It is the key dimension in the conceptualisation of strategy and organisation.	MNEs are described in their differentiation of organisational roles with regard to competencies, authority, and scope of activities
Global integration of firm	Global integration is the second main dimension in MNE strategy.	Global integration is the main focus of the process school as the degree of differentiation of the MNE is quasi taken as a given and the main challenge to be contained or resolved by the context management from the top management perspective. Exception: heterarchy	The headquarter-subsidiary perspective focuses on the integration and control of subsidiaries in the MNE network. The subsidiary perspective focuses on the level of the element rather than the level of the whole.
Global evolutionary dynamics of environment	No	No	No
Global evolutionary dynamics of firm	Teleological mechanism, VSR mechanism implicitly provides emergent elements of subsidiary.	An implicit dynamic is inherent due to the construction of the approach on the basis of of the global/local dialectic. This fact has not led to an explicit formulation of any evolutionary mechanism. Rather, dynamics were instilled by focusing on organisational processes, thus linking strategy and organisation in strategic change but evading an explanation of organisational dynamics themselves	Approaches of subsidiary evolution describe the genesis of subsidiaries from foundation to maturity. The underlying motors are teleological (intended foundation, development), life cycle (stages), dialectic (HQ/subsidiary), VSR (incremental), and autopoietic (formation of an identity).

Table 4-3: Evolutionary elements in intraorganisational network approaches

4.3 Summary

Processes of global network formation create growing interdependencies between social actors on global scale and a growing integration of their communication, activities, and structures. There are several levels on which network formation can be observed.

Interorganisational networks from local to global level dominate the external network context of a firm. On the local level, networks are nurtured by a **local milieu**, which provides the local resources, infrastructure, social capital, and innovative milieu. Local milieus are the context in which innovations and distinct capabilities can develop in a path-dependent process. Firms embedded in such a local milieu have access to the local network resources and are imprinted by the local characteristics, facilitating an innovative learning context.

Embedded in local milieus **clusters** and **industrial districts** may develop as specific local firm networks in specific businesses. Such local networks can exploit advantages from co-specialisation and collective learning, both facilitating flexible and innovative technological trajectories on local levels. Such local networks may even dominate global niche businesses and are interesting locations for innovation-seeking MNEs.

On different geographical levels **business networks** may develop, which usually comprise an entire industry or industrial niche. The industry's firms and their respective organisation sets basically constitute business networks. Business networks are thus an emergent phenomenon rather than the product of strategic choice. The contrary is true for **strategic networks**, which are based on intended co-operative relations formed for the pursuit of specific goals and purposes. Such strategic relations may even develop between competitors in selected functional or geographical areas. Different archetypes of strategic networks were developed in the 1980s, when the transnationalisation of global business nurtured an increased interorganisational orientation. While strategic networks are subject to strategic choice and planning, business networks rather represent a context for individual firm behaviour.

In all network contexts, structural and processual properties influence the evolutionary capacity of a firm. The position of a firm in a network may provide it with substantial power and informational advantages. The dynamic of a network profoundly influences the evolutionary perspectives of the individual firms that constitute it. Embeddedness and social capital in a network may provide access to strategic resources such as information or trust. Different coupling intensities may favour a more efficiency-oriented stable network fabric or a more variety generating and change-oriented network profile. Firms may explore and exploit the advantages offered by different network levels and act as bridges. Particularly globally operating firms may act as bridges between networks from local to global level and thus combine globally differentiated exploration and exploitation of competitive advantages.

The globally differentiated pursuit of competitive advantages may also be facilitated by the formation of **global intraorganisational networks**. Global network formation already emerges in the course of initial internationalisation but is traditionally the subject of MNE research. From this perspective, MNEs are conceptualised as global networks due to their **internal differentiation** and the **global dispersion** of organisational units and co-operations. Along with the dispersion emerge interdependencies and different coupling intensities between the MNE units. In this context, cross-unit learning and structural flexibility are crucial in the evolutionary interplay of strategy and structure.

The '**Process School**' of international management has basically developed the '*industry recipe*' in MNE network research. Based on the dominant duality '**global integration vs. local responsiveness**' in MNE-networks several concepts of normative **strategies** and **organisation** have been developed. The emerging **archetype** of the '*transnational*' (Bartlett 1986, Bartlett/Ghoshal 1989), '*multifocus*' (Prahalad/Doz 1987), or '*heterarchic*' (Hedlund 1986) firm balances the duality by simultaneously exploiting advantages from both extremes. The focus is on administrative mechanisms and the decision-making context. The ideal type of MNE management crystallises in '**context management**', where headquarters management provides the formal administrative context within which strategic flexibility can be exploited by the globally dispersed units. Local subsidiaries are conceptualised as '*Janus-faced*' and being integrated in both the MNE network and the respective local network. Subsidiaries may adopt different strategic roles in the context management of the MNE network depending on their resource endowments, capabilities, or criticality of the local market.

The development of such differentiated subsidiary roles has led to the development of a large stream of research on **intraorganisational roles in MNEs**. Early research in the late 1970s focused on the traditional dyadic relationship between headquarters and subsidiary. The main perspective was constituted by the duality of '*centralisation vs. subsidiary autonomy*'. In the 1980s, the focus changed to more differentiated subsidiary roles. Important starting points are **subsidiary initiatives**, which provide a basis for the assignment of subsidiary mandates and the development of subsidiary roles. Subsidiary initiatives vary in their functional and geographical scope. The most prominent **subsidiary mandates** are world product mandates but may also be directed at other specific business level. In a next step, the development of centres of excellence already implies an increased focus on strategic capabilities at subsidiary level. The strategic position of subsidiaries is generally the focus of **subsidiary role typolo-**

gies, which have been developed in abundance along a variety of dimensions such as knowledge flows between subsidiaries and headquarters or the criticality of local and MNE network resources. Subsidiary role typologies provide a basis for the development of normative subsidiary roles and subsequent strategies. However, subsidiary roles may change in the course of a subsidiary's development so that models of **subsidiary evolution** have been developed that give an idea of typical subsidiary trajectories on a basically teleological or life cycle basis. Evolutionary dynamics will now be focused in the following Chapter 5.

5 Global evolutionary processes

This chapter serves to illustrate theories, which may contribute to the explanation of evolutionary processes. As these **theories** have not been primarily developed to explain globalisation but **economic** or **social dynamics** in general, they will be adapted to globalisation whenever possible. Even without explicitly integrating globalisation phenomena in their layout, theories of social dynamics directly contribute to the understanding of one of the three basic globalisation characteristics and thus the globalisation of firms itself.

5.1 Evolutionary theories

Evolution is a word composition with roots in the Latin verb '*volvere*' (to roll) associated with '*evolvere*', indicating a forward motion. The word 'evolution' itself comes from the Latin '*evolutia*', derived from *e-* (out of) and '*volatus*' (rolled). It was used to refer to the unrolling of parchment books (Giddens 1984: 229). In the **biological context**, von Haller (1744) applied it first to describe all major structures in cells (Hodgson1993: 37). The term was further developed by the German '*Naturphilosophen*' and was introduced in the English discourse by Spencer in 1854. Spencer widened the meaning of the term and built a **universalistic theory of biological and social 'unfolding'** or evolution. It is characterised by a continuous transformation of unorganised homogeneity into organised heterogeneity. In the embryological model, the evolution from an *'indefinite incoherent homogeneity to a definite coherent heterogeneity'* takes place as a result of internal dynamics, independent of environmental contingencies. Spencer's reasoning built on Lamarck, assuming the possibility of the inheritance of acquired characters. This principle states that acquired characteristics of an individual or institution can be passed on to, or imitated by, others. The **Lamarckian perspective** hence allows for **horizontal transfer of traits** within a generation (e.g. between organisations) and learning. The Lamarckian approach is deductive with origins in sociology and philosophy.

In contrast, Darwin built his theory on empirical results in *biological research*. Inheritance is based on **genetic reproduction**, which are only passed **vertically from generation to generation**. According to Darwin, this principle is strictly biological and hence not applicable to social sciences. Three main principles of **Darwinian evolutionary theory** have to be distinguished. *First*, there must be sustained variation among members of a species or population. Variations may be blind, random, or purposive in character, but without them, as Darwin insisted, natural selection cannot operate. *Second*, there must be some principle of heredity or continuity, through which offspring have to resemble their parents more than they resemble other members of their species. There has to be a mechanism through individual characteristics can be passed on through the generations. *Third*, natural selection itself operates either because the variations or gene combinations that are preserved are those bestowing advantage in the struggle to survive (Hodgson 1993: 46, 1994: 21).

Although both Darwin and Spencer saw diversity and variety as part of evolution, these concepts played different roles in their theories. For Darwin, diversity was the essential fuel for the process of natural selection. Although Spencer also saw selection at work, for him diversity was more significant as the teleological result of the evolutionary process, rather than its crucial starting point. According to Hodgson (1994: 17), Spencer's writings contain an overriding emphasis on the supreme law of progress, the transformation '**from homogeneity to heterogeneity**', and the evolution towards ever more complex systems. Following Spencer, *'change from the homogeneous to the heterogeneous is displayed in the progress of civilization as a whole, and in the progress of every tribe or nation; and is still going on with increasing rapidity'* (Spencer 1890, 342-43). He also states a simultaneous tendency toward integration: *'In ever more or less separate part of every aggregate, integration has been, or is, in progress'* (Spencer 1890: 307). Spencer suggests that evolution means a tendency towards increasing specialisation and differentiation, combined with sufficient functional integration to ensure the coherence of the system.

A **main criticism** of evolutionary reasoning in studying the social world is based on two main arguments. First, as in the context of systems theory, the **applicability of evolutionary concepts** from biology is frequently doubted. Second, evolutionary thinking especially in the tradition of Spencer was often mixed with normative and moral biases, leading to teleological '**evolutionism**' or even to '**social Darwinism**'. Giddens (1984: xxviii-xxix) hence recommends critical attention to evolutionism based on the following **features**:

- an *irreversible series of stages* through which societies must pass through each of them to reach higher ones;
- some *conceptual linkage with biological theories of evolution*; and
- specification of *directionality through the stages* indicated, in respect of a given criterion or criteria, such as increasing complexity or expansion of the forces of production (e.g. historical materialism).

Despite this well-founded criticism of blind and unreflected evolutionism, the description of the social systems theory has shown that the application of evolutionary reasoning depends to a great deal on the methodological and conceptual adaptation of such concepts.

On balance, the **socio-economic evolution** is generally assumed to be **Lamarckian**, involving both purposeful behaviour and the inheritance of acquired characters (e.g. 'administrative heritage'). Nonetheless, the **Darwinian principles of variation, selection, and retention** have increasingly been applied to the study of human activity by changing the unit of selection from genes to *social traits and habits*. In literature on economics and strategic management, these units are *organisational routines* and *capabilities*.

From an **interpretative perspective**, the contrast between natural selection and strategic choice views crystallised in the modification of the variation-selection-retention model (Campbell 1960) by Weick (1979), which he labels **enactment-selection-retention model**. Variation in Weick's model is not principally '*blind*' as in the original evolutionary model - it is *constructed by social actors*. Similarly, *selection criteria* are not so much embodied in external environmental conditions, as they are *lodged in organisational members* themselves. Selection takes place as individuals impose meaning upon, and make sense of their enacted raw data. Those patterns of data that fit their interpretation schemes and cognitive repertoires are *selected in*; the rest is selected out (Ibid. 164). In **biology**, there is a basically *slow* '**genetic drift**'. The fundamental contrast between biological and the **social world** is that in the latter, the **generation of variety is purposeful** (Saviotti/Metcalfe 1991: 11). In socio-economic systems a much more **rapid drift** is possible through the succession of purposeful innovation, imitation, improvement, acquired character inheritance, and interpenetration of social systems (Hodgson 1993: 47). Even the *selection processes* themselves are subject to *modification* and sometimes to drastic revision. In economic evolution active selection by human agents occurs at all stages of the process (Loasby 1999: 29).

According to Baum/Singh (1994: 3-4), **evolutionary theories** have three **major foci**:

1. *entities* (e.g. routines, comps, jobs, organisations, ecosystems);
2. *processes* (e.g. replication, mutation, recombination, random drift, learning, institutionalisation, convergence, reorientation, entrepreneurship, competition, natural selection); and
3. *events* (e.g. birth, death, transformation, speciation, extinction).

The whole **evolutionary process** can be thought of as a **gigantic positive feedback loop** (Boulding 1985: 19). Evolutionary systems continually change under the impact of *mutations* – that is, changes in the parameters of the system. This produces an evolutionary process that can be defined as ecological interaction (selection) under conditions of constant change of parameters (mutation). Mutations can take the form of human artefacts in social systems through invention and discovery (Ibid. 25). Social systems arise out of the interactions of human beings and their artefacts. They arise fundamentally out of the imaging quality of the human mind and the capacity to transfer very complex images from one mind to another. They also involve **complex mutual learning processes**, not only from language and communication, but also from experiences, which also communicate. Social systems also involve evaluations, for all choice-directed behaviour involves the evaluation of alternative images of the future. The evolution of social systems involves a learning process by which we learn to produce increasingly complex objects, organisations, and people. Processes of mutation and selection are at work (Ibid. 28-29). Central to evolutionary processes in social systems are communication patterns as they are dominant in organisational structures. An organisation chart, for example, is largely a diagram of who communicates with whom (Ibid. 141). It is important to recognise that communication is not merely the transmission of information but the development and transmission of knowledge structures (Ibid. 180). As argued in the theory of social systems, evolutionary processes in organisations basically work through communications.

According to Lenski (1970: 60), four **basic phenomena** have to be explained by **theories of evolution**:

1. *continuity*: maintenance of basic fabric of social systems;
2. *innovation*: introduction of new social elements through invention, discovery, or diffusion;
3. *extinction*: on two levels: intra-systemic and inter-systemic, elements are selected as a result of choices and action of social actors;
4. *evolution*: process whereby social systems increase their capacity to mobilise energy and information in adapting to their environments (Sanderson 1990: 145).

In the following, *economic* and *social evolutionary theories* will be outlined in order to grasp the theoretical fundament explaining these phenomena within social evolutionary processes.

5.1.1 Economic evolutionary theories

'If, today, a relaxant was introduced that was physiologically addictive and could be expected to cause considerable numbers of deaths from cancer, drug regulations in most countries would inevitably prohibit it. Yet we have tobacco. If anybody today invented a sport, which ritualised physical assault intended to concur an opponent, and which resulted in cumulative brain damage and occasional deaths, there would be public outcry. Yet we have boxing. If the neo-classical theory of the firm had remained in Nirvana, and somebody today published a proposal for a theory of the firm based on omniscient owner-managers of single-product firm,

the absurdity of this concept would guarantee it a brief life cycle. Yet we have the neo-classical theory of the firm. In these examples, origins predate modern times' (Kay 1984: 189).

The shortcomings of classical and neo-classical reasoning with regard to dynamics became increasingly clear in economics. As a consequence, evolutionary economists became deeply influenced by evolutionary reasoning in biology and sociology. Marshall (1961: 241) argues: *'This increased subdivisions of functions, or 'differentiation', as it is called, manifests itself with regard to industry in such forms as the division of labour, and the development of specialised skill, knowledge and machinery: while 'integration', that is, a growing intimacy and firmness of the connections between the separate parts of the industrial organism, shows itself in such forms as the increase of security of commercial credit, and of the means and habits of communication by sea and road, by railway and telegraph, by post and printing press.'*

Marshall also expressed disillusionment with static analysis based on competitive equilibrium. He wrote that *'all sciences of life are akin to one another and are unlike physical sciences. And therefore in the later stages of economics, when we are approaching nearly the conditions of life, biological analogies are to be preferred to the mechanical, other things being equal'* (Marshall 1898: 42-43).

Veblen (1898: 393) contends that evolutionary economics must be the theory of a process of cultural growth as determined by the economic interest, a theory of a cumulative sequence of economic institutions stated in terms of the process itself. It is a cumulative growth of '**habits of thought**' (Veblen 1898: 394). According to Veblen, the **evolution of social structure** has been a process of **natural selection of institutions**. The progress, which has been made and is being made in human institutions and in human character, may be set down, broadly, to a natural selection of the fittest habits of thought and to a process of enforced adaptation of individuals to an environment which has progressively changed with the changing institutions under which men have lived. **Institutions** are not only themselves the *result of a selective and adaptive process* which shapes the prevailing or dominant types of spiritual attitude and aptitude; they are at the same time special methods of life and of human relations, and are therefore in their turn *efficient factors of selection*. The changing institutions in their turn make for a further selection of individuals endowed with the fittest temperament, and a further adaptation of individual temperament and habits to the changing environment through the formation of new institutions (Veblen 1899: 188). Veblen thus stresses the *significance of social institutions* for *socialisation, role making,* and *role distribution* in social systems. From a social systems perspective, Veblen formulates a principle of the co-evolution of individuals and social systems.

Presuming that human behaviour is dominated by habits of thought, Veblen took the view that the latter are partly rooted in instincts and were seen to represent evolutionary adaptations to changing environmental conditions. Veblen thus constructed a bridge between the emotional and cognitive level of individuals and social systems. From the concept of habits of thought, Veblen took the next step to a **definition of institutions**, which are '*settled habits of thought common to the generality of men*' (Veblen 1919, 239). The institutions are, in substance, prevalent habits of thought with respect to particular relations and particular functions of the individual and of the community. The situation of today shapes the institutions of tomorrow through a selective, coercive process, by acting upon men's habitual view of things, and so altering or fortifying a point of view or a mental attitude handed down from the past. These institutions, which have so been handed down, these habits of thought, points of view, mental attitudes and aptitudes, or what not, are therefore themselves a **conservative factor**. This is the factor of *social inertia*[2], *psychological inertia*, and *conservatism* (Veblen 1899: 190). There is a cumulative growth of customs and habits of thought, a selective adaptation of conventions and methods of life (Veblen 1899: 208).

For the purpose of economic science the process of cumulative change to be accounted for is the sequence of change in the methods of doing things – the methods of dealing with the material means of life (Veblen 1898: 387). For the description of developmental processes, when taken as items in a process of cumulative change or as items in the scheme of life, these productive goods are facts of human knowledge, skill, and predilection; that is to say, they are, substantially, prevalent habits of thought, and it is as such that they enter into the process of industrial development (Ibid.). The main focus of Veblen was not to explain '*how things stabilise themselves in a 'static state'*, but '*how they endlessly grow and change*' (Veblen 1934: 8).

Veblen had two primary reasons for the adoption of a Darwinian and evolutionary metaphor. One relates to the idea of cumulative causation and an opposition to depictions of the economic process that are consummated in equilibrium. The other is based on the formation of analogies to both the gene and the processes of natural selection in the social world. Veblen clearly saw institutions as well as individuals as units of evolutionary selection. Veblen (1899: 188) contended that institutions are both replicators and the units of selection in socio-economic evolution. Institutions and habits of thought are the units of selection.

---

[2] In economic terms, inertia is caused by sunk costs of past investments; entrenched social structures; escalation of commitment; and organisation member attachment to cognitive styles, behavioural dispositions, and decision making heuristics. The potential benefits include greater reliability in delivering sound and comprehensible products, and many economies of efficiency and routine (Lewin/Volberda 1999: 521).

'With modern hindsight, this suggests the notion that the information transmitted through learning or imitation to institutions or individuals was analogous, but different from the transmission of genetic information in the process of biological evolution. Consequently, institutions are both the replicators and the units of selection in socio-economic evolution' (Hodgson 1994: 22).

Veblen was relatively successful in establishing the basics of **Darwinian economics**. *First*, the *principle of 'idle curiosity'* became the ongoing source *of variety* or mutation in the evolutionary process. *Second*, the institution became the unit of relative stability and continuity through time, ensuring that much of the pattern and variety is passed on from one period to the next, so that selection has relatively stable units upon which to operate. *Third*, mechanisms are identified through which well-adapted institutions are imitated and replicated, and the less adapted become extinct (Hodgson 1993: 136). Similar to social systems theory, Veblen defines **meaning** (habits of thought, institutions) as the **content and driver of social evolution**. Veblen thus creates a simple model of dynamics in social evolution. On the other hand, the theoretical basis and rigour provided by the concept of autopoiesis – particularly with regard to the evolutionary motor - is missing in this model so that it reflects more a metaphor rather than a real evolutionary model of social evolution.

Veblen (1899: 190-191) also derives a first version of **institutional theory** and of **path-dependence** without terming it as such: *'The situation of today shapes the institutions of tomorrow through a selective, coercive process, by acting upon men's habitual view of things, and so altering or fortifying a point of view or a mental attitude handed down from the past ... At the same time, men's present habits of thought tend to persist indefinitely, except as circumstances enforce a change ... This is the factor of social inertial, psychological inertia, conservatism.'*

However, there is a **double relationship between institutions and evolution**: human institutions channel the evolution of economic activities, but the human institutions are themselves subject to evolution – within a broader framework and on a longer timescale (Loasby 1999: 13). The selection processes themselves are subject to modification and sometimes to drastic revision. In economic evolution, active selection by human agents occurs at all stages of the process (Ibid. 29). Evolution in economic systems depends on, if it is not constituted by, the **evolution of knowledge** (Ibid. 26). Kenneth Boulding (1978) contends that evolution itself evolves and that what evolves in evolutionary processes is know-how.

This **description of institutions** provides an important **basis for analysis** of fundamental economic activities. For example, **work** is seen as involving a degree of practical knowledge that is both acquired and routinised over time. The **industrial skill of a nation** consists of a set of relevant habits, acquired over a long time, dispersed through the work force, reflective of its culture, and deeply embedded in its practices (Hodgson 1994: 27). Economic geography illustrates such **technological trajectories** and **path-dependencies**. On the *firm level*, a central concept derived from the institutional tradition in evolutionary economics is the **organisational routine**. This concept also provides a bridge between economics and strategic management.

From the theoretical fundament provided by early evolutionary economists, several building blocks of evolutionary economics have been refined in the subsequent research. The most prominent are organisational routines, technological trajectories (path-dependence), evolutionary mechanisms, and the foundation of economic organisations. These building blocks will be described in the following paragraphs.

5.1.1.1 Organisational routines

Von Hayek (1937: 52) contends that the **central question** of all social sciences is how the **combination of fragments of knowledge** existing in different minds can bring about results, which, if they were to be brought about deliberately, would require knowledge on the part of the directing mind, which no single person can possess. It is the problem of the utilisation of knowledge not given to any one in its **totality** (von Hayek 1945: 520). Von Hayek (Ibid. 525) proposes that this problem can only be solved by some form of **decentralisation**, '*because only thus can we ensure that the knowledge of the particular circumstances of time and space will be promptly used. But the 'man on the spot' cannot decide solely on the basis of his limited but intimate knowledge of the facts of his immediate surroundings ... as he needs to fit his decisions into the whole pattern of changes of the larger economic system*' (Ibid. 524-525). In order to solve this problem, '*we must show how a solution is produced by the interactions of people each of whom possesses only partial knowledge*' (Ibid. 530).

Veblen's notion that institutions and habits are the units of selection in the social and economic evolutionary process provides the basis for the new evolutionary economics where they are termed **organisational routines** (Nelson/Winter 1982).

'*Our general term for all regular and predictable behavioural patterns of firm is 'routine' ... In our evolutionary theory, these routines play the role that genes play in evolutionary theory. They are a persistent feature of the organism and determine its possible behaviour ... they are heritable, in the sense that tomorrow's organisms generated from today's (for example, by building a new plant) have many of the same characteristics and they are selectable in the sense that organisms with certain routines may do better than others, and, if so, their relative importance in the population (industry) is augmented over time'* (Ibid. 14).

A great deal of business behaviour is **routine**. Decision-making routines produce regular and predictable behaviour based on relatively constant dispositions of strategic heuristics. A routine is a circular flow with changes in this routine itself (Schumpeter 1934: 75-76). Daily tasks are done in a customary way as routines *'because all knowledge and habit once acquired becomes as firmly rooted in ourselves as a railway embankment in the earth'* (Ibid. 84). Crises exist *'because new combinations are not evenly distributed through time but appear discontinuously in groups or swarms'* (Ibid. 253).

Evolutionary economic theory conceives **organisational capabilities** as fragmented, distributed, and embedded in organisational routines. No individual knows how the organisation accomplishes what it actually does, much less what alternatives are available, Although elements of economic choice are built into some routines, the routines themselves are not the consequence of an antecedent choice from a large menu, but of organisational learning (Winter 1994: 99).

Abstract concepts like *'profit maximisation'* are much less useful than concepts like *'routine'* and *'habitual reaction'* because they are more descriptively accurate (Winter 1975: 91-92). What corresponds to a genotype in the theory of the firm may be supposed to be a rule of action or strategy (Ibid. 97). Winter (Ibid. 101) describes his first steps in the development of evolutionary theory in economics together with his colleague Richard Nelson: The essential continuity underlying the process of evolutionary change is the continuity of routinised behaviour. **Routines in firms** are hence conceived as comparable to **genes in biology**. The role of a **business firm** is to serve as a **repository of economic capabilities**, to simply maintain and transmit through time the ability to do something useful. The institutional role is essentially that of **'remembering by doing'** (Ibid. 102). Behavioural routines change over time, in both desired and undesired ways. Such changes correspond to mutations in the biological theory, here applied to the (re-) production of routines. Winter proposes that **deliberate innovations** be counted as the most significant subset of the changes in routine behaviour. Winter argues that evolutionary theory needs a theoretical account of the **cognitive processes** involved in **innovative behaviour** (Ibid. 102-103).

Nelson/Winter view firms as possessing routines, which operate to modify over time various aspects of their operating characteristics (Ibid. 17). There is a **recursive influence of strategy** (interpretations) and **organisational structure** (capabilities) (Ibid. 37). The state of knowledge is certainly subject to change, **deliberate choice** as well as to **change by unchosen and**

unwelcome processes. It is subject to increase and decrease (Nelson/Winter 1982: 63-64). There are three **major sources of limits to the articulation of knowledge** (Ibid. 80-81):

- *feasible time rate of information transfer* along symbolic communication;
- *causal depth of knowledge* (limited depth may impede adjustment to change);
- *coherence aspect* (communication of '*complete knowledge*' between whole and parts).

All skills and routines are context-dependent in various ways but the effectiveness of planning and implementation skills is particularly dependent upon detailed features of the social context. **Operational ambiguity** influences the actual accomplishment in terms of an attempt to exercise the planned action. **Semantic ambiguity** accrues from the problem of specification, transmission and interpretation of knowledge (Nelson/Winter 1982: 87-88). This problem is particularly inherent in MNEs.

The **routinisation of activity** in an organisation constitutes the most important form of storage of the organisation's specific organisational knowledge. Organisations remember by doing – although there are some important qualifications and elaborations (Ibid. 99). Central elements of organisational knowledge are the commands of the organisational dialect, and, above all, the associations that link the incoming message to the specific performances that they call for (Ibid. 104). Nelson/Winter (Ibid. 14) think of organisations as being typically much better at the tasks of self-maintenance in a constant environment than they are at major change, and much better at changing in the direction of '*more of the same*' than they are at any other kind of change. As March/Simon (1958: 142) observed: '*Most behavior, and particularly most behavior in organisations, is governed by performance programs.*' **Behaviour programs** shape reality dramatically. Programs are not merely convenient and amenable tools that people control. Programs construct realities that match their assumptions – by influencing their users' perceptions, values, and beliefs, by dictating new programs' characteristics, by filtering information and focusing attention. Most importantly, programs act unreflectively (Starbuck 1983: 93). Research shows that programs account for almost all behaviour in non-routine positions as well. Behaviours get programmed through spontaneous habits, professional norms, education, training, precedents, traditions, and rituals as well as through formalised procedures (Starbuck 1983: 93).

Nelson/Winter (1982: 118) emphasise that **organisational routines** are **opaque**, rather than transparent. People may be purposively enacting routines without being able to articulate precisely what the routines consist of. The replication of routines across boundaries is problematic because knowledge of routines is largely tacit. Evolutionary theory thus emphasises that much of the knowledge that underlies organisational capabilities is tacit knowledge; it is not understood or communicable in symbolic form. Individual skills have large tacit components, and organisational routines involve tacit knowledge to the extent that they involve the exercise of such skills. Furthermore, **organisational knowledge is fragmented**. Its application and value depend on the interaction of individuals in order to create joint action and results (Winter 1994: 100-101).

5.1.1.2 Technological trajectories

The roots of the concept technological trajectories and path-dependence in general were developed by Veblen, who described the cumulative growth of habits of thought (Veblen 1898: 394). According to Camagni (1991: 124), the rationale for this **self-organised and ordered process** is found in the **intrinsic learning nature of technological change** occurring on the level of microeconomic learning processes (research units and firms) and social-institutional learning processes. These processes constrain the evolutionary path along ordered technological trajectories and long-term, cyclical waves. At the **macroeconomic scale**, *order* may come from socio-cultural and institutional resistances to change and from stabilising characteristics of the economic and political environment. Drivers on the **microeconomic scale** are:

- the *presence of specific technical properties*, reducing the spectrum of possible behaviours,
- the *sharing of similar problem-solving heuristics* among firms,
- the *cumulative agreement* in the society on the definition of relevant problems and targets,
- the *use of decision routines* which limit the spectrum of possible actions, and
- the *cumulative nature of incremental innovations* within each technological paradigm.

According to Camagni's approach (Ibid. 124-125), **technological change** may be interpreted in the following way:

1. It is an *irreversible, path-dependent, and evolutionary process*, stemming from the behaviour of economic agents which explore only a limited part of the theoretically possible actions, and which is strictly linked to previous innovation adoptions and to already acquired know-how.
2. It relies therefore on a *cumulative learning process*, resulting in the creation rather than the simple adoption or imitation of already existing ideas (inventions and innovations).
3. It implies *search and decision routines*, which limit the cost of information collection and uncertainty.

4. It implies *full commitment of all functions of the firm*.
5. It *cumulatively builds on tacit, firm-specific know-how and on intangible assets*, and hence difficult to transfer or to copy.
6. Its *historical path may by no means be interpreted in terms of optimality*. Once a bifurcation point is reached in the development path of a particular technology and a specific trajectory is chosen, cumulative processes reinforce and perpetuate that choice, highly reducing the spectrum of possible outcome and alternatives.

One body of economic research purports to identify a **life cycle** through which many technologies seem to go. The basic argument is that when a new technology comes to existence there is considerable uncertainty regarding which of a variety of variants will succeed. Different parties try out different ones. After a period of time and competition, one or a few of these variants come to dominate the others, and attention and resources become concentrated on these at the expense of the others. As a result, a **dominant design** emerges (Nelson 1994: 141).

Individual firms differ in their characteristics, behaviours, performances, and their propensities to commit resources to innovation and imitation. A **crucial part** of the **decision-process** is the construction, evaluation, and modification of the **frame of reference** itself. This very process can be defined as **learning**. The members' and the organisation's **information-processing capabilities** and the very **decision-making rules** cannot be postulated but are generated and co-evolve in a **process of learning and adaptation**. Organisational knowledge is neither presupposed nor derived from available information but rather emerges as a property of the learning system and is shaped by the interaction among various learning processes that constitute the organisation (Dosi/Marengo 1994: 160-162).

5.1.1.3 Evolutionary mechanisms

From the perspective of evolutionary economics, evolutionary mechanisms may be differentiated on **industry and firm level**. On the **macro-level**, Piore (1992: 442) summarises the **social division of labour** in line with the **evolutionary mechanism of differentiation and integration** as follows:

1. *Economic growth* is the product of the division of labour.
2. The division of labour involves the partitioning of economic activity. One needs to understand both the cognitive and the organisational implications of different partitioning principles.
3. The division of labour has two distinct dimensions: specialisation and integration. Cognitively, *specialisation* has two distinct functions:

- the *deepening of knowledge*, and
- *reconceptualisation*: a change in the conceptual frame itself.
  Reconceptualisation also has two dimensions:
  - *transfer*: the movement of an element from one conceptual frame to another, e.g. mechanisation of pin heading and
  - *invention*: the creation of a new conceptual frame.

Piore describes the social evolutionary process of differentiation and integration on the level of the economic subsystem. **Flexible specialisation** involves **growth through social division of labour**: the deepening of knowledge within given conceptual categories. **Network structures** facilitate both the deepening and the interaction because to better integrate with other conceptual specialities, the specialists are forced to develop their own speciality more fully. The conceptual level of understanding in this form of growth permits horizontal co-ordination, thus avoiding hierarchy, but the degree of interactions across specialities is too immense to permit a market (Ibid. 443). Piore thus also stresses the development of network building as complementing flexible specialisation in the process of economic evolution.

In her historical study on technological change, Andersen (2001: 248) observes a historical trend across technological systems, in which previously distinct industrial sectors appear to be coming together in adopting, exploiting, and developing technological systems. **Expansion of corporate technological competencies** increasingly has been **across industry boundaries**. **Industry boundaries** hence become **less well defined** (Ibid. 255). The evolution of knowledge embodied in new technological opportunities is characterised by creative, incremental, interconnected accumulation, as opposed to creative destruction, so that new technological systems with new opportunities build upon old ones rather than substitute them (Ibid. 249). Although corporate innovations evolve within technological structures, and vice versa, and although technologies and new systems are built upon old ones, the corporate and industrial scopes governed by new technological systems still substitute old ones (Ibid. 259). **Technological evolution** can be characterised by **'radical incrementalism'** or **'revolutionary gradualism'** (Ibid. 254).

Evolutionary economics states that institutions, routines, and knowledge in general are units of selection and replicators at the same time. From an efficiency perspective, the marginal cost of use of knowledge is in many cases zero. In addition, the marginal cost of new information added to the old stock of knowledge is probably very much lower when the accumulated stock is large. The more often a particular transaction is made the more information the firm may have about that transaction. Expectations based upon past experiences become more and more conditioned by probabilities inferred from past data. Over time, even secondary information settles down enough to make plans on the basis of expectations, for the accumulation of experience will enable firms to make decisions, which are correct more often in relation to uncontrolled variables. A **modus vivendi** becomes established among firms, as responses become more habituated (Malmgren 1961: 413-415).

One of the most obvious economies of social life is the '**economy of cognition**', i.e. of processes whereby the trial-and-error exploration of one member serves to save others the trouble of entering the same blind alleys. Two requisite values emerge. There is a **requirement of honesty** by communicators and there is a **requirement of trust** in communication. These are presumably universal values in human societies (Campbell 1965: 45). Institutions economise on the scarce resource of cognition, by providing us with ready-made anchors of sense, ways of partitioning the space of representations, premises for decisions, and bounds within which we can be rational or imaginative. **Institutions** represent **externally organised social capital**. Shared conventions make it easier to predict the behaviour of others, even when we cannot predict their circumstances. Conventions provide the basis for perceptions of justice (Loasby 1999: 46).

On the other hand, differences between people are primary contributors to the generation of variety and thus the evolution of economic systems (Loasby 1999: 43). Cognitive development thus becomes a social process, which exploits the variety of people's interactions with their environments (Ibid. 45). The **creation of new economic forms** is mediated cognitively in mental acts of variation and selection (Day 1987: 254). Evolutionary change is very strongly affected by the existence of '**empty niches**' (Boulding 1991: 13). But to claim that relatively fit organisms are selected to fill pre-existing niches and that optimal outcome results can be rejected for a number of reasons. First, even if such environmental niches were to exist, an infinite sequence of trials and errors would be necessary to identify the optimal match of organism and environment. Second, since an organism's environment consists of populations of other organisms, the ecological niches themselves evolve. Third, organisms actively choose their environments as to give themselves the greatest chance of survival and influence the co-evolution with the environment (England 1994: 6). '*Organisms ... do not adapt to environments; they construct them*' (Lewontin 1982: 163).

On the **micro-level**, *technological change* is increasingly understood as a **growth process**, in turn primarily driven by **endogenous processes within firms** (e.g. firm trajectories, organisational routines, searching zones) as well as **within regional settings** (e.g. industrial districts, clusters, development blocs, national trajectories). The evolutionary process involves a search for and adoption of new technologies, exploitation (voluntary dissemination) and imitation (involuntary dissemination). Pressures from competition, other new technologies and from visionary challenges posed by management seem to add impetus to the **innovation process** (Hagström/Chandler 1998: 2).

Since many of the decisions in economic selection processes are taken in firms, the study of these processes requires particular attention to the **capabilities of firms**, to the evolutionary processes by which these capabilities are developed, and to organisational structures, both formal and informal, which frame the perceptions of productive opportunities and thus help to create the selection environment (Loasby 1999: 29).

Firms are **devices for the co-ordination and use** of particular kinds of **knowledge**, including the co-ordination of knowledge generation, by the imposition of an interpretative framework on a problem area, which is treated as if it were separable from the other problem areas (Loasby 1991: 59). Knowledge is structured; it builds cumulatively and is stored in the organisation's memory to shape its future search activities. Interfirm differences in knowledge base determine the asymmetry of competing firms (Saviotti/Metcalfe 1991: 10). Each firm creates its own capabilities from its particular socially organised set of skills, which are partly inarticulate and continually changing (Loasby 1991: 60). Each firm's evolution will tend to differentiate its knowledge and capabilities from those of other firms. Within a diversified firm this process will be at work in each business unit (Ibid. 60).

Current strategies build up over time and reflect the accumulation of decisions made in the past. There is a **path-dependent nature of corporate strategies** (Kay 1997: 63). The survival rates in large firms suggest that selection processes operating at the level of the firm in such cases is typically characterised by **self-selection** (Ibid. 83). If a firm is a collection of capabilities, then the obsolescence of some of its capabilities need not imply the demise of the firm. Instead, upgrading, substitution, or replacement of capabilities will take place (Ibid. 94). Organisational change, as well as technological learning, is highly path-dependent. The strength of norms, routines, and corporate cultures resides precisely in their persistence and reproduction over time (Dosi/Marengo 1994: 176). Technical interrelatedness creates a bias toward evolutionary technological changes that are technically compatible with interrelated or complementary equipment (Cohen 1984: 788).

5.1.1.4 Foundation of organisations

While the mechanism of differentiation and integration of economic systems describes and explains the differential reproduction of economic systems, the emergence of new economic organisations has to be illustrated in more detail. **Organisational creation** can be described as a **collective, network building achievement** that centres in the inception, diffusion, and adoption of a set of ideas among a group of people who become sufficiently committed to these ideas to transform into a **social institution**. It involves the development of ideas and relationships (Bartunek/Betters-Reed 1987: 290, van de Ven et al. 1984). Bartunek/Betters-Reed (1987: 290) propose three **stages in the creation of a new organisation**, which overlap in practice. These stages are the *'first ideas'* for the organisation, *'commitments and initial planning'* during which the plan emerges, and *'implementation'* when the components of the new setting are established. The stages culminate in the official birth of the organisation. It is important to note that even the **foundation** of a new social system is an **act of social selection**. Individuals and/or other social systems select from a given range of possibilities a distinct organisation, which will be subject to reproduction and continuous selection as a whole and of its components.

Through **selective perceptions by founders** of constraints and opportunities in the environment, basic decisions are made regarding what business the firm is in and how it will compete and thus the firm's strategic orientation (Tushman/Romanelli 1985: 174). For example, the liability of resource scarcity confronts cohorts of founders in high-density periods, influencing the basic orientation (Aldrich 1999: 267). Within the critical activity domains, which are characterising organisations as they pursue a strategic orientation, core values and domain decisions set the basic premises of decisions within the firm. These premises constrain the shape and the distribution of power and the allocation of scarce resources, which, in turn, constrain choices of structures and control systems (Tushman/Romanelli 1985: 175).

Over time as the firm grows there will be the dynamic restraint that new activities take a disproportionately long time to evaluate and decide on, since there are no visible patterns of behaviour or history to rely on, but as decisions become routinised new activities can be taken on (Malmgren 1961: 419). The more heterogeneous the transactions assimilated by the firm, the greater the cost (Ibid. 420). In line with von Hayek's (1937: 36) definition of *expectational equilibrium*, *general equilibrium* can be considered in terms of the satisfaction of expectations (Malmgren 1961: 421).

Successful entrepreneurs operate in networks. These networks feed entrepreneurs with the information they require about developments in related sectors of the economy. The value of social networks is so great that entrepreneurs often play a leading role in setting them up. **Networking** is particularly significant in promoting **new channels of international trade** (Buckley 2000: 6). In general, the value of the differentiation of new capabilities may be enhanced if firms become linked in a network. Network relationships permit the transfer of ideas and also creation of new ideas through the juxtaposition of different interpretations. This is an important way in which evolution of human systems, being subject to purposeful action, differs from that of biological systems, which rely on purposeless mutation and natural selection (Loasby 1999: 142). This cumulative process of differentiation and integration, in which knowledge is generated and absorbed within and between firms, and each new division of labour enlarges some market in the economy and thereby creates the scope for fresh specialisation (Ibid. 143). The **growth of knowledge** proceeds through the differentiation and dispersion of knowledge, and the organisation of economic activity should respect the diversity of knowledge-generating systems (Loasby 1999a: 51).

During the **foundation** and later in **phases of change**, once the change process is initiated, the change process itself may become routinised and subject to inertial forces as well. This creates momentum, that is, the tendency to maintain the direction and emphasis of prior actions in current behaviour. Amburgey/Miner (1992) have identified three **types of momentum**:

1. *repetitive*, in which the same event is repeated;
2. *positional*, in which a current position is strengthened (e.g. diversified firms become more diverse); and
3. *contextual, in which organisational factors result in consistent action.*

Once initiated, momentum acts as a **selection-retention mechanism** that guides patterns of organisational variation and makes exploration of alternatives difficult (Ginsberg/Baum 1994: 129).

The **routines** to which organisations become committed tend to be determined more by initial actions than by information gained from later learning situations. Organisations are imprinted by their first actions as **self-reinforcing momentum processes** commit them to repeating routines shaped by early and often arbitrary successes. The combined influences of momentum, imprinting, forgetting, and unlearning on organisational activities provide a set of mechanisms that can produce the characteristic repetition, inaction, and reorientation of organisational evolution (Ginsberg/Baum 1994: 130). Firms grow on the basis of their ability to create new knowledge and to replicate this knowledge when entering new markets.

Management has to focus on conditions enhancing the likely value of **competence-based action** focusing on capturing value from *existing routines* (retention/exploitation) versus that of the search for *new competencies* (variation/experimentation) (Miner 1994: 85). Increasingly, empirical studies point to *recombinations of existing routines* as an important source of innovation and change (Schroeder et al. 1989).

Like evolutionary biology, evolutionary economics is much concerned with how patterns are reproduced through time in the face of continuing turnover in the population of individuals displaying the pattern (Winter 1988: 172).

5.1.2 Social evolutionary theories

Evolution is often used to refer to the processes that produce history. The development of species, individual, organisation, or society occurs through a set of **historical mechanisms**. Social order, moral, and language are outcomes of evolution. Much interest in evolution is in describing the mechanisms that generate a path of history. These include reproduction, learning, choice, imitation, and competition. For example, an organisational past can be seen as imposing itself on the present through retention of organisational experience in organisational routines and structures (March 1994: 40-41). The **gene pool of human artefacts** in general is the **whole sphere of human knowledge** (Boulding 1981: 16). Knowledge is not only a consequence of evolution, but also a central part of the very process of evolution (Wisman 1989: 650). This sphere is broadly represented by the concept of '**meaning**' in social systems theory and by '**culture**' in anthropology and ethnology, which are main areas in the research of socio-cultural evolution.

5.1.2.1 General social evolutionary theory

'*Socio-cultural evolution is, in essence, an extension of the process of organic evolution*' (Sanderson 1990: 126). Culture hence can be viewed as a system of inheritance (Boyd/Richardson 1985: 19). Thus we have in cultural transmission the analogies to reproduction and mutation in biological entities. Ideas, languages, values, behaviours, and technologies, when transmitted, undergo reproduction, and when there is a difference between the subsequently transmitted version of the original entity, and the original entity itself, '*mutation*' has occurred (Cavalli-Sforza/Feldman 1981: 10). In general, **cultural selection** may be defined as '*the differentiated social transmission of cultural variants through human decision-making, or simply as 'preservation by preference''* (Durham 1991: 198). Within the *selection by decision-making*, Durham identifies a **decision continuum** with two poles: (1) '**selection by choice**', representing the self-organisational or *autopoietic variant*, and (2) '**selection by imposition**', denoting the *allopoietic variant*, which is characterised by coercion, force, manipulation, or authority (Ibid.). The process of trait reproduction may take the form of horizontal (Lamarckian) and vertical (Darwinian) transmission. **Vertical transmission** is used to denote transmission from parent to offspring (e.g. MNE to new subsidiary) and **horizontal transmission** denotes transmission between any two actors (e.g. between subsidiaries or co-operation partners) (Cavalli-Sforza/Feldman 1981: 54).

Cultures as social systems may be conceived as systems of meaning or knowledge. The evolution of social systems or cultures then takes the form of a learning process. All processes leading to their evolution and to expansions of knowledge involve a blind-variation-and-selective-retention process. Processes, such as vision and thought, substituting for an overt trial and error are of course acknowledged. But each of these is interpreted as containing in its very workability wisdom about the environment obtained originally by the blind variation of mutation and natural selection (Campbell 1987: 111).

Three **basic requirements of variation-and-selective-retention in socio-cultural evolution** are necessary: a mechanism for introducing variation, a consistent selection process, and a mechanism for preserving and reproducing the selected variations (Campbell 1987: 92).

1. Variation:

The occurrence of variations is heterogeneous, haphazard, '**blind**', chance, random, but in any event variable. This applies to the mutation process in organic evolution and to **exploratory responses in learning**. Unlike a gene, a cultural trait can be suddenly abolished, and just as suddenly reinstated, across the whole population (Alexander 1979: 76). Cultural traits, whether practices or beliefs, can in principle provide natural selection with an equally sound variation basis (van Parijs 1981: 85). In social systems there is the unique capability of introducing fluctuations and new energy in the form of ideas, expectations, models, myths, and plans, which surface within these systems (Jantsch 1975: xvii). Genetic mutation is casual, while social evolution includes goal seeking, decisions, imitation, interpenetration of systems, and purposeful behaviour (Hodgson 1993: 216). Due to culturally determined limits to imagination, *'innovation and novelty are much more likely when these limits are being altered or broken down, such as when different cultures collide, or in periods of major socio-economic turbulence'* (Ibid. 233). The sociology of knowledge suggests that persons who have been uprooted from traditional cultures, or who have been thoroughly exposed to two or more cultures, seem to have the advantage in the range of hypotheses they are apt to consider, and through this means, in the frequency of creative innovation (Campbell 1987: 104). Too high a **mutation rate** destabilises and threatens the **preservation of complexly adapted forms**. Nonetheless, those socio-environmental setting providing the greatest range of variations, are the most likely to produce cultural advances (Campbell 1965: 28). Furthermore, innovations coming from '*intelligent*' problem solving of social actors *'is not based on 'reality' directly, but only on incomplete memory and simplified extrapolation. Even where wise, the wisdom reflects past realities, not the current or future ones directly relevant to group survival'* (Campbell 1994: 31). Campbell (1987: 96) contends that to include the knowledge process of creative thought into the general plan of blind variation and selective retention, it must be emphasised that creative thought achieves innovation, the internal emitting of thought trials one by one is blind, lacking prescience or foresight.

Organisations are generally assumed to be more likely to survive and prosper when potentially valuable innovation occurs. Unfortunately, managers cannot specify exactly in advance what needs to be discovered so that randomness still plays a significant role in the variation process of social systems. One thing organisations do to facilitate useful variation is engage in **institutionalised experimentation** (e.g. research and development). Organisations also provide direct and indirect incentives to produce valuable variation. They sometimes even tacitly acknowledge the value of **unfocused variation** or pure *'playfulness'* that develop on the basis of informality, *'skunkworks'*, and slack resources. Variation is generated on a continuum that reaches from rational planning to the permission for playfulness with almost no control and no direct involvement in its content (Miner 1994: 78). Variation is a change from current routines, competencies, and organisational forms. **Intentional variations** occur when people actively attempt to generate alternatives and seek solutions to problems. **Blind variations** occur independently of environmental or selection pressures (Aldrich 1999: 22-26). Astley (1985: 240) contends that *'selection is the regulator of evolutionary change; variation is its dynamo'*.

2. Selection:

Consistent selection criteria produce *selective elimination, selective propagation*, and *selective retention of certain types of variations*. This applies to the differential survival of certain mutations in organic evolution and the differential reinforcement of certain responses in learning. Natural selection is the mechanism that generates biological adaptation. In **cultural evolution**, there is in addition a second mode of selection, which is the result of the **capacity for decision-making** (Cavalli-Sforza/Feldman 1981: 10). Two **possible units of selection** can be chosen: (1) **bounded entities**, like groups or organisations, and (2) **routines and competencies** within the bounded entities (Aldrich 1999: 35). A distinction can be drawn between **internal selectors** and **external selectors**. One type of internal selection criterion occurs when processes of evolution build in internal selective criteria, which are vicarious representations of external selectors. Thus any social organisation tends to move in the direction of internal compatibility. **Inertia** is one end product of a process in which internal selective criteria have operated (Campbell 1965: 33). In the rational choice model of management, selection occurs through deliberate managerial choice among alternatives for future action. Goal setting, decision-making routines, and the establishment of norms and values determine corridors for the selection of organisational elements and actions. **Rational decision-making** is limited due to bounded rationality and political conflicts in organisations. On the other extreme, population ecologists argue that organisations only produce variations and are negatively selected against by the environment. From an internal perspective, selection can also occur in the form of **incremental transformations** on a basically emergent level. Internal competition resembles most the biological principle of 'survival of the fittest' and serves as a further selection mechanism (Miner 1994: 78-80). **Selection** means a **differential elimination** of certain types of variations. *External selection* is caused by forces external to an organisation that affect its routines and competencies, and structures. *Internal selection* is driven by forces internal to an organisation affecting the same traits (Aldrich 1999: 26-30). When *selection criteria shift*, some variations that previously proved more beneficial than others are no longer positively selected. An avenue is thus opened for new practices. In competitive environments, changes in the terms on which resources are available may create new selection pressures, generating changes in internal diffusion, imitation, promotion, and incentive systems (Ibid. 174). In evolutionary terms, *differences* are *crucial*. When differentiated or ambivalent threads of meaning are present in organisations, variation in routines and competencies allows for the play of selection forces within them (Ibid. 341). Networks of relations with powerful institutional actors may provide a transformational shield for organisations, buffering them against selection pressures that would otherwise induce change (Ibid. 175, Miner et al. 1990).

3.   **Retention:**

A mechanism is needed for the **preservation, duplication, or propagation of the positively selected variants**. This applies to the rigid duplication process of the chromosomegene system in plants and animals and to the memory in learning. (Campbell 1965: 27). Retention systems themselves are subject to selective-retention editing (Ibid. 34). The **crucial concept** in the retention process is **consistency across time and across units**. In rational planning, variation and selection occur in the planning phase. Implementation and control systems then constitute the retention process. Formalisation and codification of effective routines serve as retention processes. Consistency can also be sustained by organisational cultures and informal socialisation into particular values. Values therefore can serve as a selection device and as well as a retention mechanism (Miner 1994: 80-81). By retention, selected variations are preserved, duplicated, or otherwise reproduced. Retention processes allow social systems to capture value from existing routines that have proved – or been perceived as – beneficial. On a macro-level, knowledge of previously successful forms is institutionalised in the socialisation apparatus of societies (Aldrich 1999: 30-32). Retention within an organisation occurs via the preservation, duplication, and propagation of positively selected rules, policies, structures, systems, and routines that regularise behaviour. These positively selected variants constitute the organisational memory (Miller 1999: 96). Such *retention of advantageous traits and activities* may, in part, be explained by *institutionalisation theory* (Aldrich 1979: 44).

According to Miner (1994: 81), two relationships in the **continuous balance between internal evolutionary processes** are especially crucial: (1) the balance between variation and retention (e.g. radical vs. incremental variation), and (2) the balance between competition and mutualism (inter- and intra-organisational). Variation, selection, and retention occur simultaneously rather than sequentially and are linked in continuous feedback loops and cycles. The organisations and populations observed at a given moment are not the fittest in any absolute sense. Rather, their forms reflect the historical path laid down by a meandering drift of accumulated and selectively retained variations (Aldrich 1999: 33).

Selective systems constitute a **nested hierarchy** because each system is the outcome of trials at the next higher level (Anderson 1999: 138). According to Campbell (1990: 4), the laws of the higher-level selective system determine in part the distribution of lower level events and substances. Description of an intermediate level phenomenon is not complete by describing its possibility and implementation in lower level terms. Its presence, prevalence, or distribution will often require reference to law at a higher level of organisation as well. **Whole-part competition** in organisations is a **co-evolutionary problem**. That is, the organisation and its parts do not merely evolve; they co-evolve, both with each other and with a changing organisational environment (Baum 1999: 120). Campbell (1994: 38) recognised that evolutionary outcomes at different levels may undermine rather than complement each other. He contends that firm-level adaptations will be under continual undermining pressures from individual and face-to-face group preferences. At the different levels, survival of the relevant organisational entities is governed by different selection mechanisms, which are subject to many discrepancies (Rosenkopf/Nerkar 1999: 174).

In general, '...*we know little about how or why evolutionary processes in one level facilitate or constrain evolution at other levels of a nested ecological hierarchy*' (van de Ven/Grazman 1999: 189). Baum (1999: 114) assumes that evolution is faster and more effective at lower levels of organisation. The reason for this is that variation, selection, and retention processes unfold more quickly at lower levels of organisation. Romanelli (1999: 85) assumes that **subunits evolve at different paces**, sometimes faster and sometimes slower than the overall system, hence generating the need for integration because of different dynamics. As evolution is taking place in a nested hierarchy, a **greater number of variations** may be expected at **lower levels** because of a shorter time-scale, although the magnitude of these variations is likely to be smaller because of their lower level of complexity. As a consequence, even though **higher-level selection** may occur less frequently, when macro-level selection events occur, they tend to produce more **dramatic changes** than when micro-level selection events occur. Finally, selection at a given level in the hierarchy requires competition for scarce resources among entities competing at that level (van de Ven/Grazman 1999: 191-192).

In the nested hierarchical structure of social systems, organisations are viewed as evolving systems nested in other co-evolving systems at higher (e.g. industry or population) and lower (work groups or individuals) levels of analysis (Ibid. 189). There are several theoretical **implications of a nested hierarchical perspective** of organisational evolution. *First*, selection and adaptation processes can work simultaneously and differently at each level in a nested hierarchy. *Second*, relationships between levels may be both positive and negative. *Third*, the relative dominance of evolutionary processes at macro- and micro-levels is a matter of time scale and spatial variation. The rate of evolution at the micro-levels should generally exceed that at macro-levels. In terms of ecological space, micro-level selection should predominate at the macro-level because there are more variations available for selection. The scale of variations at higher-level groups is almost always greater than of those between lower-level individuals. *Fourth*, selection at a given level in the hierarchy requires competition for scarce resources among entities competing at that level. Macro-level resource scarcity constrains selection and adaptation paths by setting boundary conditions and influencing the availability of resources for lower-level evolution. The **strength of relationships between different levels** in a nested hierarchy is assumed to increase under conditions of **resource scarcity**. On balance, the emergence and persistence of branches in the lineage of any focal level are reciprocally influenced by changes in their own lineages and the lineages of other levels (Ibid. 190-192, 205).

Though Campbell (1994: 30) stresses the importance of blind variation, the model of a nested hierarchy of blind-variation-and-selective-retention mechanisms that he developed explicitly incorporates creative thought. According to Campbell (1960: 380),

1. *'A blind-variation-and-selective-retention process is fundamental to all inductive achievements, to all genuine increases in knowledge, to all increases in fit of system to environment.*
2. *The many processes, which shortcut a more full blind-variation-and-selective retention process, are in themselves inductive achievements, containing wisdom about the environment achieved originally by blind variation and selective retention.*
3. *In addition, such shortcut processes contain in their own operation a blind-variation-and selective-retention process at some level, substituting for overt locomotor exploration or the life-and-death winnowing of organic evolution'.*

If there are representatives of these three requirements at the level of social forms and customs, then a socio-cultural evolutionary process or a socio-cultural learning process is inevitable. If analogues of these three requirements are in operation, then there will occur drift pressures toward increased adaptedness, and toward increased complexity, size, and integration of social organisational units, if such increases give selective advantage (Campbell 1965: 27). More economical vicarious exploratory and selective systems have been evolved where they were possible in the course of social evolution. Each of these vicarious systems embody within themselves the three essentials of blind variation process, a selective criterion, and a retention-propagation process. Social processes of learning, as through profiting from the outcomes of another person's explorations, selective imitative tendencies, etc. can all be seen as such vicarious exploration processes (Ibid. 42).

Aldrich/Kenworthy (1999: 21) argue that in *organisations*, the *blind-variation-and-selective-retention process* described by Campbell (1960) takes the form of **organisational learning**. Variation occurs in form of exploratory responses in learning. Selection is the differentiated reinforcement of certain responses in learning. Retention generates the memory in learning (Ibid. 21-22). In the context of organisational learning, organisational variation is informed by specialised knowledge that is recombined during a process of designing a rule or a rule revision. Nevertheless organisational learning remains an evolutionary adaptive rational process since the specialists' rationality remains limited. However, **evolutionary mechanisms** are **themselves subject** to an **evolutionary process**. Organisations improve their capabilities for storing knowledge, for localising relevant knowledge, and for bringing it to bear on the generation of rule generations. Organisations thus learn to improve internal selection before external selection takes place (Kieser/Koch 2002: 254).

Through past trial-and-error learning, organisations may evolve control systems that systematically predispose an organisation toward trial of certain variations and avoidance of others. **Path-dependence** and **positive feedback loops** in social systems represent **vicarious selectors in social systems** (Romanelli 1999: 83). For Campbell, vicarious selection means that knowledge functions as a selector vicariously anticipating selection by the environment. As discussed in the social systems theory, the existing knowledge structure is itself a result of past selection and reproduction of meaning. Once firm knowledge has been retained in the form of pre-existing templates, the templates can accelerate or catalyse selection, and thus can be said to anticipate, or to vicariously represent, the naturally selected configuration. Thus, anticipatory selectors select possible actions of the system in function of the system's goal (ultimately survival) and the situation of the environment. By eliminating dangerous or inadequate actions before they are executed the **vicarious selector** foregoes selection by the environment and thus increases the chance for survival of the system. For example, venture capital may serve as a vicarious selector and one of the major factors constraining entrepreneurs who wish to start organisations (Anderson 1999: 139). In general, the **organisation of vicarious selectors is a nested hierarchy**: a retained selector itself can undergo variation and selection by another selector, at a higher hierarchical level. This allows the development of **multilevel**

cognitive organisation, leading to ever more intelligent and adaptive systems (Rao/Singh 1999: 71).

Cognitive schemata influence the kinds of variation generated and create an organisation-specific selective retention system. As a result, a **community of practice** emerges: the patterned social interaction between members that sustains organisational knowledge and facilitates its reproduction (Aldrich 1999: 141). **Learning** takes place as patterns of cognitive associations and causal beliefs are communicated and institutionalised. The learning process involves sense making, enactment, and the development and diffusion of knowledge structures and causal maps. Organisations thus evolve when members learn. **Behaviours** and **interpersonal relations**, not just cognition, catalyse the process of constructing organisational knowledge. **Procedural knowledge** learned via interaction with others may remain tacit, rather than becoming externalised as declarative knowledge (Ibid. 142). When selected routines and competencies are embedded in a web of social affiliations, the power of organisational knowledge intensifies. The web of social affiliations conveys not only cognitive knowledge but also emotional knowledge, such as affection and hatred, envy and suspicion, and trust and distrust. Knowledge thus becomes thoroughly intertwined not only with interpretations of what it means, but also with how members feel about it (Ibid. 149).

5.1.2.2 Theory of structuration (Giddens)

Giddens (1984, 1988) developed the structuration theory in order to explain the (re-) production of social structure. Structuration is defined as *'conditions governing the continuity or transformation of structures, and therefore the reproduction of systems'* (Giddens 1982: 35). According to Giddens (1982: 36), a social system is a **'structured totality'**, consisting of reproduced practices. Giddens thus adapts evolutionary theory to the sociological context without calling it by name.

Structure refers to the **structuring properties** allowing the **'binding' of time-space in social systems**, the properties which make it possible for discernibly similar social practices to exist across varying spans of time and space and which lend them **'systemic form'**. To say that structure is a **'virtual order' of transformative relations** means that social systems, as reproduced social practices, do not have **'structures'** but rather exhibit **'structural properties'** and that structure exists, as time-space presence, only in its instantiations in such practices, and as memory traces orienting the conduct of knowledgeable human agents. **Structure** is marked by an *'absence of the subject'* (Giddens 1984: 17).

'Structure, as recursively organised sets of rules and resources, is out of time and space, save in its instantiations and co-ordination as memory traces, and is marked by an absence of the

subject. The social systems, in which structure is recursively implicated, comprise the situated activities of human agents, reproduced across time and space. Analysing the structuration of social systems means studying the modes in which such systems, grounded in the knowledgeable activities of situated actors who draw upon rules and resources in the diversity of action contexts, are produced and reproduced in interaction. Crucial to the idea of structuration is the theorem of duality of structure... The constitution of agents and structures are not two independently given sets of phenomena, a dualism, but represent a duality. According to the notion of the duality of structure, the structural properties of social systems are both medium and outcome of the practices they recursively organize' (Ibid. 25).

The duality of structure in interaction relates the knowledgeable capacities of agents to structural features. Actors draw upon the modalities of structuration in the reproduction of systems of interaction, by the same token reconstituting their structural properties (Ibid. 28). **Structure** can be conceptualised abstractly as **two aspects of rules – normative elements and codes of signification** (Ibid. xxxi). Structures of signification are separable only analytically from structures of domination and legitimisation (Figure 5-1). Structure is a generic category involved in structural properties and structures (Ibid. 185). **Structures** are *rule-resource sets*, involved in the institutional articulation of social systems. **Structural properties** are *institutionalised features of social systems*, stretching across time and space. Structural properties exist in time-space only as moments of the constitution of a social system. Structural properties are hierarchically organised in terms of time-space extension of the practices they recursively organise.

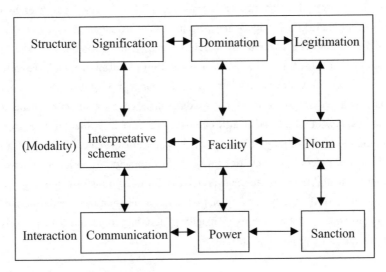

Figure 5-1: The dimensions of the duality of structure
(Source: Giddens 1984: 29)

There are basically three **forms of structural properties** in social systems: *institutions, routines,* and *resources.*

1. The most deeply embedded structural properties, implicated in the reproduction of societal totalities, are called **structural principles** by Giddens. They are principles of organisation of societal totalities. Those practices, which have the greatest time-space extension within such totalities, can be referred to as **institutions** (Ibid. 17, 184).

2. The **routine** (whatever is done habitually) is a basic element of day-to-day social activity. The repetitiveness of activities, which are undertaken in like manner day after day, is the material grounding of the recursive nature of social life. By recursive nature is meant that the structured properties of social activity – via the duality of structure – are constantly recreated out of the very resources, which constitute them. Routinisation is a source of trust and security in social life (Ibid. xxiii). Routines are not mere instruments of management control. Instead, the set of routines in an organisation represents a negotiated settlement of competing interests, a truce between potentially conflicting definitions of the situation (Kilduff 1993: 263).

3. **Resources** (focused via signification and legitimisation) are structured properties of social systems, drawn upon and reproduced by knowledgeable agents in the course of interaction. Resources are media through which power is exercised, as a routine element of the instantiation of conduct in social reproduction. Power within social systems, which enjoy some continuity over time and space, presumes regularised relations of autonomy and dependence between actors or collectivities in contexts of social interaction. But all forms of dependence offer some resources whereby those who are subordinate can influence the activities of their superiors. This is what Giddens calls the '**dialectic control**' in social systems (Giddens 1984: 16). The dialectic of control is constituted by the **reciprocal relation of autonomy and dependence** (Giddens 1982: 39). Giddens thus introduces the concept of power into the context of social evolution in the form of the guiding difference of autonomy/dependence. Resources are of two kinds: **authoritative resources**, which derive from the coordination of the activity of human agents, and **allocative resources**, which stem from control of material products or of aspects of the material world. Allocative resources refer to capabilities – or, more accurately, to forms of transformative capacity – generating command over objects, goods or material phenomena. Authoritative resources refer to types of transformative capacity generating command over persons or actors (Giddens 1984: 33).

In structuration theory structure is regarded as rules and resources recursively implicated in social reproduction; institutionalised features of social systems have structural properties in the sense that relationships are stabilised across time and space. **Rules** imply *methodological procedures of social interaction*. They relate on the one hand to the constitution of meaning, and on the other to the sanctioning of modes of social conduct (Ibid. 17). **Structure** is defined as *recursively organised rules and resources*.

Giddens assumes that social actors sustain meaning in communicative acts. But settings are also '*regionalised*' in ways that heavily influence, and are influenced by, the serial character of encounters. **Regionalisation** here is best understood not as a wholly spatial concept but as one expressing the **clustering of contexts in time-space** (Ibid. 365). *'All social interaction is situated interaction – situated in space and time'* (Ibid. 86). Time-space fixity also normally means social fixity; the substantially given character of the physical milieus of the day-to-day life interlaces with routine and is deeply influential in the contours of institutional reproduction. Regionalisation also has a strong psychological and social resonance in respect of the enclosure from view of some types of activities and some types of people and the disclosure of others (Ibid. xxv-xxvi).

A theory of structuration, which is concerned with all types of social processes, including the unconscious, must allocate a **central role to discursive and practical consciousness** – in the context of unintended consequences – **in the reproduction of social practices** (Giddens 1982: 36). This is particularly important in MNEs. One of the most obvious facts about MNEs is that subunits in different countries tend to employ different languages. The implication is that the attempt to maintain adherence to the same concepts across language boundaries is likely to prove extremely difficult to the extent that such concepts are embedded in the language patterns of particular speech communities. Within the same **MNE, managers from different cultural backgrounds** maintain **different culturally based frames of reference** and resist the homogenising effects of organisational membership. Discrepant interpretations of organisational norms can find support in the social networks through which norms are diffused (Kilduff 1993: 264-265). MNEs may thus exhibit very diverse structural properties whose reproduction is constituted by knowledgeable agents from different cultural contexts. **Organisation-wide norms, routines, and institutions** have to provide for an identity, structure, structural properties, and structural principles, which may constitute the motor of structuration - the duality of structure - **across globally dispersed units**.

Homeostatic system reproduction in human society can be regarded as involving the operation of **causal loops**, in which a range of unintended consequences of action feed back to reconstitute the initiating circumstances. But in many contexts of social life there occur processes of **selective information filtering** whereby strategically placed actors seek reflexively to regulate the overall conditions of system reproduction either to keep things as they are or to change them. The distinction between homeostatic causal loops and reflexive self-regulation in system reproduction must be complemented by the distinction between social integration and system integration. The former means systemness on the level of face-to-face interaction. System integration refers to connection with those who are physically absent in time or space (Giddens 1984: 27-28).

The **emphasis of the structuration theory** is on the **recursiveness of institutionalised reality.** Individual lives are linear in the sense that people age and die, whereas the institutions that people constitute may continue to be enacted by new generations of participants. The work of the **MNE is continually recreated** as employees engage in routinised exchanges that enact the familiar characteristics of the institution. Actors reflexively monitor both their own activities and the activities of others as part of the intentional reproduction of routine (Kilduff 1993: 264).

Social positions are constituted structurally as specific intersections of signification, domination and legitimisation, which relate to the typification of agents. A social position involves the specification of a definite **identity within a network of social relations** (Giddens 1984: 83). The positioning of actors in the regions of their daily time-space paths, of course, is their simultaneous positioning within the broader regionalisation of societal totalities and within intersocietal systems whose broadcast span is convergent with the geopolitical distribution of social systems on a global scale (Ibid. 84).

Social integration depends upon the reflexively applied procedures of knowledgeable agents. There are potential differences between knowledge of the rules and tactics of practical conduct in the milieus in which the agent moves and knowledge about those, which apply in contexts remote from his or her experience (Ibid. 90-91). In the **MNE**, the potential for **subcultures** to flourish with the support of local networks is tremendous. Intolerance or ignorance of the diversity of interpretations and behaviours can lead to unanticipated organisational conflict. Given diverse cultural premises, the **(re-)production of organisation-wide routines** may be difficult to achieve. The transmission of routines in MNEs is problematic because such routines are embedded in the interactions of specific individuals in specific places (Kilduff 1993: 269, 271).

Communicative structures like interpersonal relationships, chains-of-command, and exchange networks only survive through **constant use**. Social reproduction is even more difficult in the case of the MNE because it must be accomplished across national frontiers and cultural differences. In an **MNE** operating across many national borders with a variety of loosely coupled subsidiaries, a **large amount of resources** may have to be devoted simply to keeping **routines** and other **structured behaviours** reliable from day to day. **Inertia** in the MNC therefore is problematic: it is likely to be under continual challenge as subsidiaries open in new cultures and as the employee population becomes increasingly diverse. Paradoxically such challenges to taken-for-granted procedures may strengthen those procedures by leading to an explicit commitment by organisational members to adhere to what have hitherto been implicit norms. As MNCs may use more resources to ensure reliable reproduction of routines, they are expected to be less tolerant of heterogeneous attitudes and behaviour and among the most rigorous in enforcing procedures and norms across cultural settings (Kilduff 1993: 259).

5.1.2.3 Organisational transformation
In organisation theory, organisational transformation is basically described in terms of **organisational life cycles** and of **organisational change**.

5.1.2.3.1 Organisational life cycle
In most literature on the organisational life cycle, the latter comprises five common **stages**: birth, growth, maturity, revival, and decline (Miller/Friesen 1984: 1161). The **birth phase** shows small, young, owner-run organisations trying to establish a niche for themselves through much product innovation. The **growth phase** is characterised by larger, rapidly growing, departmentalised organisations expanding their niche in the market and evolving a more formalised organisation structure. In the **maturity phase**, organisations have stability and efficiency as their goal, their level of innovation drops, and a more bureaucratic structure is adopted. The **revival phase** is one of product market diversification, and of the adoption of a divisionalised market-based rather than function-based structure; high levels of innovation are maintained, and emphasis is given to the use of formal controls. The **decline phase** shows organisations that are beginning to stagnate as markets dry up and product lines become antiquated (Miller/Friesen 1984: 1178). The conceptual literature on the life cycle seems to oversimplify **organisational evolutionary patterns**. A study by (Miller/Friesen 1984: 1176) suggests that organisations over lengthy periods often fail to exhibit the common life cycle progression extending from birth to decline.

5.1.2.3.2 Theories of organisational change
In general, two models of organisational change have been developed. *Punctuated equilibrium models* posit long periods of organisational stability followed by short periods of comprehensive change of radical reorientation. *Incremental change models* describe fundamental organisational change as emerging over time from localised independent initiatives (Malnight 2000: 268). The larger the organisation, the greater is its structural complexity and interdependence, and the greater is the emphasis on incremental as opposed to discontinuous change (Tushman/Romanelli 1985: 192).

The **punctuated equilibrium model** represents change in a context where the relative risk of competitive failure, based on posited organisational shocks, dominates pressures for internal stability. After the *radical adjustments* and the *establishment of a new equilibrium*, the emphasis again shifts to maximising internal stability and alignment. The punctuated equilibrium model projects a *high degree of interdependence across adjustments* made within a time period. The model implicitly suggests little interdependence in adjustments across time given the movement between stable equilibrium states.

Incremental change models, by contrast, represent change in a context where the relative risk of competitive failure is small, leading to *localised adjustments* within or around *current organisational systems* (Malnight 2000: 272). The incremental change model projects an internal adjustment process characterised by *independent initiatives* distributed across the organisation over time. The model projects path-dependence in terms of interdependencies over time. The model suggests that the direction of change is emergent from the cumulative sum of localised responses (Ibid. 273).

If stable and reproducible routines are the foundation of reliable performance, then **organisational change** increases the **risk of failure** (Amburgey et al. 1993: 52). One reason is resistance by the organisational members and the effect of inertia. *'In a sense, 'people' do not resist change but, rather, patterns of interaction, relationships, bargains, negotiations, mutual adjustments, and, above all, forms of solutions or ways of handling problems resist change'* (Perrow 1970: 173).

Similarly, **organisational change** can affect the *relationship* between the *organisation* and its *environment*. Especially older, *established organisations* are likely to *suffer disruption due to change* because they have existed long enough for external linkages to develop and become routinised. In this way, change can be thought of as **'resetting' the liability-of-newness clock** (Amburgey et al. 1993: 53). The *embeddedness* of the organisation within a web of interorganisational relationships and the taken-for-granted image of the organisation are *external sources of resistance* (Ibid. 56). In an empirical study of Finnish newspapers, Amburgey et al. (Ibid. 52) found evidence that even though the **effect of change** is **more severe** for an **older organisation**, the older organisation is **more robust** before the change – the jump comes from a low base hazard rate. The organisations most likely to survive fundamental change are old organisations, not young organisations. The study suggests strong history dependence in organisational failure rates. For example, **inertia** may also imply **momentum** – an organisation in motion tends to stay in motion (Ibid. 70). In a similar vein, Aldrich (1999: 163) contends that frequent transformations may establish a momentum for change – **repetitive inertia** – that increases the likelihood of future transformations. Organisations may develop routines and competencies that make them particularly adept to certain kinds of changes (Aldrich 1999: 170). Over time, organisations develop not only operating routines but also **modification routines**: procedures for changing and creating operating routines. Typically, modification routines govern the process through which organisations search for solutions to new problems. To routinise the process of change, an organisation must gain experience in modifying operating routines. Organisations thus learn to change by changing (Amburgey et al. 1993: 54).

Tushman/Romanelli (1985) developed a model of **organisational change** that consists of three different **kinds of change**:

1. *Convergence* is defined as a process of incremental and interdependent change activities and decisions, which work to achieve a greater consistency of internal activities with a strategic orientation, and which operate to impede radical or discontinuous change.
2. *Reorientations* are defined by simultaneous and discontinuous shifts in strategy, the distribution of power, the firm's core structure, and the nature and permissiveness of control systems.
3. *Re-creations* are reorientations, which also involve a discontinuous shift in the firm's core values and beliefs. (Tushman/Romanelli 1985: 178-179).

Patterns of organisational evolution are characterised by **periods of convergence punctuated by strategic reorientation or re-creations** leading to the next convergent period. These cycles are driven by the emergence of *tension* between *organisational* and *institutional forces* for inertia and competitive, technological and legal pressures on performance, which are mediated by the perceptions and decisions of executive leadership (Tushman/Romanelli 1985: 180-181). **Reorientations** involve **substantial risk** to the organisation. To disrupt stable patterns of activities and processes, even in the face of organisation-environment inconsistencies, is to disrupt the **fabric of competence** (Tushman/Romanelli 1985: 206).

Complementing the incremental change model and the punctuated equilibrium model, Malnight (2000) develops a model of **accelerating organisational change**. The study observes a process of fundamental change occurring through a limited number of interdependent adjustments over time, a change process initially focused within a few activities and subsequently expanding in its impact across the organisation. The extent of change in early phases of the process was limited, but the rate of change increased over time. The observed process involved sequential and accelerating adjustments within the firms, whereby early, and often informal, changes minimised disruptions, and focused and enabled subsequent adjustments (Ibid. 269).

Malnight (1996, 2000) developed an evolutionary framework highlighting the **transition process of decentralised MNEs moving toward network-based approaches**. The initial focus of the process is on adjustments to such organisation, first based on informal and then formal organisation overlaying its traditional geographic structure (Malnight 1996: 55). A comparison of organisational changes at **Eli Lilly** and **Hoffmann LaRoche** between 1980 and 1994 by Malnight (2000: 285) documents such a transition process in both firms. The study shows a growing similarity in observed structures within common activities across firms and growing heterogeneity within firms across activities. In 1980, the structures of the two firms were internally consistent across activities and maximally different across firms. Within this transformational process, the firms' rates of observed change are similar despite differences in initial starting points and in the extent of total change observed. The first period (1980-1985) accounts for 5.75% of the total change in globality at Eli Lilly and 3.43% at Hoffmann LaRoche. The second period (1985-1990) accounts for 14.14% of the total change at Lilly and 12.66% of that at Roche. Finally, the third period (1990-1994) accounts for 80.11% of the total change at Lilly and 83.90% of that at Roche.

The observed change patterns suggest that *early organisational adjustments* primarily affected informal or off-line communication-related variables, with some additional adjustments to resource locations, operating decision authority, and standards and procedures. Adjustments during the *second period* continued to be concentrated in the communication variables, formalising previous adjustments, but also affected tactical decision authority and standards and procedures. During the *final period*, fundamental change occurred across all organisational variables (Malnight 2000: 294).

In both firms, the findings suggest an **initial focusing of adjustments within a limited number of activities**, then a **gradual acceleration** in both the number of activities affected and the rate of change within individual activities over time (Malnight 2000: 286-289). The findings indicate that the change process initially involved maintaining the firm's traditional success by focusing and **minimising initial organisational disruptions** while **simultaneously expanding new operations** and using off-line communication mechanisms to identify and focus subsequent adjustments. Hence, the process involved balancing the competing pressures for change and continuity (Ibid. 295). Malnight (Ibid. 285) contends that the study findings suggest a process of accelerating and drastic organisational adjustments as opposed to the incremental model.

The results of the case studies on the globalisation of activities at Eli Lilly and Hoffmann La-Roche from 1980 to 1994 provide support for the network perspective, emphasising both the firm's idiosyncratic bundles of resources, or its capacity to access dispersed and location-embedded resources, and its organisational capacity to manage and integrate those resources effectively within and across national markets. A **key finding** is that **organisational variations** occur at the **level of the activity** rather than at the *level of the firm or geographic affiliate* as projected in previous research (Ibid. 298).

A similar process could be observed in the transition of Citibank's European banking activities (Malnight 1996). The transition was marked by the changing nature of organisational linkages to initially collect and communicate information on common challenges and opportunities, to then co-ordinate activities in line with targeted markets, and eventually reallocate roles to leverage specialised activities across larger geographic markets (Ibid. 8). Rather than deliberately moving toward a known network-based structure, each phase represented a viable strategic response to then-existing challenges and opportunities. Consistency in the nature of external challenges and gradual adjustments in firm resources and organisational characteristics create new opportunities over time (Ibid. 55).

5.1.2.3.3 Concepts of dynamic organisation
Traditionally the focus in business-oriented literature on organisation has been on formal organisation structure. In the 1980s the focus changed to organisation processes while the 1990 increasingly redirected the attention to the transformational characteristics and capabilities of the whole organisation.

5.1.2.3.3.1 Relentlessly shifting organisations (Brown/Eisenhardt)
Relentlessly shifting organisations seem to have three key properties: (1) *'semistructure'* that balance between order and disorder, (2) *links in time* that direct attention simultaneously to different time frames and the ties between them, and (3) *sequenced steps*, which are the recipe by which these organisations are created over time (Brown/Eisenhardt 1997: 3).

'**Semistructures**' are organisations in which some features are prescribed or determined (e.g. responsibilities, project priorities, time intervals between projects), but others are not. Semistructures exhibit partial order, and they lie between the extremes of very rigid and highly chaotic organisation. Successfully changing organisations continuously generate '**links in time**': the explicit organisational practices that address past, present, and future time horizons and the transitions between them. Organisational change readily occurs because links in time create the direction, continuity, and tempo of change (Ibid. 28-30). Transition is facilitated by a **rhythm**, which is created when specific behaviours are combined with specific time intervals.

Rhythm, which depends on a consistent ritual of uniformly recurring behaviours, enables people to pace their work, synchronise their energies with each other, and ultimately get into a '**flow**' (Ibid. 24). The rhythm created by the transition processes may become entrained to the rhythm of the environment. Related rhythmic processes tend to synchronise with one another over time (Ibid. 25). The rhythmic transitions that Brown/Eisenhardt observed in their study of firms in high-velocity industries reveal how time-paced change may entrain organisations to their environment and, more strikingly, permit them proactively to set the tempo of their industries. In contrast, event-paced change, which is the dominant perspective in traditional thinking, emphasises reactive change in response to failure or stand-alone quantum change, e.g. by merger or extensive reorganisation (Ibid.).

Rather than ever reaching a stable equilibrium, the **most adaptive** of these complex systems keep changing continuously by remaining at the **edge of chaos** that exists between order and disorder. By staying in this intermediate zone, these systems never quite settle into a stable equilibrium but never quite fall apart. Rather, these systems exhibit the most prolific, complex, and continuous change (Brown/Eisenhardt 1997: 29).

5.1.2.3.3.2 Continuous morphing (Rindova/Kotha)

Rindova/Kotha (2001) label the process of undergoing continuously transformations '**continuous morphing**'. It may be conceived as a specific form of **dynamic morphing** of living systems as described by von Bertalanffy (1950). In their case study of the evolution of Yahoo! and Excite right from founding they observed a process of several transformations due to rapid changes in the competitive environment of the emerging industry. Rindova/Kotha (Ibid. 1264) argue that understanding how firms pursue competitive advantage in dynamic environments requires **simultaneous** understanding of **changes in function** (product, service) and **changes in form** (organisational arrangements, including structures, routines, resources, and capabilities). They suggest that organisational form is related to the **dynamic capabilities** and the **strategic flexibility** of a firm and can be used as a strategic tool to support the rapid changes in strategy required to compete in dynamic environments.

The described organisational evolution of the two companies does not only include huge variations in the offered service and underlying organisational arrangements but also various **changes of the organisational boundaries** due to expansion, reorganisation, and acquisitions of other companies. Top management of Yahoo! stated that the company has successfully developed a process of acquiring and integrating other companies. Developing this expertise was said to be a key internal goal and one that should serve well in aggressively growing business (Ibid. 1272). The whole profile of the two companies was subject to constant and disruptive variations and changes. Yahoo! and Excite repeatedly changed their function and form to respond to shifting market conditions. They continuously redefined what they were and what they offered, thus engaging in a process labelled continuous morphing (Ibid.).

Firms rely on continuous morphing to regenerate competitive advantage under conditions of rapid change. **Dynamic capabilities** and **strategic flexibility** are two organisational mechanisms that facilitate continuous morphing. As firms change what they are and what they offer through continuous morphing process, they migrate into new strategic and competitive domains. As a result to this migration, they need to regenerate competitive advantage relative to the new competitors they encounter in these domains. This change fuels the continuous morphing process again (Rindova/Kotha 2001: 1273).

5.1.2.4 Evolutionary mechanisms

Evolutionary mechanisms drive the reproduction of systems in a dynamic world. While a **static world** is based on the notions of **equilibrium** and of a dualism between **irreconcilable opposites**, an **evolutionary world** of processes resolves the **dualism between opposites** (Jantsch 1975: 289). Opposites in the form of **distinctions are the basis for any kind of observation** and hence of any theory as well. A dynamic theory hence should be able to describe a given phenomenon by describing the dynamic dualism of opposites. The relation between opposites and their dynamic interplay has also been the explicit basis for the construction of the **dialectical theory**. Hegel developed the foundations of dialectical theory, designing an image of history as moving forward as the result of a continuous series of negations and synthesis (Sanderson 1990: 126). Providing a different perspective, post-modern discourse analyses social life in terms of paradox and indeterminacy, thus rejecting the human agent as the centre of rational control and understanding.

More specifically, Benson (1977) develops a **dialectical view of organisations**. The dialectical approach places at the centre of analysis the process through which organisational arrangements are produced and maintained. Analysis is guided by four basic principles - social construction, totality, contradiction, and praxis (Ibid. 1). Dialectical theory offers an explanation of the processes involved in the production, the reproduction, and the destruction of particular organisational forms and social orders (Benson 1977: 2).

Benson (1977: 3) describes the **building blocks of the dialectical view**:

1. *Social construction*: The production of social structure occurs within a social structure.
2. *Totality*: Dialectical analysis, while looking at wholes, stresses the partial

		autonomy of the components. The principle of totality expresses a commitment to study social arrangements as complex, interrelated wholes with partially autonomous parts.
3.	*Contradiction*:	Radical breaks with the present order are possible because of contradictions.
4.	*Praxis*:	People can be agents of free and creative reconstruction of social arrangements.

From a dialectical perspective, concrete social life consists of an intricate interplay between form and content, between structure and process, and the like (Ibid. 9). **Change** and **stability** co-exist in **dialectical synthesis** (Starbuck 1983: 99, Giddens 1979: 131-164). In an evolutionary inquiry have to be included the dialectics of learning processes and organisational context that drive organisational evolution (Pautzke 1989: 265). As contexts vary internationally, there are **differences in cultural structures of meaning and learning**. For example, **Westerners** have a tendency to perceive stimuli in terms of **dichotomies** and **dualisms** rather than paradoxes or holistic pictures (Osland/Bird 2000: 68). If we accept that cultures are paradoxical, then it follows that learning another culture occurs in a dialectical fashion (Ibid. 73).

Contradictions feed into the **social construction process** in several ways. *First*, contradictions provide a continuing source of tensions, conflicts, and the like which may, under some circumstances, shape consciousness and action to change the present order. *Second*, contradictions set limits upon and establish possibilities for reconstruction at any given time. *Third*, contradictions may produce crises, which enhance possibilities for reconstruction. *Fourth*, contradictions are important as defining limits of a system (Benson 1977: 16).

Major changes in interpretative schemes occur through **dialectical processes** in which old and new ways of understanding interact, resulting in a synthesis. The process of change in interpretative schemes is in a reciprocal relationship with changes in structure (Bartunek 1984: 355). This process is analogous to the development of more cognitively complex understanding in individuals. It implies both processes of differentiation and integration, in that different perspectives are encountered and synthesised in a new understanding. Because this process is dialectical, it necessarily involves **conflict between perspectives** and between **groups holding the different perspectives**. The resolution of the process will depend in part on the comparative power of these different groups to have their perspectives heard (Ibid. 365). The dialectical process that occurs does not take place solely on the level of interpretative schemes. Both original and antithetical ways of understanding are expressed in actions taken by organisational members (Ibid. 365).

Structural change is more directly linked to action that results from change in interpretative schemes than to the changing interpretative schemes themselves (Ibid. 366). The order's experience of the dialectical processes, which are typical in organisations undergoing second-order change, is not devoid of feeling: second-order change in interpretative schemes has a strong affective component (Ibid. 367).

Van de Ven (1992: 176-181) and van de Ven/Poole (1995: 513-519, 525) introduce four basic **theories** that may serve as **building blocks for explaining processes of change** in organisations: life cycle, teleology, dialectics, and evolution.

1. **Life cycle theory** is the most common explanation of development in the management literature and assumes that *change* is *immanent*, that is, the developing entity contains an underlying logic, programme, or code that regulates the process of change. The **trajectory** to the final state is prefigured and requires a specific **historical sequence** of events. The typical progression of change events in a life-cycle model is a unitary sequence, which is cumulative (characteristics acquired in earlier stages are retained) and conjunctive (stages are related and derived from a common underlying process). The condition for a life cycle motor is that a singular discrete entity exists that undergoes change yet maintains its identity throughout the process. The entity passes through stages distinguishable in form or function. A programme, routine, rule, or code exists in nature, social institutions, or logic that determines the stages of development and governs progression through the stages.

2. **Teleology** is a philosophical doctrine that **purpose of goal** is the **final cause for guiding movement of an entity**. This approach underlies many organisational theories of change, including functionalism, decision-making, voluntarism, social construction, and most models of strategic planning and goal setting. According to teleology, development of an organisational entity proceeds toward a goal or an end state. It is assumed that the developing entity is purposeful and adaptive; by itself or in interaction with others, the entity constructs an envisioned end state, takes action to reach it, and monitors the progress. Teleological models rely on *voluntarism* as the explanatory principle. Development is movement toward attaining a purpose, goal, function, or desired end state. The condition for a teleological motor is that an individual or group exists that acts as a singular, discrete entity, which engages in reflexive monitored action to socially construct and cognitively share a common end state or goal. The entity may envision its end state of development before or after actions it may take, and the goal may be set explicitly or implicitly. The process of social construction or sense making, decision-making, and goal setting must be identifiable. A set of requirements and con-

straints exist to attain the goal, and the activities and developmental transitions undertaken by the entity contribute to meeting these requirements and constraints.

3. **Dialectical theory** begins with the Hegelian assumption that the organisational entity exists in a particularistic world of colliding events, forces, or contradictory values that compete with each other for domination and control. In this process, an entity may subscribe to a **thesis** *(A)* challenged by an opposing entity with an **antithesis** *(Not-A)*, and the resolution of the conflict produces a **synthesis** *(which is Not-Not-A)*. Over time, this *synthesis* can become the *new thesis* as the dialectical process continues. **Stability and change** are explained by the **relative balance of power** between opposing forces. Change occurs when these opposing forces go out of balance. Different patterns for resolving dialectical oppositions can push an organisation to flow toward equilibrium, to oscillate in cycles between opposites, or to bifurcate far from equilibrium and spontaneously create revolutionary changes. The **condition for a dialectical motor** is that at least two entities exist that oppose or contradict one another. The **opposing entities** must confront each other and engage in a conflict or struggle through some physical or social venue, in which the opposition plays itself out. The outcome of the conflict must consist either of a new entity that is different from the previous two, or the defeat of one entity by the other, or a stalemate among the entities.

4. **Evolutionary theory** focuses on *cumulative changes* in structural forms of populations of organisational entities across communities or society at large. Change proceeds through a **continuous, cumulative cycle of variation, selection, and retention**. Alternative theories of organisational evolution can be distinguished in terms of how traits are inherited, the rate of change, and the unit of analysis. In **Darwinian** evolution traits are inherited through *intergenerational processes*, whereas the **Lamarckian** concept argues that traits are acquired within a generation through *learning and imitation*. A Lamarckian view on the acquisition of traits appears more appropriate than strict Darwinism for organisation and management applications (Ibid.). The condition for an evolutionary motor is that a population of entities exists in a commensalistic relationship. Identifiable mechanisms exist for variation, selection, and retention of entities in the population. Macro-population characteristics set the parameters for micro-level variation, selection, and retention mechanisms (Ibid.).

Life cycle and teleological theories are predictive. Dialectical and evolutionary theories centre on the means of action themselves; i.e. the dynamic process of social construction and transformation of alternative forms within and across generations of competing organisational routines, forms, and institutions. Dialectical and evolutionary theories explain only how change and development occur. They are not predictive and thus explanatory theories (van de Ven 1992: 180-181). A prescribed mode of change as inherent in life cycle and teleological theories channels the development of entities in a prespecified direction. On the other hand, a constructive mode of change generates unprecedented, novel forms that, in retrospect, often are discontinuous and unpredictable departures from the past (van de Ven/Poole 1995: 519-523).

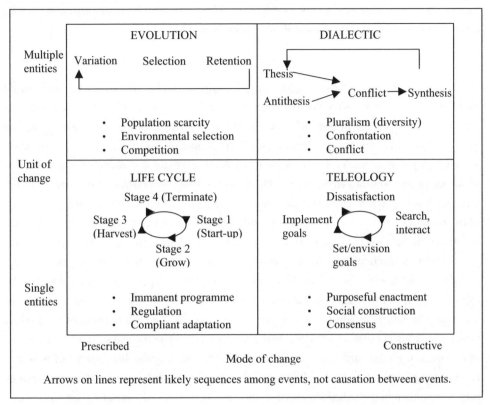

Figure 5-2: Evolutionary motors
(Source: van de Ven/Poole 1995: 520)

An **integrative perspective** may provide a **framework of change** linking (1) *prescriptive elements* that are *voluntarily controllable* within the limits of bounded rationality and (2) *constructive elements*, which provide *emergent properties* to organisations.

In each of the four theories (a) process is viewed as a *different cycle of change events*, (b) which is governed by a *different 'motor' or generating mechanism* that (c) operates on a *different unit of analysis* and (d) represents a *different mode of change* (Ibid. 519-520). Figure 5-1 categorises the four theories on the basis of the **two dimensions** '*unit of change*' and '*mode of change*'. From the angle of '**units of change**', there are *two levels*: (1) the *internal devel-*

opment of a single organisational entity by examining its historical processes of change, adaptation, and replication, and (2) the *relationships between numerous entities* to understand ecological processes of competition, co-operation, conflict, and other forms of interaction. Figure 5-3 illustrates the four evolutionary motors. It is possible that more than one of the **four motors** comes into play because the organisational context of development and change extends over space and time in any specific case. There may also be some degree of *nesting*, *timing/sequencing* and *complementarity of motors* (Ibid. 534).

In addition to the four motors of organisational change identified by van de Ven and van de Ven/Poole, a *fifth motor* is the described **autopoietical motor** provided by the social systems theory. In this mode, the **process of differentiation and integration** drives change in and of social systems. Meaning is reproduced on the basis of guiding differences. New differentiated meaning may also be implemented on the action level and enter the **co-evolutionary process of meaning and action reproduction**. On the other hand, emergent actions may enter the meaning level by observation and learning, entering as well this co-evolutionary interplay. Thus, **intended** (prescriptive) as well as **unintended** (emergent or constructive) elements constitute the autopoietical motor in social systems. In addition to the explanation of emergence and reproduction of individual entities like routines or organisational forms as explained by biological or social evolutionary theories, the autopoietical theory provides the explicit explanation of the relational aspect in the evolution of systems by the inclusion of integration of entities as a basic change mechanism. The development of complexity of social systems hence is not merely a casual result of probabilistic variation and selective retention or of teleological mechanisms like rational planning. On the contrary, **integration of new differentiations** within, between, and across evolving systems is introduced as the **complementary mechanism** to the variation, selection, and retention of new differentiated entities. Social change and reproduction thus is driven by the **mechanism of recursively processing differences**: (1) on **two ontological levels** (meaning and action) (2) by **two complementary processes** (differentiation and integration), (3) by **two drivers** (autopoietic and allopoietic), and (4) on the basis of **two levels of initiation** (intended and unintended).

5.1.2.5 Management of evolution

Lovas/Ghoshal (2000) conceptualised strategy as '**guided evolution**'. The model has *five main elements*. *First*, there are strategic initiatives and human and social capital as the two units of selection (Ibid. 875). Social capital may act as a significant buffer from selection pressures (Levinthal 1992: 437). *Second*, the firm's strategic intent defines the objective function. *Third*, administrative systems serve to facilitate the replication of a natural selection environment inside the firm. *Fourth*, the sources of variation include everyone who may have the relevant knowledge of the issues in question. *Fifth*, the agents of selection and retention are multiple, and effectively include everyone who works on a strategic initiative (Lovas/Ghoshal 2000: 875-876). Strategic initiatives and human and social capital are viewed as the units of selections and tied together in a co-evolutionary process; that is, as the genealogical entities of replication, human, and social capital are embodied in individuals. These individuals in turn, interact in both an external and an internal ecological environment, and through this interaction human and social capital is produced, replicated, or destroyed (Ibid. 891). On balance, the model explains the **development and reproduction of strategic initiatives and human/social capital** but is far from being evolutionary. There is no self-reproductive mechanism and no theoretical underpinning of the evolutionary process.

Similarly, McKern (1993: 351) posits an **active role for management** in adapting the competencies of the firm, a process analogous to learning and its transmission between generations. The firm's fitness depends therefore not only on its inheritance in the form of routines and operational competencies, but also on its ability to effect adaptive changes in its behaviour, or its strategic competencies. McKern assigns an important role to **selection forces outside the firm** in the industry environment and to **internal inertial forces**, but argues that processes within the firm can effect adaptation within a time period relevant to the speed of environmental change (Ibid.).

Differences between national environments select for differences between countries in the general **fitness of firms** for international competition (Ibid. 352). **Management** faces three **major tasks**: determining businesses or environmental niches in which to operate, developing and deploying the skills necessary for success, and managing strategic change. In evolutionary terms, the firm's drive for profitability is analogous to the concept of homeostasis (Ibid. 354-355).

Routines themselves are not the basis for lasting differences in competitive strength among firms. Instead, **distinctive organisational competencies** are the **discriminators**. Organisational competencies are operational and strategic. Operational competencies provide the ability to integrate routines and perform them in a consistent manner (Ibid. 357). **Strategic competencies** reflect a firm's processes for detecting environmental change, deciding what adaptation is needed, and shifting resources so as to develop new routines and operational competencies for implementing new strategies (Ibid. 358). Strategic competence includes variety generation, a selection mechanism and a retention process (Ibid. 366). Successful international diversifiers are more likely to have developed a strategic competence, which is sensitive to new opportunities, allocates resources for experimentation and investigation of new markets, and facilitates consideration of challenging proposals. These processes encourage strategic variety (Ibid. 363).

5.1.2 Contribution to an evolutionary perspective

Evolutionary theories directly provide a **link between social organisation and evolutionary mechanisms**. Social traits in social evolutionary theories and habits of thought or routines in economics take the role of genes or replicators in social reproduction. While a Lamarckian type of horizontal reproduction is assumed to take place across organisations, the Darwinian mechanism of variation and selective retention provides the evolutionary dynamics in these theories. As already remarked in the context of the social systems theory, the adaptation of the biological concepts of evolution to a different ontological level (social evolution) is only achieved at a metaphorical level and marks a basic theoretical flaw in these approaches. Therefore, social and economic evolutionary theories become theoretically consistent only on the basis of autopoietical concepts provided by social systems theory, again documenting the necessity of a social systems framework of globalisation as a process of social evolution.

Evolutionary economics facilitated a quantum leap from an economic world dominated by the models of static equilibria towards a dynamic economic perspective. Firms are conceived as bundles of routines, institutions, and other habits of thought, or knowledge, which are both units and replicators of selection in firms. Specialisation and co-specialisation in industries lead to the differentiation of knowledge and institutions, thus driving the evolutionary process. Firms specialise in order to develop competitive advantages and thus cumulatively provoke the path-dependent differentiation and diffusion of institutions, thus driving the technological trajectory in the industry. In turn, the individual firms have to react to this process of innovation on industry level by beginning the recursive interplay of differentiation again. Evolutionary dynamics are basically driven by VSR processes (blind and learning) but also based on teleological mechanisms (decision-making) and dialectical processes, e.g. by the continuous choice between market and hierarchy. Evolutionary economics have not been directly adapted to globalisation processes but provide one building block for the development of the knowledge-based view described in Chapter 5.2.

The roots of socal evolutionary theories may be found in anthropology (culture) and sociology (organisations). **Social evolution** may be conceived as a **VSR process** working on **social traits**, which may be inherited vertically between generations (*Darwinian*) or horizontally between social actors (*Lamarckian*). From a **sociological perspective**, the evolution of social structures and particularly of organisations may be described as a **process of structuration**, driven by the duality of structure as a pattern of relationships and institutions and as the provider of evolutionary, autopoietic change. The structural properties of social systems are both medium and outcome of the practices they recursively organise. **MNEs** may exhibit very **diverse structural properties** whose reproduction is constituted by actors from **different cultural contexts**. Organisation-wide routines and institutions have to provide for identity, structure, structural properties, and principles, which may constitute the motor of structuration across dispersed units. Organisation theory further provides different **forms** and **drivers for organisational transformation and change.** Models of life cycles, incremental change, punctuated equilibrium, or continuous change provide a rich perspective on the reproduction of organisations. The sociological perspective even allows for the identification of four distinct **motors of change** (life cycle, teleological, dialectic, VSR), which may be complemented by the autopoietic motor defined by social systems theory. Except for a few publications, **evolutionary theories** still await their **adaptation to the global context** but have entered the discourse in the knowledge-based view, which increasingly serves as a melting pot for the observation of change in organisational meaning systems (Chapter 5.2). Table 5-1 summarises the inclusion of evolutionary principles in globalisation processes by economic and social evolutionary theories. Of course, these theories provide together with social systems theory the building blocks for the evolutionary perspective but are still to be adapted to the context of globalisation.

	Economic evolutionary theories	**Social evolutionary theories**
Foundation	Firms are created by individuals with a shared interest to pursue their individual interest with this organisation. Once in place, the evolutionary process sets in, with habits of thought, institutions, routines or other knowledge as entities and replicators of evolution.	Collective process that centres in the inception, diffusion, and adoption of a set of ideas among individuals who become sufficiently committed to transform these ideas into a social institution. Once in place, the organisation develops momentum for change.
Co-evolution of firm and environment	Co-evolution on the basis of economic interaction and diffusion and of the learning of institutions, routines, and other knowledge.	Shared culture and social systems drive diffusion of traits and institutions by learning and influencing.
Global differentiation of firm	Differentiation takes the form of specialisation and co-specialisation in an industry. Differentiation works on evolutionary entities of institutions and knowledge.	Differentiation of cultural traits and social structures is the main driver of social evolution.
Global integration of firm	Co-specialisation creates a conceptual level of knowledge, which allows for co-ordination (e.g. institutions, routines, industry recipes). Path-dependence induces institutionalised integration.	Integration by shared cultural traits, goals, and decision-making.
Global evolutionary dynamics of environment	Institutions, habits of thought, routines, and other knowledge are the units and replicators of evolution and induce technological path-dependence in industries. Mechanisms are VSR, decision-making, and dialectical (market vs. hierarchy)	Culture can be viewed as a system of inheritance. Cultural evolution occurs by differentiated social transmission of cultural variants through VRS (Lamarckian and Darwinian) and decision-making. The decision continuum reaches from *'selection by choice'* to *'selection by imposition'*. Power positions in social relations also induce dialectical mechanisms. In addition, structuration theory provides an autopoietic mechanism by the duality of structure. Organisational change can also be described by life cycles.
Global evolutionary dynamics of firm	Knowledge-based units and replicators of evolution drive the firm's competitive and technological path. Mechanisms are VSR, decision-making, and dialectical (market vs. hierarchy).	Similar to its social environment, the evolutionary dynamics of a firm may be driven by all five mechanisms.

Table 5-1: Evolutionary principles in economic and social evolutionary theories

5.2 The knowledge-based view of management

Globalisation has been described as an evolutionary process, leveraging the reproduction of social systems to a worldwide level. Social systems are basically characterised by the reproduction of meaning by communication and action. Given that thinking and acting are mutual and intertwined processes (Lindell et al. 1998: 77), de Geus (1988: 11) argues: *'The globalisation process and the learning process are inextricably bound together. Globalisation requires more flexibility in learning, more extensive learning and more learning from sources previously overlooked by most organisations'*. In a similar vein, Archiburgi/Lundvall (2001: 2) emphasise how the **'learning economy'** and the **'globalising economy'** are strictly connected in a circular process. On the one hand, the development of an integrated world economy has allowed for the acquisition of information, expertise, and technology at a faster pace and often at lower costs than in the past. On the other hand, the current phase of globalisation has been nurtured by a generation of new technologies. The learning and the globalising dimensions of the world economy strongly enforce each other. The globalisation of firms may hence be basically conceived as the extension of the firm's evolution, in particular of the constituting action and meaning system, to a worldwide scale.

In literature, knowledge has been a topic in cognitive psychology, sociology, and management, particularly in the context of organisational learning. With the development of the new **evolutionary economics** with its focus on **routines** (Nelson/Winter 1982) and the development of the '*resource-based view*' in strategic management (Penrose 1959, Wernerfelt 1984), knowledge has gained central prominence in management literature. The **resource-based view** emphasises the firm-specific resource base as a source for sustained competitive advantage, thus stressing the given action system of a firm. The **knowledge-based view** emerged from the resource-based view and focuses on the firm's *intangible resources*. Knowledge is conceived as the basic source of sustained competitive advantage, thus stressing capabilities and competencies embedded in the underlying meaning system. However, conceiving of knowledge as an asset is not new. For example, sixteenth-century alchemists protected intensively the secrets of their craft. In the nineteenth century, Britain imposed restrictions on the migration of its skilled craftsmen in order to protect its competitive advantages in industrial machinery against competition from Continental Europe. New since the late twentieth century is that knowledge assets are coming to constitute the very basis of post-industrial economies (Boisot 1998: 2).

Resource-based or knowledge-based theories of the firm have attracted much attention in recent years. They portray a business firm as a collection of firm-specific resources, organisational routines, capabilities and competencies, which may explain interfirm differences in competitiveness, as well as intertemporal dynamics (i.e. evolution) of business-enterprise systems (Fujimoto 1998: 15). Both theories will be outlined in the following in order to complete the bridge between the more abstract system-theoretical framework and recent management-oriented research.

5.2.1 Theoretical roots: resource-based and knowledge-based view

The knowledge-based view may be regarded as an offspring of the *resource-based view*, which has been developed as a **complementary perspective** to the **market-based view**. It has been refined and integrated further theoretical elements, particularly from the literature on organisational learning.

5.2.1.1 The roots of the resource-based view

The roots of the resource-based view are generally ascribed to Penrose (1959). According to Penrose, it is not only that resources with which a particular firm is accustomed to working with shape the productive services its management is capable of rendering, but also the experience of management affects the productive services that all its other resources are capable of rendering. In order to focus attention on the *crucial role of a firm's 'inherited' resources*, the *environment* is treated, in the first instance, as an '*image*' in the entrepreneur's mind of the possibilities and restrictions with which he or she is confronted (Ibid. 5). With the maturing of the firm, organisational structures and procedures evolve, which ensure a high degree of consistency among decisions, providing co-ordination in the environmental adaptation process (Ibid. 17).

Penrose (Ibid. 10) contends that it is difficult to define the **identity of a firm** except with reference to what it does or what is done within it. It is hence the '*area of co-ordination*' and the '*area of authoritative communication*' (Barnard 1938) that define the boundaries of the firm (Ibid. 20). The firm is conceived as *'a collection of productive resources the disposal of which between different uses and over time is determined by administrative decision'* (Ibid. 24). Penrose distinguishes physical resources and human resources (Ibid. 24-25). '*Strictly speaking, it is never resources themselves that are the 'inputs' in the production process, but only the services that the resources can render*' (Ibid.). From a social systems perspective, it is their use in meaningful action by the actors. Penrose hence draws a central distinction, indicating that the value of resources is not only determined by the market but also by their use in the value-added process.

Since the services from *'inherited'* managerial resources control the amount of new managerial resources that can be absorbed, they create a fundamental and inescapable limit to the amount of expansion a firm can undertake at any time (Ibid. 48). Penrose (Ibid. 31) defines the '**productive opportunity**' as comprising all of the productive possibilities that entrepreneurs see and can take advantage of. Productive opportunities can hence be objective and subjective (perception of entrepreneur). An increase in knowledge not only causes the productive opportunity of a firm to change in ways unrelated to changes in the environment, but also contributes to the '**uniqueness**' of the opportunity of each individual firm (Ibid. 52). It is likely that increases in knowledge can always increase the range or amount of services available for any resource (Ibid. 76). On the other hand, '*in a very significant sense unused productive services are a selective force in determining the discretion of expansion*' (Ibid. 87).

Though Penrose may have laid the theoretical basis, Wernerfelt (1984) explicitly formulated the resource-based view as such. By **resource** Wernerfelt means anything, which could be thought of as a strength or weakness of a given firm. More formally, a firm's resources at a given time could be defined as those tangible and intangible assets, which are tied semipermanently to the firm (Ibid. 172). Resources are any assets that are actually available to an organisation to use in pursuit of its goals and include external assets that can be accessed when needed by the firm (Nonaka et al. 2000: 21). Firm resources include all assets, capabilities, organisational processes, firm attributes, information, knowledge, etc. controlled by a firm that enable it to conceive of and implement strategies that improve its efficiency and effectiveness (Barney 1986: 101).

Fladmoe-Lindquist/Tallman (1994: 53) suggest five major types of **firm-specific resources of MNE**: *physical, human, organisational*, and also *financial* and *political resources*. In their *resource-based model of MNE strategy*, the authors particularly focus on the potential for identifying home country resources with competitive advantage in MNEs. In their specific model, *home country characteristics* provide the basis for *firm-specific resources* (FSR), which may constitute competitive advantages. This perspective basically alludes to the principle of organisational imprinting. With increasing importance of internal and external networking, sustainable competitive advantages will be derived from different positions within the network. MNEs develop FSRs as they absorb assets from the global environment. Therefore, MNEs faced with pressures from global competition and exposed to international markets for resources will develop FSRs unique to their particular experiences as global firms, such as particular skills in managing subsidiaries. Similar capabilities will be developed in local institutional adaptation and networking on different geographical levels.

Of course, not all aspects of these resources are strategically relevant. Therefore, Barney (1986) defines four basic **empirical indicators** of the **potential of firm resources** to generate **sustained competitive advantage**: (a) a firm resource must be *valuable* by exploiting opportunities or neutralising threat, (b) it must be *rare* among a firm's current and potential competition, (c) it must be *imperfectly imitable*, and (d) there *cannot be strategically equivalent substitutes* for this resource that are valuable but neither rare or imperfectly imitable (Ibid. 105-112). Imperfect imitability is primarily a result of firm-specific unique historical conditions, causal ambiguity, and social complexity (Ibid.). Further determinants of the sustainability of competitive advantage are durability, transparency, transferability, and replicability (Grant 1991: 124).

From a resource-based perspective, **firms** are *heterogeneous* with respect to their **resource and capabilities endowments**. These, in turn, are *sticky* as firms lack the organisational capacity to develop new capabilities quickly. Furthermore, some assets, like tacit knowledge or reputation, are not tradable. Even when an asset can be purchased, firms may stand little to gain by doing so (Teece et al. 1990: 7-8). From a competitive perspective, resource position barriers are partially analogous to entry barriers. *'What a firm wants is to create a situation where its own resource position directly or indirectly makes it more difficult for others to catch up'* (Wernerfelt 1984: 173). The resource-based view hence provides a complementary view to the market-based view that heretofore had been dominating strategic management from the 1970s onward. The market-based view stresses the adaptational perspective to the market environment culminated in the *'market structure – conduct – performance paradigm'* with derived normative strategies (e.g. Porter 1986).

From the resource-based perspective, the **capturing of rents on scarce, firm-specific resources** is central to strategy. The first **strategic dimension** therefore is the **exploitation of existing firm-specific assets**. The second dimension is the consideration of **strategies for developing new capabilities**. Similarly, Ghoshal et al. (2002: 285) define the ability to perceive potential resource combinations and exchanges as *'entrepreneurial judgement'* and the ability to carry out any combination and exchange as *'organisational capability'*. Both capabilities together constitute the *'management competence'*, which ultimately resides in any organisational member. From this perspective, management is the activity of exploring new and exploiting disposable resource combinations. In the competitive process, maintaining an appropriate balance between exploration of new resource combinations and exploitation of already available ones is a primary factor in a firm's survival and prosperity (March 1991: 71). In this regard, the resource-based view has been traditionally more concentrated to understand how firms prolong their competitive advantages, rather than seeking an understanding of how they create advantages in the first place (Mathews 2002: 114). A logical step in the development of a more dynamic perspective has been the development of the knowledge-based view by integrating more dynamic theoretical concepts.

5.2.1.2 The roots of the knowledge-based view

The knowledge-based view or competence-based view has been refined from the more general resource-based view. It suggests that a firm's abilities in the creation of new knowledge may be more important determinants of competitive success in dynamic markets than the firm's current endowment of resources (Murray/Worren 2001: 142). In an attempt to define a *'knowledge-based theory of the firm'*, Grant (1996: 109) conceptualises the **firm as an institution for integrating knowledge**. Firms are distributed knowledge systems in a strong sense: they are decentred systems. A firm's knowledge cannot be surveyed as a whole; it is not self-contained; it is inherently indeterminate and continually reconfiguring. The firm can be described as a set of local forms of knowledge structured through doing and the recurrent activity of problem solving (Tsoukas 1996: 13).

The **knowledge-based view** has been enriched by literature on **organisational learning** and **evolutionary economics**. From the latter perspective, **firms** perform their function as **repositories of knowledge** largely by virtue of the extension in time of the association of inputs, especially human service inputs, with the firm. At any particular time, the network of transacting patterns already in place substantially influences the costs and benefits of adjustments in governance modes for particular classes of transactions. Thus, the process of change in a firm's ways of doing things most typically involves incremental adjustment in a complex, interdependent system. Such a process may well produce progress, but it does not produce an *'answer to any well-specified question of a list of questions about how activity should be organised'* (Winter 1988: 177).

From the complementary **learning perspective**, the **firm** takes on the features of a '**pool of forms of knowledge**'. The representation of these forms of knowledge and the way in which they are generated, selected, and modified thus becomes the focus for analysis. The focus is on the **learning activities** taking place within the firm and the **historical and local nature** of the **knowledge creation process**. Organisations learn and their experience is encoded in routines or develops in capabilities. Firms are built on the cumulative growth of knowledge, sometimes depicted as the repertoire of persistent patterns of behaviour, sometimes described in terms of capabilities that build on one another through time (Turvani 2002: 199).

The perspective of firms in terms of a pool of knowledge holds that *firms remember and know by doing - thus integrating action and knowledge in a recursive interplay*. Firm's routines and capabilities serve as a repertoire of abilities and skills that may be used within the firm. They describe what the firm knows and how it knows it, but they also frame the way by which the environment is perceived and interpreted. The routines and capabilities can therefore be interpreted as the '**cognitive apparatus**' or '**cognitive model**' of the firm. This *'lens'* filters what the firm perceives in the environment and how it monitors and interprets its internal evolution (Ibid.). Kogut/Zander (1993: 625) conceive of **firms** as '*social communities that specialise in the creation and internal transfer of knowledge*'. Firms are social communities, which use their relational structure and shared coding schemes to enhance the transfer and communication of new skills and capabilities (Zander/Kogut 1995: 76). According to Nonaka et al. (2000: 26), a **knowledge-creating organisation** with such **autonomy** can be depicted as an **autopoietic system**.

Due to the open-ended nature of knowledge, the pool of knowledge within the firm is developed by means of discretion and of judgement in carrying out individual cognitive activities. These spaces for discretion and judgement grow with the complexity of both the knowledge that individuals hold and the different possible uses within the firm. The process by which knowledge is developed offers the firm a **degree of 'liquidity' in the stock of knowledge** and provides *variations for the production of new knowledge*. The construction of shared mental cognitive models and their renewal is itself a cognitive activity in which all individuals participate, creating dense communication networks (Turvani 2002: 203-205). In a next step, different forms and concepts of knowledge will be differentiated before its generation, development, and diffusion in social systems are outlined.

5.2.2 Knowledge in the global context

Globalisation in recent history has been particularly marked by the *extension and integration of informational and knowledge processes on a worldwide scale*. For example, MNEs are establishing and expanding R&D abroad, benefiting from the possibilities offered by information and communication technologies to internationalise the learning processes along the whole of the value chain (Cohendet/Joly 2001: 63, 80). As described in Chapter 2, the emergence of global communication and knowledge networks is part of the evolution of society in general and of economy as a social subsystem in particular. From the perspective of the main social actors, i.e. organisations it is important to reflect the individual embeddedness in such a stream of globalisation forces while pursuing the own, individual genesis and value generation. In the following, knowledge in the global context hence will be analysed from both the integrative economic perspective and the individual firm perspective.

5.2.2.1 Knowledge in the global economy

Chapter 2 showed that globalisation is driven by self-fuelling dynamics. As a consequence, the **'geography' of the production of knowledge** is going to be drastically modified. In general, exploiting global markets further enhances globalisation. Development and introduction of innovations, particularly when done with speed and regularity, further contribute to environmental dynamism (Hitt et al. 1998: 39). In recent years the *interconnections between geo-*

graphically different parts of the world have considerably increased and this has also *multiplied learning opportunities*. The learning and the globalising dimensions of the world economy strongly reinforce each other (Archibugi/Lundvall 2001: 2), leading to the integration, expansion, and creation of social systems on the global level. Historically, however, most social systems have national origins and thus encountered **nationally based imprinting** at their founding. An observation of knowledge in the globalising economy has to include the national origins its constituting social systems.

5.2.2.1.1 National origins

Patel/Pavitt (1991: 17) suppose that the **production of technology** remains *far from globalised*. Large firms' technological performance is still assumed to be strongly dependent on the performance of the home country, and not independent of it. What happens in home countries still matters greatly in the creation of global technological advantage on the firm level. Nation-states often deliberately create discontinuities at their borders in order to foster a sense of identity among their citizens. Language, laws, currencies, traditions, and institutional practices thus differ on either side of the border. Firms do likewise. Technologies, institutional practices, traditions, and internal regulations will differ from one firm to the next, giving rise to distinctive corporate cultures. They are important to offer a firm a differential advantage in the accumulation of knowledge assets. The rigidity of organisational boundaries differs significantly between nations as a comparison of organisational networks like Chaebol, Keiretsu, or Western MNCs clearly document.

First, from the *perspective of evolutionary economics*, knowledge and innovation are the key forces determining the competitiveness of firms and countries and that are developed through search and learning across firm functions, sectors, and institutions. The feedback from users or access to complementary expertise from competing firms or other institutions is the central driving force of knowledge development and innovation in this respect. For example, within the framework of '**national innovation systems**', national institutions are important for developing and diffusing knowledge in society. The key idea behind the innovation system concept is that the innovative capacity of an economy depends on more than the sum of its organisations but on their interaction in knowledge development, diffusion, and use (Nyholm et al. 2001: 266).

Second, from a *resource-based perspective*, Fladmoe-Lindquist/Tallman (1994: 47) suggest that a key source of the unique resources for MNEs is their home country competitive context. Firm-specific resources can arise due to the firm's interactions with external inputs or pressures from social, financial, and political institutions in their home countries. Such factors as differences in culture, education and training of the workforce, and in the physical infrastructures of countries have major effects on the types of firm-specific resources developed in MNEs from different nations (Ibid. 55). For example, the strong scientific culture of Germany has facilitated the development of firms in those industries that have strong technological components (Ibid. 68).

Similarly, strategic behaviour differs across nations. Noorderhaven/Harzing (2003) ascribe these differences to the '**country-of origin-effect'**. It *'consists of that part of the differences in internationalisation strategies and international control strategies of MNCs that can be ascribed to the different national origins of these MNCs, rather than to variations in their task environment'* (Ibid. 54). For example, Kagono et al. (1985) found national differences between Japanese, European, and American firms in their approach to strategy formulation. The *Japanese approach* is described as *'evolutionary'*, while the *Western approach* is described as *'strategic planning'*. On the organisational level, Harzing et al. (2002) found large differences between German and British MNEs in nearly all aspects of the headquarters-subsidiary relationship. On the more general level of the meaning system, a study by Schneider/de Meyer (1991: 318) showed that national culture influences interpretations and responses to strategic issues. More specifically, national culture influences *'crisis'* and *'threat'* interpretations and proactive responses, both internally and externally oriented.

In resource-based terms, **home country origin** should affect the **distribution** of at least some **firm-specific resources** among MNEs of different national affiliations within an industry (Fladmoe-Lindquist/Tallman 1992: 8). Collis (1991: 51) argues that the historical evolution of a firm constrains its strategic choice and that complex social phenomena, or invisible assets can be a source of sustainable competitive advantage. A firm's country of origin will hence directly affect its **choice of strategy**. Even as a firm internationalises, it remains imprinted by its early developmental history and domestic environment (Kogut 1993: 137). From a knowledge-based perspective, FDI is the extension of organising principles and capabilities of the firm across countries. Intangible assets represent the cumulated capabilities of the firm. Part of the capabilities of a firm consists of its relationships with other firms and institutions. In the early history of firms, the predominant factor in these relationships is that they are usually contained within borders of a single country (Ibid. 143). Once a start-up firm begins to grow, its reliance on the collection of technological skills of individuals shifts to the important task of creating organising recipes. These recipes are adopted from the current agreement on what constitutes best practice. The disposition of the availability of knowledge is determined by the structure of social relations. In an international study, Lane (2001) describes different **national learning styles** characterising supplier networks in Germany, Great Britain, Japan, and the U.S. with different predispositions within dualities such as internal/external learning, centralisation/decentralisation, and symbiosis/arm-length style. Supplier networks in these countries expose idiosyncratic learning styles with some opening and convergence due to globalisation forces (Ibid. 711).

Zaheer/Zaheer (1997) showed that both national industry arrangements and national cultural factors account for **country level effects on information seeking** leading to the conclusion that *'one cannot underestimate the influence of country-level effects on firm behaviour'* (Ibid. 95-97). A study by McKendrick (2001: 307) suggests that firms from the same nation are likely to adopt similar global strategies initially, but that, over time, the industry as a whole converges on the same blueprint for action. At the same time, however, strategic focus and organisational characteristics moderate national influences. Through processes of selective imitation, firms from the same nation will initially adopt similar global strategies but over time the industry as a whole converges on the same blueprint for action. Yet the emergent global strategy is likely to be pioneered and transmitted by only a subset of national firms that operate in the same strategic space and possess similar organisational characteristics. By contrast, late adopters share similar characteristics regardless of nationality (McKendrick 2001: 331). Bensedrine/Kobayashi (1998: 51) make a similar observation on the level of industry evolution. In their empirical study of the chlorofluorocarbons (CFCs) industry firms' strategies differed most of the time but homogenised when national institutional contexts converged.

5.2.2.1.2 Cultural differences

A basic influence on the (re-) production of knowledge in the global context is caused by different national or ethnic cultures. **Knowledge** itself is a symbolic representation of meaning and therefore directly an **element of culture**. The traditionally dominating influence of national, ethnically, or religious-based cultures has been increasingly complemented by the impact of professional, scientific, or other subcultures. Nonetheless, socialisation of individuals and imprinting of organisations are still dominated by these general building blocks of social meaning structures.

Culture involves far more than general values and knowledge that influence tastes and decisions; it defines the ontological value of actor and action (Meyer et al. 1994: 18). Cultural differences often seem to be a residual category to which people attribute problems in the absence of a supportive context (Kanter/Corn 1998: 42). This gives rise to **questions about the usefulness of the 'cultural differences' approach**:

1. When people of different national cultures interact, they can be remarkably adaptive.

2. Technical orientation can override national orientation. Similar educational experiences, e.g. of specialists, can erase ideological differences. Those within the same profession tend to espouse similar values regardless of nationality.
3. Tensions often have more structural than cultural causes.
4. Cultural value issues and issues of 'difference' in general are more apparent at early stages of relationships than later, before people come to know each other more holistically.
5. Central country values are often reported at a high level of generality (e.g. global subcultures) and are often more important from abroad than from within (Kanter/Corn 1998: 24-26).

Cultural distance affects managerial decisions (Tse et al. 1988), work values (Ralston et al. 1997), patterns of negotiations (Bangert/Pirzada 1991), conflict within and failure of international joint ventures, overseas entry mode (Kogut/Singh 1988), degree of partner reciprocity, and transaction costs (Gomez-Meija/Palich (1997). Hamilton/Kashlak (1999: 175) propose that the **degree of cultural distance** between home country and host countries will influence an **MNE's parent-subsidiary performance ambiguity** and **task definition**. As a result, task programmability and output measurability will decline.

Boundaries of the firm are determined, in part by the need for cognitive proximity, next to reduction of transaction costs. There is a trade-off between cognitive distance, needed for variety and novelty of cognition, and cognitive proximity, needed for mutual understanding (Nooteboom 2001: 44).

From a resource-based perspective, the very **ability to bridge cultural distance** confers a unique advantage (Shenkar 2001: 522). The transfer of managers seems to present a solution to half of the dilemma of co-ordination in MNEs: the co-ordination between headquarters and the foreign branch. However, the other half of the dilemma of co-ordination, which is the co-ordination between expatriate groups and local employees within foreign branch units, still remains to be solved. For example, difficulties in managing local employees in foreign subsidiaries of Japanese MNEs have been attributed to the transfer of Japanese management practices based on harmony, groupism, and consensus, not common in Western countries (Chikudate 1995: 28). Jun et al. (2001: 369) found evidence that satisfaction of expatriates with the host culture influences the expatriate's commitment to the local operation and to the parent company.

Processing of knowledge is highly influenced by the cultural context. Empirical studies suggest that the international context multiplies the difficulties in knowledge transfer (Bendt

2000: 111, 184). As the basic cause of such intercultural difficulties, **perception gaps** are defined as '*a difference between managerial perceptions regarding a subsidiary's capability to solve its operative problems effectively*' (Arvidsson 1999: 96). There are two kinds of perception gaps. First, **hierarchical gaps** may exist between a corporate and a subsidiary manager. Second, **horizontal gaps** may exist between two subsidiary managers from different subsidiaries. A study by Arvidsson (Ibid. 197) on the evaluation and transfer of marketing capabilities in Swedish MNEs proved the existence of hierarchical perception gaps. These are mainly caused by selective attention and bounded rationality of corporate managers. In addition, there were indications that corporate managers actually were culturally biased in their evaluations of subsidiary capability. Position and knowledge hierarchies were proved to be two separate internal structures of the MNE (Ibid.).

An important instrument for the creation of more **cross-cultural flexibility** is the training of cultural adaptation within new cultural contexts. Cultural adaptation is a social cognitive process that reduces uncertainty and an affective process that reduces anxiety. The outcomes of cultural adaptation include psychological well-being and satisfaction as well as social competence. Uncertainty reduction involves the creation of proactive explanations about the behaviour of oneself and others. Accurate interpretation of behaviours can be gained through learning about the host culture (Jun et al. 2001: 370).

Within the **internationalisation dimension**, new, culturally distant engagements have to be integrated in the evolving meaning and activity structure. A common assumption about internationalisation processes is that firms initially operate locally and that their knowledge reflects their operations in their local contexts. This knowledge is embedded in the routines and administrative structure developed to manage domestic operations. When they go abroad, firms base their activities on these established routines and on their embedded knowledge, which frequently does not aid in the understanding of situations and conditions in specific foreign markets (Eriksson et al. 2001: 23). In the final stage of the sequential internationalisation process, the learning from the foreign market is transferred internationally and influences the accumulation and recombination of knowledge throughout the network of subsidiaries, including the home market (Kogut/Zander 1993: 636). In its more advanced evolution, the **internationalisation process** alters the **global knowledge of the firm** and may result in its transformation towards a network of subsidiaries characterised by the **cross-border transfer of learning** (Ibid. 640). However, a globalising firm's path of learning should not only consider cultural distance but also the mode and ownership of foreign expansions. Firms learn from their previous experience more when following a centrifugal expansion pattern than a random strategy. When starting a new venture, firms benefit more from previous experience with expansions in the same country. Learning from previous FDI largely concerns learning about foreign organisational cultures (Barkema et al. 1996: 155, 163). After globalisation has become fully institutionalised, the **role of cultural barriers and learning** may become less prominent (Ibid.).

MNEs with their **cultural diversity** therefore have to facilitate the **transfer of knowledge** across distances, different organisational, cognitive and normative maps, and different technical systems. The capacity for transfer and absorption of knowledge is particularly important for MNEs. The development of a structure of relationships is a central element in the transfer process, which can be promoted by augmenting the density and depth of relationships, the development of intercultural and communicative competence, communication media, and transfer instruments (Bendt 2000: 193).

Within this context, **intercultural teams** are central pivots in the co-ordination across subsidiaries or co-operations. In a study of a German-Japanese management team, Salk/Brannen (2000: 200) found prove that wide gaps between the cultures of team members do not doom a team or organisation to suffer poor performance or other developmental pathologies. The results suggest that differences themselves do not cause problems; rather, it is how a team's context and individual team members' orientations to local (team) norms channel these differences. In this case, cultural knowledge is still limited because of relatively infrequent interaction between Europeans and Japanese in general (Chikudate 1995: 29). German managers are known for placing high reliance on expertise and formal individual responsibility, and Japanese managers are known for having a generalist and diffuse view of responsibility. Establishing and maintaining interpersonal contact and harmony on an emotional level is vital for daily team functioning for Japanese people but not for Germans. German co-workers may have no social relations outside the work place while this is quite common for Japanese. Both, however, are likely to share a group or organisational orientation rather than an individualistic orientation (Salk/Brannen 2000: 193).

In the process, Japanese and German managers described the norms surrounding emergent decision-making processes in the same way. Certain decision-making issues – specifically the values of consensus, speed, and efficiency – surfaced in all interviews (Salk/Brannen 2000: 194). The team was reasonably well integrated and did not show a legacy of having two different national cultures. The results show that **context and process dimensions of intercultural teams** may be much **more decisive** and emergent phenomena than thinking in static dimensions of **cultural differences** (Ibid.).

Tsang (2001) describes the process of managerial learning in foreign invested enterprises of China, providing some examples of failing **intercultural adaptation**. For example, Chinese tend to place more emphasis on technical rather than management expertise. A person without a relevant technical background is regarded as a layman ('*waihang*' in Chinese), no matter how much management experience has. In China, 'waihang' leading people who are experts in the trade ('*neihang*') is not considered as an appropriate arrangement. Chinese quite simply are less motivated to learn from such expatriate managers and to accept their authority. The same problem occurs in the case of missing seniority of managing or consulting expatriates. Another case of intercultural conflict may arise when Chinese may feel that their technical expertise is challenged, e.g. when a foreign investor tries to introduce a new organisational technology (Ibid. 39-41).

5.2.2.2 Globalisation knowledge of firms

Globalisation knowledge of firms may be differentiated along the three basic dimensions of globalisation: internationalisation, networking, and evolutionary dynamics. As the perspective in this Chapter is that of evolutionary dynamics, the implications for globally operating firms have been provided in the respective thematical parts. In the following, internationalisation and network knowledge of firms will be discussed in the global context.

5.2.2.2.1 Internationalisation knowledge

Factors such as the duration of foreign operations (Erramilli 1991), the firms' size and age, and the number of foreign countries in which they operate (Barkema/Vermeulen 1998) seem to influence the accumulation of knowledge. In a series of articles, Eriksson et al. (1997, 2000, 2001) expanded the concept of experiential knowledge and integrated research from organisational learning and the knowledge-based view of the firm.

For example, an empirical study of 362 service firms by Eriksson et al. (1997) delivered proof for the assumption that the **level of risk perception of international activities** is continuously decreasing along the **internationalisation process**. The analysis shows that a firm's experience of the internationalisation process influences the perceived cost in this process. This implies that some **experiential knowledge** is located in the firm, in its decision-making routines and structures (Ibid. 352). Such routines and structures are first developed by a firm to manage operations in the home market, but are not sensitive to stimuli origination from overseas (Eriksson et al. 2000: 29). The findings indicate that **accumulated internationalisation experience** that affects both business knowledge and institutional knowledge is not related to specific country markets. It is a firm-specific experience relevant to all markets. It seems to be reasonable to regard it as a kind of **procedural knowledge** concerning, for instance, what kind of knowledge a firm needs in different situations.

The study indicates that the perceived costs of internationalisation by decision-makers tend to decrease continuously with increasing experience of the firm in international business. The authors conclude that **international experiential knowledge** is learned organisationally and that it is institutionalised in decision-routines and the organisation structure. The international learning process is not confined to the individual experiences of decision-makers but is accompanied by an **institutionalisation process of international management** (Eriksson et al. 1997: 352). The study further indicates that knowledge has to be gained not only on foreign markets but also on the internal resources of a firm and what the firm is capable of when exposed to new and unfamiliar conditions. A firm therefore must develop structures and routines that are compatible with its internal resources and competence, and that can guide the search for experiential knowledge about foreign markets and institutions. '*On a different level, this can be viewed as the need to develop a cognitive framework showing what further knowledge about foreign markets is relevant*' (Ibid. 353).

Eriksson et al. (2000) examine the effect of variations in the geographical scope of international business operations on experiential knowledge development in the internationalisation of the firm. **Experiential knowledge** is assumed to have three interrelated **components**: *internationalisation knowledge, business knowledge,* and *institutional knowledge* (Ibid. 26). While internationalisation knowledge concerns the firm's strategy with regard to internationalisation, business knowledge and institutional knowledge concern specific foreign markets (Eriksson et al. 2001: 26). The study by Eriksson et al. (2000) demonstrates that internationalisation knowledge is a key variable that mediates the effect of variation on the other knowledge variables.

'**Internationalisation knowledge**' reveals a firm's capability and resources to engage in international operations (Eriksson et al. 2000: 26, 2001: 23). It operates as a repository in which knowledge may be retained for a period of time and supplies decisional stimuli and responses that are preserved in the firms and have behavioural consequences when revealed. Internationalisation knowledge captures the firm's '*absorptive capacity*' (Cohen/Levinthal 1990) in *internationalisation*. It highlights the fact that when firms first go abroad, they are likely to be ethnocentric (Perlmutter 1969) because their absorptive capacity is domestic market based. In the context of experiential knowledge development in the internationalisation process, internationalisation knowledge can be regarded as the firm's theory-in-use with regard to international business strategy. Lack of internationalisation knowledge is perceived when the theory-in-use is vague, ill defined or irrelevant (Eriksson et al. 2001: 24). The study of Eriksson et al. (2001) gives rise to the assumption that some *basic restructuring of internationalisation knowledge* occurs over time. There seems to be a discontinuity of internationalisation knowledge.

'**Business knowledge**' concerns competitive situations in specific markets and clients in these markets. In international markets, a lack of knowledge about a particular client's way of making decisions and his idiosyncratic requirement regarding products and services is problematic. Operations in a market allow the internationalising firm to accumulate the kind of institutional and business knowledge it requires and to interpret the information in a firm-specific context. Most firms are aware that business conditions are complex, fluid, and equivocal. They know that the acquisition of foreign knowledge will require interaction with actors abroad. The perceived lack of foreign business knowledge is reduced over time through ongoing foreign operations (Eriksson et al. 2001: 37).

'**Institutional knowledge**' is information about the governance structures in specific countries and their rules, regulations, norms, and values. The accumulation of knowledge drives internationalisation (Eriksson et al. 2000: 29-30). Lack of institutional knowledge has a significant effect on the cost of international business. With respect to institutional knowledge, firms are strictly ethnocentric when first going abroad. This ethnocentricity decreases over time as the firms learn about the equivocality of the institutional setting of foreign business (Eriksson et al. 2001: 37). The early years of foreign operations appear to be characterised primarily by a feeling of growing knowledge which as outcomes of operations realised, is replaced after some years by a growing awareness of a lack of institutional knowledge and that institutions are more complex than initially expected (Eriksson et al. 2000: 37-38). The psychic distance paradox exemplified by study of O'Grady/Lane (1996) about the entry of Canadian retailers in the US market seems to be attributable to unexpected complexity relating to institutional conditions in a country that was initially expected to be quite similar. The perception of a country as having a small psychic distance from one's own can lead decision-makers to a number of faulty assumptions - creating an inability to learn about the country (Ibid. 310).

In an empirical study of Swedish service firms, Eriksson et al. (2001) showed that firms with a long and a short duration in foreign markets differ substantially with regard to knowledge accumulation. Duration was proved to have a much stronger effect in the short than in the long duration group. This shows that *learning* is particular intense in the *early stages of internationalisation*. The development of internationalisation knowledge appears to be a *discontinuous, stepwise process*. With regard to business knowledge, most firms are already aware that business conditions are complex, fluid, and equivocal (Ibid. 35-37). The kinds of experimental knowledge developed at the outset of internationalisation led to the same kinds of knowledge being further developed in any subsequent internationalisation. Experiential knowledge types not developed in the early stages of internationalisation are not developed later (Eriksson et al. 2000: 323).

The behaviour of the international firm is path- or history-dependent because its internationalisation process is based on the stock of the firm-specific tacit or experimental knowledge in the firm. The existing stock of knowledge and the operating environment limit and direct the evolution of the firm (Ibid. 307-8). **Path-dependence** is the incremental process where the pattern of behaviour by firms is contingent upon and a function of its past international experience. Benito/Gripsrud (1992: 475) found that there is a strong interrelation between the locations of subsequent FDI by firms, although rather in form of an iterating pattern than a centrifugal unfolding of international activities. Barkema et al. (1996: 163) showed that **acquisitions and joint ventures** are the types of ventures where firms reduce **cultural barriers** through learning, with the **success of later ventures** increasing with the **amount of previous FDI** of the firm. Learning from previous FDI largely concerns learning about foreign organisational cultures. Andersson et al. (1997: 81) further argue that there are two contextual dimensions impacting on acquisition behaviour and its consequences: extent of previous relationships between the acquiring and the acquired companies and psychic distance.

Exposure to variation enables internationalising firms to accumulate knowledge from a richer variety of business and institutional actors, so that a **double-loop learning process** more easily evolves in such firms. Exposure to a richer set of business actors and institutional environments may set in motion a process whereby the internationalising firm's current assumptions regarding business and institutional actors are confronted with a new reality. The feedback process from this questioning may force the firm to reconsider and amend its existing theory-in-use as well as its organisational practices and strategies, compelling it to develop new technological solutions, products, and ideas. A **richer knowledge set** has a positive effect on the **future internationalisation** of the firm, because there is a higher probability that the new knowledge required for a new situation may bear some similarity to the current stock of knowledge at the firm (Ibid. 30-31).

Bilkey (1978) and Naidu/Rao (1993) argue that the experiential knowledge that firms gain in the early years of internationalisation is extremely important for their subsequent resource commitments in the international market. Sullivan/Bauerschmidt (1990) found that managers' perceptions of barriers hinge on their past experience. Managers' knowledge of international conditions, information gaps of international transactions, and characteristics of foreign markets shape internationalisation. *'The gestalt of managers' objective and experiential knowledge drives internationalisation'* (Ibid. 26). Path-dependence therefore can be expected to have a strong effect on resource commitment in foreign markets (Eriksson et al. 308).

5.2.2.2.2 Network knowledge in MNEs

MNEs are international traders in information (Magee 1977: 334). MNEs are also networks of capital, product, and knowledge transactions (Gupta/Govindarajan 1991: 770). Nonetheless, or '*curiously, there has been little explicit attention given to the resource based view of the firm in the MNE literature*' (Birkinshaw 2001: 387).

Kogut/Zander (1993: 625) view firms as '*social communities that specialise in the creation and internal transfer of knowledge*'. MNEs hence arise out of their superior efficiency as an organisational vehicle by which to transfer this knowledge across borders. In a similar vein, Oliveira/Child (1999: 3) conceive of companies as '**stocks of knowledge**' as well as '**flows of knowledge**'. MNEs then represent '**dynamic learning networks**' (Ibid. 8). From this perspective, what will determine the firm's success is its efficiency in the knowledge management and learning process. Lessard/Amsden (1998: 67) define a **global learning organisation** as '*one that has global cognitive scope*'. Following this definition, learning on a local-for-local basis in a variety of locations does not qualify as global organisational learning. The firm must somehow be able to exploit the multi-point nature of learning and transform it into an economy of scope. MNEs as '*multi-country firms*' operate in a variety of markets and technological contexts and face especially high costs, as well as potentially high benefits, related to integrating and diffusing knowledge that is culturally, geographically, and politically disparate (Ibid. 69). The **MNE** is potentially a **unique learning organisation** because of its exposure to multiple learning stimuli and knowledge contexts, where learning tends to be more tacit than explicit and, therefore, more in need of learning-by-doing than formal arm's-length instruction (Ibid. 71).

The international setting is interesting as it illustrates the difficulty of learning when the requisite institutional mechanisms are not well developed. This difficulty is greater when new **organising practices** must be learned, as opposed to the imitation of technologies, because these practices are likely to be embedded in the **social network and values of individual countries**. The learning of new organising principles is both more transparent and yet more difficult across the borders of a country than of a firm (Kogut 1993: 148).

MNEs establish **international networks** to support process of technological accumulation and **learning**. An interactive view of MNE affiliates replaces a system of satellites or miniature replicas (Cantwell 1995: 37). Tacit capability embodied in the collective skills and organisational routines of the firm is the product of continual problem-solving and learning which is enhanced in a MNE through combining complementary awareness of technological development in an international network. While technological advantage or competence forms the essential basis of the competitiveness of MNEs in world markets, the international networks of MNEs help to reinforce such capability through mutually oriented learning between affiliates, and an enhanced ability to engage in purposeful R&D (Cantwell 1995: 46).

Two basic questions in international business concern the acquisition of local knowledge by MNEs and the contribution of the latter to the local technological process. The results of an empirical study by Almeida (1996: 162) confirm the local character of both learning and contributing by MNEs. The findings suggest that foreign firms are aware of the difficulty of learning from afar, and use local plants to upgrade the technological ability in fields, which may be weak in their home countries. The findings also suggest that foreign firms may not be targeting just regions but specific firms in their learning efforts. The study also confirmed the suggestion that **MNEs** contribute to **local technological development** in the form of **knowledge exchange** (Ibid. 163). For example, a study by Ernst (2001: 107-108) shows that inward FDI played an important role for knowledge creation during the critical early phase of the development of Taiwan's electronics industry. It exposed Taiwanese workers and managers to new organisational techniques while not necessarily best practice, contributed to the development of a successful management culture.

If industry-specific knowledge tends to be localised and if each industry has multiple geographical clusters throughout the world, then the multinational enterprise has an advantage over national enterprises in its ability to access knowledge in multiple location (Almeida et al. 1998: 121). A basic question is *'how much the MNE knows about what it knows'* (Arvidsson 1999: 8). As we move into a knowledge economy the benefits MNEs gain from multinationality hence will be far more a function of their ability to manage practices across borders than activities (Eriksson et al. 2001: 38). Kogut/Kulatilaka (1994: 4) distinguish between two kinds of MNE's strategic responses with regard to different locations: **'within-country growth option'** through the introduction of new products and activities and **'across-country switching option'** through locational migration of activities and products. MNEs are likely to pursue upgrading in a location where the potential of existing local capabilities for advanced activities is big enough to override the disadvantage caused by unfavourable events such as local wage hikes.

The uniqueness of the MNE as an organisational form arises from the fact that its different constituent units, which form the intraorganisational network, operate in different environments (Campbell/Verbeke 2001: 194). The *MNE creates value from knowledge* not only through its ability to exploit economies of scale and scope in knowledge from deploying its knowledge assets in multiple geographical markets but from its ability to acquire knowledge in different locations and to combine these different types of knowledge (Almeida et al. 1998: 121). Hence, the greater the **complexity of the product or service** being delivered, the more likely is it that the **MNE** is the preferred **organisational form of knowledge transfer** (Ibid. 137).

Still, MNCs face the problems and opportunities inherent in globally distributed knowledge. Thinking and acting parts of the corporation are both geographically diffused, and the scattered '*brain*' proves a significant obstacle to clear hierarchical structure. **Internationalisation** means a **quantum leap** in uncertainty and change. This makes a '*freezing*' of the structure more difficult (Hagström/Hedlund 1998: 171). Weick/van Orden (1991: 49) contend that globalisation involves at least two basic themes: making sense of turbulence, and creating processes that keep resources moving. As MNEs may confront dangers that arise from two major forces, cognition (incomprehensibility) and structure (tight coupling), the search for remedies needs to focus on ways to facilitate sense making and comprehension, and on organisational form and design (Ibid. 50). The MNC has to be able to shift the perspective between, for example, product, technological, and geographical foci, as the situation so requires (Hagström/Hedlund 1998: 171).

The **ability to leverage core competencies** across geographic and product business units helps firms to achieve economies of scale and scope (Hitt et al. 1998: 28). A study by Mauri/Phatak (2001: 246) confirms that the main driver behind the international integration of company operations is the *firm's desire to leverage its specific competencies* with local immobile resources to produce competitive advantage. This process hinges on three **basic pillars**:

1. A successful international knowledge combining process must find itself in harmony with the organisational structure of the company as a whole.
2. Network structures seem to be more effective than hierarchical forms.
3. Central management may be successfully implemented for information, but not so successfully for knowledge (Arvidsson 1999: 231).

Hagström/Hedlund (1998: 176-182) and Arvidsson (1999: 54) differentiate three **internal structures** instead of a formal hierarchy: positional, knowledge, and action structure.

- *Positional structure* denotes the ordering of individuals and organisational units in terms of formal status, location, and authority.
- *The knowledge structure* combines different elements laterally. It is fleeting and ever changing as knowledge is structured relatively horizontally, flatly, temporarily, and circularly. The knowledge structure serves to define relationships, behaviours, and actions for organisational members. It is socially constructed and relies on consensus or

agreement (Lyles/Schwenk 1997: 53). Changes in the knowledge structure occur as a result of the impact of the interpretation of environmental events, results of past organisational actions, the influence of key decision makers, and the advocacy position of coalitions within the firm agreement (Lyles/Schwenk 1997: 55).

- The *action structure* is flexible, flat, and temporary. The archetypal action unit becomes the multiskilled, multiknowledgeable, and temporary project team. The action structure is by and large a mirror of the knowledge one.

The **sequencing of the knowledge management process** is a further determinant of success. An important managerial task is to place attention on organising *feedback* from the *peripheral units* engaged in international operations to the more *central units* where feedback from different units can be integrated. Such feedback is not primarily a matter of standardised information systems, but rather of routines for listening to the experiences of boundary managers. This is particularly critical in the early phase of internationalisation (Eriksson et al. 2001: 38). An effective transfer process requires that managers in the firm know the proficiency of each subsidiary in regard to the particular capability being leveraged (Arvidsson 1999: 8).

Barriers to knowledge and knowledge frontiers may constitute serious obstacles for knowledge management in MNEs (Buckley/Carter 1999: 11). From the perspective of the behavioural theory of the firm, limits to time and attention, levels of aspiration, and characteristics of the search process are vital in determining the effectiveness of efforts to integrate geographically dispersed knowledge. Moreover, when the geographical aspect, the fact that the search area consists of globally dispersed units, is considered, limits to time and attention, ability, and different levels of aspiration become forceful, binding constraints on achieving effective use of globally dispersed resources (Arvidsson 1999: 43). Bounded and local rationality means that each local unit will make decisions based on local knowledge. Thus, locally set goals become independent constraints that units strive toward satisficing (Ibid. 45). Successful implementation requires the creation of a common language, knowledge, and understanding for and by the participants in the process (Buckley/Carter 1999: 11).

5.2.2.2.2.1 Knowledge creation in MNEs

Eriksson et al. (2001: 38) assume that applied resources, i.e. capabilities or practices represent the real competitive edge for MNEs. Given that such practices typically emerge in a local setting, and that they are therefore *sticky*, Eriksson et al. (Ibid. 38) believe that '*the ability to apply, adapt, or transfer practices on a world-wide basis is what separates the unsuccessful MNEs from the less successful*'. Activities are what a firm does; practices are how the firm does it. This local, path-dependent, and highly embedded technological change is a strong and positive driver of globalisation on the output side, precisely because it supplies scarce resources to the global economy in the form of temporarily unique knowledge embedded in products or services. (Ibid. 49)

In evolutionary terms, **MNEs** have three basic **advantages** in the **evolution of their meaning system** or, in terms of the knowledge-based view, in knowledge creation:

1. *generation of variety*: variety in environmental stimuli: MNEs as '**global scanners**'
2. *joint knowledge creation*: MNEs as '**knowledge creating networks**' (Westney 2001: 147-148),
3. *dispersed innovation centres*: MNEs as '**global selection regimes**' (Ibid.), and
4. *implementation and diffusion of innovation*: MNEs as '**global retention mechanisms**'.

The study by Arvidsson (Ibid. 30) showed that (1) the overall knowledge management tended to be predominantly hierarchically controlled while deliberately leaving room for decentralised initiatives and action, (2) integration efforts are restricted largely to particular regions, (3) there were few formal incentives for sharing knowledge, and (4) socialisation as a mechanism for knowledge transfers was preferred for sharing knowledge.

In a study by McKenney et al. (1992: 285), face-to-face communications were found to serve as a **context-creating medium**, while e-mail proved to be a **context-reliant medium**. Face-to-face interaction and observation is a better mechanism for the transfer of tacit knowledge and taken-for-granted understandings than electronic media often relied on heavily to co-ordinate geographically dispersed teams (Argote 1999: 111, Nonaka 1991). Electronic media are more effective at augmenting existing relationships (Argote 1999: 181). Nohria/Eccles (1992: 304) argue that network organisations cannot be built on electronic networks alone. At the core, the network organisation depends on a network of relationships forged on the basis of face-to-face interaction. This network of relationships serves as the substrate on which the electronic network can float or be embedded. **Intercultural differences** make **networking** even more difficult so that '**rich media**' should be used to build a consensual basis across important network positions.

5.2.2.2.2.2 Diffusion of knowledge in the global network

MNEs that are able to learn from the globally dispersed subsidiaries achieve a higher performance (Tienessen et al. 1997: 386). In contrast to some established literature on MNEs, Sölvell/Zander (1998) suggest that MNEs are not particularly well equipped to continuously transfer technological knowledge across national borders and that their contribution to the international diffusion of knowledge has been overestimated. The nature of the innovation process suggests that all international innovation projects are associated with increasing costs and lengthened development times. As the MNE becomes more firmly established in foreign (local) innovation systems, a process by which **large and well-established subsidiaries** become less prone to share and diffuse their **core capabilities** accompanies this process of local adaptation. As subsidiaries develop their own unique resources and capabilities, the formation of **global product mandates** is promoted at the **expense of knowledge exchange** across geographically dispersed units (Ibid. 404-405).

Andersson et al. (2001: 1013) stress that recent research on the competitive advantage of MNEs has emphasised the importance of the ability of subsidiaries to assimilate new knowledge from their external environment. The authors assume that the **processes behind competence development within an MNE** are located at three different **levels**:

1. *Business relationship level*: It focuses on the extent to which interactions between the subsidiary and individual exchange partners serve as sources of new knowledge for the subsidiary. A high embeddedness in the social context particularly facilitates the assimilation of non-codified, tacit knowledge.
2. *Subsidiary level*: It is concerned with how the subsidiary manages not only to assimilate knowledge from the environment but also to commercialise it to achieve increased market performance. The innovative capacity of a firm is contingent on its ability to absorb new knowledge from the environment and is positively related to the exchange of complex knowledge through relationships with specific actors in the environment. Buckley et al. (2003) distinguish '**reverse knowledge transfer**', when new knowledge is returned to the parent firm and '**secondary knowledge transfer**', which is defined as the transfer of knowledge from the primary affiliate of the foreign investor to a secondary affiliate, that is, one controlled by the primary affiliate (Ibid. 68).
3. *Corporation level*: competence is transferred within the corporation, from one subsidiary to other units, thereby upgrading the competence of the whole MNE. Differences in embeddedness between an MNE's subsidiaries create differences in their level of competence, which in turn create differences in the roles the subsidiaries can play within the corporate system. The transfer of knowledge is supposed to be easier to accomplish within organisations. The main competitive advantage of MNEs hence is the possibility to '*harvest*' practices and to transfer and combine knowledge among subsidiaries located in different countries and contexts.

Particularly internationally operating firms often complain that they have lost sight of their internal competencies and knowledge assets in important areas. The understanding of the relevant knowledge environment is also critical in this case (Probst et al. 2000: 70-71). Instruments like knowledge maps, knowledge topographies, maps of knowledge assets and a geographical information system may facilitate the integration of **'islands of knowledge'** (Ibid 75-77).

With regard to **knowledge diffusion**, empirical studies prove that (1) articulated knowledge is more easily transferred internationally, (2) the absorptive capacity of the recipient is crucial for transfers, (3) causal ambiguity hinders transfer, and (4) actual implementation and use of transferred practices depend on the recipients' internalisation of the basic meaning of the transferred capability (Arvidsson 1999: 30).

Gupta/Govindarajan (1991) develop a **subsidiary role typology** with the knowledge perspective as the underlying framework. Subsidiaries can be arrayed along the following two-dimensional space: (1) the extent to which the subsidiary engages in knowledge inflows from the rest of the corporation, and (2) the extent to which the subsidiary engages in knowledge outflows to the rest of the corporation (Ibid. 773-775). Figure 5-3 shows the resulting typology.

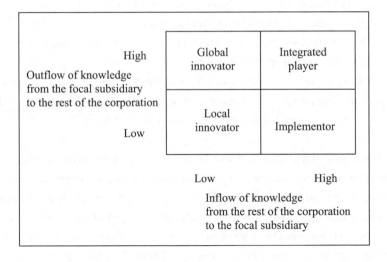

Figure 5-3: Variations in subsidiary strategic contexts based on knowledge flows
(Source: Gupta/Govindarajan 1991: 774)

In the *global innovator role*, the subsidiary serves as the fountainhead of knowledge for other units. The *integrated player role* is similar to the global innovator role because it also implies a responsibility for creating knowledge that can be utilised by other subsidiaries. Unlike the global innovator, though, an integrated player subsidiary is not self-sufficient in the fulfilment of its own knowledge needs. In the *implementor role*, the subsidiary engages in little knowledge creation of its own and relies heavily on knowledge inflows from either the parent or peer subsidiaries. The *local innovator role* implies that the subsidiary has almost complete local responsibility for the creation of relevant know-how in all key functional areas. This knowledge is seen as too idiosyncratic to be of much competitive use outside of the country in which the subsidiary is located (Gupta/Govindarajan 1991: 773-775).

Gupta/Govindarajan (1993: 331) further propose a **knowledge-based framework of variations in subsidiary strategic contexts**. The two dimensions are (1) 'inflow of knowledge from the rest of the corporation to the focal subsidiary', and (2) 'outflow of knowledge from the focal subsidiary to the rest of the corporation'. The typology is basically the same as the one developed by the authors described above. The results show that

1. *local innovator subsidiaries* are involved minimally in formal lateral integration mechanisms with other subsidiaries and have the lowest intensity of communication with peer subsidiaries and the headquarters;
2. *implementor subsidiaries* are headed by presidents who exhibit the lowest degree of internal control and have the highest degree of corporate socialisation;
3. *integrated player subsidiaries* exhibit the maximum use of formal lateral integration mechanisms and also have the highest intensity of communication with peer subsidiaries as well as the parent corporation;
4. *global innovator subsidiaries* exhibit moderately high intensity of communication with the parent corporation but not with sister subsidiaries. Subsidiary presidents show the lowest degree of corporate socialisation (Ibid. 342-343).

Subsidiaries with a global innovator role by definition serve as crucial sources of creativity and innovation for the whole corporation – measured by high knowledge outflows to and little inflow from the rest of the corporation. It is remarkable, that the study provided strong evidence that this role is not assigned from headquarters as part of top-down induced strategic processes. Instead, it seems that this role is carved out by enterprising subsidiary managers as part of bottom-up autonomous strategic processes (Ibid.). This finding again shows the value of evolutionary, self-organisational elements in knowledge management.

In a study by Arvidsson (1999: 240), the selection of capability transfer sources was only related to subsidiaries' self-evaluations. Subsidiaries seeing themselves as being capable had more outward transfers than other units. A recommendation would be to base the selection of sources in the transfer process on a combination of multiple evaluations by corporate managers and subsidiary managers from different subsidiaries, rather than from individual management perspectives (Ibid.). The results indicate corporate management plays an unimportant role in the transfer process (Ibid. 258).

Given the restricted reach of central direction and influence in knowledge transfer, Gupta et al. (1999: 206) stress the importance of **feedback-seeking behaviour** in MNEs. Feedback from other organisational units in an MNE is regarded essential for innovation and co-ordination. Feedback faces **obstacles** caused by **differences in the task contexts** of different subsidiaries but is even more important so. Differences are driven by (1) heterogeneity across countries, (2) heterogeneity across the strategic charters assigned to various subsidiaries, and (3) heterogeneity in the consensus and clarity of the roles assigned to subsidiary presidents (Ibid. 207). Studies by Simonin (1999, 1999a) point to the critical role played by knowledge ambiguity as a full mediator of tacitness, experience, complexity, and cultural and organisational distance on knowledge transfer. When knowledge is not or cannot be codified in a meaningful way, learning from experience and learning by doing in the presence of knowledgeable partners become a sine qua non for circumventing ambiguity and favouring knowledge transfer (Simonin 1999a: 611, 614).

Oliveira/Child (1999: 3) propose that the **role of subsidiaries** is basically the ability in enhancing the **knowledge flow** within and among the multinational units, and therefore developing a **dynamic learning network**. The network of subsidiaries provides a firm with incremental learning (inclusive of foreign practices) and the option to co-ordinate operation flexibly in response to difficult-to-forecast events (e.g., exchange rates, innovations, or government policies) (Kogut 1993: 150). The transfer of knowledge from subsidiary to network is difficult, but it is a key part of the architectural knowledge of the successful MNE network (Tallman/Fladmoe-Lindquist 2002: 131).

A study by Gupta/Govindarajan (2000: 473) showed that **knowledge outflows** from a subsidiary are positively associated with the value of the subsidiary's knowledge stock, its motivational disposition to share knowledge, and the richness of transmission channels. They further found evidence that **knowledge inflows** into a subsidiary are positively associated with the richness of information channels, motivational disposition to acquire knowledge, and the capacity to absorb incoming knowledge.

The empirical study by Andersson et al. (2001: 1028) showed that an **MNE subsidiary's external network** constitutes an important part of its **core competence**, with direct consequences for its expected market performance. The subsidiary's technical embeddedness further proved to predict its role as a contributor to competence development in other MNE units. The subsidiary's ability to contribute to other units' competence development is not counterbalanced by the problem of transferring knowledge form one subsidiary to other subsidiaries due to context specificity (Ibid.). However, if the subsidiary's network consists only of highly embedded relationships, there is a risk that it will be closed off from new and innovative processes, because there are hardly any non-redundant links to outside members (Ibid. 1030, Burt 1992). The more context-specific solutions are, the more difficult it will be to apply that knowledge within the business context of another unit. Andersson et al. (2001: 1019) assume that the subsidiary network embeddedness is positively related to competence development, but also to context specificity, leading to a trade-off between embeddedness and the possibility to transfer knowledge to other corporate units.

5.2.2.2.3 Knowledge-based theory of the MNE

Kogut/Zander (1993: 625) promote a view that the *'firm as specialising in the transfer of knowledge and recombination of knowledge is the foundation to an evolutionary theory of the multinational corporation'*. The MNC is no longer seen as a repository of its national imprint. Instead, it is an instrument whereby learning is transferred across subsidiaries, which are responding, and adapting to different environment pressures (Kogut 1993: 149).

Firms grow on their ability to create new knowledge and to replicate this knowledge so as to expand their market (Kogut/Zander 1993: 639). The evolutionary process of firm growth often begins with the establishment of exporting facilities. The initial market entry with FDI then serves as a platform that recombines the firm's knowledge acquired in its home market with the gradual accumulation of learning in the foreign market. In a final stage of this process, the learning from the foreign market is transferred internationally and influences the accumulation and recombination of knowledge throughout the network of subsidiaries, including the home market (Ibid. 636).

From a knowledge perspective, FDI is the transfer of the organisational principles, or knowledge, of the firm from one country to another (Ibid. 626). Co-operation within an organisation leads to a set of capabilities that are easier to transfer within the firm than across organisations and constitute the ownership advantage. These capabilities consist as well of the capacity to grow and develop through the recombination of existing elements of the knowledge of the firm and its members. It is the notion of the firm as a repository of social knowledge that structures co-operative action that lies at the foundation of an evolutionary theory of the MNE (Ibid. 627).

5.2.3 Contribution to an evolutionary perspective

The knowledge-based view of management provides a rich tool kit for the conceptualisation and description of evolution on the level of the meaning system. A broad variety of knowledge-related properties of organisations and organisational facilitators offer concepts for the conceptualisation and operationalisation of the firm's meaning system from a rational, allopoietic perspective. Other levels of meaning, which are more tied to the level of emotions, motivations, interpretations, or expectations are not explicitly included in this canon of concepts and may appear as a residual in the category of '*implicit*' knowledge. However, these meaning levels may be increasingly complemented in future research in order to complete the scope of meaning systems described by the knowledge-based approach. A further strength of the knowledge-based view is that a link between the meaning and the action system is facilitated by a couple of concepts such as capabilities, routines, communities of practice, or absorptive capacity. Even the learning process is often described as being structurally linked in an interplay with action, e.g. learning-by-doing, and thus corresponds with evolutionary and system-based approaches. Its already eclectic character allows for the integration of concepts from complementary theories, which may provide more theoretical scope and rigour to the main pillars of the knowledge-based view.

On the level of international business, the knowledge-based view does not only offer the possibility to apply dynamic concepts to the global level (e.g. global diffusion of best practices) but also provides valuable contributions to internationalisation and global network perspectives. Internationalisation has already been described as a learning process by the learning-based stage model. Internationalisation may be conceived as an extension and differentiation of the meaning or knowledge system to the global level. FDI may be conceived as the extension of the firm-specific knowledge base to other countries and internalisation of foreign firms as the internalisation of foreign knowledge. On the level of global networks, MNEs may be conceived as global learning networks with all properties and processes differentiated on global level. Table 5-2 provides an overview over the inclusion of global evolutionary principles in the knowledge-based view.

Foundation	No explanation
Co-evolution of firm and environment	Firms acquire knowledge from the environment in order to develop competencies and capabilities, which constitute competitive advantages. Firms are actively embedded in co-operations and networks, which may serve as organisational facilitators for knowledge evolution. Collective knowledge structures and communities of practice may develop in such relations. Globally operating firms are themselves differentiated in a differentiated global environment. Boundary-spanning units such as subsidiaries are bridges in the transfer of knowledge from the local context and from the MNE network. The development of interpenetration and consensual domains across globally dispersed units and environments allows for a co-evolutionary interplay of organisational units internally and with the respective environments.
Global differentiation of firm	Globally operating firms develop differentiated knowledge structures on global and local level. These globally differentiated knowledge structures and the underlying learning processes overlap and are interlinked. The evolution of knowledge structures itself is driven by the process of differentiation and integration and provides variations by internal generation of variety in terms of innovation and learning or by import of external knowledge. Globally operating firms may be termed global learning networks as variations emerge in different local contexts and units and may be propelled across the global network.
Global integration of firm	The integration of globally differentiated organisational units and knowledge structures may be facilitated by mechanisms of knowledge creation (externalisation, internalisation, socialisation, combination), standardisation, diffusion of best practices, or formalisation. In addition, organisational properties such as absorptive capacity, communities of practice, collective minds, and collective knowledge structures may provide a robust fundament for knowledge evolution. This presupposes the development of means for interpenetration and of consensual areas across the globally differentiated units.
Global evolutionary dynamics of environment	Due to the underlying firm perspective, evolutionary dynamics of the environment are not explained and conceived as a given. No mechanisms are defined. An exception is the intended interplay of co-operation and network partners, which serve as interorganisational facilitators of knowledge evolution. The underlying mechanism is teleological due to the intentional character of such relations. Evolutionary and dialectical mechanisms may also emerge in external relations but are not defined.
Global evolutionary dynamics of firm	Evolutionary dynamics emerge particularly on the basis of teleological processes as the intentional creation and exploitation of competitive advantages is the basic principle from the knowledge-based perspective. Due to the assumption of path-dependence, evolutionary must be at work but are explained only exceptional cases. The development of concepts like dynamic capabilities shows that authors in the field of the knowledge-based view strive for a more dynamic layout of the theoretical framework but do not explain mechanisms of evolutionary dynamics. The description of learning processes does not really explain the scope of evolutionary dynamics. Particularly the autopoietic motor may provide theoretical rigor to the rather eclectic conceptual framework of the knowledge-based view.

Table 5-2: Inclusion of evolutionary principles in the knowledge-based view

5.3 Summary

Processes of evolutionary dynamics drive the differentiation and integration of social systems on global scale. **Social** and **economic evolutionary theories** adapt principles of biological evolution to social structures. Traits in sociological theories and routines in evolutionary economics take the role of genes in biological reproduction. Social evolution is much more dynamic due to intended evolution and the speed of horizontal (Lamarckian) reproduction by communication and learning as compared to vertical (Darwinian) reproduction along hereditary trajectories between generations. Nonetheless, evolutionary dynamics are conceived to be caused by the Darwinian mechanism of variation and selective retention. Gidden's **theory of structuration** explains the (re-)production of social structure on the basis of social practices. According to the notion of the *duality of structure*, the structural properties of social systems are both medium and outcome of the practices they recursively organise. Social structure and social practices are reproduced in a recursive interplay, reflecting the evolutionary interplay of the meaning and action system in social systems theory.

Social evolutionary theories conceptualise **organisational transformation** in terms of life cycles and different phases of continuous or discontinuous change. Such change processes may also take the form of a punctuated equilibrium with stable phases of incremental change punctuated by phases of radical change. Such change intervals differ in terms of duration (e.g. epochs or episodes) and intensity (e.g. deep structure or surface structure). On the basis of their inherent dynamics, organisations may even be characterised as relentlessly shifting or continuously morphing. In general, social evolutionary theory identifies four distinct evolutionary mechanisms (life cycle, teleological, dialectical, and Darwinian) that are driving organisational transformation and serve as a building block in the evolutionary theory of the globalisation of firms. These four mechanisms are complemented by the motor of autopoietic reproduction of social systems.

The **knowledge-based view** of management provides a rich tool kit for the evolution of social systems. In the **global context**, knowledge structures and modes of knowledge processing may vary significantly across different local contexts. Such differences in national cultures produce the *'country-of-origin effect'*. Firms are imprinted with characteristic of the national culture and develop culture-specific international strategies and structures as well as different learning and information behaviour. In the process of **internationalisation**, firms extend their knowledge structure and integrate global variety, thus facilitating the institutionalisation of international management and global knowledge structures. **Global network knowledge** accumulates along a path-dependent trajectory in the evolving multinational learning network.

MNEs may be conceived as global scanners, knowledge creating networks, global selection regimes, and global retention mechanisms. In MNEs, learning processes and particularly knowledge diffusion across dispersed subsidiaries are central a symbiotic evolution. Knowledge how to cope with **global evolutionary dynamics** is accumulated in the process of globalisation and retained in capabilities of global dynamic morphing. Though teleological motors are dominating the dynamics of MNEs, all evolutionary motors are critical for its reproduction and the organisation at least implicitly learns how to balance the different dynamics, which may adopt quite different forms in different geographical and organisational regions.

6 Evolutionary theory of firm globalisation

In the previous chapters, the **three basic characteristics of globalisation** and their reflection as capabilities of globalising firms have served to provide a **framework for the integration and application of specialised theories**, which explain different aspects of the three overarching phenomena. In the final chapter, however, an **evolutionary theory** of firms will in turn be generated on the basis of the discussed theoretical building blocks, which have been assembled within the framework of the three basic globalisation characteristics or capabilities, respectively. The theoretical perspective generated this way is itself recursive as it leads to an evolutionary perspective of globalisation based on the theoretical insights gained in the previous chapters. In part, this circle has already been closed once as globalisation has been described in terms of an evolutionary process at the beginning. The development of this book, however, has been passing circles continuously so that the concluding chapter may serve as well as the introducing chapter.

The **theoretical framework** is developed on the basis of the *social systems theory* as it provides a general framework, which allows for a commensurable integration of individual theories explaining different aspects of the global evolution of social systems. Without an integrative framework, integration would only be possible as an eclectic approach as the assumptions of the individual theories are fundamentally different. For example, any kind of intention or choice is at best irrelevant in population ecology. Similarly, in institutionalisation theory there is no concept explaining innovation. Nonetheless, concepts like choice and innovation are central to social evolution and have to be integrated in an explanatory approach. In the chosen framework, the individual theories explain distinct elements within the global evolution of firms.

Two levels of the framework have to be differentiated. *First*, a general framework for the foundation and evolution of firms as social systems has to be outlined. In a *second* step, this framework has to be continually adapted to the context of the globalising environment. Individual concepts developed and outlined in the previous chapters are used as inputs for the construction of this two-level framework.

In this study, the description began with the **macro-perspective**. In Chapter 2, **globalisation** was described as a historical social process characterised by a process of increasing differentiation and integration of social systems on a geographical and functional level. The Chapters 3, 4, and 5 described **theories** contributing to an understanding of the **globalisation process of organisations**. These theories were organised in the specific framework of the **three basic**

dimensions of globalisation of social systems identified in Chapter 2: internationalisation, global network building, and evolutionary properties. From the **micro-level perspective**, these characteristics may represent both **properties** and **capabilities**. The underlying assumption in this study clearly is that these three capabilities are critical for the evolution of individual organisations.

Individual theories from different disciplines have been integrated within this framework, as no integrating framework existed yet that would allow for an integration of these specific and highly idiosyncratic theories in the context of globalisation. An integration of these theories within a single framework is facilitated by the more general **social systems theory**, which subsequently has been termed *meta-theory* (Scott 1986, Luhmann 1995) and the evolutionary theories. The latter provide different perspectives on the mechanisms of social evolution while social systems theory allows for the application of evolutionary principles developed in other disciplines (e.g. neurobiology) to social systems and particularly to organisations. General systems theory provides the means to describe basic properties of living systems. Social systems theory even provides the means to describe social systems and specifically organisations in terms of meaning-based autopoietic systems. It allows for a comprehensive conceptualisation of the evolution of social systems and their co-evolution with their social environment, particularly of the dynamics and mechanisms driving this process. This **guiding difference** allows for the observation of social system evolution within the context of globalisation, which can be conceptualised as a historical process of social evolution. The guiding difference '*parts vs. whole*' further allows for the observation of **social systems as networks**, both inter- and intra-organisationally. The **principles of 'recursiveness'** and '**self-similarity**' facilitate the perspective of social systems as a nested hierarchy of systems, from the level of society as a whole to the basic units (roles), driven by the same principles. The guiding difference '*element vs. relation*' allows for the distinction between '*structure*' and '*organisation*' (in Maturana's autopoietic sense) and thus for the distinction between '**allopoiesis**' and '**autopoiesis**', which both characterise social systems. The **evolutionary principle of differentiation and integration** captures the basic evolutionary dynamics of social systems, with the **processing of meaning by guiding differences** as the mechanism or **motor** driving this evolutionary process. As the social systems theory provides integrative terminology and explanation from the level of the individual ('*psychic system*') to organisational units, organisations, networks, and even the society as a whole, it allows for the integration of all theories describing organisations or social evolution. It even allows for an integration of the basic ontological guiding difference '*intersubjective vs. systemic*' dominating the conceptualisation of social systems as it dynamically integrates individual (psychic system) and social system as well as element and whole (system).

Due to different basic assumptions and design, many of the described **specific theories** would be **incommensurable** or even incompatible without such a **comprehensive framework**. Due to the lack of a joint theoretical and conceptual basis, the theories have been described individually in order to allow for an understanding of their idiosyncratic perspectives within the given framework. An integration of these diverse theories from the start may have led to confusion and an ignorance of their idiosyncratic context. Each theory has been developed on the basis of *idiosyncratic assumptions and perspectives* that do not allow for a simple import of individual propositions without a commensurable context. In addition, the *succinctness of theoretical arguments* might have gone lost without a description within the respective theoretical context.

The depth of the individual theories could also be used to adapt them to the context of globalisation. By means of the social and evolutionary theories, it is now possible to integrate the different perspectives into a joint theoretical framework of globalisation. The **basic phenomena** to be explained by an **evolutionary perspective on globalisation of firms** in the sense of social systems are their **foundation** (emergence) and **reproduction in the context of social globalisation**. Social systems theory provides the basic framework to integrate literature explaining biological and social evolution with organisation theory and thus with management literature on international and strategic management. Entities from the society as a whole to organisational units as basic elements can be described in terms of systems and subsystems, integrated by autopoietic and allopoietic social organisation and being commensurable due to the principles of self-similarity and recursiveness.

Firms or other organisations are *instrumental, goal-directed social systems*. As such, they are subject to different interests and political action. **Organisations** can thus be observed at **two levels**:

1. As **allopoietic**, or syn-referential systems, they are constituted by individuals as the basic organisational actors who dispose of a resource base in order to conduct the primary activities of the organisation to achieve its goals.
2. On a secondary, enacted level, organisations are **autopoietic** systems, which reproduce themselves independent of distinct individual actors. Organisations as autopoietic social systems emerge from the stream of social evolution and hence they are not part of the vertical chain of inheritance of general social traits along generations of human beings with only minor, incremental variety of changes. As enacted, second-level social systems, they are both subject to voluntary, intentional change and emergent, evolutionary change.

As described in Chapter 2, the **process of globalisation** is characterised by emergent, evolutionary change. No individual society or other social system is able to control or even plan this process. For organisations, it therefore represents the **relevant environment**, in which co-evolution takes place. Globalisation is a social phenomenon, producing a global level of society, which heretofore did not exist across different societies and organisations. It reflects the formation of differentiated social systems with global reach. Social systems, which become global themselves, internalise such global complexity as a *whole* (e.g. MNEs) or become themselves *part* of a global system (e.g. global strategic network).

Social systems theory is particularly valuable in the explanation of the three **basic dimensions of globalisation**:

1. **Internationalisation** of a social system can be conceived as changes in its geographical or cultural extension. Both changes in the extension of the meaning and the action system may induce internationalisation. Global media have provided the basis for a general internationalisation of meaning systems. More important, however, is the internationalisation of system-specific meaning. In a strict sense, internationalisation only takes place, when also the activity system is subject to changes in the geographical and/or cultural extension. Studies by Schulte (2002) and Borghoff/Schulte (2003) show that internationalising SMEs often do not have a symmetrical behaviour in this regard. The studies indicate that SMEs often build activity structures abroad without sufficient adaptation of the meaning structure or vice versa. Internationalisation literally induces changes in the system's boundaries and its relationship with its environment. In the case of expansion, environmental complexity increases, inducing an increase of the system's internal complexity and requisite variety as well.
2. **Network formation** is a process, which reflects both changes in the relations between subsystems and thus the system's autopoietic organisation, and changes in the amount and extension of structural coupling with other systems. The formation and reproduction of relations and social acts between internal subsystems and with external systems becomes much more complex when these are located in different cultural environments. Symbolic codes (e.g. language) and interpretational schemes in communication may be different, i.e. the interpenetration of systems and the development and reproduction of consensual domains may be very difficult. The same applies to the activity level, where path-dependent developments and endowments may produce incompatible structures and processes of production and interaction between systems of different contexts.
3. **Evolutionary dynamics** become more complex as systems in different local environments may expose different forms and levels of evolutionary motors. For example, the

well-known study by Hofstede showed that different cultures may have different attitudes toward uncertainty. This may cause a preference of teleological mechanisms like formal planning as compared to more emergent evolutionary mechanisms. In addition to different internal dynamics, the environments of systems may expose different degrees of complexity and rates of change. A globally acting system hence may have to integrate and equilibrate the co-evolution of different subsystems, which may be structurally coupled with local environments that have different rates of change. Globally differentiated systems have to buffer different modes and rhythms of change across their subsystems and respective environments.

In a first step, a general framework of firms as social system is developed before it is used to illuminate the three characteristics of globalisation and their manifestation as properties and respective capabilities of firms as social systems.

6.1 Properties of firms as social systems

An evolutionary perspective on the globalisation of firms has to be embedded within a conceptual framework that allows for the application of evolutionary principles to the firm level. In order to have evolutionary properties, a firm has to be autonomous in its reproduction. This means it has to be self-reproducing. The traditional instrumental perspective of organisations does not allow for such an approach because individuals as the elements of an organisation do not reproduce themselves in the organisation. Neither, they are exclusively elements of one organisation. Hence, an application of evolutionary principles within the instrumental perspective is not possible. However, the application of evolutionary principles to organisations is possible when the latter are conceived as autopoietic systems as will be argued in the following. In a first step, basics in systems theory will provide a basis for the conceptualisation of firms as autopoietic social systems.

6.1.1 Theoretical basis of a social systems perspective

Systems theories provide a general framework for the observation of social evolutionary processes. **General systems theory** provides basic properties and mechanisms characterising natural systems, e.g. the basic design of production and regulation processes or the inherent tendency for growth. **Theories of living systems** already describe the transition of systems toward states of higher order and differentiation. Such organic forms are considered as the expression of processes of an ordered system of forces, constituting a process of *dynamic morphing* (von Bertalanffy 1950: 26-27). A living system is characterised by autopoietic reproduction. **The theory of autopoiesis** developed in cognitive biology marks the watershed in the integration of autopoietic principles in social systems theory because cognitive and emotional processes are the basis for social processes. The three levels of systems theory are outlined briefly in the following.

6.1.1.1 Firms as open systems: General systems theory

General systems theory is a kind of *meta-theory* that serves to integrate various theories from natural to social sciences. The *roots* were developed in the *natural sciences* by von Bertalanffy (1950), von Hayek (1945), and other chemists, physics, and biologists. General systems theory was enhanced by contributions from social sciences and established a common language and concepts to describe and observe different kinds of systems. While the general systems theory provides some common basis for all kinds of systems, several streams of this theoretical approach were adapted to more specific research areas.

Systems can be differentiated into closed and open systems. **Closed systems**, like machines, have no elements of self-organisation and exchange with their environment. In contrast, **open systems** like organisations are in a continuous exchange with their environment (Katz/Kahn 1978: 125-126). Katz/Kahn further define nine properties of open systems (Table 6-1):

1.	Importation of energy	Open systems import energy from the external environment.
2.	Through-put	Open systems transform the energy available to them.
3.	Output	Open systems export some product into the environment.
4.	Cycles of events	The pattern of activities has a cyclic character.
5.	Negative entropy	Open systems must move to arrest the entropic process. They must acquire negative entropy (organised complexity).
6.	Information input and negative feedback	Inputs furnish signals to the structure about the environment and about its own functioning in relation to the environment. Negative feedback enables the system to correct deviations from the course.
7.	Steady state and dynamic homeostasis	The importation of energy to arrest entropy operates to maintain some constancy in energy exchange. At more complex levels the steady state preserves the character of the system through growth and expansion.
8.	Differentiation	Open systems move towards differentiation and elaboration.
9.	Equifinality	A system can reach the same final state from differing initial conditions and by a variety of paths (von Bertalanffy 1950: 25).

Table 6-1: Properties of open systems
(Source: Katz/Kahn 1966: 20-25)

In contrast to physics (2nd law of thermodynamics), **biological and social evolution** is accompanied by **progressive structuration** such as that introduced by the division of labour in the history of human societies (Prigogine 1976: 94). The basic principle of the biological and social universe is increase of diversification, heterogeneity, and symbiotisation. *'What survives is not the strongest, but the most symbiotic'* (Maruyama 1976: 202).

Self-regulating, equilibrium-based, and thus *deviation-counteracting systems* were the object in the first phase of cybernetic thinking, termed **Cybernetics I** by Mayurama (1963). **Cybernetics II**, on the other hand, focuses on *circular processes*, which constitute *autonomous, self-referential units* with the capacity for *self-structuration* and *self-organisation* (Schulz 1993: 44). The difference between Cybernetics I and II is that the *deviation-counteracting system* has mutual *negative feedback* between the elements in it while the *deviation-amplifying system* has mutual *positive feedback* between the elements in it (Mayurama 1963: 166). Inherent in this perspective is the **principle of learning**, i.e. the increase in the adaptability and self-complexity of the system. Cybernetics II is focused on change, instability, and self-reinforcing processes as well as evolution and co-evolution (Schulz 1993: 26). Summarising different perspectives, Jantsch/Waddington (1976) identify *twelve characteristics of evolving systems* in general and human systems in particular, constituting their dynamics (Table 6-2).

1.	A state of sufficient nonequilibrium is maintained with the system and in its relations with the environment. The state of a system at a moment of time is the set of relevant properties, which that system has at that time (Ackoff 1971: 662).
2.	Functions (the relations with the environment) and structure determine each other; they are complementary.
3.	Deterministic and stochastic (random) features are interdependent in a process view.
4.	There exist multiple stable regions, or dynamic regimes, for the system. In switching between them, the system has the capability of qualitative change.
5.	Evolution implies an ordered succession of such transitions. Autocatalysis at many levels seems to be a principal *'driving mechanism'*.
6.	Resilience, or persistence, is high near the boundaries of a stable regime, where fluctuation is abound and stability is low. Inversely, high stability implies low resilience - a system geared to short-term efficiency and productivity.
7.	The thrust of evolution seems to favour flexibility at all levels. The development of a capability to deal with the unexpected is favoured over short-term efficiency and productivity.
8.	By virtue of this flexibility, the evolutionary processes work through evolutionary experimentation at many levels of an open learning hierarchy.
9.	The result of evolution is a progressive correlation between genotypes and environments.
10.	A basic principle of this correlation is symbiotisation of heterogeneity.
11.	High resilience through high fluctuation may be assumed to imply an enhanced capability for long-term viability through transformability.
12.	Evolutionary processes imply open development and not static optimisation.

Table 6-2: Dynamic-constituting characteristics of evolving systems
(Source: Jantsch/Waddington, 1976: 6-7)

The properties of firms as open, evolving systems provide important hints to **general behavioural traits of firms**. For example, firms are characterised by an inherent drive towards growth and increasing complexity. This explains the traditional trend towards large, diversified firms. The growth principle exerts a strong influence on the evolution of a firm if not addressed consciously by decision-makers, e.g. in order to stress profitability or flexibility rather than size. On a macro-level, globalisation itself is a result of this inherent drive of social systems towards growth and increasing extension.

General systems theory also provides the basic **building blocks** in the constitution of systems. There is a basic production or transformation process, which provides the necessary resources in co-evolution with the environment. The internal organisation is based on equifinal and adaptable structures and regulatory processes based on information. Globally operating firms develop a maximum complexity with dispersed and differentiated subsystems, each characterised by its own production and regulatory processes and embedded in a co-evolution with both the integrating internal MNE context and the external local context. A globally operating firm thus is subject to fluctuations on multiple levels and depending on a resource exchange with multiple other systems in different local contexts.

6.1.1.2 Theory of living systems

The next step from the general systems theory to social organisations is the living systems theory. Living systems theory is a general systems theory of the organisation (Duncan 1972: 518). Living systems are open systems, maintaining themselves in exchange of materials with the environment, and in continuous building up and breaking down of their components. Such systems are never in true equilibrium, but in a **steady state**. In a steady state, an open system may attain a time-independent state where the system remains constant as a whole and in its phases, though there is a continuous flow of the component materials (von Bertalanffy 1950: 23). Contrary to closed systems, which are subject to the second law of thermodynamics ('*entropic death*' of systems), in organic development and evolution, a transition toward states of higher order and differentiation seems to occur (Ibid. 26). Organic forms are considered as the expression of processes of an ordered system of forces, constituting a process of '**dynamic morphing**' (Ibid. 27).

A living system is characterised only as a network of processes of production of components that is continuously, and recursively, generated and realised as a concrete entity (unity) in the physical space, by the interaction of the same components that it produces as such a network (Maturana 1975: 313). A basic premise in the conceptualisation of living systems is the fact that *'all the distinctions that we handle, conceptually or concretely, are made by us as observers: everything said is said by an observer to another observer'* (Maturana 1975: 315). It is principally a decision of the **observer** to choose the criteria for the definition of a system and its boundaries (zu Knyphausen 1988: 213).

The **internal logic of a system** cannot necessarily be observed externally. On the contrary, each observer creates the observations on the basis of his or her individual organisation of cognition (knowledge, experience, form of perception). The result is that everything said might indicate more about the observer than about the described object, which will be perceived and described differently by each observer. Perception and cognition varies more across biological species but even within social systems **strong differences** exist due to **cultural** and **individual differences**. Our cognitive system completes the image by means of memory. This explains the phenomenon that new things in a familiar milieu are often overlooked – which can have disastrous consequences (Roth 1980: 50). Living systems are historical systems and their **realities** are a **result of a historical process** (Hejl 1984: 68).

Maturana (1975: 315) defines some **common properties of living systems** in order to make an objective discourse about them more probable:

- A '*unity*' is any entity (concrete or conceptual) separated from a background by a concrete conceptual operation of distinction. The 'unity' of a globally operating firm is subject to centrifugal forces due to the high degree of global differentiation. Integration by network formation and identity building hence are central tasks in such firms.
- '*Space*' is the domain of all the possible relations and interaction of a collection of elements that the properties of these elements define. Globally operating firms r occupy the maximum and globally differentiated space.
- '*Organisation*' refers to the relations between components, which define a system as a unity. Globally operating firms may be characterised both by allopoietic and autopoietic organisation. Their global differentiation makes the co-evolution of subsystems critical in both the internal global and the external local context critical.
- '*Structure*' refers to the actual components and to the actual relations, which these must satisfy in their participation in the constitution of a given unity. Globally operating firms may develop subsystems with very different structures and are capable to adapt to changing environments.
- A '*consensual domain*' is a domain of interlocked sequences of states, established and determined through ontogenetic interactions between structurally plastic state-determined systems (Ibid.). A consensual domain is a domain with overlapping behaviours resulting from the ontogenetic reciprocal coupling of systemic structures. Interaction and the interchange of elements between two distinct systems become possible

after the establishment of such consensual domains (Maturana 1985: 256). Living systems are interacting systems, which construct consensual domains as socially accepted reality (Schmidt 1986: 34). Globally operating firms have to develop consensual domains both externally with systems in their global environment. And internally between and across their dispersed organisational units. These, in turn, have to develop consensual domains with their respective local and global environment.

- A *'domain of structural coupling'* has been established through the recurrent mutual structural selection of the participating organisms and reveals their present operationally congruent structures (Maturana 1980: 15). Structural coupling between organisms leads to the creation of isomorphic structures and of a consensual space (Fischer 1991: 78). Globally operating firms have to develop structural coupling on the activity level in the same way as they have to do it develop consensual domains on the meaning level. Both are necessary to establish and maintain the co-evolutionary interplay between systems and their environment (including other systems and subsystems).

In terms of living systems, firms develop idiosyncratic properties in structural terms. They develop an identity and an individual form of organisation, which manifests itself in changing structural arrangements. Behaviour and structure of a firm is recursively linked to other systems in its social environment. Consensual domains and structural coupling allow for the co-evolution of these systems. In the **global context**, the organisation, structure, consensual domains, and structural couplings are subject to cultural and contextual differences that call for the differentiation of internal structures and the development of integration mechanisms.

6.1.1.3 Theory of autopoietic systems

With the concept of autopoietic systems entered the element of evolution into systems theory. Autopoietic systems are capable of self-reference, self-organisation, and self-reproduction. Autopoiesis is a term of Greek derivation and means self (*auto*) production (*poiesis; poein*) (von Krogh/Roos 1995: 33). Maturana (1975: 317-318) defines '**autopoietic systems**' as follows:

'There is a class of mechanical systems in which each member of the class is a dynamic system defined as a unity by relations that constitute it as a network of processes of production of components which: a) recursively participate through their interactions in the generation and realisation of the network of processes of production of components which produced them; and (b) constitute this network of processes of production of components as a unity in the space in which they (the components) exist by realizing its boundaries. Such systems I call autopoietic systems: the organization of an autopoietic system is the autopoietic organisation.'

The evolution of autopoietic systems exposes the following characteristics:

- The result of the establishment of the *dynamic structural correspondence* between an autopoietic unity and its medium, or *structural coupling*, is the effective correspondence of changes of state of the unity with the recurrent changes of state of the medium while the unity remains autopoietic (Ibid. 320).
- A *fragmentation of the autopoietic unity* (self-division or self-reproduction) produces at least two new autopoietic unities that have identical or different structures (Ibid. 323).
- Two plastic systems become *structurally coupled* as a result of sequential interaction when their respective structures undergo sequential changes without loss of identity (Ibid. 326).
- *Evolution* can be conceived as the reproduction of circular organisation with changes in each stage of reproduction (Maturana 1985: 37).

Contrary to autopoietic systems, in 'allopoietic' systems, the organisation itself does not produce the elements and processes constituting it as a unity (Maturana 1985: 177). **Allopoiesis** is defined as a *production of something else than itself*. In management theory, it resembles the traditional *perspective of purposive, rational planning* and *implementation*, including the construction of formal hierarchical organisation, in which lower levels are designed and controlled. Informal and emergent properties from this view are excluded or invisible. Allopoietic systems are undoubtedly the precursors of autopoiesis in social systems – '*allopoiesis is the framework, a condition, within which autopoiesis can take place*' (Zeleny 1981: 95-96). Autopoiesis and allopoiesis are *complementary* rather than exclusive characterisations for a system (Varela 1981: 39).

A basic principle of social systems is that each social system is embedded in a wider social system in a recursive way while all are autopoietic. Social systems are hence characterised by the '**principle of recursiveness**'. A social system and its subsystems all have the *same basic structural properties*. Therefore, they are also characterised by the '**principle of self-similarity**' (Malik 1984: 104). *All subsystems* therefore are '*wholes*' with boundaries and all characteristics of a social system. For example, within an organisation, all *organisational units* have defining boundaries, a formal and an informal structure, an identity, thus leading to comparable, **self-similar principles of organisation**. Within such a *layered* or *multi-level structure*, allopoietic organisation has to define arenas for self-organisation (zu Knyphausen 1988: 309). Adapted to firms this would mean that units at hierarchically lower levels are purposively structured and given orders by higher levels while maintaining their self-organisation within defined limits and residual spaces. Such a conscious **context management** has proved to be particularly valuable in international management as shown in Chapter 4.2.2. The task of management is to stimulate the growth of a network of decision processes, systems, programs, and rules, that is to say, an organisation, which may be considered effective in attaining institutional objectives. One basic objective is to develop the *autonomous dynamic unity of the organisation* (i.e. an autopoietic operation). The network of decision processes must produce components capable of recursively generating the same network through their interactions. In this sense, a manager is the catalyst rather than the designer of an organisation (Zeleny/Pierre 1976: 161).

Individuals are the nodes between several social systems (Maturana 1985: 178). A cognitive or social system can create *consensual linguistic fields* and *self-consciousness* by orientational interaction with similar systems and with itself (Maturana 1985: 71). The fact is that **information** does not exist independent of a **context of organisation** that generates a cognitive domain, from which an observer community can describe certain elements as informational and symbolic (Varela 1981: 45). **Globally operating firms** thus have to cope with **multiple diverse consensual domains** on different geographical and business-oriented levels. As observers know and create their environment through interactions with it (Uribe 1981: 51), such firms have to develop their consensual domains in an **evolutionary interplay** with their respective **local and business environments** while maintaining an overlapping consensual domain vis-à-vis their **global environment** as a whole.

6.1.1.4 The dual character of social systems

Despite the conceptual problems in the adaptation of the theory of autopoietic systems to social systems, Jantsch (1986: 161) contends that *'genetic, epigenetic, social, and socio-cultural evolution appear to be connected by homologous, and not only analogous principles – principles which in different variations and on different levels of evolution are of the same type as they all stem from the same origin.'* In a similar vein, Malik (1993: 101) contends that genetic, epigenetic, social, and socio-cultural evolution are linked through homologous principles and expose an astonishing coherence in form of circular logics of trial-and-error processes. According to Malik (1993: 99) it is important to note that *'...it was not human reason that produced social institutions in order to pursue certain objectives but rather that human reason emerged as a consequence of the evolution of social institutions'*.

A conception of social systems as constituted by individuals as elements would allow for an allopoietic perspective. It may hence provide a **teleological approach** to the evolution of systems. This is an important contribution as intended influences on the reproduction of a social system from outside the system's boundaries always have allopoietic connotations. Due to the *principle of recursiveness and self-similarity*, this also applies to influences from other *subsystems* within the same system, e.g. the influence of headquarters on subsidiaries in MNEs. Both headquarters and subsidiaries are organisational units and as such constitute themselves a social system in the **nested hierarchy of social systems**.

In contrast to the allopoietic approach, which still assumes individuals to be the elements of social systems, the **adaptation of the concept of autopoiesis to social evolution** appears to be conceptually possible by an adaptation of the mechanism of the *reproduction of components*. **Social acts** as communication, legal acts etc, may be *components of self-referential*, but not of autopoietic systems: they do not exist independent from the existence of acting individuals and in physical-biological sense communicative acts do not produce new communicative acts themselves but trigger them in individuals. A social system may only be regarded as being *autopoietic* by an **ontological change** of the system level. This implies (1) a complete exclusion of acting and communicating individuals from the concept of social system, and (2) a conceptualisation of social acts (communications, actions) as the only components of the social system. It is thus possible to develop an ontology of systems, in which the states adopted by the components of an allopoietic system become the components of an *ontologically higher system*, which may be regarded as a *social system of a second level or order* (Roth 1986: 212). A **primary social system** in terms of a population - e.g. a society, or tribe – may be conceived as an autopoietic system *constituted by individuals* as their elements. Organisations are primary social systems that are allopoietic as individuals do not 'reproduce' themselves. *Functional social systems* and *organisations*, however, are autopoietic systems of a *second level*, or **secondary social systems**, as they are *constituted by social acts* as their elements. The individuals constituting a social system by their social acts do not enter the system as elements. Rather, they may be conceived as stakeholders and primary resources, which provide all necessary tangible and intangible resources by communication and action.

> *The elements of the autopoietic social system are all communications and actions on its behalf and from its perspective - not the constituting individuals.*

Members of a social system constitute a **primary, allopoietic social system**, which serves as the basis for the formation of a **secondary, autopoietic social system**. The latter is constituted by social acts on its behalf and from its perspective, which may consequently also be provided by individuals that are no formal members of the primary system. As individuals are not exclusive elements of one social system, they can contribute to the autopoietic reproduction of various secondary social systems by providing them with actions and communications belonging to their path-dependent reproduction. On balance, **social systems** are both **autopoi-**

etic in their underlying meaning-based reproduction and **allopoietic**, as they depend on the intentions of the individual stakeholders. Social systems emerge on the basis of consensual domains formed and implemented by the founding individuals. They grow as other individuals or social actors increasingly contribute to their reproduction internally, or externally as exchange partners.

6.1.2 Properties of firms as allopoietic systems

The view of **organisations** as allopoietic social systems is the *traditional view of purposeful, instrumental, and goal-directed systems constituted by individuals*. It has traditionally been dominating organisation and management theory. With the exception of ecological organisation theories and institutionalisation theory, the perspective is basically voluntaristic and functional. The focus has traditionally been on formal organisation. Elements of organisation are formal roles and organisational units. The function of the organisation is to attain the formulated purpose and specific goals by means of specialisation and co-ordination of organisational processes, roles, and units.

From the allopoietic perspective, **teleological processes** of planning and decision-making drive evolution. All properties of organisations, which may not be observed by this formal and instrumental perspective, basically become a residual in the shadow of this lens. For example, Tichy (1981: 225) noted that '*the prescribed organization structure provides the pegs upon which the emergent networks hang*', thus putting all organisational properties, which are not formally intended and prescribed into the '*informal*' drawer. This '*unknown organisational world*' may be '*contained*' or even integrated by '*context management*' but remains a black box - theoretically and in managerial practice. '**Emergent**' strategies may '*occur*' and shadow options may exist but are not part of the standard repertoire in management. Informal organisation hence often remains a residual task for the human resource management as most efforts to explain it have been made by concepts of motivation, incentives, and social cohesion. Organisational aspects themselves are basically '*out of sight*' of the allopoietic perspective, as – even by definition – it cannot explain organisation from within and by its own logic.

On the other hand, the allopoietic perspective provides directly **applicable knowledge** for those who have an **instrumental stake in organisations**. It provides insights about how goal attainment, instrumental and intentional behaviour as well as efficient organisational structures and processes may be designed and implemented. This literature comprises both **organisation theory** (e.g. contingency theory) and **management literature**, particularly on organisation structure and design. Systems theory has been applied explicitly only in form of the cybernetic concepts, which focus on control and regulation based on negative feedback loops.

While the designs of **formal organisation structure** and processes **traditionally** have been the main targets of **organisation research**, the focus is increasingly on **dynamic meaning-related organisation** as reflected by the knowledge-based view. *Routines, capabilities, best practices, and core competencies* have become main concepts in theoretical and instrumental organisation literature. Particularly in the global context such a reorientation may be very inspiring as it directs more attention to underlying differences and basic levers in the organisation of dispersed organisational units. For example, Egelhoff (1993: 204-205) contends that a key function of formal MNC structure is that managers across the company know where specific sources of knowledge and capability lie. As long as the locations tend to be fairly stable, managers are generally familiar with how to access them. With **increasing dynamics in transnational structures**, *formal structure* begins to lose its value as an accurate and stable directory of where knowledge and capability reside and how they can be accessed. A **shift** in the focus from **formal regulations** to a **dynamic knowledge perspective** thus provides more flexibility also for the instrumental, allopoietic perspective of organisation in the global context.

6.1.3 Properties of firms as autopoietic systems

Autopoietic systems are capable to reproduce themselves. In this view, firms are not only instruments to achieve the goals of the stakeholders but they take a life on their own (Selznick 1947). An evolutionary perspective of social systems can only be based on an autopoietic view as it allows conceiving firms as autonomous systems reproducing themselves. Of course, a conceptualisation of firms as autopoietic social systems presupposes a definition of respective properties. The most important difference between allopoietic and autopoietic social system level is that the latter is constituted by meaning and social acts rather than by individuals as their elements.

6.1.3.1 Meaning as the basis of social systems

While **psychic systems** are constituted on the basis of a unified (self-referential) *nexus of conscious states*, **social systems** are constituted on the basis of a unified (self-referential) *nexus of communications*. The **co-evolution of both** has led to the common evolutionary achievement of **meaning**, employed by psychic as well as social systems. Both kinds of systems are ordered according to it, and for both it is binding as the indispensable, undeniable form of their complexity and self-reference (Luhmann 1995: 59). Meaning extracts differences to enable a **difference-based processing of information** (Ibid. 63). **The processing of meaning** follows the principles of '**distinction**' and '**indication**' (Spencer-Brown 1972: 3). The mechanism for the construction and description of a form (an object) is therefore: *'Draw a distinction!'* (Ibid.) While doing this in a plane is quite simple (a line drawn between two objects may be sufficient), social systems expose a high degree of complexity so that the introduction of central guiding differences is critical to co-ordination of decision-makers and of globally dispersed activities. **Globally operating firms** have to identify the most important **guiding differences** in their heterogeneous context in order to augment their evolutionary capability. Intercultural comparisons may be difficult because **cultures** diverge in the **semantics** of the very first proceeding of this compulsion to self-change (Luhmann 1995: 64). This causes serious implications for globally operating firms. The **meaning-based structure of social systems** does not only *differ* with regard to *content* but also in the *process of selective reproduction*. Selection mechanisms and criteria may be different between cultural contexts and respective social systems.

Differences in meaning structures do not only exist between cultures. *Meaning* is always *system-specific*. Only shared meaning allows for interaction and communication between systems. Meaning may be incorporated in worldviews, values, norms, roles, etc. It is produced and negotiated in ongoing interactions (Willke 1994a: 175). Meanings are open, have no ultimate origin or ultimate truth. *'Meanings are bounded by socio-cultural limits'* (Dachler/Hosking 1995: 9). For example, *'efficient'* management structures and practices differ in many important respects because business environments do so as well (Whitley 1992: 122). The socially constructed nature of firms and markets implies that they are meaningful entities whose nature and operations vary according to differences in meaning systems and dominant rationalities. Thus, *'rules of the game'* *'business recipes'*, and economic rationalities may vary considerably between countries (Ibid. 122, 125). No set of rules can ever be self-contained and complete. Every act of human understanding is essentially based on unarticulated background of what is taken for granted. It is when we lack a common background that misunderstandings arise, in which case we are forced to articulate the background, and explain it to ourselves and to others (Tsoukas 1996: 16). A recipe, e.g. an industry recipe (Spender 1989), consists of a set of background distinctions tied to a particular field of experience. It is learned within the context of discursive practices (Tsoukas 1996: 20-21).

The world of social systems is brought forth in language. For example, Eskimos have some thirty words for different kinds of snow because their world is, to a large extent, made up of snow (von Krogh/Roos 1995: 95). The language we use influences how we experience our world and thus how we know our world. Organisational languaging presupposes socialised organisational knowledge and gives rise to distinctions that form an integral part of the concept of organisation. The organisation has no substance except for being a self-similar, autopoietic system of knowledge and distinctions. *'It demands of its members to continue to language about it on all scales in order for it to survive, or in other words, continue its autopoiesis'* (Ibid. 98). Particular usage of words tend to be specific to national cultures, to regional sub-groups within a nation, as well as to organisations and are embedded in specific contexts of meaning. The same applies to professions. For instance, everybody participating in a medical operation knows the meaning when the surgeon shouts *'scalpel'*. Therefore, the **interpretation** even of individual words is based on *highly contextual knowledge* and might vary between *different contexts*. Socialised organisational knowledge allows for less to be said than what is known (Ibid. 119).

In international management, a basic precondition is to develop differentiated discursive practices that allow for **global discourse across all units**. Specialised discursive practices on a *geographical level* (e.g. local subsidiaries and networks) and on a *professional level* (communities of practice) should complement the system-wide discourse. **Globally operating firms** have to provide for *nested consensual domains* and *common evolutionary motors across the dispersed units* including a framework that allows for a *co-evolution of subsidiaries and local environments*. **Meaning** provides **stability** in the form of organisational memory, structures, and routines but is also subject to a continuous process of new meaning generation. The variety of the internal and external context of globally operating firms provides a high self-complexity and rich source for the generation of new meaning. In management literature this is a central aspect in innovation and knowledge-based approaches.

Meaning may be conceptualised quite differently dependent on the **theoretical perspective**. *Evolutionary economics* concentrate on routines and technologies. *Social evolutionary theories* observe social traits and culture, Campbell (1960) even stresses knowledge and learning. *Population ecologists* focus on *'comps'* as an equivalent to genes in biological evolutions. Institutional theories illuminate economic regulations (institutional economics), sense (interpretative view), and institutions (institutionalisation theory), respectively. In management theory, meaning has always played a role in form of information, technology, patents, and others. An explicit and consistent approach to explore the meaning level of firms is being developed in the *knowledge-based view of management*. Due to the underlying instrumental management perspective, meaning is observed basically in terms of rational meaning, though tacit knowledge may represent a bridge to interpretational or emotional levels of meaning. The knowledge-based view developed a rich vocabulary and conceptual pool, which may provide the raw material for an increasingly consistent approach to the meaning level in organisations, particularly in firms. In general, the concept of meaning allows for the use and transfer of knowledge across different disciplines and theoretical perspectives.

6.1.3.2 Evolutionary mechanism of social systems
In terms of Waddington (1976: 11), *'man's development of language as a means of communicating information and instructions ... provided him with an enormously powerful mechanism of evolution'*. **Social evolution** is much faster than biological evolution as is is based on the

processing of meaning. Even in the global context the unit acts of this process increasingly proceed on a zero-time basis due to information and communication technologies. The basic **evolutionary mechanism of social systems** is the operation of meaning on the basis of guiding differences. **Guiding differences** are distinctions that steer the possibilities of processing information. For example, these guiding differences can acquire the property of a dominating paradigm if they organise a supertheory in such a way that in practice all information processing proceeds according to them. For example, Darwin channelled the supertheory evolution into the difference between variation and selection (Luhmann 1995: 4).

While most economic and management theories are instrumental and focused on normative issues in order to provide managers with means to pursue their goals, evolutionary theories explain mechanisms of change. They are open-ended and not directed towards the achievement of defined goals. The latter only applies to the teleological mechanism. The processing of meaning on the basis of distinctions, i.e. opposites, drives social evolution. In **formal (static) logic**, **contradiction** has the connotation of *falsity*. That is, a contradiction proposes that something is both the case and not the case at the same time and is, therefore, logically impossible because '*tertium non datur*' (Hatch 1997: 321). From a **temporal perspective**, however, the dialectic tension between two opposites provides the evolutionary motor that instils social systems with dynamics. Guiding differences are central *sources of variation* and *selective retention* as they provide the basis for the recursive interaction between meaning processing and action. For example, business organisations may be driven by the temporal needs for more expansion (e.g. diversification), then (as a consequence) for more consolidation and selective focusing (e.g. concentration on core competencies). **Firms** hence are floating between the extreme points of guiding differences, which are constitutive for their evolution. In the **global context**, a critical task of firms thus is to define and to actualise the **guiding differences** that are most important for their economic and reproductive success. These guiding differences provide the **basis for perception, interpretation, and decision-making**. They direct the attention and preferences of decision-makers and are decisive for the pattern of self-organisation.

> *The processing of meaning, actions, and decisions by guiding differences constitutes the autopoietic evolutionary motor of social systems. Globally operating firms have to develop the requisite self-complexity and resonance capacity to facilitate the autopoietic reproduction across dispersed units in a globally differentiated and nested hierarchy of social systems.*

Globally operating firms are subject to internal and external pressures for **local adaptation and global integration**. This paradox must not be neglected but appear as a **dominating guiding difference**, which has to be *balanced dynamically*. The more a firm understands and manages the dominant paradoxes underlying its business, the higher is its self-complexity and evolutionary capability.

6.1.3.3 Complexity of social systems

A **major task** in globalisation processes is the creation and reproduction of **organised complexity across the globally differentiated units** produced by internationalisation activities. In effect, complexity means being forced to select; being forced to select means contingency; and contingency means risk. Each complex state of affairs is based on a selection of relations among its elements, which it uses to constitute and maintain itself. The focus in business organisations with globally dispersed units therefore is on the **relational structure among these units**, or, in other terms, the internal network of relations among the units and the external network of relations with the organised environment.

Clearly, systems lack the **requisite variety** that would enable them to react to every state of the environment, that is to say, to establish an environment exactly suited to the system. There is *no point-for-point correspondence* between *system* and *environment* (such a condition would even abolish the difference between system and environment). The system's inferiority in complexity must be counter-balanced by **strategies of selection** (Luhmann 1995: 25). Particularly the differentiated *global context* provides an immense complexity. Firms have to develop the capacity for the dynamic selection and design of their networks of relations or, in terms of systems theory, their '*Eigenkomplexität*' ('**self-complexity**').

Resulting from the historical accumulation of system states like knowledge and experience, self-complexity is the capability of a system not only to reduce the unlimited environmental complexity, but also to transform it into a specific order by using rules, which depend on the conditions of reproduction and co-ordination provided by the existing self-complexity (Willke 1994: 103). The accompanying '*Resonanzfähigkeit*' ('**resonance capacity**') is the capability of a social system to equilibrate, respond, and absorb external perturbations and to act with regard to them. In the knowledge-based view of strategic management, a similar concept was developed in the knowledge-based view of strategic management and termed '*absorptive capacity*' (Cohen/Levinthal 1990).

Social systems are characterised by the principles of '**recursiveness**' and '**self-similarity**'. A social system and its subsystems are self-similar and linked in a recursive interplay (Malik 1984: 104). All subsystems are '*wholes*' with boundaries and all characteristics of a social system linked by self-similar principles of organisation. In this layered structure, **allopoietic organisation** has to define **arenas for self-organisation** in the form of **context management**, which proved to be particularly valuable in international management (Bartlett/Ghoshal 1986). The explanatory value of self-organisation and autonomy is particularly high in international business because of the differences in environmental conditions. **Self-similarity reduces structural complexity**, and makes transparency, communication, and substitutability of elements easier. Self-similar and recursive structures may also facilitate information processing (e.g. data structures, algorithms) and knowledge management (e.g. knowledge integration and distribution). Self-similar structures may be designed on the basis of subsidiaries or other types of organisational units (Schiemenz 1994: 304).

In firms, no matter where it is or how small it is, when the scale for observation is changed, (e.g., when studying learning processes at individual, group, or SBU level), new processes are revealed, each resembling the overall process. They are always similar but never identical (von Krogh/Roos 1995: 82). For example, MNEs pursuing a *'multinational' strategy* are characterised by a *duplication of activities across countries* and local autonomy. Subsidiaries are given equal treatment and develop similar activities along the whole value chain. Despite local differences, these subsidiaries will exhibit a great similarity. **Decision-making in organisations**, including rational choice models, bureaucratic models and political models of decision making, can also be said to be *self-similar* as it can applied to all organisational levels (von Krogh/Roos 1995: 82). How an individual autopoietically produces new knowledge (new distinctions) is similar to the way a SBU produces knowledge, which in turn, is similar to the way an organisation produces knowledge. This may even be extended to interorganisational and societal levels. At various levels of scales of observations, the individual, group, or organisation are autonomous, simultaneously open and closed, self-referential, and observing systems. In general, **globalisation** leads to an increase in the complexity of decision-making (Schiemenz 1994: 286). The design of self-similar structures is a main instrument to reduce global complexity.

6.1.3.4 Interpenetration of system and environment

A particularly neglected research area in strategic and international management is the **dynamic coupling of organisational actors** and the interaction between individual level understanding and organisational action (Lyles/Schwenk 1997: 52). From a knowledge-based perspective, *complex organisations* are conceived as *'repositories of knowledge'* and exist as communities in which varieties of functional expertise can be communicated and combined by a common language and organising principles. A *firm's functional expertise* is nested within a higher-order set of recipes that act as *organising principles*. A firm's knowledge may also consist of the information of other actors in a network, as well as the procedures by which resources are gained and transactions and co-operation are conducted (Kogut/Zander 1992: 384). *Such a view* is pragmatically appealing but lacks *theoretical foundation*, as the ontological status of a *'firm'* remains unclear. A *'repository'* cannot dispose of *evolutionary capabilities*. It may only be subject to transformation on the basis of rational choice from *'outside'*. Thus, viewing firms as repositories of knowledge, who will decide as no individuals or organisational actors are included as elements?

In the social systems view, however, *'interpenetration'* provides the *basis for structural coupling, consensual domains*, and the *co-evolution of psychic and social systems*. Interpenetration is an intersystem relation between systems that are environment for each other. While **penetration** exists when a system makes its own complexity available for constructing another system, **interpenetration** exists when this occurs *reciprocally*, that is, when both systems enable each other by introducing their own complexity into each other (Luhmann 1995: 213).

Interpenetration may emerge (1) externally *between distinct systems* (e.g. organisations), (2) internally *between distinct parts of a system* (e.g. organisational units), and (3) *between systems of different ontological levels* (psychic and social systems). Psychic systems (individual actors) constitute social systems on the basis of meaning. **The interpenetration of psychic and social systems is based on meaning**. Psychic systems supply social systems with adequate disorder and vice versa. The construction of social systems follows the principle of *'order from noise'*. Social systems come into being on the basis of the noise that psychic systems create in their attempts to communicate (Luhmann 1995: 214). Actions are simultaneously the actions of human beings and the possible building blocks of social systems (Ibid. 215). From this perspective, human beings constitute the environment of social systems. Psychic systems – or cognitive systems (in terms of Maturana) – are subsystems of human beings and belong to the environment of social systems (Ibid. 255). Psychic systems are autopoietic systems based on consciousness, not on life (Ibid. 262). Psychic systems and social systems come into being in the course of co-evolution (Ibid. 271). The relationship of human beings to social system is one of interpenetration (Ibid. 240). Only those **stocks of meaning** in the consciousness of individuals that *'belong' to a social system* are **parts** of it. The same applies to communications and actions by the individuals on behalf of the system.

☞ **The relation between individuals and social systems**

From the autopoietic perspective and akin to management approaches, **individuals** (e.g. employees) are **not elements** of the organisation but may be regarded as resources, providing labour to conduct necessary activities, and to process meaning in terms of innovation, planning, decision-making, and control. Individuals act as stakeholders, catalysts, and means for the foundation and maintenance of autopoietic social systems. They contribute to the reproduction of autopoietic social systems but are not part of them.

This enables individuals to participate in the reproduction of various different social systems without becoming extinct when any one system '*dies*'. Only what an individual '*invests*' in terms of acting (working) and meaning processing (planning, thinking, ideas, desires, expectations, etc.) on behalf of the system becomes part of it. All other aspects of an individual's life remain outside of the system but will certainly be recursively influenced by it. On the other hand, individuals do not only receive **direct incentives** from the social system but also **valuable meaning** and **access to relations**. As argued in the case of born globals, founders invest the meaning (knowledge, experiences, intuition) and the relationships generated in their professional history as founding capital in the new venture. As DiMaggio/Powell (1983) contend, the building blocks for the formation of social systems have become virtually littered in the social space. Founders of born globals appear to have collected enough such building blocks on global scale to set-up new ventures viable in this context.

Individuals also take **boundary-spanning roles**, facilitating the interpenetration of social system, their structural coupling, and the development of consensual domains between them. They provide the autopoietic system with the capability to import information and other necessary resources, and to export its products in exchange. From the institutionalisation perspective, individuals act as '**isomorphic ventilators**', instilling the social system with meaning from the social environment and communicating meaning generated by the system to their social environment. Individuals are the generators and transmission belts for the recursive interplay of meaning and action. The autopoietic system thus depends on the *organisation* of this recursive interplay but not on the concrete *structure* at any given point in time (Maturana 1985).

As the firm or other organisation provides the means to achieve the goals of social actors, it attracts them to participate. Due to double contingency and interdependencies with exchange partners, the probability of structural coupling with other social actors rises as more individuals put their stakes and resources into the organisation. Individual motivations of stakeholders and double contingency with other social actors constitute the inherent tendency for growth, which is typical for living systems. In the **global context**, individuals in terms of psychic systems are socialised quite differently and intercultural differences may demand more efforts in the development of shared meaning and activity structures. Both more conscious efforts and learning-by-doing may become necessary to bridge cultural and contextual differences by developing globally nested consensual domains between and across dispersed organisational units.

6.1.3.5 Recursive interplay of action and meaning structure

A social system is constituted as an action system, but must presuppose the communicative context of action. Both action and communication are necessary, and both must constantly co-operate in order to enable reproduction out of the elements of reproduction. Reproduction means only production out of what has been produced; for autopoietic systems this means that the system does not end through its actual activity, but goes on. This going on depends on the fact that actions (whether intentionally or not) have communicative value. Communication and action are recursively related (Luhmann 1995: 169).

> *The evolution of a social system is driven by the recursive interplay of its activity structure and its meaning structure. Actions and communications are the unit acts in this process.*

The **autopoietic organisation** of a social system is constituted by the **recursive interplay between meaning and action level**. The basic social acts are communication and action - both on the basis of a path-dependent structure, which reflects the underlying organisation. A social system is constituted as an action system, but must presuppose the communicative and meaning-based context of action. Communication and action are recursively related and the elements of the autopoietic system (Luhmann 1995: 169). Through communication, organised action can occur despite differences of interpretation among organisational members. Communication enables members to create equifinal meaning, from which organised action can follow (Donnellon et al. 1986: 43).

Communication or processing of meaning in general recursively drive the **reproduction** of the underlying **meaning structure**, which is first imprinted by the **founding stakeholders** and then begins its **autopoietic reproduction**. The same applies to the **action level**, where actions recursively drive the autopoietic reproduction of the activity structure. The elements of an autopoietic social system hence are meaning and social acts – not individuals.

The **autopoietic system** is dependent on the interpenetration and **structural coupling with individuals** who provide their contribution in form of necessary **resources** - including the capacity of meaning processing and activity conduct - and who in turn receive the expected incentives by the autopoietic system. As long as the social system '*finds*' individuals (stakeholders) who participate in this interplay, the autopoietic system will survive. The system may even change its purpose, its technology, or products as long as it maintains its reproduction, i.e. its autopoietic organisation.

Giddens assumes that *social actors sustain meaning in communicative acts*. But settings are also 'regionalised' in ways that heavily influence, and are influenced by, the serial character of encounters. **Regionalisation** here is best understood not as a wholly spatial concept but as one expressing the **clustering of contexts in time-space** (Giddens 1984: 365). All social interaction is situated in space and time (Ibid. 86). In addition, meaning inherently forces itself to change. One must be careful about **intercultural comparisons** because cultures diverge in the **semantics** of the very first proceeding of this compulsion to **self-change** (Luhmann 1995: 64). This causes serious implication for globally operating firms. The meaning-based structure of social systems does not only differ with regard to content but also to the process of selective reproduction. **Selection mechanisms** and criteria may be different between **cultural contexts** and respective **social systems**. Globally operating firms have to provide for a common **evolutionary motor** across the dispersed units and a framework on meaning and action level that allows for a **co-evolution of subsidiaries** with both the **MNE network** and **local environments**.

6.1.4 Change and reproduction of global social systems

The **structure of elements and relations** in social systems is **basically stable** over a certain period of time. A given **organisational structure** restricts the amount of possible choices and relations among elements and behaviours and consists of a **structure of expectations** regulating legitimated behaviour (Luhmann 1995: 283). Expectations are the autopoietic requirement for the reproduction of actions. There are no other structural possibilities for social systems because social systems temporalise their elements as action-events. **Expectations** translate meaning into intended action and its implementation. **Decisions** legitimate expectations and make them explicit. An action therefore is always oriented by expectations. **Routinisation** and **institutionalisation** can reduce the need for decision-making as expected actions are stabilised. Routine and institutionalised actions thus lose the character of a decision (Ibid. 293-295). They reflect **organised complexity** and reduce the amount necessary decisions but may also become rigid and dysfunctional.

In **globally differentiated systems**, the complexity and dynamics would call for routines and institutionalised action in order to reduce the complexity of decision-making. However, as local contexts and expectations may differ profoundly, such standardisation may be difficult to achieve. One basic solution is the minimisation of interdependencies by decentralisation; another is the development of **consensual domains between and across globally differentiated units**. The latter allows for a **commensurability of expectations across the units**, providing a **joint orientation** towards intended actions and transformations. As a minimum condition, the units have to develop equifinal meaning (e.g. expectations) by communication, which allows for directed organised action - even though there are diverging interests, motives, and interpretations.

As structures of social systems, expectations acquire social relevance and suitability only if they can be anticipated. Only in this way can double contingency be ordered. **Expectations** must become **reflexive across the subunits** involved. The anticipation of expectations induces all participants to take up orientations that reciprocally overlap in time and are, in this sense structural. This prevents social systems from being formed as mere chains of reactions (Luhmann 1995: 303, 305). A basic condition in globally operating firms is the development of interculturally suitable communication and meaning structures, which may provide the necessary transparency and direction.

The **historical law** governing the structural development of action systems is the **increase of functional differentiation** (Ibid. 349). A theory of evolution then focuses on the formulation of causes and effects of the differentiation of evolutionary mechanisms. When the mechanisms are differentiated more sharply, structural change becomes more probable and the social system increases its speed of transformation (Ibid. 152). **Intentional changes** are always embedded in an evolutionary process, which assimilates and 'deforms' them. Choice and planning are components of the evolution of social systems but a planning system has to be capable to observe itself in the system's evolution (Luhmann 2000: 185, 353). Given that uncertainty rather than certainty is continuously characterising the situation of an organisation, **evolutionary rationality** in planning is reflected in an **organisation's robustness** rather than in the efficiency of optimisation (Luhmann 1988: 122). From a systems perspective, it would be reasonable and a precondition of robustness to design an organisation in a way that allows it to grow and shrink within a certain range (Luhmann 2000: 310). This argument also supports the position that internationalisation processes involve both increases and decreases in the geographic and cultural extension of a firm. **Management in complex global systems** therefore includes the *increase in the global requisite variety*, in the *capability of organisational resonance in globally differentiated environments,* and the *respective processing of contingencies* in terms of the behavioural potential of the system (Müller 1996: 73). A process of global differentiation and integration drives the development of these organisational properties and capabilities.

6.1.4.1 Differentiation and integration

Historically, the first move on the way from a mechanistic general systems theory to a theory of social systems is the replacement of the traditional **difference between whole and part** by that between **system and environment**. This transformation (von Bertalanffy 1950) enables to interrelate the theory of the organism, thermodynamics, and evolutionary theory, constituting the theory of system differentiation (Luhmann 1995: 6). System differentiation is the repetition of the difference between system and environment. Through it, the whole system uses itself as environment in forming its own subsystems (Ibid. 7). The **functional differentiation** of social systems increases the pace in the evolution of social action in societies substantially (Kieser 1989: 178). In terms of population ecology, it produces **new niches** in which **new organisational forms** may emerge and develop. From an evolutionary perspective, differentiation facilitates the structural implementation of the mechanisms of variation. It facilitates systemic change through the **division of subsystems** so that not each change in a subsystem induces adaptation in other subsystems as well (Luhmann 1975: 62). In economic terms, differentiation and subsequent integration of social relations in the differentiated systems constitutes **functional specialisation**. The evolutionary process of differentiation and integration therefore creates variation (innovation) and more efficiency in the functional systems. For example, the global market economy based on the generalised medium 'money' provides much more variety and efficiency than ancient forms of economic organisation. The same applies to the organisations working within the economic subsystem.

Differentiation and integration, i.e. the **evolutionary motor** of social systems, is constituted by the continuous, **recursive interaction** between their two constituting levels of **meaning and action**. In the course of its evolution, the interpretation of perceptions of a system determines its activities. The activities of a system, in turn, determine the interpretations of its perceptions. Such a circular explanation is necessary and valid because it infuses a system with its dynamic (von Foerster 1985: 47).

After the **founding process** of a new social system, the **process of differentiation and integration** sets in *internally* and with regard to the *coupling with the environment*. Internally, the social system differentiates new subsystems (e.g. organisational units), which are themselves social systems due to the principle of self-similarity. The social system unfolds an internal nested hierarchy of social systems. The **self-similarity** of these **(sub-)systems** allows for consistent communication, action, and organising principles. In the **process of globalisation**, the social system encounters perturbations, as individuals belonging to other national or cultural systems – living and socialised in a different cultural context - constitute new differentiated subsystems.

Activity and meaning structures and even **modes of meaning processing** are different and represent a serious obstacle to the integration of **globally differentiated subsystems** in the evolutionary path of the overall system. **Consensual domains** have to be developed both between individual subsystems (e.g. two subsidiaries) and on system level (e.g. MNE). The system has to develop meaning structures and processes, which facilitate the **generation and**

diffusion of meaning across all subsystems, at least in those areas that are vital for the system as a whole.

As argued in Chapter 2, globalisation is characterised by the expansion of social systems and the development of network relations on global scale. Globalisation thus provides a fertile context for the increasing formation, expansion, and linking of social systems in a recursive, self-fuelling process. The **principle of differentiation and integration** leads to **complementary processes of globalisation** on organisation level, here exemplified by the difference of global vs. local:

1. It may be argued that **global systems** like MNEs differentiate subsystems (e.g. subsidiaries), which adapt to local conditions and act as bridges to build consensual domains and structural couplings with systems in the local environment. The **MNE** thus may gain access to local resources and options to export the systems' products. The MNE differentiates own subunits but also develops external interdependencies on global scale, further increasing the probability of system formation and differentiation. In order to maintain their steady state and autopoietic reproduction, MNEs commit substantial resources to the integration of their subsystems. With increasing internal differentiation and external interdependencies, the complexity of relations increases. Besides the mere quantity of relations, it is the variety of environments and the resulting differentiation of internal subsystems, external interdependencies and consensual domains, which produces the immense complexity of MNEs. These have to develop the requisite variety in form of organised complexity in order to maintain their identity and their autopoiesis. This induces the import and integration of organised complexity in the form of meaning. MNEs must dispose of a variety of knowledge of the diverse social spaces in which they act and must develop the capacity to integrate this knowledge in the internal process of meaning generation and reproduction. The generation and diffusion of knowledge at both system level (global) and subsystem level (e.g. local) becomes a critical capability of MNEs in order to maintain the evolutionary interplay between meaning and action levels across all subsystems.

2. Contrary to MNEs, many **local organisations**, such as **SMEs**, do not dispose of globally dispersed resources and interdependencies. Such local firms have not reached the global level by internal differentiation and integration and thus these two subprocesses of social evolution still await geographic extension. Local firms may follow the course of internationalisation by internal differentiation, i.e. FDI, or by the establishment of interdependencies with other, globally dispersed organisations. In the first case, integration is primarily focused on internal relations. In the second case, the harmonisation of globally differentiated consensual domains becomes a main task in order to

maintain a symbiotic co-evolution with the now geographically and culturally differentiated environment. Though circular in a recursive perspective, differentiation precedes and even induces integration in a sequential perspective. Internationalisation efforts of SMEs therefore often concentrate on the entrepreneurial side, i.e. differentiation, and neglect the integrative aspect of globalisation.

3. Complementary to the single firm or *intraorganisational globalisation perspective*, which distinguishes *global firms* (MNEs) and *local firms* (majority of SMEs), the local vs. global difference may also be applied to **interorganisational networks**. As shown in Chapter 4, there are strong competitive advantages of both local and global networks. **Local networks** provide advantages of flexible specialisation, innovative milieus, cultural homogeneity, and social capital from local embeddedness. As in the case of MNEs, **global interorganisational networks** provide substantial advantages from global variety, global co-specialisation, and co-ordination. Contrary to MNEs, they dispose of more flexibility and possibilities of niche specialisation by individual firms. While global interorganisational networks certainly dispose of a higher variety and a higher capacity to exploit location advantages and to leverage competitive advantages, their integration is very difficult and may impede more complex forms of activities. *Local networks*, on the other hand, are much easier to co-ordinate due to their local embeddedness but do not dispose of the global diversity of their global counterparts. Increasingly, local networks seem to develop relations with global networks, and vice versa. **Globalisation** thus induces the **formation of multi-layered networks from the local to the global level**.

The described global differentiation and integration of MNEs, the internationalisation of MNEs, and the emergence of multi-layered networks on global scale induce the '**liquefaction of global competition**', which sets the standards for the global evolution of firms in the context of economic globalisation.

6.1.4.2 Evolutionary motors

The **basic principle of evolution** is not teleological, towards some however defined higher perfection. Rather, the basic principle is '**to get out of the way**'. In biology, this means to get out of the way of competitors, predators, and other environmental threats. In societies, social systems encounter such restriction in terms of other social systems, i.e. organisations, and legitimacy. The irony with the process of globalisation is that the globalisation itself strictly limits the possibility to get out of the way. **Globalisation** *causes a* '**domestication**' **of the global arena**. While '*discoveries*' and geographic expansion in ancient times basically reflected a spatial extension of a social system, they now lead to changes within the **increasingly dense fabric of global networks**. In addition to the principle to get out of the way in order to find a stable supply with resources and to pursue the basic function and goals of the system, social systems have also been described as being designed for the pursuit of individual goals of the stakeholders. As such, they are also instruments and subject to allopoietic reproduction. As shown in Chapter 5, there are basically four **mechanisms of change** in social systems identified by organisation theory. In addition, the mechanism of meaning processing by guiding differences by social system may be regarded as a fifth mechanism. All the five mechanisms provide the **dynamics** that drive the **principle of differentiation and integration in social evolution**.

☞ **Life cycle mechanisms**

Life cycle mechanisms are the **most common holistic explanation** of transformation in the **management literature**. The typical progression of change events in a life-cycle model is a unitary sequence, which is cumulative and conjunctive. A singular discrete entity exists that undergoes change yet maintains its identity throughout the process. The entity passes through stages distinguishable in form or function. A program, routine, rule, or code exists in nature, social institutions, or logic that determines the stages of development and governs progression through the stages. The **logic of life cycle models** is appealing as social systems have a '*birth*' in terms of foundation, growth, and often, even death. An important restriction is the missing consistency of what happens between birth and death. There are no consistent overarching principles or phases applying to all organisations or other social systems. On the contrary, population ecology showed that contrary to biology, the probability of death in the case of organisations decreases with increasing age. The same applies to transformation processes. A study by Singh et al (1986: 606) suggests that organisational changes made earlier in the life cycle are more likely to influence the hazard of death. The life cycle has been explicitly chosen by Vernon (1966) as the motor for change in his **international product life cycle model**. Life cycle mechanisms are also underlying all other stage models of internationalisation, though in combination with other mechanisms.

☞ **Teleological mechanisms**

Teleological mechanisms drive the development of an organisational entity toward a **goal** or an **end state**. The organisational entity is purposeful and adaptive; by itself or in interaction with others, the entity constructs an envisioned end state, takes action to reach it, and monitors the progress. Such a mechanism perfectly fits in the case of organisations as rational, purposive, and goal-directed social systems. Consequently, the teleological mechanisms dominate the management perspective due to their instrumental value. The **purpose of an organisation** is first defined by the **founders** and imprinted at foundation. Later, the respective stakeholders continuously renegotiate the purpose and the specific goals dependent on their power positions. Strategic contingency theory, exchange theory, and resource dependence theory provide a great variety of arguments in this regard. The **basic means** of social teleological mechanisms are **decision-making processes**. Decision-making is not only necessary to make expectations explicit in order to implement the intended activities. In addition, negated possibilities may determine the system more than pursued possibilities because they cannot be corrected or adapted by learning. They influence the '**structural drift**' of the system much more than the accepted possibilities, which can be modified by further decisions. Consequently, it may be a reasonable maxim to decide in a way that decisions extend the decisional space and autonomy of the system (Luhmann 2000: 199). Structures in organisations have the function of premises for decisions and hierarchies are thus priori decisions on how decisions shall be made (Luhmann 1971: 69).

Decision-making has received extensive attention in literature on international business with regard to strategy-making under the perspective '**centralisation vs. decentralisation**' (Garland/Farmer 1986, Ronen 1986) and particularly in the Process School of international business, which put the decision-making context – particularly between MNE headquarters and subsidiaries - at the centre of the transnational model.

☞ **Dialectical mechanisms**

Dialectical mechanisms develop in systems, which are subject to **contradictory** or **colliding forces**. Historically, such mechanisms have particularly been identified in contexts of **political and power struggle**, e.g. in historical materialism (work vs. capital). In the operation of dialectical mechanisms, initially opposing **thesis** and **antithesis** are fused by a **synthesis**, which becomes a stable compromise for a period of time and can become the new and challenged thesis as the dialectical process continues. **Change** and **stability** thus co-exist in **dialectical synthesis**. The dialectical view particularly applies to the context of globalisation and particularly to MNEs, which already internalised the basic dialectic of local adaptation vs. global integration.

☞ **Evolutionary mechanisms**

The evolutionary motor causes **cumulative changes** in social systems. Change proceeds through a continuous cycle of variation, selection, and retention. In contrast to **Darwinian** evolution where traits are inherited through intergenerational processes, the **Lamarckian** concept argues that traits are acquired within a generation through learning and imitation. A Lamarckian view thus appears to be more reasonable in the case of social evolution. In contrast to blind Darwinian evolution, which applies to biology, active selection by human agents occurs at all stages of the process of social evolution. Evolution in social systems is constituted by the evolution of knowledge (Loasby 1999a, Boulding 1981, Veblen 1899). The VSR mechanism is consequently the first evolutionary mechanisms used to explain evolutionary dynamics by the knowledge-based view.

☞ **Autopoietic mechanisms**
A fifth motor not included by van de Ven/Poole is the autopoietic motor of meaning processing by guiding differences in social systems. The evolutionary mechanism of social systems is the **recursive reproduction of meaning and action** on the basis of '*guiding differences*' (Luhmann 1995: 4). Such guiding differences allow for the organisation of meaning by building dynamic relations. For example, as shown by Ghoshal (1987), the distinction of global integration vs. local adaptation may be applied to organise knowledge from the industry level, to firms, and even to individual activities. A basic task in the evolution of an organisation is to identify the most critical guiding differences for their successful reproduction. The evolution of the organisational meaning structure and consensual domains across units and with external partners thus may be facilitated. The **guiding differences** provide the basis for perception, interpretation, and decision-making. They direct the attention and preferences of decision-makers and are decisive for the pattern of self-organisation. In the process of globalisation, a system has to develop the requisite organised complexity by integration of guiding differences, which allow for a viable perception and meaning processing in the globally differentiated context. Generally, more than one motor comes into play because the organisational context of development and change extends over space and time in any specific case. There may also be some degree of nesting, timing/sequencing, and complementarity of motors.

6.1.5 Co-evolution of social systems and their environment

The **basic condition** for the **co-evolution of social systems** is their capability to communicate, to interact, and to understand and interpret the communication and actions of each other. When these conditions are given and interaction is taking place, this is called interpenetration. **Interpenetration** exists when two systems enable each other by introducing their own complexity into each other (Luhmann 1995: 213). Social systems do this by means of **meaningful communication and action**. As argued above, individuals act as catalysts and channels for the flow of such social acts. **Interpenetration** provides the basis for **structural coupling**, **consensual domains**, and the **co-evolution of systems**. Meaning enables psychic and social system formations to interpenetrate, while protecting their autopoiesis (Ibid. 232).

Interpenetration of social systems from **different cultural environments** is much more difficult than within a homogeneous context. *First*, the basic means of communication, language, is different. Communication may be simply impossible, but even qualified personnel may not perceive minute connotations of communications formulated in the language of the foreign partner. *Second*, different cultures have different preferences, norms, interpretations, habits, and even different modes of meaning reproduction. The interchange of meaning, ranging from simple information to the transfer of best practice or technology thus represents a major obstacle to international or even global interaction. Particularly more dynamic and complex forms of interchange like innovation processes may be very difficult between culturally different systems.

The **co-evolution of social systems** thus presupposes a **parallelisation of structural elements and acts** in their reproduction. A set of temporalised expectations, intentions, and actions must be identical in their references to system and environment, for an even flow of time is required to compensate for the lack of certainty and stability. The increasing differentiation of social systems and the resulting dynamics in the globalisation process may lead to **asymmetrical ageing** in the co-evolution of structurally coupled organisations and even of their subunits. Structural elements and relations become temporally more differentiated. Their dynamic integration may be facilitated by **intentional 'mutual ageing'** (Schütz 1932: 111), which becomes a key to successful co-specialisation and co-operation.

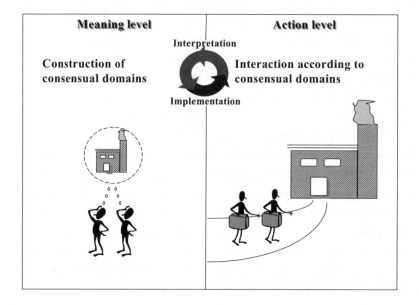

Figure 6-1: Construction of consensual domains

As the basic structural means for the co-evolution of social systems, the **construction of consensual domains** can be viewed as the **central demand** resulting from **globalisation processes** (Figure 6-1, 6-2). New organisational units or co-operation partners have to be integrated into the ongoing structures and operations, so that the construction of a shared reality may be the fundament for successful interaction. New operations have to be negotiated and therefore to be constructed into the open space of options. Globally dispersed activities lead to an increasing necessity of consensual domain construction and integration. Local subsidiaries have to develop their consensual domains and structural couplings in their local context and that way they may be the source of innovative processes for the whole network. The co-operation with local partners can lead to the construction of innovative products, practices, etc. as well.

On the other hand, **standardised knowledge** in form of best practices, standardised processes, and products or structural arrangements have to be conveyed to new units and partners to guarantee efficiency and continuation as well as a boundary-spanning fit with existing structures and processes. The development of **transparency** in the **own structures and operations** is therefore a very important step to develop the ability to communicate and construct new realities with partners, co-operation partners as well as other internal organisational units.

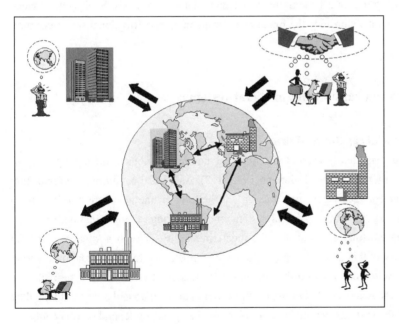

Figure 6-2: Integration of local and global consensual domains

Particularly the **variety of consensual domains on the global scale** can be viewed as the **central challenge** to the **management of globalisation**. It can be the source of conflicts and misunderstanding as well as a source of new ideas and innovations and thus exerts a fundamental impact on the evolution of a company.

As **globally differentiated subsystems** are constituted primarily by **local individuals**, they are instilled with **meaning** generated in the **local context**. A large variety of meaning and interpretations is thus imported into the local subsidiary due to the interpenetration of social and psychic systems. Local subsidiaries are rich sources of new meaning and interpretation. At the same time, **individuals from the local context** have to be instilled with system- or **firm-specific meaning**. This includes the transfer of knowledge and organisational culture. **Individuals** are the linking pins between the local environment and the subsidiary and are the **means of local interpenetration** and the development of **local consensual domains**.

In addition, they act as linking pins between the local sub-system (subsidiary) and the network of globally dispersed subsystems generating and reproducing the respective interpenetrations and consensual areas. Individuals in subsystems thus have to develop a **'Janus-faced' role**, which allows for a dynamic balancing of the two perspectives. Once again, the principle of evolution by the processing of guiding differences becomes apparent. Individuals may be trained and sensitised to focus on such central guiding differences in order to allow for a common orientation on a heterarchic rather than hierarchical basis. Such general capabilities of system members provide the fundament for the more specific globalisation capabilities.

6.2 Globalisation capabilities of social systems

6.2.1 Entrepreneurial capability of firms

Social systems are formed only where the actions and communications of different psychic or social systems are interdependent (Luhmann 1995: 113). As a basic condition, the **formation of a social system** emerges when the situation and **actions** of one actor are **contingent** on those of the other and vice versa. A social system emerges through the fact that both partners experience **double contingency** and that the indeterminability of such a situation for both partners in any activity that then takes place possesses significance for the formation of structures (Ibid. 108). Actors can try to influence what they observe by their own action and can learn further from the feedback. This way, an **emergent order** can arise that is conditioned by the complexity of the systems that make it possible but that does not depend on this complexity being calculated or controlled. This emergent order is a social system. Successively, autopoietic reproduction, action out of action, emerges. The absorption of uncertainty runs its course by **stabilising expectations**, not by stabilising behaviour, and this naturally presupposes that **behavioural selections** are not selected without orientation and expectations. In the context of double contingency, expectations thus acquire structural or *'connective value'* for building emergent systems and a certain kind of reality. The development of social systems and their consensual domains hinges on a **parallelisation of meaning and expectations**, which generate actions in a co-evolutionary interplay.

With recurrent interaction, **'condensed meaning'** crystallises and forms the foundation for the formation of consensual domains and structures on the meaning and action level. **Power differences** between interdependent social actors instil the formation context of social systems with an asymmetry of influence with regard to the development of the **purpose, profile,** and **boundary- and self-definition** of the emerging new social system. The **formation process of a social system** may be conceived as **allopoietic** as the founding actors '*construct*' a new system and instil it with a negotiated purpose and initial characteristics. On the level of the wider social context, it may be conceived as **autopoietic** as the system emerges from a social fabric of social structures, interdependencies, and double contingencies. For example, with the liquefaction of global competition, the **formation of new global systems** becomes more probable - independent from the individual case. The **initial formation process** ends when both the meaning and action level begin their co-evolutionary interplay and thus their **autopoietic reproduction within established boundaries**. Once in motion, the new system orients itself by the question if potential partners will accept interaction and have a positive motivation in interactions in order to develop viable activity structures.

After the foundation, founders of a social system may act as internal and/or external actors constituting the system. In the **initial autopoietic formation** of its identity and boundaries, a social system can **define its boundaries** as more or less open and permeable, but it must then internally determine the **rules of selection** by whose help themes can be accepted or rejected. Through the connection between selections and further selections in the course of communication, a **domain** of what is to be accepted and expected condenses. **Roles** and **organisational units** are formed as collages of expectations, functioning as points of reference for further selections within the system (Luhmann 1995: 127). **In the beginning** of the autopoietic formation, the **founders** still have a **dominating influence on the imprinting of the new system**. The system continues to be malleable and receptive to intended changes by decision-makers but once the system has a history, **change** becomes **increasingly path-dependent** and embedded in the **co-evolution with the social environment**.

In the **process of globalisation**, the **multitude** and the **connectedness of social actors** increase on the global level so that **situations of double contingency** increase as well. Globalisation induces the formation of a multilevel network competition in a **process of liquefaction** of the global competition. It may be assumed that the number and forms of new social systems formed in this context will also increase - particularly in the new social spaces that emerge in social and economic evolution on the global level and between different geographical levels. This tendency has been proved historically for organisations in the sense of purposefully created and goal-directed social systems. As argued in Chapter 2, the globalisation of social systems in the economic functional system is quite advanced while in other functional systems of society the situation is still '*inter-national*' at best.

> ***The process of globalisation induces increasing interdependencies between local and global social contexts and systems. These interdependencies cause double contingencies between globally dispersed social actors – leading to an increase in the formation of new social systems in the global context.***

The increase in interdependencies and double contingencies also fuels interactions between globally dispersed social systems, their co-operation, and network building. A third aspect is the internalisation of global activities by social systems by processes of internal internationalisation.

6.2.1.1 Foundation of organisations

Organisations are founded as **individual founders** develop an idea and a consensual domain on the **meaning level** with regard to a joint new venture, which may provide the means to achieve the desired goals. The new venture then is implemented on the **action level**, and once in place, the existence and evolution of the **second-level, autopoietic system** sets in. The autopoietic system forms and stabilises its **identity** and its **boundaries** until it occupies a **position** in its social ecological **niche**. After a process of initial imprinting, a *meaning structure crystallises* and the *activity structure* based on the resource endowment *stabilises*. After this initial process of foundation, the autopoietic system becomes increasingly independent from the constituting primary (allopoietic) social system. Formal job and authority structures abstract from the individual level and make individual members increasingly substitutable. The organisation diminishes the character of an instrument for the achievement of the original founders' goals and may become even independent of them. Once in place, stakeholders and even the owners may change without seriously influencing the reproduction of the autopoietic system. The organisation thus may take a '*life on its own*' (Selznick 1947: 26).

Due to the liabilities of newness, smallness, and foreignness, **new organisations** find more serious **obstacles** in their development and are more likely to die than old organisations. The founding of an organisation has an especially influential effect on the structure, processes, and strategy the organisation develops and continues to exhibit over time and on the orientations organisations adopt in implementing goals (Boeker 1988: 33). The dates and social conditions of their founding have strong and continuing influence on the orientations that organisations adopt in implementing goals. The environment at founding, the personality of the founder, and the nature of initial decisions have all lasting effects on organisational structure and behaviour (Tucker et al. 1990: 184). The **founding** of an organisation is an **overriding factor in moulding** and constraining the **organisation's behaviour** during the subsequent stages of its **life cycle**. In the process of foundation, decisions about the organisation's initial purpose, activities, and geographical extension are made. The initial stage entails a learning process that results in decision-making patterns, an authority structure, and rules and procedures that are relatively permanent and evoke pressures toward organisational inertia. While organisations undergo modifications and display varying degrees of flexibility, foundation casts them into a mould that is discernible in all subsequent stages of their life cycle (Pennings 1980: 254). In the **global context**, this also implies that the **initial imprinting by the home culture** may create **stable cultural patterns** within the organisation itself, which may still be perceived in old MNEs.

☞   **Foundation of organisations in the context of globalisation**
Globalisation is a **self-fuelling process** causing a **compression of social time and space**. The evolution of global structures provides actors with consciousness and expectations developed in the globalising social context. Professional education, media, travelling, and international work experience provide entrepreneurs increasingly with knowledge and experiences urging them to define their '*playground*' as global. The globe becomes the reference point for self-conscious identity formation. This applies to individuals and to social systems. If the foundation of a start-up is global depends to a decreasing degree on the cognitive constructs available and on the personal relations with actors from other locations. Even this obstacle is becoming easier to resolve as international mobility of students and professionals is increasing. **Foundation of global systems** becomes **more probable**.Nonetheless, and despite the increasing emergence of international new ventures, Chapter 3 showed that in traditional theories of internationalisation the **foundation of firms** is viewed as occurring in a **culturally homogeneous context** before internationalisation sets in. It may be assumed that the vast majority of firms still will be founded in a local context due to the advantages of **social milieus** but that their internationalisation – when taking place – will not display the traditional incremental form. **In the long run** it may be expected that **foundations** of firms will emerge **more evenly distributed across the differentiated geographical landscape** of social functional systems. Born globals and traditional internationalisers thus should not be conceived as opposites but as beginning on the globalisation path from different starting points.

The **globalisation capabilities**, which were illustrated in Figure 2-5, may best serve to explore the different starting points of born globals and traditional internationalisers. These competencies apply to the development and evolution of global activities in the context of global diversity. But they can also be generalised for a '**diversity-free**' context by conceptualising them as **general evolutionary capabilities** (Figure 6-3). The '*internationalisation capability*' can be conceived of as the '*entrepreneurial capability*' in the globalisation process. Similarly, the '*global network capability*' can be generalised as a '*network capability*' that applies also for the evolutionary process in culturally homogeneous settings. The '*capability of global evolutionary dynamics*' can also be generalised so that it also applies to the case of restricted local or regional niches. This capability is crucial in the early years of a start-up firm because of the amount and intensity of rapid changes and adaptations that are necessary to establish a new firm in the market.

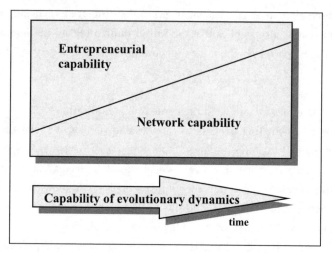

Figure 6-3:   General evolutionary capabilities of firms

The **dynamics of change** (both external an internal) induce the development of corporate structures, which may not remain optimal for long. Those firms, which adapt strategically and manage to surf along the dynamics of change, are more likely to make it to the shores of economic success (Etemad 1999: 101).

In contrast to the traditional firms, **born globals** have **no temporal differentiation in their global capability development** so that their entrepreneurial capability is global right from the start as are their network capability and their capability of evolutionary dynamics. The entrepreneurial capability of born globals hence includes the internationalisation component right from inception. The network capability and the capability of evolutionary dynamics contain the global components as well. The **global dimensions** of the three competencies represent part of the '**founding capital**' of such new ventures.

Firms that follow the **traditional, incremental path of internationalisation** are characterised by a **two-step globalisation**. In a first step, they establish a home market base on the basis of the general evolutionary competencies. After a successful development and stabilisation in the home market, the firm begins its internationalisation process. The explanatory approach of internationalisation theories begins with this second step into international markets while the foundation of a firm and the process of imprinting in the national context never were included in the stage theories of internationalisation. The two-step process underlying the logic of the stage theories of internationalisation is illustrated in Figure 6-4.

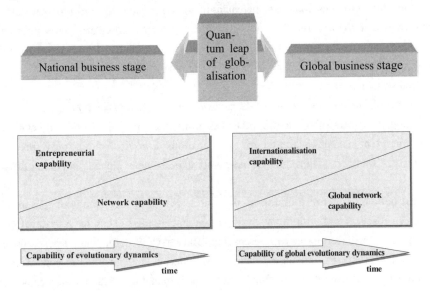

Figure 6-4: Two-step globalisation

In the **context of increasing globalisation**, however, it may be assumed that **organisations will be increasingly founded on an international basis from the start**. Within the global network competition, it is increasingly probable that actors from different countries found start-ups with international funding, using internationally dispersed technology and resources, and aiming at global markets (particularly niches). This does not mean that all criteria have to apply. While the use of globally dispersed resources may be restricted to inputs and the supply of different local markets may be confined to marketing, the main question with regard to born globals is the formation of a global social system. The question is how a self-referential system of meaning and action with global extension comes into being. In other words, how do actors from different countries form a joint system of meaning, expectations, and actions, which develops a life of its own?

One **basic condition** is the **availability of meaning** *(knowledge, institutions, and routines)* about the **global context** and of **relations and consensual areas with the respective actors** in it. The incremental process appears quite reasonable when local founders lack these resources at the time of foundation and in the first years of activity. Gradually they have to acquire the knowledge and to build relations with international partners. On the other hand, founders of born globals seem to dispose of these resources quasi from the start. Two aspects seem to **support** the **development of knowledge and relations in the global context**:

1. Globalisation provides founders increasingly with the *means to acquire respective knowledge and to build relations with globally dispersed actors*. Particularly information and communications technologies, formation of globally linked networks and brokering institutions provide founders with the means to acquire and to build up the needed structures and resources.
2. The *founders themselves dispose of the relevant knowledge and relations* at the time of founding. Founders often have experiences from their previous work and relations with important stakeholders in the relevant locations. Empirical studies prove that the majority of founders of born globals have work experience in globally operating firms.

In the **process before the act of foundation**, the founders have to develop a joint consensual area between themselves and with the most important stakeholders. They have to develop a shared imagination of the firm that will be enacted. They have to define the purpose, objectives, value-added processes, structures, identity, boundaries, and intended structural couplings with other actors, usually documented in a business plan. Only with a shared construct it is possible to put such a new firm into being. The resulting **meaning system** has to be complemented by an **action system** in order to form a social system. In a recursive process, the intended system is put into action. It is typical that the implementation of the generated meaning system by action is not a smooth process. Usually, there are **dramatic adaptations** of the meaning system when action provides feedback from the environment. The **evolutionary motor** of variation and selective retention is **extremely active** both internally (new ideas, concepts, solutions) and externally (changing partners, relations, maybe even '*death*' of the new venture). Studies about the liability of newness (externally) and continuous morphing (internally) confirm the **high rate of transformation in the founding process**. The implementation of the meaning system on the activity level is termed '*imprinting*', producing the initial structures, processes, and routines of the new firm. With the constitution of the new firm in economic reality, the autopoietic reproduction of the new social system begins. Action provides feedback in the form of meaning, providing variety to the meaning system, which is processed, selected, and retained in a process of learning. New expectations are formed, providing momentum to further actions and decisions. *The recursive interplay of action and meaning processing is set in motion.*

Local start-up firms implement their action system only in the **local context**, providing the meaning system only with feedback in the national context. **Meaning and activity structures** *are national and* **culture-bound**. Any international element is new and appears to be '*foreign*'. Even existing meaning, for example about the firm's value-added processes and its products is culture-bound. With the beginning of international interaction (internationalisation), each meaning item has to be translated and adapted to the new context. Therefore, internationalisation is such a tremendous step in the initial phases as even items like documentation and information for clients have to be translated to the international context.

Born globals start this **recursive reproduction of meaning and action** on **global level right from the start** as the founders instil the social system with their individual global knowledge, experience, and relations. These are part of the founding capital and the resource base. The enacted meaning system is global right from the start. The same applies to the **enacted global environment**, which also allows for an implementation of the action system on the global level. The new venture can generate globally generalised as well as locally adapted subsystems of meaning and action, thus fuelling a globally differentiated process. There is no implicit process in which the national and the '*other*' or the '*foreign*' have to converge in a long process – many large MNEs are still nationally dominated – but a consistent global evolution from the start. Nonetheless it should be stressed that even many of the born globals described in literature internationalised rapidly but were not founded globally.

Born globals may exploit their advantage of being **embedded in different local networks**. They have **access** to local, particularly implicit knowledge, social capital, and network relations. The local contexts provide a **huge amount of variety**, fuelling innovation and globally differentiated learning processes. Compared to '*traditional internationalisers*', born globals may be expected to dispose of a **greater innovative capacity** and **transformational flexibility**. A **globally differentiated learning process** drives born globals from the start (and even before). The learning process is provided with a global variety of impulses, regulated by globally differentiated selectors and may diffuse positively selected products and routines across globally dispersed markets.

6.2.1.2 Foundation of networks

Interorganisational networks may be termed **'third-level' social systems**, as they are founded by organisations, which are based on first- and second-level social systems. Interorganisational networks generally are **more loosely coupled** than organisations, which are characterised by strong identities and boundaries based on strong formal regulation concerning membership and ownership. Interorganisational networks therefore are by definition formed on the basis of co-operative relations between independent organisations. They are formed by organisations already in place and thus are easier to put into action but similarly easier to disband, thus inducing a much weaker coherence and stability. Therefore, **interorganisational networks** develop such a **lower level of autopoietic organisation than organisations**. On the contrary, (1) **strategic networks** are usually formed for the pursuit of specific goals and consequently subject to allopoietic organisation and rational planning, (2) **industrial networks** are linked by existing interdependencies resulting from industry structure, thus exposing relations but no organisation in the strict sense, and (3) **local networks** are bound by sharing a joint *social milieu* without providing a uniting organisation and identity.

However, interorganisational networks expose elements of evolutionary reproduction. **Industrial networks** develop some form of co-specialisation and the system of production as a whole is reproduced though individual firms may be substituted, added, or eliminated from the network. Industrial networks develop an **underlying meaning structure** in terms of '**industry recipes**' and a shared view of what business the network is in and how the co-specialisation basically works. Both meaning and activity structures are reproduced on a broad level. This reproduction is more characterised by technological path-dependence than by deliberate reproduction. Reproduction on industry level is more autopoietic than allopoietic.

Strategic networks are intended constructions of organisations in order to pursue defined objectives by co-specialisation. The reproduction thus is primarily allopoietic though autopoietic traits emerge, e.g. by developing consensual domains, common codes, and expectations. Once in place, even joint ventures may be established, providing a stronger structural coupling between the partners.

Like an industrial network, a **local network** is not the result of purposive action. Rather, it emerges incrementally and is more defined by social embeddedness than by intended, explicit co-operation. On the level of the social milieus, reproduction is basically autopoietic with regard to symbiotic relations and social traits. Co-specialisation is the result of an incremental co-evolutionary process and thus does not even need much allopoietic organisation in order to continue. This may be different in the case of internationalisation of the local network, when more intentionally co-ordinated behaviour among organisations becomes vital.

Industrial and local networks emerge from **autopoietical processes** rather than from rational, intended action on behalf of social actors. Exceptions may be dominant firms capable to '*invent*' an industry or national and local governments that try to build industrial districts from a blueprint. While industrial and local networks generally emerge from historical processes of technological path-dependencies or the evolution of local social milieus, respectively,

strategic networks may be **founded intentionally**. The foundation of a strategic network may be described by using a **three-stage model** (Baum/Ingram 2002: 197-205) describing the dynamics of network organisations, i.e. the emergence, spread, and institutionalisation of network organisations:

Phase 1:   Firm-level embedding
When two actors perceive their activities as being interdependent, they are inclined to start an exchange with each other. Subsequently, they learn about each other's capabilities and needs. As they learn, they utilise and strengthen the interdependencies of their activities. It is resulting in a circular causality between activity interdependencies and exchange relations. These are embedded in other relations of the wider web of industrial activities performed in the network (Håkansson/Johansson 1993: 40). Firm-level embedding may be differentiated into a structural and a cognitive perspective.

Firm-level structural embedding comprises relational and third-party embedding. Relational embedding highlights effects of dyadic ties between firms on subsequent co-operation between them (Gulati/Gargiulo 1999). Third-party embeddedness incorporates the local structure of partners' relations around firms and their tendency to co-operate with one another (Granovetter 1985).

Firm-level cognitive embedding occurs in the form of routinisation. Organisational routines are socially constructed programs of action that embody the knowledge, capabilities, beliefs, values, and memory of the organisation and the decision-makers. They are products of a process of incremental updating of routines based on the interpretation of experience, and the short-run focus of organisational decision-making and action. Organisational routines both enable and constrain organisational action by conserving the cognitive capabilities of decision makers and by limiting and channelling political conflict. Action encoded in routines is thus more likely to be attended to and accepted by organisational decision-makers (Baum/Ingram 2002: 198).

Phase 2:   Network-level embedding
Similar to firm-level embedding, a differentiation into a structural and a cognitive perspective may also be observed on the network level.

Network-level structural embedding comprises the position in the network and the formation of cliques. Interfirm networks are the evolutionary outcome of structurally and cognitively embedded organisational action in which relations are increasingly embedded in the very same network that shaped the organisational decisions to create them. This dynamic between organisational action and network structure that results from that action drives a progressive structural differentiation of the interfirm network. **Structural differentiation** refers to the extent to which firms in a network occupy an identifiable set of self-reproducing network positions characterised by distinct relational profiles. **Positional embeddedness** captures the impact of the positions firms occupy in the overall structure on their decisions about co-operative ties. Status flows through interconnections between firms. Ties to higher-status firms enhance one's own status, while ties to lower-status firms detract from it (Baum/Ingram 2002: 200). In addition to self-reproducing firms' positions, self-reproducing cliques of repeatedly co-operating sets of firms – network organisations – also emerge as embedded organisational action increasingly reinforces repeated ties among firms (Ibid. 201)

Network-level cognitive embedding refers to mental models and interorganisational imitation. When a particular mental model becomes shared by decision-makers from several firms, the joint focus of these firms' decision-makers on each other creates a market in which firms are engaged in reciprocal monitoring and mutual adjustments. Mental models are defined by firms' decision-makers and are sustained through a self-reinforcing reciprocal process of cognition and enactment through which firms' decision-makers both respond to and create their environments. Convergence on a shared mental model institutionalises behaviour among competing firms by creating common beliefs about the meaning and appropriateness of organisational structures, practices, strategies, actions, and networks of relations. This facilitates interorganisational imitation by enabling firms' decision-makers to interpret and give meaning to information about other firms and their behaviour (Ibid. 201-202).

Phase 3: Network organisation: performance feedback and group selection.

Once performance differentials appear around network organisations and become salient, these differentials may provoke firms' decision-makers to rethink and alter their pattern of interfirm relationship. Patterns of interdependence among firms initiate patterns of relational and third-party embeddedness among firms. If **patterns of interfirm interdependence** remain stable, relational, and third-party embeddedness take over as dynamics, driving a progressive structural differentiation that shapes positional embeddedness, the status of the firms occupying the positions, and the formation of repeatedly co-operative cliques, or network organisations. As **interorganisational relations** proliferate, interorganisational knowledge created through firms' mutual monitoring and interaction institutionalises the network organisational form as a shared mental model, and provides a further impetus for imitative partnering. The emergent structure of the network, positions of firms, and network organisations within it will tend to remain stable, reproduced over time through embedded interfirm interactions unless salient performance differences emerge among competing network organisations.

Then, decision-makers may revisit their network organisation models, renewing their focus on interdependence considerations, engendering firm-level efforts to reconfigure interorganisational networks, and a reshaping of network organisations (Ibid. 204-205).

Foundation of global networks

The **formation of industrial networks** basically depends on the dominating characteristics of the industry. For example, **local industries** may emerge and develop basically independently of global interdependencies, while particularly many new industries of highly complex and specialised products are global from inception – basically for the same reasons as their counterparts on the organisation level, i.e. the born globals. In **global industries**, MNEs generally try to develop activities in all major markets and in all regions providing location advantages in the acquisition of resources and particularly knowledge. In addition, co-operations among MNE-units and internationalising SMEs increase the density of network relations, further fuelling the liquefaction of competition in global industries.

The trend of **networking and co-specialisation on global scale** also leads to an increasing **bridging of local networks**. This process is usually not a joint effort of the network as a whole but the result of the activities of global players. For example, a firm in the photonics industry of the Boston Area may invest in a subsidiary in Eastern Germany, where it may find a region with substantial know-how in optical and photo technology, which may be an important source of innovation and complementary capabilities. Globalisation of local networks therefore is generally an emergent phenomenon based on the efforts of individual firms rather of concerted action on network level. Local networks as a loosely coupled social system do not pursue the formation of global networks, as they do not have the properties of a social actor due to a missing organisation and identity of the '*whole*'.

Strategic networks are very prominent instruments for the pursuit of objectives on global scale. Particularly the complexity of the global environment and the amount of resources necessary to internalise global activities often even impede a '*go it alone*' perspective. For SMEs, strategic networks offer access to global markets and to complementary resources. SMEs may act globally by co-specialisation. **Strategic networks** and **network-building** in general increasingly represents a **distinct form of internationalisation**. For **MNEs**, strategic networks offer **access** to globally dispersed knowledge and markets, the possibility of flexibilisation, risk reduction, collusion, and the financing of resource-intensive projects. On the **global level**, the development of strategic networks is heavily dependent on **intercultural skills** and the **development of consensual domains**. As shown in Chapter 5, particular expectations as well as communication and learning styles may differ significantly between cultures so that a parallelisation in these properties is a basic condition for the creation of a win-win situation.

6.2.2 Internationalisation

Similar to the foundation process, internationalisation may be observed on **firm and network level**. As discussed in Chapter 3, both levels are intertwined, as network building may be an important lever in the internationalisation process of a firm. However, internationalisation processes of and in interorganisational networks did not receive considerable attention in literature.

6.2.2.1 Internationalisation of firms

Internationalisation indicates processes that lead to a **change in the geographical and cultural extension of the firm's meaning and action system**. It includes forward and backward processes of de- and re-internationalisation. These processes drive both traditional internationalisers and born globals as they change their extension in their reproduction. The momentum in the internationalisation processes is instilled by external environmental changes as well as by the dynamics provided by the pursuit of motives and objectives of the stakeholders. In the firm trajectory, the meaning structure influences actions, which induces changes in the resource configuration and activity system. The resulting changes provide momentum for further variation and adaptation in the meaning system. In the course of increasing extension, the focus changes from geographical expansion to the leverage of dispersed resources. Studies by Schulte (2002) and Borghoff/Schulte (2003) provide evidence that the **internationalisation process of SMEs** is often characterised by **asymmetries between the 'internationalisation' of the meaning system and of the action system**.

For example, there are many SMEs entering international markets more or less '*by accident*' as global clients demand their products or even co-operation. A second reason may be the emergent and more or less casual decision of the owner-manager to invest in a country due to personal contacts or preferences. In such instances, activity structures are built without the requisite knowledge, experience, and analysis necessary for a reasonable decision and activity. Such activities may be successful when the actors '*learn to swim*' rapidly or find a capable local manager. If not, they may lead to unexpected failures due to missing context knowledge, resulting in de-internationalisation and often even pathological consequences with regard to further international activities. On the other extreme, SMEs may prefer an extensive preparation for the first internationalisation steps, including extensive information gathering and analysis. Such firms may end up puzzled and incapable to decide due to extensive complexity and thus frustrated with the complications and resource-intensiveness associated with internationalisation. The result may be extensive internationalisation knowledge, which may become pathological, as it does not enter the recursive interplay with action. In both cases, (1) **action without knowledge**, and (2) **knowledge without action**, firms may not achieve the development of an effective evolutionary interplay between meaning and action level on global scale. An early closing of the meaning/action cycle on international level seems to be a central demand in internationalisation in order to create viable autopoietic subsystems in this context.

The **process of internationalisation** thus is characterised by the **geographical and cultural extension on the meaning and action level of the firm**. At the same time, the evolution of an individual firm is *embedded in the evolution of its respective environment*, i.e. the competition, which itself is driven by the pace of globalisation. Firms and their environments find themselves in a co-evolutionary interplay that is marked by processes of differentiation and integration, which are reinforced by the decreasing rigidity of boundaries. This process leads to an expanding and intensifying **network-competition**. Firms have to cope with their **structural couplings** on the level of all their organisational units. The **global differentiation** of activities leads to an **exponential increase in different contextual demands** so that a firm has to develop the **requisite variety** and **resonance capacity**.

In order to exemplify the globalisation process of a firm, **three key characteristics of a firm's globalisation process** are reflected in a **three-stage model** (Figure 6-5). The *first stage* represents the start as a national company that in a *second stage* builds up individual business activities in the international context, which are increasingly embedded in global network relations in the *third stage*. The observation of this process from a systemic perspective can be ensured by the **conceptualisation of organisations** and **organisational units** as **social systems** with structural and functional (processual) properties, which are evolving in an **interplay** with their internal and external **environments**. In order to observe the co-evolution of different systems and their environment, a conceptualisation of system properties has to be developed. **Each social system** must consist of the **same basic properties** to ensure a consistent observation of their respective evolution. The **principle of self-similarity** ensures a consistent conceptualisation of social (sub-)systems. This is also necessary to describe evolutionary changes and innovations, their institutionalisation, and their diffusion via **structural coupling** (isomorphism). Globalisation thus can be described as the co-evolutionary process of differentiation and integration of social systems, their environment, and their (social) subsystems. For reasons of comparability of in reality very different systems, the broadest common ground has to be developed for a characterisation of social systems. In order to describe the evolution of firms, these are conceptualised as social systems. **Firms**, other **organisations**, as well as the respective **organisational subunits** (subsidiaries, departments, and job position) are all **conceptualised as 'organisational units'** with the same (self-similar) general **properties** fundamental to an evolutionary perspective. These properties are:

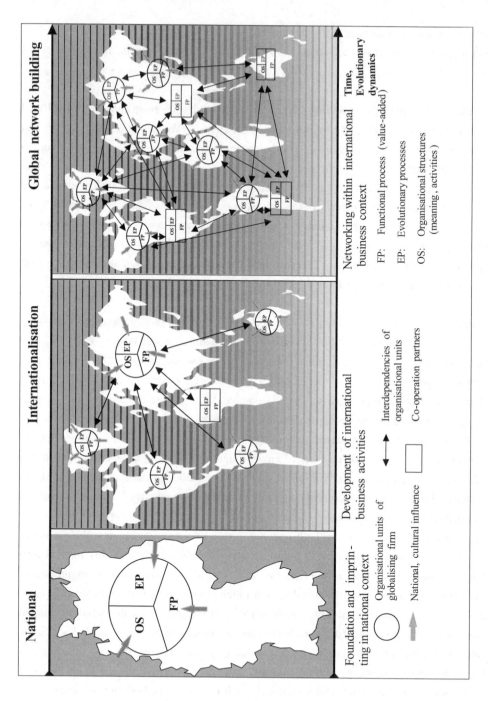

Figure 6-5: Globalisation process of a firm

☞ **Functional processes (FP)**

Functional processes include the **execution** and the **regulation** of the necessary activities to produce the unit's product or service. They serve to pursue the **instrumental purpose** and the specific goals of the firm. Each organisational unit is primarily characterised by a functional task it has to do. In firms, these tasks may be generally termed '**value-added activities**'. This may be the production of products or services on the level of the whole firm or business unit, the development of strategic alternatives in case of a planning staff or the calculation of deferred payments in the case of an individual job position in a controlling department. Functional processes constitute the basis for interdependencies between organisational units (internal and external). **Functional processes** also include **regulatory processes** to organise, plan, and control the primary processes within and across units. This seems clear on higher organisational levels, but even on the level of individual job positions this happens in form of self-regulation, e.g. in individual work organisation. In the context of internationalisation, functional processes may be differentiated on the global level. There may be a process of co-specialisation or of mere reproduction into new contexts. Due to different environmental conditions (e.g. technologies, values, or legislation), both the primary processes of production and the regulatory processes may have to be adapted and integrated across the different local contexts.

☞ **Evolutionary processes (EP)**

Evolutionary processes constitute the autopoietic organisation of a firm. These processes drive the **reproduction** and **transformation** of the firm on system and subsystem level. Evolutionary processes are those processes, which produce **changes in the meaning and action structure**, both **intended** and **unintended**. Decision-making processes within and across units basically drive intended evolutionary processes. Unintended processes may be stimulated by the interpenetration with the system's environment or by emergent internal variations. Firms are also subject to dialectical forces, which induce continuous or discontinuous morphing. On a fundamental level, the continuous processing of guiding differences by the constituting psychic and social systems drives the evolution of the meaning system. On balance, however, evolutionary processes are all processes, which drive the process of differentiation and integration of the firm. In the context of internationalisation, the evolutionary processes are subject to a quantum leap as they have to be extended to other contexts and to integrate new types of processing from these contexts. For example, a mutual adaptation of decision-making is necessary to facilitate a symbiotic co-evolution. In addition, due to the '*dual character of structure*' (Giddens 1984), the transformation of the processes themselves develops in a recursive interplay with the global transformation of the organisational structure.

☞ **Organisation structure (OS)**

The organisation structure can be differentiated into a **meaning structure** and an **activity structure**. It has been argued that internationalisation can begin at both levels. Due to the diffusion of global information by global media and due to travelling, it may be assumed that the meaning system of the firm contains global elements as it is enriched by the interpenetration with its individual members. Before internationalisation sets in, however, the firm may not dispose of own, autopoietic, firm-specific global knowledge. **Internationalisation** thus may be conceived as an act of **entrepreneurship** as the development of global meaning and activity structures begin from the start. In this process, (1) consensual domains have to be developed across internal actors and with actors in foreign local environments, and (2) these consensual domains on meaning level have to be implemented as structural coupling on the action level in order to constitute autopoietic reproduction. Once the autopoietic reproduction begins on international level, the recursive reproduction of meaning and activity structure in the global context sets in.

> *Functional processes, evolutionary processes, and organisation structures are the constituting properties of social systems. These properties and the relations between the (sub-)systems are evolving in a co-evolutionary interplay of differentiation and integration on a global basis.*

While **born globals** start their evolution directly on the **global level** (third stage in Figure 6-5), the by far **largest part of new ventures** begins on the **local or national level**. In the first stage, the imprinting during the foundation and national positioning of these firms is characterised by the culture of the home country. Studies of start-up firms by Welge/Borghoff (2000) and Borghoff/Welge (2003) show how national start-ups first constitute their autopoiesis and develop their identity and competitive positioning within the local context. Personal networking, a very dynamic development of consensual domains and dynamic morphing are key characteristics during this stage. After some time of stabilisation, a part of the new ventures begins the internationalisation stage illustrated by Figure 6-5, while others keep focused on the national market.

Those firms that begin the process of internationalisation increasingly internalise national and cultural boundaries. Firm boundaries are further blurred by international co-operations. As **internationalisation** is an **entrepreneurial process**, it provides a **large amount of variations on the meaning and the action level**. Internationalisation as a **process of global differentiation** thus provides the **basis for the selection forces in globalising firms**. Internal selection pressures arise from the increasing scale, growing complexity, and internal diversity, and intensifying co-ordination requirements that accompany international expansion (Westney/Zaheer 2001: 351). The range of meanings, activities, and globally differentiated structural coupling provides a huge input for selection processes. A main task in the course of globalisation is the development of the **requisite variety** in the **processing of global complexity**. This applies to processes of innovation, decision-making, and to processes of implementation and diffusion of selected options.

Systemic differentiation and integration processes induce the need for **mutual adaptation processes** because of **structural coupling** between (sub-) systems, described as **isomorphism** in institutionalisation theory. The **entry-mode choice** is influenced by the host country institutional environment and the internal institutional environment, which crystallises in the process of internationalisation. The primary channel by which the internal institutional environment can influence entry mode choice is **intraorganisational imprinting** (Lu 2002: 22). Firms may prefer high control modes of market entry by establishing wholly-owned subsidiaries, thus increasing the ability to co-ordinate activities and strategies across dispersed units and, thereby, reinforce **internal isomorphism**. Isomorphism may be enforced on the meaning level by means of communication and socialisation or on the activity level by diffusing best practices and technology. Initial imprinting causing a '*mirror-effect*' of new subsidiaries is the strongest means to enforce internal isomorphism. Firms may also prefer low-control modes of market entry. The focus here is not on the creation of a strong internal isomorphism and control but on a symbiotic relation with foreign environments. This presupposes the development of consensual domains with individuals and social systems within and across local contexts. Internationalisation from this perspective is based on the **co-evolution in multi-layered global and local contexts**.

A study on structural inertia, imitation, and foreign expansion of South Korean firms and business groups in China by Guillén (2002: 521) shows that business group experience and imitation among firms from the same home-country industry increase the rate of foreign expansion. Industry imitation effects tend to decrease after a firm makes its first foreign entry. An internationalising firm may obtain information and legitimacy from interacting with other firms in its home country environment. Those interactions enable the firm to identify foreign opportunities, build the knowledge necessary to pursue them, tackle internal and external resistance, and feel confident of being able to compete against domestic firms familiar with the local environment in the host country. By learning from each other's foreign experiences, firms reduce the uncertainty surrounding foreign expansion and enhance legitimacy of pursuing international opportunities (Ibid. 510).

Focusing on the underlying dynamics of the globalisation process of firms, literature on organisational transformation shows that the necessary adaptations are not entirely implemented on an incremental basis. **Evolutionary tensions** between organisational units and their environment are often accumulated because of organisational inertia. This leads to **'quantum leaps' of organisational change** (Miller/Friesen 1980, Kutschker 1996, Macharzina/Engelhard 1991). Not only tensions but also the involuntary decay of organisational relations can result from evolutionary changes. Particularly in the **global context** this might happen because of **lacking transparency and commensurability between globally dispersed systems.**

6.2.2.2 Internationalisation of networks

The **liquefaction of global competition** both drives and is driven by increasing interdependencies and network formation. It is astonishing, though, that in contrast to the formation of strategic networks on global level, the internationalisation of already existing local or national networks still did not receive considerable explicit attention. Nonetheless, there is evidence of its significance on different levels.

Locally founded firms first develop their organisation and network embeddedness in the local context. This process leads to the development of **network positions within local networks** and/or **industrial and strategic networks on the national level**. Internationalisation thus may be focused not only on the internationalisation of individual firms but also on the **internationalisation of such nationally bounded networks**. For example, a study of 19 industrial districts in Italy by Corò/Grandinetti (1999: 117) provided evidence of a key transformation in all observed districts. The traditionally rather closed local networks are all opening-up and increasingly relating with external holders of knowledge and resources. It is helpful in outlining the idea of local not on the basis of a rigid dichotomy between local (district) enterprises and non-local enterprises (MNEs), but between different forms and intensities of embeddedness (Varaldo 1995: 28):

1. For the **district enterprise**, *embeddedness will be natural* (connected to its entire life cycle), totalising (involving the entire network of its articulations, knowledge, and culture) and thus dependent on local external economies.
2. For the **MNE**, it will assume a *planned character* (strategic choice), selective, and interdependent (on global network level).

As reflected by the liquefaction of competition, both large and small enterprises are in a process of **'double convergence'** (Conti 1997: 24). Growing environmental complexity induces both SMEs and MNEs to search different styles of behaviour (in time and space), aimed at constructing more effective interactive relations, both with other firms and with the relevant socio-cultural context. In global competition, diversity becomes the basis of competitive advantage and the instrument for the production of economic value (Conti 1995: 3-4). The most effective management of local resources occurs through culturally decentralised organisation, capable of interacting and co-evolving with the local environment. **Key capabilities in the network environment** are what Asanuma (1989) calls '**relation-specific skills**'. They constitute a key economic basis of external accumulation of know-how in these networks. **Agglomerated learning capability** becomes a condition for both dominating the relevant global economic networks and securing the **cumulative industrial development** of the 'home base', by attracting and supporting the best quality domestic and overseas firms (Amin/Thrift 1995: 275). Industrial districts can thus be sustained as '**learning regions**'. Traditional contextual knowledge and the codified knowledge of the global economy may thus be integrated in a framework of territorially embedded regional systems of innovation. Such learning regions are supposed to be in a much better position than traditional industrial districts to avoid a '*lock-in*' of development caused by localised path-dependence (Asheim 1997: 165-166). Porter/Stern (2001: 29) stress the importance of the common innovation infrastructure and especially of the cluster-specific environment for innovation in core industries of an economic region.

Chapter 3 also provided evidence that **local or national networks of SMEs** already established on local or national scale may provide the drive and means towards **co-specialised** or **co-financed internationalisation**, e.g. by establishing a joint production site or by sharing sales representatives and facilities. On balance, the internationalisation of networks is an under-researched field that may be worth more attention.

6.2.3 Global network capability

The global network capability may be differentiated in two levels. Intrasystemic networking comprises all networking efforts within a system, i.e. across the system's subunits. Intersystemic networking applies to the interorganisational level and thus to co-operations and external networks.

6.2.3.1 Intrasystemic networking

With increasing internationalisation, the degree of dispersion and differentiation of the firm's meaning and activity structure increases. Each **new activity or unit created in the internationalisation process** calls for its **integration into the firm's existing context**. Interdependencies with existing structures have to be analysed and organised. The firm has to import and develop the requisite '*organised complexity*' in order to secure a balanced and coherent evolution in the global context. With increasing differentiation the need for integration increases as well. The guiding difference '**differentiation vs. integration**' provides the system with **dynamics** as one of the two elements changes. In a dynamic view, a change in one direction induces a change in the other direction in a recursive interplay, thus instilling the system with dynamics. This recursive interplay of system constituting differences must be conceived as constitutive for the development of organised complexity as it means nothing more than complexity with selective relations among its elements (Luhmann 1995: 20, 24).

A critical consequence in globalisation processes is the creation and reproduction of **organised complexity across the differentiated units** formed in the course of internationalisation. The focus in business organisations with globally dispersed units therefore is on the relational structure among these units, or, in other terms, the internal network of relations among the units and the external network of relations with the organised environment. The differentiated global context provides an immense complexity. Firms have to develop the capacity for the dynamic selection and design of their networks of relations or, in terms of systems theory, their self-complexity.

While **internationalisation** is basically a process of **differentiation on global level**, **global networking** is a process of **integration** of systems and subsystems. There is both an intrasystemic or intraorganisational level and an intersystemic or interorganisational level. On the intrasystemic level, networking is organised on multiple levels, from the level of the '*whole*' to the level of the '*parts*' or subsystems, which in firms are organisational units. Organisational units may appear as actors. **Networking** comprises the development and reproduction of relations and interaction patterns among the constituting subsystems of a system. It comprises the intentional design of interdependencies and their organisation.

The process of **internationalisation** provides the meaning and activity structure of system with **global variety**. **Global networking** integrates the new elements in the path-dependent meaning and activity structure and allows for the **creation of organised global complexity**. Internationalisation provides new elements on the global level, while global networking integrates them in the ongoing reproduction. As networks of individuals and social systems are themselves social systems, the analytical toolkit provided by network analysis may serve to analyse the relational structure of social systems. Network analysis may be applied from the level of the individual to the level of inter-organisational network due to the principle of self-similarity. Other network theories may be applied according to their level of observation.

Networking has to provide and to sustain basic systemic properties. The relational networks among the subunits have to be linked by *structural coupling*. *Interdependencies* between subunits are established by *interaction patterns*, which provide the means for the reproduction of communication and actions. *Structural coupling* is facilitated by the *interpenetration of subunits on the basis of meaning*. A basic condition for the integration of subunits is the *development of consensual domains*. Shared structures of meaning, expectations, and activities allow for a co-evolution of the subunits.

In its **process of globalisation**, a social system has to develop the *capability for structural coupling, interpenetration, and consensual domains on the global level*. The basic means to facilitate the effective development of interpenetration, structural coupling, meaning structures, and consensual domains is communication. The **co-evolution of globally differentiated subsystems and local contexts** may be facilitated by the development of *isomorphic structures, loose coupling, and particularly a requisite amount of communication*. A basic **obstacle** to complex global systems like firms or networks is that *communicative structures* such as interpersonal relationships, chains-of-command, and exchange networks *only survive through constant use*. Social reproduction is even more difficult in the case of global systems because it must be accomplished across national frontiers and cultural differences. In a system operating across many national borders with a variety of loosely coupled subsystems (e.g. subsidiaries), a large amount of resources may have to be devoted to keeping routines and other structured behaviours reliable. **Stability and equilibrium in global systems** therefore is **problematic**: it is likely to be under continual challenge as subsystems are founded in new cultures and as worldwide staff becomes increasingly diverse.

On the **meaning level**, the system has to develop the linguistic and interpretational basis in order to facilitate interpenetration of subsystems. As interpenetration is the capability of a system to instil another system with its own complexity, in social systems it depends on the capability to instil other social systems with meaning. There are three **basic conditions for viable interpenetration**:

1. The subunits need a *common platform for communication*, i.e. a common language and other necessary codes of communication, such as norms or standards. In international business, the standard language is English but may vary between regions. International standards such as those of the International Standardisation Organisation (ISO) or the International Accounting Standards (IAS) facilitate the exchange of information and create transparency and comparability.
2. The subunits need the *mutual background knowledge* in order develop adequate interpretations. A basic obstacle for globally operating firms is that there are potential differences between knowledge of the rules and tactics of practical conduct in the local context of an actor and knowledge about those, which apply in contexts remote from the actor's experience (Giddens 1984: 90-91). The diversity of interpretations and be-

haviours can even lead to unanticipated organisational conflict. The (re-) production of organisation-wide meaning may be difficult to achieve due to diverse cultural premises (Kilduff 1993: 269, 271).

3. The subunits need the *communicative skills and capabilities* in order to facilitate continuous communication. Such skills may be developed cumulatively by experience or by intercultural training of the actors. In addition, rich communication media and agreed upon standards of communication may increase the efficiency of communication.

In addition to the *communicative capability*, the **capability for structural coupling** further presupposes the *technological capabilities and skills* that are necessary to facilitate mutual interaction. The use of basically different technologies or resources may impart recurrent interaction. With an increasing degree of globalisation, the amount and variety of local contexts rises so that the intensity of possible interaction with some subunits may be quite limited. In addition, organising logics vary substantially in different social milieus (Biggart/Guillén 1999:725). **MNEs** try to increase the capability of structural coupling by *standardisation, diffusion of best practices,* and the *definition of core activities,* which allow for *efficient co-specialisation*. In this context, the exploration and exploitation of global synergies is an important aspect of the capability of structural coupling (Achenbach/Borghoff 2004).

Structural coupling generates **isomorphic forces**, which lead to the development of isomorphic structures internally among subsystems and externally between subsystems and the respective environment. For example, **MNE subsidiaries** participate in two organisational fields, one defined by the MNE network of which they are part and one defined by the host country environment. Therefore, subsidiaries of MNEs face **dual pressures** from the local institutional environment and the MNE network. Internally, pressures for isomorphism may emerge through attempts to transfer best practices. The local context may influence how MNEs' management practices transfer across business systems and with what outcomes (Sharpe 2001: 196). Subsidiaries are not only concerned with establishing legitimacy with both the external host country institutional environment and the internal environment of the MNE, but also may find it difficult to reconcile these two institutional pressures (Kostova/Roth 2002: 220). **MNEs as a whole** confront a **multitude** of different and possibly conflicting **institutional pressures** and have to develop **globally differentiated and multi-layered institutional structures** that allow for both internal and external structural coupling.

Structural coupling facilitates the development of similar organisational structures and processes. This '*mirror effect*' is caused, as the **MNE organisation** is a **source of strong isomorphic pulls** toward similarity between organisational units. These isomorphic pulls may be both emergent due to the strong internal isomorphic forces resulting from interdependencies or a matter of conscious choice or imposition, e.g. by imprinting the mirror effect at the foundation of a new subsidiary. The establishment of foreign subsidiaries often follows a process of **replication**, as organisations enact existing routines and standard operating procedures when setting up new operations. From this perspective, Kogut (1993: 137) contends that FDI embodies the **extension of organising principles across borders**.

The **basis for consensual domains** is provided by a **successful interpenetration**. Globally dispersed subunits have to develop shared knowledge structures, interpretational patterns, and structures of expectations in order to stabilise the co-evolutionary process and to develop coordinated and directed action. In the **global context**, the development of **commensurable interpretations and expectations** is much more difficult due to different **cultural and geographical contexts**. It can be facilitated by rich communication patterns allowing for the communication of explicit and implicit meaning. The latter may also be enhanced by socialisation processes or personal contacts in general. An important aspect in the development of consistent expectations is the design of **decision-making processes** as these make expectations explicit and ready for implementation. The participation of all units concerned by intended actions into the decision-making process in a form that is perceived as '*procedurally just*' may enhance the acceptance and efforts of participating units (Kim/Mauborgne 1993).

6.2.3.2 Intersystemic networking

Globalising systems enter new contexts and have to develop **relations with local partners**. This requires the development of interpenetration, structural coupling, and consensual domains with the new partners. The conditions and problems, which may arise, are the same as for the development in the intraorganisational context. However, there are big differences in the actual achievement as there are **no hierarchical means to promote the coupling of units**. On the contrary, there are even **more obstacles** to the development of co-evolutionary relations due to *different competitive behaviour, business practices* or *legislature*. Therefore, it may be much more difficult to develop mutual certainty and trust than within a hierarchy or among co-operation partners in a culturally homogeneous context. While investments in a common *social 'hard- and software'* are much more common in hierarchical contexts, the loose coupling between global co-operation partners may produce obstacles in the development of the partnership. For example, partners may not be willing to invest in the qualification of employees or in the development of an informational infrastructure. **Global networks** therefore may need much **more commitment by the partners** in order to be built and reproduced.

Interpenetration may be impaired by *differences in language, interpretation or communicative style*. It may be further affected by mutual prejudices, fears, and missing trust and background knowledge. **Structural coupling** may be additionally degraded by *different technological standards or resource bases*. Literature on knowledge and internationalisation has shown that the transfer of complex technological knowledge is very difficult in the global context and usually internalised. Therefore, MNE activity has been concentrated in the more technologically progressive industries with higher rates of R&D and where technology transfer poses greater difficulties (Williamson 1985: 296). Of course, this presupposes effective and efficient **globalisation capabilities of the MNEs**.

Globally operating firms have to cope with **multiple and diverse consensual domains** on *different geographical* and *business-oriented levels*. Such firms have to develop their consensual domains in an evolutionary interplay with their respective local and business environments while maintaining an integrating and overlapping consensual domain vis-à-vis their global internal and external environment as a whole. Like the system itself, consensual domains may form nested hierarchies, with basic structures being similar across all units but exposing isomorphism also with the social environment of the respective unit's local context. Thus, interpenetration and structural coupling both on local and on system level may be achieved.

The **external linkages** of the globally dispersed subsystems are associated with specific pressures for similarity or **isomorphic pulls**. The various pulls arising from the multiple external networks may be **complementary** or **conflicting** and may have a varying degree of consistency with the firm's existing **administrative heritage**. The pressures exerted from multiple networks span all relevant actors in the firm's networks, thus exerting pressures at multiple geographic levels. The multiple network challenge consists of responding appropriately to pulls exerted by multiple actors at multiple geographic levels on the dispersed subsystems.

As an example of **strategic options** for the handling of **globally differentiated isomorphic pulls**, Campbell/Verbeke (2001: 199) identify two distinct MNE responses in form of '*isomorphic flexibility*' and '*institutionalisation*'. **Isomorphic flexibility** implies the adaptation of internal processes to the pressures exerted by various external networks. This strategy implies the adaptation of the intraorganisational network to conform to the conflicting isomorphic pulls prevailing in the various organisational units. On the contrary, **institutionalisation** is based on efforts to actively change the external networks to conform to existing intraorganisational patterns and internal processes. For example, MNEs may cause mimetic or coercive isomorphism. They are key agents in the diffusion of practices across national borders because they transfer organisational techniques and standards to subsidiaries and to other organisations in the foreign host countries in which they operate.

6.2.4 Capability of global evolutionary dynamics

The evolutionary dynamics of social systems are evoked by the principle of differentiation and integration. The **process of globalisation** itself may be described as a *process extending the process of differentiation and integration of social systems to the global level*. In the context of globalisation, this **principle of social evolution** increasingly **extends to the global level** as (1) local systems internationalise, (2) global systems develop internal differentiated networks, (3) multiple social actors build co-operations and inter-organisational networks, (4) new social systems are founded with global scale from inception, and (5) communication and activity structures emerge on global scale. The **process of differentiation and integration in globalisation** is generally observed in terms of *'globalisation vs. localisation'* or *'global integration vs. local adaptation'* though these dualities only catch distinct aspects of globalisation. In general, the globalisation of the process of differentiation and integration of social systems induces an **exponential increase of complexity** by the number of different local contexts that become integrated. Each property and act of the system becomes subject to a myriad of possible interpretations, expectations, and modes of implementation under continuation of its unity and identity. The five motors of change evoke the dynamics of social systems. The description of these dynamics in globalisation will be described by using the five motors of change in social systems.

6.2.4.1 The life cycle motor

Life cycle mechanisms are underlying and dominating all **stage models of internationalisation**. All these models are based on the assumption that firms begin their internationalisation on the basis of an already established business in the home country. Depending on the individual model, internationalisation begins with pre-export activities or later with actual market entry. In a **sequence of several stages**, the internationalising firm then increases the scope and complexity of international activities. However, the sequential character of internationalisation processes has been widely criticised due to the increasing emergence of born globals, interorganisational networks, leapfrogging of stages, and outpacing strategies. Life cycle models therefore *loose their explanatory capacity* on the organisation level with *increasing environmental dynamic* and thus with *globalisation*.

Life cycle mechanisms may be *more meaningful* in case of more *specific properties of organisations* rather than the evolution of the whole system. For example, life cycles of products or technologies have been described successfully. In general, life cycle models are difficult to apply to globalisation, as it is a process generating new forms of social systems by differentiation and integration instead of reproducing stable forms of existing entities.

6.2.4.2 The teleological motor

Teleological mechanisms drive the '*unfolding*' of a system towards a desired or pre-defined end-state. For example, all **stage theories** also include teleological elements as the open-ended life cycle of **internationalisation** culminates in the **emergence of a multinational enterprise** as an **end state**. Internationalisation in stage theories generally ends with the acquisition of the MNE characteristic. Internationalisation from this perspective is a **teleological process** describing the **evolutionary path from a local SME to an MNE**.

Besides such an unfolding conceived as being inherent to the internationalisation process, teleological mechanisms particularly provide the **dynamics on the allopoietic level** of organisations as these are *founded in order to pursue the goals* (desired end-states) of the shareholders. On this level, individual stakeholders and decision-makers define the purpose, and specific goals of the system. From a political perspective, this process is characterised by both conflict and negotiation among the decision-makers about the definition of the desired end states. From a functional perspective, the process is characterised by **decision-making** under bounded rationality. Decision-makers define the system's goals, analyse the internal and external environment, develop strategies to achieve the stated goals, and implement the strategies on the action level. Decision-making hence defines all forms of **intended goal-directed action of the system**. All emergent meaning and behaviour of the system thus can neither be explained nor directed and controlled by decision-making. Decisions and intended behaviour can only be prepared and conducted on the basis of already available meaning and action structures.

It becomes apparent that **internationalisation** of the system implies the *exploration of new contexts,* thus *radically diminishing* the *potential of already existing decision-making capabilities*. Due to missing managerial capacity in terms of personnel, knowledge, and experiences the basis for intended actions is seriously limited. Internationalisation activities thus are characterised by a high degree of risk and uncertainty for the system. It is a main condition for the foundation of **born globals** that the founders dispose of the requisite global variety in their decision-making capability. Consequently, **traditional internationalisers**, as systems missing such requisite global variety in their meaning-, activity-, and decision-making structures have to begin a *learning process*, which is at the centre of stage models of internationalisation.

With increasing global differentiation and integration of the system, decision-making structures themselves are subject to this process. As **decision-making** itself fulfils the function of the **selection mechanism** in the system's evolution, initial decision-making structures manifest themselves as inertial forces. The **country-of-origin character of decision-making structures** therefore is typical for the first phase of internationalisation and often still imprinted in older MNEs. The **development of decision-making structures** capable of **balancing the dominating dualities** induced by **globalisation** is one of the *most critical constructions in the globalisation of the system*. For example, in terms of the Process School, the evasion of integrative decision-making is reflected in *multinational* structures, while a *globally centralised* structure reflects the evasion of globally differentiated decision-making mechanisms.

Bartlett/Ghoshal (1986) stress the importance of the formal organisational context and of **'context management'** in MNEs, which provide a structure of decision-making based on autopoietic self-organisation within a pre-defined allopoietic context within and across globally dispersed units. Due to processes of differentiation and integration of globally dispersed social systems, **globalisation** leads to an increase in the **complexity of decision-making**. On the firm level, individual firms are embedded in a competitive environment that is increasingly dense with regard to relations due to the **liquefaction of global competition**. The increasing number and dynamic of interdependencies induce more structural and strategic flexibility internally and externally. Consensual domains have to be constructed and adapted in a way that allows for flexible but consistent decision-making. Due to the liquefaction of competition, individual firms have to *'dynamise'* their properties and behaviours.

Decision-making in the traditional time-consuming mode of synoptic planning is increasingly complemented by directed and permanent **dynamic morphing**, thus *fusing strategy and organisation* in a more *symbiotic recursive interplay* than in the old *'structure follows strategy'* paradigm. Globally differentiated systems have **organisational 'regions'** with **different dynamics** due to different internal and external influences and logics, for example depending on products, markets, or technologies. A viable co-evolution of globally differentiated subsystems in globally differentiated contexts therefore becomes more a **process of dynamic 'co-organisation'** than of centralised or decentralised *synoptic decision-making*.

Decision-making as the **mechanism for intended evolution** becomes *highly differentiated in globally differentiated systems* – even more so as it has to take the other **emergent mechanisms of change** into account:

1. It has to evaluate the **influence of life cycles on different levels** such as products or technologies into account. The decision-making in globalising systems is itself subject to some kind of maturing, as initial personal leadership by the founders is complemented and later substituted by more complex forms of decision-making. Generally beginning with a home-based bias (with the notable exception of born globals), decision-making becomes increasingly differentiated in the globalising system. In contrast to life cycle models, though, one may speak of the formation of a global system and its decision-making mode rather than of a complete cycle. Once extended to the global level, decision-making is generally dominated by the principle of global differentiation and integration rather than by decay and death.

2. It has to identify the most influential **internal and external dialectics**, which instil the system with *underlying dynamics*. The most general dialectic in globalisation is global integration vs. local adaptation. A globally differentiated system has to develop the requisite variety and organised complexity to regulate power distribution and conflict internally and with the globally differentiated environment.

3. It is itself the intentional selector within the evolutionary mechanism of variation and selective retention and thus self-referential. As the intentional selection mechanism in social reproduction it also defines **how decision-making itself is reproduced**. Individuals and other social actors who contribute to decision-making thus also influence their own influence in the future while those who do not participate are only subject to such selections. Global differentiation of systems therefore calls for the global differentiation of decision-making also in its organisational manifestation in order to make itself more viable. *Decision-making has to reflect on itself* as only one component driving the dynamics in reproduction. Therefore, the **main task** from an evolutionary view is to **identify dynamics of the other mechanisms of change** because they are the *most influential objects of intentional action*. By definition, the non-teleological mechanisms cannot be directed or controlled but may be perturbed to work towards an intended direction, for example by changing organisational properties and processes.

4. **Decision-making** is the *mechanism* by which the *autopoietic social systems develop shared explicit expectations* and thus influences both the **meaning and the activity structure**. As a mode of meaning processing, *decision-making itself* is a process based on the **processing of meaning on the basis of guiding differences**. For example, the use of portfolios, scales, or similar techniques based on guiding differences in decision-making illustrates this mode. It also exemplifies the importance of the set of **guiding differences dominating decision-making** as they define the corridor of (1) what can be perceived, (2) what enters into decision-making, (3) how it is interpreted, and (4) which preferences will influence decisions. Strategic management literature provides a rich field of articles on '**strategic issue arrays**' (Dutton/Duncan 1987),

'**cognitive maps**' (Lei et al. 1996), and similar concepts. In addition, *decision-making is autopoietic as it reproduces itself*. First, on the action generating level of decision content, decisions already create the need for further decisions. Second, the structure of decision-making reproduces itself as well. Decision-makers thus have to be aware that they define themselves what enters decision-making and how decision-making works. They enact the environment, the domain, and the capacity for intentional reproduction of the system. In globally differentiated systems, the requisite variety in decision-making thus should reflect the complexity of the system. From a system perspective, the **requisite variety** may be developed by the **inclusion of globally differentiated meaning**, by global differentiation and integration of the process itself and of the constituting actors.

6.2.4.3 The dialectical motor

The whole discourse on the **phenomenon of globalisation** is dominated by the **dialectic of global integration vs. local adaptation**. The study of social systems already reproducing themselves on that level thus will be automatically strongly influenced by this dialectic. The dominance of this dialectic stems from the defining characteristic of globalisation itself, namely the extension of the formation and reproduction of social systems from the local to the global level. As exemplified by the example of Ghoshal, who applies this dialectic from the industry to the activity level, all properties and acts of **global or globalising social systems** thus may be observed and analysed from the **perspective of this basic dialectic**. In the realm of this dominating dialectic, there are also accompanying dialectics such as *centralisation vs. decentralisation* traditionally dominating the headquarters-subsidiary relations or *culture-free vs. culturalist* approaches in the realm of intercultural management. The dialectics distinctive for the phenomenon of globalisation itself emerge from the cultural and geographic differentiation of social systems from local to global levels.

At the **beginning of the internationalisation process**, the firm will be confronted with the basic dialectic of **home country vs. foreign**. Generally, internationalising firms are *eager to exert substantive power on subsidiaries abroad*. On the other hand, the lack of managerial resources and international experience of headquarters provides local managers with substantive advantages. In addition, **local managers** may dispose of **informational advantages** and **local network capital**, providing them with the **power of boundary-spanners** controlling environmental uncertainty. Foreign subsidiaries of MNEs dispose of a larger power basis than affiliates of purely national firms as the knowledge and control of contingencies increase their power. The capacity for uncertainty reduction has the greatest influence on the power of a subunit, may be assumed to be located primarily in boundary units, and is even augmented by the global dispersion of these units. As **foreign subsidiaries** have a **greater distance to**

headquarters, they are **less controllable** and **substitutable** when there is a high embeddedness of the subsidiaries in both their local and their business networks. The **embeddedness of a subsidiary in a local network** may provide the subsidiary with an **exceptional power basis** when its local context is the source of a high percentage of global sales, of technology, and other capabilities. The power of subsidiaries may be reflected in their respective roles (Chapter 4).

The **dialectics of globalisation** thus only emerge with increasing internationalisation. Before internationalisation, **general entrepreneurial dialectics** like *stability vs. flexiblity* or *diversification vs. single-product* may dominate the evolutionary dynamics. With increasing internationalisation, however, the **global dialectics are increasingly internalised** and dominate the emerging internal and external organisational complexity. Dialectics like *headquarters vs. foreign subsidiary* or *FDI vs. co-operation* increasingly influence activities and the processing of meaning in globalising firms.

Studies by Bartlett (1989) and Martinez/Jarillo (1989) prove that the **genesis of MNEs** has been highly influenced by the **dialectic of global integration vs. local adaptation**. While MNEs between 1920-1950 preferred as their **thesis** the *multinational model* (decentralised units, local adaptation), MNEs between 1950 and 1980 generally preferred the **antithesis** of the *global model* of global integration and centralisation. Bartlett and Martinez/Jarillo then introduce the **synthesis** of the *transnational model*, which normatively integrates the models of multinational adaptation and global integration. In future research, this transnational model itself may become the challenged thesis and an antithesis may hold that a thinking still based on national borders has become outdated and a more symbiotic approach should be found.

MNEs are subject to *dialectics*, which are *reflected in power distribution*. From an evolutionary perspective, power provides social actors with means to influence or even determine variation and selective retention of organisational objectives, elements, and properties. The *perception and strategic control of external contingencies* is of *particular importance for MNEs* as they face a higher internal and external complexity and dynamic. **Power positions** beyond the control of headquarters may emerge due to the given variety and amount of interdependencies, which may not be completely overviewed and controlled by headquarters. This process increases the ferocity of dialectical dynamics between headquarters and subsidiaries.

It is a **basic dilemma of MNEs** that (1) environmental diversity leads to the *dispersion of activities*, providing advantages of local adaptation and the exploitation of global diversity and (2) *specialisation of foreign subsidiaries* in the handling of strategic contingencies provides the latter with *significant bases of power*. As assumed in strategic contingency theory, *political conflict, negotiation, and self-organisation* thus may *increase with increasing global complexity*.

Pautzke (1989: 265) argues that in an **evolutionary inquiry** has to be included the **dialectics of learning processes** and **organisational context** that drives organisational evolution. Pautzke thus applies the systemic difference of system vs. environment to describe the recursive process of system learning. As contexts vary internationally, there are differences in cultural structures of meaning and learning. The **dialectical mechanism** may even apply to **learning itself**. For example, Westerners have a tendency to perceive stimuli in terms of dichotomies and dualisms rather than paradoxes or holistic pictures (Osland/Bird 2000: 68). Conceiving culture as paradoxical, it follows that learning about another culture occurs in a dialectical fashion (Ibid. 73). Learning processes thus depend on recursive processes, which reproduce meaning structure and differentiate them by recursive contact with variation, e.g. with other cultures. **Retained meaning structures** in *form of theses* may be differentiated by confronting them with *antitheses* from the environment, which provide opportunities for learning. The **globally differentiated context** therefore offers the **maximum opportunity for learning**.

Major **changes in interpretative schemes** occur through **dialectical processes** in which old and new ways of understanding interact, resulting in a synthesis. The process of change in interpretative schemes is in a reciprocal relationship with changes in formal structure (Bartunek 1984: 355). This process implies both *processes of differentiation and integration*, in that different perspectives are encountered and synthesised in a new understanding. Because this process is dialectical, it necessarily involves **conflict between perspectives** and between **globally dispersed groups** holding the different perspectives. The resolution of the process will depend in part on the comparative power of these different groups to have their perspectives heard. The **dialectical process** does not take place solely on the level of interpretative schemes. Both original and antithetical ways of understanding are expressed in actions taken by organisational members (Ibid. 365). Dialectical processes induce changes in structures. Several authors even call for the **institutionalisation of conflict** in organisations in order to generate a **maximum flexibility** and **learning capability** (Hedberg et al. 1976). Due to the **internalisation of global complexity**, globally operating firms confront a huge amount of **dialectical tensions**, which may cause **conflicts** but may also be sources and drivers of **learning processes**.

6.2.4.4 The Darwinian motor
Once founded, the evolutionary motor of social systems sets in. The initially imprinted system becomes driven by **variation and selective retention**. In social systems, variation may be

'*blind*', as propagated by the '*garbage can model*' or population ecology, or intentional, as assumed in strategic choice models. **Variation** may be produced *internally or imported* due to the *meaning-based interpenetration* of social and psychic systems. Particularly institutionalisation theory provides ample evidence of the diffusion of meaning-based variations (here: institutions) across organisations in a particular field. In literature on global business, variations emerge in the form of innovation, technological change, and environmental adaptation.

In the **strategic choice model**, selection occurs through deliberate choice among alternatives of future action. Goal setting, decision-making routines, and the establishment of norms and values determine corridors for the selection of organisational elements and actions. Rational decision-making is limited due to bounded rationality and political conflicts in organisations. On the other extreme, **population ecologists** argue that organisations only produce '*blind*' variations, which are selected against by the environment. Similarly, internal competition may also resemble the biological principle of '*survival of the fittest*' and serve as a further selection mechanism (Miner 1994).

On **industry level**, selection may resemble the **'blind' mode** of population ecology or may be based on political struggle and power positions. On **organisation level**, global firms may be viewed as '**global selection regimes**' of innovations, individual dispersed units, and locations. In MNEs, the different subsystems have to adapt to different local ecological niches while at the same time collectively creating and adapting to the global environment of the MNE as a whole. **MNEs** are subject to environmental **variations in diverse local environments**. The process of **global adaptation** may be viewed as a **process of creation and elimination** of whole **local subsidiaries**, or **elements of subsidiaries** such as businesses, activities, or competencies. By selecting globally dispersed elements, the MNE constitutes the evolution of its structure over time.

The **crucial concept** in the retention process is **consistency across time and across units**. In rational planning, variation and selection constitute the planning phase. Implementation and control systems then constitute the retention process. Formalisation, codification, and diffusion of effective routines serve as retention processes. **Globalisation** leads to a **rapid diffusion of new social traits and practices on global level**. Successful diffusion of new knowledge and practices therefore has become *critical to the success of globally operating firms*. Another factor is the **organisational resonance capacity**, allowing for a rapid and effective identification, interpretation, adoption, adaptation, and diffusion of new knowledge and practices.

Baum (1999) and Romanelli (1999) assume that **subunits** evolve at **different paces**, sometimes faster and sometimes slower than the overall system, hence generating the need for integration because of different dynamics. This constitutes the **challenge of 'mutual ageing'** as formulated by Michels (1932). While more variations may be expected to occur on lower hierarchical levels, selection and diffusion is usually centralised on higher system levels, providing them with a stronger influence on the system's evolution. Similarly, more variations and thus more evolutionary dynamics may emerge in certain **geographical regions** while the **'centre of gravitation'** in terms of selection may remain stable in the home country of a firm due to path-dependence. MNEs often try to equilibrate this asymmetry by assigning different roles to subsidiaries, for example those in technological or market-oriented lead countries.

Boulding (1978) and Aldrich/Kenworthy (1999) argue that in **organisations, evolutionary processes** emerge as **organisational learning**. Variation generates new knowledge. Selection is the differentiated reinforcement of new knowledge and retention generates the memory in learning, i.e. the knowledge structure. Evolutionary mechanisms are themselves subject to an evolutionary process. Organisations improve their capabilities for storing knowledge, for localising relevant knowledge, and for its application in viable activities. Organisations thus learn to improve internal selection before external selection takes place (Kieser/Koch 2002). From a **social systems view**, such a **learning perspective** is extended to the **evolution of meaning**, which is more comprehensive than knowledge and includes expectations and emotional states.

In the **globally differentiated network** of globally operating systems, there is a **huge variety of levels** on which **selection** may work. It ranges from *organisational units* to *local markets* and *individual activities* or *capabilities*. MNEs thus are increasingly described as global knowledge networks or dynamic learning networks (Oliveira/Child. 1999: 3).

In such a globally differentiated network, **evolutionary mechanisms** may be *identified* with regard to their **path-dependent dynamics**, *locating their effects* on the level of subsystems, core capabilities, or routines, and particularly possible directions of the dynamics. The **generated transparency** about the effects and extension of evolutionary mechanisms then may provide the **means to apply teleological mechanisms** in order to nurture, direct, or contain these **emergent dynamics**.

Such an *analysis* may be *facilitated by longitudinal,* e.g. **historical analyses of the system's most critical properties**, such as products, clients, underlying capabilities and processes. An understanding of the underlying dynamics particularly in the co-evolutionary interplay with the environment may provide the means to allocate resources to processes, which produce the most forceful effects rather than to waste them in processes that are contrary or simply not fitting the system's identity and evolutionary dynamics. In this context, it may be reasonable to speak of sustainable capabilities and processes, which reflect the core identity and evolutionary dynamics of the system. Their identification may allow for a more efficient allocation of resources and a strengthening of the system's evolutionary robustness.

6.2.4.5 The autopoietic motor

The **processing of meaning** on the basis of **guiding differences** constitutes the autopoietic mechanism in social systems. This mechanism drives the **recursive reproduction** of the **meaning and the action system**. Both meaning itself and action can only constitute their co-evolution on the basis of meaning. Action is conducted on the basis of meaning in the form of knowledge, expectations, and intentions. Action can only feed back to the formation of further intended action in the form of meaning. As a consequence, only meaningful action is autopoietic, not any kind of casual behaviour. The latter may only enter the autopoietic reproduction when it appears as a blind variation, with meaning ascribed to it after happening.

As all observations and thinking are made on the basis of distinctions, a self-referential social system has to explore and define the most critical distinctions for its successful reproduction. These critical distinctions are guiding differences dominating the meaning structure and processing and thus decision-making. In general, evolutionary processes and thus globalisation comprise five constitutive guiding differences (Luhmann 1995):

- system – environment   e.g. subsidiary – local market,
- element – whole   e.g. subsidiary – MNE network,
- element – relation   e.g. organisational units – interdependencies,
- identity – difference   e.g. co-operation – firm vs. firm
- autopoiesis - allopoiesis   e.g. management – national legislation.

Organising and communicating along such basic distinctions may facilitate the **evolution of consensual domains** and a shared orientation. Of course, each social system has to identify the distinctions critical to its individual context. The five general distinctions above only serve as a basic framework for the general description of evolution of social systems adapted to the context of globalisation.

6.2.4.5.1 System – environment

Social systems are formed by the development of a consensual domain among the founders and its implementation on the action level. Once in place, the evolutionary process of differentiation and integration sets in. In the **founding phase**, the system has to develop its own identity and autopoietic organisation. Is also has to define its boundaries and its environment. The environment is socially organised and provides all necessary resources. The system has to establish structural couplings with systems in its environment in order to import necessary resources and to export its products, thus creating interdependencies. The purpose of the system and the chosen domain of activity already determine basic environmental stakeholders like clients and suppliers but these have to be specified and structural couplings have to be developed. The foundation phase is characterised by high dynamics in the adaptation of the own identity, boundaries, structural couplings, and consensual areas until the system stabilises and finds a stable position in its niche. **Born globals** already develop a high degree of global differentiation from inception. They already *internalise geographical and cultural boundaries from the start* and enact a globally differentiated environment. **Traditional internationalisers** begin their identity and boundary formation in a local culturally homogeneous context and *begin later with the development of global complexity*.

After the foundation phase, the system begins to *differentiate specialised subsystems*. The system *continuously* has to *redefine* the own identity, its boundaries, and structural couplings with other social systems. In its globalisation process, the system **globally differentiates its subsystems**. Each of the *dispersed subsystems* becomes *embedded in a local environment* characterised by different cultural and other contextual standards. The subsystems develop **structural couplings** and **consensual domains** with other systems in their **local environments** and become subject to **local isomorphic forces** based on **interpenetration**. The globalising system increasingly has to *balance local and global isomorphic forces*. Each subsystem faces two relevant environments, the internal environment based on co-specialisation and the external, both global and local environment. The co-evolution with a globally differentiated environment therefore presupposes the continuous formation, reproduction, and elimination of functional and geographical subsystems, their interpenetration, structural coupling, and consensual domains. The globalising system may even form third-level social systems in terms of external networks. As stated above, the formation and reproduction of identity, organisation, and boundaries of the network are even more dynamic due to its loose coupling.

As social systems may be conceived as **nested hierarchies of self-similar social systems**, boundary definition becomes a central capability to be developed by the system in its globalisation process. The **definition of identities and boundaries** becomes necessary internally between the differentiated subsystems, and externally between the system or its subsystems and the respective environment. Particularly **subsidiaries** have often been described in their **dual role** towards the internal and the external environment. Conceiving social systems as nested hierarchies of self-similar social systems, the difference system/environment overlaps with the second difference of element and whole. A basic task of all subsystems is a clear definition of identity, boundaries, and the network properties as expressed by interpenetration, structural coupling, and consensual domains.

6.2.4.5.2 Element – whole

As the globalising system becomes increasingly differentiated, the relation between elements and whole become more complex. Looking at a **nested hierarchy of systems**, on *each level* there may appear other *relations of element and whole*. The **distinction headquarters vs. subsidiary** dominates the discussion in international business but in reality, there may appear more or less dense **organisational regions** in the system on the basis of local, regional, global, functional, or product-based interdependencies. **Each subsystem** therefore has to carefully examine the most significant **relations of element and whole**. In organisations, an element may be any kind of organisational unit, from a job role to a division. In a similar vein, a whole may be everything from a project group to the firm or even the strategic or local network. **Clear positioning** by definitions and self-definitions of the organisational units and their relations to the most critical **elements and wholes** becomes vital in order to develop organised global complexity. The **self-similarity** and **recursiveness** of the units' properties allow for a **coherent structuration** on the global level.

Due to the complexity of element-whole relations, these should not be reduced to hierarchical or value-added interdependencies. Elements and wholes should be defined on the basis of all vital evolutionary properties such as knowledge generation. Different **element/whole relations** are the **source of different roles and expectations**. For example, a **subsidiary** may perceive itself as part of a **local network** or as an element of the **MNE network**. It may be useful to develop clear definitions of such dualities in order to provide the means for transparency and clear expectations. Possible conflicts due to fuzzy mutual knowledge and expectations thus may be avoided.

Seen as a heterarchy or holographic network, **all core subsystems** should be instilled with the basic properties of the whole and share the same **holistic identity**. As specialised subsystems, which are adapted to a local context, they also dispose of traits of the local context, itself being a social whole. Again, the similarity between the dualities of system/environment and element/whole becomes apparent. The **first duality** captures the boundary between inside and outside the system, while the **second duality** differentiates entities within a system. As social systems are not made of individuals but of meaning and action, it is a **question of the perspective** what is defined as **in or out, element or whole**. Globally operating systems may try to make such differing perspectives and possible role conflicts conscious for the actors in order to instil a viable amount of the whole in and across the subsystems and to allow for their adaptation to the environment without passing the boundary.

6.2.4.5.3 Element – relation

In most social evolutionary approaches, the focus is on the reproduction of elements, e.g. traits, routines, or organisational units. From the autopoietic perspective, however, the focus is on the reproduction of the autopoietic organisation. Elements may be substituted and structures may change as long as the reproduction of the autopoietic organisation is maintained. A **main focus of autopoietic reproduction** is not only on the **positioning of elements** but also on their **relational fabric**. The reproduction of an autopoietic social system depends on the recursive relation between meaning and action. It further depends on the *interpenetration, structural coupling, and consensual domains* among the constituting elements, subsystems, and with the environment. The global context is particularly marked by different forms and qualities ascribed to relations. For example, as preferred by many MNEs, products, best practices, or technologies may be '*cloned*' across several locations. Though patterns of relations are already integrated in a '*package*' and transferable as a blueprint, the implementation may be difficult due to different market or technological infrastructures, i.e. different relational embeddedness.

It may be valuable to differentiate relations according to their contents, intensity, or other critical properties. **Network analysis** and **organisation theories** (exchange theory, contingency theory, and resource dependence theory) provide a rich set of instruments and concepts how to describe and study relations. It may also be fruitful to identify if relations are restricted to operational interdependencies or critical to the evolutionary capabilities.

6.2.4.5.4 Identity – difference

Depending on the theoretical perspective, there are different **interpretations of identity**. In **economics**, identity is usually explained by some form of *asset specificity* (Williamson 1998: 28). In **sociology**, identity may be conceived as a no more than *relatively stable construction in an ongoing process of social activity* (Calhoun 1991: 52, 59). In **social systems theory**, the *difference between identity and difference* is necessary in order to work out a theory of self-referential systems that incorporates system/environment theory. **Self-reference** can be realised in the actual operations of a system only when a self can be identified through itself and set off as different from others. Conceived as a **hierarchy of nested systems**, there are **myriads** of ways to define **identities** or **differences** within the system. This is most visible in situations, when members of an organisational unit talk of '*we*' and '*they*'. Such identity formation does *not only depend on formal organisational units*. It may also emerge across professional or cultural subgroups, information groups, and even interorganisationally by the formation of networks or communities of practice. Again, *a clear self-definition and self-positioning of subsystems is the basis for unambiguous behaviour and clear mutual knowledge and expectations.*

The **difference of 'identity vs. difference'** constitutes the **basis for dynamics in social systems**. Seen from a **static view**, distinctions such as globalisation vs. localisation may be perceived as *opposites* calling for decisions either for the one or the other end of the scale. From a **dynamic view**, a distinction provides the dynamics as the *emphasis on one extreme* after a while *provoke the emphasis on the other*. For example, increasing levels of global integration after a while provoke increasing levels of local adaptation. *Change can only be thought and implemented by processing distinctions.* Distinctions serve as a means to observe and to create new meaning. An emphasis on the static and competitive view on dualities inhibits change and may only cause short-term gains. The distinction of identity vs. difference is driving the **change of meaning and action structures** as it dynamically (re-)defines boundaries and identities.

6.2.4.5.5 Allopoiesis – Autopoiesis

The difference of allopoiesis and autopoiesis is basically dependent on the level of observation. For example, management can be seen as the basic mechanism of self-organisation on system level but may appear as allopoietic organisation from the perspective of the subsystems. **Allopoietic organisation** is organisation imposed on the system by its environment. From the **perspective of the firm as a whole**, this may be the national legislature, limiting the space of options or directly imposing the institutionalisation of structural elements (e.g. supervisory boards) or control mechanisms (e.g. accounting principles). **Within the firm**, allopoietic organisation is generally **institutionalised between hierarchical levels** and is based on *formal authority*. **Autopoietic organisation** emerges within the defined frontiers of a system or subsystem. While **allopoietic organisation** provides the 'pegs' of **instrumental, prescribed organisation** described by Tichy (1981), the **autopoietic organisation** fills **emerging organisational space** with complementary and sometimes even conflicting meaning and action.

In the **process of global differentiation and integration** of social systems, the **degree of self-complexity** increases to a **point of equilibrium of global extension** where the *reproduction of global complexity* becomes more dominant than its *generation by internationalisation processes*. In the process of increasing global complexity, both allopoietic and autopoietic organisation become more differentiated. The **globalising firm** develops **complex hierarchies** for the distribution and reproduction of **allopoietic organisation** and a **large variety of autopoietic contexts** within and across the dispersed subsystems. In addition, the differentiated global system becomes *subject to allopoietic influences* from its *globally differentiated environment*, particularly from its stakeholders. The **global system** therefore does not only have to identify and define the **allopoietic influences and structures** but particularly the **organisational regions** in which **autopoietic reproduction** takes place and the units facilitating this process. MNEs have various options to achieve this. For example, global firms try to identify core capabilities and the units participating in their exploration and exploitation. They form *strategic business units* in order to bundle strategic sense and action across formal units. MNEs also facilitate the formation and reproduction of *communities of practice* in order to form a niche for the reproduction of distinct areas of knowledge. There are multiple means to facilitate and nurture autopoietic reproduction by allopoietic means. More generally, **autopoietic organisation** may be nurtured by all means *facilitating communication and interaction* in the system.

In the **course of a firm's evolution**, it is critical to reflect on the **basic guiding differences** in order to prevent '*pathological reproduction*'. In a changing environment, if a firm continues to formulate the same distinctions without change, it is not learning, but only reproducing itself in a pathological manner (von Krogh/Vicari 1993: 400). For example, an industry recipe (Spender 1989) consists of a set of background distinctions tied to a particular field of experience. Such a recipe may become useless due to technological or market change, thus inducing the construction of a new set of background distinctions. Similarly, while **born globals** are characterised by a polyglot culture and meaning structure from the start, **traditional internationalisers** are imprinted with a unicultural pattern, which becomes more multicultural in the process of internationalisation. The basic frontier between the national home culture and everything '*foreign*' may still remain a faltline in the firm's meaning and action system when the firm does not unlearn the distinction between '*we*' and '*foreign*'. According to autopoiesis theory, the way a firm can stimulate the **self-reproductive process** is to create **new distinctions** by producing new information internally or by importing it (von Krogh/Vicari 1993: 401-402).

Jantsch (1986: 189) argues that when evolution is conceived as the **evolution of organisation** *rather than of entities* as proposed by autopoietic theory, it can be viewed as the **evolution of knowledge**. Knowledge is information that is transformed into dynamic, self-organising complexity. The **processing of meaning by guiding differences** drives this *transformation*. The *autopoietic mechanisms* therefore may also provide a valuable *theoretical basis for organisation theories and the knowledge-based view* as well. In turn, concepts of knowledge evolution (teleological and evolutionary) may be used to describe the autopoietic reproduction of global firms.

6.3 A management perspective on the globalisation of firms

6.3.1 Management of global foundation

An **evolutionary perspective on the globalisation of firms** may already begin with the **foundation**. Depending on the business the founders want to get in, it may be reasonable to create an **international new venture**, for example in small, specialised niches of high-technology industries. In this case, the founders have basically two sources to instil the new venture with properties and capabilities required by the global competitive context. First, they may have own network capital, knowledge, and experiences in global business and may invest it as part of their founding capital of the international new venture. Second, they may exploit already existing institutionalised knowledge of international business and use it as building blocks of the new venture. Though **imprinted with globalisation capabilities from inception**, the emerging new global firm is generally starting small and has to *develop organised complexity on the global level*. The firm has to develop the requisite globalisation capabilities similarly as traditional internationalisers but has the advantage that the **basic layout of action and meaning system** is already **globally differentiated**. The born global firm therefore has to learn globalisation like all firms have to do in their globalisation process, particularly regarding the **firm-specific capabilities** as compared to general ones. However, the born global can advance more smoothly and homogenically in its **accumulation of globalisation knowledge** while **traditional internationalisers** encounter a **quantum leap of internationalisation** and, at least for a considerable time, a faltline between the core structure imprinted by their home-culture and the foreign periphery.

The **globalisation process of born globals** is also characterised by the development of such global complexity by differentiation and integration of subsystems and of system-specific globalisation capabilities. Thus, born globals still have everything to learn and to develop as start-ups in the global context, but they have the possibility to develop the underlying meaning and activity structure with a global basic layout.

In contrast, **local start-ups** build a *home-based and culturally homogeneous meaning and activity structure* that in the process of globalisation later has to be extended and transformed to get a global outlook. **International new ventures** may shortcut the development of a *global basic layout* in their organisation but have to learn it from inception, which may provoke serious difficulties in the foundation phase. Founders of international new ventures face the challenge to create a new firm with a global fabric while managers of traditional internationalisers face the challenge of a quantum leap when the firm has to transform its structures from national to global levels.

6.3.2 Management of global differentiation

The management of global differentiation may be basically conceived as a process that evokes **changes** in the **global differentiation of meaning and activity structures** of firms. It comprises the **traditional internationalisation perspective**, which describes a process of a positive, increasing global differentiation, extension, and amount of activities. It also comprises processes of **de-internationalisation** and **re-internationalisation**. For MNEs, it may not be even necessary to draw such a distinction as their reproduction is marked by a constant flow of increases and decreases in the global differentiation of meaning and activity structures, e.g. in form of FDI, re-locations, and learning.

From the **traditional internationalisation perspective**, there is **abundant literature** on internationalisation theory, internationalisation forms and strategies, entry modes and learning processes. From an **evolutionary perspective**, it remains to add that the management of **global differentiation** in firms may be particularly stimulated by internal and external **variations**. **External variety** may be explored by an *increase in the firm's resonance capacity*, and particularly in the absorptive capacity. Environmental scanning, information and communication systems, a '*curious*' organisational culture, and social capital are examples of means that may contribute to a viable resonance capacity. **Internal variation** may be enhanced by innovation programmes, co-specialisation, communities of practice, or the internalisation of different contexts, e.g. by FDI. It has already been stressed that **MNEs** may be conceived as *global ventilators for innovative impulses*.

As **evolutionary dynamics** in social systems hinge on the evolutionary interplay between meaning and action, the **mechanism of differentiation and integration** may be nurtured by **strengthening learning from existing activities** and efforts and by **transforming meaning into action**. Only when the interplay between meaning and action level is in motion, there is differentiation and progress. Only by acting and learning by doing progress can be made by differentiation of meaning and activity structures. Therefore, it is neither practicable to develop a **comprehensive master plan** before initiating first internationalisation steps nor is it efficient to end up in **actionist behaviour** with dispersed but uncoupled or inconsistent activities. The *first extreme* may end in frustration and wasting of resources as the master plan may encounter an environment that does not react as expected. The *second extreme* may result in sunk costs of investments that do not fit in a coherent pattern and inhibit learning. It may be better to create a context with a frequent and continuous circle in the interplay between meaning and action level in order to facilitate both learning and the development of viable activity structures on global scale. Of course, the fastest way to generate global differentiation is the **internalisation of globally dispersed social systems** or **individuals**, providing the global system with the requisite variety and establishing the co-evolutionary interplay of the meaning and activity structure on global scale. Such shortcuts may be valuable facilitators of internationalisation, making **big steps** possible. In the **long run**, however, it is important to **balance internationalisation steps in a healthy flow**. The underlying guiding differences may help the firm to find orientation and direction for a **robust internationalisation**.

6.3.3 Management of global network capabilities

The **key to a successful co-evolution** with the environment can be found in the *construction, institutionalisation, and evolutionary adaptation* of **consensual domains** and **structural couplings**. International differentiation of organisational units and activities of international operating companies, as well as the resulting interdependencies, lead to the particular demands on the management of globalisation. **Each organisational unit** has to develop **transparency** in its **self-definition** and **self-positioning** in its internal and external context. This comprises several **components in systemic positioning**:

- *definition of the core competence and core function of the unit*, particular in relation to its internal and external context,
- *definition of the role the unit shall play* in the company and the environmental context,
- *definitions of the boundaries* with the internal and external environment and respective subsystems,
- *design of the corresponding interpenetration and structural couplings* with interaction partners,
- *creation of customised and complementary consensual domains* with interaction partners, and
- *establishment of interaction patterns* that are either limited or evolutionary conceptualised.

Structural couplings of systems lead to the development of **isomorphic structures**, which are the necessary precondition of communications and therefore of construction of consensual cognitive domains (Fischer 1991: 78). Within the **internal and external networks** there may develop **organisational regions of different densities** and with different **degrees of couplings**. The main focus from a **network perspective** is on the **relations** and **interdependencies** between network elements. It has also been the main focus of MNE literature since the 1980s with a strong emphasis on co-ordination. From a management perspective, the concepts cumulate in the **context management of multinational networks** as coined by Bartlett/Ghoshal. In this view, **allopoietic organisation** represented by **headquarters** provides a **context** of management structures and processes in which **autopoietic organisation** may take place. Models of MNEs as holographic organisations or multi-centre structures already relativated the traditional headquarters-subsidiary perspective and introduced a more differentiated picture of relations and interdependencies in MNEs.

Conceiving **global firms** and their environments as **nested hierarchies of social systems** allows for a much more flexible definition and organisation of these multinational structures. **Social systems** may be *defined around meaning structures* (e.g. core competencies), *activities,* or *organisational actors*. Co-ordination and the design of mechanisms for information, communication, and decision-making may thus be oriented to a higher degree at the task to instill the firm with the drive and flexibility that allows for **dynamic morphing** in a **dynamic global context**. Of course, this includes the capability to exploit the classical advantages of global firms. In addition, a main advantage of creating transparency by looking at social systems instead of focusing on formal units exclusively may be the **localisation of central motors of evolutionary dynamics** in different **organisational regions** and the potential to trigger or even direct them to a certain degree.

6.3.4 Management of global evolutionary dynamics

The management of globalisation dynamics focuses on the **intentional efforts** to direct the global evolutionary processes within the firm. Managers of globalisation face a **basic dilemma**: while they control the allopoietic reproduction of the firm, they only have a limited impact on the dynamics generated by four of the five basic evolutionary motors. Managers can use decision-making and authority structures to develop the teleological and intentional drive of the firm in terms of objectives and goals, formal organisational structures, strategic and operational processes, and organisational change. The other four mechanisms, however, managers cannot directly influence and control. A **basic challenge** for the management of globalisation is to accept the limits of possible control and to accept the role of **managers as catalysts** rather than of the rational designers of the firm. This challenge grows with increasing levels of globalisation and organisational complexity. Of course, management should do its utmost to create efficient communication, decision-making, and activity structures with all instruments of intended, allopoietic organisation. But the faults and flaws of management due to uncertainty, ambiguity, and bounded rationality increase erratically when management is based on the ignorance of the other four **evolutionary motors**. The allocation of resources and development of activities may be highly inefficient when they are not harmonised with the dynamics inflicted by the other mechanisms and the forces of historical path-dependence. A basic challenge of globalisation management is to discover the *'force of history'*, as most global firms still are more likely to be compared to huge oil tankers navigating in deep seas rather than with flexible new ventures. Even the latter have to understand the historical dynamics of the competitive and general context in which they are embedded. Particularly such new and small ventures are subject to very dynamic processes of **dynamic morphing** in their globalisation process in order to position themselves in their environment and to develop the symbiotic rhythm in their co-evolutionary process.

6.3.5 Management of differences in globalisation

Differences have traditionally been a main focus in the study of international business. For example, Wiesmann (1993) initiated a discussion about a theoretical framework in international management that could be based upon the concepts of complexity and difference. Wiesmann even proposes a view of international management as a *'management of differences'*. From this perspective, differences across national markets and cultures are viewed as a basic constituent of the complexity in international management. Each firm therefore should explore the differences critical to its global evolution. As the central demand typical for international management, Wiesmann (1993) and Brauchlin/Wiesmann (1992) view the boundary-spanning character of activities. Boundaries in this respect are interpreted as **'specific differences'** that can be grouped to (Wiesmann 1993: 109-110):

- geographical differences,
- cultural differences, and
- systemic differences (political, legal, infrastructure, etc.).

Wiesmann (1993) and Dülfer (1991) propose that culture-based differences for perceptions are exceptionally increasing the complexity. A further increase of complexity is caused by differentiated roles of internationally dispersed organisational units (Wiesmann 1993: 115-116).

Evans/Doz (1992) propose an appropriate **balance of 'dualities'** in international management as the fundament of an equilibrated evolution of enterprises. While in a dualism, we confront a dichotomy – two distinct and opposed positions, processes, or entities, dualities involve single positions, processes, or entities whose various aspects may be temporarily bracketed (Weaver/Gioia 1994: 578). Evans/Doz thus propose that the balance between complementary dualities should be regarded as dynamic; asymmetry should never oppress the other pole totally because this would lead to organisational degeneration and crises. The maintenance of a duality, e.g. in case of the temporary concentration on one pole, can be sustained by **'cultural layering'**. Dualities can thus be integrated into management processes and culture, so that a rich structure of differentiated perceptions, cognitive orientations, relations, and networks is created, that especially serves to enrich the decision-process (Evans/Doz 1992: 90-97).

Cameron (1986: 545-546) assumes an even deeper necessity in the development of a **'Janusian thinking'**, together with the cultivation of flexibility and of the adaptability by manifesting paradoxes, like the parallel presence of loose coupling (sustains innovation, flexibility) and tight coupling (sustains implementation competence). Empirical research by Bourgeois/Eisenhardt (1988) showed, that in a turbulent environment, the decision-process of successful companies were characterised by the balancing of different dualities at the same time (Eisenhardt 1989: 555-558)

Differences are a basic characteristic of the global social context and of global social systems. From a static comparative perspective, there are differences on geographical, cultural, or institutional level. Management has to cope with different business practices, national legislatures, infrastructures, local consumer preferences, etc.. At any given point in time, globally operating firms have to facilitate the conduct of globally differentiated processes and the function of globally differentiated structures. Interpenetration is based on different languages and codes, structural couplings with interaction partners may have to be designed differently, and consensual domains may expose very different contents and forms. On the individual level, much emphasis is put on intercultural capabilities and training in order to facilitate the consistent reproduction of meaning and activity structures.

From a **dynamic perspective**, differences dominate the globalisation and global evolution of social systems in terms of dialectics and guiding differences. Management has to identify, contain, and balance underlying dialectics such as global integration vs. local adaptation with resulting positions and power bases of organisational actors, which evoke negotiations and conflicts with external stakeholders and between internal organisational actors.

A reasonable formation of roles and expectations on the basis of such fundamental guiding differences as element/whole, system/environment, or identity/difference may provide the necessary transparency and orientation across internal and external actors in order to sustain a coherent evolutionary process. The exploration of the most critical **guiding differences** and their actualisation allows for the most effective and efficient evolution of the meaning structure, which in turn allows for the development of the most promising activities.

6.4 Contribution to an evolutionary perspective

The evolutionary approach outlined in Chapter 6 provides several basic **building blocks** for the explanation of the globalisation of firms:

1. Firms as social systems may be conceived as both *action* and *meaning systems* based on the interplay of both levels.

2. The approach allows for an observation of the *whole evolutionary process* of a firm as a social system. It serves to explain the whole process from foundation to allopoietic and autopoietic reproduction.
3. Firms may be observed as both *allopoietic* and *autopoietic social systems*, allowing for the application of different evolutionary mechisms and perspectives.
4. The approach includes the basic principle of social evolution, i.e. the *process of differentiation and integration* of social systems. It thus provides the basic principle of globalisation as a historical process of social evolution.
5. The approach includes five *evolutionary mechanisms* and adapts the Darwinian mechanism of variation and selective retention to social systems in a theoretically correct way. Only social systems approaches currently resolve the ontological problem of this adaptation.
6. The processing of meaning by *guiding differences* provides a strong indicator on how social systems reproduce themselves, particularly by decision-making.
7. The *co-evolutionary interplay* between whole and parts or system and environment is conceptualised by the concepts of interpenetration, structural coupling, and consensual domains. Such a theoretical foundation is missing in most organisation and management theories.
8. The principles of *recursiveness* and *self-similarity* allow for the adaptation of the underlying concepts to all system levels, from job role to organisation and society.
9. This general applicability allows for a *commensurable integration* of all evolutionary theories, organisation theories, and management approaches.

Table 6-3 provides an overview over the contribution to an explanation of the evolutionary principles underlying the globalisation of firms (Chapter 2).

	Allopoietic social systems	**Autopoietic social systems**
Foundation	Social systems are founded by individuals	Social systems emerge in situations of interdependence and double contingency between psychic systems.
Co-evolution of firm and environment	Individuals act as nodes in which different social systems overlap and their interactions and parallelised cognitive states mark the boundary. Co-evolution is thus facilitated by the participation of individuals in different social systems.	The co-evolution of autopoietic systems and their environment is based on interpenetration, structural coupling, and consensual domains. Every change in a system increases the complexity of the environment for all other systems.
Global differentiation of firm	Differentiation on the basis of interaction and parallelised cognitive states.	Differentiation and integration of social systems on the level of meaning and action is the main principle of social evolution.
Global integration of firm	Integration on the basis of interaction and parallelised cognitive states.	Differentiation and integration of social systems on the level of meaning and action is the main principle of social evolution. Subsystems are integrated in a structure on the basis of their autopoietic organisation
Global evolutionary dynamics of environment	Dynamics emerge by interaction between systems and as individuals transfer perturbations in cognitive states across the social systems in which they participate.	The evolutionary principle of differentiation and integration of social systems drives social evolution. 5 evolutionary motors provide the dynamics
Global evolutionary dynamics of firm	Systems continuously undergo a process of ontogenetic change. This circular process of (1) interactions, (2) modulation of state, and (3) definition of a new reality generates a shared common reality on action and meaning level.	Life cycles, dialectical processes, processes of VSR, autopoiesis, and decision-making fuel the differentiation and integration of social systems.

Table 6-3: Inclusion of evolutionary principles on allopoietic and autopoietic level

6.5 Summary

The evolutionary theory developed in this chapter is built on two conceptual levels. First, a general evolutionary theory of the firm has to be developed before it can be adapted to the level of globalisation as an evolutionary process.

Organisations may be conceptualised as allopoietic or autopoietic systems. As **allopoietic**, or *syn-referential systems,* they are constituted by individuals as the basic organisational actors. They dispose of a resource base and conduct the primary activities of the organisation in order to achieve the stated goals. Allopoietic systems are instruments and subject to teleological, intended change. Organisations may also be conceptualised as **autopoietic** *systems*, which reproduce themselves independent of distinct individual actors. Organisations as autopoietic social systems emerge from the stream of social evolution. As enacted, second-level social systems, they are both subject to voluntary, intentional change and emergent, evolutionary change. In globally operating firms, it is important to identify the idiosyncratic properties of the globally differentiated systems and their relations in order to develop transparency and profiles (identities), which may provide the means for a more symbiotic and directed global evolutionary across all units.

Change and reproduction of social systems is based on the evolutionary interplay of the constituting meaning and action system. This interplay is driven by a **process of differentiation and integration**, providing the system with complexity, adaptability, and dynamic. The process of differentiation and integration is fuelled by the five different motors of evolutionary change (life cycle, teleological, dialectical, Darwinian VSR, and social autopoietic). The Principle of differentiation and integration and the five evolutionary motors are subject to differences in the global context. Therefore, there may develop organisational regions within a globally operating firm with different dynamics and different relative effects of the individual motors.

The evolution of a social system is structurally coupled with the evolution of its environment. Therefore, the globalisation of a firm has to be observed in its co-evolutionary interplay with the environment. The global differentiation of systems leads to a variety of local and global co-evolutionary contexts between units of the globally operating firm and the respective environments. Subsidiaries are classical examples of dual isomorphic pressures resulting from differentiated structural coupling.

Social systems develop four principle capabilities of globalisation, which reflect the three basic dimensions of globalisation. The fourth dimension results from the extraction of the **entrepreneurial capability** from the **internationalisation capability** in order to focus explicitly on the phenomenon of global system foundation. Entrepreneurial, internationalisation, global network, and global evoutionary capabilities are all applied to a firm and to an external network level.

The **foundation of firms** on global level becomes more probable due to the globalisation of communication and activity structures. Situations of double contingency and interdependencies between entrepreneurs and organisational actors increase so that the global foundation of new firms becomes a logical consequence. A further reason is the global knowledge and experience of the founders, who already dispose of the ingredients for a successful international new venture. Facilitators of global foundations such as banks, clients, and venture capitalists are part of the developing global context for foundations. The **foundation of global networks** may occur on two levels. First, the foundation of global business networks is driven by an emergent process, which leads to the development of global industries. On the other hand, strategic networks are founded to facilitate the intentional pursuit of competitive advantages by exploiting network resources in specific functional, product, or geographic areas.

The **internationalisation of firms** is marked by the extension of the culturally homogeneous meaning and action structure to other contexts. In this process, the meaning and action structure become globally differentiated, producing an immense pressure to develop the requisite interpenetrations, structural couplings, and consensual domains on a globally differentiated basis. Meaning and action structure may develop asymmetrically, leading to serious discontinuities in the internationalisation process of the firm.

The **internationalisation of networks** may be differentiated on three levels. *Local networks* may begin a process of internationalisation similar to that of firms but based on collective action. Important brokers for access to global networks may be MNEs, which establish subsidiaries in such local networks. Another driver may be the concentration of the local network on a global niche market. *Business networks* may internationalise both by integration and expansion of formerly national business networks. *Strategic networks* founded in a national or regional context may be internationalised in order to exploit competitive advantages on global scale.

The **global network capability** comprises *intrasystemic networking* and *intersystemic networking*. **Intrasystemic networking** may be observed on two levels. Internationalising firms have to integrate the new activities generated by their entry in new markets into their ongoing operations and structures. They have to develop a globally differentiated network capability to integrate globally dispersed activities that are all characterised by different local contexts. MNEs already dispose of globally dispersed activities and may be conceived as an intraorganisational network.

Intersystemic networking has a different character on the three external network levels. In *local networks*, firms are embedded in a common social context, which provides a high degree of isomorphism, social capital, trust, and implicit co-ordination based on local trajectories. Networking emerges in a symbiotic way and is driven by both co-operative and competitive forces. *Global business networks* are linked by technological and other business related interdependencies and are co-ordinated by a global industry recipe, industry trajectories, and a common institutional context. *Strategic networks* are driven by goal-oriented decision-making and formal co-ordination. One or few powerful MNEs may dominate a strategic network and design it to extend their own value-added chain by inclusion of complementary firms such as suppliers into the global network.

The **capability of global evolutionary dynamics** facilitates the successful global reproduction of the firm on the basis of the principle of global differentiation and integration. The five evolutionary motors fuel this process. In the process of current globalisation, **life cycles** of products, practices, and organisational forms become shorter and call for a more innovative and flexible flow of organisational adaptations. **Dialectical processes** become more globally differentiated and are particularly influenced by the dominating duality of global vs. local. With the globalisation of organisational actors, dialectical processes between them globalise as well. **Teleological processes** of intentional evolutionary change have to be facilitated by the development of globally differentiated decision contexts, which are embedded in symbiotically nested consensual domains. **Darwinian VSR processes** extend to global scale as boundaries between formerly isolated social niches become blurred, causing a spillover of variations and selective retention in the global context. The **social autopoietic reproduction** is extended to global scale and leads to the formation and reproduction of global systems. This process is fuelled by the emergence of global communication and meaning structures.

The management of globalisation has to pay tribute to these developments and to strengthen the individual globalisation properties and capabilities and their symbiotic interplay. Of particular importance is the dynamic management of differences and variety across organisational units and contexts in the flow of globalisation.

7 Conclusions

Globalisation induces a liquefaction of global competition, which culminates in a dynamic global network competition. Research on globalisation has produced a quite amorphous landscape of literature, in which the term is used to describe different phenomena on different levels of social life. Within the business context, globalisation is described as both a contingency driving global competition towards increasing complexity and dynamic and as a process of firms adapting to this process by developing global strategies and structures. Completely missing is a perspective, which integrates both the globalisation process and the globalisation of individual firms, pariculary in form of a co-evolutionary interplay.

Particularly this very scattered and heterogeneous research landscape provides the motivation for the **overarching objective** of this study, which has been to provide a **comprehensive framework** for the identification and explanation of properties, characteristics, and mechanisms of globalisation processes both of individuals firms and of their co-evolutionary interplay with their globalising environment. Therefore, a basic framework has been developed that allows for the explanation of the globalisation of the firm and its environment as an evolutionary process and that provides the possibility to symbiotically integrate existing specialised approaches, which explain certain aspects of globalisation. This basic framework has been developed on the basis of social evolutionary theories and allows for the integration of knowledge from more specialised theories.

A *second objective* derived from this holistic approach has been the **explanation of the whole evolutionary process of the firm**; as such a perspective is completely missing. The *third objective* has been to outline **specific theories** contributing to an understanding of **global evolutionary processes** in detail in order to generate a comprehensive and in-depth knowledge base on globalisation processes. A *fourth objective* of this study has been the identification and description of **motors of global evolutionary change** and a *fifth* the description and explanation of the **co-evolutionary interplay** of **globalisation as a social phenomenon** and the **globalisation of individual firm** within this stream of social evolution.

The *main objective* of this study thus has been **theory building** in order to develop a **holistic, evolutionary approach to the globalisation of firms**, which also offers free space for specific theories contributing to such a perspective.

On a general level, three **subprocesses** constitute **globalisation**: internationalisation, global network formation, and global evolutionary dynamics. Organisations expose the same constitutive processes in their individual globalisation and develop respective capabilities within their co-evolutionary interplay. Literature in the realm of globalisation has been organised along these three basic characteristics in order to provide in-depth knowledge within each perspective and to discover knowledge, which may contribute to an integration of the three basic perspectives. The description of the three globalisation dimensions on firm level is much more comprehensive, when it is embedded in the relevant context where the globalisation of individual firms takes place.

Observation of a phenomenon is only possible on the basis of distinctions. The observation of a *'moving target'* - as in the case of globalising firms - presupposes a definition of the relevant background in order to identify any kind of process. This background is provided by a description of globalisation as a historical process in which the globalisation of individual firms takes place. Consequently, **Chapter 2** showed that globalisation is a social evolutionary process in which social system formation extends to global scale. It is a historical process that has been unfolding for thousands of years. While international trade already took place in ancient cultures, the formation of social systems with global interdependencies began with technological and organisational innovations in the 15th century. From this perspective, globalisation is an underlying social process including subprocesses such as internationalisation or transnationalisation. The latter concepts presuppose activities between nation states (internationalisation) or across nation states (transnationalisation), which were first founded in the 16th century. Historically, both phenomena are much more specific and temporally bounded than the underlying globalisation process. Globalisation is the historical process in which the evolutionary principle of social differentiation and integration is principally not any more restricted to national or cultural boundaries but **extended to global scale**. It extends from locally dispersed to globally nested social systems from local to global level. Especially the economic system has become independent of national or regional boundaries because of the technological and social developments in recent decades. The result is a process of increasing differentiation and integration on a now principally global basis. Within the global business context this dialectical process is particularly apparent in the duality of global integration vs. local responsiveness.

As argued above, globalisation is constituted by three subprocesses *First*, **processes of internationalisation** induce changes in the global extension of social systems by a spatial differentiation of social actors on global scale and by the formation of social systems with worldwide extension (e.g. *'born globals'*). *Second*, **processes of global network formation** create growing interdependencies between social actors on global scale and a growing integration of their communication, activities, and structures. *Third*, **processes of evolutionary dynamics** cause a compression of social time and space and drive the differentiation and integration of social systems on global scale.

The three subprocesses of globalisation apply to all kinds of social systems, from society to to the level of organisational units and constitute the globalisation of social systems. On the level of the individual social system, they are reflected in the respective internationalisation capability, global network capability, and capability of global evolutionary dynamics. From a system's perspective it is thus possible to derive evolutionary principles, which should be explained by an evolutionary theory of the globalisation of firms. Such a theory should capture the whole evolutionary process including the firm's '*birth*' (foundation), its co-evolutionary interplay with its environment, and its reproduction. Accordingly, the evolutionary principles to be explained are (1) **foundation of firms**, (2) **co-evolution of firm and environment**, (3) **global differentiation and integration of firms**, and (4) **global evolutionary dynamics of environment and firm**. Evolutionary dynamics follow the principle of differentiation and integration. Five distinct evolutionary motors, which are explained in Chapter 5.1.2.4, may drive this principle (life cycle, teleological, dialectical, Darwinian variation and selective retention 'VSR', and social autopoietic). The basic evolutionary principles have served as a framework to evaluate the contribution of all theoretical perspectives outlined in this publication to an evolutionary perspective of globalisation.

Chapter 3 illuminated **internationalisation processes** as the first of the three underlying subprocesses of globalisation. Basically two streams of literature may be identified within the realm of the internationalisation of firms: internationalisation strategy and internationalisation theory.

Internationalisation strategies may be differentiated in *market entry strategies* with a focus on international differentiation and a focus on the individual market entry and *international business strategies*, which generally balance differentiation and integration of business activities in the global context.

Internationalisation has been subject to theoretical research since the 1950s. Several **internationalisation theories** have been developed meanwhile. **Processual internationalisation** theories provide such a dynamic perspective but generally do so without conceptualisation of an evolutionary motor or mechanism, leading to a basically teleological and predefined course of internationalisation with fixed stages. The **international life cycle** described by Vernon (1966) is constituted by stages documenting the life of a business from its birth to its death along fixed stages. **Stage models of organisational structures** describe the development and change of organisational structures in the course of internationalisation, usually from a simple to a complex from.

The most comprehensive view on internationalisation processes is conveyed by the **learning-based stage theories** developed by Uppsala School, Helsinki School (together Scandinavian School), and the Innovation School. While the Scandinavian model comprises the whole internationalisation process from first steps to the genesis of a multinational enterprise along fixed stages, the innovation model is restricted to an export perspective. All models conceive internationalisation as an incremental, learning-based process along fixed stages in a centrifugal way with an increasing psychic and business distance to the explored markets. While the innovation model ends with fully developed export activities, the Scandinavian model begins with exports from the home base and ends with the formation of a MNE with subsidiaries in different national markets. Though based on a learning perspective, the models do not provide an explanation for global evolutionary dynamics and suffer from several restrictions. The underlying logic of the models is intriguing and captured very well the context of the 1970s but encounters limitations with increasing dynamics, skipping of stages, decreasing importance of distances, and the emergence of born globals as firms being global from inception rather than expanding in a rings-in-the-water mode.

Literature on born globals is still in its infancy and has to develop a complementary position vis-à-vis traditional internationalisation theory. Born globals are observed with a dominant focus on entrepreneurship and personal networks. The emergence of born global firms is already well researched. Still missing is an observation of globalisation processes after the global emergence. This perspective would be quite interesting as born globals are imprinted with globalisation capabilities from inception and are not marked by a distinction between home-culture and '*foreign*' markets but still are start-ups that have to develop their global activity and meaning structure, particularly with regard to firm-specific capabilities. Therefore, they have to develop globalisation capabilities just like traditional internationalisers, too, with the marked difference that the latter have to overcome the faltline between home-based and globally differentiated activities and structures.

The **discontinuous stage theories** provide an interesting and complementary perspective to the incremental stage models. The **GAINS paradigm** ('*Gestalt approach*') derives different internationalisation profiles but was not developed any further. The **dynamic internationalisation theory** provides a more differentiated view due to the integration of different organisational change concepts from deep structure to surface structure and from episodical to epochal change. The underlying **strategic process** perspective offers a quite sophisticated spectrum of change concepts. On a stand-alone basis, the discontinuous stage theories represent innovative concepts in the area of internationalisation by import of concepts from organisational change literature but have not matured to consistent theories explaining internationalisation processes. This may also be attributed to a missing adoption of the approaches by other researchers in the international business community.

The **knowledge-based theory of internationalisation** is only emerging and still represents more an extension of economic and learning-based internationalisation theories. It may thus serve as an approach integrating these two distinct research streams. The eclectic character of the knowledge-based view may sustain the development of a more integrative approach to internationalisation. Such an integrative approach to internationalisation may serve as a theoretical '*region*' filling the internationalisation perspective in the evolutionary framework of globalisation developed in the course of this study. Particularly the conceptual closeness between a knowledge-based approach and the meaning-based layout of the evolutionary framework allow for a close and complementary integration.

On balance, the described approaches to internationalisation cover important aspects of internationalisation processes. Learning-based stage theories and literature on SMEs, born globals, and international business strategy also include aspects of network formation as a facilitator of internationalisation. Learning-based stage theories are implicitly based on learning as an evolutionary driver but none of the internationalisation approaches defines or conceptualises network capabilities or evolutionary mechanisms explicitly.

Chapter 4 focused on **processes of global network formation**, which are described on several levels. **Interorganisational networks** from local to global level dominate the external network context of a firm. On the local level, networks are nurtured by a **local milieu**, which provides the local resources, infrastructure, social capital, and innovative milieu. Local milieus are the context in which innovations and distinct capabilities can develop in a path-dependent process. Firms embedded in such a local milieu have access to the local network resources and are imprinted by the local characteristics, facilitating an innovative learning context.

Embedded in local milieus may develop **clusters** and **industrial districts** as specific local firm networks in specific businesses. Such local networks can exploit advantages from co-specialisation and collective learning, both facilitating flexible and innovative technological trajectories on local levels. Such local networks may even dominate global niche businesses and are interesting locations for innovation-seeking MNEs.

On different geographical levels may develop **business networks**, which usually comprise an entire industry or industrial niche. The industry's firms and their respective organisation sets basically constitute the business network. Business networks are thus an emergent phenomenon rather than the product of strategic choice. The contrary is true for strategic networks, which are based on intended co-operative relations formed for the pursuit of specific goals and purposes. Such strategic relations may even develop between competitors in selected functional or geographical areas. Different ideal types of strategic networks were developed in the 1980s, when the transnationalisation of global business nurtured an increased interorganisational orientation. While strategic networks are subject to strategic choice and planning, business networks rather represent a context for individual firm behaviour.

In all network contexts, structural and processual properties influence the evolutionary capacity of a firm. The position of a firm in a network may provide it with substantial power and informational advantages. The dynamic of a network profoundly influences the evolutionary perspectives of the individual firms that constitute it. Embeddedness and social capital in a network may provide access to strategic resources such as information or trust. Different coupling intensities may favour a more efficiency-oriented stable network fabric or a more variety generating and change-oriented network profile. Firms may explore and exploit the advantages offered by different network levels and act as bridges. Particularly globally operating firms may act as bridges between networks from local to global level and thus combine globally differentiated exploration and exploitation of competitive advantages.

The globally differentiated pursuit of competitive advantages may also be facilitated by the formation of **global intraorganisational networks**. Global network formation already emerges in the course of initial internationalisation but is traditionally the subject of MNE research. From this perspective, MNEs are conceptualised as global networks due to their **internal differentiation** and the **global dispersion** of organisational units and co-operations. Along with the dispersion emerge interdependencies and different coupling intensities between the MNE units. In this context, cross-unit learning and structural flexibility are crucial in the evolutionary interplay of strategy and structure.

The '**Process School**' of international management has basically developed the '*industry recipe*' in MNE network research. Based on the dominant duality '**global integration vs. local responsiveness**' in MNE-networks several concepts of normative **strategies** and **organisation** have been developed. The emerging **ideal type** of the '*transnational*' (Bartlett 1986, Bartlett/Ghoshal 1989), '*multifocus*' (Prahalad/Doz 1987) or '*heterarchic*' (Hedlund 1986) firm balances the duality by simultaneously exploiting advantages from both dimensions. The focus is on administrative mechanisms and decision-making contexts. The ideal type of MNE management crystallises in '**context management**', where headquarters provides the formal administrative context within which strategic flexibility can be exploited by the globally dispersed units. Local subsidiaries are conceptualised as '*Janus-faced*' and integrated in both the MNE network and the respective local network. Subsidiaries may adopt different strategic roles in the context management of the MNE network depending on their resource endowments, capabilities, or criticality of the local market.

The development of such differentiated subsidiary roles has led to the development of a large stream of research on **intraorganisational roles in MNEs**. Early research in the late 1970s focused on the traditional dyadic relationship between headquarters and subsidiary. The main perspective was constituted by the duality of '*centralisation vs. subsidiary autonomy*'. In the 1980s, the focus changed to more differentiated subsidiary roles. Important starting points are **subsidiary initiatives**, which provide a basis for the assignment of subsidiary mandates and the development of subsidiary roles. Subsidiary initiatives vary in their functional and geographical scope. The most prominent **subsidiary mandates** are world product mandates but may also be directed at other specific business levels. In a next step, the development of centres of excellence already implies an increased focus on strategic capabilities at subsidiary level. The strategic position of subsidiaries is generally the focus of **subsidiary role typologies**, which have been developed in abundance along a variety of dimensions such as knowledge flows between subsidiaries and headquarters or the criticality of local and MNE network resources. Subsidiary role typologies provide a basis for the development of normative subsidiary roles and subsequent strategies. However, subsidiary roles may change in the course of a subsidiary's development so that models of **subsidiary evolution** have been developed that give an idea of typical subsidiary trajectories on a basically teleological or life cycle basis.

Chapter 5 provided a perspective on global evolutionary dynamics. **Social** and **economic evolutionary theories** adapt principles of biological evolution to social structures. Traits in sociological theories and routines in evolutionary economics take the role of genes in biological reproduction. Social evolution is much more dynamic due to intended evolution and the speed of horizontal (Lamarckian) reproduction by communication and learning as compared to vertical (Darwinian) reproduction along hereditary trajectories between generations. Nonetheless, evolutionary dynamics are conceived to be caused by the Darwinian mechanism of variation and selective retention. Gidden's **theory of structuration** explains the (re-)production of social structure on the basis of social practices. According to the notion of the *duality of structure*, the structural properties of social systems are both medium and outcome of the practices they recursively organise. Social structure and social practices are reproduced in a recursive interplay, reflecting the evolutionary interplay of the meaning and action system in social systems theory.

Social evolutionary theories conceptualise **organisational transformation** in terms of life cycles and different phases of continuous or discontinuous change. Such change processes may also take the form of a punctuated equilibrium with stable phases of incremental change punctuated by phases of radical change. Such change intervals differ in terms of duration (e.g. epochs or episodes) and intensity (e.g. deep structure or surface structure). On the basis of their inherent dynamics, organisations may even be characterised as relentlessly shifting or continuously morphing. In general, social evolutionary theory identifies four distinct evolutionary mechanisms (life cycle, teleological, dialectical, and Darwinian) that are driving organisational transformation and serve as a building block in the evolutionary theory of the globalisation of firms. These four mechanisms are complemented by the motor of autopoietic reproduction of social systems.

The **knowledge-based view** of management provides a rich tool kit for the evolution of social systems. The reproduction of knowledge can be described by means of the identified evolutionary mechanisms. *First*, knowledge may be subject to **life cycles**, particularly in technology-related areas. The existence of such regular life cycles in knowledge reproduction in different industries or areas may have a significant impact on organisational form and transformation. *Second*, **teleological knowledge reproduction** takes generally place in the form of knowledge management, i.e. the intentional evolution of knowledge by deliberate learning processes. Models of the learning process itself are generally akin to the traditional decision-making sequence in a recursively-closed form. Learning processes may be nurtured on different levels and by the means of different strategies.

Increasingly, the **Darwinian evolutionary motor** of variation and selective retention is integrated into learning models in order to import evolutionary dynamics into the knowledge perspective. Variation may basically take the form of imitation (isomorphism) or innovation (internal or external). Selection is generally based on an internal decision-making process or external selection of evolutionary '*fit*' knowledge. Retention resembles very much the process of institutionalisation, specifically in form of codification and diffusion. Retention of knowledge may also take the form of implementation when knowledge is retained at the action level.

Dialectical reproduction of knowledge is particularly ingrained in MNEs due to the huge differences in knowledge structures and processing styles. As stated by Wiesmann (1993), international management is the management of differences and as such a forum for learning processes. Besides the dominating dualities of global vs. local and headquarters vs. subsidiary, all relations between internal and external actors adopt a dialectical form of learning as different positions and expectations lead to a continous process of mutual learning. In this process, dialectics are continuously adapted and updated along the process of evolutionary change.

The **autopoietical reproduction** of knowledge, which describes the cognitive process of learning itself by the processing of meaning on the basis of guiding differences still has not been adopted explicitly but is implicitly apparent in the concepts of path-dependence and trajectories in the knowledge evolution independent of teleological influence.

In the **global context**, knowledge structures and modes of knowledge processing may vary significantly across different local contexts. Such differences in national cultures produce the *'country-of-origin effect'*. Firms are imprinted with characteristics of the national culture and develop culture-specific international strategies and structures as well as different learning and information behaviour. In the process of **internationalisation**, firms extend their knowledge structure and integrate global variety, thus facilitating the institutionalisation of international management and global knowledge structures. **Global network knowledge** accumulates along a path-dependent trajectory in the evolving multinational learning network. MNEs may be conceived as global scanners, knowledge creating networks, global selection regimes, and global retention mechanisms. In MNEs, learning processes and particularly knowledge diffusion across dispersed subsidiaries are central to a symbiotic evolution. Knowledge how to cope with **global evolutionary dynamics** is accumulated in the process of globalisation and retained in capabilities of global dynamic morphing. Though teleological motors are dominating the dynamics of MNEs, all evolutionary motors are critical for its reproduction and the organisation at least implicitly learns how to balance the different dynamics, which may adopt quite different forms in different geographical and organisational regions.

The evolutionary theory developed in **Chapter 6** is built on two conceptual levels. A general evolutionary theory of the firm has been developed before this, in turn, has been adapted to the level of globalisation as an evolutionary process.

Organisations may be conceptualised as allopoietic or autopoietic systems. As **allopoietic**, or *syn-referential systems,* they are constituted by individuals as the basic organisational elements. They dispose of a resource base and conduct the primary activities of the organisation in order to achieve the stated goals. Allopoietic systems are instruments and subject to teleological, intended change. Organisations may also be conceptualised as **autopoietic** *systems*, which reproduce themselves independent of distinct individual actors. Organisations as autopoietic social systems emerge from the stream of social evolution. As enacted, second-level social systems, they are both subject to voluntary, intentional change and emergent, evolutionary change. In globally operating firms, it is important to identify the idiosyncratic properties of the globally differentiated systems and their relations in order to develop transparency and profiles (identities), which may provide the means for a more symbiotic and directed global evolutionary across all units.

Change and reproduction of social systems is based on the evolutionary interplay of the constituting meaning and action system. This interplay is driven by a **process of differentiation and integration**, providing the system with complexity, adaptability, and dynamic. The process of differentiation and integration is fuelled by the five different motors of evolutionary change (life cycle, teleological, dialectical, Darwinian VSR, and social autopoietic). The Principle of differentiation and integration and the five evolutionary motors are subject to differences in the global context. Therefore, there may develop organisational regions within a globally operating firm with different dynamics and different relative effects of the individual motors.

The evolution of social systems is structurally coupled with the evolution of its environment. Therefore, the globalisation of a firm has to be observed in its **co-evolutionary interplay** with the environment. The global differentiation of systems leads to a variety of local and global co-evolutionary contexts between units of the globally operating firm and the respective environments. Subsidiaries are classical examples of dual isomorphic pressures resulting from differentiated structural coupling.

Social systems develop four principal capabilities of globalisation, which reflect the three basic dimensions of globalisation. The fourth dimension results from the extraction of the **entrepreneurial capability** from the **internationalisation capability** in order to focus explicitly on the phenomenon of global system foundation. Entrepreneurial, internationalisation, global network, and global evolutionary capabilities are all applied to a firm and to an external network level.

The **foundation of firms** on global level becomes more probable due to the globalisation of communication and activity structures. Situations of double contingency and interdependencies between entrepreneurs and organisational actors increase so that the global foundation of new firms becomes a logical consequence. A further reason is the global knowledge and experience of the founders, who already dispose of the ingredients for a successful international new venture. Facilitators of global foundations such as banks, clients, and venture capitalists are part of the developing global context for foundations. The **foundation of global networks** may occur on two levels. First, the foundation of global business networks is driven by an emergent process, which leads to the development of global industries. On the other hand, strategic networks are founded to facilitate the intentional pursuit of competitive advantages by exploiting network resources in specific functional, product, or geographic areas.

The **internationalisation of firms** is marked by the extension of the culturally homogeneous meaning and action structure to other contexts. In this process, the meaning and action structure become globally differentiated, producing an immense pressure to develop the requisite interpenetrations, structural couplings, and consensual domains on a globally differentiated basis. Meaning and action structure may develop asymmetrically, leading to serious discontinuities in the internationalisation process of the firm.

The **internationalisation of networks** may be differentiated on three levels. *Local networks* may begin a process of internationalisation similar to that of firms but based on collective action. Important brokers for access to global networks may be MNEs, which establish subsidiaries in such local networks. Another driver may be the concentration of the local network on a global niche market. *Business networks* may internationalise both by integration and expansion of formerly national business networks. *Strategic networks* founded in a national or regional context may be internationalised in order to exploit competitive advantages on global scale.

The **global network capability** comprises *intrasystemic networking* and *intersystemic networking*. **Intrasystemic networking** may be observed on two levels. Internationalising firms have to integrate the new activities generated by their entry in new markets into their ongoing operations and structures. They have to develop a globally differentiated network capability to integrate globally dispersed activities that are all characterised by different local contexts. MNEs already dispose of globally dispersed activities and may be conceived as an intraorganisational network.

Intersystemic networking has a different character on the three external network levels. In *local networks*, firms are embedded in a common social context, which provides a high degree of isomorphism, social capital, trust, and implicit co-ordination based on local trajectories. Networking emerges in a symbiotic way and is driven by both co-operative and competitive forces. *Global business networks* are linked by technological and other business related interdependencies and are co-ordinated by a global industry recipe, industry trajectories, and a common institutional context. *Strategic networks* are driven by goal-oriented decision-making and formal co-ordination. One or few powerful MNEs may dominate a strategic network and design it to extend their own value-added chain by inclusion of complementary firms such as suppliers into the global network.

The **capability of global evolutionary dynamics** facilitates the successful global reproduction of the firm on the basis of the principle of global differentiation and integration. The five evolutionary motors fuel this process. In the process of current globalisation, **life cycles** of products, practices, and organisational forms become shorter and call for a more innovative and flexible flow of organisational adaptations. **Dialectical processes** become more globally differentiated and are particularly influenced by the dominating duality of global vs. local. With the globalisation of organisational actors, dialectical processes between them globalise as well. **Teleological processes** of intentional evolutionary change have to be facilitated by the development of globally differentiated decision contexts, which are embedded in symbiotically nested consensual domains. **Darwinian VSR processes** extend to global scale as boundaries between formerly isolated social niches become blurred, causing a spillover of variations and selective retention in the global context. The **social autopoietic reproduction** is extended to global scale and leads to the formation and reproduction of global systems. This process is fuelled by the emergence of global communication and meaning structures.

The management of globalisation has to pay tribute to these developments and to strengthen the individual globalisation properties and capabilities and their symbiotic interplay. Of particular importance is the dynamic management of differences and variety across organisational units and contexts in the flow of globalisation.

☞ **Implications for globalisation as a historical process**
As discussed in the general systems theory, natural systems are characterised by a growth mechanism, which results from striving for the maintenance of autonomy and survival. The expansion proceeds on the basis of autopoietic processes that are continuously extended by the differentiation and integration of the system's functions and structure. Due to the described historical process of increasing complexity and extension of the system '*human society*', which has already reached the geographic extension of the environment '*earth*', the latter has to be conceived as the *relevant niche*. As the influence of the human society on the structure, fluctuations, and reproduction processes within the meta-system earth is increasing progressively, so is increasing its relevance for the order and reproductive capacity of the whole system. Consequently, the share of the human society in the meta-system's autopoietic organisation should increase, as its influence is decreasingly balanced and complemented by other, natural subsystems. Competition with other natural systems is quasi extinct and the allocation of resources is controlled by the human society. As a result, the possibility to equilibrate the proportionally increasing share of human society in the total terrestrial entropy

by import of free resources is shrinking. This leads to serious problems as the social transformation processes developed in the course of industrialisation are only to a very limited degree cyclic and sustainable, causing a process of increasing uncertainty and dynamics – not to mention the enormous loss of ecological variety and resources.

A current central problem is the basically autonomous reproduction of differentiated social subsystems. For example, the actors in the economic subsystem may always recur to the internal logic of economic efficiency and make it an imperative to reproduce autonomously with only a negligible consciousness to define efficiency not only as a whole on this subsystem level but also as a *'part'* within the social fabric of the *'whole'* (society). Globalisation is characterised by very asymmetrical levels of intensity, providing economic actors with maximum leverage while other functional systems are still basically national or locally bounded. The next step in globalisation thus is not to impede the internal logic and thus reproductive capacity of individual subsystems but to provide more symmetrical levels of globalisation and global mechanisms of structural coupling in order to facilitate a symbiotic reproduction of the global society as a whole in its natural environment.

The increasing relative importance of the human society as a subsystem of the *'blue planet'* induces its increasing importance for the reproduction of the meta-system and thus the necessity of an increasing requisite variety and self-organisation, which parallel proportionally the increasing differentiation and expansion. This is necessary to safeguard the dynamic equilibrium. Resulting from the logic of the system theory is the expectation of an **increasing importance of the self-organisational capacity of social systems** – particularly of the intended evolution. Without a profound learning process and the human society's acceptance of its responsibility for the reproduction of itself and of the meta-system, human society will expand uncontrolled, consuming excessively available negative entropy and implode after resources have been consumed. This also applies to society's subsystems like organisations due to the principles of self-similarity and recursiveness.

The subsystem *'economy'* regulates the transformation and exchange of resources and productive services in the society so that it embodies the most influential social function regarding the co-evolution with the natural environment. Calls for economic freedom hence should take into account that the accompanying responsibility for the results of economic activity is internalised as well. Should this be impossible, as in the case of public goods, mechanisms of social integration between the society's functional systems have to be established in order to equilibrate entropic processes caused by the economy. Ignorance of society's responsibility to provide negentropy would leave the whole task of selection to an environment marked by a decreasing variety and complexity and increasing entropy (i.e. pollution and extinction) due to human intervention. A still expanding human population characterised by an enormous consumption of natural resources does its best to minimise the own evolutionary capacity. On balance, the functional differentiation of social systems increases the efficiency within these functions. But the evolutionary motor also asks for an effective integration of these differentiated subsystems when effects caused by one systems spill over to other subsystems. The need for social integration seems to increase progressively, as the intrasystemic principle of competition within the economy even increases the forces of differentiation. This development led Terreberry (1968: 69) as early as 1968 to the question *'as to whether man actually has the capacity to cope with the turbulence that he has introduced into the environment'*. Therefore, the basic evolutionary capability of systems is increasingly not only that of organisation in terms of production or resource control but also that of self-organisation and self-control both as a part and as a whole. Globalisation leads to a domestication of the global social context and increasingly impedes the export of internal problems to external systems. Social actors have to globalise their worldview consequently further in order to identify potentials and responsibilities for the reproduction of human society as a whole, which may now be identified as a global society. In the inter-national world, such a holistic view was impossible due to competition between nation states and cultures. With an emerging identity as a *'whole'*, global society may be increasingly able to resolve problems fundamentally as there is no escape across borders.

☞ **Implication for the globalisation of firms**

As argued above, the liquefaction of global competition culminates in a global network competition, with globally differentiated and nested organisational actors as the main players. The process of differentiation and integration of social systems on global level will continue so that the evolutionary principles of the globalisation of firms may provide a good orientation for the main directions of globalisation tendencies.

Firstly, it is probable that the **foundation of firms** will be increasingly initiated by founders from different nations and cultures. This means an increase in the number of born globals and globally dispersed stakeholders. The global economy may be conceived as a rich new niche in which a '**new zoology**' is emerging (Mathews 2002). This means that not only the **form of foundation** will be increasingly taking place on global level but also that new **forms of organisations** will emerge, leading to the development of new organisational populations.

Secondly, the **co-evolution of firm and environment** is going to be globally differentiated so that evolutionary interplays of firms and their environment may be taking place from an exclusively local level like in many services, to a purely global level like in global industries and global niche markets. Between these two extremes there is a nested interplay of globally differentiated social environments and organisations so that simply the variety of evolutionary forms and contexts will increase. What becomes increasingly impossible is to conceive a social context as isolated because even the most remote tribes and social systems are in reach of global influences. Even localisation is increasingly dominated by choice rather than by missing means and alternatives for expansion. With an increasing symmetry between the globalisation degrees of different social functional subsystems, there will also be more symbiotic interplays between organisational actors from these subsystems. For example, there is already an increased co-operation between firms and universities in R&D or firms and local communities in the development of industrial districts.

Thirdly, **global differentiation and integration of firms** will lead to a sustained liquefaction of global competition. Inter- and intraorganisational networks will probably become both more differentiated with regard to specialisation and to the design of relations. A further blurring of boundaries on geographical, cultural, and organisational level may also be expected along with more flexible couplings between organisational actors. Increasing differentiation and integration of firms will increase the innovative capacity of firms and society, providing both with a larger variety of products, servives, and organisational forms. In turn, the increasing variety calls for requisite selection mechanisms, which are likely to be increasingly self-organisational.

Fourthly, **global evolutionary dynamics of environment and firm** already have propelled social systems to a level of complexity, which calls for increasing levels of self-organisation. **Life cycles** are getting shorter, calling for more variation and a more symbiotic flow in reproduction processes. This applies to both products and organisational fabric of firms. **Teleological processes** become more dynamic and complex, calling for the design of flexible and differentiated decision contexts within and across organisations. **Dialectical processes** may become more dynamic and accentuated due to the increasing velocity in the change of social systems and more differentiated due to the increasing global differentiation of organisational actors. **Darwinian dynamics** of variation and selective retention are deeply influenced by the blurring of boundaries as there are less isolated and protected niches. Globalisation itself means an expansion of social system reproduction from a local to a globally differentiated level, leading to spillovers of variations across different geographical and organisational niches. **Autopoietic dynamics** increase along with the increasing global expansion of communication and meaning processing. Social systems emerge on a globally differentiated level and begin their autopoietic reproduction in this environment. Organisational actors have to provide the means to facilitate the reproduction of globally differentiated systems with diverse meaning structures and modes of meaning processing. Globally differentiated systems have to develop the requisite interpenetrations, structural couplings, and consensual areas for a symbiotic reproduction of heterogeneous and globally dispersed units. These means are provided by the three global evolutionary capabilities.

☞ Implications for further research

A main demand resulting from the perspective developed in the course of the given approach is the adaptation to an **empirical level**. Such empirical adaptation may be pursued on quite different levels as the approach comprises the maximum extension of evolutionary processes. It may be interesting to sketch historical cases from a firm's foundation along its whole globalisation process, describing its internationalisation, the integration of the created global variety in network structures, and the evolutionary mechanisms dominating this process in different phases and organisational regions. Such a dynamic perspective may also be applied to shorter periods of organisational change or limited to specific units of observation. A particular application may be the observation of the emergence of born globals and their 'compressed globalisation process'. The same applies to a comparison between the globalisation process of born globals and traditional internationalisers whose internationalisation process appears to be increasingly compressed as well.

In large MNEs, the evolutionary approach may serve to identify basic dynamics in the reproduction of already existing global organisations. The approach may particularly help to capture the complexity of these processes and reduce it due to its nested design. MNEs may be observed as both selection and selected mechanism. This may be done on an inter- or intraorganisational basis. The conceptualisation of self-similar and nested social systems allows for a consistent application of concepts across all organisational levels. In addition, the conceptualisation of individuals as being part of both the firm and its environment also allows for an integration of the social context in the globally differentiated reproduction of MNEs. It may also be possible to identify organisational regions in MNEs, which differ in their constitution and their evolutionary drive.

On a **theoretical level**, the approach is designed to serve as a framework for the crystallisation of globalisation knowledge from different disciplines. In turn, it may serve as a source of theoretical variety and underpinnings for the more specialised approaches. As argued above, the conceptualisation of the co-evolutionary interplay between firms and their environment and the recursive reproduction of meaning and action system provide valuable concepts, which may enrich other theories. For example, evolutionary theories may find a theoretical underpinning for the adaptation of the Darwininan mechanism to the reproduction of social traits or routines, which is still done only metaphorically. The same applies to the knowledge-based view, which has neither a solid intersubjective nor systemic theoretical fundament with regard to reproduction and evolutionary processes in firms. Dynamic organisational theories may find it easier to use knowledge across theoretical boundaries when embedded in a common evolutionary framework. In such a framework, theories then represent different regions of knowledge linked by bridges rather than divided by faltlines based on different assumptions and conceptualisations, which do not allow the transfer of knowledge to another framework.

From a globalisation perspective, it is particularly important to have a framework that allows for the observation of the whole evolutionary process and not only of certain aspects. To remain in a traditional metaphor: it is important to know that the elephant is running and not only waving his tail.

References

Achenbach, S./Borghoff, T. (2004): *Exploration and exploitation of synergies in the context of a 'liquefaction' of global competition – Approach towards a better understanding of the relationship between immaterial resources as the basis for 'synergy management' representing a core dynamic capability*, Paper presented at the 4th EURAM-Conference in St. Andrews, Scotland

Ackoff, R. L. (1971): Towards a system of systems concepts, *Management Science*, Vol. 17, No. 11, pp. 661-671

Acs, Z.J./Preston, L. (1997): Small and medium-sized enterprises, technology, and globalization: Introduction to a special issue on small and medium-sized enterprises in the global economy, *Small Business Economics*, Vol. 9, No. 1, pp. 1-6

Aharoni, Y. (1966): *The foreign investment decision process*, Boston, MA: Harvard Graduate School of Business Administration

Aharoni, Y. (1993): Ownerships, networks and coalitions; in: Aharoni, Y. (ed.): *Coalitions and competition*, New York: Routledge, pp. 121-142

Aharoni, Y. (1993a): Globalization of professional business services; in: Aharoni, Y. (ed.): *Coalitions and Competition*, New York, NY: Routledge, pp. 1-19

Albrow, M. (1992): Globalization; in: Bottomore, T.B./Outhwaite, W. (eds.): *The Blackwell dictionary of twentieth century social thought*, Oxford: Basil Blackwell

Albrow, M. (1997): *The global age: State and society beyond modernity*, Stanford, CA: Stanford University Press

Aldrich, H.E. (1979): *Organizations and environments*, Englewood Cliffs, NJ: Prentice-Hall

Aldrich, H.E. (1999): *Organisations evolving*; London: Sage Publications

Aldrich, H.E./Kenworthy, A.L. (1999): The accidental entrepreneur: Campbellian antinomies and organizational foundings; in: Baum, J.A.C./McKelvey, B. (eds.): *Variations in organization science*, Thousand Oaks, CA: Sage Publications, pp. 19-34

Aldrich, H.E./Rosen, B./Woodward, W. (1987): The impact of social networks on business foundings and profit in a longitudinal study; in: Churchill, N.C./Hornaday, J.A./Kirchhoff, B.A./Krasner, O.J./Vesper, K.H. (eds.): *Frontiers of entrepreneurship research*, Wellesley, MA: Babson College, pp. 154-168

Aldrich, H.E./Zimmer, C. (1986): Entrepreneurship through social networks; in: Donald, S.L./Raymond, W.S. (eds.): *The art and science of entrepreneurship*, Cambridge, MA: Ballinger, pp. 3-24

Alexander, E.R. (1979): The design of alternatives in organizational contexts, a pilot study, *Administrative Science Quarterly*, Vol. 24, pp. 382-404

Almeida, P. (1996): Knowledge sourcing by foreign multinationals: Patent citation analysis in the U.S. semiconductor industry, *Strategic Management Journal*, Vol. 17, Special Issue Winter, pp. 155-165

Almeida, P./Grant, R.M./Song, J. (1998): The role of the international corporations in cross-border knowledge transfer in the semiconductor industry; in: Hitt, M.A./Ricart, I./Costa, J.E./Nixon, R.D. (eds.): *Managing strategically in an interconnected world*, Chichester et al.: John Wiley & Sons, pp. 119-148

Altmann, N./Sauer, D. (1989): *Integrative Rationalisierung und Zulieferindustrie*, Frankfurt a.M./New York: Campus

Alvesson, M. (1990): Organization: From substance to image?, *Organization Studies*, Vol. 11, No. 3, pp. 373-394

Alvesson, M. (1995): *Management of knowledge-intensive companies*, Berlin: De Gruyter

Amburgey, T.L./Kelly, D./Barnett, W.P. (1993): Resetting the clock: The dynamics of organizational change and failure, *Administrative Science Quarterly*, Vol. 38, No. 1, pp. 51-73

Amburgey, T.L./Miner, A.S. (1992): Strategic momentum: The effects of repetitive, positional, and contextual momentum on merger activity, *Strategic Management Journal*, Vol. 13, No. 5, pp. 335-348

Amburgey, T.L./Rao, H. (1996): Orgnizational ecology: Past, present, and future directions, *Academy of Management Journal*, Vol. 39, No. 5, pp. 1265-1286

Amin, A./Robins, K. (1991): These are not Marshallian times; in: Camagni, R. (ed.): *Innovation networks: Spatial perspectives*, London: Belhaven Press, pp. 105-120

Amit, R./Shoemaker, P.J.H. (1993): Strategic assets and organizational rent, *Strategic Management Journal*, Vol. 14, No. 1, pp. 33-46

Anand, J./Delios, A. (1997): Location specificity and the transferability of downstream assets to foreign subsidiaries, *Journal of International Business Studies*, Vol. 28, No. 3, pp. 579-603

Andersen, B. (2001): *Technological change and the evolution of corporate innovation: The structure of patenting 1890-1990*, Cheltenham, UK/Northampton, MA: Edward Elgar

Andersen, O. (1993): On the internationalization process of firms: A critical analysis, *Journal of International Business Studies*, Vol. 24, No. 2, pp. 209-231

Andersen, O. (1997): Internationalization and market entry mode: A review of theories and conceptual frameworks, *Management International Review*, Vol. 37, Special Issue 2, pp. 27-42

Anderson, P. (1999): Venture capital dynamics and the creation of variation through entrepreneurship; in: Baum, J.A.C./McKelvey, B. (eds.): *Variations in organization science*, Thousand Oaks, CA: Sage Publications, pp. 137-154

Andersson, Å.E. (1985): Creativity and regional development, *Papers of the Regional Science Association*, Vol. 56, pp. 5-20

Andersson, S. (2000): The internationalization of the firm from an entrepreneurial perspective, *International Studies of Management & Organization*, Vol. 30, No. 1, pp. 63-92

Andersson, U./Forsgren, M. (2000): In search of centres of excellence: Network embeddedness and subsidiary roles in multinational corporations, *Management International Review*, Vol. 40, No. 4, pp. 329-350

Andersson, U./Forsgren, M./Holm, U. (2001): Subsidiary embeddedness and competence development in MNCs: A multi-level analysis, *Organization studies*, Vol. 22, No. 6, pp. 1013-1034

Andersson, U./Forsgren, M./Holm, U. (2002): The strategic impact of external networks: Subsidiary performance and competence development in the multinational corporation, *Strategic Management Journal*, Vol. 23, pp. 979-996

Andersson, U./Johanson, J./Vahlne, J.-E. (1997): Organic acquisitions in the internationalisation process of the business firm, *Management International Review*, Vol. 37, Special Issue 2, pp. 67-84

Antonelli, C. (1998): Localized technological change and the evolution of standards as economic institutions; in: Chandler, A.D./Hagström, P./Sölvell, Ö. (eds.): *The dynamic firm*, Oxford: Oxford University Press, pp. 78-100

Archibugi, D./Lundvall, B.-Å. (2001): Introduction: Europe and the learning economy; in: Archibugi, D./Lundvall, B.-Å. (eds.): *The globalizing learning economy*, Oxford: Oxford University Press, pp. 1-20

Argote, L. (1999): *Organizational learning: Creating, retaining and transferring knowledge*, Boston, MA et al.: Kluwer Academic Publishers

Arvidsson, N. (1999): *The ignorant MNE: The role of perception gaps in knowledge management*, Stockholm: IIB Stockholm School of Economics

Asanuma, B. (1989): Manufacturer-supplier relationships in Japan and the concept of relation-specific skill, *Journal of the Japanese and International Economies*, Vol. 3, No. 1, pp. 1-30

Asheim, B.T. (1997): "Learning regions" in a globalised world economy: Towards a new competitive advantage of industrial districts?; in: Taylor, M./Conti, S. (eds.): *Interdependent and uneven development: Global-local perspectives*, Aldershot, UK: Ashgate Publishing, pp. 143-176

Astley, W.G. (1985): The two ecologies: Population and community perspectives on organizational evolution, *Administrative Science Quarterly*, Vol. 30, No. 2, pp. 224-241

Audretsch, D.B. (1997): Technological regimes, industrial demography and the evolution of industrial structures, *Industrial and Corporate Change*, Vol. 6, No. 1, pp. 49-82

Axelrod, R./Dion, D. (1988): The further evolution of cooperation, *Science*, Vol. 242, pp. 1385-1390

Axtman, R. (ed.) (1998): *Globalization and Europe: Theoretical and empirical investigations*, London: Pinter

Ayal, I./Raban, J. (1987): Export management structure and successful high technology innovation; in: Reid, S.D./Rosson, P.J. (eds.): *Managing export entry and expansion*, New York, NY: Praeger

Baer, J.B./Saxon, O.G. (1949): *Commodity exchanges and futures trading*, New York: Harper & Brothers

Bahrami, H./Evans, S. (1987): Stratocracy in high-technology firms, *California Management Review*, Vol. 30, No. 1, pp. 51-65

Ball, D.A./McCulloch, Jr./Wendell, H. (1999): *International business: The challenge of global competition*, International edition, 7th ed., Boston, MA: Irwin/McGraw-Hill

Bamberger, I./Evers, M. (1996): Internationalisierungsverhalten von Klein- und Mittelunternehmen; in: Engelhard, J./Rehkugler, H. (eds.): *Strategien für nationale und internationale Märkte*, Wiesbaden: Gabler

Bangert, D.C./Pirzada, K. (1991): *Culture and negotiation*, Working Paper 1991-4, University of Hawaii, College of Social Sciences, Matsunage Institute for peace: Program on conflict resolution

Barber, B.R. (1995): *Jihad vs McWorld*, New York, NY: Times Books

Barkema, H.G./Bell, J.H.J./Pennings, J.M. (1996): Foreign entry, cultural barriers, and learning, *Strategic Management Journal*, Vol. 17, No. 2, pp. 151-166

Barkema, H.G./Vermeulen, F. (1998): International expansion through start-up or acquisition: A learning perspective, *Academy of Management Journal*, Vol. 41, No. 1, pp. 7-26

Barnard, C.I. (1938): *The functions of the executive*, Cambridge, MA: Harvard University Press

Barney, J.B. (1986): Strategic factor markets: Expectations, luck and business strategy, *Management Science*, Vol. 32, pp. 1231-1241

Baron, J.N./Hannan, M.T./Burton, M.D. (1999): Building the iron cage: Determinants of managerial intensity in the early years of organizations, *American Sociological Review*, Vol. 64, No. 4, pp. 527-547

Bartlett, C. (1981): Multinational structural change: Evolution versus reorganization; in: Otterbeck, L. (ed.): *The management of headquarters-subsidiary relationships in MNCs*, New York: Saint Martin's Press, pp. 121-145

Bartlett, C. (1986): Building and managing the transnational: The new organizational challenge; in: Porter, M.E. (ed.): *Competition in global industries*, Boston, MA: Harvard University Press, pp. 367-401

Bartlett, C./Ghoshal, S. (1986): Tap your subsidiaries for global reach, *Harvard Business Review*, Vol. 64, No.6, pp. 87-94

Bartlett, C./Ghoshal, S. (1987): Managing across borders: New strategic requirements, *Sloan Management Review*, Vol. 28, No. 4, pp. 7-17

Bartlett, C./Ghoshal, S. (1988): Organizing for worldwide effectiveness: The transnational solution, *California Management Review*, Vol. 31, No. 1, pp. 54-74

Bartlett, C./Ghoshal, S. (1989*): Managing across borders: The transnational solution*, Boston, MA: Harvard Business School Press

Bartlett, C./Ghoshal, S. (1991): Global strategic management: Impact on the frontiers of strategy research, *Strategic Management Journal*, Vol. 12, No. 4, pp. 5-16

Bartunek, J.M. (1984): Changing interpretive schemes and organizational restructuring: The example of a religious order, *Administrative Science Quarterly*, Vol. 29, No. 3, pp. 355-372

Bartunek, J.M./Betters-Reed, B.L. (1987): The stages of organizational creation, *Americam Journal of Community Psychology*, Vol. 15, No. 3, pp. 287-303

Baum, J.A.C. (1999): Whole-part coevolutionary competition in organizations; in: Baum, J.A.C./McKelvey, B. (eds.): *Variations in organization science*, Thousand Oaks, CA: Sage Publications, pp. 113-136

Baum, J.A.C./Ingram, P. (2002): Interorganizational learning and network organization: Toward a behavioral theory of the interfirm; in: Augier, M./March, J.G. (eds.): *The economics of choice, change and organization: Essays in memory of Richard M. Cyert*, Cheltenham, UK: Edward Elgar, pp. 191-218

Baum, J.A.C./Singh, J. (1994): Organizational hierarchies and evolutionary processes: Some reflections on a theory of organizational evolution; in: Baum, J.A.C./Singh, J. (eds.): *Evolutionary dynamics of organizations*, New York/Oxford: Oxford University Press, pp. 3-20

Bauman, Z. (1998): *Globalization: The human consequences*, Cambridge: Polity Press

Bäurle, I. (1996): *Internationalisierung als Prozessphänomen*, Wiesbaden: Gabler

Beamish, P.W. (1999): The role of alliances in international entrepreneurship; in: Rugman, A.M./Wright, R.W. (eds.): *International entrepreneurship: Globalization of emerging businesses*, Stanford, CT: JAI Press, pp. 43-62

Becattini, G./Rullani, E. (1994): Sistema locale e mercato globale; in: Becattini, G./Vaccà, S. (eds.): Prospettive degli studi di politica industriale in Italia, Milano: Franco Angeli, pp. 21-39

Beechler, S./Bird, A./Taylor, S. (1998): Organisational learning in Japanese MNCs: Four affiliate archetypes, in: Birkinshaw, J./Hood, N. (eds.): *Multinational corporate evolution and subsidiary development*, Houndmills, Basingstoke: Macmillan Press, pp. 333-367

Bell, J./Young, S. (1998): Towards an integrative framework of the internationalization of the firm; in: Hooley, R./Loveridge, R./Wilson, D. (eds.): *Internationalization: Process, context and markets*, London: Macmillan Press, pp. 5-28

Bendt, A. (2000): *Wissenstransfer in multinationalen Unternehmungen*, Wiesbaden: Gabler

Benito, G.R.G./Gripsrud, G. (1992): The expansion of foreign direct investment: Discrete rational location choices or a cultural learning process?, *Journal of International Business Studies*, Vol. 23, No. 3, pp. 461-476

Benito, G.R.G./Welch, L.S. (1997): De-internationalization, *Management International Review*, Vol. 37, Special Issue 2, pp. 7-25

Bensedrine, J./Koayashi, H. (1998): Firms' strategies and national institutional environments; in: Hitt, M.A./Ricart, I./Costa, J.E./Nixon, R.D. (eds.): *Managing strategically in an interconnected world*, Chichester: John Wiley & Sons, pp. 39-54

Benson, J.K. (1975): The interorganizational network as a political economy, *Administrative Science Quarterly*, Vol. 20, No. 2, pp. 229-249

Benson, J.K. (1977): Organizations: A dialectical view, *Administrative Science Quarterly*, Vol. 22, No. 1, pp. 1-21

Berger, P.L. (2002): *Many globalizations: cultural diversity in the contemporary world*, New York: Oxford University Press

Berra, L./Piatti, L./Vitali, G. (1995): The internationalization process in the small and medium sized firms: A case study on the Italian clothing industry, *Small Business Economics*, Vol. 7, No. 1, pp. 67-75

Best, M.H. (2002): *Regional growth dynamics: a capabilities perspective*, Oxford: Oxford University Press, pp. 179-194

Bettman, J.R./Weitz, B. (1983): Attributions in the board room: Causal reasoning in corporate annual reports, *Administrative Science Quarterly*, Vol. 28, No. 2, pp. 165-183

Beyer, J.M. (1981): Ideologies, values, and decision-making in organizations; in Nystrom, P.C./Starbuck, W.H. (eds.): *Handbook of organizational design, Vol. II*, Oxford: Oxford University Press, pp. 166-202

Biggart, N.W./Guillén, M.F. (1999): Developing difference: Social rise of the auto industries in South Korea, Taiwan, Spain and Argentina, *Sociological Review*, Vol. 4, No. 5, pp. 722

Biggart, N.W./Orrù, M./Hamilton, G.G. (1997): *The economic organization of East Asian capitalism*, Thousand Oaks: Sage Publications

Bilkey, W.J. (1978): An attempted integration of the literature on the export behavior of firms, *Journal of International Business Studies*, Vol. 9, No. 1, pp. 33-46

Bilkey, W.J./Tesar, G. (1977): The export behavior of smaller Wisconsin manufacturing firms, *Journal of International Business Studies*, Vol. 8, No.1, pp. 93-98

Birkinshaw, J. (1994): *Global centres of excellence*, Paper presented at the Academy of International Business Annual Meeting, Boston, MA

Birkinshaw, J. (1994a): *Entrepreneurial behaviour in multinational subsidiaries*, Paper presented at Academy of Management Annual Meeting, Dallas, TX

Birkinshaw, J. (1994b): Approaching heterarchy: A review of the literature on multinational strategy and structure, *Advances in International Comparative Management*, Vol. 9, pp. 111-144

Birkinshaw, J. (1996): How multinational subsidiary mandates are gained and lost, *Journal of International Business Studies*, Vol. 27, No. 3, pp. 467-495

Birkinshaw, J. (1997): Entrepreneurship in multinational corporations: The characteristics of subsidiary initiatives, *Strategic Management Journal*, Vol. 18, No. 3, pp. 207-229

Birkinshaw, J. (2000): Multinational corporate strategy and organization: An internal market perspective; in: Hood, N./Young, S. (eds.): *The globalization of multinational enterprise activity and economic development*, Houndsmills, Basingstoke: Macmillan, pp. 55-79

Birkinshaw, J. (2000a): *Entrepreneurship in the global firm*, London: Sage Publications

Birkinshaw, J. (2001): Strategy and management of MNE subsidiaries; in: Rugman, A.M./Brewer, T.L. (eds.): *The Oxford handbook of international business*, Oxford: Oxford University Press, pp. 380-401

Birkinshaw, J. (2002): Managing internal R&D networks in global firms, *Long Range Planning*, Vol. 35, No. 3, pp. 245-267

Birkinshaw, J./Fry, N. (1998): Subsidiary initiatives to develop new markets, *Sloan Management Review*, Vol. 39, No. 3, pp. 51-61

Birkinshaw, J./Hood, N. (1998): *Multinational corporate evolution and subsidiary development*, Macmillan, pp.1-15

Birkinshaw, J./Hood, N. (2000): Characteristics of foreign subsidiaries in industry clusters, *Journal of International Business Studies*, Vol. 31, No. 1, pp. 141-154

Birley, S. (1985): The role of networks in the entrepreneurial process, *Journal of Business Venturing*, Vol. 1, No. 1, pp. 107-117

BIS (1996): *International Banking and Financial Market Developments*, Basle: Bank for International Settlements

BIS (1998): *68th Annual Report*, Basle: Bank for International Settlements

Blankenburg Holm D./Eriksson, K./Johanson, J. (1996): Business networks and cooperation in international business relationships; in: Beamish, P.W./Killing, J.P. (eds.): *Cooperative strategies: European perspectives*, San Francisco, CA: The New Lexington Press, pp. 242-266

Boeker, W.P. (1988): Organizational origins: Entrepreneurial and environmental imprinting at the time of founding; in: Carroll, G. R. (ed.): *Ecological models of organisation*, Cambridge, MA: Ballinger Publishing Company, pp. 33-51

Boettcher, R. (1996): *Global Network Management*, Wiesbaden: Gabler

Boettcher, R./Welge, M.K. (1996): Global strategies of European firms, *The International Executive*, Vol. 37, No. 2

Boettcher, R./Paul, T./Welge, M.K. (1993): Global networks: Toward a conceptual framework, in: Sokoya, S.K. (ed.): Proceeding of the 1993 Conference of the Association for Global Business, Chicago: Association of Global Business, pp. 87-96

Boisot, M.H. (1998): *Knowledge assets*, Oxford: Oxford University Press

Borghoff, T./Schulte, A. (2003): International capabilities of born globals and traditional small and medium-sized enterprises, Achenbach, S./Borghoff, T./Schulte, A. (2003): *Strategische und internationale Perspektiven des Managements*, Lohmar: Eul-Verlag, pp. 253-290

Borghoff, T./Welge, M.K. (2000): *The globalization of SMEs in the global network competition*, Paper presented at the 4th RENT-Conference in Prague

Borghoff, T./Welge, M.K. (2001): Globalization: The evolution of enterprises in the global network competition, *Organizações & Sociedade*, Vol. 8, No. 22, pp. 137-160

Borghoff, T./Welge, M.K. (2003): Die Globalisierung der Netzwerkbildung von professionellen Dienstleistungsunternehmen: Fallbeispiele von drei Start-up-Unternehmen, in: Bruhn, M./Stauss, B. (eds.): *Dienstleistungsnetzwerke*, Wiesbaden: Gabler, pp. 131-158

Boulding, K.E. (1978): *Ecodynamics: A new theory of societal evolution*, Beverly Hills, CA: Sage

Boulding, K.E. (1981): *Evolutionary economics*, Beverly Hills, CA: Sage Publications

Boulding, K.E. (1985): *The world as a total system*, Beverly Hills, CA: Sage Publications

Boulding, K.E. (1991): What is evolutionary economics?, *Journal of Evolutionary Economics*, Vol. 1, pp. 9-17

Bourgois, L.J./Eisenhardt, K.M. (1988): Strategic decision processes in high velocity environments: Four cases in the microcomputer industry, *Management Science*, Vol. 34, pp. 816-835

Bower, J.L. (1970): *Managing the resource allocation process: A study of corporate planning and investment*, Boston, MA: Harvard Business School Press

Boyd, R./Richerson, P.J. (1985): *Culture and the evolutionary process*, Chicago, IL: University of Chicago Press

Brandt, W.K./Hulbert, J.M. (1976): Pattern of communication in the multinational corporation: An empirical study, *Journal of International Business Studies*, Vol. 7, No. 1, pp. 57-64

Brooke, M.S./Remmers, H.L. (1978): *The strategy of multinational enterprise*, 2nd ed., London: Pitman

Brouthers, K.D./Brouthers, L.E. (2001): Explaining the national cultural distance paradox, *Journal of International Business Studies*, Vol. 32, No. 1, pp. 177-189

Brown, S.L./Eisenhardt, K.M. (1997): The art of continuous change: Linking complexity theory and time-paced evolution in relentlessly shifting organizations, *Administrative Science Quarterly*, Vol. 42, No. 1, pp. 1-34

Buckley, P.J. (2000): Models of multinational enterprise: A new research agenda; in: Casson, M. (ed.): *Economics of international business: A new research agenda*, Cheltenham, UK: Edward Elgar Publishing, pp. 1-29

Buckley, P.J./Carter, M.J. (1999): *International strategies to capture value from knowledge: Four company case studies*, Paper presented at the Carnegie Bosch Conference on 'The impact of the global information revolution', San Francisco, October 21-23, 1999

Buckley, P.J. /Casson, M (1998): Analysing foreign market entry strategies: Extending the internalisation approach, *Journal of International Business Studies*, Vol. 29, No. 3, pp. 539-562

Buckley, P.J./Casson, M. (1998a): Models of the multinational enterprise, *Journal of International Business Studies*, Vol. 29, No. 1, pp. 21-44

Buckley, P.J./Clegg, J./Forsans, N./Reilly, K.T. (2001): Increasing the size of the 'country': Regional economic integration and foreign direct investment in a globalised world economy, *Management International Review*, Vol. 41, No. 3, pp. 251-274

Buckley, P.J./Clegg, J. /Tan, H. (2003): The art of knowledge transfer: secondary and reverse transfer in China's telecommunications manufacturing industry, *Management International Review*, Vol. 43, Special Issue, 2003/2, pp. 67-94

Buckley, P.J./Ghauri, P.N. (eds.) (1999): *The internationalization of the firm*, 2nd ed., London: International Thompson Business Press

Burkhardt, M.E./Brass, D.J. (1990): Changing patterns or patterns of change: The effects of a change in technology on social network structure and power, *Administrative Science Quarterly*, Vol. 35, No. 1, pp. 104-127

Burmester, B. (1998): Book review on Eleonore Kofman and Gillian Youngs: Globalization: Theory and practice, *The American Journal of Islamic Social Sciences*, Vol. 15, No.3, pp. 136-138

Burt, R.S. (1992): *The social structure of competition*, Cambridge, MA: Harvard University Press

Burton-Jones, A. (1999): Knowledge capitalism, Oxford: Oxford University Press

Calhoun, C. (1991): The problem of identity in collective action; in: Huber, J. (ed.): *Macro-micro linkages in sociology*, Beverly Hills, CA: Sage, pp. 51-75

Calof, J.L./Beamish, P.W. (1994): The right attitude for international success, *Business Quarterly*, Vol. 59, No. 1, pp. 105-110

Calvet, A.L. (1981): A synthesis of foreign direct investment theories and theories of the multinational firm, *Journal of International Business Studies*, Vol. 12, No. 1, pp. 43-59

Camagni, R. (1991): Introduction: From local 'milieu' to innovation through cooperation networks; in: Camagni, R. (ed.): *Innovation networks: Spatial perspectives*, London: Belhaven Press, pp. 1-9

Camagni, R. (1991a): Local 'milieu', uncertainty and innovation networks: Towards a new dynamic theory of economic space; in: Camagni, R. (ed.): *Innovation networks: Spatial perspectives*, London: Belhaven Press, pp. 121-144

Camagni, R./Capello, R. (2002): Milieux innovateurs and collective learning: From concepts to measurement; in: Acs, Z.J./Groot, H.L.F./Nijkamp, P. (eds.): *The emergence of the knowledge economy*, Amsterdam: Springer pp. 15-46

Cameron, K. (1986): Effectiveness as paradox, *Management Science*, Vol. 32, No. 5, pp. 539-552

Campbell, A./Verbeke, A. (2001): The multinational management of multiple external networks; in: van den Bulcke, D./Verbeke, A. (eds.): *Globalization and the small open economy*, Cheltenham, UK: Edward Elgar, pp. 193-209

Campbell, D.T. (1960): Blind variation and selective retention in creative thought as in other knowledge processes, *Psychological Review*, Vol. 67, No. 6, pp. 380-400

Campbell, D.T. (1965): Variation and selective retention in socio-cultural evolution; in: Barringer, H.R. (ed.): *Social change in developing areas*, Cambridge: Schenkman, pp. 19-49

Campbell, D.T. (1987): Evolutionary epistemology, rationality and the sociology of knowledge, in: Radnitzky, G./ Popper, K.R., (eds.): *Blind variation and selective retention in creative thought as in other knowledge processes,* La Salle, Ill.: Open Court, pp. 91-114

Campbell, D.T. (1990): Levels of organization, downward causation, and the selection-theory approach to evolutionary epistemology, in Greenberg, G./Tobach, E. (eds.), *Theories of the evolution of knowing*, Hillsdale, NJ: Lawrence Erlbaum, pp. 1-17

Campbell, D.T. (1994): How individual and face-to-face-group selection undermine firm selection in organizational evolution; in: Baum, J.A.C./Singh, J. (eds.): *Evolutionary dynamics of organizations*, Oxford: Oxford University Press, pp. 23-38

Cantwell, J. (1989): *Technological innovation and multinational corporations*, Oxford: Basil Blackwell

Cantwell, J. (1991): The theory of technological competence and its application to international production; in: McFetridge, D. (ed.): *Foreign investment, technology and economic growth*, Calgary: University of Calgary Press, pp. 33-67

Cantwell, J. (1995): Multinational corporations and innovatory activities; in: Molero, J. (ed.): *Technological innovation, multinational corporations and new international competitiveness: The case of intermediate countries*, Singapore: Harwood Academic Publishers, pp. 21-57

Cantwell, J. (1998): The globalization of technology: What remains of the product-cycle model?, in: Chandler, A.D./Hagström, P./Sölvell, Ö. (eds.): *The dynamic firm*, Oxford: Oxford University Press, pp. 263-288

Cantwell, J. (2001): Innovation and information technology in MNE; in: Rugman, A.M./Brewer, T.L. (eds.): *The Oxford handbook of international business*, Oxford: Oxford University Press, pp. 431-456

Cantwell, J. (2001a): Introduction; in: Cantwell, J. (ed.): *Foreign direct investment and technological change, Vol. I: Theories of technological change*, Cheltenham, UK: Edward Elgar Publishing, pp. ix-xxiv

Cantwell, J./Piscitello, L. (1999): The emergence of corporate international networks for the accumulation of dispersed technological competences, *Management International Review*, Vol. 39, Special Issue 1, pp. 123-147

Cantwell, J.A./ Piscitello, L. (2000): Accumulating technological competence: Its changing impact upon corporate diversification and internationalization, *Industrial and Corporate Change*, Vol.9, No. 1, pp. 21-51

Cappellin, R. (1991): International networks of cities; in: Camagni, R. (ed.): *Innovation networks: Spatial perspectives*, London: Belhaven Press, pp. 230-244

Carsrud, L.A./Gaglio, G.M./Olm, K.W. (1987): Entrepreneurs: Mentors, networks, and successful new venture development: An exploratory study; in: Churchill, N.C./Hornaday, J.A./Kirchhoff, B.A./Krasner, O.J./Vesper, K.H. (eds.): *Frontiers of entrepreneurship research*, Wellesley MA: Babson College, pp. 229-243

Casson, M. (1982): Transaction costs and the theory of the multinational enterprise; in: Rugman, A.M. (ed.): *New theories of the multinational enterprise*, New York: St. Martin's Press, pp. 24-43

Casson, M. (1990): *Enterprise and competitiveness*, Oxford: Oxford University Press

Castells, M. (1996): *The rise of the network society*, Malden, MA: Blackwell Publishers Inc.

Cateora, P.R./Graham, J.L. (1999): *International Marketing*, International edition, 10th ed., Boston, MA: Irwin/McGraw-Hill

Cavalli-Sforza, L.L./Feldman, M.W. (1981): *Cultural transmission and evolution: A quantitative approach*, Princeton, NJ: Princeton University Press

Caves, R.E./Porter, M.E. (1976): Barriers to exit; in: Qualls, P.D./Masson, R. (eds.): *Essays in industrial organization in honor of Joe Bain*, Cambridge: Ballinger, pp. 36-69

Cavusgil, S.T. (1980): On the internationalisation process of firms, *European Research*, Vol. 8, pp. 273-281

Cavusgil, S.T. (1982): Some observations on the relevance of critical variables for internalization stages; in: Czinkota, M.R./Tesar, G. (eds.), *Export management – an international context*, New York, pp. 276-286

Cavusgil, S.T. (1984): Organisational characteristics associated with export activity, *Journal of Management Studies*, Vol. 21, No. 1, pp. 3-22

Cavusgil, S.T./Bilkey, W.J./Tesar, G. (1979): A note on the export behavior of firms: Exporter profiles, *Journal of International Business Studies*, Vol. 10, No. 1, pp. 91-97

Chamberlin, E. (1939): *The theory of monopolistic competition*, Cambridge, MA: Harvard University press

Chandler, A.D., Jr. (1977): *The visible hand*, Cambridge, MA/London: The Belknap Press of Harvard University Press

Chandler, A.D., Jr. (1986): Technological and organizational underpinnings of modern industrial multinational enterprise: The dynamics of competitive advantage; in: Teichova, A./Lévy-Leboyer, M./Nussbaum, H. (eds): *Multinational enterprise in historical perspective*, Cambridge, MA: Cambridge University Press, pp. 30-54

Chandler, A.D., Jr. (1990): *Scale and scope – The dynamics of industrial capitalism*, Cambridge, MA/London: The Belknap Press of Harvard University Press

Chandler, A.D., Jr./Amatori, F./Hikino, T. (eds.) (1997): *Big business and the wealth of nations*, Cambridge, MA: Cambridge University Press

Chandler, A.D., Jr./Hikino, T. (1997): The large industrial enterprises and the dynamics of modern economic growth; in: Chandler, A.D., Jr./Amatori, F./Hikino, T (eds.): *Big business and the wealth of nations*, Cambridge, MA: Cambridge University Press, pp. 24-57

Chang, S.-J./Rosenzweig, P.M. (1998): Functional and line of business evolution processes in MNC subsidiaries: Sony in the USA, 1972-1995; in: Birkinshaw, J./Hood, N. (eds.): *Multinational corporate evolution and subsidiary development*, Houndmills, Basingstoke: Macmillan Press, pp. 299-332

Charbit, C. (1996): Inter-firm cooperation: A mode for the internationalisation of SME; in: Vence-Deza, X./Metcalfe, J. S. (eds.): *Wealth from diversity*, Amsterdam: Kluwer Academic Publishers, pp. 241-266

Chen, H./Chen, T.-J. (1998): Network linkages and location choice in foreign direct investment, *Journal of International Business Studies*, Vol. 29, No. 3, pp. 445-468

Chesnai, F. (1994) : *La mondialisation du capital*, Paris: Syros

Chesnai, F. (1995): World oligopoly: Rivalry between 'global firms' and global corporate competitiveness; in: Molero, J. (ed.): *Technological innovation, multinational corporations and new international competitiveness: The case of intermediate countries*, Singapore: Harwood Academic Publishers, pp. 75-107

Chikudate, N. (1995): Communication network liaisons as cultural interpreters for organizational adaptation in Japan-Europe business environments, *Management International Review*, Vol. 35, Special Issue 2, pp. 27-38

Choi, C.J./Lee, S.H. (1997): A knowledge-based view of cooperative interorganisational relationships; in: Beamish, P.W./Killing, J.P. (eds.): *Cooperative strategies: European perspectives*, San Francisco, CA: The New Lexington Press, pp. 33-58

Clark, I. (1999): *Globalization and international relations theory*, Oxford: Oxford University Press

Clark, K. (1987): Investment in new technology and competitive advantage; in: Teece, D.J. (ed.): *The competitive challenge: Strategies for industrial innovation and renewal*, Cambridge: MA: Ballinger Publishing, pp. 59-82

Cohen, A.J. (1984): Technological change as historical process: The case of the U.S. pulp and paper industry, 1915-1940, *Journal of Economic History*, Vol. XLIV, No.3, pp. 775-799

Cohen, W.M./Levinthal, D. (1990): Absorptive capacity: A new perspective on learning and innovation, *Administrative Science Quarterly*, Vol. 35, No. 2, pp. 128-152

Cohendet, P./Joly, P.-B. (2001): The production of technological knowledge: New issues in a learning economy; in: Archibugi, D./Lundvall, B.-Å. (eds.): *The globalizing learning economy*, Oxford: Oxford University Press, pp. 63-82

Colberg, W. (1989): *Internationale Präsenzstrategien von Industrieunternehmen*, Kiel: Wissenschaftsverlag Vauk

Collis, D.J. (1991): A resource-based analysis of global competition: The case of the bearings industry, *Strategic Management Journal*, Vol. 12, Special Issue, pp. 49-68

Conti, S. (1995): *The industrial enterprise and its environment: Spatial perspectives*, Aldershot, UK: Avebury

Conti, S. (1997): Global-local perspectives: A review of concepts and theoretical proposals; in: Tayler, M./Conti, S. (eds.): *Interdependent and uneven development: Global-local perspectives*, Aldershot, UK: Ashgate, pp. 15-56

Conti, S./Enrietti, A. (1995): *The Italian automobile industry and the case of Fiat: one country, one company. One market? Towards a new map of automobile manufacturing in Europe?*, Berlin: Springer, pp. 117-145

Cooke, P. (1996): Building a twenty-first century regional economy in Emilia-Romagna, *European Planning Studies*, Vol. 4, No. 1, pp. 53-62

Coriat, B./Dosi, G. (1998): Learning how to govern and learning how to solve problems: On the co-evolution of competences, conflicts, and organisational routines; in: Chandler, A.D./Hagström, P./Sölvell, Ö. (eds.): *The dynamic firm*, Oxford: Oxford University Press, pp. 103-133

Corò, G./Grandinetti, R. (1999): Evolutionary patterns of Italian industrial districts, *Human Systems Management*, Vol. 18, No. 2, pp. 117-129

Coviello, N.E./McAuley, A. (1999): Internationalisation and the smaller firm: A review of contemporary empirical research, *Management International Review*, Vol. 39, No. 3, pp. 223-256

Coviello, N./ Munro, H.(1992) : *Internationalizing the entrepreneurial technology-intensive firm*: Growth through linkage development, Paper presented at the Babson Entrepreneurship Research, INSEAD, France

Coviello, N.E./Munro, H. (1997): Network relationships and the internationalization process of small software firms, *International business Review*, Vol. 6, No. 4, pp. 114-135

Coviello, N.E./Munro, H. (1999): Internationalizing the entrepreneurial technology-intensive firm: Growth through linkage development, *Paper presented at the Babson Entrepreneurship Research Conference, INSEAD, France*

Cox, R.W. (1996): A perspective on globalization; in: Mittelman, J.H. (ed.): *Globalization: Critical reflections*, Boulder, CO: Lynne Rienner Publishers, pp. 21-30

Cray, D. (1984): Control and coordination in multinational corporations, *Journal of International Business Studies*, Vol. 15, No. 3, pp. 85-98

Cyert, R.D./March, J.G. (1963): *A behavioral theory of the firm*, Englewood Cliffs, NJ: Prentice-Hall

D'Cruz, J.R. (1986): Strategic management of subsidiaries; in: Etemad, H./Dulude, L.S. (eds.): *Managing the multinational subsidiary: Response to environmental changes and to host nation R&D policies*, London: Croom Helm, pp. 75-89

Dachler, H.P./Hosking, D.M. (1995): The primacy of relations in socially constructing organisational realities; in: Dachler, H.P./Hosking, D.-M./Gergen, K.J. (eds.): *Management and organization: Relational alternatives to individualism*, Aldershot, UK: Avebury, pp. 1-28

Daniels, J.D./Pitts, R.A./Tretter, M.J. (1984): Strategy and structure of U.S. multinationals: An exploratory study, *Academy of Management Journal*, Vol. 27, No. 2, pp. 292-307

Daniels, J.D./Pitts, R.A./Tretter, M.J. (1985): Organizing for dual strategies of product diversity and international expansion, *Strategic Management Journal*, Vol. 6, No. 3, pp. 223-237

Davidson, W.H./Hapeslagh, P. (1982): Shaping a global product organization, *Harvard Business Review*, Vol. 60, No. 4, pp. 125-132

Davis, P.S./Harveston, P.D. (2000): Internationalization and organizational growth: The impact of internet usage and technology involvement among entrepreneur-led family businesses, *Family Business Review*, Vol. XIII, No. 2, pp. 107-120

Day, R.H. (1987): The evolving economy, *European Journal of Operational Research*, Vol. 30, No. 3, pp. 251-257

De Geus, A. (1988): Planning as learning, in: *Harvard Business Review*, Vol. 66, No. 2, pp. 70

Delany, E. (1998): Strategic development of multinational subsidiaries in Ireland; in: Birkinshaw, J./Hood, N. (eds.): *Multinational corporate evolution and subsidiary development*, Houndmills, Basingstoke: Macmillan, pp. 239-267

Delany, E. (2000): Strategic development of the multinational subsidiary through subsidiary initiative-taking, *Long Range Planning*, Vol. 33, No. 2, pp. 220-244

Deng, K.G. (1997): The foreign staple trade of China in the pre-modern era, *International History Review*, Vol. 19, No. 2, pp. 253-283

Denis, J.E./Depeltreau, D. (1985): Market knowledge, diversification, and export expansion, *Journal of International Business Studies*, Vol. 16, No. 3, pp. 77-89

Dicken, P./Thrift, N. (1992): The organisation of production and the production of organization: Why business enterprises matter in the study of geographical industrialization, *Transactions of the Institute of British Geographers*, New Series, Vol. 17, pp. 279-289

Dicken, P. (1986): *Global shift – Industrial change in a turbulent world*, London: Harper and Row

Dicken, P. (1994): Global-local tensions: Firms and states in the global space-economy, *Advances in Strategic Management*, Vol. 11, pp. 217-247

Dierickx. I./Cool, K. (1989): Asset stock accumulation and sustainability of competitive advantage, *Management Science*, Vol. 35, No. 12, pp. 1504-1511

DiMaggio, P.J./Powell, W.W. (1983): The iron cage revisited: Institutional isomorphism and collective rationality in organizational fields, *American Sociological Review*, Vol. 48, No. 2, pp. 147-160

Donnellon, A./Gray, B./Bougnon, M.G. (1986): Communication, meaning, and organized action, *Administrative Science Quarterly*, Vol. 31, No. 1, pp. 43-55

Doremus, P.N./Keller, W.W./Pauly, L.W./Reich, S. (1998): *The myth of the global corporation*, Princeton, NJ: Princeton University Press

Dosi, G. (1997): Organizational competences, firm size, and the wealth of nations: Some comments from a comparative perspective; in: Chandler, A.D., Jr./Amatori, F./Hikino, T. (eds.): *Big business and the wealth of nations*. Cambridge, MA: Cambridge University Press, pp. 465-479

Dosi, G./Marengo, L. (1994): Some elements of an evolutionary theory of organizational competences; in: England, R.W. (ed.): *Evolutionary concepts in contemporary economics*, Ann Arbor, MI: The University of Michigan Press, pp. 157-178

Doz, Y.L. (1980): Strategic management in multinational companies, *Sloan Management Review*, Vol. 21, No. 2, pp. 27-46

Doz, Y.L. (1986): *Strategic management in multinational companies*, Oxford: Pergamon Press

Doz, Y.L./Bartlett, C.A./Prahalad, C.K. (1981): Global competitive pressures and host country demands: Managing tensions in MNCs, *California Management Review*, Vol. 23, No. 3, pp. 63-74

Doz, Y.L./Prahalad, C.K. (1981): Headquarters influence and strategic control in MNCs, *Sloan Management Review*, Vol. 23, No. 1, pp. 15-29

Doz, Y.L./Prahalad, C.K. (1986): Controlled variety: A challenge for human resource management in the MNC, *Human Resource Management*, Vol. 25, No. 1, pp. 55-71

Doz, Y.L./Prahalad, C.K. (1987): A process model of strategic redirection in large complex firms: The case of multinational corporations; in: Pettigrew, A.M. (ed.): *The management of strategic change*, Oxford: Basil Blackwell, pp. 62-83

Doz, Y.L./Prahalad, C.K. (1991): Managing DMNCs: A search for a new paradigm, *Strategic Management Journal*, Vol. 12, Special Issue Summer, pp. 145-164

Doz, Y.L./Prahalad, C.K. (1993): Managing DMNCs: A search for a new paradigm; in: Ghoshal, S./Westney, D.E. (eds.): *Organizational theory and the multinational corporation*, Houndsmill/London: Macmillan, pp. 24-50

Dubini, P./MacMillan, I.C. (1999): Getting there by lurches: The rugged road to globalization; in: Hitt, M.A./Clifford, P.G./Nixon, R.D./Coyne, K.P. (eds.): *Dynamic strategic resources: Development, diffusion and integration*, Chichester et al.: John Wiley & Sons, pp. 191-220

Dülfer, E. (1991): *Internationales Management in unterschiedlichen Kulturbereichen*, München/Wien/Oldenburg: Oldenbourg

Duncan, R.B. (1972): Characteristics of organizations, *Administrative Science Quarterly*, pp. 313-327

Dunning, J.H. (1977): Trade, location of economic activities and the MNE: A search for an eclectic theory; in: Ohlin, B./Hesselborn, P.O./Wijkman, P.M. (eds.): *The international allocation of economic activity*, London: Holmes and Meier, pp. 395-431

Dunning, J.H. (1993): *The globalization of business – The challenge of the 1990s*, London: Routledge

Dunning, J.H. (1997): A business analytic approach to governments and globalization; in: Dunning, J.H. (ed.): *Governments, globalization, and international business*, Oxford: Oxford University Press, pp. 114-131

Dunning, J.H. (1997a): *Alliance capitalism and global business*, London/New York: Routledge

Dunning, J.H. (ed.) (1997b): *Governments, globalization, and international business*, Oxford: Oxford University Press

Dunning, J.H. (1997c): Governments and the macro-organization of economic activity: A historical and spatial perspective; in: Dunning, J.H. (ed.): *Governments, globalization, and international business*, Oxford: Oxford University Press, pp. 31-72

Dunning, J.H. (1998): Location and the multinational enterprise: A neglected factor?, *Journal of International Business Studies*, Vol. 29, No. 1, pp. 45-66

Dunning, J.H. (2000): Globalization and the theory of MNE activity; in: Hood, N./Young, S. (eds.): *The globalization of multinational enterprise activity and economic development*, New York: Palgrave Macmillan, pp. 21-52

Durham, W.H. (1991): *Coevolution: Genes, culture, and human diversity*, Stanford, CA: Stanford University Press

Easton, G./Araujo, L. (1996): Characterizing organizational competences: An industrial networks approach; in: Sanchez, R./Heene, A./Thomas, H. (eds.): *Dynamics of competence-based competition: Theory and practice in the new strategic management*, Oxford: Elsevier Science, pp. 183-208

Egelhoff, W.G. (1988): Strategy and structure in multinational corporations: A revision of the Stopford and Wells model, *Strategic Management Journal*, Vol. 9, No. 1, pp. 1-14

Egelhoff, W.G. (1993): Information processing theory and the multinational corporation; in: Ghoshal, S./Westney, D.E. (eds.): *Organizational theory and the multinational corporation*, Houndsmill/London: Macmillan, pp. 182-211

Eisenhardt, K.M. (1989): Making fast strategic decisions in high velocity environments, *Academy of Management Journal*, Vol. 32, No. 3, pp. 543-578

England, R.W. (1994): Time and economics: An introductory perspective; in: England, R.W. (ed.): *Evolutionary concepts in contemporary economics*, Ann Arbor, MI: The University of Michigan Press, pp. 3-8

Engwall, L./Wallenstal, M. (1988): Tit for tat in small steps: The internationalization of Swedish banks, *Scandinavian Journal of Management*, Vol. 4, No. 3-4, pp. 147-155

Eriksson, K./Johanson, J./Majkgard, A./Sharma, D.D. (1997): Experiential knowledge and cost in the internationalization process, *Journal of International Business Studies*, Vol. 28, No. 2, pp. 337-360

Eriksson, K./Johanson, J./Majkgard, A./Sharma, D.D. (2000): Effect of variation on knowledge accumulation in the internationalization process, *International Studies of Management and Organization*, Vol. 30, No. 1, pp. 26-44

Eriksson, K./Johanson, J./Majkgard, A./Sharma, D.D. (2001): Time and experience in the internationalization process, *Zeitschrift für Betriebswirtschaft (ZfB)*, Vol. 71, No. 1, pp. 21-43

Eriksson, K./Majkgard, A./Sharma, D.D. (2000): Path dependence and knowledge development in the internationalization process, *Management International Review*, Vol. 40, No. 4, pp. 307-328

Ernst, D. (2001): Small firms competing in globalized high-tech industries: The co-evolution of domestic and international knowledge diffusion; in: Guerrieri, P./Iammarino, S./Pietrobelli, C. (2001): *The global challenge to industrial districts: Small- and medium-sized enterprises in Italy and Taiwan*, Cheltenham, UK: Edward Elgar, pp. 95-130

Ernst, D./Guerrieri, P./Iammarino, S./Pietrobelli, C. (2001): New challenges for industrial clusters and districts: Global production networks and knowledge diffusion; in: Guerrieri, P./Iammarino, S./Pietrobelli, C. (2001): *The global challenge to industrial districts: Small- and medium-sized enterprises in Italy and Taiwan*, Cheltenham, UK: Edward Elgar, pp. 131-144

Erramilli, M.K. (1991): The experience factor in foreign market entry behavior of service firms, *Journal of International Business Studies*, Vol. 22, No. 3, pp. 479-501

Erramilli, M.K./Rao, C.P. (1990): Choice of foreign market entry modes by service firms: Role of market knowledge, *Management International Review*, Vol. 30, No. 2, pp. 135-150

Erramilli, M.K./Rao, C.P. (1993): Service firms' international entry-mode choice: A modified transaction-cost analysis approach, *Journal of Marketing*, Vol 57, No. 3, pp. 19-38

Erramilli, M.K./Srivastava, R./Kim, S.-S. (1999): Internationalization theory and Korean multinationals, *Asia Pacific Journal of Management*, Vol. 16, No. 1, pp. 29-45

Etemad, H. (1999): Globalisation and small-to-medium-sized enterprises: Search for potent strategies, *Global focus*, Vol. 11, No. 3, pp. 85-104

Etemad, H./Wright, R.W./Dana, L.P. (2001): Symbiotic international business networks: Collaboration between small and large firms, *Thunderbird International Business Review*, Vol. 43, No. 4, pp. 481-499

Etzioni, A. (1968): *The active society*, London/New York: Free Press

Euroclear (2000): *1999: Another record year as Euroclear market share shows marked increase*, Euroclear Press Release, February 16th

Evans, P.H.L./Doz, Y. (1992): Dualities; in: Pucik, V./Tichy, N.M./Barnett, C.K. (eds.): *Globalizing management*, New York, NY: John Wiley & Sons

Fahey, L./Narayanan, V.K. (1989): Linked changes in revealed causal maps and environmental change: An empirical study, *Journal of Management Studies*, Vol. 26, No. 4, pp. 361-378

Fahy, J. (1998): The role of resources in global competition; in: Hooley, G./Loveridge, R./Wilson, D. (eds.): *Internationalization: Process, context and markets*, Houndsmill, Basingstoke, UK: Macmillan

Fannin, W.R./Rodrigues, A.F. (1986): National or global? – Control vs flexibility, *Long Range Planning*, Vol. 19, No. 5, pp. 84-88

Featherstone, M./Lash, S./Robertson, R. (eds.) (1995): *Global modernities*, London: Sage Publications

Fischer, H.R. (1991): Information, Kommunikation und Sprache; in: Fischer, H.R. (ed.): *Autopoiesis*, Heidelberg: Carl-Auer-Systeme Verlag, pp. 67-98

Fladmoe-Lindquist, K./Tallman, S. (1992): *Resource-based strategy and competitive advantage among multinationals*, Paper presented at the Academy of International Business, Brussels/Belgium

Fladmoe-Lindquist, K./Tallman, S. (1994): Resource-based strategy and competitive advantage among multinationals, *Advances in Strategic Management*, Vol. 10A, pp. 45-72

Foreman-Peck, J. (1998): *Historical foundations of globalization*, Cheltenham, UK: Edgar Elgar

Forsgren, M. (1989): *Managing the internationalization process: The Swedish case*, London: Routledge

Forsgren, M./Holm, U. (1993): Internationalization of management: Dominance and distance, in: Buckley, P.J./Ghauri, P.N. (eds.), *The Internationalization of the firm*, High Holborn, London: International Thomson Business Press, pp. 336-349

Forsgren, M./Holm, U./Johanson, J. (1991): Internationalisering av andra graden, in: Andersson et al. (eds.): *Internationalisering, företagen och det lokala samhället*, Stockholm: SNS Förlag

Forsgren, M./Holm, U./Thilenius, P. (1997): Network infusion in the multinational corporation; in: Björkman, I./Forsgren, M. (eds.): *The nature of the international firm - Nordic contributions to international business research*, Copenhagen: Copenhagen Business School Press, pp. 475-494

Forsgren, M./Johanson, J. (1992): Managing internationalization in business networks; in: Forsgren, M./Johanson, J. (eds.): *Managing networks in international business*, Philadelphia, PA: Gordon and Breach, pp. 1-18

Forsgren, M./Johanson, J. (1992a): Managing in international multi-centre firms; in: Forsgren, M./Johanson, J. (eds.): *Managing networks in international business*, Philadelphia, PA: Gordon and Breach, pp. 19-31

Franko, L.G. (1976): *The European multinationals*, London: Harper & Row

Franko, L.G. (1976a): Organizational structures and multinational strategies of Continental European enterprises; in: Ghertman, M./Leontiades, J. (eds.): *European research in international business*, Amsterdam: North-Holland, pp. 111-140

Fratocchi, L./Holm, U. (1998): Centres of excellence in the international firm; in: Birkinshaw, J./Hood, N. (eds.): *Multinational corporate evolution and subsidiary development*, Houndmills, Basingstoke: Macmillan, pp. 189-209

Frese, E. (1994): Internationalisierungsstrategie und Organisationsstruktur; in: Schiemenz, B./Wurl, H.-J. (eds.): *Internationales Management*, Wiesbaden: Gabler, pp. 3-22

Friedman, J. (1995): Global system, globalization and the parameters of modernity; in: Featherstone, M./Lash, S./Robertson, R. (ed.): *Global modernities*, London: Sage Publications, pp. 69-90

Frost, T.S. (2001): The geographic sources of foreign subsidiaries' innovations, *Strategic Management Journal*, Vol. 22, No. 2, pp. 101-123

Frost, T.S./Birkinshaw, J.M./Ensign, P.C. (2002): Centers of excellence in multinational corporations, *Strategic Management Journal*, Vol. 23, pp. 997-1018

Fujimoto, T. (1998): Reinterpreting the resource-capability view of the firm: A case of the development-production systems of the Japanese auto-makers; in: Chandler, A.D./Hagström, P./Sölvell, Ö. (eds.): *The dynamic firm*, Oxford: Oxford University Press, pp. 15-44

Fujita, M. (1998): *The transnational activities of small- and medium-sized enterprises*, Dordrecht/NL: Kluwer Academic Publishers

Gaba, V./Pan, Y./Ungson, G.R. (2002): Timing of entry in international market: An empirical study of U.S. Fortune 500 firms in China, *Journal of International Business Studies*, Vol. 33, No. 1, pp. 39-55

Gallo, M.A./Pont, C.G. (1996): Important factors in family business internationalisation, *Family Business Review*, Vol. 9, No. 1, pp. 45-60

Gankema, H.G.J./Snuif, H.R./Zwart, P.S. (2000): The internationalization process of small- and medium-sized enterprises: An evaluation of stage theory, *Journal of Small Business Management*, Vol. 38, No. 4, pp. 15-27

Garfinkel, H. (1967): *Studies in ethnomethodology*, Englewood Cliffs, NJ: Prentice-Hall

Garland, J./Farmer, R. (1986): *International dimensions of business policy and strategy*, Boston: Kent Publishing

Garnier, G.H. (1982): Context and decision making autonomy in the foreign affiliates of U.S. multinational corporations, *Academy of Management Journal*, Vol. 25, No. 4, pp. 893-908

Gates, S.R./Egelhoff, W.G. (1986): Centralization in headquarters-subsidiary relationships, *Journal of International Business Studies*, Vol. 17, No. 2, pp. 71-92

Geertz, C. (1998): The world in pieces: Culture and politics at the end of the century, *Focaal: Tijdschrift voor Antropologie*, Vol. 32, pp. 91-117

Genosko, J. (1997): Networks, innovative milieux and globalization: Some comments on a regional economic discussion, *European Planning Studies*, Vol. 5, No. 3, pp. 283-297

Gereffi, G. (1996): The elusive last lap in the quest for development: Country states; in: Mittelman, J.H. (ed.): *Globalization: Critical reflections*, Boulder, CO: Lynne Rienner Publishers, pp. 53-81

Gerlach, L.P./Palmer, G.B. (1981): Adaptation through evolving interdependence; in: Nystrom, P.C./Starbuck, W.H. (eds.): *Handbook of organizational design*, Vol. 1, Oxford: Oxford University Press, pp. 323-381

Germann, H./Raab, S./Setzer, M. (1999): Messung der Globalisierung: Ein Paradoxon; in: Steger, U. (ed.): *Facetten der Globalisierung*, Berlin: Springer-Verlag, pp. 1-28

Ghauri, P.N. (2001): Using cooperative strategies to compete in a changing world; in: Rao, C.P. (ed.): *Globalisation and its managerial implications*, Westport, CT: Quorum Books, pp. 29-43

Ghauri, P.N. (1990): Emergence of new structures in Swedish multinationals, *Advances in International comparative Management*, Vol. 5

Ghemawat, P./Kennedy, R./Khanna, T. (1998): Competitive policy shocks and strategic management; in: Hitt, M.A./Ricart, I./Costa, J.E./Nixon, R.D. (eds.): *Managing strategically in an interconnected world*, Chichester et al.: John Wiley & Sons, pp. 15-38

Ghoshal, S. (1987): Global strategy: An organizing framework, *Strategic Management Journal*, Vol. 8, No. 5, pp. 425-440

Ghoshal, S./Bartlett, C. (1988): Creation, adoption, and diffusion of innovations by subsidiaries of multinational corporations, *Journal of International Business Studies*, Vol. 19, No. 3, pp. 365-388

Ghoshal, S./Bartlett, C. (1990): The multinational corporation as an interorganizational network, *Academy of Management Review*, Vol. 15, No. 4, pp. 603-625

Ghoshal, S./Bartlett, C. (1993): The multinational corporation as an interorganizational network, in: Ghoshal, S./Westney, D.E. (eds.): *Organizational theory and the multinational corporation*, Houndsmill/London: Macmillan, pp. 77-104

Ghoshal, S./Hahn, M./Moran, P. (2002): Management competence, firm growth and economic progress; in: Pitelis. C. (ed.): *The growth of the firm: The legacy of Edith Penrose*, Oxford: Oxford University Press, pp. 279-308

Ghoshal, S./Westney, D.E. (1993): Introduction and overview; in: Ghoshal, S./Westney, D.E. (eds.): *Organizational theory and the multinational corporation*, Houndsmill/London: Macmillan, pp. 1-23

Giddens, A. (1979): *Central problems in social theory: Action, structure and contradiction in social analysis,* Cambridge: Cambridge University Press

Giddens, A. (1982): *The constitution of society: Outline of the theory of structuration*, Berkeley: University of California Press

Giddens, A. (1984): *The constitution of society*, Cambridge, MA: Polity Press

Giddens, A. (1990): *The consequences of modernity*, Stanford, CA: Stanford University Press

Giddens, A. (1991): *Modernity and self-identity*, Cambridge, MA: Polity Press

Giddens, A. (2000): *Runaway world: How globalization is reshaping our lives*, New York, NY: Routledge

Gilpin, R. (1987): *The political economy of international relations*, Princeton, NJ: Princeton University Press

Ginsberg, A./Baum, J.A.C. (1994): Evolutionary processes and patterns of core business change; in: Baum, J.A.C./Singh, J. (eds.): *Evolutionary dynamics of organization*, New York/Oxford: Oxford University Press, pp. 127-151

Gomes-Casseres, B. (1997): Alliance strategies of small firms, *Small Business Economics*, Vol. 9, No. 1, pp. 33-44

Gomez-Meija, L. (1992): Structure and process of diversification, compensation strategy, and firm performance, *Strategic Management Journal*, Vol. 13, No. 5, pp. 381-397

Gordon, R. (1991): Innovation, industrial networks and high-technology regions; in: Camagni, R. (ed.): *Innovation networks: Spatial perspectives*, London: Belhaven Press, pp. 174-195

Grabher, G. (1993): Rediscovering the social in the economics of interfirm relations; in: Grabher, G. (ed.): *The embedded firm: On the socioeconomics of industrial networks*, London: Routledge, pp. 1-31

Grabher, G. (1993a): The weakness of strong ties: The lock-in of regional development in the Ruhr area; in: Grabher, G. (ed.): *The embedded firm: On the socioeconomics of industrial networks*, London: Routledge, pp. 255-277

Granovetter, M. (1985): Economic action and social structure: The problem of embeddedness, *American Journal of Sociology*, Vol. 91, No. 3, pp. 481-510

Grant, R.M. (1991): The resource-based theory of competitive advantage: Implications for strategy formulation, *California Management Review*, Vol. 33, No. 3, pp. 114-135

Grant, R.M. (1996): Prospering in dynamically-competitive environments: Organizational capability as knowledge integration, *Organization Science*, Vol. 7, No. 4, pp. 375-387

Greiner, L.E. (1972): Evolution and revolution in organizations' growth, *Harvard Business Review*, Vol. 50, No. 4, pp. 35-46

Guillén, M.F. (2001): Is globalization civilizing, destructive or feeble? A critique of five key debates in the social science literature, *Annual Review of Sociology*, Vol. 27, No. 1, pp. 235-260

Guillén, M.F. (2001a): *The limits of convergence: Globalization and organizational change in Argentina, South Korea, and Spain*, Princeton, NJ: Princeton University Press

Gulati, R. (1995): Social structure and alliance formation patterns: A longitudinal analysis, *Administrative Science Quarterly*, Vol. 40, No. 4, pp. 619-652

Gulati, R./Gargiulo, M. (1999): Where do interorganizational networks come from?, *American Journal of Sociology*, Vol. 104, No. 5, pp. 1439-1493

Gupta, A.K./Govindarajan, V. (1991): Knowledge flows and the structure of control within multinational corporations, *Academy of Management Review*, Vol. 16, No. 4, pp. 768-792

Gupta, A.K./Govindarajan, V. (1993): Coalignment between knowledge flow patterns and strategic systems and processes within MNCs; in: Lorange, P./Chakravarthy, J./Roos, J./van Veen, A. (eds.): *Implementing strategic processes: Change, learning and cooperation*, Oxford: Basil Blackwell, pp. 329-346

Gupta, A.K./Govindarajan, V. (1994): Organizing for knowledge flows within MNCs, *International Business Review*, Vol. 3, No. 4, pp. 443-457

Gupta, A.K./Govindarajan, V. (2000): Knowledge flows within multinational corporations, *Strategic Management Journal*, Vol. 21, No. 4, pp. 473-496

Gupta, A.K./Govindarajan, V./Malhotra, A. (1999): Feedback-seeking behavior within multinational corporations, *Strategic Management Journal*, Vol. 20, No. 3, pp. 205-222

Gustavsson, P./Melin, L./Macdonald, S. (1994): Learning to glocalize, *Advances in Strategic Management*, Vol. 10b, pp. 255-288

Habib, M./Victor, B. (1991): Strategy, structure, and performance of U.S. manufacturing and service MNCs: A comparative analysis, *Strategic Management Journal*, Vol. 12, No. 8, pp. 589-606

Hagström, P./Chandler, A.D. (1998): Perspectives on firm dynamics; in: Chandler, A.D./Hagström, P./Sölvell, Ö. (eds.): *The dynamic firm*, Oxford: Oxford University Press, pp. 1-12

Hagström, P./Hedlund, G. (1998): A three-dimensional model of changing internal structure in the firm; in: Chandler, A.D./Hagström, P./Sölvell, Ö. (eds.): *The dynamic firm*, Oxford: Oxford University Press, pp. 166-191

Håkansson, H. (1990): Technological collaboration in industrial networks, *European Management Journal*, Vol. 8, No. 3, pp. 371-379

Håkansson, H./Johanson, J. (1988): Formal and informal cooperation strategies in international industrial networks; in: Contractor, F.J./Lorange, P. (eds.): *Cooperative strategies in international business*, Lexington, MA: Lexington Books, pp. 369-379

Håkansson, H./Johanson, J. (1993): The network as a governance structure: Interfirm cooperation beyond markets and hierarchies; in: Grabher, G. (ed.): *The embedded firm*, London/New York: Routledge, pp. 35-51

Håkansson, H./Snehota, I. (1989): No business is an island: The network concept of business strategy, *Scandinavian Journal of Management*, Vol. 5, No. 3, pp. 187-200

Hamel, G./Prahalad, C.K. (1983): Managing strategic responsibility in the MNC, *Strategic Management Journal*, Vol. 4, No. 4, pp. 341-351

Hamel, G./Prahalad, C.K. (1989): Strategic intent, *Harvard Business Review*, Vol. 67, No. 3, pp. 63-76

Hamilton, R.D./Kashlak, R.J. (1999): National influences on multinational corporation control system selection, *Management International Review*, Vol. 39, No. 2, pp. 167-189

Hargittai, E./Centeno, M.A. (2001): Introduction: Defining a global geography, *American Behavioral Scientist*, Vol. 44, No. 10, pp. 1545-1560

Harvey, D. (1989): *The condition of postmodernity*, Oxford: Basil Blackwell

Harzing, A.W. (2000): An empirical analysis and extension of the Bartlett and Ghoshal typology of multinational companies, *Journal of International Business Studies*, Vol. 31, No. 1, pp. 101-120

Harzing, A.W./Sorge, A.M./Paauwe, J. (2002): HQ-subsidiary relationships in multinational companies: A British-German comparison, in: Geppert, M./Matten, D./Williams, K. (eds.): *Challenges for European management in a global context – experiences from Britain and Germany*, Basingstoke, London, New York: Palgrave, pp. 96-118

Hasenkamp, U. (1994): Internationale Aspekte des Informationsmanagements; in: Schiemenz, B./Wurl, H.-J. (eds.): *Internationales Management*, Wiesbaden: Gabler, pp. 147-160

Hatch, M.J. (1997): *Organization theory: Modern, symbolic, and postmodern perspectives*, Oxford: Oxford University Press

Hedberg, B.L.T./Nystrom, P.C./Starbuck, W.H. (1976): Camping on seasaws: Self-designing organization, in: *Administrative Science Quarterly*, Vol. 21, pp. 41-57

Hedberg, B./Dahlgren, G./Hansson, J./Olve, N.-G. (1997): *Virtual organizations and beyond: Discover imaginary systems*, Chichester: John Wiley & Sons

Hedlund, G. (1981): Autonomy of subsidiaries and formalization of headquarters: Subsidiary relationships in Swedish MNCs; in: Otterbeck, L. (ed.): *The management of headquarters: Subsidiary relationships in multinational corporations*, Hampshire, UK: Gower, pp. 25-78

Hedlund, G. (1986): The hypermodern MNC – a heterarchy?, *Human Resource Management*, Vol. 25, No. 1, pp. 9-35

Hedlund, G. (1993): Assumptions of hierarchy and heterarchy, with applications to the management of the multinational corporation; in: Ghoshal, S./Westney, D.E. (eds.): *Organizational theory and the multinational corporation*, Houndsmill/London: Macmillan, pp. 211-236

Hedlund, G./Kverneland, A. (1985): Are strategies for foreign markets changing? The case of Swedish investment in Japan, *International Studies of Management and Organization*, Vol. 15, No. 2, pp. 41-51

Hedlund, G./Ridderstråle, J. (1997): Toward a theory of the self-renewing MNC; in: Toyne, B./Nigh, D. (eds.): *International business: An emerging vision*; Columbia, SC: University of South Carolina Press, pp. 329-354

Hejl, P.M. (1984): Towards a theory of social systems: Self-organization and self-maintenance, self-reference and syn-reference; in: Ulrich, H./Probst, G.J.B. (eds.): *Self-organization and management of social systems: Insights, promises, doubts, and questions*, Berlin: Springer-Verlag, pp. 60-78

Held, D./McGrew, A./Goldblatt, D./Perraton, J. (1999): *Global transformations: Politics, economics and culture*, Cambridge, UK: Polity Press

Henzler, H./Rall, W. (1986): Facing up the globalization challenge, *The McKinsey Quarterly*, Winter Issue, pp. 52-68

Hinings, B./Greenwood, R. (1988): The normative prescription of organizations; in: Zucker, L. (ed.): *Institutional patterns and organizations: Culture and environment*, Cambridge, MA: Ballinger Publishing, pp. 53-70

Hippel, E. (1998): Economics of product development by users: The impact of 'sticky' local information, *Management Science*, Vol. 44, No. 5, pp. 629-644

Hirsch-Kreinsen, H./Schulte, A. (2002): Internationalisierung von Unternehmen: Das Phänomen der Rückverlagerung, *WSI Mitteilungen der Hans Böckler Stiftung*, Vol. 55, July, pp. 389-396

Hirst, P./Thompson, G. (1996): *Globalization in question*, Cambridge, UK: Polity Press

Hitt, M.A./Keats, B.W./DeMarie, S.M. (1998): Navigating in the new competitive landscape: Building strategic flexibility and competitive advantage in the 21st century, *Academy of Management Executive*, Vol. 12, No. 4, pp. 22-42

Hodgson, G.M. (1993): *Economics and evolution*, Cambridge, UK: Polity Press

Hodgson, G.M. (1994): Precursors of modern evolutionary economics: Marx, Marshall, Veblen, and Schumpeter; in: England, R.W. (ed.): *Evolutionary concepts in contemporary economics*, Ann Arbor, MI: The University of Michigan Press, pp. 9-38

Hood, N./Young, S. (2000): Globalization, multinational enterprises and economic development, in: Hood, N./Young, S. (eds.): *The globalization of multinational enterprise activity and economic development*, Houndmills, Basingstoke, Hampshire: Macmillan, pp. 3-241

Houston, T./Dunning, J.H. (1976): *British industry abroad*, London, UK: Financial Times

Hulbert, J.M./Brandt, W.K. (1980): *Managing the multinational subsidiary*, New York: Holt Rinehart and Winston

Hurry, D. (1994): Shadow options and global exploration strategies, *Advances in Strategic Management*, Vol. 10A, pp. 229-248

Hymer, S.H. (1960): *The international operations of national firms: A study of direct foreign investment*, Cambridge, MA: MIT Press

Hymer, S.H. (1976): *The international operations of national firms: A study of direct foreign investment*, Cambridge, MA: MIT Press

IMF (1993): *International financial statistics yearbook*, Washington, DC: International Monetary Fund

IMF (1996): *Annual Report*, Washington, DC: IMF

Jantsch, E. (1975): *Design for evolution*, Boston, MA: George Braziller

Jantsch, E. (1986): *Die Selbstorganisation des Universums: Vom Urknall zum menschlichen Geist*, München: Deutscher Taschenbuch-Verlag

Jarillo, J.C. (1987): *Sustaining networks*, Institute of Management Sciences, Vol.17, No. 5, pp. 82-91

Jarillo, J.C. (1988): On strategic networks, *Strategic Management Journal*, Vol. 9, No. 1, pp. 31-41

Jarillo, J.C./Martinez, J.I. (1990): Different roles for subsidiaries: The case of multinational corporations in Spain, *Strategic Management Journal*, Vol. 11, No. 7, pp. 501-512

Jarillo, J.C./Martinez, J.I. (1991): The international expansion of Spanish firms; in: Mattson, L.-G./Stymme, B. (eds.): *Corporate and industry strategies for Europe*, Amsterdam: Elsevier, pp. 283-302

Jepperson, R.L. (1991): Institutions, institutional effects, and institutionalism; in: Powell, W.W./DiMaggio, P.J.: *The new institutionalism in organizational analysis*, Chicago, IL/London: University of Chicago Press, pp. 143-163

Johannisson, B. (1995): Local and international networking as strategy for adaptation to globalizing markets for small- and medium-sized firms; in: Bamberger, I. (ed.): *Anpassungsstrategien kleiner und mittlerer Unternehmen an die Globalisierung der Märkte*, Working paper No. 7, Faculty of Organisation & Planning, University of Essen/Germany, pp. 35-47

Johanson, J. (1985): Marketing instruments and market investments in industrial networks, *International Journal of Research in Marketing*, Vol. 2, No. 3, pp. 185-195

Johanson, J. (1989): Business relationships and industrial networks; in: Institute of Economic Research (ed.): *Perspectives on the economics of organization*, Lund: Lund University Press

Johanson, J./Mattson, L.G. (1986): International marketing and internationalisation processes: A network approach; in: Paliwoda, S./Turnbull, P.W. (eds.): Research in international marketing, London: Croom Helm, pp. 234-265

Johanson, J./Mattson, L.G. (1987): Interorganisational relations in industrial systems: A network approach compared with the transaction-cost approach, *International Studies of Management & Organization*, Vol. 17, No. 1, pp. 34-48

Johanson, J./Mattson, L.G. (1988): Internationalisation in industrial systems: a network approach; in: Hood, N./Vahlne, J.E. (eds.): *Strategies in global competition*, London: Croom Helm, pp. 287-314

Johanson, J./Mattsson, L.G. (1993): Strategic adaptation of firms to the European single market – a network approach, in : Mattsson, L.G./Stynne, B. (eds.): *Corporate and industry strategies for Europe*, Amsterdam: Elsevier, pp. 263-281

Johanson, J./Vahlne, J.-E. (1977): The internationalization process of the firm: A model of knowledge development and increasing foreign market commitments, *Journal of International Business Studies*, Vol. 8, No. 1, pp. 23-32

Johanson, J./Vahlne, J.-E. (1990) : The mechanism of internationalisation, *International Marketing Review*, Vol. 7, No. 4, pp. 11-24

Johanson, J./Wiedersheim-Paul, F. (1975): The internationalization of the firm: Four Swedish cases, *Journal of Management Studies*, Vol. 12, No. 3, pp. 305-322

Johnson, P. (1991): *The birth of the modern – world society 1815-1830*, London: George Weidenfeld & Nicolson

Jones, R.E./Jacobs, L.W./van't Spijker, W. (1992): Strategic decision processes in international firms, *Management International Review*, Vol. 32, No. 3, pp. 219-236

Jun, S./Gentry, J.W./Hyun, Y.J. (2001): Cultural adaptation of business expatriates in the host marketplace, *Journal of International Business Studies*, Vol. 32, No. 2, pp. 369-377

Kagono, T./Nonaka, S.K./Okumura, A. (1985): *Strategic vs evolutionary management: A U.S.- Japan comparison of strategy and organization*, Amsterdam: North Holland

Kanter, R.M./Corn, R.I. (1998): Do cultural differences make a business difference?; in: Keys, J.B./Fulmer, R.M. (eds.): *Executive development and organisational learning for global business*, New York: International Business Press, pp. 23-48

Karagozoglu, N./Lindell, M. (1998): Internationalization of small- and medium-sized technology-based firms: An exploratory study, *Journal of Small Business Management*, Vol. 36, No. 1, pp. 44-59

Kaufmann, F. (1993): *Internationalisierung durch Kooperation*, Wiesbaden: DUV

Katz, D./Kahn, R. (1978): *The social psychology of organisations*, 2nd ed., New York: John Wiley & Sons

Katz, D./Kahn, R. (1966): Open-system theory, in: Maurer, J.G. (ed.): *Open-system approaches,* New York: Random Hause, pp. 11-30

Kay, N.M. (1984): *The emergent firm: Knowledge, ignorance and surprise in economic organisation*, London: Macmillan

Kay, N.M. (1997): *Pattern in corporate evolution*, Oxford: Oxford University Press

Kelley, M.R./Helper, S. (1997): *The influences of agglomeration economies and local institutions on the technology adoption decisions of US manufacturing enterprises*, Paper presented at the EUNIT international conference on 'Industry, innovation and territory', Lisbon, 20-22 March

Kellner, D. (2000): Theorizing globalization critically; in: Suess, A. (ed): *Globalization: A scientific issue?,* Vienna: Passagen Verlag, pp. 73-107

Keys, J.B./Fulmer, R.M. (1998): Introduction; in: Keys, J.B./Fulmer, R.M. (eds.): *Executive development and organisational learning for global business*, New York: International Business Press, pp. 1-10

Khondker, H.H. (1996): Globalization theory: A critical appraisal, *The Journal of Social Studies (Dhaka),* Vol. 19, pp. 44-68

Khor, M. (2001): *Rethinking globalization*, London: Zed Books

Kick, E.L./Davis, B.C. (2001): World-system structure and change, *American Behavioral Scientist*, Vol. 44, No. 10, pp. 1561-1578

Kieser, A. (1989): Entstehung und Wandel von Organisationen; in: Bauer, L./Matis, H.: *Evolution - Organisation - Management. Zur Entwicklung und Selbststeuerung komplexer Systeme*; Berlin: Duncker & Humblot, pp. 161-194

Kieser, A./Koch, U. (2002): Organizational learning through rule adoption: From the behavioral theory to transactive organizational learning; in: Augier, M./March, J.G. (eds.): *The economics of choice, change and organization: Essays in memory of Richard M. Cyert*; Cheltenham, UK: Edward Elgar, pp. 237-258

Kilduff, M. (1993): The reproduction of inertia in multinational corporations; in: Ghoshal, S./Westney, D.E. (eds.): *Organizational theory and the multinational corporation*, Houndsmill/London: Macmillan, pp. 259-274

Kilminster, R. (1997): Globalization as an emergent concept; in: Scott, A. (ed.): *The limits of globalization: Cases and arguments*, London: Routledge, pp. 257-83

Kim, W.C./Hwang, P. (1992): Global strategy and multinationals' entry mode choice, *Journal of International Business Studies*, Vol. 23, No. 1, pp. 29-54

Kim, W.C./Mauborgne, R. (1991): The role of procedural justice, *Strategic Management Journal*, Vol. 12, No. 4, pp. 125-143

Kim, W.C./Mauborgne, R. (1993): Effectively conceiving and executing multinationals' worldwide strategies, *Journal of International Business Studies*, Vol. 24, No. 3, pp. 419-444

Kim, W.C./Mauborgne, R. (1993a): Procedural justice theory and the multinational corporation; in: Ghoshal, S./Westney, D.E. (eds.): *Organizational theory and the multinational corporation*, Houndsmill/London: Macmillan, pp. 237-255

King, A./Schneider, B. (1992): *Die erste globale Revolution: Ein Bericht des Rates des Club of Rome*, Frankfurt: Horizonte Verlag

Kipping, M. (2002): Trapped in their wave: The evolution of management consultancies; in: Clark, T./Fincham, R. (eds.): *Critical consulting*, Oxford: Blackwell, pp. 28-49

Kipping, M./Sauviat, C. (1996): *Global management consultancies: Their evolution and role*, The University of Reading, Discussion Papers in Business International Business and Investment Studies, Series B, Vol. IX, No. 221

Kirzner, I.M. (1973): *Competition and entrepreneurship*, Chicago, IL: University of Chicago Press

Knickerbocker, F.T. (1973): *Oligopolistic reaction and multinational enterprise*, Boston, MA: Harvard University Publications

Knight, G.A. (1997): *Emerging paradigm for international marketing: The born global firm*, Dissertation, Michigan State University

Knight, G.A./Cavusgil, S.T. (1996): The born global firm: A challenge to traditional internationalization theory, *Advances in International Marketing*, Vol. 8, pp. 11-26

Knudsen, C. (1995): The competence view of the firm: What can modern economists learn from Philip Selznick's sociological theory of leadership?; in: Scott, W.R./Christensen, S. (eds.): *The institutional construction of organizations: International and longitudinal studies*, Thousand Oaks, CA: Sage Publications, pp. 135-163

Kobrin, S.J. (1988): Strategic integration in fragmented environments: Social and political assessment by subsidiaries of multinational firms; in: Hood, H./Vahlne, J.E. (eds.): *Strategies in global competition*, London: Croom Helm, pp. 104-120

Kobrin, S.J. (1991): An empirical analysis of the determinants of global integration, *Strategic Management Journal*, Vol. 12, No. 4, pp. 17-31

Kobrin, S.J. (1997): The architecture of globalization: State sovereignty in a networked global economy; in: Dunning, J.H. (ed.): *Governments, globalization, and international business*, Oxford: Oxford University Press, pp. 146-71

Kobrin, S.J. (2001): Territoriality and the governance of cyberspace, *Journal of International Business Studies*, Vol. 32, No. 4, pp. 687-704

Kodama, F. (1992): Technological fusion and the new R&D, *Harvard Business Review*, Vol. 70, No. 3, pp. 70-78

Koestler, A. (1978): *Janus – a summing up*, New York: Random House

Koestler, A. (1967): *The ghost in the machine*, New York: Macmillan Company

Kogut, B. (1985): Designing global strategies: Comparative and competitive value-added chains, *Sloan Management Review*, Vol. 26, No. 4, pp. 15-28

Kogut, B. (1985a): Designing global strategies: Profiting from operational flexibility, *Sloan Management Review*, Vol. 27, No. 1, pp. 27-38

Kogut, B. (1989): Research notes and communications: A note on global strategies, *Strategic Management Journal*, Vol. 10, No. 3, pp. 383-389

Kogut, B. (1990): The permeability of borders, and the speed of learning among countries, *Globalization of firms and the competitiveness of nations*, Crafoord Lectures, University of Lund

Kogut, B. (1991): Country capabilities and the permeability of borders, *Strategic Management Journal*, Vol. 12, No. 4, pp. 33-47

Kogut, B. (1993): Learning, or the importance of being inert: Country imprinting and international competition; in: Ghoshal, S./Westney, D.E. (eds.): *Organizational theory and the multinational corporation*, Houndsmill/London: Macmillan, pp. 135-154

Kogut, B. (1996): National organizing principles of work and the erstwhile dominance of the American multinational corporation; in: Dosi, G./Malerba, F. (2001): *Organization and strategy in the evolution of the enterprise*, London: Macmillan, pp. 246-287

Kogut, B. (2000): The network as knowledge: Generative rules and the emergence of structure, *Strategic Management Journal*, Vol. 21, No. 3, pp. 405-425

Kogut, B./Kulatilaka, N. (1994): Operating flexibility, global manufacturing and the option value of multinational network, *Management Science*, Vol. 40, pp. 123-139

Kogut, B./Singh, H. (1988): The effect of national culture on the choice of entry mode, *Journal of International Business Studies*, Vol. 19, No. 3, pp. 411-432

Kogut, B./Zander, U. (1992): Knowledge of the firm, combinative capabilities, and the replication of technology, *Organization Science*, Vol. 3, No. 3, pp. 383-397

Kogut, B./Zander U. (1993): Knowledge of the firm and the evolutionary theory of the multinational corporation, *Journal of International Business Studies*, Vol. 24, No. 4, pp. 625-645

Kolde, E. J./Hill, R.E. (1967): Conceptual and normative aspects of international management, *Academy of Management Journal*, Vol. 10, No. 2, pp. 119-128

Korsgaard, O. (1993): Internationalization and globalization, *Adult Education and Development*, Vol. 49, pp. 9-28

Kostova, T./Roth, K. (2002): Adoption of an organizational practice by subsidiaries of multinational corporations: Institutional and relational effects, *Academy of Management Journal*, Vol. 45, No. 1, pp. 215-233

Kotha, S./Rindova, V.P./Rothaermel, F.T. (2001): Assets and actions: Firm-specific factors in the internationalisation of U.S. internet firms, *Journal of International Business Studies*, Vol. 32, No. 4, pp. 769-791

Krasne, S.D. (1983): *International Regimes*, Ithaca, NY: Cornell University Press

Kreikebaum, H. (1998): Unternehmensethik und Globalisierungsstrategien; in: Handlbauer, G./Matzler, K./Sauerwein, E./Stumpf, M.: *Perspektiven im strategischen Management*, Berlin: Walter de Gruyter, pp. 167-182

Kriger, M.P. (1988): The increasing role of subsidiary boards in MNCs: An empirical study, *Strategic Management Journal*, Vol. 9, No. 4, pp. 347-360

Kristensen, P.H./Zeitlin, J.A. (2001): The making of a global firm: Local pathways to multinational enterprise, in: Morgan, G./Kristensen, P.H./Whitley, R. (eds.): *The multinational firm: Organizing across institutional and national divides*, Oxford: Oxford University Press, pp. 172-196

Krugman P.R. (1991): *Geography and trade*, Cambridge, MA: MIT Press

Krystek, U./Zur, E. (2002): Internationalisierung als Herausforderung für die Unternehmensführung; in: Krystek, U./Zur, E. (eds.): *Handbuch Internationalisierung*, Berlin: Springer, pp. 3-20

Kustin, R.A. (1994): A special theory of globalization: A review and critical evaluation of the theoretical and empirical evidence, *Journal of Global Marketing*, Vol. 7, No. 3, pp. 79-101

Kutschker, M. (1994): Dynamische Internationalisierungsstrategie; in: Engelhard, J./Rehkugler, H. (eds.): *Strategien für nationale und internationale Märkte*, Wiesbaden: Gabler, pp. 221-248

Kutschker, M. (1994a): Strategische Kooperationen als Mittel der Internationalisierung; in: Schuster, L. (ed.): *Die Unternehmung im internationalen Wettbewerb*, Berlin: Erich Schmidt Verlag, pp. 121-158

Kutschker, M. (1996): Evolution, Episoden und Epochen: Die Führung von Internationalisierungsprozessen; in: Engelhard, J. (ed.): *Strategische Führung internationaler Unternehmen*, Wiesbaden: Gabler, pp. 1-38

Kutschker, M./Bäurle, I. (1997): Three + one: Multidimensional strategy of internationalization, *Management International Review*, Vol. 37, No. 2, pp. 103-125

Kutschker, M./Bäurle, I./Schmid, S. (1997): International evolution, international episodes, and international epochs: Implications for managing internationalization, *Management International Review*, Vol. 37, Special Issue 2, pp. 101-124

Kuznets, S. (1967): Quantitative aspects of the economic growth of nations: Level and structure of foreign trade: Long term trends, *Economic Development and Cultural Change*, Vol. 15, No. 2, pp. 1-140

Lau, H.F. (1992): Internationalization, internalization, or a new theory for small, low-technology multinational enterprise, *European Journal of Marketing*, Vol. 26, No. 10, pp. 17-31

Lawrence, P.R./ Lorsch, J.W. (1967): *Organization and environment*, Boston, MA: Harvard University Press

Leamer, E.E./Storper, M. (2001): The economic geography of the internet age, *Journal of International Business Studies*, Vol. 32, No. 4, pp. 641-665

Le Heron, R./Park, S.O. (1995) : Introduction: Geographies of globalization; in: Le Heron, R./Park, S.O. (eds.): *The Asian Pacific Rim and globalization*, Aldershot, UK: Avebury, pp. 1-16

Lei, D./Hitt, M.A./Bettis, R. (1996): Dynamic core competences through meta-learning and strategic context, *Journal of Management*, Vol. 22, No. 4, pp. 549-569

Lenski, G.E. (1970): *Human societies: a macrolevel introduction to sociology*, New York: McGraw-Hill

Leonidou, L.C./Katsikeas, C.S. (1996): The export development process: An integrative review of empirical models, *Journal of International Business Studies*, Vol. 27, No. 3, pp. 517-551

Leontiades, J. (1986): Going global: Global strategies vs. national strategies, *Long Range Planning*, Vol. 19, No. 6, pp. 96-104

Lessard, D.R./Amsden, A.H. (1998): The multinational enterprise as a learning organization; in: Cohen, D. (ed.): *Trade, payments and debt*, Basingstoke, Hampshire: Macmillan, pp. 65-81

Levinthal, D. (1992): Surviving Schumpeterian environments: An evolutionary perspective, *Industrial and Corporate Change*, Vol. 1, No. 3, pp. 427-443

Lewin, A.Y./Volberda, H.W. (1999): Prolegomena on co-evolution: a framework for research on strategy and new organization forms, *Organization Science*, Vol. 10, No. 5, pp. 519-534

Lewontin, R. (1982): Organism and environment; in: Plotkin, H. (ed.): *Learning, development, and culture*, Chichester: John Wiley & Sons, pp. 151-170

Liebermann, M.B./Montgomery, D.B. (1998): First mover (dis)advantages: Retrospective and link with the resource-based view, *Strategic Management Journal*, Vol. 19, No. 12, pp. 1111-1125

Lindell, P./Melin, L./Gahmberg, H.J./Hellqvist, A./Melander, A. (1998): Stability and change in a strategist's thinking; in: Eden, C./Spender, J.C. (eds.): *Managerial and organizational cognition: Theory, methods and research*, London: Sage Publications, pp. 76-93

Lindert, P.H./Morton, P.J. (1989): How sovereign debt has worked; in: Sachs, J.D. (ed.): *Developing country debt and the world economy*, Chicago, IL/London: The University of Chicago Press, pp. 225-236

Lippman, S.A./ Rumelt, R.P. (1982): Uncertain imitability: *An analysis of interfilm differences in efficiency under competition*, Bell J. Economics Vol. 13, pp. 418-438

Loasby, B.J. (1991): *Equilibrium and evolution: An exploration of connecting principles in economics*, Manchester: Manchester University Press

Loasby, B.J. (1999): *Institutions and evolution in economics*, London: Routledge

Loasby, B.J. (1999a): *Knowledge, institutions and evolution in economics*, London: Routledge

Lorange, P./Probst, G. (1990): Effective strategic planning process in the multinational corporation; in: Bartlett et al. (eds.): *Managing the global firm*, New York: Routledge, pp. 145-163

Lord, M.D./Ranft, A. (2000): Organizational learning about new international markets: Exploring the internal transfer of local market knowledge, *Journal of International Business Studies*, Vol. 31, No. 4, pp. 573-598

Lovas, B./Ghostral, S. (2000): Strategy as guided evolution, *Strategic Management Journal*, Vol. 21, pp. 875-896

Lovelock, C.H./Yip, S. (1996): Developing global strategies for service businesses, *California Management Review*, Vol. 38, No. 2, pp. 64-86

Løwendahl, B./Haanes, K. (1997): The unit of activity: A new way to understand competence building and leveraging; in: Sanchez, R./Heene, A. (eds.): *Strategic learning and knowledge management*, Chichester, UK: John Wiley & Sons, pp. 19-38

Lu, J.W. (2002): Intra- and inter-organizational imitiative behavior: institutional influences on Japanese firms' entry mode choice, *Journal of International Business Studies*, Vol. 33, No. 1, pp. 19-37

Lu, J.W./Beamish, P.W. (2001): The internationalization and performance of SMEs, *Strategic Management Journal*, Vol. 22, No. 6/7, pp. 565-586

Lübbe, H. (1996): Zur Theorie der zivilisatorischen Evolution; in: Biskup, R. (ed.): *Globalisierung und Wettbewerb*, Bern: Verlag Paul Haupt, pp. 39-64

Luhmann, N. (1971): *Politische Planung, Aufsätze zur Soziologie von Politik und Verwaltung*, Opladen: Westdeutscher Verlag

Luhmann, N. (1975): Weltzeit und Systemgeschichte; in: *Soziologische Aufklärung Band* 2, Opladen: Westdeutscher Verlag, pp. 103-133

Luhmann, N. (1988): *Die Wirtschaft der Gesellschaft*, Frankfurt a. M.: Suhrkamp Verlag

Luhmann, N. (1995): *Social systems*, Stanford, CA: Stanford University Press

Luhmann, N. (2000): *Organisation und Entscheidung*, Opladen/Wiesbaden: Westdeutscher Verlag

Lundvall, B.Å. (ed.) (1992): *National systems of innovation: Towards a theory of innovation and interactive learning*, London: Pinter Publishers

Luostarinen, R. (1980): *Internationalization of the firm*, Helsinki: Acta Academicae Oeconomicae Helsingiensis

Luostarinen, R. (1994): *Internationalization of Finnish firms and their response to global challenges*, Helsinki: UNU World Institute for Economics Research

Luostarinen, R./Hellman, H. (1994): *The internationalization process and strategies of Finnish family firms*, Helsinki: HSE Press

Luostarinen, R./Marschan-Piekkari, R. (1999): *Strategic evolution of foreign-owned subsidiaries in a host country: The case of Finland*, Paper presented at the 25th Annual Conference of EIBA, Manchester

Lyles, M. (1990): A research agenda for strategic management in the 1990s, *Journal of Management Studies*, Vol. 27, No. 4, pp. 363-375

Lyles, M./Schwenk, C.R. (1997): Top management, strategy and organizational knowledge Structures; in: Prusak, L.(ed.,):, Newton, MA: Butterworth- Heimann

Macdonald, S. (1992): Information networks and the exchange of information; in: Antonelli, C. (ed.): *The economics of information networks*, Amsterdam: Elsevier Science, pp. 51-69

Macharzina, K. (1992): Internationalisierung und Organisation, *Zeitschrift für Führung und Organisation*, Vol. 61, No. 1, pp. 4-11

Macharzina, K. (1993): Organisation der internationalen Unternehmensaktivität; in: Kumar, B.N./Haussmann, H. (eds.): *Handbuch der internationalen Unternehmenstätigkeit*, München, pp. 592-608

Macharzina, K. (1996): Globalisierung als Unternehmensaufgabe: Strategien und Organisation: Kriterien für Standortentscheidungen; in: Steger, U. (ed.): *Globalisierung der Wirtschaft*, Berlin: Springer-Verlag, pp. 199-215

Macharzina, K./Engelhard, J. (1991): Paradigm shift in international business research: From partist to eclectic approaches to the GAINS paradigm, *Management International Review*, Vol. 31, No. 4, Special Issue, pp. 23-43

Madhok, A. (1997): Cost, value and foreign market entry mode: The transaction and the firm, *Strategic Management Journal*, Vol. 18, No. 1, pp. 39-61

Madsen, K.T./Servais, P. (1995): *The internationalization of born globals: an evolutionary process?*, Working paper, Odense: Odense University Department of Marketing

Madsen, K.T./Servais, P. (1997): The internationalization of born globals: An evolutionary process?, *International Business Review*, Vol. 6, No. 6, pp. 561-583

Magee, S.P. (1977): Multinational corporations, the industry technology cycle and development, *Journal of World Trade Law*, Vol. 11, No. 4, pp. 297-321

Mahini, A. (1988): *Making decisions in multinational corporations*, New York: John Wiley & Sons

Maillat, D. (1996): Regional productive systems and innovative milieux; in: OECD (ed.): *Networks of enterprises and local development*, pp. 67-80

Maira, A.N. (1998): Connecting across boundaries: The fluid-network organization, *Prism (Arthur D. Little)*, Vol. 9, No. 1, pp. 23-35

Malik, F. (1984): *Strategie des Managements komplexer Systeme*, Bern: Verlag Paul Haupt

Malik, F. (1989): Elemente einer Theorie des Managements sozialer Systeme; in: Bauer, L./Matis, H. (ed.): *Evolution - Organisation - Management. Zur Entwicklung und Selbststeuerung komplexer Systeme*; Berlin: Duncker & Humblot, pp. 131-143

Malik, F. (1993): *Systemisches Management, Evolution, Selbstorganisation: Grundprobleme, Funktionsmechanismen und Lösungsansätze für komplexe Systeme*, Bern: Verlag Paul Haupt

Malmberg, A. (1997): Industrial geography: Location and learning, *Progress in Human Geography*, Vol. 21, No. 4, pp. 573-582

Malmberg, A./Sölvell, Ö. (1997): Localised innovation processes and the sustainable competitive advantage of firms: A conceptual model; in: Taylor, M./Conti, S. (eds.): *Interdepend-

ent and uneven development: Global-local perspectives, Aldershot, UK: Ashgate Publishing, pp. 119-142

Malmgren, H.B. (1961): Information, expectations and the theory of the firm, *Quarterly Journal of Economics*, Vol. 75, No. 3, pp. 399-421

Malnight, T.W. (1995): Globalization of an ethnocentric firm: An evolutionary perspective, *Strategic Management Journal*, Vol. 16, No. 2, pp. 119-141

Malnight, T.W. (1996): The transition from decentralized to network-based structures: An evolutionary perspective, *Journal of International Business Studies*, Vol. 27, No. 1, pp. 43-66

Malnight, T.W. (2000): Toward a model of accelerating organizational change: Evidence from the globalization process; in: Earley, P.C./Singh, H. (eds.): *Innovations in international and cross-cultural management*, Thousand Oaks, CA: Sage Publications, pp. 267-310

March, J.G./ Simon, H.A. (1958): *Organizations*, New York: Wiley

March, J.G. (1981): Footnotes on organizational change, *Administrative Science Quarterly*, Vol. 26, pp. 563-597

March, J.G. (1991): Exploration and exploitation in organizational learning, *Organization Science*, Vol. 2, No. 1, pp. 71-87

March, J.G. (1994): The evolution of evolution; in: Baum, J.A.C./Singh, J. (eds.): *Evolutionary dynamics of organization*, New York/Oxford: Oxford University Press, pp. 39-49

Mariotti, S./Piscitello, L. (2001): Localized capabilities and the internationalization of manufacturing activities by SMEs, *Entrepreneurship & Regional Development*, Vol. 13, No. 1, pp. 65-80

Markusen, A. (1996): Sticky places within slippery space: A typology of industrial districts, *Economic Geography*, Vol. 72, No. 3, pp. 293-313

Marshall, A. (1898): Distribution and exchange, *The Economic Journal*, Vol. 8, March, pp. 37-59

Marshall, A. (1961): *The principles of economics*, 9th ed., London: Macmillan

Martinez, J.I./Jarillo, J.C. (1989): The evolution of research on coordination mechanisms in multinational corporations, *Journal of International Business Studies*, Vol. 20, No. 3, pp. 489-514

Maruyama, M. (1963): The second cybernetics: Deviation-amplifying mutual causal processes, *General Systems*, Vol. 8, pp. 233-241

Maruyama, M. (1976): Toward cultural symbiosis; in: Jantsch, E./Waddington, C.H. (eds.): *Evolution and consciousness*, Reading, MA: Addison-Wesley, pp. 198-213

Maskell, P./Eskelinen, H./Hannibalsson, I./Malmberg, A./Vatne, E. (1998): *Competitiveness, localised learning and regional development: specialisation and prosperity in small open economies*, London: Routledge

Mathews, J.A. (2002): *Dragon multinational, a new model for global growth*, Oxford: Oxford University Press

Mattsson, L.G. (1998): Dynamics of overlapping networks and strategic actions by the international firm; in: Chandler, A.D./Hagström, P./Sölvell, Ö. (eds.): *The dynamic firm*, Oxford: Oxford University Press, pp. 242-259

Mattsson, L.G. (1989): Development of firms in networks: Positions and investments; in: Hallén, L./Johanson, J. (eds.): *Networks of relationships in international industrial marketing*, Greenwich: JAI Press, pp. 121-140

Maturana, H.R. (1975): The organization of the living: A theory of the living organization, *International Journal of Man-Machine Studies*, Vol. 7, pp. 313-332

Maturana, H.R. (1980): Man and society; in: Benseler, F./Hejl, P.M./Köck, W.K. (eds.): *Autopoiesis, communication, and society*, Frankfurt a.M.: Suhrkamp, pp. 11-32

Maturana, H.R. (1985): *Erkennen: Die Organisation und Verkörperung von Wirklichkeit*, 2nd ed., Braunschweig: Friedrich Vieweg & Sohn

Matusik, S.F./Hill, C.W.L. (1998): The utilization of contingent work, knowledge creation, and competitive advantage, Academy of Management Review, Vol. 23, No. 4, pp. 680-697

Mauri, A.J./Phatak, A.V. (2001): Global integration as inter-area product flows: The internalisation of ownership and location factors influencing product flows across MNC units, *Management International Review*, Vol. 41, No. 3, pp. 233-249

Mazlish, B. (1993): An introduction to global history; in: Mazlish, B./Buultjens, R. (eds). *Conceptualizing global history*, Boulder, CO: Westview Press, pp. 1-24

McAdam, D. (1986): Recruitment to high-risk activism: The case of freedom summer, *American Journal of Sociology*, Vol. 92, No. 1, pp. 64-90

McDonald, F./Burton, F. (2002): *International business*, London: Thompson

McDougall, P.P./Oviatt, B.M. (1991): Global start-ups: New ventures without geographic limits, *Entrepreneurship Forum*, Winter 1991, pp. 1-5

McDougall, P.P./Shane, S./Oviatt, B.M. (1994): Explaining the formation of international new ventures: The limits of theories from international business research, *Journal of Business Venturing*, Vol. 9, No. 6, pp. 469-487

McGrew, A. (ed.) (1997): *The transformation of democracy? Globalization and territorial democracy*, Cambridge, MA: Polity Press

McGrew, A. (1997a): Globalization and territorial democracy: An introduction; in: McGrew, A. (ed.): *The transformation of democracy? Globalization and territorial democracy*, Cambridge, MA: Polity Press, pp. 1-24

McKelvey, B. (1978): Organizational systematics: Taxonomic lessons from biology, *Management Science*, Vol. 24, No. 13, pp. 1428-1440

McKendrick, D.G. (2001): Global strategy and population-level learning: The case of hard disk drives, *Strategic Management Journal*, Vol. 22, No. 4, pp. 307-334

McKenney, J.L./Zack, M.H./Doherty, V.S. (1992): Complementary communication media: A comparison of electronic mail and face-to-face communication in a programming team; in: Nohria, N./Eccles, R.G. (eds.): *Networks and organizations*, Boston, MA: Harvard Business School Press, pp. 262-287

McKern, B. (1993): An evolutionary aproach to strategic management in the international firm; in: Lorange, P./Chakravarthy, J./Roos, J./van Veen, A. (eds.): *Implementing strategic processes: Change, learning and cooperation*, Oxford: Basil Blackwell, pp. 349-372

McLuhan, M. (1964): *Understanding Media,* London: Routledge

McNaughton, R.B./Bell, J.D. (1999): Brokering networks of small firms to generate social capital for growth and internationalisation; in: Rugman, A.M./Wright, R.W. (eds.): *International entrepreneurship: Globalization of emerging businesses,* Stanford, CT: JAI Press, pp. 63-82

McNee, R.B. (1960): Towards a more humanistic economic geography: The geography of enterprise, *Tijdschrift voor Economische en Sociale Geografie,* Vol. 51, pp. 201-205

Mead, G.H. (1962): *Mind, self, and society,* Chicago, IL: University of Chicago Press

Meffert, H. (1986): *Multinationales oder globales Marketing,* in: Gaugler, E./Meissner, H.G./Thom, N. (eds.): , pp.191-209

Meffert, H. (1993): Wettbewerbsstrategische Aspekte der Globalisierung: Status und Perspektiven länderübergreifender Intergration; in: Haller, M./Bleicher, K./Brauchlin, E./Pleitner, H.-J./Wunderer, R./Zünd, A. (eds.): *Globalisierung der Wirtschaft: Einwirkungen auf die Betriebswirtschaftslehre,* Bern: Verlag Paul Haupt, pp. 23-48

Meissner, H.G./Gerber, S. (1980): Die Auslandsinvestition als Entscheidungsproblem, *Betriebswirtschaftliche Forschung und Praxis,* Vol. 32, No. 3, pp. 217-228

Melin, L. (1992): Internationalization as a strategy process, *Strategic Management Journal,* Vol. 13, No. 8, pp. 99-118

Mendenhall, M./Punnett, B.J./Ricks, D. (1995): *Global Management,* Cambridge, MA: Blackwell Publishers

Meyer, J.W./John, B./Thomas, G.M. (1994): *Ontology and rationalization in the Western cultural account, institutional environments and organizations,* Thousand Oaks, CA: Sage Publications, pp. 9-27

Michels, R. (1932): *Introduzione alla storia delle dottrine economiche e politiche con un saggio sulla economia classica italiana e la sua influenza sulla scienza economica,* Bologna: Zanichelli, Vol. XIII, pp. 310

Miles, R./Snow, C.C. (1986): Organizations: New concepts for new forms, *California Management Review,* Vol. 28, No. 3, pp. 62-73

Miller, D. (1999): Selection processes inside organisations: The self-reinforcing consequences of success; in: Baum, J.A.C./McKelvey, B. (eds.): *Variations in organization science,* Thousand Oaks, CA: Sage Publications, pp. 93-112

Miller, D./Friesen, P.H. (1978): Archetypes of strategy formulation, *Management Science,* Vol. 24, No. 9, pp. 921-933

Miller, D./Friesen, P.H. (1980): Archetypes of organizational transition, *Administrative Science Quarterly,* Vol. 125, No. 2, pp. 268-299

Miller, D./Friesen, P.H. (1982): Structural change and performance, *Academy of Management Journal,* Vol. 25, No. 4, pp. 867-892

Miller, D./Friesen, P.H. (1984): *Organizations: A quantum view,* Englewood Cliffs, NJ: Prentice-Hall

Millington, A.I./Bayliss, B.T. (1990): The process of internationalisation: UK companies in the EC, *Management International Review,* Vol. 30, No. 2, pp. 151-161

Miner, A.S. (1994): Seeking adaptive advantage: Evolutionary theory and managerial action; in: Baum, J.A.C./Singh, J. (eds.): *Evolutionary dynamics of organization*, New York/Oxford: Oxford University Press, pp. 76-89

Miner, A.S./Amburgey, T.L./Stearns, T.M. (1990): Interorganizational linkages and population dynamics: Buffering and transformational shields, *Administrative Science Quarterly*, Vol. 35, pp. 689-713

Mintzberg, H. (1987): The strategy concept I: Five Ps for strategy, *California Management Review*, Vol. 30, No. 1, pp. 11-23

Mittelman, J.H. (1996): The dynamics of globalisation; in: Mittelman, J.H. (ed.): *Globalization: Critical reflections*, Boulder, CO: Lynne Rienner, pp. 1-20

Mittelman, J.H. (ed.) (1996): *Globalization: Critical reflections*, Boulder, CO: Lynne Rienner

Mlinar, Z. (2000): Globalization, individualization and territorial identities; in: Suess, A. (ed.): *Globalization: A scientific issue?*, Wien: Passagen Verlag, pp. 135-149

Moore, K. (2001): A strategy for subsidiaries: Centres of excellence to build subsidiary specific advantages, *Management International Review*, Vol. 41, No. 3, pp. 275-290

Moore, K./Birkinshaw, J. (1998): Managing knowledge in global service firms: Centers of excellence, *Academy of Management Executive*, Vol. 12, No. 4, pp. 81-92

Moore, K./Heeler, R. (1998): A globalization strategy for subsidiaries: Subsidiary specific advantages; in: Mucchielli, J.L./Buckley, P.J./Cordell, V.V. (eds.): *Globalization and regionalization: Strategies, policies, and economic environments*, Binghampton, NY: International Business Press, pp. 1-14

Moore, K./Lewis, D. (1998): The first multinationals: Assyria circa 2000 B.C., *Management International Review*, Vol. 38, No. 2, pp. 95-107

Morgan, G. (2001): *The multinational firm: organizing across institutional and national divides*; in: Morgan, G./Kristensen, P.H./Whitley, R. (eds.): *The multinational firm: Organizing across institutional and national divides*, Oxford: Oxford University Press, pp. 1-26

Morsink, R.L.A. (1998): *Foreign direct investment and corporate networking*, Cheltenham, UK: Edward Elgar

Mueller, F. (1994): Societal effect, organizational effect and globalization, *Organization Studies*, Vol. 15, No. 3, pp. 407-428

Müller, U. (1996): Systemtheorie – Ein interdiszipinärer Ansatz zum Verständnis von Globalisierung?; in: Steger, U. (ed.): *Globalisierung der Wirtschaft*, Berlin: Springer-Verlag, pp. 56-82

Murray, F./Worren, N. (2001): Why less knowledge can lead to more learning: Innovation processes in small vs. large firms; in: Sanchez, R. (ed.): *Knowledge management and organizational competence*, Oxford: Oxford University Press, pp. 137-156

Nachum, L. (1999): *The origins of international competitiveness of firms*, Cheltenham, UK: Edward Elgar

Naidu, G.M./Rao, T.R. (1993): Public sector promotion of exports: A needs-based approach, *Journal of Business Research*, Vol. 27, No. 1, pp. 85-101

Neal, L. (1985): Integration of international capital markets: Quantitative evidence from the eighteenth to twentieth centuries, *Journal of Economic History*, Vol. XLV, No. 2, pp. 219-226

Nederveen Pieterse, J.P. (1995): Globalization as hybridisation; in: Featherstone, M./Lash, S./Robertson, R. (eds.): *Global modernities*, London: Sage Publications, pp. 45-68

Nelson, R.R. (1994): The coevolution of technologies and institutions; in: England, R.W. (ed.): *Evolutionary concepts in contemporary economics*, Ann Arbor, MI: The University of Michigan Press, pp. 139-156

Nelson, R.R./Winter, S.G. (1982): *An evolutionary theory of economic change*, Cambridge, MA: Belknap Press

Neumann, J. (1999): *The impact of the global information revolution on international management*, Speech at the Carnegie Bosch Institute Conference, October 22, 1999, San Francisco, USA

Newbould, G.D./Buckley, P.J./Thurwell, L. (1978): *Going international: The experience of smaller companies overseas*, London: Associated Business Press

Newell, S./Swan, J. (2000): Trust and inter-organizational networking, *Human Relations*, Vol. 53, No. 10, pp. 1287-1328

Nilsson, J.V./Dicken, P./Peck, J. (eds.) (1996): *The internationalization process: European firms in global competition*, London: Paul Chapman Publishing Ltd.

Nohria, N./Garcia-Pont, C. (1991): Global strategic linkages and industry structure, *Strategic Management Journal*, Vol. 12, Special Issue, pp. 105-124

Nohria, N./Ghoshal, S. (1994): Differentiated fit and shared values: Alternatives for managing headquarters-subsidiary relations, *Strategic Management Journal*, Vol. 15, No. 6, pp. 491-502

Nonaka, I. (1991): The knowledge-creating company, *Harvard Business Review*, Vol. 69, No. 6, pp. 96-109

Nonaka, I./Toyama, R./Konno, N. (2000): SECI, ba and leadership: A unified model of dynamic knowledge creation, *Long Range Planning*, Vol. 33, No. 1, pp. 5-34

Noorderhaven, N.G./Harzing, A.W. (2003): The 'country-of-origin' effecting multinational corporations: sources, mechanisms and moderating conditions, *Management International Review*, Vol. 43, Special issue, Vol. 2, pp. 47-66

Nooteboom, B. (2001): From evolution to language and learning; in: Foster, J./Metcalfe, J.S. (eds.): *Frontiers of evolutionary economics: Competition, self-organization and innovation policy*, Cheltenham, UK: Edward Elgar, pp. 41-69

Nordström, K.A. (1991): *The internationalisation process of the firm*, Dissertation for the Doctors Degree in Business Administration, Institute of International Business, Stockholm School of Economics

O'Brian, R. (1992): *Global financial integration: The end of geography*, London: Pinter

O'Grady, S./Lane, H.W. (1996): The psychic distance paradox, *Journal of International Business Studies*, Vol. 27, No. 2, pp. 309-333

Obrecht, J.J. (1994): Die Bedeutung der KMU im Rahmen der internationalen wirtschaftlichen Beziehungen; in: Institut für Mittelstandsforschung der Universität Mannheim (ed.): *Internationale Aktivitäten mittelständischer Unternehmen*, Mannheim, pp. 18-29

OECD (1997): *Globalisation and small and medium enterprises*, Paris: OECD

Oesterle, M.J. (1997): Time-span until internationalisation: Foreign market entry as a built-in-mechanism of innovations, *Management International Review*, Vol. 37, Special Issue 2, pp. 125-149

Oliveira, M. Jr./Child, J. (1999): *Knowledge sharing in multinational advertising companies: Empirical findings from a case study in three countries*, Paper presented at the 19th Annual International Strategic Management Society Conference 1999, Berlin

Osborn, R.N./Hagedoorn, J./Denekamp, J.G./Duysters, G./Baughn, C. (1998): Embedded patterns of international alliance formation, *Organization Studies*, Vol. 19, No. 4, pp. 617-638

Osland, J.S./Bird, A. (2000): Beyond sophisticated stereotyping: Cultural sensemaking in context, *Academy of Management Executive*, Vol. 14, No. 1, pp. 65-79

Oviatt, B.M./McDougall, P.P. (1994): Toward a theory of international new ventures, *Journal of International Business Studies*, Vol. 25, No. 1, pp. 45-64

Oviatt, B.M./McDougall, P.P. (1995): Global start-ups: Entrepreneurs on a world-wide stage, *Academy of Management Executive*, Vol. 9, No. 2, pp. 30-44

Oviatt, B.M./McDougall, P.P. (1997): Challenges for internationalization process theory: The case of international new ventures, *Management International Review*, Vol. 37, Special Issue 2, pp. 85-99

Oviatt, B.M./McDougall, P.P. (1999): A framework for understanding accelerated international entrepreneurship; in: Rugman, A.M./Wright, R.W. (eds.): *International entrepreneurship: Globalization of emerging businesses*, Stanford, CT: JAI Press, pp. 23-40

Padmanabhan, P./Cho, K.R. (1996): Ownership strategy for a foreign affiliate: An empirical investigation of Japanese firms, *Management International Review*, Vol. 36, No. 1, pp. 45-65

Park, S.O. (1996): Networks and embeddedness in the dynamic types of new industrial districts, *Progress in Human Geography*, Vol. 20, No. 4, pp. 476-493

Patel, P./Pavitt, K. (1991): Large firms in the production of the world's technology: An important case of 'non-globalisation', *Journal of International Business Studies*, Vol. 22, No. 1, pp. 1-21

Patel, P./Pavitt, K. (1998): The wide (and increasing) spread of technological competencies in the world's largests firms: A challenge to conventional wisdom; in: Chandler, A.D./Hagström, P./Sölvell, Ö. (eds.): *The dynamic firm*, Oxford: Oxford University Press, pp. 192-213

Pautzke, G. (1989): *Die Evolution der organisatorischen Wissensbasis*, Munich: Verlag Barbara Kirsch

Pavitt, K. (1987): International patterns of technological accumulation; in: Hood, N./Vahlne, L.E. (eds.): *Strategies in global competition*, London: Croom Helm

Peiers, B. (1995): *Informed traders, intervention and price leadership: A deeper view of the microstructure of the foreign-exchange market*, Los Angeles, CA: Mimeo

Pennings, J.M. (1980): *Interlocking directorates*, San Francisco: Jossey-Bass

Penrose, E. (1959): *The theory of the growth of the firm*, London: Basil Blackwell

Perlitz, M. (1994): Die internationale Wettbewerbsfähigkeit: Internationalisierungsstrategien kleiner und mittlerer Unternehmen; in: Institut für Mittelstandsforschung der Universität Mannheim (ed.): *Internationale Aktivitäten mittelständischer Unternehmen*, Mannheim, pp. 30-52

Perlitz, M. (1995): *Internationales Management*, 2nd ed., Stuttgart/Jena: Gustav Fischer Verlag

Perlmutter, H.V. (1969): The tortuous evolution of the multinational corporation, *Columbia Journal of World Business*, Vol. 10, No. 1, pp. 9-18

Perrin, J.-C. (1991): Reseaux d'innovation – milieux innovatuers: développement territorial, *Revue d'économie régionale et urbaine*, pp. 343-374

Perrow, C. (1970): *Organisational analysis*, London: Tavistock Publications

Perrow, C. (1992): Small-firm networks; in: Nohria, N./Eccles, R.G. (eds.): *Networks and organizations*, Boston, MA: Harvard Business School Press, pp. 445-470

Pettigrew, P.S. (2000): Globalization vs. internationalisation, *Vital Speeches of the Day*, Vol. LXVI, No. 20, pp. 610-616

Piore, M.J. (1992): Fragments of a cognitive theory of technological change and organisational structure; in: Nohria, N./Eccles, R.G. (eds.): *Networks and organizations*, Boston, MA: Harvard Business School Press, pp. 430-445

Pitelis, C. (2002): Edith's garden and a glass half full: further issues; in: Pitelis, C. (ed.): *The growth of the firm: The legacy of Edith Penrose*, Oxford: Oxford University Press, pp. 309-321

Polanyi, M. (1966): *The tacit dimension*, Garden City, NY: Doubleday

Porter, M.E. (1986): *Competition in global industries*, Boston, MA: Harvard University Press

Porter, M.E. (1986a): Changing patterns of international competition, *California Management Review*, Vol. XXVIII, No. 2, pp. 9-40

Porter, M.E. (1990): *Wettbewerbsstrategie*, 6th ed., Frankfurt a.M.: Suhrkamp Verlag

Porter, M.E. (1993): *Nationale Wettbewerbsvorteile: erfolgreich konkurrieren auf dem Weltmarkt*, Special Edition, Wien: Springer-Verlag

Porter, M.E. (1997): Response to letters to the editor, *Harvard Business Review*, Vol. 75, No. 4, pp. 162-163

Porter, M.E. (2001): Strategy and the Internet, *Harvard Business Review*, Vol. 79, No. 3, pp. 62-77

Porter, M.E./Fuller, M.B. (1986): Coalitions and global strategy; in: Porter, M.E. (ed.): *Competition in global industries*, Boston, MA: Harvard University Press

Porter, M.E./Stern, S. (2001): Innovation: Location matters, *Sloan Management Review*, Vol. 42, No. 4, pp. 28-36

Powell, W.W. (1990): Neither market nor hierarchy: Network forms of organisation; in: Staw, B./Cummings, L.L. (eds.): *Research in organisational behavior*, Greenwich, CT: JAI Press, pp. 295-336

Powell, W.W./Brantley, P. (1992): Competitive cooperation in biotechnology: Learning through networks?; in: Nohria, N./Eccles, R.G. (eds.): *Networks and organizations*, Boston, MA: Harvard Business School Press, pp. 366-394

Powell, W.W./Koput, K.W./Smith-Doerr, L. (1996): Interorganizational collaboration and the locus of innovation: Networks of learning in biotechnology, *Administrative Science Quarterly*, Vol. 41, No. 1, pp. 116-145

Poynter, T.A./Rugman, A.M. (1982): World product mandates: How will multinationals respond?, *Business Quarterly,* Autumn, pp. 54-61

Poynter, T.A./White, R.E. (1990): Making the horizontal organization work, *Business Quarterly*, Winter, pp. 73-77

Prahalad, C.K. (1976): Strategic choices in diversified MNCs, *Harvard Business Review*, Vol. 54, No. 4, pp. 67-78

Prahalad, C.K./Bettis, R.A. (1986): The dominant logic: A new linkage between diversity and performance, *Strategic Management Journal*, Vol. 7, No. 6, pp. 485-501

Prahalad, C.K./Doz, Y.L. (1981): An approach to strategic control in MNCs, *Sloan Management Review,* Vol. 22, No. 4, pp. 5-13

Prahalad, C.K./Doz, Y.L. (1987): *The multinational mission: Balancing local demands and global vision*, New York: The Free Press

Prigogine, I. (1976): Order through fluctuation: self-organization and social systems, in: Jantsch, E./Waddington, C.H. (eds.): *Evolution and consciousness*, Reading, MA: Addison-Wesley, pp. 93-126

Probst, G./Raub, S./Romhardt, K. (2000): *Managing knowledge: Building blocks for success*, West Sussex, UK: John Wiley & Sons

Quévit, M. (1991): Regional development trajectories in the attainment of the European internal market, Louvain-de-Neuve: Rider

Quinn, J.B. (1980): *Strategies for change: Logical incrementalism*, Homewood, IL: Irwin

Ralston, D.A./Holt, D.H./Terpstra, R.H./Yu, K. (1997): The impact of national culture and economic ideology on managerial work values: A study of the United States, Russia, Japan and China, *Journal of International Business Studies*, Vol. 28, No. 1, pp. 177-207

Ramaswamy, K./Kroeck, K.G. (1995): Measuring the degree of internationalization of firm: A comment, *Journal of International Bussiness Studies*, Vol. 27, No. 1

Ramaswamy, K./Kroeck, K.G./Renforth, W. (1996): Measuring the degree of internationalization of a firm: A comment, *Journal of International Business Studies*, Vol. 27, No. 1, pp. 167-177

Randøy, T./Li, J. (1998): Global resource flows and MNE network integration, In: Birkinshaw, J./Hood, N. (eds.): *Multinational corporate evolution and subsidiary development*, Houndmills, Basingstoke: Macmillan Press, pp. 76-101

Rao, H./Singh, J.V. (1999): Types of variation in organizational populations: The speciation of new organizational forms; in: Baum, J.A.C./McKelvey, B. (eds.): *Variations in organization science*, Thousand Oaks, CA: Sage Publications, pp. 63-78

Reed, R./DeFillippi, R.J. (1990): Causal ambiguity, barriers to imitation, and sustainable competitive advantage, *Academy of Management Review*, Vol. 15, No. 1, pp. 88-102

Regnier, P. (1996): The dynamic Asian economies: Local systems of SMEs and internationalisation; in: OECD (ed.): *Networks of enterprises and local development*, pp. 225-236

Reid, S.D. (1983): Firm internationalization, transaction costs and strategic choice, *International Marketing Review*, Vol. 1, No. 2, pp. 45-56

Reiser, O.L./Davies, B. (1944): *Planetary democracy: An introduction to scientific humanism and applied semantics*, New York: Creative Age Press

Rennie, M.W. (1993): Born global, *McKinsey Quarterly*, No. 4, pp. 45-52

Reuber, A.R./Fischer, E. (1997): The influence of the management team's international experience on the internationalization behaviors of SMEs, *Journal of International Business Studies*, Vol. 28, No. 4, pp. 807-825

Rindova, V.P./Kotha, S. (2001): Continuous 'morphing': Competing through dynamic capabilities, form, and function, *Academy of Management Journal*, Vol. 44, No. 6, pp. 1263-1280

Roberts, S.M. (1995): Small place, big money: The Cayman Islands and the international financial system, *Economic Geography*, Vol. 71, No. 3, pp. 237-56

Robertson, R. (1992): *Globalization: Social theory and global culture*, London: Sage Publications

Robertson, R. (1995): Globalization: Time-space and homogeneity-heterogeneity; in: Featherstone, M./Lash, S./Robertson, R. (eds.): *Global modernities*, London: Sage Publications, pp. 24-44

Robinson, W.T./Fornell, C./Sullivan, M. (1992): Are market pioneers intrinsically stronger than later entrants?, *Strategic Management Journal*, Vol. 13, No. 8, pp. 609-624

Robock, S.A./Simmonds, K. (1989): *International business and multinational enterprise*, Burr Ridge, IL: Irwin

Rodrik, D. (1997): *Has globalization gone too far?* Washington, DC: Institute for International Economics

Rogers, E.M. (1962): *Diffusion of innovations*, New York: The Free Press

Romanelli, E. (1999): Blind (but not unconditioned) variation: Problems of copying in sociocultural evolution; in: Baum, J.A.C./McKelvey, B. (eds.): *Variations in organization science*, Thousand Oaks, CA: Sage Publications, pp. 79-92

Ronen, S. (1986): *Comparative and multinational management*, New York: John Wiley & Sons

Ronstadt, R.C. (1988): The corridor principle, *Journal of Business Venturing*, Vol. 3, No. 1, pp. 31-40

Roos, J./Veie, E./Welch, L.S. (1992): A case study of equipment purchasing in Czechoslowakia, *Industrial Marketing Management*, Vol. 21, No. 3, pp. 257-263

Root, F. (1987): *Entry strategies for international markets*, Lexington, MA: Lexington Books

Rosenkopf, L./Nerkar, A. (1999): On the complexity of technological evolution: Exploring coevolution within and across hierarchical levels in optical disc technology; in: Baum, J.A.C./McKelvey, B. (eds.): *Variations in organization science*, Thousand Oaks, CA: Sage Publications, pp. 169-184

Rosenzweig, P.M./Nohria, N. (1994): Influences on human resource management practices in multinational corporations, *Journal of International Business Studies*, Vol. 25, No. 2, pp. 229-251

Rosenweig, P.M./Singh, J.V. (1992): Organizational environments and the MNC, in: Root, F.R./Visudtibhan, K. (eds.): *International strategic management*, New York: Taylor and Francis, pp. 141-160

Roth, G. (1980): Cognition as a self-organising system, in: Benseler, F. (ed.): *Autopoiesis, communication, and society: The theory of autopoietic systems in the social sciences*, Frankfurt a.M./New York: Campus-Verlag, pp. 45-52

Roth, G. (1986): Selbstorganisation und Selbstreferentialität als Prinzipien der Organisation von Lebewesen, *Dialektik*, Vol. 12, pp. 195-213

Roth, K. (1992): International configuration and coordination archetypes for medium-sized firms in global industries, *Journal of International Business Studies*, Vol. 23, No. 3, pp. 533-549

Roth, K./Nigh, D. (1992): Headquarters-subsidiary relationships: The role of coordination, control, and conflict, *Journal of Business Research*, Vol. 25, No. 4, pp. 277-301

Routledge, B./von Amsberg, J. (1997): *Endogenous social capital*, GSIA Working Papers from Carnegie Mellon University, Graduate School of Industrial Administration

Rothwell, R. (1994): Industrial innovation: Success, strategy, trends; in: Dogson, M./Rothwell, R. (eds.), *The handbook of industrial innovation*, Aldershot: Edward Elgar Publishing

Rowe, W./Schelling, V. (1991): *Memory and modernity: Popular culture in Latin America*, London: Verso

Rugman, A.M. (2001): *The end of globalisation*, New York: AMACOM

Rugman, A.M./D´Cruz, J.R. (2000): *Multinationals as flagship firms*, Oxford: Oxford University Press

Rugman, A.M./Verbeke, A. (2001): Location, competitiveness, and the multinational enterprise; in: Rugman, A.M./Brewer, T.L. (eds.): *The Oxford handbook of international business*, Oxford: Oxford University Press, pp. 150-180

Sachs, J.D. (1989): *Developing country debt and the world economy*, Chicago, IL/London: The University of Chicago Press

Salk, J.E./Brannen, M.Y. (2000): National culture, networks, and individual influence in a multinational management team, *Academy of Management Journal*, Vol. 43, No. 2, pp. 191-202

Sanderson, S.K. (1990): *Social evolutionism: A critical history*, Cambridge, MA: Basil Blackwell

Sandström, M. (1992): The culture influence on international business relationships; in: Forsgren, M./Johanson, J. (eds.): *Managing networks in international business*, Philadelphia, PA: Gordon and Breach, pp. 47-60

Santangelo, G.D. (1999): *Multi-technology, multinational corporations in a new socio-economic paradigm based on information and communications technology (ICT): The European ICT industry*, Doctoral thesis, University of Reading

Sargeant, L.W. (1990): Strategic planning in a subsidiary, *Long Range Planning*, Vol. 23, No. 2, pp. 43-54

Saviotti, P.P./Metcalfe, J.S. (1991): Present developments and trends in evolutionary theories; in: Saviotti, P.P./Metcalfe, J.S. (eds.): *Evolutionary theories of economic and technological change*, Chur, CH: Harwood Academic Publishers, pp. 1-30

Schiemenz, B. (1994): Hierachie und Rekursion im nationalen und internationalem Management von Produktion und Information; in: Schiemenz, B./Wurl, H.J. (eds.): *Internationales Management*, Wiesbaden: Gabler, pp. 285-306

Schmid, S./Bäurle, I./Kutschker, M. (1998): *Tochtergesellschaften in international tätigen Unternehmungen: Ein 'state-of-the-art' unterschiedlicher Rollenypologien*, Diskussionsbeiträge der Wirtschaftswissenschaftlichen Fakultät Ingolstadt, No. 104

Schmidt, G. (1986): Einverständnishandeln - ein Konzept zur 'handlungsnahen' Untersuchung betrieblicher Entscheidungsprozesse; in: Seltz, R./Mill, U./Hildebrandt, E. (eds.): *Organisation als Sozialsystem*, Berlin: Springer-Verlag

Schmidt, M. (1987): Autopoiesis von sozialen Systemen; in: Haferkamp, H./Schmidt, M. (eds.): *Sinn, Kommunikation und soziale Differenzierung*, Frankfurt a.M.: Suhrkamp Verlag, pp. 25-50

Schmidt, S.J. (1987): Der radikale Konstuktivismus: Ein neues Paradigma im interdisziplinären Diskurs; in: Schmidt, S.J. (ed.): *Der Diskurs des radikalen Konstruktivismus*, Frankfurt a.M.: Suhrkamp Verlag, pp. 11-89

Schmitz, H. (1992): On the clustering of small firms, *IDS Bulletin*, Vol. 23, No. 1, pp. 64-69

Schneider, S.C./de Meyer, A. (1991): Interpreting and responding to stragic issues: The impact of national culture, *Strategic Management Journal*, Vol. 12, No. 4, pp. 307-320

Scholte, J. A. (2000): *Globalization: A critical Introduction*, Houndsmills, UK: Palgrave

Schuler, R.S./Fulkerson, J.R./Dowling, P.J. (1991): Strategic performance measurement and management in multinational corporations, *Human Resource Management*, Vol. 30, No. 3, pp. 365-392

Schulte, A. (2002): *Das Phänomen der Rückverlagerung: Internationale Standortentscheidungen kleiner und mittlerer Unternehmen*, Wiesbaden: Gabler

Schulz, D.E. (1993): *Ordnung und Chaos in der Wirtschaft: Zur strategischen Lenkbarkeit von Organisationen aus systemtheoretischer Sicht*, München: VVF

Schumpeter, J.A. (1934): *The theory of economic development*, Cambridge, MA: Harvard University Press

Schütz, A. (1932): *Der sinnhafte Aufbau der sozialen Welt: Eine Einleitung in die verstehende Soziologie*, Wien: Passagen

Schwarzer, B. (1993): *Empirische Ergebnisse zum IT-Einsatz in ausgewählten Prozessen deutscher multinationaler Unternehmen*, Stuttgart: Lehrstuhl für Wirtschaftsinformatik, University of Hohenheim

Scott, W.R. (1986): *Grundlagen der Organisationstheorie*, Frankfurt a.M.: Suhrkamp-Verlag

Selznick, P. (1947): Foundations of the theory of the organization, in: *American Sociological Review*, pp. 25-35

Shapira, Z. (1994): Evolution, externalities and managerial action; in: Baum, J.A.C./Singh, J. (eds.): *Evolutionary dynamics of organization*, New York/Oxford: Oxford University Press, pp. 117-127

Sharma, D.D. (2001): A resource-based model of the internationalisation process of the firm; in: Rao, C.P. (ed.): *Globalisation and its managerial implications*, Westport, CT: Quorum Books, pp. 75-97

Sharma, D.D./Johanson, J. (1987): Technical consultancy in internationalisation, *International Marketing Review*, Vol. 4, No. 4, pp. 20-29

Sharpe, D. R. (2001): Globalization and change: Organizational continuity and change within a Japanese multinational in the UK; in: Morgan, G./Kristensen, P.H./Whitley, R. (eds.): *The multinational firm*, Oxford: Oxford University Press, pp. 196-224

Shenkar, O. (2001): Cultural distance revisited: Towards a more rigorous conceptualisation and measurement of cultural differences, *Journal of International Business Studies*, Vol. 32, No. 3, pp. 519-535

Shimizu, H. (1995): Ba-principle: New logic for the real-time emergence of information, *Holonics*, Vol. 5, No. 1, pp. 67-79

Shrader, C.B./Lincoln, J.R./Hofman, A.N. (1989): The network structures of organizations: Effects of task contingencies and distributional form, *Human Relations*, Vol. 42, No. 1, pp. 43-66

Siegfried, J.J./Evans, L.B. (1994): Empirical studies of entry and exit: A survey of the evidence, *Review of Industrial Organization*, Vol. 9, pp. 121-155

Simon, H.A. (1962): The architecture of complexity, *Proceedings of the American Philosophical Society*, Vol. 106, pp. 467-482

Simonin, B.L. (1999): Transfer of marketing know-how in international strategic alliances: An empirical investigation of the role and antecedents of knowledge ambiguity, *Journal of International Business Studies*, Vol. 30, No. 3, pp. 463-490

Simonin, B.L. (1999a): Ambiguity and the process of knowledge transfer in strategic alliances, *Strategic Management Journal*, Vol. 20: pp. 595-623

Singh, J.V./House, R.J./Tucker, D.J. (1986): Organizational change and organizational mortality, *Administrative Science Quarterly*, Vol. 31, No. 4, pp. 587-611

Smith, A. (1776): *Inquiry into the nature and causes of the wealth of nations*, London: Encyclopaedia Britannica

Snehota, I. (1990): *Notes on a theory of business enterprise*, Doctoral dissertation, Department of Business Studies, Uppsala: Uppsala University

Snow, C.C./Miles, R.E./Coleman, H.J., Jr. (1992): Managing 21st century network organisations, *Organizational Dynamics*, Vol. 20, No. 3, pp. 5-20

Sölvell, Ö./Birkinshaw, J. (2000): Multinational enterprises and the knowledge economy: Leveraging global practices; in: Dunning, J.H. (ed.): *Regions, globalization, and the knowledge-based economy*, Oxford: Oxford University Press, pp. 82-106

Sölvell, Ö./Zander, I. (1995): Organization of the dynamic multinational enterprise: The home-based and the heterarchical MNE, *International Studies of Management & Organization*, Vol. 25, No. 1-2, pp. 17-38

Sölvell, Ö./Zander, I. (1998): International diffusion of knowledge: Isolating mechanisms and the role of the MNE; in: Chandler, A.D./Hagström, P./Sölvell, Ö. (eds.): *The dynamic firm*, Oxford: Oxford University Press, pp. 402-416

Spencer, H. (1890): *First principles*, 5th ed., London: Williams and Norgate

Spencer Brown, G. (1972): *Laws of form*, New York: Julian Press

Spender, J.C (1989): *Industry Recipes: The nature and sources of managerial judgement*, Basil Blackwell, Oxford

Staber, U. (1998): Inter-firm cooperation and competition in industrial districts, *Organization Studies*, Vol. 19, No. 4, pp. 701-724

Starbuck, W.H. (1983): Organizations as action generators, *American Sociological Review*, Vol. 48, No. 2, pp. 91-102

Steger, U. (1996): Einleitende Zusammenfassung: Globalisierung verstehen und gestalten; in: Steger, U. (ed.): *Globalisierung der Wirtschaft*, Berlin: Springer-Verlag, pp. 3-17

Steger, U. (ed.) (1996): *Globalisierung der Wirtschaft*, Berlin: Springer-Verlag

Steger, U. (1999): *Facetten der Globalisierung: ökonomische, soziale und politische Aspekte*, Berlin: Springer-Verlag

Steinmann, H./Kumar, B./Wasner, A. (1977): *Internationalisierung von Mittelbetrieben*, Wiesbaden: Gabler Verlag

Steinmann, H./Kumar, B./Wasner, A. (1981): Der Internationalisierungsprozess von Mittelbetrieben; in: Pausenberger, E. (ed.): *Internationales Management*, Stuttgart: Poeschel Verlag, pp. 108-127

Stinchcombe, A.L. (1965): Social structure and organisations; in: March, J. (ed.): *Handbook of organizations*, Chicago, IL: Rand McNally, pp. 142-193

Stopford, J.M./Wells, L.T. Jr. (1972): *Managing the multinational enterprise*, New York: Basic Books

Storper, M. (1992): The limits to globalization: Technology districts and international trade, *Economic Geography*, Vol. 68, No. 1, pp. 60-93

Storper, M. (2000): Globalization and knowledge flows: An industrial geographer's perspective; in: Dunning, J.H. (ed.): *Regions, globalization, and the knowledge-based economy*, Oxford: Oxford University Press, pp. 42-61

Strati, A. (1998): Organizational symbolism as a social construction: A perspective from the sociology of knowledge, *Human Relations*, Vol. 51, No. 11, pp. 1379-1402

Stratos Group (1991): *Strategic orientations of small European business*, Aldershot, UK: Ashgate Publishing

Suess, A. (ed.) (2000): *Globalization. A scientific issue?*, Wien: Passagen Verlag

Sullivan, D. (1994): The 'threshold of internationalization': Replication, extension, and reinterpretation, *Management International Review*, Vol. 34, No. 2, pp. 165-186

Sullivan, D./Bauerschmidt, A. (1990): Incremental internationalization: A test of Johanson's and Vahlne's thesis, *Management International Review*, Vol. 30, No. 1, pp. 19-30

Surlemont, B. (1998): A typology of centres within multinational corporations: An empirical investigation, In: Birkinshaw, J./Hood, N. (eds.): *Multinational corporate evolution and subsidiary development*, Houndmills, Basingstoke: Macmillam, pp. 162-188

Swoboda, B. (1997): *Internationalisierungsstufen von Klein- und Mittelunternehmen*, Saarbrücken: Institut für Handel und Internationales Marketing

Sydow, J. (1991): Strategische Netzwerke in Japan, *Zeitschrift für betriebswirtschaftliche Forschung*, Vol. 43, No. 3, pp. 238-254

Sydow, J. (1992): *Strategische Netzwerke*, Wiesbaden: Gabler

Sydow, J./Windeler, A. (1998): Organizing and evaluating interfirm networks: A structurationist perspective on network processes and effectiveness, *Organization Science*, Vol. 9, No. 3, pp. 265-284

Sydow, J./ Windeler, A. (2000): Steuerung von und in Netzwerken; in: Sydow, J./Windeler, A. (eds.): *Steuerung von Netzwerken*, pp. 1-24

Taggart, J.H. (1997): Autonomy and procedural justice: A framework for evaluating subsidiary strategy, *Journal of International Business Studies*, Vol. 27, No. 1, pp. 51-76

Taggart, J.H. (1998): Identification and development of strategy at subsidiary level; in: Birkinshaw, J./Hood, N. (eds.): *Multinational corporate evolution and subsidiary development*, Houndmills, Basingstoke: Macmillan, pp. 23-49

Tallman, S./Fladmoe-Lindquist, K. (2002): Internationalization, globalization, and capability-based strategy, *California Management Review*, Vol. 45, No. 1, pp. 116-135

Taylor, M./Conti, S. (eds.) (1997): *Interdependent and uneven development: Global-local perspectives*, Aldershot, UK: Ashgate Publishing

Taylor, M./Conti, S. (1997a): Introduction: Perspectives on global-local interdependencies; in: Taylor, M./Conti, S. (eds.): *Interdependent and uneven development: Global-local perspectives*, Aldershot, UK: Ashgate Publishing, pp. 1-14

Taylor, M./Ekinsmyth, C./Leonard, S. (1997): Global-local interdependencies and conflicting spatialities: 'Space' and 'place' in economic geography; in: Taylor, M./Conti, S. (eds.): *Interdependent and uneven development: Global-local perspectives*, Aldershot, UK: Ashgate Publishing, pp. 57-80

Teece, D.J./Pisano, G./Shuen, A. (1990): *Firm capabilities, resources and the concept of strategy*, Working Paper EAP-38, Berkeley, CA: University of California

Teece, D.J./Rumelt, R./Dosi, G./Winter, S. (1994): Understanding corporate coherence, *Journal of Economic Behavior and Organization*, Vol. 23, No. 1, pp. 1-30

Terrebery, S. (1968): The evolution of organizational environments, *Administrative Science Quarterly*, Vol.12, No.4, pp. 590-613

The Economist (2002): Is it at risk?, *The Economist*, February 2nd, pp. 61-63

Thiessen, J.H./Merrilees, B. (1999): An entrepreneurial model of SME internationalisation; in: Rugman, A.M., Wright, R.W. (eds.): *International entrepreneurship: Globalization of emerging businesses*, Stanford, CT: JAI Press, pp. 131-156

Thompson, J.D. (1967): *Organisations in action*, New York: McGraw-Hill

Thorelli, H.B. (1986): Networks: Between markets and hierarchies, *Strategic Management Journal*, Vol. 7, No. 1, pp. 37-51

Thornton, P.H. (1995): Accounting for acquisition waves: Evidence from the U.S. college publishing industry; in: Scott, W.R./Christensen, S. (eds.): *The institutional construction of organizations: international and longitudinal studies*, Thousand Oaks, CA: Sage Publications, pp. 199-225

Tichy, N.M. (1981): Networks in organizations; in: Nystrom, P./Starbuck, W. (eds.): *Handbook of organizational design*, Vol. II, Oxford: Oxford University Press, pp. 225-249

Tienessen, I./Lane, H.M./Crossan, M.M./Inkpen, A.C. (1997): Knowledge management in international joint ventures; in: Beamish, P.W./Killing, J.P. (eds.): *Cooperative strategies: North American perspectives*, San Francisco, CA: The New Lexington Press, pp. 370-402

Troub, R.M. (1982): A general theory of planning: The evolution of planning and the planning of evolution, *Journal of Economic Issues*, Vol. 16, No. 2, pp. 381-390

Tsang, E.W.K. (2001): Managerial learning in foreign-invested enterprises of China, *Management International Review*, Vol. 41, No. 1, pp. 29-51

Tse, D.K.C. (1988): Does culture matter? - A cross-cultural study of executives' choice, decisiveness and risk adjustment in international marketing, *Journal of Marketing*, Vol. 52, No. 4, pp. 81-95

Tsoukas, H. (1996): The firm as a distributed knowledge system: A constructionist approach, *Strategic Management Journal*, Vol. 17, Winter Special Issue, pp. 11-25

Tucker, D.J./Singh, J.V./Meinhard, A.G. (1990): Founding characteristics, imprinting, and organizational change; in: Singh, J.V. (ed.): *Organizational evolution: New directions*, Newbury Park, CA: Sage Publications, pp. 182-200

Turnbull, P.W. (1987): A challenge to the stages theory of the internationalization process; in: Rosson, P./Reid, S.D.(eds.): *Managing export entry and expansion*, New York: Praeger, pp. 21-40

Turvani, M. (2002): Mismatching by design: Explaining the dynamics of innovative capabilities of the firm with a Penrosean mark; in: Pitelis, C. (ed.): *The growth of the firm: The legacy of Edith Penrose*, Oxford: Oxford University Press, pp. 195-213

Tushman, M.L./Romanelli, E. (1985): Organizational evolution: A metamorphosis model of convergence and reorientation, *Research in Organizational Behavior*, Vol. 7, pp. 171-222

UNCTAD (1993): United Nations Conference on Trade and Development. *World Investment Report 1993: Transnational corporations and integrated international production,* (ST/CTC/156), New York: United Nations

UNCTAD (1993a): *Small- and medium-sized transnational corporations: Role impact and policy implications,* (ST/CTC/160), New York: United Nations

UNCTAD (1997): *World Investment Report 1997,* Geneva: United Nations

UNCTAD (2001): *World Investment Report 2001,* New York: United Nations

UNCTAD (2002): *World Investment Report 2002,* New York: United Nations

Uribe, R.B. (1981): Modeling autopoiesis; in: Zeleny, M. (ed.): *Autopoiesis,* New York: Elsevier North Holland, pp. 51-62

Van de Ven, A.H. (1992): Suggestions for studying strategy process: a research note, *Strategic Management Journal,* Vol. 13, Summer Special Issue, pp. 169-188

Van de Ven, A.H./Grazman, D.N. (1999): Evolution in a nested hierarchy: A genealogy of twin cities health care organizations, 1853-1995; in: Baum, J.A.C./McKelvey, B. (eds.): *Variations in organization science,* Thousand Oaks, CA: Sage Publications, pp. 185-212

Van de Ven, A.H./Hudson, R./Schroeder, D.M. (1984): Designing new business startups: Entrepreneurial, organizational, and ecological considerations, *Journal of Management,* Vol. 10, No. 1, pp. 87-107

Van de Ven, A.H./Poole, M.S. (1995): Explaining development and change in organizations, *Academy of Management Review,* Vol. 20, No. 3, pp. 510-540

Van de Ven, A.H./Walker, G. (1984): The dynamics of interorganizational coordination, *Administrative Science Quarterly,* Vol. 29, No. 4, pp. 598-621

Van Parijs, P. (1981): *Evolutionary explanation in the social sciences: An emerging paradigm,* London/New York: Tavistock Publications

Varaldo, R. (1995): Dall impresa localizzata all impresa radicata, *Economia,* Vol. 14, No. 1, pp 3-25

Varela, F.J. (1981): Describing the logic of living; in: Zeleny, M. (ed.): *Autopoiesis,* New York: Elsevier North Holland, pp. 36-47

Vatne, E. (1995): Local resource mobilisation and internationalization strategies in small and medium sized enterprises, *Environment and Planning,* Vol. 27, No. 1, pp. 63-80

Vaupel, J.W./Curhan, J.P. (1969): *The making of the multinational enterprise: A sourcebook of tables based on a study of 187 major U.S. manufacturing corporations,* Boston, MA: Harvard University Graduate School of Business Adminstration

Veblen, T. (1898): Why is economics not an evolutionary science?, *The Quarterly Journal of Economics,* Vol. 12, No. 4, pp. 373-397

Veblen, T. (1899): *The theory of the leisure class: An economic study of institutions,* New York: Macmillan

Veblen, T. (1919): *The place of science in modern civilisation and other essays,* New York: Huebsch

Veblen, T. (1934): *Essays on our changing order,* New York: Viking Press

Vernon, R. (1966): International investment and international trade in the product cycle, *Quarterly Journal of Economics*, Vol. 80, No. 2, pp. 190-207

Vernon, R. (1979): The product life cycle hypothesis in a new international environment, *Oxford Bulletin of Economics and Statistics*, Vol. 41, No. 4, pp. 255-267

Von Bertalanffy, L. (1950): The theory of open systems in physics and biology, *Science*, Vol. 111, pp. 23-29

Von Foerster, H. (1985): *Sicht und Einsicht*, Braunschweig: Friedrich Vieweg & Sohn

Von Hayek, F.A. (1937): Economics and knowledge, *Economica*, February, pp. 33-54

Von Hayek, F.A. (1945): The use of knowledge in society, *The American Economic Review*, Vol. 19, No. 4, pp. 519-530

Von Hippel, E. (1988): *The sources of innovation*, New York: Oxford University Press

Von Hippel, E. (1998): 'Sticky information' and the locus of problem solving: Implications for innovation; in: Chandler, A. D./Hagström, P./Sölvell, Ö. (eds.): *The dynamic firm*, Oxford: Oxford University Press, pp. 60-77

Von Krogh, G./Roos, J. (1995): *Organizational epistemology*, New York: St. Martin's Press

Von Krogh, G./Vicari, S. (1993): An autopoiesis approach to experimental strategic learning; in: Lorange, P./Chakravarthy, J./Roos, J./van Veen, A. (eds.): *Implementing strategic processes: Change, learning and cooperation*, Oxford: Basil Blackwell, pp. 394-410

Vygotski, L.S. (1962): *Thought and language*, Cambridge, MA: MIT Press

Waddington, C.H. (1976): Evolution in the sub-human world, in: Jantsch, E./Waddington, C.H. (eds.): *Evolution and consciousness*, Reading, MA: Addison-Wesley, pp. 11-15

Wallerstein, I. (1974): *The modern world-system*, New York: Academic Press

Waters, M. (1995): *Globalization*, London: Routledge

Waters, M. (2001): *Globalization*, 2nd ed., London: Routledge

Weaver, G.R./Gioia, D.A. (1994): Paradigms lost - incommensurability versus structurationist inquiry, *Organization Studies*, Vol. 25, No. 4, p. 26

Webster, N. (1961): *Webster's third new international dictionary of the English language unabridged*, Springfield, MA: Merriam

Weggeman, M. (1996): Knowledge management: The modus operandi for a learning organization; in: Schreinemakers, J.F. (ed.): *Knowledge management: Organization, competence and methodology*, Würzburg: Ergon-Verlag, pp. 175-188

Weick, K.E. (1979): Cognitive processes in organizations, *Research in Organizational Behavior*, Vol. 1, pp. 41-74

Weick, K.E./van Orden, P.W. (1991): Organizing on a global scale: A research and teaching agenda, *Human Resource Management*, Vol. 29, No. 1, pp. 49-61

Welch, L.S. (1996): Information behaviour and internationalisation, *International Journal of Technology Management*, Vol. 11, No. 1/2, pp. 179-191

Welch, L.S./Luostarinen, R. (1988): Internationalization: Evolution of a concept, *Journal of General Management*, Vol. 14, No. 2, pp. 36-64

Welge, M.K. (1981): The effective design of headquarters-subsidiary relationships in German multinational corporations; in: Otterbeck, L. (ed.): *The management of headquarters-subsidiary relationships in MNCs*, New York: Saint Martin's Press, pp. 79-106

Welge, M.K. (1989): Desinvestitionen, internationale; in: Macharzina, K./Welge, M.K. (eds.): *Handwörterbuch Export und Internationale Unternehmung*, Stuttgart: Schäffer-Poeschel, Columns 276-289

Welge, M.K. (1990): Globales Management; in: Welge, M.K. (ed.): *Globales Management: Erfolgreiche Strategien für den Weltmarkt*, Stuttgart: Schäffer-Poeschel, pp. 1-16

Welge, M.K. (1992): Strategien für den internationalen Wettbewerb zwischen Globalisierung and lokaler Anpassung; in: Kumar, B.N./Haussmann, H. (eds.): *Handbuch der internationalen Unternehmenstätigkeit*, München: Beck, pp. 569-589

Welge, M.K./Al-Laham, A. (2003): *Strategisches Management*, 4th ed., Wiesbaden: Gabler

Welge, M.K./Boettcher, R./Paul, T. (1996): Netzwerkmanagement in globalen Unternehmungen: Eine empirische Studie in europäischen MNUs, Working Paper No. 21 of the Chair for Strategic and International Management, University of Dortmund

Welge, M.K./Boettcher, R./Paul, T. (1998): *Das Management globaler Geschäfte: Grundlagen–Analyse–Handlungsempfehlungen*, München/Wien: Hanser Verlag

Welge, M.K./Borghoff, T. (1999): *An evolutionary perspective on the globalization of enterprises in the global network competition*. Paper presented at the 25th EIBA-Conference in Manchester.

Welge, M.K./Borghoff, T. (2003): Innovation processes in local and global network; in: Peske, T./Schrank, R. (eds.): *Strategie, Innovation und Internationalisierung*, Lohmar: Eul-Verlag, pp. 313-339

Welge, M.K./Borghoff, T. (2003a): Die Globalisierung der Netzwerkbildung von professionellen Dienstleistungsunternehmen; in: Bruhn, M./Stauss, B. (eds.): *Dienstleistungsnetzwerke*, Wiesbaden: Gabler, pp. 131-158

Welge, M.K./Holtbrügge, D. (2003): *Internationales Management*, 3rd ed., Stuttgart: Schäffer-Poeschel

Wells, P.E./Cooke, P.N. (1991): The geography of international strategic alliances, *Environment and Planning A*, Vol. 23, No. 1, pp. 87-106

Wernerfelt, B. (1984): A resource-based view of the firm, *Strategic Management Journal*, Vol. 5, No. 2, pp. 171-180

Westney, D.E. (2001): Multinational enterprises and cross-border knowledge creation; in: Nonaka, I./Nishiguchi, T. (eds.): *Knowledge emergence*, Oxford: Oxford University Press, pp. 147-175

Westney, D.E./Zaheer, S. (2001): The multinational enterprise as an organisation; in: Rugman, A.M./Brewer, T.L. (eds.): *The Oxford handbook of international business*, Oxford: Oxford University Press, pp. 349-379

White, R.E./Poynter, T.A. (1984): Strategies for foreign-owned subsidiaries in Canada, *Business Quarterly*, Vol. 2, pp. 59-69

White, R.E./Poynter, T.A. (1989): Achieving worldwide advantage with the horizontal organization, *Business Quarterly*, Autumn, pp. 55-60

Whitley, R. (1992): The social construction of organizations and markets: The comparative analysis of business recipes; in: Reed, M./Hughes, M. (eds.): *Rethinking organization*, London: Sage Publications, pp. 120-143

Whitley, R. (2001): How and why are international firms different? The consequences of cross-border managerial coordination for firm characteristics and behaviour; in: Morgan, G./Kristensen, P.H./Whitley, R. (eds.): *The multinational firm: Organizing across institutional and national divides*, Oxford: Oxford University Press, pp. 27-68

Wiesmann, D. (1993): *Komplexität und Differenz*, Konstanz: Universitätsverlag

Wilkins, M. (1970): *The emergence of multinational enterprise: American business abroad from the colonial era to 1914,* Cambridge, MA/London, UK: Harvard University Press

Wilkins, M./Hill, F.E. (1964): *American business abroad: Ford on six continents*, Detroit, MI: Wayne State University Press

Wilkins, M. (1974): *The maturing of multinational enterprise: American business abroad from 1914 to 1970*, Cambridge, MA/London: Harvard University Press

Williamson, J.G. (1995): *Globalization, convergence, and history*, Working Paper 5259, Cambridge, MA: National Bureau of Economic Research

Williamson, O.E. (1985): *The economic institutions of capitalism*, New York: Free Press

Williamson, O.E. (1998): *Transaction cost economics and organization theory*; in: Dosi, G./Teece, D.J./Chytry, J. (eds.): *Technology, organization and competitiveness*, Oxford: Oxford University Press, pp.17-66

Willke, H. (1994): *Interventionstheorie: Grundzüge einer Theorie der Intervention in komplexe Systeme*, Stuttgart/Jena: Gustav Fischer Verlag

Willke, H. (1994a): Systemtheoretische Strategien des Erkennens: Wirklichkeit als interessierte Konstruktion; in: Götz, K. (ed.): *Theoretische Zumutungen: Vom Nutzen der systemischen Theorie für die Managementpraxis*, Heidelberg: Carl-Auer-Systeme Verlag, pp. 97-116

Wind, Y./Douglas, S.P./Perlmutter, H.V. (1979): Guidelines for developing international marketing strategies; in: Jain, S.C./Tucker, L.R. (eds.): *International marketing: Managerial perspectives*, Boston, MA: CBI Publishing, pp. 410-419

Winter, S.G. (1975): Optimization and evolution in the theory of the firm; in: Day, R.H./Groves, T. (eds.): *Adaptive economic models*, New York: Academic Press, pp. 73-118

Winter, S.G. (1987): Knowledge and competence as strategic assets; in: Teece, D.J. (ed.): *The competitive challenge: Strategies for industrial innovation and renewal*, Cambridge, MA: Ballinger Publishing, pp. 159-184

Winter, S.G. (1988): On Coase, competence, and the corporation, *Journal of Law, Economics, and Organization*, Vol. 4, No. 1, pp. 163-180

Winter, S.G. (1994): Organizing for continuous improvement: Evolutionary theory meets the quality revolution; in: Baum, J.A.C./Singh, J. (eds.): *Evolutionary dynamics of organization*, New York/Oxford: Oxford University Press, pp. 90-108

Yip, G.S. (1989): Global strategy...In a world of nations?, *Sloan Management Review*, Vol. 31, No. 1, pp. 29-41

Zack, M.H. (1999): Developing a knowledge strategy, *California Management Review*, Vol. 41, No. 3, pp. 125-145

Zack, M.H. (1999a): Managing codified knowledge, *Sloan Management Review*, Vol. 40, No. 4, pp. 45-58

Zaheer, S. (1995): Overcoming the liability of foreignness, *Academy of Management Journal*, Vol. 38, No. 2, pp. 341-363

Zaheer, S. (2000): Time zone economies and managerial work in a global world; in: Earley, P.C./Singh, H. (eds.): *Innovations in international and cross-cultural management*, Thousand Oaks, CA: Sage Publications, pp. 339-354

Zaheer, S./Manrakhan, S. (2001): Concentration and dispersion in global industries: Remote electronic access and the location of economic activities, *Journal of International Business Studies*, Vol. 32, No. 4, pp. 667-686

Zaheer, S./Mosakowski, E. (1997): The dynamics of the liability of foreignness: A global study of survival in financial services, *Strategic Management Journal*, Vol. 18, No. 6, pp. 439-464

Zaheer, A./Zaheer, S. (1997): Catching the wave: Alertness, responsiveness, and market influence in global electronic networks, *Management Science*, Vol. 43, No. 11, pp. 1493-1509

Zander, U./Kogut, B. (1995): Knowledge and the speed of the transfer and imitation of organizational capabilities: An empirical test, *Organization Science*, Vol. 6, No. 1, pp. 76-92

Zeleny, M. (1981): *Autopoiesis: A theory of living organizational*, New York: Elsevier North Holland, pp. 3-307

Zeleny, M./Pierre, N.A. (1976): *Simulation of self-renewing systems,* in: Jantsch, E./Waddington, C.H. (eds.): Evolution and consciousness, Reading, MA: Addison-Wesley, pp. 150-165

Zu Knyphausen, D. (1988): *Unternehmungen als evolutionsfähige Systeme: Überlegungen zu einem evolutionären Konzept für die Organisationstheorie*, Munich: Verlag Barbara Kirsch

International Business immer aktuell

Kostenloses Probeheft unter:
Tel. 06 11.78 78-129
Fax 06 11.78 78-423

mir
Management International Review

- **mir** wendet sich an Sie als Wissenschaftler und Führungskraft, die sich auf internationale Wirtschaft spezialisiert hat.

- **mir** verbreitet die aktuellen Ergebnisse der internationalen angewandten Forschung aus Unternehmensführung und Betriebswirtschaftslehre.

- **mir** fördert den Austausch von Forschungsergebnissen und Erfahrungen zwischen Wissenschaft und Praxis.

- **mir** zeigt, wie Sie wissenschaftliche Modelle und Methoden in die Praxis umsetzen können.

- **mir** bietet Ihnen als Leser die Möglichkeit, in einem speziell dafür vorgesehenen „Executive Forum" zu den wissenschaftlichen Beiträgen und zu aktuell interessierenden Problemen aus der Sicht der Praxis Stellung zu nehmen.

- **mir** erscheint 4x jährlich.

Wenn Sie mehr wissen wollen:
www.uni-hohenheim.de/~mir
www.mir-online.de

Änderungen vorbehalten. Stand: Januar 2005.
Gabler Verlag · Abraham-Lincoln-Str. 46 · 65189 Wiesbaden · www.gabler.de

mir Special Issues

New Aspects of International Activity

This special issue is devoted to the topic of globalization, one of the most emotionally charged terms in international business today. While globalization is not really a new phenomenon, advances in transportation and communications technology as well as decreasing trade barriers have increased the pace and magnitude of cross border interactions, bringing them to the forefront of discussion for scholars.

Shirley J. Daniel /
Wolf Reitsperger (Eds.)
Challenges of Globalization
mir Special Issue
2004, 172 p. Pb., EUR 72,90
ISBN 3-409-12644-9

Studies on International Entrepreneurship

The rapid globalization of the environment, the liberalization of trade and investments, and the rapid advances in technology have led to the emergence of the inter-disciplinary field of International Entrepreneurship. The papers in this special issue break new ground in a variety of ways by explaining the challenges associated with entrepreneurial firms that take advantage of opportunities on a global scale.

Alan M. Rugman /
Alain Verbeke (Eds.)
The Limits to Globalization and the Regional Strategies of Multinational Enterprises
mir Special Issue
2005, 168 p. Pb., EUR 72,90
ISBN 3-409-14240-1

Selective Approaches to Internationalization

Internationalization is a well-understood concept at the macro-level: it refers to the increasing economic interdependence among nations. Unfortunately, in the past two decades, many authors from academia and the public sphere made a conceptual quantum leap, equating internationalization with globalization, i.e., the idea that the world is a fully integrated market place. The problem with such a perspective on globalization is that it negates the necessity of selectivity in internationalization. Such selectivity is to some extent introduced at the macro-level, but even more importantly, selectivity in internationalization is a firm-driven phenomenon.

Hamid Etemad (Ed.)
Aspects of the Internationalization Process in Smaller Firms
mir Special Issue
2005, 168 p. Pb., EUR 79,90
ISBN 3-8349-0060-5

Änderungen vorbehalten.
Stand: Juli 2005.

Gabler Verlag · Abraham-Lincoln-Str. 46 · 65189 Wiesbaden · www.gabler.de

Mit einem Klick alles im Blick

- Tagesaktuelle Informationen zu Büchern, Zeitschriften, Online-Angeboten, Seminaren und Konferenzen

- Leseproben - z. B. vom Gabler Wirtschaftslexikon -, Online-Archive unserer Fachzeitschriften, Aktualisierungsservice und Foliensammlungen für ausgewählte Buchtitel, Rezensionen, Newsletter zu verschiedenen Themen und weitere attraktive Angebote, z. B. unser Bookshop

- Zahlreiche Servicefunktionen mit dem direkten Klick zum Ansprechpartner im Verlag

- **Klicken Sie mal rein: www.gabler.de**

Abraham-Lincoln-Str. 46
65189 Wiesbaden
Fax: 06 11.78 78-400

KOMPETENZ IN
SACHEN WIRTSCHAFT